Visit classzone
and get conne...

Online resources provide instruction, practice, and learning support correlated to your text.

- **Guided Web activities** introduce students to real-world French.

- **Audio flashcards** provide review of vocabulary and pronunciation.

- **Self-scoring quizzes** help students assess comprehension.

- **Writing workshops** invite students to share their creations online.

- **Teaching resources** offer answer keys and other support.

You have immediate access to *ClassZone's* teacher resources.

MCDTESCODFRZ

Use this code to create your own username and password.

Also visit *ClassZone* to learn more about these innovative online resources.

- Online Workbook
- eTest Plus Online
- EasyPlanner Plus Online

Now
click

CLASSZONE

McDougal

Visit classzone
and get conne

Online resources provide instruction, practice, and learning support correlated to your text.

- **Guided Web activities** introduce students to real-world French.

- **Audio flashcards** provide review of vocabulary and pronunciation.

- **Self-scoring quizzes** help students assess comprehension.

- **Writing workshops** invite students to share their creations online.

- **Teaching resources** offer answer keys and other support.

You have immediate access to *ClassZone's* teacher resources.

MCDTESCODFRZ

Use this code to create your own username and password.

Also visit *ClassZone* to learn more about these innovative online resources.

- Online Workbook
- eTest Plus Online
- EasyPlanner Plus Online

Now it all clicks!™

CLASSZONE.COM

McDougal Littell

BLEU
1a

Première
partie

TEACHER'S
EDITION

Discovering
FRENCH
Nouveau!

Jean-Paul Valette
Rebecca M. Valette

McDougal Littell
A HOUGHTON MIFFLIN COMPANY
Evanston, Illinois • Boston • Dallas

From the Authors

DEDICATION

On June 6, 1944, shortly after 6:30 a.m., Private John Nedelka of the 16th Regiment, First Division (the Big Red One), came ashore on a stretch of the Normandy Coast now known as Omaha Beach. Pinned down under a deluge of fire, he spent the next hour crawling his way to the relative safety of a seawall just one hundred yards inland. As he scrambled up the cliffs off the beach later that afternoon, he suddenly realized that he was one of the few survivors of his company.

This book is dedicated to our friend John Nedelka, to the hundreds of thousands of young Americans who, like him, risked their lives, and, above all, to the tens of thousands who lost theirs in the liberation of France.

IN MEMORIAM

Roger Coulombe (*1940–2001*)

We would like to dedicate **Discovering French, Nouveau!** to the memory of our long-time associate, Roger Coulombe. For twenty-five years, he provided his editorial guidance and focused his artistic flair on the production and design of our language books—books which have encouraged millions of American young people to discover the beauty of French language and culture. May his commitment to quality and education inspire new generations of foreign language editors.

Jean-Paul Valette   *Rebecca M. Valette*

Printed in the United States of America

ISBN: 0-618-03216-9   3 4 5 6 7 8 9 10 - VJM - 07 06 05 04

Dear French Teachers,

We take this opportunity to welcome you to **Discovering French, Nouveau!** In fact, this is really your program, for it has been revised and expanded thanks to the suggestions, critiques, and encouragement we have received from the many hundreds of secondary school teachers who have enjoyed success getting their students to communicate with *Discovering French*.

Discovering French, Nouveau! emphasizes communication with accuracy and stresses meaningful cultural contexts. With **Discovering French, Nouveau!** your students will:

- **Experience France and the Francophone world**
- **Communicate with confidence**
- **Extend and enhance their learning through integrated technology**

As you look through the book you will discover new features, such as the end-of-unit *Tests de contrôle* and the addition of thematic vocabulary lists.

In conclusion, we would like to stress that our program is a flexible one, which allows teachers to take into account the needs of their students and build their own curriculum focusing on specific skills or topics.

We wish you the best of success with **Discovering French, Nouveau!** It is our hope that for you and your students, teaching and learning French with this program will be an enjoyable as well as a rewarding experience.

Jean-Paul Valette   Rebecca M. Valette

Contents

Program Overview T6

Program Resources T8

Easy Articulation T10

Book Organization T12

Scope and Sequence T14

Walkthrough T28

Cultural Reference Guide T52

Professional Development T56

Professional Reference Information T64

Program Consultants

- Dan Battisti
- Dr. Teresa Carrera-Hanley
- Bill Lionetti
- Patty Murguía Bohannan
- Lorena Richins Layser

Discovering
FRENCH *Nouveau!*

Discovering French *Nouveau!*

Explore French-speaking cultures with the proven leader.
A program that offers:

Culture
• Experience France and the Francophone World

Skills and Strategies
• Communicate with confidence

Integrated Technology
• Extend and enhance learning

1. Jean-Pierre
Paris
Sophie
Strasbourg
2. Paul
3. Éric
Lyon
5. Nicole
Bordeaux
4. Michèle
Nice
Marseille

Discovering FRENCH *Nouveau!*

Explores France and the distinctive French-speaking cultures

- Photos and illustrations reflect the cultural diversity of the French-speaking world.

- *Connexions* offer real-world activities that promote cultural awareness.

- *En bref* features familiarize students with the wide variety of countries in the French-speaking world.

- *Notes culturelles* provide more in-depth cultural information about France and the French-speaking world.

Builds skills and develops strategies for more accurate communication

- Strategies for developing reading and writing skills are included in each unit.

- Writing hints provide further support to help students write accurately in French.

- Learning about Language features provide strategies for communication and help students understand how language functions.

Integrates technology for engaging, real-world instruction

- Extensive video program presents and practices vocabulary and grammar in authentic cultural contexts.

- Online *Activités pour tous* Workbook offers leveled practice on the Internet.

- EasyPlanner CD-ROM and Test Generator CD-ROM give teachers the flexibility of having all ancillaries available in an electronic format.

- ClassZone.com presents a variety of engaging resources, from WebQuests to test preparation tools, all correlated to *Discovering French, Nouveau!*

Program Resources

Extensive resources tailored to the needs of today's students!

TEACHER'S RESOURCE PACKAGE

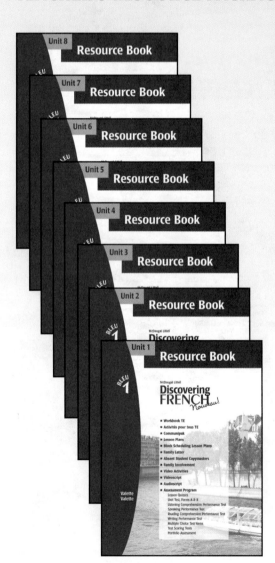

Unit Resource Books

Per Lesson -
Workbook TE
Activités pour tous TE
Lesson Plans
Block Scheduling Lesson Plans
Absent Student Copymasters
Family Involvement
Video Activities
Videoscripts
Audioscripts
Lesson Quiz

Per Unit -
Family Letter
Communipak
Activités pour tous TE Reading
Workbook TE Reading and Culture Activities
Lesson Plans for *Images*
Block Scheduling Lesson Plans for *Images*

Assessment Options
Portfolio Assessment
Unit Test Form A
Unit Test Form B
Unit Test Part III (Alternate) Cultural Awareness
Listening Comprehension Performance Test
Speaking Performance Test
Reading Comprehension Performance Test
Writing Performance Test
Multiple Choice Test Items
Test Scoring Tools
Audioscripts
Answer Keys

Block Scheduling Copymasters

Teacher to Teacher Copymasters

TEACHER'S EDITION

ADDITIONAL RESOURCES

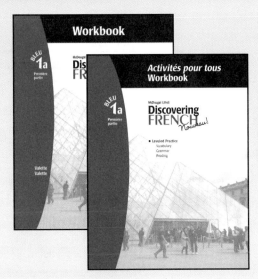

Overhead Transparencies & Copymasters

Student Workbooks
- **Workbook**
- *Activités pour tous*

INTERNET RESOURCES

- **Online Workbook**
  leveled, self-scoring practice
- **eTest Plus Online**
  Complete Test Generator functionality, plus
  administer tests online
- **EasyPlanner Plus Online**
  Complete EasyPlanner functionality, plus
  view or print standards with each lesson
- **ClassZone.com**
  WebQuests, test preparation, flashcards
  and more

MIDDLE SCHOOL RESOURCES

- **Middle School Bridging Packet**
  - Reprise Workbook TE
  - Reprise Audioscript
  - Middle School Copymasters
  - Middle School Audio CD

TECHNOLOGY RESOURCES

- **Audio CD Program**
- *Chansons* **Audio CD**
- **Video Program (videotape / DVD)**
- **Test Generator CD-ROM**
- **EasyPlanner CD-ROM**
- **Power Presentations CD-ROM**

Easy Articulation

▶ *Discovering French, Nouveau!* is a carefully articulated three-level sequence of French instruction. Each level has its own special focus, which builds a spiraling progression across levels.

	CONVERSATION	DESCRIPTION	NARRATION	EXPLANATION
BLEU	Basic communication with learned phrases; simple questions and answers	Simple descriptions of people and things	Simple narration in the present; introduction to past narration	Simple explanations as to why something is done
BLANC	Creative conversation; asking and answering questions	More detailed descriptions, including simple comparisons	Basic narration in the past (*passé composé* and imperfect) and future	Expression of personal wishes and needs
ROUGE	Extended conversation using complex sentences and appropriate pronouns	More complex comparisons of people, things and actions	Extended narration of past, present and future events and corresponding conditions	Expression of emotions, wishes and hypotheses in complex sentences

▶ This chart shows the articulation of basic communication themes and topics across levels. (Only the major entry and reentry points are shown.) These themes and topics are recycled throughout the program in the various exercises, readings and communication activities.

THEMES AND TOPICS	BLEU *première partie* and *deuxième partie*	BLANC	ROUGE
Greeting and meeting people	Unit 1 *première partie*	Reprise: Rappel 1	—
Time and weather	Unit 2 *première partie*	Reprise: Rappel 1	Unit 3
Family and friends; Family relationships	Unit 1 *première partie*	Unit 1	Reprise A; Unit 9
Food and restaurants	Unit 2 *première partie* Unit 8 *deuxième partie*	Units 1, 3	Reprise A
Money and shopping	Unit 2 *première partie* Unit 6 *deuxième partie*	Reprise: Rappel 2	Reprise B; Unit 4
School and education	Images: À l'école en France *première partie*	Reprise: Faisons connaissance	Unit 10
Daily activities	Unit 3 *première partie*	Reprise: Rappel 3	Reprise A
Getting around the city	Unit 3 *première partie* Unit 5 *deuxième partie*	Unit 2	Unit 8
Describing oneself	Unit 4 *première partie*	Units 1, 7	Unit 1
Home and furnishings	Unit 4 *première partie* Unit 5 *deuxième partie*	Unit 6	Unit 6
Possessions and their description	Unit 4 *première partie*	Reprise: Rappel 2 Unit 2	Reprise A; Unit 2
Sports, fitness, daily routine	Unit 5 *deuxième partie*	Units 5, 8	Unit 1
Medical and dental care	—	Unit 5	Unit 7
Clothing and personal appearance	Unit 6 *deuxième partie*	Unit 7	Reprise A; Unit 4
Leisure activities, music, entertainment	Unit 7 *deuxième partie*	Unit 4	Interlude 4
Vacation and travel	Unit 7 *deuxième partie*	Unit 8	Reprise B; Unit 3
Transportation	Unit 7 *deuxième partie*	Units 8, 9	Unit 5
Jobs and professions	—	Unit 1	Units 2, 10
Helping around the house	—	Unit 2	Unit 2
Nature and the environment	—	Unit 2	Unit 3
Services and repairs	—	—	Unit 4
Hotel accommodations	—	—	Unit 6

FUNCTION	BLEU	BLANC	ROUGE
Greeting people and socializing	Units 1, 2 première partie	Reprise: Rappel 1	–
Talking about the present Asking and answering questions Describing people, places and things Describing future plans (Simple description)	Units 3, 4, 5, 6 première partie, deuxième partie	Reprise: Rappels 2, 3; Unit 1	Reprise A
Narrating past events (Simple narration)	Unit 7 deuxième partie	Unit 2	Reprise B
Discussing daily routines (Simple narration)	–	Unit 5	Unit 1
Describing people, places, things (Extended description)	Unit 8 deuxième partie	Units 3, 4, 5	Reprise C Units 2, 4
Describing past conditions and narrating past events (Extended narration)	–	Unit 6	Reprise B Units 3, 7
Comparing and discussing people, things and actions (Complex description)	–	Unit 7	Units 6, 9
Discussing future events (Extended narration)	–	Unit 8	Units 5, 8
Discussing hypothetical conditions and events (Complex discussion)	–	Unit 8	Units 5, 8
Expressing wishes and obligations (Direct statements)	–	Unit 9	Unit 2
Expressing doubts and emotions (Complex discussion)	–	–	Unit 7
Expressing cause and purpose (Complex discussion)	–	–	Unit 10

Book Organization
Discovering French, *Nouveau!* BLEU Première partie

Basic Structure The Student Text contains four units and one *Images* photo essay. The *Invitation au français* section (Units 1-2) builds student confidence and quickly develops basic conversation skills. Units 3-4 complete the study of level 1A, focusing on the formal development of language for accurate communication.

INTRODUCTION

Invitation au français emphasizes speaking and listening to French.

UNITÉ 1 • **Faisons connaissance** *To make knowledge*

UNITÉ 2 • **La vie courante** *In everyday life*

TOPICS COVERED
- greeting people
- introducing oneself
- talking about friends and family
- ordering in a café
- numbers 0–100
- telling time
- days of the week
- months and dates
- weather and seasons

CORE MATERIAL

These units provide the linguistic base needed for basic communication skills.
Emphasis is on asking and answering questions. (Students should complete these units.)

UNITÉ 3 • **Qu'est-ce qu'on fait?**

IMAGES *À l'école en France*

UNITÉ 4 • **Le monde personnel et familier**

TOPICS COVERED
- discussing daily activities and leisure pastimes
- talking about people and possessions

INVITATION AU FRANÇAIS

UNITÉ 1 Faisons connaissance · CULTURAL CONTEXT Meeting people

PREMIÈRE PARTIE

COMMUNICATION: FUNCTIONS AND ACTIVITIES COMPREHENSION AND SELF-EXPRESSION	COMMUNICATION TOPICS THEMATIC VOCABULARY	LINGUISTIC GOALS ACCURACY OF EXPRESSION
Meeting people • Introducing oneself (**Leçon 1A**) • Spelling one's name (**Leçon 1A**) • Asking someone's name (**Leçon 1A**) • Saying where you are from (**Leçon 1B**)	• Adjectives of nationality (**Leçon 1B**)	• **L'alphabet (Leçon 1A)** • **Français / française (Leçon 1B)**
Greeting people • Saying hello (**Leçon 1A**) • Asking how people feel (**Leçon 1C**) • Saying good-bye (**Leçon 1C**)	• Expressions with ça va (**Leçon 1C**) • Counting 0 to 10 (**Leçon 1A**) • Counting 10 to 20 (**Leçon 1B**) • Counting 20 to 60 (**Leçon 1C**)	
Talking about other people • Pointing people out (**Leçon 2A**) • Finding out someone's name (**Leçon 2B**) • Saying where a person is from (**Leçon 2B**)	• People (**Leçon 2A**)	• **Un garçon / une fille (Leçon 2A)** • **Le garçon / la fille (Leçon 2B)**
Introducing one's family • Giving their names (**Leçon 2B**) • Giving their ages (**Leçon 2C**)	• Family members (**Leçon 2C**) • Counting 60 to 79 (**Leçon 2A**) • Counting 80 to 100 (**Leçon 2B**)	• **Mon cousin / ma cousine (Leçon 2C)** • **Ton cousin / ta cousine (Leçon 2C)**

UNITÉ 2 La vie courante · CULTURAL CONTEXT Having a snack in France

PREMIÈRE PARTIE

Saying you are hungry • Offering a friend something to eat (**Leçon 3A**) • Asking a friend for something to eat (**Leçon 3A**)	• Foods (**Leçon 3A**)	• **Un sandwich / une pizza (Leçon 3A)**
Saying you are thirsty • Ordering a beverage in a café (**Leçon 3B**) • Asking an adult for something to eat or drink (**Leçon 3B**)	• Beverages (**Leçon 3B**)	• **S'il te plaît / s'il vous plaît (Leçon 3B)**
Paying at a café in France • Asking what something costs (**Leçon 3C**) • Asking a friend to lend you money (**Leçon 3C**)		
Talking about time • Asking for the time (**Leçon 4A**) • Indicating the time (**Leçon 4A**) • Saying when certain events are scheduled (**Leçon 4A**)	• Expressions of time (**Leçon 4A**)	
Talking about dates • Asking the day of the week (**Leçon 4B**) • Giving the date (**Leçon 4B**) • Talking about birthdays (**Leçon 4B**)	• Days of the week (**Leçon 4B**) • Months of the year (**Leçon 4B**)	
Talking about the weather	• Weather expressions (**Leçon 4C**) • Seasons (**Leçon 4C**)	

UNITÉ 3 Qu'est-ce qu'on fait? • CULTURAL CONTEXT Daily activities at home, at school, on weekends

PREMIÈRE PARTIE

COMMUNICATION: FUNCTIONS AND ACTIVITIES COMPREHENSION AND SELF-EXPRESSION	COMMUNICATION TOPICS THEMATIC VOCABULARY	LINGUISTIC GOALS ACCURACY OF EXPRESSION
Describing daily activities • What people do and don't do (**Leçon 5**) • What people like to do and don't like to do (**Leçon 5**) • What you want and don't want to do (**Leçon 5**)	• Daily activities (**Leçon 5**) • Expressions with **faire** (**Leçon 8**)	• Subject pronouns (**Leçon 6**) • The negative **ne... pas** (**Leçon 6**) • Verb + infinitive (**Leçon 7**) • Regular **-er** verbs (**Leçon 7**) • The verb **faire** (**Leçon 8**)
Talking about where people are	• Places (**Leçon 6**)	• The verb **être** (**Leçon 6**)
Finding out what is going on • Asking yes/no questions (**Leçon 6**) • Asking information questions (**Leçon 8**)	• Question words (**Leçon 8**)	• Yes/no questions with **est-ce que** (**Leçon 6**) • Information questions with **est-ce que** (**Leçon 8**) • Questions with inversion (**Leçon 8**)
Inviting friends to do things with you • Extending an invitation (**Leçon 5**) • Accepting an invitation (**Leçon 5**) • Turning down an invitation (**Leçon 5**)		• Verb + infinitive (**Leçon 7**)
Expanding one's conversational skills • Answering yes/no questions (**Leçon 6**) • Expressing approval or regret (**Leçon 7**) • Expressing mild doubt or surprise (**Leçon 8**)	• Affirmative and negative expressions (**Leçon 6**)	

UNITÉ 4 Le monde personnel et familier • CULTURAL CONTEXT People and their possessions

PREMIÈRE PARTIE

Describing yourself and others • Physical appearance (**Leçon 9**) • Age (**Leçons 9, 10**) • Character traits (**Leçon 11**) • Nationality (**Leçon 11**)	• People (**Leçon 9**) • Adjectives of physical description (**Leçon 9**) • Adjectives of personality (**Leçon 11**) • Adjectives of nationality (**Leçon 11**) • Adjectives of aspect (**Leçon 12**)	• Singular and plural nouns (**Leçon 10**) • Definite and indefinite articles (**Leçon 10**) • The expression **avoir... ans** (**Leçon 10**) • Adjective formation (**Leçon 11**) • Adjective position (**Leçons 11, 12**) • Use of **c'est** and **il est** (**Leçon 12**)
Describing your room • What is in it (**Leçon 9**) • Where things are located (**Leçon 9**)	• Room furnishings (**Leçon 9**) • Prepositions of place (**Leçon 9**)	• The expression **il y a** (**Leçon 9**)
Talking about possessions • Things that one owns and doesn't own (**Leçons 9, 10**) • Whether they work or not (**Leçon 9**) • Where they were made (**Leçon 11**) • What they look like (**Leçon 12**)	• Everyday objects (**Leçon 9**) • Color (**Leçon 12**) • Aspect (**Leçon 12**)	• The verb **avoir** (**Leçon 10**) • The negative article **pas de** (**Leçon 10**)
Expanding one's conversational skills • Getting someone's attention (**Leçon 12**) • Making generalizations (**Leçon 10**) • Expressing opinions (**Leçon 12**) • Talking about regular events (**Leçon 10**) • Contradicting a negative statement or question (**Leçon 10**) • Introducing a conclusion (**Leçon 11**)	• Attention getters (**Leçon 12**) • Expressions of opinion (**Leçon 12**)	• Use of the definite article: in general statements to indicate repeated events (**Leçon 10**) • Impersonal **c'est** (**Leçon 12**)
optional: Talking about past events (**Leçons 10, 11, 12**)		• Conversational introduction: answering questions in the **passé composé** (**Leçons 10, 11, 12**)

REPRISE Bonjour! • CULTURAL CONTEXT Getting reacquainted

COMMUNICATION: FUNCTIONS AND ACTIVITIES COMPREHENSION AND SELF-EXPRESSION	COMMUNICATION TOPICS THEMATIC VOCABULARY	LINGUISTIC GOALS ACCURACY OF EXPRESSION
Talking about school and classes (Bonjour: Et vous) **Talking about self and family (Bonjour and Et vous)**	Personal and family characteristics School subjects (**Faisons connaissance!**)	
Expressing oneself on familiar topics • Giving the date (**R-4**) • Telling time (**R-4**) • Describing the weather (**R-4**)	• Review: numbers 1-100 (**App. A**) • Review: days, months (**App. A**) • Review: times of day (**App. A**) • Review: weather (**App. A**)	
Talking about places and things • Describing things you own (**R-2**) • Saying where things are (**R-2**) • Pointing things out (**R-2**) • Expressing preferences (**R-3**)	• Review: place names (**App. A**)	• Review: possessive adjectives (**App. A**)
Carrying out simple conversations • Asking and answering questions (**R-1**) • Talking about daily activities (**R-1**) • Talking about places where you go (**R-3**) • Saying what you like (**R-3**)	• Review: question words (**R-3**) • Review: common verbs (**App. A**)	• Review: present tense of regular verbs (**App. A**) • Review: interrogative and negative constructions (**App. A**)

UNITÉ 5 En ville • CULTURAL CONTEXT City life—the home, the family and urban activities

Describing your city • Streets and public buildings (**Leçon 13**) • Places you often go to (**Leçon 14**) • How you get around (**Leçon 14**)	• City places and buildings (**Leçon 13**) • Transportation (**Leçon 14**)	• The verb **aller** (**Leçon 14**) • Contractions with **à** (**Leçon 14**)
Finding your way around • Asking and giving directions (**Leçon 13**) • Indicating the floor (**Leçon 16**)	• Giving directions (**Leçon 13**)	• Ordinal numbers (**Leçon 16**)
Describing your home and your family • Your address (**Leçon 13**) • The inside and outside of your home (**Leçon 13**) • Your family (**Leçon 16**)	• Neighborhood (**Leçon 13**) • Rooms of the house (**Leçon 13**) • Family members (**Leçon 16**)	• The expression **chez** (**Leçon 14**) • Stress pronouns (**Leçon 15**) • The construction noun + **de** + noun (**Leçon 15**) • Possession with **de** (**Leçon 16**) • Possessive adjectives (**Leçon 16**)
Making plans to do things in town • What you are going to do (**Leçon 14**) • Asking others to come along (**Leçon 15**) • Saying where you have been (**Leçon 15**)	• Activities: sports, games, etc. (**Leçon 15**)	• **Aller** + infinitive (**Leçon 14**) • The verb **venir** (**Leçon 15**) • Contractions with **de** (**Leçon 15**)
Expanding one's conversational skills: • Contradicting someone (**Leçon 15**) • Expressing doubt (**Leçon 16**) • Expressing surprise (**Leçon 15**)		
optional: Talking about past events (**Leçons 13, 14, 15, 16**)		• Conversational introduction: answering questions in the **passé composé** (**Leçons 13, 14, 15, 16**)

UNITÉ 6 Le shopping • CULTURAL CONTEXT Buying clothes

Talking about clothes • What people are wearing (**Leçon 17**) • Whether the clothes fit (**Leçon 17**) • What they look like (**Leçons 17, 19**) • What one's preferences are (**Leçon 17**)	• Clothing and accessories (**Leçon 17**) • Descriptive adjectives (**Leçon 17**) • Adjectives **beau, nouveau, vieux** (**Leçon 19**) • Expressions of opinion (**Leçon 17**)	• The verb **mettre** (**Leçon 18**) • The verb **préférer** (**Leçon 18**) • The demonstrative **ce** (**Leçon 18**) • The interrogative **quel?** (**Leçon 18**)
Discussing shopping plans • Where to go (**Leçons 17, 20**) • What to buy (**Leçon 18**)	• Stores that sell clothes (**Leçon 17**) • Verbs like **vendre** (**Leçon 20**)	• The verb **acheter** (**Leçon 18**) • Regular -**re** verbs (**Leçon 20**) • The pronoun **on** (**Leçon 20**)

UNITÉ 6 (continued)

DEUXIÈME PARTIE

COMMUNICATION: FUNCTIONS AND ACTIVITIES COMPREHENSION AND SELF-EXPRESSION	COMMUNICATION TOPICS THEMATIC VOCABULARY	LINGUISTIC GOALS ACCURACY OF EXPRESSION
Buying clothes • Asking for help (**Leçon 17**) • Finding out prices (**Leçons 17, 20**) • Deciding what to choose (**Leçon 19**) • Comparing items (**Leçon 19**) • Talking about what you need and what you like (**Leçon 20**) • Giving advice (**Leçon 20**)	• Numbers 100–1000 (**Leçon 17**) • Money-related expressions (**Leçon 20**) • Verbs like **choisir** (**Leçon 19**) • Expressions **avoir besoin de** and **avoir envie de** (**Leçon 20**)	• Regular **-ir** verbs (**Leçon 19**) • The verb **payer** (**Leçon 20**) • Comparisons (**Leçon 19**) • The imperative (**Leçon 20**)
Expanding one's conversational skills • Emphasizing a remark (**Leçon 18**) • Indicating approval (**Leçon 20**) • Introducing an opinion (**Leçon 19**)		
optional: Talking about past events (**Leçons 17, 18, 19, 20**)		• Conversational introduction:answering questions in the **passé composé** (**Leçons 17, 18, 19, 20**)

UNIT 7 Le temps libre • CULTURAL CONTEXT Leisure-time activities

DEUXIÈME PARTIE

Discussing leisure activities • Going out with friends (**Leçon 21**) • Sports (**Leçon 21**) • Helping around the house (**Leçon 21**) • How you and others feel (**Leçon 22**) • Things you never do (**Leçon 24**)	• Common weekend activities (**Leçon 21**) • Individual summer and winter sports (**Leçon 21**) • Household chores (**Leçon 21**)	• **Faire de** + sport (**Leçon 21**) • Expressions with **avoir** (**Leçon 22**) • **Ne … jamais** (**Leçon 24**)
Describing vacation travel plans • Travel dates (**Leçons 21, 24**) • How to travel (**Leçon 21**) • How long to stay (**Leçons 21, 23**) • What to see (**Leçon 23**)	• Means of transportation (**Leçon 21**) • Divisions of time (**Leçon 21**) • Periods of future time (**Leçon 23**) • Verbs of movement (**Leçon 24**)	• The verb **voir** (**Leçon 23**)
Narrating what happened • What you did and didn't do (**Leçons 22, 23**) • Where you went and when you returned (**Leçon 24**) • The sequence in which you did these things (**Leçon 22**) • Remaining vague about certain details (**Leçon 24**)	• Adverbs of sequence (**Leçon 22**) • Periods of past time (**Leçon 23**)	• **Passé composé** of **-er** verbs (**Leçon 22**) • **Passé composé** of **-ir** verbs (**Leçon 23**) • **Passé composé** of **-re** verbs (**Leçon 23**) • **Passé composé** of irregular verbs (**Leçon 23**) • **Passé composé** with **être** (**Leçon 24**) • **Quelqu'un, quelque chose** and their opposites (**Leçon 24**)

UNITÉ 8 Les repas • CULTURAL CONTEXT Food and meals

DEUXIÈME PARTIE

Talking about your favorite foods • What you like and don't like (**Leçon 25**) • What you can, should and want to eat (**Leçons 25, 26, 27**)	• Names of foods and beverages (**Leçon 25**) • Verbs of preference (**Leçon 25**)	• The verb **vouloir** (**Leçon 26**) • The verbs **pouvoir** and **devoir** (**Leçon 27**)
Shopping for food • Making a shopping list (**Leçon 25**) • Interacting with vendors (**Leçon 25**) • Asking prices (**Leçon 25**)	• Quantities (**Leçon 25**) • Fruits and vegetables (**Leçon 25**)	• Partitive article (**Leçon 26**)
Planning a meal • Asking others to help you (**Leçon 27**) • Setting the table (**Leçon 25**)	• Meals (**Leçon 25**) • Verbs asking for service (**Leçon 27**) • Place setting (**Leçon 25**)	• Pronouns **me, te, nous, vous** (**Leçon 27**) • Pronouns with commands (**Leçon 27**)
Eating out with friends • Ordering food (**Leçon 25**) • Asking the waiter/waitress to bring things for others (**Leçon 28**) • Talking about people you know (**Leçon 27**) • Talking about what others have said or written (**Leçon 28**)	• Verbs using indirect objects (**Leçon 28**)	• The verb **prendre** (**Leçon 26**) • The verb **boire** (**Leçon 26**) • The verb **connaître** (**Leçon 28**) • The verbs **dire** and **écrire** (**Leçon 28**) • Pronouns **le, la, les, lui, leur** (**Leçon 28**)

REPRISE (REVIEW) Entre amis • CULTURAL CONTEXT Getting acquainted

COMMUNICATION: FUNCTIONS AND ACTIVITIES COMPREHENSION AND SELF-EXPRESSION	COMMUNICATION TOPICS THEMATIC VOCABULARY	LINGUISTIC GOALS ACCURACY OF EXPRESSION
Talking about school and classes (Faisons connaissance!)	• School subjects (**Faisons connaissance!**)	
Expressing oneself on familiar topics • Giving the date (**Rappel-1**) • Telling time (**Rappel-1**) • Describing the weather (**Rappel-1**)	• Review: numbers 1-100 (**Appendix A**) • Review: days, months (**Appendix A**) • Review: times of day (**Appendix A**) • Review: weather (**Appendix A**)	
Talking about places and things • Describing things you own (**Rappel-2**) • Saying where things are (**Rappel-2**) • Pointing things out (**Rappel-2**) • Expressing preferences (**Rappel-2**)	• Review: common objects and items of clothing (**Appendix A**) • Prepositions of location (**Rappel-2**) • Review: place names (**Appendix A**)	• Review: articles and contractions, **ce** and **quel** (**Appendix A**) • Review: possessive adjectives (**Appendix A**)
Carrying out simple conversations • Asking and answering questions (**Rappel-3**) • Talking about daily activities (**Rappel-3**) • Talking about places where you go (**Rappel-3**) • Saying what you like (**Rappel-3**)	• Review: question words (**Rappel-3**) • Review: common **–er, -ir, -re** verbs (**Appendix A**)	• Review: present tense of regular verbs (**Appendix A**) • Review: interrogative and negative constructions (**Appendix A**) • Review: subject pronouns and stress pronouns (**Rappel-3**) • Review: the imperative (**Appendix A**)

UNITÉ 1 Qui suis-je? • CULTURAL CONTEXT Oneself and others

Presenting oneself and others • Providing personal data (**Leçon 1**) • Identifying one's family (**Leçon 1**) • Talking about professions (**Leçon 1**)	• Adjectives of nationality (**Leçon 1**) • Family and friends (**Leçon 1**) • Professions (**Leçon 1**)	• The verb **être** (**Leçon 2**) • **C'est** and **il est** (**Leçon 2**)
Interacting with others • Introducing people (**Leçon 1**) • Making phone calls (**Leçon 1**) • Reading birth and wedding announcements (**Leçon 1**)		
Talking about oneself and others • Describing looks and personality (**Leçon 2**) • Talking about age (**Leçon 3**) • Describing feelings and needs (**Leçon 3**)	• Descriptive adjectives (**Leçon 2**) • Expressions with **avoir** (**Leçon 3**) • Expressions with **faire** (**Leçon 3**)	• Regular and irregular adjectives (**Leçon 2**) • The verb **avoir** (**Leçon 3**) • The verb **faire** (**Leçon 3**) • Inverted questions (**Leçon 3**)
Describing one's plans • Saying where people are going and what they are going to do (**Leçon 4**) • Saying where people are coming from (**Leçon 4**) • Saying how long people have been doing things (**Leçon 5**)	• Expressions with **depuis** (**Leçon 4**)	• The verb **aller** (**Leçon 4**) • The construction **aller** + infinitive (**Leçon 4**) • The verb **venir** (**Leçon 4**) • The present with **depuis** (**Leçon 4**)

READING Getting the gist

UNITÉ 2 Le week-end, enfin! • CULTURAL CONTEXT Weekend activities

COMMUNICATION: FUNCTIONS AND ACTIVITIES COMPREHENSION AND SELF-EXPRESSION	COMMUNICATION TOPICS THEMATIC VOCABULARY	LINGUISTIC GOALS ACCURACY OF EXPRESSION
Talking about weekend plans • Describing weekend plans in the city (**Leçon 5**) • Planning a visit to the country (**Leçon 5**)	• Going out with friends (**Leçon 5**) • Helping at home (**Leçon 5**) • The country and the farm (**Leçon 5**) • Domestic and other animals (**Leçon 5**) • Expressions of present and future time (**Leçon 7**)	• The verbs **mettre**, **permettre**, and **promettre** (**Leçon 6**) • The verb **voir** (**Leçon 7**) • The verbs **sortir**, **partir**, and **dormir** (**Leçon 8**)
Getting from one place to another • Getting around in Paris (**Leçon 5**) • Visiting the countryside (**Leçon 5**)	• Getting around by subway (**Leçon 5**)	• The verb **prendre** (**Leçon 6**)
Narrating past weekend activities • Talking about where one went (**Leçons 7, 8**) • Talking about what one did and did not do (**Leçons 6, 7, 8**)	• Expressions of past time (**Leçon 6**)	• The **passé composé** with **avoir** (**Leçons 6, 7**) • The **passé composé** with **être** (**Leçons 7, 8**) • Impersonal expressions: **quelqu'un**, **quelque chose**, **personne**, **rien** (**Leçon 7**) • **Il y a** + elapsed time (**Leçon 8**)

READING Recognizing word families

UNITÉ 3 Bon appétit! • CULTURAL CONTEXT Meals and food shopping

Planning a meal • Talking about where to eat (**Leçon 9**) • Setting the table (**Leçon 9**)	• Meals (**Leçon 9**) • Place setting (**Leçon 9**)	
Going to a café • Ordering in a café (**Leçon 9**)	• Café foods and beverages (**Leçon 9**)	• The verb **boire** (**Leçon 11**)
Talking about favorite foods • Discussing preferences (**Leçon 9**) • Expressing what one wants (**Leçon 12**)	• Mealtime foods and beverages (**Leçon 9**) • Fruits and vegetables (**Leçon 9**)	• The verb **préférer** (**Leçon 11**) • The verb **vouloir** (**Leçon 10**)
Shopping for food at a market • Interacting with vendors and asking prices (**Leçon 9**) • Asking for specific quantities (**Leçon 9**) • Discussing what one can get (**Leçon 12**) • Talking about what one should buy or do (**Leçon 12**)	• Common quantities (**Leçon 12**) • Expressions of quantity (**Leçon 12**)	• Partitive article (**Leçon 10**) • The verbs **acheter** and **payer** (**Leçon 11**) • Expressions of quantity with **de** (**Leçon 12**) • The adjective **tout** (**Leçon 12**) • The verbs **devoir** and **pouvoir** (**Leçon 10**) • The expression **il faut** (**Leçon 12**)

READING Reading by phrase groups

UNITÉ 4 Loisirs et spectacles! • CULTURAL CONTEXT Free time and entertainment

COMMUNICATION: FUNCTIONS AND ACTIVITIES COMPREHENSION AND SELF-EXPRESSION	COMMUNICATION TOPICS THEMATIC VOCABULARY	LINGUISTIC GOALS ACCURACY OF EXPRESSION
Planning one's free time • Going out with friends (**Leçon 13**) • Extending, accepting, and turning down invitations (**Leçon 13**) • Talking about concerts and movies (**Leçon 13**)	• Places to go and things to do (**Leçon 13**) • Types of movies (**Leçon 13**)	
Talking about your friends and your neighborhood • Describing people and places you know (**Leçon 15**)		• The verb **connaître** (**Leçon 15**) • Object pronouns **le**, **la**, **les** (**Leçon 15**) • The verb **savoir** (**Leçon 16**)
Discussing relations with others • Asking others for assistance (**Leçon 14**) • Describing services of others (**Leçon 16**)	• Verbs asking for a service (**Leçon 14**) • Verbs using indirect objects (**Leçon 16**)	• Object pronouns **me**, **te**, **nous**, **vous** (**Leçon 14**) • Object pronouns **lui**, **leur** (**Leçon 16**) • Object pronouns in commands (**Leçon 14**) • Double object pronouns (**Leçon 16**)
Reading and writing about daily events • Writing a letter to a friend (**Leçon 14**) • Discussing what you like to read (**Leçon 16**) • Talking about what others have written or said (**Leçon 16**)	• Expressions used in letters (**Leçon 14**) • Reading materials (**Leçon 16**)	• The verbs **écrire**, **lire**, and **dire** (**Leçon 16**)
Narrating what happened • Talking about losing and finding things (**Leçon 15**)	• Verbs used to talk about possessions (**Leçon 15**)	• Object pronouns in the **passé composé** (**Leçon 15**)

READING Inferring meaning

UNITÉ 5 Vive le sport! • CULTURAL CONTEXT Sports and health

Discussing sports • Finding out what sports your friends like (**Leçon 17**) • Talking about where you practice sports and when (**Leçon 18**) • Giving your opinion (**Leçon 18**)	• Individual sports (**Leçon 17**) • Adverbs of frequency (**Leçon 18**) • Expressions of opinion (**Leçon 18**)	• The verb **courir** (**Leçon 17**) • The expression **faire du** (**Leçon 17**) • The pronouns **en** and **y** (**Leçon 18**)
Discussing fitness and health • Describing exercise routines (**Leçon 17**) • Describing common pains and illnesses (**Leçon 17**)	• Parts of the body (**Leçon 17**) • Health (**Leçon 17**)	• The expression **avoir mal à** (**Leçon 17**) • Definite article with parts of the body (**Leçon 19**)
Talking about one's daily activities • Describing the daily routine (**Leçon 19**) • Caring for one's appearance (**Leçon 19**) • Giving others advice (**Leçon 20**) • Asking about tomorrow's plans (**Leçon 20**)	• Daily occupations (**Leçon 19**) • Hygiene and personal care (**Leçon 19**)	• Reflexive verbs: present tense (**Leçon 19**) • Reflexive verbs: imperative (**Leçon 20**) • Reflexive verbs: infinitive constructions (**Leçon 20**)
Narrating past activities • Describing one's daily routine in the past (**Leçon 20**)	• Common activities (**Leçon 20**)	• Reflexive verbs: **passé composé** (**Leçon 20**)

READING Recognizing prefixes

Gr 9.

UNIT 6 Chez nous • CULTURAL CONTEXT House and home

COMMUNICATION: FUNCTIONS AND ACTIVITIES COMPREHENSION AND SELF-EXPRESSION	COMMUNICATION TOPICS THEMATIC VOCABULARY	LINGUISTIC GOALS ACCURACY OF EXPRESSION
Discussing where you live • Describing the location of your house or apartment (**Leçon 21**) • Explaining what your house or apartment looks like (**Leçon 21**)	• Location of one's home (**Leçon 21**) • Rooms of the house (**Leçon 21**) • Furniture and appliances (**Leçon 21**)	• The verb **vivre** (**Leçon 22**)
Renting an apartment or house • Reading classified ads (**Leçon 21**) • Asking about a rental (**Leçon 21**) • Giving more complete descriptions (**Leçon 22**)		• Relative pronouns **qui** and **que** (**Leçon 22**)
Talking about the past • Explaining what you used to do in the past and when (**Leçon 23**) • Describing ongoing past actions (**Leçon 23**) • Giving background information about specific past events (**Leçon 24**)	• Prepositions of time (**Leçon 23**) • An accident (**Leçon 24**)	• The imperfect (**Leçon 23**) • Contrasting the imperfect and the **passé composé** (**Leçons 23, 24**)

READING Recognizing partial cognates

UNITÉ 7 Soyez à la mode! • CULTURAL CONTEXT Clothes and accessories

Talking about clothes • Saying what people are wearing (**Leçon 25**) • Describing clothes and accessories (**Leçon 25**)	• Clothes and accessories (**Leçon 25**) • Colors (**Leçon 25**) • Fabric, design, materials (**Leçon 25**)	
Shopping for clothes • Talking with the sales clerk (**Leçon 25**) • Expressing opinions (**Leçon 25**)	• Types of clothing stores (**Leçon 25**) • Sizes, looks, and price (**Leçon 25**) • Numbers 100–1,000,000 (**Leçon 26**) • Adjectives **beau, nouveau, vieux** (**Leçon 26**)	
Comparing people and things • Ranking items in a series (**Leçon 26**) • Expressing comparisons (**Leçon 27**) • Saying who or what is the best (**Leçon 27**) • Referring to specific items (**Leçon 28**)	• Descriptive adjectives (**Leçon 27**)	• Ordinal numbers (**Leçon 26**) • Comparisons with adjectives (**Leçon 27**) • Superlative constructions (**Leçon 27**) • Pronouns **lequel?** and **celui** (**Leçon 28**)
Talking about how things are done • Describing how things are done (**Leçon 26**) • Comparing how things are done (**Leçon 27**)	• Common adverbs (**Leçon 27**)	• Adverbs ending in **-ment** (**Leçon 26**) • Comparisons with adverbs (**Leçon 27**)

READING Understanding the context

UNITÉ 8 Bonnes vacances • CULTURAL CONTEXT Travel and summer vacations

COMMUNICATION: FUNCTIONS AND ACTIVITIES COMPREHENSION AND SELF-EXPRESSION	COMMUNICATION TOPICS THEMATIC VOCABULARY	LINGUISTIC GOALS ACCURACY OF EXPRESSION
Discussing summer vacations • Talking about vacation plans **(Leçon 29)** • Planning a camping trip **(Leçon 29)**	• Destinations, lodging, travel documents **(Leçon 29)** • Foreign countries **(Leçon 29)** • Camping equipment **(Leçon 29)**	• Prepositions with names of countries **(Leçon 30)** • The verbs **recevoir** and **apercevoir** **(Leçon 30)**
Making travel arrangements • Buying tickets **(Leçon 29)** • Checking schedules **(Leçon 29)** • Expressing polite requests **(Leçon 32)**	• At the train station, at the airport **(Leçon 29)**	• The use of the conditional to make polite requests **(Leçon 32)**
Talking about what you would do under various circumstances	• Verbs followed by infinitives **(Leçon 30)**	• The constructions verb **+ à +** infinitive, verb **+ de +** infinitive **(Leçon 30)**
Making future plans • Talking about the future **(Leçon 31)** • Setting forth conditions **(Leçon 31)**		• The future tense **(Leçon 31)** • The future with **si**-clauses **(Leçon 31)** • The future with **quand** **(Leçon 31)**
Talking about what one would do under certain circumstances • Discussing what would occur **(Leçon 32)** • Describing conditions **(Leçon 32)**		• The conditional **(Leçon 32)** • The conditional with **si**-clauses **(Leçon 32)**

READING Recognizing false cognates

UNITÉ 9 Bonne route • CULTURAL CONTEXT Getting around by car

Talking about cars • Describing cars **(Leçon 33)** • Having one's car serviced **(Leçon 33)** • Getting one's license **(Leçon 33)** • Rules of right of way **(Leçon 33)**	• Types of vehicles **(Leçon 33)** • Parts of a car **(Leçon 33)** • Car maintenance **(Leçon 33)**	• The verbs **conduire** and **suivre** **(Leçon 33)**
Expressing how one feels about certain events		• Adjective **+ de +** infinitive **(Leçon 34)**
Talking about past and present events • Describing purpose and sequence **(Leçon 34)** • Describing simultaneous actions and cause and effect **(Leçon 34)**	• Prepositions **pour, sans, avant de,** and **en** **(Leçon 34)**	• Preposition **+** infinitive **(Leçon 34)** • Present participle constructions **(Leçon 34)**
Discussing what has to be done • Expressing necessity and obligation **(Leçon 35)** • Letting others know what you want them to do **(Leçon 36)**	• **Il faut que** **(Leçon 35)** • **Je veux que** **(Leçon 36)**	• Present subjunctive: regular forms **(Leçon 35)** • Present subjunctive: irregular forms **(Leçon 36)**

READING Recognizing figures of speech

REPRISE • OBJECTIVE Light Review of Basic Material (from Levels One and Two)

BASIC REVIEW		CULTURE AND READING
STRUCTURES	**VOCABULARY**	**VACATION OPTIONS** Travel, sports, archaeology, helping others
A. La vie courante Describing the present • Present of regular verbs • **Être, avoir, aller, faire, venir** and expressions used with these verbs • Other common irregular verbs • Use of present with **depuis** • Regular and irregular adjectives • Use of the partitive article	• Daily activities • Food and beverages	The French-speaking world: Its people
B. Hier et avant Describing the past • **Passé composé** with **avoir** and **être** • Imperfect and its basic uses	• Clothes	The French-speaking world: Cultural background
C. Nous et les autres Referring to people, things, and places • Object pronouns • Negative expressions • **Connaître** and **savoir** • Other irregular verbs		**Lecture:** *Les trois bagues*

UNITÉ 1 Au jour le jour • MAIN THEMES Looking good; one's daily routine

COMMUNICATION OBJECTIVES		READING AND CULTURAL OBJECTIVES		Interlude Culturel 1
COMMUNICATION: FUNCTIONS AND CONTEXTS LE FRANÇAIS PRATIQUE	**LINGUISTIC GOALS** LANGUE ET COMMUNICATION	**DAILY LIFE** INFO MAGAZINE	**READING** LECTURE	Le monde des arts GENERAL CULTURAL BACKGROUND
Describing people • Their physical appearance **Caring for one's appearance** • Personal care and hygiene • Looking good **Describing the various aspects of one's daily routine** **Expressing how one feels and inquiring about other people**	**Describing people and their ailments** • The use of the definite article **Describing what people do for themselves** • Reflexive verbs **Explaining one's daily activities** • Reflexive verbs: different tenses and uses	**How important is personal appearance for French young people and what do they do to enhance it?** • The importance of **le look** • Clothing and personal style **How have artists expressed their concept of beauty?** **How do people begin their daily routine?**	Ionesco, *Conte pour enfants de moins de trois ans*	**French modern art** • **Impressionism** and impressionist artists: **Monet, Degas, Renoir, Manet, B. Morisot** • Artists of the **post-impressionist** era: **Van Gogh, Gauguin, Matisse, Rousseau, Toulouse-Lautrec** • **Surrealism** as an artistic and literary movement: **Magritte** **Poems** • Desnos, *La fourmi* • Prévert, *Pour faire le portrait d'un oiseau*

UNITÉ 2 Soyons utiles! • MAIN THEME Being helpful around the house

COMMUNICATION OBJECTIVES		READING AND CULTURAL OBJECTIVES		Interlude Culturel 2
COMMUNICATION: FUNCTIONS AND CONTEXTS LE FRANÇAIS PRATIQUE	**LINGUISTIC GOALS** LANGUE ET COMMUNICATION	**DAILY LIFE** INFO MAGAZINE	**READING** LECTURE	**Les grands moments de l'histoire de France (jusqu'en 1453)**
Helping around the house • In the house itself • Outside **Asking for help and offering to help** • Accepting or refusing help • Thanking people for their help **Describing an object** • Shape, weight, length, consistency, appearance, etc. • The material it is made of	**Explaining what has to be done** • **Il faut que** + subjunctive **Telling people what you would like them to do** • **Vouloir que** + subjunctive	**Why do French people enjoy do-it-yourself activities?** • What is **bricolage**? • What is **jardinage**? **How should you take care of your plants?** **How do French young people earn money by helping their neighbors?**	***La Couverture*** *(Une fable médiévale)*	GENERAL CULTURAL BACKGROUND **Early French history** • Important events The Roman conquest The Holy Roman Empire The Norman Conquest of England The Hundred Years War • Important people **Vercingétorix** **Charlemagne** **Guillaume le Conquérant** **Aliénor d'Aquitaine** **Jeanne d'Arc** **Literature:** *La Chanson de Roland*

UNITÉ 3 Vive la nature! • MAIN THEMES Vacation and outdoor activities; the environment and its protection

				Interlude Culturel 3
Talking about outdoor activities • What to do • What not to do **Describing the natural environment and how to protect it** **Talking about the weather and natural phenomena** **Relating a sequence of past events** **Describing habitual past actions**	**Talking about the past** • The **passé composé** • The imperfect • The **passé simple** • Contrastive uses of the **passé composé** and the imperfect **Narrating past events** • Differentiating between specific actions (**passé composé**) and the circumstances under which they occurred (imperfect) • Providing background information (imperfect)	**How do the French feel about nature and their land?** • What is **le tourisme vert**? • What is an **éco-musée**? **How do the French protect their environment?** • What rules to observe on camping trips • What young people do to protect the environment • Who was **Jacques-Yves Cousteau**? **Why do the French people love the sun?**	Sempé / Goscinny, ***King***	**Les grands moments de l'histoire de France (1453-1715)** GENERAL CULTURAL BACKGROUND **The classical period of French history** • Important periods: **la Renaissance, le Grand Siècle** • Important people: **François Ier, Louis XIV** • French castles, as witnesses of French history **Literature** • La Fontaine, *Le Corbeau et le renard* • Prévert, *Soyons polis* **Film:** Rostand, *Cyrano de Bergerac*

UNITÉ 4 Aspects de la vie quotidienne • MAIN THEME Going shopping and asking for services

COMMUNICATION OBJECTIVES		READING AND CULTURAL OBJECTIVES		Interlude Culturel 4
				Vive la musique!
COMMUNICATION: FUNCTIONS AND CONTEXTS LE FRANÇAIS PRATIQUE	LINGUISTIC GOALS LANGUE ET COMMUNICATION	DAILY LIFE INFO MAGAZINE	READING LECTURE	GENERAL CULTURAL BACKGROUND
Shopping for various items • in a stationery store • in a pharmacy • in a convenience store **Buying stamps and mailing items at the post office** **Having one's hair cut** **Asking for a variety of services** • at the cleaners • at the shoe repair shop • at the photo shop	**Answering questions and referring to people, things, and places using pronouns** • Object pronouns • Two-pronoun sequence **Talking about quantities** • The pronoun **en** • Indefinite expressions of quantity **Describing services that you have done by other people** • The construction **faire + infinitive**	**How are certain aspects of daily life different in France?** • Shopping on the Internet • Shopping in a supermarket • Services at the post office • When to tip and not to tip	*Histoire de cheveux*	**The musical landscape of France and the French-speaking world** • Classical musicians: **Lully, Chopin, Bizet, Debussy** • Historical overview of French songs • Famous French singers of yesterday and today • The multicultural aspect of music from the francophone world: **zouk** (Antilles); **raï** (North Africa); **cajun, zydéco** (Louisiana) **Song: Vigneault,** *Mon pays* **Opera: Bizet,** *Carmen*

UNITÉ 5 Bon voyage! • MAIN THEME Travel

				Interlude Culturel 5
				Les grands moments de l'histoire de France (1715-1870)
				GENERAL CULTURAL BACKGROUND
Planning a trip abroad **Going through customs** **Making travel arrangements** • Purchasing tickets **Travel in France** • at the train station • at the airport	**Making negative statements** • Affirmative and negative expressions **Describing future plans** • Future tense • Use of future after **quand** **Hypothesizing about what one would do** • Introduction to the conditional	**What are the advantages of visiting France by train?** • The **TGV** • The **Eurotunnel** **Why do French people like to travel abroad and what do they do on their vacations?** • Impressions of young people visiting the United States	*Le mystérieux homme en bleu*	**The historical foundation of modern France** • Important periods the **French Revolution** the **Napoleonic era** • Important contemporary French institutions • Important people **Louis XVI et Marie-Antoinette Napoléon** **Song: Rouget de Lisle,** *La Marseillaise* **Literature: Victor Hugo,** *Les Misérables*

UNITÉ 6 Séjour en France • MAIN THEME Hotels and other places to stay when traveling

COMMUNICATION OBJECTIVES		READING AND CULTURAL OBJECTIVES		Interlude Culturel 6
COMMUNICATION: FUNCTIONS AND CONTEXTS LE FRANÇAIS PRATIQUE	LINGUISTIC GOALS LANGUE ET COMMUNICATION	DAILY LIFE INFO MAGAZINE	READING LECTURE	Les grands moments de l'histoire de France (1870 au présent)
Deciding where to stay when traveling Reserving a room in a hotel Asking for services in a hotel	Comparing people, things, places and situations • The comparative • The superlative Asking for an alternative • The interrogative pronoun **lequel?** Pointing out people or things • The demonstrative pronoun **celui** Indicating possession • The possessive pronoun **le mien**	What inexpensive accommodations are available to students? • Auberges de jeunesse • Séjour à la ferme How does one use the *Guide Michelin* when traveling in France? • To find a hotel • To choose a restaurant	*Une étrange aventure*	**GENERAL CULTURAL BACKGROUND** **France in the 20th century** • Important events the two World Wars the economic union of Europe • Important people **Marie Curie** **Charles de Gaulle** **Simone Veil** Literature: **Éluard**, *Liberté* Film: **L. Malle**, *Au revoir, les Enfants*

UNITÉ 7 La forme et la santé • MAIN THEME Health and medical care

				Interlude Culturel 7
Going to the doctor's office • Describing your symptoms • Explaining what is wrong • Giving information about your medical history • Understanding the doctor's prescriptions Going to the dentist Going to the emergency ward	Expressing how you and others feel about certain facts or events • Use of the subjunctive after expressions of emotion Expressing fear, doubt or disbelief • Use of the subjunctive after expressions of doubt and uncertainty Expressing feelings or attitudes about past actions and events • The past subjunctive	How do the French take care of their health? • How does the French health system work? • What is the **Sécurité sociale?** • Why do the French consume so much mineral water? • What is **thermalisme?** How do French doctors participate in humanitarian missions around the world? • What is **Médecins sans frontières?**	Maupassant, *En voyage*	Les Français d'aujourd'hui **GENERAL CULTURAL BACKGROUND** **Modern France as a multi-ethnic and multi-cultural society** • The French as citizens of Europe • The new French mosaic: the impact of immigration on French society • The **Maghrébins** – their culture and their religion • **SOS Racisme** • Two French humanitarians: **L'abbé Pierre** and **Coluche** Song: *Éthiopie*

UNITÉ 8 En ville • MAIN THEME Cities and city life

				Interlude Culturel 8
Making a date and fixing the time and place Explaining where one lives and how to get there Discussing the advantages and disadvantages of city life	Narrating past actions in sequence • The pluperfect Formulating polite requests • The conditional Hypothesizing about what one would do under certain circumstances • The conditional and its uses • The past conditional • Sequence of tenses in **si**-clauses	What does a typical French city look like? • Its historical development • Its various neighborhoods • Its buildings • The **villes nouvelles** Why do French people love to stroll in the streets? • Various street shows • Sculptures to view while walking in Paris	Theuriet, *Les Pêches*	Les Antilles francophones **GENERAL CULTURAL BACKGROUND** **The French-speaking Caribbean islands** • Historical background • Important people **Toussaint Louverture** **Joséphine de Beauharnais** **Aimé Césaire** • Haitian art as an expression of life Literature: **Césaire**, *Pour saluer le Tiers-Monde* Film: **Palcy**, *Rue Cases-nègres*

UNITÉ 9 Les relations personnelles • MAIN THEME Personal relationships, friendships, and family life

COMMUNICATION OBJECTIVES		READING AND CULTURAL OBJECTIVES		Interlude Culturel 9
COMMUNICATION: FUNCTIONS AND CONTEXTS LE FRANÇAIS PRATIQUE	**LINGUISTIC GOALS** LANGUE ET COMMUNICATION	**DAILY LIFE** INFO MAGAZINE	**READING** LECTURE	L'Afrique dans la communauté francophone
Describing degrees of friendship **Expressing different feelings towards other people** **Discussing the state of one's relationship with other people** **Congratulating, comforting, and expressing sympathy for other people** **Describing the various phases of a person's life**	**Describing how people interact** • Reciprocal use of reflexive verbs **Describing people and things in complex sentences** • Relative pronouns • Relative clauses	**How important are friends and family to French people?** • The meaning of friendship • Family relationships **How socially concerned are French young people and what type of social outreach do they do?** **What is a typical French wedding like?** • Where French spouses meet one another • Planning the wedding • A French wedding ceremony	**M. Maurois, *Le Bracelet***	**GENERAL CULTURAL BACKGROUND** **The place of Western and Central Africa in the francophone world** • Historical periods and events: prehistory, the **African empires**, colonization, and independence • Basic facts about Western Africa language and culture religions and traditions • **African art** and its influence on European art **African Fable: *La Gélinotte et la Tortue*** **Literature** • D. Diop, *Afrique* • Dadié, *La légende baoulé*

UNITÉ 10 Vers la vie active • MAIN THEME University studies and careers

				Interlude Culturel 10
				La France et le Nouveau Monde
Deciding on a college major • University courses **Planning for a career** • Professions • The work environment • Different types of industries **Looking for a job** • Preparing a résumé • Describing one's qualifications at a job interview	**Describing simultaneous actions** • The present participle **Explaining the purpose of an action** • **Pour** + infinitive • **Pour que** + subjunctive **Explaining the timing, conditions, and constraints of an action** • The use of the infinitive or the subjunctive after certain prepositions and conjunctions	**How important is academic success to French young people?** • The French school system: high schools and universities • **Le bac:** its history and its importance **What does one do after graduation?** • Choosing a profession • **Le service militaire** **How does one interview for a job?** • Preparing for the interview • Writing a résumé in French	**Thériault, *Le Portrait***	**GENERAL CULTURAL BACKGROUND** **The French presence in North America** • Historical background The French in Canada and Louisiana • Important people **Jacques Cartier, Jeanne Mance, Cavelier de La Salle** • Why certain American cities have French names **Song: Richard, *Réveille*** **Literature: La Fayette, *Lettre à sa femme***

Setting the Stage for Communication

The Unit Opener presents the unit theme and communicative objectives.

○ There are **four thematically-linked lessons** in each unit. Vocabulary presented in the first lesson (*Le français pratique*) is then used throughout the next three lessons as structure is taught, reinforcing the unit theme.

○ **Unit Theme and Objectives** preview for the students what they will be able to do at the end of the unit.

UNITÉ 3

Qu'est-ce qu'on fait?

LEÇON 5   LE FRANÇAIS PRATIQUE: Mes activités

LEÇON 6   Une invitation

LEÇON 7   Une boum

LEÇON 8   Un concert de musique africaine

THÈME ET OBJECTIFS

Daily activities

In this unit, you will be talking about the things you do every day, such as working and studying, as well as watching TV or playing sports.

You will learn ...

- to describe some of your daily activities
- to say what you like and do not like to do
- to ask and answer questions about where others are and what they are doing

You will also learn ...

- to invite friends to do things with you
- to politely accept or turn down an invitation

  WEBQUEST CLASSZONE.COM

70   soixante-dix
Unité 3

soixante et onze 71
Unité 3

Opener photo highlights the people and places of the new culture.

Discovering
FRENCH
Nouveau!

Strengthen proficiency

The Lesson Opener provides cultural and linguistic background through text and photos and a visual briefing of the communicative contents of the lesson.

- *Le français pratique* presents the communicative focus and functional language of the unit. Students immediately get and give information in French.

- The **thematic presentation** introduces students to the lesson content. The video program provides additional cross-cultural interactions.

LEÇON 5

LE FRANÇAIS PRATIQUE
VIDÉO DVD AUDIO

Vocabulaire et Culture

Mes activités

Accent sur ... Les activités de la semaine

French teenagers spend a great deal of time on their studies since they and their families consider it important to do well in school. They have a longer class day than American students and are given more homework.

However, French teenagers do not study all the time. They also enjoy listening to music, watching TV, and playing computer games. Many participate in various sports activities, but to a lesser extent than American students. On weekends, they like to go out with their friends to shop or see a movie. They also go to parties and love dancing.

Mélanie est à la maison. Elle écoute un CD.
Mélanie: J'aime le rock anglais.

Marc, Élodie et David sont au stade. Ils jouent au foot.
Marc: Nous jouons au foot.
Élodie: Nous jouons aussi au basket.
David: Nous aimons les sports.

Olivier est en ville. Il téléphone.
Olivier: J'aime téléphoner.
Je téléphone à une copine.

Zaïna joue aux jeux vidéo.
Zaïna: J'aime jouer aux jeux vidéo.
J'aime aussi regarder la télé.

Vocabulaire et Culture LEÇON 5

72 soixante-douze
Unité 3

soixante-treize 73
Leçon 5

- **Video, DVD and audio** icons indicate the variety of resources that support lesson content.

- Students are introduced to the **language patterns** of the unit **in context**.

The *Vocabulaire et communication* sections of *Le français pratique* lessons present new conversational patterns by function.

New vocabulary and related conversational patterns are introduced in **thematic context**. All vocabulary is coded in yellow; functions are highlighted with a red triangle and darker yellow band.

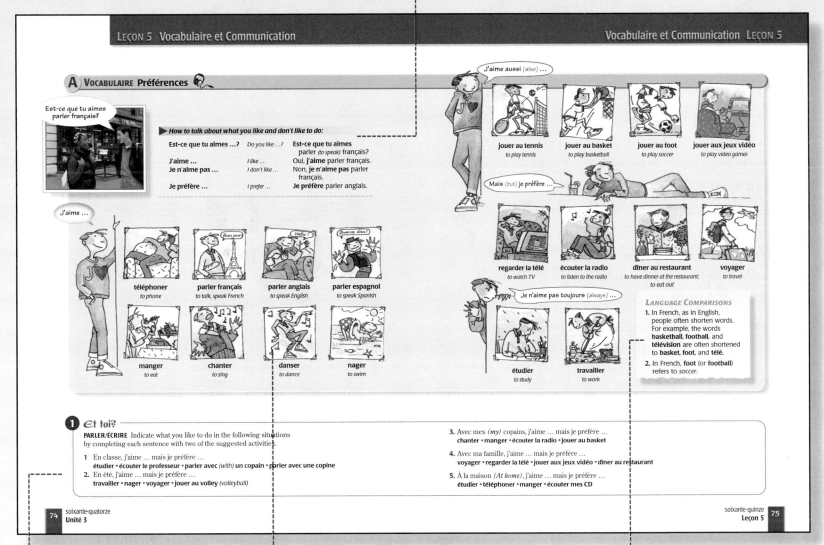

Student-centered activities practice new vocabulary in contexts ranging from structured to open-ended self-expression.

Art-cued vocabulary is used to help the visual learner and provide a functional cultural context. Since the artists used in *Discovering French, Nouveau!* are actually French, students are exposed to authentic cultural detail in every drawing.

Language comparisons help students understand how language functions.

Each *Le français pratique* lesson moves through
functional introduction of language practice activities, and
culminates in the *À votre tour* review section.

○ *Objectifs* remind students
of what they've learned
and why.

2 Tu
PARLE
▶ cha

○ *À votre tour* activities
recombine material from each
lesson as well as previous units.
These open-ended activities
allow students to demonstrate
what they can do with the
language and to monitor their
own progress through critical
thinking and self-expression.

À votre tour!

OBJECTIFS

Now you can …
• talk about activities you like and do not like
• extend and accept invitations
• give an excuse when you cannot accept

1 *Écoutez bien!* -------

ÉCOUTER You will hear French young people telling you what they like to do.
Listen carefully to each activity. If it is illustrated in the picture on the left,
mark A. If it is illustrated in the picture on the right, mark B.

A  **B**

	A	B
1.		
2.		
3.		
4.		
5.		
6.		

4
PARLER
following
cannot a

▶ jouer a

1. jouer a
2. mange
3. regard
4. jouer a
5. dîner a
6. jouer a

5 Expr
PARLER/
Complet
in the f

▶ En hi
En hi
la t
J'aim
Je n'a

2 Communication -------

ÉCOUTER You have invited a French friend to spend the weekend at your house.
Ask your friend …

• if he/she likes to watch TV
• if he/she wants to play video games
• if he/she likes to listen to the radio
• if he/she wants to eat a pizza

A classmate will play the role of your French friend and answer your questions.

6
ÉCRIRE
going to
France.
correspo
written a
and don'
vacation
Respond
answerin

3 Conversation dirigée -------

PARLER Trinh is phoning Céline. Write out their conversation according to
the directions. You may want to act out the dialogue with a classmate.

Trinh				Céline
	asks Céline how she is	→ ↙	answers that she is fine	
	asks her if she wants to eat out	→ ↙	asks at what time	
	says at 8 o'clock	→ ↙	says that she is sorry but that she has to study	
	says it is too bad (**Dommage!**)			

80 quatre-vingts
Unité 3

n'aimes pas?

ether or not you like to do the following things.

Est-ce que tu veux jouer
au tennis avec moi?

Non, je ne peux pas.
Je dois travailler.

ialogue

es if they want to do the
They will answer that they
the excuses below.

EXCUSES:

téléphoner à une copine

étudier   travailler

parler avec ma mère

dîner avec ma cousine

chanter avec la chorale (choir)

nelle

ke to do often depends on the circumstances.
low saying what you like and don't like to do

der

1. En été ...
2. En automne ...
3. Le samedi (On Saturdays) ...
4. Le dimanche ...

5. Le soir (In the evening) ...
6. En classe ...
7. Avec mes (my) amis ...
8. Avec ma famille ...

basket.

ce

re
n

e

,

STRATEGY Writing

1. Make a list of activities you
   like and do not like. Use only
   vocabulary that you know.

   ☺   ☹

2. Write your e-mail.   Cher Vincent,
                        En vacances, j'aime ...

3. Read over your letter to be sure you
   have used the right verb forms.

LESSON REVIEW
CLASSZONE.COM

B VOCABULAIRE Souhaits (Wishes)

Je voudrais voyager
en France.

▶ **How to talk about what you want, would like, and do not want to do:**

Je veux ...	I want ...	**Je veux** parler français.
Je voudrais ...	I would like ...	**Je voudrais** voyager en France.
Je ne veux pas ...	I don't want ...	**Je ne veux pas** étudier aujourd'hui.

5 Ce soir (Tonight)

PARLER/ÉCRIRE Say whether or not you
want to do the following things tonight.

▶ étudier?
  Oui, je veux étudier.
  (Non, je ne veux pas étudier.)

1. parler français?
2. travailler?
3. jouer aux jeux vidéo?
4. chanter?
5. danser?
6. regarder la télé?
7. écouter la radio?
8. dîner avec une copine?
9. manger une pizza?
10. téléphoner à mon cousin?

6 Week-end

PARLER/ÉCRIRE Léa and her friends are
discussing their weekend plans. What do
they say they would like to do?

▶ LÉA: Je voudrais jouer au tennis.

Léa   1. Jérôme   2. Monique

3. Jean-Louis   4. Caroline   5. Patrick

7 Trois souhaits (Three wishes)

ÉCRIRE Read the list of suggested activities and select the three that you would like to do most.

parler français
parler espagnol
parler avec (with) Oprah Winfrey
dîner avec le Président
dîner avec Matt Damon

voyager avec ma cousine
voyager en France
chanter comme (like) Britney Spears
jouer au tennis comme Venus Williams
jouer au basket comme Shaquille O'Neal

▶ Je voudrais parler espagnol.
  Je voudrais chanter comme Britney Spears.
  Je voudrais voyager en France.

⊙ Writing strategies
offer important tips for
improving writing skills.

⊙ The writing activities
encourage students to express
their own thoughts and ideas
and may be included in
students' writing portfolios.

⊙ Web icons guide students to relevant
online materials at ClassZone.com

Build accuracy

Conversation et Culture lesson openers present reading and culture as they recycle the communicative functions of *Le français pratique* vocabulary and provide grammar support and explanation.

○ The opening **reading and/or video dialog** provides a context for the communicative functions and presentation of linguistic structures. You may vary your presentation of the new language according to the needs of your students, addressing a variety of learner types.

○ **Comprehension checks** allow students to self-check their comprehension (both reading and listening) as receptive skills are developed.

LEÇON 7

Conversation et Culture

Une boum AUDIO

Jean-Marc has been invited to a party. He is trying to decide whether to bring Béatrice or Valérie.

LEÇON 6

Conversation et Culture

Une invitation VIDÉO DVD AUDIO

It is Wednesday afternoon. Antoine is looking for his friends but cannot find anyone. Finally he sees Céline at the Café Le Bercy and asks her where everyone is.

Antoine:	Où est Léa?		*Where*
Céline:	Elle est à la maison.		*at home*
Antoine:	Et Mathieu? Il est là?		*here*
Céline:	Non, Il n'est pas là.		
Antoine:	Où est-il?		
Céline:	Il est en ville avec une copine.		*in town*
Antoine:	Et Julie et Stéphanie? Est-ce qu'elles sont ici?		*here*
Céline:	Non, elles sont au restaurant.		
Antoine:	Alors, qui est là?		*So*
Céline:	Moi, je suis ici.		
Antoine:	C'est vrai, tu es ici! Eh bien, puisque tu es là,		*true / since*
	je t'invite au cinéma. D'accord?		*I'll invite you to the movies.*
Céline:	Super! Antoine, tu es un vrai copain!		*real*

Compréhension

Indicate where the following people are by selecting the appropriate completions.

1. Léa est …   3. Julie et Stéphanie sont …   au café   en ville
2. Mathieu est …   4. Antoine et Céline sont …   à la maison   au restaurant

NOTE culturelle

Le mercredi après-midi

French middle school students do not usually have class Wednesday afternoons. Some young people use this free time to go out with their friends or to catch up on their homework. For other students, Wednesday afternoon is the time for music and dance lessons as well as sports activities. Many students play soccer with their school te with their local sports club. Other popular activities inclu tennis, skateboarding, and in-line skating.

COMPARAISONS CULTURELLES

How does the school week in France compare to the school week in the United States?
• Do you see any differences in the ways French and American teenagers spend their free time? Explain.
• Do American and French teenagers like the same sports? Explain.

LEÇON 8

Conversation et Culture

Un concert de musique africaine

VIDÉO DVD AUDIO

Nicolas is at a café with his new friend Fatou. He is interviewing her for an article in his school newspaper.

Conversation et Culture LEÇON 7

NOTE *culturelle*

Une boum

On weekends, French teenagers like to go to parties that are organized at a friend's home. These informal parties have different names according to the age group of the participants. For students at a **collège** (middle school), a party is sometimes known as **une boum** or **une fête.** For older students at a **lycée** (high school), it is called

...ents are usually around to help out and set up a
...en features items contributed by the guests. Pizza
...ry popular. There may also be homemade
...Chinese food. Preferred beverages are sodas and

...ng people like to dance and listen to their favorite music.
...drawn into the latest video games. Others simply enjoy
... to talk about the week's events. For everyone, it is a way
...o spend a relaxing evening with friends.

---

et Culture LEÇON 6

COMPARAISONS CULTURELLES
How do French parties compare to parties that you and your friends organize? Explain.

quatre-vingt-treize **93**
Leçon 7

NOTE *culturelle*

Le Sénégal
★ Dakar

EN BREF: Le Sénégal
Capitale: Dakar
Population: 10 000 000
Langue officielle: français

Dakar, Sénégal

A former French colony, Senegal became an independent republic in 1960. Its population is divided into about a dozen ethnic groups, each with its own language, the most important being **wolof** and **pulaar.**

Des jeunes Sénégalais

Youssou N'Dour
Youssou N'Dour is an internationally known musician from Senegal who combines traditional African music with pop, rock, and jazz. He sings in French and English, as well as in three Senegalese dialects. His lyrics promote African unity and human dignity. In many of his songs, he also plays the **tama**, a traditional Senegalese drum covered with reptile skins.

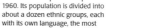
Le tama

CONNEXIONS Senegal and African Music
- As a class project, make a display board on Senegal, using information and pictures from travel brochures or from the Internet.
- Obtain a CD of Youssou N'Dour or of music from another French-African country and play your favorite selection for the class.

cent cinq **105**
Leçon 8

● *Connexions* offer real world activities that engage students and promote cultural awareness.

quatre-vingt-trois **83**
Leçon 6

● *Notes culturelles,* coded in blue throughout the program, expand on the cultural content of the lesson opener. Further cultural expansion is also available on video, correlated at point-of-use in the Teacher's Edition.

Langue et communication pages present grammatical structures in a variety of formats appropriate to varied learning styles, including model sentences, visual representations, cartoons, summary boxes, and charts.

Listening icons highlight the listening strand in the student books.

Coded in green, the structure sections clearly and concisely summarize essential grammar points. Sample sentences are provided to present material in meaningful context.

Pair and group activities allow students to communicate and exchange information while practicing new structures in both guided and open-ended activities.

B Les

To ask ab

LEÇON 8 Langue et Communication

A Les questions d'information

The questions below ask for specific information and are called INFORMATION QUESTIONS.
The INTERROGATIVE EXPRESSIONS in heavy print indicate what kind of information is requested.

—**Où** est-ce que tu habites?	**Where** do you live?
—J'habite **à Nice.**	I live **in Nice.**
—**À quelle heure** est-ce que vous dînez?	**At what time** do you eat dinner?
—Nous dînons **à sept heures.**	We eat **at seven.**

→ In French, information questions may be formed according to the pattern:

INTERROGATIVE EXPRESSION	+ **est-ce que**	+ SUBJECT	+ VERB ... ?
À quelle heure	**est-ce que**	vous	travaillez?

→ **Est-ce que** becomes **est-ce qu'** before a vowel sound.

Quand **est-ce qu'**Alice et Roger dînent?

→ In information questions, your voice rises on the interrogative expression and then falls until the last syllable.

Quand est-ce que tu travailles?   **À quelle heure** est-ce que vous dînez?

Observation In casual conversation, French speakers frequently form information questions by placing the interrogative expression at the end of the sentence. The voice rises on the interrogative expression.

Vous habitez **où?**   Vous dînez **à quelle heure?**

VOCABULAIRE Expressions interrogatives

où	where?	**Où** est-ce que vous travaillez?
quand?	when?	**Quand** est-ce que ton copain organise une boum?
à quelle heure?	at what time?	**À quelle heure** est-ce que tu regardes la télé?
comment?	how?	**Comment** est-ce que tu chantes? Bien ou mal?
pourquoi?	why?	—**Pourquoi** est-ce que tu étudies le français?
parce que	because	—**Parce que** je veux voyager en France.

→ **Parce que** becomes **parce qu'** before a vowel sound.
Juliette invite Olivier **parce qu'**il danse bien.

1

STRAT
Underst
attentio
express
informa

ÉCOUTER
hear can
only one
Listen ca
and selec

a. à sept
b. à Paris

VOCABUL

How to exp

Ah bon

3

PARLER
his plans

▶ organi

1. organi
2. dîner à
3. dîner
4. regard
5. inviter

4 *Ques*

1. Où es
2. Où es
3. À quel
4. À que
5. Quan

○ **Listening strategies** give students a variety of tips to improve their listening skills.

Langue et Communication

Langue et Communication **LEÇON 8**

nterrogatives avec *qui*

n speakers use the following interrogative expressions:

Qui est-ce que tu invites au concert?

Langue et Communication **LEÇON 8**

2 **Curiosité**

PARLER At a party in Paris, Nicolas meets Béatrice, a Canadian student. He wants to know more about her. Play both roles.

▶ où / habiter? (à Québec)

NICOLAS: **Où est-ce que tu habites?**
BÉATRICE: **J'habite à Québec.**

1. où/étudier? (à Montréal)
2. où/travailler? (dans [*in*] une pharmacie)
3. quand/parler français? (toujours)
4. quand/parler anglais? (souvent)
5. comment/jouer au tennis? (bien)
6. comment/danser? (très bien)
7. pourquoi/être en France? (parce que j'aime voyager)
8. pourquoi/être à Paris? (parce que j'étudie ici)

ions pour la conversation

ld doubt:

—Stéphanie organise une soirée.
—**Ah bon?** Quand?

 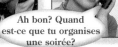

J'organise une soirée.

Ah bon? Quand est-ce que tu organises une soirée?

Samedi.

to tell her about

nd? samedi)

(quand? dimanche)
d? lundi)
au restaurant Belcour)
elle heure? à 9 heures)
concert)

6. parler espagnol (comment? assez bien)
7. étudier l'italien (pourquoi? je veux voyager en Italie)

elles **PARLER/ÉCRIRE**

(*name of your city*)
(*name of your school*)
tu dînes?
tu regardes la télé?
s? (en été? en hiver?)

6. Quand est-ce que tu joues au volley? (en mai? en juillet?)
7. Comment est-ce que tu chantes? (bien? très bien? mal?)
8. Comment est-ce que tu nages?

cent sept
Leçon 8 107

---

7 **Questions**

PARLER/ÉCRIRE For each illustration, prepare a short dialogue with a classmate using the suggested cues.

où?
—Où est-ce que tu dînes?
—Je dîne à la maison.
à la maison

1. à quelle heure?
à 8 heures

2. quand?
en septembre

3. comment?
BONJOUR!
très bien

4. avec qui?
avec Denise

5. à qui?
à mon cousin

6. de qui?
BLA BLA BLA...
de toi

7. pour qui?
pour M. Lambert

C ***Qu'est-ce que?***

Note the use of the interrogative expression **qu'est-ce que** *(what)* in the questions below.

Qu'est-ce que tu regardes? Je regarde un match de tennis.
Qu'est-ce qu'Alice mange? Elle mange une pizza.

To ask <u>*what people are doing*</u>, the French use the following construction:

qu'est-ce que + SUBJECT + VERB + ...?	Qu'est-ce que tu regardes?
qu'est-ce qu' (+ VOWEL SOUND)	Qu'est-ce qu'elle mange?

8 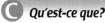 **À la FNAC**

PARLER People in Column A are at the FNAC, a store that sells books and recordings. Use a verb from Column B to ask what they are listening to or looking at. A classmate will answer you, using an item from Column C.

A	**B**	**C**
tu	écouter?	un livre de photos
vous	regarder?	un poster
Alice		un CD de rock
Éric		un CD de jazz
Antoine et Claire		un album de Youssou N'Dour

Qu'est-ce qu'Éric écoute?

Il écoute un album de Youssou N'Dour.

cent neuf
Leçon 8 109

○ Whenever possible, **authentic French drawings, photos, and realia** are used to increase comprehension and success for all students.

After students have become comfortable with material in context, **formal charts** help them analyze forms and structure.

Supplementary vocabulary, coded in yellow, offers students communicative functions for immediate implementation in dialogs.

D Le verbe *faire*

Faire *(to do, make)* is an IRREGULAR verb. It is used in many French expressions. Note the forms of **faire** in the present tense.

faire *(to do, make)*	
je **fais**	Je **fais** un sandwich.
tu **fais**	Qu'est-ce que tu **fais** maintenant?
il/elle **fait**	Qu'est-ce que ton copain **fait** samedi?
nous **faisons**	Nous **faisons** une pizza.
vous **faites**	Qu'est-ce que vous **faites** ici?
ils/elles **font**	Qu'est-ce qu'elles **font** pour la boum?

VOCABULAIRE Expressions avec *faire*

faire un match	*to play a game (match)*	Mes cousins **font un match** de tennis.
faire une promenade	*to go for a walk*	Caroline **fait une promenade** avec Olivier.
faire un voyage	*to take a trip*	Ma copine **fait un voyage** en France.
faire attention	*to pay attention*	Je **fais attention** quand le prof parle.

9 La boum de Léa

PARLER/ÉCRIRE Léa's friends are helping her prepare food for a party. Use the verb **faire** to say what everyone is doing.

▶ Je … une crêpe.

Je fais une crêpe.

1. Nous … une salade.
2. Tu … une salade de fruits.
3. Vous … une tarte *(pie)*.
4. Cécile et Marina … un gâteau *(cake)*.
5. Christine … une pizza.
6. Marc … un sandwich.
7. Patrick et Thomas … une omelette.
8. Pierre et Karine … une quiche.

10 Qu'est-ce qu'ils font?

PARLER/LIRE Read the descriptions below and say what the people are doing. Use the verb **faire** and an expression from the list.

> un voyage
> une promenade
> une pizza
> un match
> attention

▶ Madame Dumont est en Chine.
 Elle fait un voyage.

1. Léa travaille dans *(in)* un restaurant.
2. Nous sommes en ville.
3. Céline et Jean-Paul jouent au tennis.
4. Je suis dans la cuisine *(kitchen)*.
5. Marc est dans le train Paris-Nice.
6. Vous jouez au volley.
7. Je suis dans le parc.
8. Monsieur Lambert visite Tokyo.
9. Nous écoutons le prof.

Langue et Communication LEÇON 8

E L'interrogation avec inversion

LEARNING ABOUT LANGUAGE

In conversational French, questions are usually formed with **est-ce que.** However, when the subject of the sentence is a pronoun, French speakers often use inversion, that is, they invert or reverse the order of the subject pronoun and the verb.

REGULAR ORDER: **Vous parlez** français.   INVERSION: **Parlez-vous** anglais?
SUBJECT VERB   VERB   SUBJECT

The pairs of questions below ask the same thing. Compare the position of the subject pronouns.

Est-ce que **tu** parles anglais?	Parles-**tu** anglais?	*Do you speak English?*
Est-ce que **vous** habitez ici?	Habitez-**vous** ici?	*Do you live here?*
Où est-ce que **nous** dînons?	Où dînons-**nous**?	*Where are we having dinner?*
Où est-ce qu'**il** est?	Où est-**il**?	*Where is he?*

Inverted questions are formed according to the patterns:

YES/NO QUESTION	VERB / SUBJECT PRONOUN	...?	
	Voyagez-vous	souvent?	

INFORMATION QUESTION	INTERROGATIVE EXPRESSION + VERB / SUBJECT PRONOUN	...?	
	Avec qui	**travaillez-vous**	demain?

→ In inversion, the verb and the subject pronoun are connected by a hyphen.

Observation In inversion, liaison is required before **il/elle** and **ils/elles.** If a verb in the singular ends on a vowel, the letter **"t"** is inserted after the verb so that liaison can occur:

Où travaille-**t**-il?   Où travaille-**t**-elle?   Avec qui dîne-**t**-il?   Avec qui dîne-**t**-elle?

11  Conversation

PARLER Ask your classmates a few questions, using inversion.

▶ où / habiter? —**Où habites-tu?**
                  —**J'habite à (Boston).**

1. à quelle heure / dîner?
2. à quelle heure / regarder la télé?
3. avec qui / parler français?
4. à qui / téléphoner souvent?
5. comment / nager?
6. avec qui / étudier?
7. où / jouer aux jeux vidéo?
8. comment / chanter?

PRONONCIATION   /y/

La voyelle /y/

The vowel sound /y/ – represented by the letter "u" – does not exist in English.

Super!

To say **super,** first say the French word **si.** Then round your lips as if to whistle and say **si** with rounded lips: /sy/. Now say **si-per.** Then round your lips as you say the first syllable: **super!**

Répétez: /y/   **s<u>u</u>per   t<u>u</u>   ét<u>u</u>die   bien s<u>û</u>r**
                   L<u>u</u>cie   L<u>u</u>c
                   T<u>u</u> ét<u>u</u>dies avec L<u>u</u>cie.

cent onze
Leçon 8   **111**

O Learning about language notes focus on strategies for authentic language production, explain terminology, and help students understand how language functions.

O *Prononciation* features give students the opportunity to practice single "key" words and then to use them in context. All pronunciation sections, coded in purple, are available on the audio program.

Culminating the lesson, the *À votre tour* activities provide opportunities for self assessment in a variety of contextualized formats.

- Culminating **listening and speaking activities** are ideal for expanding students' use of language beyond the classroom setting.

À votre tour!

OBJECTIFS

Now you can …
- ask and answer information questions
- ask about what people are doing

1 Allô!

PARLER Fatou is phoning some friends. Match her questions on the left with her friends' answers on the right.

1. Qu'est-ce que tu fais?
2. Qu'est-ce que vous faites samedi?
3. Où est ton père?
4. Quand est-ce que tu veux jouer au tennis avec moi?
5. Qui est-ce que tu invites au cinéma?
6. Pourquoi est-ce que tu étudies l'anglais?

a. Il fait une promenade.
b. Ma cousine Alice.
c. Dimanche. D'accord?
d. J'étudie.
e. Nous faisons un match de tennis.
f. Parce que je voudrais habiter à New York.

2 Les questions

LIRE/PARLER The following people are answering questions. Read what they say and figure out what questions they were asked.

Je chante très mal.

▶ Comment est-ce que tu chantes?

1. J'habite à Québec.
2. Je dîne à sept heures.
3. Nous dînons à l'Hippopotame.
4. Je mange une pizza.
5. Je regarde un film.
6. J'invite Catherine.

3 **Créa-dialogue**

PARLER Ask your classmates what they do on different days of the week. Carry out conversations similar to the model. Note: "??" means you can invent your own answers.

▶ —Qu'est-ce que tu fais <u>lundi</u>?
—Je <u>joue au tennis</u>.
—Ah bon? À quelle heure est-ce que tu <u>joues</u>?
—<u>À deux heures</u>.
—Et avec qui?
—Avec <u>Anne-Marie</u>.

	lundi	mardi	mercredi	jeudi	vendredi	samedi	dimanche
ACTIVITÉ						??	??
À QUELLE HEURE?	2 heures	6 heures	??	??	??	??	??
AVEC QUI?	avec Anne-Marie	avec un copain	??	??	??	??	??

4 **Faisons connaissance!** *(Let's get acquainted!)*

PARLER/ÉCRIRE Get better acquainted with a classmate. Ask five or six questions in French. Then write a summary of your conversation and give it to the friend you have interviewed.

▶ Mon ami(e) s'appelle ...
Il/elle habite ...

You might ask questions like:

- Where does he/she live?
- Does he/she speak French at home? With whom?
- Does he/she watch TV? When? What programs (**quelles émissions**)?
- Does he/she play video games? When? With whom?
- Does he/she play soccer (or another sport)? Where? When?
- Does he/she like to swim? When? Where?
- What does he/she like to do on weekends? When? Where? With whom?

5 **Curiosité**

ÉCRIRE Imagine that a French friend has just made the following statements. For each one, write down three or four related questions you could ask him or her.

Je joue au foot demain.

• Avec qui est-ce que tu joues?
• Où est-ce que vous jouez?
• À quelle heure est-ce que vous jouez?
• Pourquoi est-ce que vous jouez au foot?

LESSON REVIEW
CLASSZONE.COM

cent treize
Leçon 8 113

○ The *Créa-dialogue* provides models to guide but not limit students' creative language use. Recombination and re-entry of previously learned material provide students with opportunities to demonstrate how well they can communicate in French.

○ **Writing activities** encourage students to present their thoughts and ideas in written form and provide material for student portfolios.

Follow up with Diagnostic Review

Tests de contrôle provide comprehensive review activities that students can use to check their comprehension.

The **"learning tabs"** in the side column help students self diagnose and review what they can do and where to go for help.

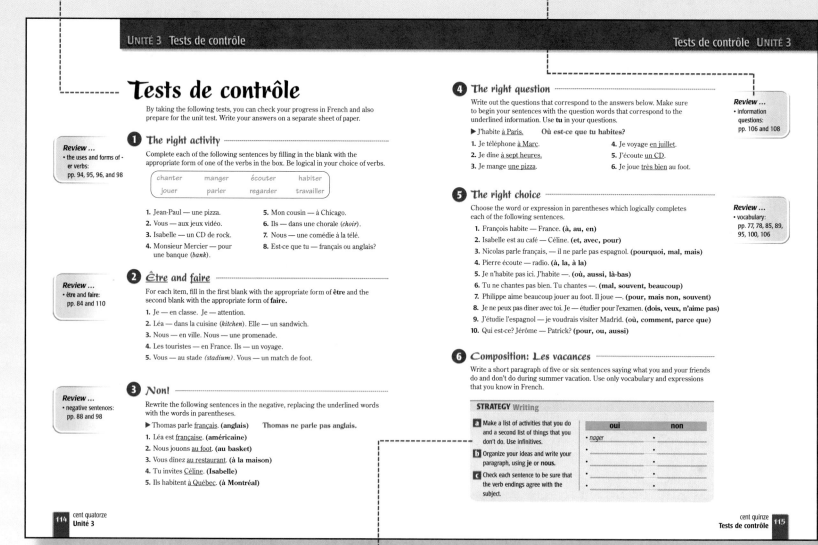

Tests de contrôle

By taking the following tests, you can check your progress in French and also prepare for the unit test. Write your answers on a separate sheet of paper.

Review ...
• the uses and forms of -er verbs:
pp. 94, 95, 96, and 98

1 The right activity

Complete each of the following sentences by filling in the blank with the appropriate form of one of the verbs in the box. Be logical in your choice of verbs.

| chanter | manger | écouter | habiter |
| jouer | parler | regarder | travailler |

1. Jean-Paul — une pizza.
2. Vous — aux jeux vidéo.
3. Isabelle — un CD de rock.
4. Monsieur Mercier — pour une banque (*bank*).
5. Mon cousin — à Chicago.
6. Ils — dans une chorale (*choir*).
7. Nous — une comédie à la télé.
8. Est-ce que tu — français ou anglais?

Review ...
• être and faire:
pp. 84 and 110

2 Être and faire

For each item, fill in the first blank with the appropriate form of **être** and the second blank with the appropriate form of **faire.**

1. Je — en classe. Je — attention.
2. Léa — dans la cuisine (*kitchen*). Elle — un sandwich.
3. Nous — en ville. Nous — une promenade.
4. Les touristes — en France. Ils — un voyage.
5. Vous — au stade (*stadium*). Vous — un match de foot.

Review ...
• negative sentences:
pp. 88 and 98

3 Non!

Rewrite the following sentences in the negative, replacing the underlined words with the words in parentheses.

▶ Thomas parle <u>français</u>. **(anglais)**   Thomas ne parle pas anglais.

1. Léa est <u>française</u>. **(américaine)**
2. Nous jouons <u>au foot</u>. **(au basket)**
3. Vous dînez <u>au restaurant</u>. **(à la maison)**
4. Tu invites <u>Céline</u>. **(Isabelle)**
5. Ils habitent <u>à Québec</u>. **(à Montréal)**

4 The right question

Write out the questions that correspond to the answers below. Make sure to begin your sentences with the question words that correspond to the underlined information. Use **tu** in your questions.

▶ J'habite <u>à Paris</u>.   **Où est-ce que tu habites?**

1. Je téléphone <u>à Marc</u>.
2. Je dîne <u>à sept heures</u>.
3. Je mange <u>une pizza</u>.
4. Je voyage <u>en juillet</u>.
5. J'écoute <u>un CD</u>.
6. Je joue <u>très bien</u> au foot.

Review ...
• information questions:
pp. 106 and 108

5 The right choice

Choose the word or expression in parentheses which logically completes each of the following sentences.

1. François habite — France. **(à, au, en)**
2. Isabelle est au café — Céline. **(et, avec, pour)**
3. Nicolas parle français, — il ne parle pas espagnol. **(pourquoi, mal, mais)**
4. Pierre écoute — radio. **(à la, à la)**
5. Je n'habite pas ici. J'habite —. **(où, aussi, là-bas)**
6. Tu ne chantes pas bien. Tu chantes —. **(mal, souvent, beaucoup)**
7. Philippe aime beaucoup jouer au foot. Il joue —. **(pour, mais non, souvent)**
8. Je ne peux pas dîner avec toi. Je — étudier pour l'examen. **(dois, veux, n'aime pas)**
9. J'étudie l'espagnol — je voudrais visiter Madrid. **(où, comment, parce que)**
10. Qui est-ce? Jérôme — Patrick? **(pour, ou, aussi)**

Review ...
• vocabulary:
pp. 77, 78, 85, 89, 95, 100, 106

6 Composition: Les vacances

Write a short paragraph of five or six sentences saying what you and your friends do and don't do during summer vacation. Use only vocabulary and expressions that you know in French.

STRATEGY Writing

a Make a list of activities that you do and a second list of things that you don't do. Use infinitives.

b Organize your ideas and write your paragraph, using **je** or **nous.**

c Check each sentence to be sure that the verb endings agree with the subject.

oui	non
• *nager*	•
•	•
•	•
•	•
•	•

Pre-writing strategies and **graphic organizers** help students become successful writers.

Thematic French-English vocabulary presentation brings together all unit vocabulary for easy review.

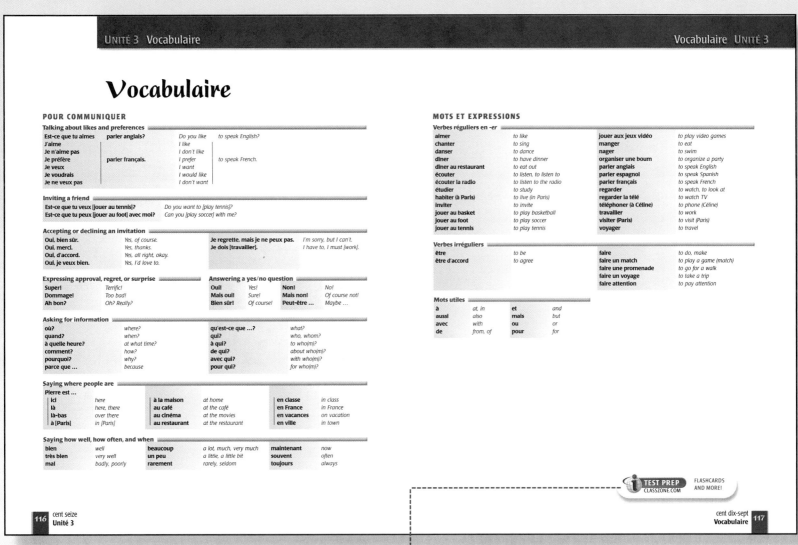

UNITÉ 3 Vocabulaire

Vocabulaire UNITÉ 3

Vocabulaire

POUR COMMUNIQUER

Talking about likes and preferences

Est-ce que tu aimes	parler anglais?	Do you like	to speak English?
J'aime		I like	
Je n'aime pas		I don't like	
Je préfère	parler français.	I prefer	to speak French.
Je veux		I want	
Je voudrais		I would like	
Je ne veux pas		I don't want	

Inviting a friend

Est-ce que tu veux [jouer au tennis]?	Do you want to [play tennis]?
Est-ce que tu peux [jouer au foot] avec moi?	Can you [play soccer] with me?

Accepting or declining an invitation

Oui, bien sûr.	Yes, of course.	Je regrette, mais je ne peux pas.	I'm sorry, but I can't.
Oui, merci.	Yes, thanks.	Je dois [travailler].	I have to, I must [work].
Oui, d'accord.	Yes, all right, okay.		
Oui, je veux bien.	Yes, I'd love to.		

Expressing approval, regret, or surprise

Super!	Terrific!
Dommage!	Too bad!
Ah bon?	Oh? Really?

Answering a yes/no question

Oui!	Yes!	Non!	No!
Mais oui!	Sure!	Mais non!	Of course not!
Bien sûr!	Of course!	Peut-être ...	Maybe ...

Asking for information

où?	where?	qu'est-ce que ...?	what?
quand?	when?	qui?	who, whom?
à quelle heure?	at what time?	à qui?	to who(m)?
comment?	how?	de qui?	about who(m)?
pourquoi?	why?	avec qui?	with who(m)?
parce que ...	because	pour qui?	for who(m)?

Saying where people are

Pierre est ...

ici	here	à la maison	at home	en classe	in class
là	here, there	au café	at the café	en France	in France
là-bas	over there	au cinéma	at the movies	en vacances	on vacation
à [Paris]	in [Paris]	au restaurant	at the restaurant	en ville	in town

Saying how well, how often, and when

bien	well	beaucoup	a lot, much, very much	maintenant	now
très bien	very well	un peu	a little, a little bit	souvent	often
mal	badly, poorly	rarement	rarely, seldom	toujours	always

MOTS ET EXPRESSIONS

Verbes réguliers en -er

aimer	to like	jouer aux jeux vidéo	to play video games
chanter	to sing	manger	to eat
danser	to dance	nager	to swim
dîner	to have dinner	organiser une boum	to organize a party
dîner au restaurant	to eat out	parler anglais	to speak English
écouter	to listen, to listen to	parler espagnol	to speak Spanish
écouter la radio	to listen to the radio	parler français	to speak French
étudier	to study	regarder	to watch, to look at
habiter (à Paris)	to live (in Paris)	regarder la télé	to watch TV
inviter	to invite	téléphoner (à Céline)	to phone (Céline)
jouer au basket	to play basketball	travailler	to work
jouer au foot	to play soccer	visiter (Paris)	to visit (Paris)
jouer au tennis	to play tennis	voyager	to travel

Verbes irréguliers

être	to be	faire	to do, make
être d'accord	to agree	faire un match	to play a game (match)
		faire une promenade	to go for a walk
		faire un voyage	to take a trip
		faire attention	to pay attention

Mots utiles

à	at, in	et	and
aussi	also	mais	but
avec	with	ou	or
de	from, of	pour	for

TEST PREP
CLASSZONE.COM
FLASHCARDS AND MORE!

○ **Online test prep** at ClassZone.com prepares students to be successful test takers.

Develop Reading Skills and Experience French and Francophone Culture

Ce week-end, à la télé

Le week-end, les jeunes Français regardent souvent la télé. Ils aiment regarder les films et le sport. Ils regardent aussi les jeux et les séries américaines et françaises. Les principales chaînes° sont TF1, France 2, France 3, Cinquième Arte, M6 et Canal Plus. Voici le programme de télévision pour ce week-end.

chaînes *channels*

Note In French TV listings, times are expressed using a 24-hour clock. In this system, 8 p.m. is 20.00 (**vingt heures**), 9 p.m. is 21.00 (**vingt et une heures**), 10 p.m. is 22 heures (**vingt-deux heures**), etc.

SÉLECTION DE LA SEMAINE	VENDREDI	SAMEDI
TF1	**20.50** Magazine **SUCCÈS** Émission présentée par Julien Courbet et Anne Magnien **23.15** MAGAZINE • **Célébrités**	**20.50** Jeu **QUI VEUT GAGNER DES MILLIONS?** avec Jean-Pierre Foucault **21.50** SÉRIE • **Les Soprano**
2 *France*	**20.55** Série **HÔTEL DE POLICE** **Le gentil Monsieur** de Claude Barrois avec Cécile Magnet **23.20** DOCUMENTAIRE • **Histoires Naturelles**	**21.00** Variétés **CHAMPS-ÉLYSÉES** Invités: Ricky Martin, Juliette Binoche, Ben Affleck **22.35** SÉRIE • **Buffy contre les Vampires**
france 3	**21.00** Film **LE CINQUIÈME ÉLÉMENT** de Luc Besson avec Bruce Willis et Milla Jovovich **22.15** CONCERT • **Viva Latino**	**20.40** Série **INSPECTEUR BARNABY** avec Daniel Casey **22.50** SPORT • **Grand Prix d'Italie** Motocyclisme
france 5 arte	**20.45** Documentaire **CATHÉDRALES** de Jean-François Delassus **22.20** FILM • **Quasimodo, le bossu de Notre Dame**	**20.50** Documentaire **ARCHITECTURES** La Tour Eiffel **20.05** CONCERT • **Le Philharmonique de Vienne**
M6	**20.50** Variétés **GRAINES DE STAR** émission présentée par Laurent Boyer **22.20** THÉÂTRE • **Rhinocéros**	**20.35** Film **LE MARIAGE DE MON MEILLEUR AMI** avec Julia Roberts **22.15** SÉRIE • **Police District**
CANAL+	**20.50** Football **MARSEILLE-NICE** Championnat de France **22.50** FILM • **Air Force One** avec Harrison Ford	**20.45** Film **MON PÈRE, CE HÉROS** avec Gérard Depardieu **23.15** RUGBY • **Toulouse-Biarritz**

○ *Entracte: Lecture et Culture* supports the development of reading skills, cultural awareness, and vocabulary in context.

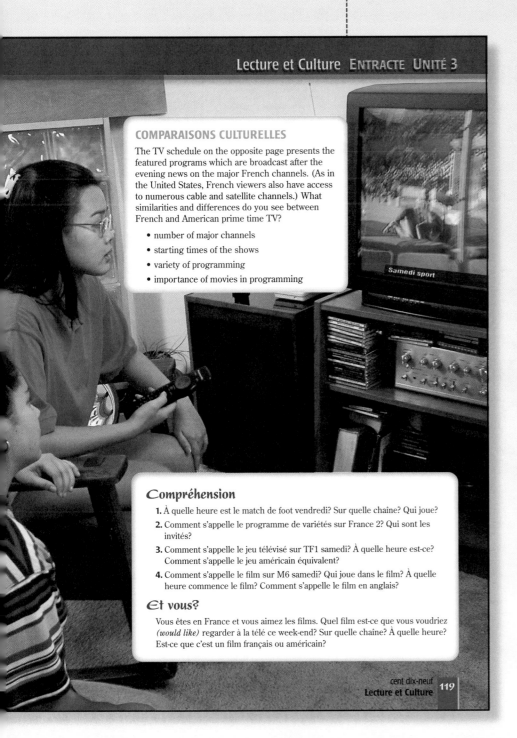

Lecture et Culture **ENTRACTE UNITÉ 3**

COMPARAISONS CULTURELLES

The TV schedule on the opposite page presents the featured programs which are broadcast after the evening news on the major French channels. (As in the United States, French viewers also have access to numerous cable and satellite channels.) What similarities and differences do you see between French and American prime time TV?

- number of major channels
- starting times of the shows
- variety of programming
- importance of movies in programming

Compréhension

1. À quelle heure est le match de foot vendredi? Sur quelle chaîne? Qui joue?

2. Comment s'appelle le programme de variétés sur France 2? Qui sont les invités?

3. Comment s'appelle le jeu télévisé sur TF1 samedi? À quelle heure est-ce? Comment s'appelle le jeu américain équivalent?

4. Comment s'appelle le film sur M6 samedi? Qui joue dans le film? À quelle heure commence le film? Comment s'appelle le film en anglais?

Et vous?

Vous êtes en France et vous aimez les films. Quel film est-ce que vous voudriez *(would like)* regarder à la télé ce week-end? Sur quelle chaîne? À quelle heure? Est-ce que c'est un film français ou américain?

cent dix-neuf
Lecture et Culture 119

L'INTERNET, c'est cool!

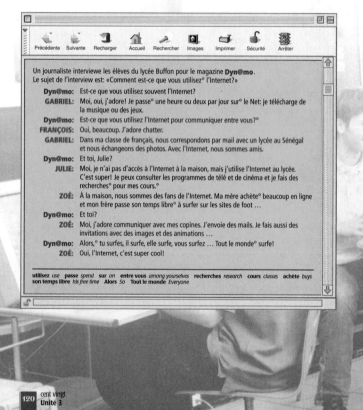

Un journaliste interviewe les élèves du lycée Buffon pour le magazine **Dyn@mo**.
Le sujet de l'interview est: «Comment est-ce que vous utilisez° l'Internet?»

Dyn@mo: Est-ce que vous utilisez souvent l'Internet?

GABRIEL: Moi, oui, j'adore! Je passe° une heure ou deux par jour sur° le Net: je télécharge de la musique ou des jeux.

Dyn@mo: Est-ce que vous utilisez l'Internet pour communiquer entre vous?°

FRANÇOIS: Oui, beaucoup. J'adore chatter.

GABRIEL: Dans ma classe de français, nous correspondons par mail avec un lycée au Sénégal et nous échangeons des photos. Avec l'Internet, nous sommes amis.

Dyn@mo: Et toi, Julie?

JULIE: Moi, je n'ai pas d'accès à l'Internet à la maison, mais j'utilise l'Internet au lycée. C'est super! Je peux consulter les programmes de télé et de cinéma et je fais des recherches° pour mes cours.°

ZOÉ: À la maison, nous sommes des fans de l'Internet. Ma mère achète° beaucoup en ligne et mon frère passe son temps libre° à surfer sur les sites de foot …

Dyn@mo: Et toi?

ZOÉ: Moi, j'adore communiquer avec mes copines. J'envoie des mails. Je fais aussi des invitations avec des images et des animations …

Dyn@mo: Alors,° tu surfes, il surfe, elle surfe, vous surfez … Tout le monde° surfe!

ZOÉ: Oui, l'Internet, c'est super cool!

utilisez *use* **passe** *spend* **sur** *on* **entre vous** *among yourselves* **recherches** *research* **cours** *classes* **achète** *buys*
son temps libre *his free time* **Alors** *So* **Tout le monde** *Everyone*

NOTE culturelle

Les jeunes Français et l'Internet
French people are technologically very sophisticated. They developed the **Minitel**, a precursor of the Internet, many years before this newer system of transmitting information became universally adopted.

At school, French students learn how to use the Internet in their computer science classes (**les cours d'informatique**). Many have Internet connections at home. Those who do not can go to a **cybercafé** where they can surf the Net while having a sandwich or a soda.

PETIT DICTIONNAIRE DE L'INTERNET

Télérama
le site internet

- **chatter** = *to chat*
- **envoyer un mail (un mél)** = *to send an e-mail*
- **surfer sur l'Internet (le Net)** = *to surf the Internet*
- **télécharger** = *to download*
- **être en ligne** = *to be online*

COMPARAISONS CULTURELLES

Read the **Dyn@mo** interview again and make a list of the different ways students at the lycée Buffon use the Internet. Then list the ways in which you use the Internet. Do you engage in some of the same activities as the French teenagers?

les jeunes Français	moi
•	•
•	•
•	•

● **Cultural comparisons** help students appreciate the similarities and differences between American and French cultures.

Bonjour, Trinh!

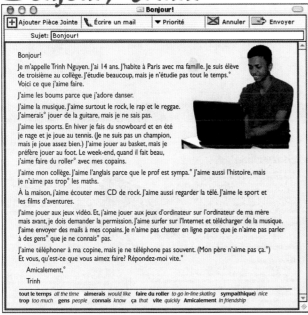

🖂 Bonjour!

✚ Ajouter Pièce Jointe | ✎ Écrire un mail | ▼ Priorité | ✖ Annuler | ➡ Envoyer

Sujet: Bonjour!

Bonjour!

Je m'appelle Trinh Nguyen. J'ai 14 ans. J'habite à Paris avec ma famille. Je suis élève de troisième au collège. J'étudie beaucoup, mais je n'étudie pas tout le temps.°
Voici ce que j'aime faire.

J'aime les boums parce que j'adore danser.

J'aime la musique. J'aime surtout le rock, le rap et le reggae. J'aimerais° jouer de la guitare, mais je ne sais pas.

J'aime les sports. En hiver je fais du snowboard et en été je nage et je joue au tennis. (Je ne suis pas un champion, mais je joue assez bien.) J'aime jouer au basket, mais je préfère jouer au foot. Le week-end, quand il fait beau, j'aime faire du roller° avec mes copains.

J'aime mon collège. J'aime l'anglais parce que le prof est sympa.° J'aime aussi l'histoire, mais je n'aime pas trop° les maths.

À la maison, j'aime écouter mes CD de rock. J'aime aussi regarder la télé. J'aime le sport et les films d'aventures.

J'aime jouer aux jeux vidéo. Et, j'aime jouer aux jeux d'ordinateur sur l'ordinateur de ma mère mais avant, je dois demander la permission. J'aime surfer sur l'Internet et télécharger de la musique. J'aime envoyer des mails à mes copains. Je n'aime pas chatter en ligne parce que je n'aime pas parler à des gens° que je ne connais° pas.

J'aime téléphoner à ma copine, mais je ne téléphone pas souvent. (Mon père n'aime pas ça.°)
Et vous, qu'est-ce que vous aimez faire? Répondez-moi vite.°

Amicalement,°

Trinh

tout le temps *all the time* **aimerais** *would like* **faire du roller** *to go in-line skating* **sympa(thique)** *nice*
trop *too much* **gens** *people* **connais** *know* **ça** *that* **vite** *quickly* **Amicalement** *In friendship*

STRATEGY Reading

Cognates You have already discovered that there are many words in French that look like English words and have similar meanings. These are called cognates. Cognates let you increase your reading comprehension effortlessly. Be sure to pronounce them the French way!

- Sometimes the spelling is the same, or almost the same:

  un champion *champion*
  la permission *permission*

- Sometimes the spelling is a little different:

  les maths *math*

Activité écrite: Une lettre à Trinh

You are writing an e-mail to Trinh in which you introduce yourself and explain what you like to do. Be sure to use only vocabulary that you know in French. You may tell him:

- if you like music (and what kind)
- what sports you like to do in fall or winter
- what sports you like to do in spring or summer
- which school subjects you like and which you do not like
- what you like to do at home
- which programs you like to watch on TV
- what you like to do on the Internet and what you do not like to do

Writing Hint Use Trinh's letter as a model.

NOTE *culturelle*

Les Vietnamiens en France

Vietnam and other Southeast Asian countries like Laos and Cambodia have a long civilization. For a period of about eighty years until the mid-1950s, these countries were occupied and administered by France which established schools and promoted the use of the French language among their populations.

In recent years, many Vietnamese people like Trinh's family have emigrated to France. Vietnamese restaurants are very popular with French students because of their fine yet inexpensive cuisine.

○ Reading Strategies develop students' skills by emphasizing different ways to approach a variety of texts.

○ *Note culturelle* features the variety of cultures that make up the French-speaking world.

Implement ideas and lesson plans easily and effectively

The Expansion Activities, Planning Guide and Pacing Guide in the Teacher's Edition offer outstanding support to make teaching French adaptable to every situation.

● **Expansion Activities** spark students' excitement with new ways to learn language and culture.

UNITÉ 3 Expansion activities PLANNING AHEAD

Games

• Charades
Divide the class into two or three teams. Choose one of the vocabulary words from pages 74–75, and tell one member from each team the word for that round. These team members alternate acting out clues until one team guesses the correct word. The first team to guess the word gets a point and starts the next round with a new member from each team as performer. Set a 1-minute time limit for each round. The team with the most points is the winner.

Pacing Suggestion: Upon completion of Leçon 5.

• Mais non!
First, have each student draw a quick illustration of a person in one of the places taught in **Vocabulaire** on page 85. Ask students to write a true or false caption for their illustration. For example, if a student draws a boy near the Eiffel Tower, the caption might read either **Jean est à Paris** (true), or **Jean est à la maison** (false). Then divide the class into two teams. Have a student from one team show his or her illustration to the class and read the caption aloud. The first student to raise his or her hand gets the opportunity to respond «**Oui, c'est vrai**» or «**Mais non!**» If they respond «**Mais non!**» they must correct the sentence using **ne . . . pas** and name the place the illustration really portrays to earn a point. Have teams alternate presenting their drawings.

Pacing Suggestion: Upon completion of Leçon 6.

Projects

• Invitation à une boum
Have students create a party invitation. The invitations should tell when and where the party will be and who is throwing the party. Using vocabulary they have learned, students may wish to list the refreshments that will be served. The invitations should be decorated with markers, stickers, glitter, beads, etc. As a variation, you may want to have students create invitations online.

Pacing Suggestion: Upon completion of Leçon 7.

• Le Sénégal
Divide the class into small groups. Have each group find information about Senegal. Groups may:
* create a map that shows where Senegal is located
* find information about activities that are common among young people in Senegal
* find or create illustrations that show what Senegal looks like
* find information about the weather, people, politics, industry, etc., of Senegal

Each group should create a colorful booklet or pamphlet they can use to present the information they obtained to the rest of the class. Students can create these by hand or on the computer.

Pacing Suggestion: Upon completion of Leçon 8.

Bulletin Boards

• La musique francophone
Have students search the Internet to find out what singers, musical groups, and songs are currently popular in France or in francophone countries. (You could assign a different country to pairs or groups of students and suggest specific Web sites for their search.) Ask students to find photos of some of these artists and create a bulletin board about francophone music. You can expand the activity by having students draw comparisons between their findings and some of their favorite popular music groups and performers in the United States.

Pacing Suggestion: Upon completion of Leçon 5.

Storytelling

• Une mini-histoire
Model a brief conversation in which you call a friend. Invite your friend to do something you both enjoy, acting out the conversation with stuffed animals or puppets. Pass out copies of your conversation and say it aloud with pauses, allowing students to repeat after you, or fill in the words. Then have them work in pairs to expand on their versions. Ask students to write out their conversations, practice them for intonation, and perform them for the class.

Pacing Suggestion: Upon completion of Leçon 6.

• Écrire un poème
Explain to students that French is rich in rhyme. (You can point out, for example, that the infinitive form of all verbs ending in -er rhyme.) Have students brainstorm some rhyming words they have learned in French. Then have them use their lists of words to create a short poem. You may wish to ask for volunteers to share their poems with the class.

MODEL: Je n'aime pas nager, je préfère danser.
Mais je veux bien parler français.
Maintenant je ne peux pas nager,
Je ne peux pas danser.
Je dois étudier le français!

Pacing Suggestion: Upon completion of Leçon 7.

Recipe

• Fondue au chocolat
Fondue, which originated in Switzerland, is a typical French party food. Fondue can be made of melted cheese, chocolate, caramel, etc. You may wish to tell students that fondue is traditionally served in a fondue pot and that guests dip their foods using fondue forks.

Pacing Suggestion: Upon completion of Leçon 7.

Hands-on Crafts

• Le tama
Have pairs of students make a collage inspired by the **tama**, a traditional Senegalese drum, like the one pictured on this page. Suggest that students begin with colored or construction paper as a base. Ask them to bring in twine, rope, and other decorative materials to build up their two-dimensional drum designs into layers. When they have finished, have students set up a display of their drums.

Pacing Suggestion: Upon completion of Leçon 8.

End of Unit

• C'est moi!
Each student will create a poster to tell about his or her activities. First, have students write several sentences with their name, age, and several activities in which they participate. Then ask them to exchange papers with a classmate. Once they have corrected any errors, have students write their sentences on a poster, and use magazine photos or drawings to illustrate each sentence. You may want to have students give oral presentations to the class using their posters. As an alternative, have students act out and videotape their self-portraits.

Rubric   A = 13–15 pts. B = 10–12 pts. C = 7–9 pts. D = 4–6 pts. F = < 4 pts.

Criteria	Scale				
Vocabulary Use	1	2	3	4	5
Grammar/Spelling Accuracy	1	2	3	4	5
Creativity	1	2	3	4	5

Fondue au chocolat

Ingrédients
• 250 grammes de chocolat ou chocolat au lait
• 40 cl lait concentré sucré
• 10 cl lait
• des morceaux de gâteau et de fruits

Préparation
1. Cassez le chocolat en morceaux et mettez-le dans une casserole.
2. Ajoutez le lait et le lait concentré sucré.
3. Mélangez bien.
4. Ajoutez plus de lait si la fondue devient trop épaisse.
5. Piquez le fruit et le gâteau avec une fourchette et trempez-les dans le chocolat.

Pour huit personnes.

Ingredients
• approx. 8 oz. dark or milk chocolate
• approx. 1 cup sweetened condensed milk
• approx. 1/4 cup milk
• squares of cake and chunks of assorted fruit for dipping

Directions
1. Break the chocolate into pieces and melt it in a Crock-Pot.
2. Add regular milk and condensed milk.
3. Stir well.
4. Add extra milk if the mixture becomes too thick.
5. Use forks or skewers to dip cake or fruit into the chocolate.

Serves eight.

● **Easy-to-prepare recipes** give students a delicious opportunity to experience cuisine from France and the French-speaking world.

At-a-glance overviews outline the objectives and program resources for at-a-glance support.

Listening scripts in the Teacher's Edition provide the practical information needed for easier lesson preparation.

UNITÉ 3 — Student Text Listening Activity Scripts
AUDIO PROGRAM

▶ **LEÇON 5** LE FRANÇAIS PRATIQUE Mes activités

• **Préférences** *p. 74* CD 2, TRACK 1

How to talk about what you like and don't like to do. Écoutez et répétez.

Est-ce que tu aimes...? #
J'aime...#
Je n'aime pas...#
Je préfère...#

Now practice the names of the activities.

téléphoner #
parler français #
parler anglais #
parler espagnol #
manger #
chanter #
danser #
nager #
jouer au tennis #
jouer au basket #
jouer au foot #
jouer aux jeux vidéo #
regarder la télé #
écouter la radio #
dîner au restaurant #
voyager #
étudier #
travailler #

Est-ce que tu aimes parler français? #
Oui, j'aime parler français. #
Non, je n'aime pas parler français. #
Je préfère parler anglais. #

J'aime téléphoner. #
J'aime parler français. #
J'aime parler anglais. #
J'aime parler espagnol. #
J'aime manger. #
J'aime chanter. #
J'aime danser. #
J'aime nager. #
J'aime aussi jouer au tennis. #
J'aime aussi jouer au basket. #
J'aime aussi jouer au foot. #
J'aime aussi jouer aux jeux vidéo. #
Mais je préfère regarder la télé. #
Mais je préfère écouter la radio. #
Mais je préfère dîner au restaurant. #
Mais je préfère voyager. #
Je n'aime pas toujours étudier. #
Je n'aime pas...

• **Créa-dialogue** *p. 81* CD 2, TRACK 5

Listen to the following dialogues and match the invitations with the excuses.

Modèle: —Est-ce que tu veux jouer au tennis avec moi?
—Non, je ne peux pas. Je dois travailler.

1. —Est-ce que tu veux jouer au basket avec moi?
—Non, je ne peux pas. Je dois téléphoner à une copine. #
2. —Est-ce que tu veux manger une pizza?
—Non, je ne peux pas. Je dois dîner avec ma cousine. #
3. —Est-ce que tu veux regarder la télé?
—Non, je ne peux pas. Je dois parler avec ma mère. #
4. —Est-ce que tu veux jouer au ping-pong?
—Non, je ne peux pas. Je dois étudier. #
5. —Est-ce que tu veux dîner au restaurant?
—Non, je ne peux pas. Je dois chanter avec la chorale. #

▶ **LEÇON 6** Une invitation

• **Une invitation** *p. 82*

A. **Compréhension orale** CD 2, TRACK 6

Please turn to page 82 for complete *Compréhension orale* text.

B. **Écoutez et répétez.** CD 2, TRACK 7

You will now hear a paused version of the dialog. Listen to the speaker and repeat right after he or she has completed the sentence.

▶ **LEÇON 7** Une boum

• **Une boum** *p. 92*

A. **Compréhension orale** CD 2, TRACK 11

Please turn to page 92 for complete *Compréhension orale* text.

B. **Écoutez et répétez.** CD 2, TRACK 12

You will now hear a paused version of the dialog. Listen to the speaker and repeat right after he or she has completed the sentence.

• **Écoutez bien!** *p. 99* CD 2, TRACK 13

You will now hear French young people tell you what they do and do not like. Listen carefully to what they each say and determine if they do the following activities.

Modèle: Je ne joue pas au foot. Je joue au basket.

Let's begin.

1. Je parle anglais. Je ne parle pas espagnol. #
2. Je n'habite pas à Tours. J'habite à Paris. #
3. Je dîne à la maison. Je ne dîne pas au restaurant. #
4. Je téléphone à un copain. Je ne téléphone pas à une copine. #
5. Je ne mange pas une pizza. Je mange un sandwich. #
6. J'étudie l'espagnol. Je n'étudie pas l'anglais. #
7. Je n'écoute pas la radio. J'écoute un CD. #

• **Prononciation** *p. 101* CD 2, TRACK 14

Les voyelles /i/ et /u/

Écoutez: /u/ où? /i/ ici!

Be sure to pronounce the French "i" as in *Mimi*.

Répétez: /i/ # ici # Philippe...

1. Où est-ce que tu habites? #
2. À quelle heure est-ce que vous dînez? #
3. Comment est-ce que vous parlez français? #
4. Quand est-ce que vous visitez Dakar? #
5. Où est-ce que vous visitez Dakar? #
6. Quand est-ce que ton copain travaille? #
7. À quelle heure est-ce que ton copain voyage en France? #
8. Comment est-ce que tu chantes? #

• **Prononciation** *p. 111* CD 2, TRACK 20

La voyelle /y/

Écoutez: Super!

The vowel sound /y/—represented by the letter "u"—does not exist... first say the French word *si.* Then round your lips as if to whistle an... lips: /sy/. Now say *si-per.* Then round your lips as you say the first s...

Répétez: /y/ # super # tu # étudie # bien sûr # Lucie # Luc #

À votre tour!

• **Allô!** *p. 112* CD 2, TRACK 21

Fatou is phoning some friends. Match her questions on the left wi... answers on the right.

1. Qu'est-ce que tu fais?
2. Qu'est-ce que vous faites samedi?
3. Où est ton père?
4. Quand est-ce que tu veux jouer au tennis...

UNITÉ 3 — Planning Guide CLASSROOM MANAGEMENT

OBJECTIVES

Communication
- Describe some of your daily activities *pp. 72–73, 95*
- Say what you like and do not like to do *pp. 74–75, 77*
- Ask and answer questions about where others are and what they are doing *pp. 85–86, 89*
- Invite friends to do things with you *p. 78*
- Politely accept or turn down an invitation *p. 78*

Grammar
- Le verbe *être* et les pronoms sujets *pp. 84–85*
- Les questions à réponse affirmative ou négative *pp. 86–87*
- La négation *p. 88*
- Les verbes en *-er*: le singulier *p. 94*
- Les verbes en *-er*: le pluriel *p. 96*
- Le présent des verbes en *-er*: forme affirmative et forme négative *p. 98*
- La construction: verbe + infinitif *p. 101*
- Les questions d'information *p. 106*
- Les expressions interrogatives avec *qui p. 108*
- *Qu'est-ce que? p. 109*
- Le verbe *faire p. 110*
- L'interrogation avec inversion *p. 111*

Vocabulary
- Préférences *pp. 74–75*
- Souhaits *p. 77*
- Invitations *p. 78*
- Où? *p. 85*
- Expressions pour la conversation *pp. 87, 100, 107*
- Mots utiles *pp. 89, 100*
- Les verbes en *-er p. 95*
- Expressions interrogatives *p. 106*
- Expressions avec *faire p. 110*

Pronunciation
- La voyelle /a/ *p. 89*
- Les voyelles /i/ et /u/ *p. 101*
- La voyelle /y/ *p. 111*

Culture
- Le téléphone *p. 79*
- Le mercredi après-midi *p. 83*
- Une boum *p. 93*
- Le Sénégal *p. 105*
- Les jeunes Français et l'Internet *p. 121*
- Les Vietnamiens en France *p. 123*

PROGRAM RESOURCES

Print
- Workbook PE, *pp. 59–84*
- *Activités pour tous* PE, *pp. 33–49*
- Block Scheduling Copymasters, *pp. 33–64*
- Teacher to Teacher Copymasters
- Unit 3 Resource Book
  Lesson 5–8 Resources
  Workbook TE
  Activités pour tous TE
  Lesson Plans
  Block Scheduling Lesson Plans
  Family Letter
  Absent Student Copymasters
  Family Involvement
  Video Activities
  Videoscripts
  Audioscripts
  Assessment Program
  Unit 3 Resources
  Communipak
  Activités pour tous TE Reading
  Workbook TE Reading and Culture Activities
  Assessment Program
  Answer Keys

Audiovisual
- Audio Program PE CD 2 Tracks 1–23
- Audio Program Workbook CD 7 Tracks 1–21
- *Chansons* Audio CD
- Video Program Modules 5, 6, 7, 8
- Overhead Transparencies
  15 Où sont-ils?;
  12 Menu from "Le Select";
  16 Subject Pronouns;
  14a, 14b, 17 *-er* Verbs;
  16 Subject Pronouns;
  6 Clock face *Quelle heure est-il?*;
  8 Expressions with *faire*

Technology
- Online Workbook
- ClassZone.com
- eTest Plus Online/Test Generator CD-ROM
- EasyPlanner Plus Online/EasyPlanner CD-ROM
- Power Presentations on CD-ROM

Assessment Program Options
- Lesson Quizzes
- Portfolio Assessment
- Unit Test Form A
- Unit Test Form B
- Unit Test Part III (Alternate)
  Cultural Awareness
  Listening Comprehension Performance Test
  Speaking Performance Test
  Reading Comprehension Performance Test
  Writing Performance Test
- Multiple Choice Test Items
- Test Scoring Tools
- Audio Program CD 14 Tracks 1–16
- Answer Keys
- eTest Plus Online/Test Generator CD-ROM

Pacing Guide SAMPLE LESSON PLAN

DAY	DAY	DAY	DAY	DAY
1 Unité 3 Opener / Leçon 5 • Vocabulaire et Culture–Mes activités • Vocabulaire–Préférences	**2** Leçon 5 • Vocabulaire–Préférences (continued) • Vocabulaire–Souhaits	**3** Leçon 5 • Vocabulaire–Invitations • Note culturelle–Le téléphone	**4** Leçon 5 • À votre tour!	**5** Leçon 6 • Une invitation • Note culturelle–Le mercredi après-midi • Le verbe *être* et les pronoms sujets
6 Leçon 6 • Vocabulaire–Où? • Les questions à réponse affirmative ou négative	**7** Leçon 6 • Vocabulaire–Expressions pour la conversation • La négation	**8** Leçon 6 • La négation (continued) • Vocabulaire–Mots utiles • Prononciation–Le voyelle /a/	**9** Leçon 6 • À votre tour!	**10** Leçon 7 • Une boum • Note culturelle–Une boum • Les verbes en *-er*: le singulier • Vocabulaire–Les verbes en *-er*
11 Leçon 7 • Vocabulaire–Les verbes en *-er* (continued) • Les verbes en *-er*: le pluriel	**12** Leçon 7 • Le présent des verbes en *-er*: forme affirmative et forme négative	**13** Leçon 7 • Vocabulaire–Mots utiles • Vocabulaire–Expressions pour la conversation • La construction: verbe + infinitif	**14** Leçon 7 • Prononciation–Les voyelles /i/ et /u/ • À votre tour!	**15** Leçon 8 • Un concert de musique africaine • Note culturelle–Le Sénégal • Les questions d'information
16 Leçon 8 • Vocabulaire–Expressions interrogatives • Vocabulaire–Expressions pour la conversation	**17** Leçon 8 • Les expressions interrogatives avec *qui* • *Qu'est-ce que?*	**18** Leçon 8 • Le verbe *faire* • Vocabulaire–Expressions avec *faire* • L'interrogation avec inversion	**19** Leçon 8 • Prononciation–La voyelle /y/ • À votre tour!	**20** • Tests de contrôle
21 • Unit 3 Test	**22** • Entracte: Lecture et culture			

Time-saving lessons present sequenced teaching suggestions.

Suggests practical teaching ideas

The comprehensive Teacher's Edition and resource materials provide the support you need to introduce, explain, and expand your lessons.

○ **Point-of-use** references to program components help you integrate a variety of resources into your lessons with ease.

○ **Practical suggestions** for tailoring and enhancing your lessons help you meet the learning needs of all your students.

SECTION A

Communicative function
Identifying people and where they are

Teaching Resource Options

PRINT
Workbook PE, pp. 65–68
Unit 3 Resource Book
  Communipak, pp. 128–143
  Video Activities, pp. 50–51
  Videoscript, p. 53
  Workbook TE, pp. 33–36

AUDIO & VISUAL
Overhead Transparencies
15 *Où sont-ils?*

TECHNOLOGY
Power Presentations

VIDEO PROGRAM

VIDEO DVD
MODULE 6

6.2 Mini-scenes: Je suis en classe
(13:29–13:51 min.)

6.3 Mini-scenes: Où sont-ils?
(13:52–15:05 min.)

Teaching notes
Why begin with **être**?
The conjugation of the verb **être** is presented in Leçon 6, ahead of the **-er** verbs for the following reasons:
• **Être** is the most frequently used verb in the French language.
• Students are introduced to the concept of conjugation (in the affirmative, negative and interrogative) with a single verb. In Leçon 7, students will learn about infinitives, stems and endings.

♻ **Re-entry and review**

Remind students that they have already been using the singular forms of être:
  Je suis américain.
  Tu es français.
  Il est canadien.

Pronunciation note There is usually liaison after **est**: Elle **est** ici. Liaison is optional after other forms of **être**: Ils **sont** ici. or Ils **sont** ici.

84 · Langue et Communication
Unité 3 Leçon 6

A Le verbe *être* et les pronoms sujets

Être *(to be)* is the most frequently used verb in French. Note the forms of **être** in the chart below.

	être	to be	
SINGULAR	je **suis**	*I am*	Je **suis** américain.
	tu **es**	*you are*	Tu **es** canadienne.
	il/elle **est**	*he/she is*	Il **est** anglais.
PLURAL	nous **sommes**	*we are*	Nous **sommes** à Paris.
	vous **êtes**	*you are*	Vous **êtes** à San Francisco.
	ils/elles **sont**	*they are*	Ils **sont** à Genève.

→ Note the liaison in the **vous** form:
  Vous êtes français?

→ Note the expression **être d'accord** *(to agree)*:
  —Tu **es** d'accord   *Do you agree*
    avec moi?   *with me?*
  —Oui, je **suis** d'accord! *Yes, I agree!*

TU or VOUS?
When talking to ONE person, the French have two ways of saying *you*:

• **tu** ("familiar *you*") is used to talk to someone your own age (or younger) or to a member of your family
• **vous** ("formal *you*") is used when talking to anyone else

When talking to TWO or more people, the French use **vous**.

♻ **RAPPEL** You should use ...
• **vous** to address your teacher
• **tu** to address a classmate

LEARNING ABOUT LANGUAGE
• The words **je** *(I)*, **tu** *(you)*, **il** *(he)*, **elle** *(she)*, etc. are called SUBJECT PRONOUNS.
  • SINGULAR pronouns refer to one person (or object).
  • PLURAL pronouns refer to two or more people (or objects).
• The VERB **être** *(to be)* is IRREGULAR because its forms do not follow a predictable pattern.
• A chart showing the subject pronouns and their corresponding verb forms is called a CONJUGATION.

 Tu es français?   Vous êtes français?   Vous êtes français?

84 quatre-vingt-quatre
Unité 3

TEACHING NOTE Adapting instruction

To meet the needs of different learners, **Discovering French, *Nouveau!*** presents French structures in several ways:

▶ Structures in context (in dialogues)—for those who learn best by hearing and repeating.

▶ Charts and brief explanations—for those who need to understand a pattern before practicing it.

▶ Cartoon drawings (where appropriate)—for those who find it helpful to visualize a concept in picture form.

Langue et Communication LEÇON 6

ILS or ELLES?

The French have two ways of saying *they*:

* **ils** refers to two or more males or to a mixed group of males and females
* **elles** refers to two or more females

Ils sont à Paris. Ils sont à Bordeaux.

Ils sont à Lyon. Elles sont à Nice.

1 En France

PARLER/ÉCRIRE The following students are on vacation in France. Which cities are they in?

▶ Sophie … à Nice.   **Sophie est à Nice.**

1. Antoine … à Tours.
2. Nous … à Toulouse.
3. Vous … à Marseille.
4. Je … à Strasbourg.
5. Julie et Marie … à Lille.
6. Éric et Vincent … à Lyon.
7. Ma cousine … à Paris.
8. Tu … à Bordeaux.

VOCABULAIRE Où?

Où est Cécile?	*Where is Cécile?*
Elle est …	**ici** *(here)*
	à Paris *(in Paris)*
	en classe *(in class)*
	en vacances *(on vacation)*
	au café *(at the café)*
	à la maison *(at home)*

là *(here, there)*
à Boston
en ville *(in town)*
en France *(in France)*
au restaurant

là-bas *(over there)*
à Québec

au cinéma *(at the movies)*

2 À Tours

PARLER/ÉCRIRE You are spending your summer vacation in Tours at the home of your friend Léa. Ask the following people questions using **Tu es** or **Vous êtes** as appropriate.

▶ *(the mailman)* … français?   **Vous êtes français?**

1. *(Léa's mother)* … de Tours?
2. *(Léa's best friend)* … française?
3. *(Léa's brother)* … en vacances?
4. *(a lady in the park)* … française?
5. *(Léa's cousin)* … de Paris?
6. *(a little girl)* … avec ta mère?
7. *(Léa's teacher)* … strict?
8. *(a tourist)* … américain?

quatre-vingt-cinq **85**
Leçon 6

COMPREHENSION In France

PROPS: signs: Paris, Bordeaux, Lyon, Nice
Place signs dividing class into 4 "cities."
Voici Paris. Voici Bordeaux. etc.

Ask in which city students are.
Où est X? [À Bordeaux.]
Où sont Y et Z? [À Paris.]

Then have students move around.
X, où es-tu? [À Bordeaux.]
Lève-toi et va à Nice.
Où es-tu maintenant? [À Nice.] …
Y et Z, levez-vous et allez à Lyon.
Où êtes-vous? [À Lyon.] …

Optional, with full answers:
[Je suis à Nice.]

If students ask The pronouns **il** and **elle** may also mean *it*. Remind them that in **Invitation au français** they used sentences like:

[le sandwich] **Il coûte 5 euros.**

Learning aid Always use **vous** with people you address as **Monsieur**, **Madame**, or **Mademoiselle**.

Teaching tip Use **Transparency 16** (Subject pronouns) as a visual aid to present and practice verb forms throughout this program.

1 PRACTICE saying where people are

1. Antoine est à Tours.
2. Nous sommes à Toulouse.
3. Vous êtes à Marseille.
4. Je suis à Strasbourg.
5. Julie et Marie sont à Lille.
6. Éric et Vincent sont à Lyon.
7. Ma cousine est à Paris.
8. Tu es à Bordeaux.

> **Middle School Copymasters**
> Worksheet 1: *Où?*, p. 37

2 COMPREHENSION using tu and vous

1. Vous êtes de Tours?
2. Tu es française?
3. Tu es en vacances?
4. Vous êtes française?
5. Tu es de Paris?
6. Tu es avec ta mère?
7. Vous êtes strict?
8. Vous êtes américain?

If students ask In French, the word for vacation (**les vacances**) is always plural.

Comprehension Variation Use places from the **Vocabulaire** section: en classe, au café, au cinéma, à la maison …

Langue et Communication
Unité 3 LEÇON 6 · **85**

Answers for every activity are included in the wrap.

Cultural Reference Guide

Discovering French, *Nouveau!* BLEU Première partie

Note: *Page numbers in bold type refer to the Teacher's Edition.*

ANIMALS
domestic animals   35, **35**, 36, **36**, **187**
wild animals   175, 187

ARTS
French contributions   **5**

ATTITUDES AND VALUES
cars   173
cuisine and food   45, 54
friendship   26, 27, 136
money   52, 136
music   32
school   72

BIRTHDAYS   37, 62

CAFÉS   43, 44, 45, **45**, **48**, 49, **104**
ordering beverages   49
tipping   49

CARS   **171**, 173, 181
driver's license   173
parking   **146**

CINEMA
movies   72

CITIES
Chamonix, France   **4**
Dakar, Sénégal   105
Fort-de-France, Martinique   19
Montréal, Canada   31, **31**, **107**
Paris, France   **105**
Port-au-Prince, Haïti   151
Savigny-sur-Orge   124–126
Toulouse, France   191, **191**

CITY LIFE
châteaux   5
See also: Cafés, Museums,
    Restaurants

COMMUNICATIONS
l'Internet   120–121, 147
le Minitel   121
telephone   79
writing letters   123, 191

CONCERTS See Music

CURRENCY See Money

CYCLING See Sports

DAILY ACTIVITIES   79
See also: School, Leisure activities

ETHNIC DIVERSITY   6, 123

EXCHANGE PROGRAMS   **32**

FAMILY
family members   34, 35, **35**
family occasions   35, **35**
vacations   35

FAST FOODS AND SNACKS
la boulangerie   43
fast food restaurants   43, **43**, 45, **45**
la pâtisserie   43
street vendors   43, 44
See also: Cafés

FOOD   45
beverages   49–50, **49–50**
les crêpes   45
un croque-monsieur   **46**
ice cream   **45**
les pizzas   **44**
sandwiches   45–46, **46**, **104**
See also: Cafés, Fast food,
    Restaurants, School cafeteria

FRANCE   4
See also: Cities, Geography,
    Population, Regions

FRENCH CANADA
"Alouette"   69, **69**
Canadian flag   40
French language in Canada   17, 21, **61**, 173
See also: Cities: Montréal, Québec,
    French-speaking world: Québec

FRENCH-SPEAKING WORLD   **9**
Algeria   9, **9**, 40
Belgium   9
Cambodia   9
Cameroun   41
Côte d'Ivoire   9, **9**, 41
flags   40–41
Haïti   8, 40, 151
Lebanon   9

Louisiana   8
Luxembourg   9, 40
Madagascar   9, **9**
Mali   41
Morocco   9, **9**, 41
New England   8
North Africa   9, **9**
Québec   8, 31
République démocratique du Congo   9, 41
Sénégal   9, **9**, 41, **104**, 105
Switzerland   9, 40
Tunisia   9, **9**
Vietnam   9, 123
See also: Regions and departments
    of France

FRIENDS See Interpersonal relations

GEOGRAPHY
Alps   **4**, 5, **65**
beaches   4
France   4
Pyrénées   4, **4**

GREETINGS
la bise   13
formality   23, **23**, 84
forms of address   23
greetings   13, **15**, 23, **23**, 24
handshake   13

HISTORY AND HISTORICAL SITES
Gallo-Roman Period   **5, 16, 61**
Vikings   **29**

HOLIDAYS AND TRADITIONS
birthdays   37, 62
French flag   6
le Quatorze Juillet   89, **89**
French houses   5

INDUSTRY
automobile   173, **173**

INTERPERSONAL RELATIONS
compliments and insults   186
formality   23, **23**, 84
friendship   26, 27, **27**, 163
invitations   78
See also: Greetings

LANGUAGE

créole	19
French language in Canada	**17, 21, 61, 173**

LEISURE ACTIVITIES

after school	72, 83
dancing	93
parties	93, **93**
preferences	122

See also: Cafés, Cinema, Family, Holidays and traditions, Music, Reading, Sports, Television

MONEY

currency of French-speaking countries	6, **52**
French currency	6, 52, **53**

MOVIES See Cinema

MUSEUMS

le Louvre	2

MUSIC AND CONCERT HALLS

hi-fi equipment	**142**
Youssou N'Dour	105

NAMES

African and North African names	10–11
French names	10-11, **10-11**, 15, **15**, 26, **26**

PARIS

Eiffel Tower	20
le Louvre	2
Montmartre	5
l'Opéra	2
Saint-Germain-des-Prés	**172**
la Sorbonne	3

PEOPLE AND PERSONALITIES

Astérix	16
Bartholdi, Auguste	**20**
Baudelaire	**5**
Camus, Albert	**5**, 63
Colette	**5**
Corot, Jean-Baptiste	126
Debussy, Claude	**5**
Eiffel, Gustave	**20**
Gauguin, Paul	**5**
Hugo, Victor	**5**

Matisse	**5**
Youssou N'Dour	105
Ravel	**5**
Rampal, Jean-Pierre	**5**
Renoir, Auguste	**5**
Rousseau	**5**
Sartre, Jean-Paul	**5**
Voltaire	**5**

QUÉBEC

description and population	31

RADIO **108**

READING AND LITERATURE

comics	16
French literature	**5**

REGIONS AND DEPARTMENTS OF FRANCE 4

Alsace	4
Bretagne	4
DOM-TOM	**19**
French Guiana	**5, 21**
Guadeloupe	8
Martinique	8, **18**, 19, **19**
New Caledonia	8
Normandie	8, **29**
Provence	4, 5
Tahiti	8
Touraine	4

RESTAURANTS

Guide Michelin	**54**
ordering from a menu	**49**
types of restaurants	54

SCHOOL

le bac	128
cafeteria	18, 127, 162
classes, class schedules	**15**, 72, 130–131
le collège	**15**, 93, 128, **138**
foreign languages	130
homework	72
le lycée	93, 126–131, **138**
la rentrée	14-15
Wednesday afternoon	83

SHOPPING FOR CLOTHES

Les Galeries Lafayette	**154**

SPORTS

cycling	28
snowboarding	5
soccer	72
Tour de France	28, **28**

TECHNOLOGY

Airbus	191
Ariane rockets	**5, 21**, 191
cell phones	79
computers	120–121, 147
Internet	120–121, 147
le Minitel	121
satellites	5
TGV	3

TELEPHONE

cell phones	79
French phone numbers	**29**, 33, **33**
making phone calls	79
Quebec phone numbers	**17**

TELEVISION

French programs	118–119, **118–119**

TIME

French calendar	**61, 63, 159**
official time	**57**, 118
telling time	56, 58

TRADITIONS See Holidays and traditions

TRANSPORTATION AND TRAVEL

automobiles	173, **173**
bicycle	136
la contractuelle	**146**
mopeds	**143**, 188–189, **188–189**
scooters	**143**, 188–189, **188–189**
trains	3, 59

UNITED STATES

French attitudes toward	32
Statue of Liberty	20, **20**

VALUES See Attitudes and values

WEATHER 65, **65**

WEEKENDS AND VACATIONS **85**

Cultural Reference Guide

Discovering French, *Nouveau!* BLEU Deuxième partie

Note: *Page numbers in bold type refer to the Teacher's Edition.*

ANIMALS
domestic animals   **227**

ATTITUDES AND VALUES
cuisine and food   362, 387, **387**
fashion   256, 276, 302
money   285, 308
music   **323**, 341
quality of life   308, 319
school   **309**

BIRTHDAYS   349

CAFÉS   **387**
ordering beverages   **367**

CINEMA
movies   240–241, 308

CITIES
Bordeaux, France   194
Bruxelles, Belgium   242
Chamonix, France   265
Deauville, France   260, **373**
Fort-de-France, Martinique   359
Grenoble, France   194
Lille, France   194
Lyon, France   194, **194**
Marseille, France   194, **194**
Montréal, Canada   264, **264**, **321**
Nantes, France   194
New Orleans, Louisiana   **212**
Nice, France   194, 265
Paris, France   194, **194**, 205, **218**, 246–253
Port-au-Prince, Haïti   359
Québec, Canada   **198**, **287**, 358
Strasbourg, France   194
Toulon, France   194
Toulouse, France   194
Tours, France   195, **196**
Trois Îlets, Martinique   **415**
Versailles, France   391

CITY LIFE
apartment buildings   **201**, 226–227, 252
châteaux   195
churches   **197**, 248–249
neighborhoods   197
public buildings   195, 197, **197**, **202**, 205, 246–251
street names   196, **199**
See also Cafés, Museums, Restaurants

CLOTHING AND PERSONAL APPEARANCE
fashion   256, **258**, 276, 300–304
shopping for clothes   258–260, **258**, **260**, 262, 266

COMMUNICATIONS
post office   197
telephone   230

CONCERTS See Music

CUISINE
Creole cuisine   415
French terminology   364, 387
making crêpes   **386**, 416–417

CURRENCY See Money

CYCLING See Sports

EARNING A LIVING
part-time jobs   285

ETHNIC DIVERSITY   **235**

FAMILY
family members   229, **229**
family occasions   319
helping at home   308

FASHION
clothing   256, 258–260, 266, 276, 300–301

FAST FOODS AND SNACKS
la crêperie   416
fast food restaurants   **365**, 387
See also: Cafés

FOOD   **363**, 366–367, **366-367**, 371, 375, **375**, **385**, **397**
beverages   367, **367**
les crêpes   416, **416**, 417
desserts   367
ice cream   367
le pâté   397
les pizzas   413, **413**
See also: Cafés, Fast food, Restaurants, School cafeteria

FRANCE
See also: Cities, Geography, Population, Regions

FRENCH CANADA   **363**
le château Frontenac   **287**

French language in Canada 196, 258, 310, **364**, **367**
La Ronde   **321**
Mont Ste Anne   **313**
See also: Cities: Montréal, Québec, French-speaking world: Québec

FRENCH-SPEAKING WORLD
Algeria   242, 305
Belgium   242–243
Cameroun   **235**
Congo   **235**
Côte d'Ivoire   **235**
Haïti   359
Mali   **235**
Morocco   357, 358
North Africa   305, 358
Québec   358, 356, **363**
Sénégal   **235**
See also: Regions and departments of France

FRIENDS See Interpersonal relations

GEOGRAPHY
Alps   265

HISTORY AND HISTORICAL SITES
Gallo-Roman Period   **194**

HOLIDAYS AND TRADITIONS
birthdays   **349**
la Fête de la Musique   341
holidays   312, **312**, **313**
le Quatorze Juillet   **313**

HOUSING AND THE HOME
apartment buildings   **201**, 226, 227
floor plan   201, **201**
French houses   200, **200**, **416**
numbering of floors   227

INTERPERSONAL RELATIONS
meeting people   **218**
See also: Greetings

LANGUAGE
French language in Canada 196, 258, 310, **363**, **367**

LEISURE ACTIVITIES
after school   217, 308
dancing   308
parties   319

picnics	397, **397**
preferences	308, 319

See also: Cafés, Cinema, Family, Holidays and traditions, Music, Reading, Sports, Television

MARKETS

le marché	371, **371**

MEALS

le déjeuner	362, **362-363,** 366
le dîner	363, **363,** 366
le goûter	363, **363**
le petit déjeuner	362, **363, 366,** 414–415
picnics	397
typical French meals	**364,** 366–367, 375, 412, 414–415

See also: Fast foods and snacks, Restaurants, School cafeteria

MONEY

part-time jobs	285
spending money	285

MOVIES See Cinema

MUSEUMS

le Louvre	247, 250, 332
Mona Lisa	212, 250
le musée d'Orsay	247, 250, 332
le musée Picasso	332, 400

MUSIC AND CONCERT HALLS

concerts	**209,** 308, 341, **341**
la Fête de la Musique	341
hi-fi equipment	341
MC Solaar	245
preferences	**323,** 341
le Zénith	340

NAMES

Arab names	**304**

NEWSPAPERS AND MAGAZINES 324, 344

PARIS

administration	246
l'Arc de Triomphe	246, **247,** 249, 332
le bateau-mouche	**247,** 253
le Centre Pompidou	204–205, **205,** 247, 250, **250,** 252, 332
les Champs-Elysées	204–205, **205, 247,** 249
la Défense	251
Eiffel Tower	**247–248**
les Invalides	**246–247**
le jardin des Tuileries	**246**
le jardin du Luxembourg	**219**
le Louvre	247, 250, 332

Montmartre	249
monuments	209, 247, **247, 253**
le musée d'Orsay	247, 250, 332
le musée Picasso	332
Notre Dame	247, **247** 332
l'Opéra	**209, 246,** 247
le palais Omnisports Paris Bercy	247, 251
le parc de la Villette	204–205, **205,** 251
la Place de la Concorde	**246**
le Quartier latin	**219,** 247, 249, 252, 332
le Sacré Coeur	247–249
la Seine	246, 253

PEOPLE AND PERSONALITIES

Boucicaut, Aristide	266
Cardin, Pierre	256
Chanel, Coco	256
Dior, Christian	256
Hugo, Victor	196
La Fayette	196
Masséna	**199**
Molière	**199**
Monet, Claude	250, **250**
Moulin, Jean	**199**
Napoléon	**219,** 249, **249**
Pascal, Blaise	**199**
Pompidou, Georges	**250**
Renoir, Auguste	250, **250**
Saint Laurent, Yves	256
Solaar, MC	245
Sully, Duc de	**199**
Tintin	242–243
Toulouse-Lautrec, Henri de	250, **250**

QUÉBEC **280,** 340, **347**

READING AND LITERATURE

comics	242–243
Paris-Match	**324**
reading for pleasure	242–243, 308

REGIONS AND DEPARTMENTS OF FRANCE

Bretagne	416
Guadeloupe	**235,** 356, 415
Martinique	**235,** 309, 415
Normandie	260
Touraine	**196**

RELIGION **196**

RESTAURANTS

ordering from a menu	368, 413, **415**
types of restaurants	**373,** 387

SCHOOL

le bac	**309**
cafeteria	375, **375**

entrance exams	**309**
homework	**331, 389**

SHOPPING FOR CLOTHES 258–260, **258-260** 262, 276, 300–301

catalog shopping	275, 300–301
clothing stores and boutiques	256–257, **264, 276**
department stores	256, **264,** 266, **267,** 273
discount stores	256
Les Galeries Lafayette	**219,** 232, **247**
le Marché aux puces	256, 263, 276, 302
sales	303
shopping on the Internet	300–301

SHOPPING FOR FOOD **370**

les grandes surfaces	256
le marché	256, 371, **371**
specialty shops	**371**
supermarkets	371, 384

SHOPPING FOR VARIOUS ITEMS

les grandes surfaces	256

SPORTS 221, **312, 344**

participation	308
rollerblading	354–355
skiing	**312,** 313
snowboarding	309, 313
soccer	**220, 331**
Tour de France	**205**
windsurfing	**308**

TECHNOLOGY

cell phones	230

TELEPHONE

cell phones	230

TELEVISION

viewing habits	331

TRADITIONS See Holidays and traditions

TRANSPORTATION AND TRAVEL

le bateau-mouche	**247,** 253
buses	**210,** 253
le métro	253
taxis	253

VALUES See Attitudes and values

WEATHER **325**

WEEKENDS AND VACATIONS **309, 336**

summer vacation	308, **309**
weekends	308, 318–319, 356

WEIGHTS AND MEASURES

metric system	371, **371**

Universal Access in the Foreign Language Classroom

by Linda Carnine and Doug Carnine

Instructional Goal

The goal for all foreign language students in today's world is to learn to **speak** the language as well as to read and write it. Everyone can learn a foreign language as long as the instruction is explicit, direct, and systematic, and the learner is well placed. Forty years ago, foreign language instruction was mostly geared to the study of literature in the target language. More recently, due to more economical air travel, large waves of immigration, and more advanced technology, the emphasis has shifted to promoting spoken proficiency in the language studied. Students can advance to reading and writing according to their skill level, which is usually related to their skills in their native languages. Students who begin foreign language study in middle school or earlier (in immersion programs, for example) have an opportunity to study the culture, geography, history, and even dialects of the language. Nonetheless, the first expectation of instruction is that students will learn how to speak the language.

Adjusting Instruction for Diverse Learners

In this section we suggest strategies teachers can use to adjust instruction for diverse groups of students. Because research on teaching foreign language to diverse learners is quite limited, the suggestions are usually extrapolations from findings and practices in other areas. The student texts for *Discovering*

French, Nouveau! are designed for students near grade level. Instructional strategies provided in this section allow teachers to provide universal access to all students. Teachers may find it helpful to view students as members of four basic groups, namely, advanced learners, grade level learners, students with learning difficulties—including special education students—and Heritage learners. As a general guideline, the proficiency level students possess in their native language will determine how much differentiated instruction they need.

Three key strategies are recommended to meet the needs of students in all four groups:

1. **Frequent assessment** allows you to determine what each student does and does not know and provides the basis for instructional planning.
2. **Flexible grouping** strategies facilitate the management of a variety of achievement levels and learning needs (Learning Environments/ Teaching Strategies).
3. **Planned modifications in instruction** - planning ahead of time allows you to differentiate as the need arises during instruction.

Frequent Assessment

Assessment is an important way to create strong language students. Likewise, providing students with feedback via clear, well-articulated grading procedures also fosters strong language learners. Assessing foreign language

STRATEGIES BY STUDENT GROUP

STRATEGIES FOR ADVANCED GROUP Advanced students will be placed in accelerated classes in 9th grade and in Sophomore Honors, take the AP Language test (SAT-II) at the end of Junior year, and take the AP Literature test (SAT-II) at the end of Senior year. They will progress rapidly through the basics of the oral language and begin studying literature.	1. Involve students in a Pen Pal project to develop communication skills with peers in foreign countries. 2. Schedule meetings between Foreign Language and English teachers to develop common rubrics for literary analysis. 3. If taught in a heterogeneous class, substitute more challenging assignments for easier ones. 4. Make sure instruction is sufficiently complex and in-depth.
STRATEGIES FOR GRADE LEVEL GROUP Grade level students are usually college-oriented, have an adequate foreign language reading level, but need lots of visuals for instruction.	1. Assess what these students already know and adjust the rate of introduction of new material based on frequent assessments during instruction. 2. Provide cumulative review of sound/symbol relationships, vocabulary and grammatical forms taught; use flash cards for class and partner review. 3. Progress through *Discovering French, Nouveau!* at the recommended pace and sequence.
STRATEGIES FOR STUDENTS WITH LEARNING DIFFICULTIES GROUP Learners have the lowest functional vocabulary level, are very visual learners, and need more cumulative review.	1. Assess what these students already know and adjust rate of introduction of new material based on frequent assessments during instruction. 2. Focus primarily on oral language. 3. Explicitly teach sound/symbol relationships, separating difficult discriminations in introduction. 4. Introduce vocabulary through drawings and personalized vocabulary. 5. Provide daily oral practice through group responding, partner practice, and short presentations.
STRATEGIES FOR STUDENTS NEEDING INTENSIVE HELP (SPECIAL EDUCATION) Intensive needs students are those whose performance is two or more standard deviations below the mean on standardized measures. These students will probably be eligible for special education services. This is a very small percentage of the general population.	1. Determine reading level in English to guide the introduction of oral language content. 2. Follow the guidelines given for Students with Learning Difficulties. 3. Use a very visual approach and concentrate on oral language. 4. Directly teach sound/symbol relationships and vocabulary by clustering vocabulary words using sound/symbol relationship. 5. Place these students in lower grade level material if at all possible.

skills can be time consuming and demanding. *Discovering French, Nouveau!* offers multiple avenues for efficient assessment, including Lesson Quizzes, Unit Tests, and Proficiency Tests for Reading, Writing, Listening and Speaking. Complete guidelines for implementing Portfolio Assessment are also provided. Scoring criteria/rubrics accompany the Speaking and Writing Proficiency tests.

At the initial stages of language instruction, assessment can include simple tasks based on vocabulary students have learned, such as having students respond appropriately to greetings and simple classroom instructions. In addition to checking for listening comprehension, written comprehension tasks are also appropriate at the initial stages. For example, having students write a list of their 5 favorite foods (or 5 pieces of clothing) can serve as a quick writing assessment.

At the advanced levels, assessment of written work is structured by each classroom teacher. Grammatical structures and themes to be evaluated can be highlighted in the assessment directions and in the rubrics. If students are writing an essay based on a literary piece that they have read, allow the students to bring 3 x 5 cards to the test. These cards are prepared by the students to include quotes, verb forms, or special vocabulary they wish to include in their essay. No paragraphs should be allowed on the cards.

At a very formal level, national foreign language assessments provide schools with a summative evaluation of the advanced foreign language program. The SAT II is a traditional grammar and literature test. If your students take the SAT II in the fall, it will have a listening component. Advanced Placement tests in language and literature also provide program evaluation information. The Advanced Placement exams have a speaking component, whereas the SAT II does not.

Flexible Grouping Strategies

For large district implementations, flexible homogenous groupings are recommended.

Most districts organize foreign language students into three groups: the advanced/honors group, the grade level group, and the students with learning difficulties group. The emphasis for the scholarly, advanced group will be on literature and writing after the initial instruction in the spoken language. These students are usually expected to take both the SAT II language and literatures exams. The grade level, college-bound groups will progress at a less accelerated pace, taking the SAT II language test at the end of their senior year. The last group, students with learning difficulties, will have a primary emphasis on the spoken language during the high school program. Heritage learners may fit into any of the groups, but are more likely to be on or above grade level in their French class.

Planned Modification: Learning Environments and Teaching Strategies

For all types of students, one way to improve achievement is by providing high-quality, well-paced instruction. Depending on the learning activity, different seating arrangements may be desirable. Moveable chairs with an attached writing surface provide optimal flexibility. They allow for rearranging the room depending on the activity. For teacher-directed instruction in sound/symbol relationships, vocabulary, or grammar conventions, a large U shaped arrangement can work well. This allows you to observe all students, maximize active participation, and provide frequent feedback and quick pacing for familiar instructional routines.

Previous success in an area is a strong predictor of motivation. We also know that below-grade level students perform better when they are given the opportunity to have a higher rate of correct responses. Seating strategic learners closer to you may allow you to focus on their success rate and to give corrective feedback when confusions/errors occur.

Whenever possible, allow students to respond to a partner. The advantage of peer responses is that partnering fulfills students' desire to talk to each other. Besides having a social benefit, it provides a safe opportunity to respond as well as to receive feedback. The more opportunities students have to verbalize their answers and to receive feedback, the better they will be able to develop their oral language skills.

Planned Modifications for Vocabulary Development

Use visuals as much as possible, and have students bring in visuals to talk about. Anything from family photos to a video of their bedrooms will enhance and personalize oral communication, plus offer a supplement to the activities provided in the text. This emphasis on visuals is effective across all groups and levels, and will support the learning of all students, regardless of the diversity of their background knowledge.

The more personal the teacher can make vocabulary instruction, the more meaningful the response of the student. For example, in the classroom with students with learning difficulties, you may act out a dialog between friends eating at a sidewalk cafe. A quick discussion of the similarities and differences between eating at a sidewalk café and a food court in a shopping mall will personalize the vocabulary and the setting. In an advanced class, as students read a literary piece about a king who threatens capital punishment, the class can debate the pros and cons of capital punishment. Personalize your class activities and support them with visuals.

Students with learning difficulties, including special education students, will require the most frequent cumulative review. This can be done efficiently using flash cards. When initially introducing a new sound/symbol relationship or term, add the new item much more frequently among the review cards to provide massed practice. Once students are responding correctly 100% of the time, review the new items less frequently. Try to separate the introduction of difficult-to-discriminate symbols and words.

For grade level learners as well as strategic learners, set up all new vocabulary on cards, using either a picture, an English word or symbol, or a cue for an idiomatic expression. Students also benefit from having their own deck of cards, which can then be used in partner review in the classroom. For advanced learners, the cards can be extended to include lists of vocabulary and summarize grammatical structures and cultural notes. For all students, pictures can be drawn on large oak tag (8 x 10) to elicit stories.

GENERAL BACKGROUND: Questions and Answers

What are the Goals and Standards for Foreign Language Learning?

Over the past several years, the federal government has supported the development of Standards in many K-12 curriculum areas such as math, English, fine arts, and geography. These Standards are "content" standards and define what students should "know and are able to do" at the end of grades 4, 8 and 12. Moreover, the Standards are meant to be challenging, and their attainment should represent a strengthening of the American educational system.

In some subject matter areas, these Standards have formed the basis for building tests used in the National Assessment of Education Progress (NAEP). At that point, it was necessary to develop "performance" standards which define "how well" students must do on the assessment measure to demonstrate that they have met the content standards.

As far as states and local school districts are concerned, both implementation of the Standards and participation in the testing program are voluntary. However, the very existence of these standards is seen as a way of improving our educational system so as to make our young people more competitive on the global marketplace.

How are the Goals and Standards for Foreign Language Learning defined?

The Goals and Standards for Foreign Language Learning contain five general goals which focus on communication, culture, and the importance of second language competence in enhancing the students' ability to function more effectively in the global community of the 21st century. These five goals, each with their accompanying standards, are shown in the chart below. In the formal report, these standards are defined in greater detail with the addition of sample "benchmarks" or learning outcomes for grades 4, 8 and 12, and are illustrated with sample learning scenarios.

STANDARDS FOR THE LEARNING OF FRENCH

GOAL 1: **Communication** Communicate in French	**Standard 1.1 Interpersonal Communication** Students engage in conversations or correspondence in French to provide and obtain information, express feelings and emotions, and exchange opinions. **Standard 1.2 Interpretive Communication** Students understand and interpret spoken and written French on a variety of topics. **Standard 1.3 Presentational Communication** Students present information, concepts, and ideas in French to an audience of listeners or readers.
GOAL 2: **Cultures** Gain Knowledge and Understanding of the Cultures of the Francophone World	**Standard 2.1 Practices of Culture** Students demonstrate an understanding of the relationship between the practices and perspectives of the cultures of the francophone world. **Standard 2.2 Products of Culture** Students demonstrate an understanding of the relationship between the products and perspectives of the cultures of the francophone world.
GOAL 3: **Connections** Use French to Connect with Other Disciplines and Expand Knowledge	**Standard 3.1 Making Connections** Students reinforce and further their knowledge of other disciplines through French. **Standard 3.2 Acquiring Information** Students acquire information and recognize the distinctive viewpoints that are available through francophone cultures.
GOAL 4: **Comparisons** Develop Insight through French into the Nature of Language and Culture	**Standard 4.1 Language Comparisons** Students demonstrate understanding of the nature of language through comparisons of French and their native language. **Standard 4.2 Cultural Comparisons** Students demonstrate understanding of the concept of culture through comparisons of francophone cultures and their own.
GOAL 5: **Communities** Use French to Participate in Communities at Home and Around the World	**Standard 5.1 School and Community** Students use French both within and beyond the school setting. **Standard 5.2 Lifelong Learning** Students show evidence of becoming life-long learners by using French for personal enjoyment and enrichment.

Teaching to the Standards

The new Standards for Foreign Language Learning focus on the outcomes of long K-12 sequences of instruction. In most schools, however, French programs begin at the Middle School or Secondary level. With **Discovering French, *Nouveau!*** teachers can effectively teach toward these goals and standards while at the same time maintaining realistic expectations for their students.

*With **Discovering French, Nouveau!** teachers can effectively teach towards these goals and standards while at the same time maintaining realistic expectations for their students.*

GOAL ONE: Communicate in French

From the outset, **Discovering French, *Nouveau!*** students learn to communicate in French. In the *Invitation au français* opening section of **DFN-Bleu**, the focus is on understanding what French young people are saying (on video, DVD, and audio) and on exchanging information in simple conversations. In units 3–6, the oral skills are supplemented by the written skills, and students learn to read and express themselves in writing.

As students progress through **DFN-Blanc** and **DFN-Rouge**, they learn to engage in longer conversations, read and interpret more challenging texts, and understand French-language films and videos. Teachers who incorporate portfolio assessment into their programs will have the opportunity to keep samples of both written and recorded student presentations.

GOAL TWO: Gain Knowledge and Understanding of the Cultures of the Francophone World

In **Discovering French, *Nouveau!*** students are introduced to the diversity of the French-speaking world. In **DFN-Bleu**, the emphasis is on contemporary culture — in France, of course, but also in Quebec, the Caribbean, and Africa. Students learn to observe and analyze cultural differences in photographs and on the video program.

GOAL THREE: Use French to Connect with Other Disciplines and Expand Knowledge

It is especially in **DFN-Rouge** that students have the opportunity to use the French language to learn about history, art, music, social concerns and civic responsibilities. Topics suggested in the student text can be coordinated with colleagues across the school curriculum.

GOAL FOUR: Develop Insight through French into the Nature of Language and Culture

From the outset, **Discovering French, *Nouveau!*** draws the students' attention to the way in which French speakers communicate with one another, and how some of these French patterns differ from American ones (for example, shaking hands or greeting friends with a *bise*). Notes in the Teacher's Edition provide suggestions for encouraging cross-cultural observation. English and French usage are also compared and contrasted, as appropriate.

GOAL FIVE: Use French to Participate in Communities at Home and Around the World

In **Discovering French, *Nouveau!*** beginning students are invited to exchange letters with French-speaking pen pals. In addition, students are encouraged to participate in international student exchanges. The Teacher's Edition has a listing of addresses of organizations that can provide these types of services. In addition, teachers are given information on where to obtain French-language publications for their classes, and where to find French-language material on the Internet. In **DFN-Rouge**, students are invited to discover French-language videos which in many parts of the country can be found in a local video store. As students experience the satisfaction of participating in authentic cultural situations, they become more confident in their ability to use their skills in the wider global community.

For more information on the National Standards project and its publications, contact: **National Standards in Foreign Language Education, 6 Executive Plaza, Yonkers, NY 10701-6801; phone: (914) 963-8830 or on the Internet go to: www.actfl.org**

Since young adolescents have their own specific learning needs, an effective foreign language program for the middle level must provide both age-appropriate and developmentally-appropriate materials and activities. Teaching French to middle school students presents a special challenge: many types of learners as well as varying developmental ability levels need to be addressed. With **Discovering French, Nouveau!** the middle school language classroom can become an exciting environment that provides opportunities for success for all students.

Teaching French at the Middle School level

What are the primary educational goals in Middle School?

The primary educational goals at the middle level are similar to those at any stage of early language introduction. Students should be given the opportunity to:

- learn successfully
- develop critical thinking skills
- become better global citizens

How are these goals best reached?

It is at the "how" level that teachers at the middle level need to establish age-appropriate learning environments and select developmentally appropriate learning experiences. In particular, effective Middle School programs...

- focus on process, rather than memorization of content
- use a full range of communication skills
- integrate technology into the subject area
- organize the curriculum around meaningful themes
- incorporate a variety of methodologies linked to differing learning styles
- encourage active participation of all students in the learning process
- provide opportunities for authentic assessment

In what way can these goals be realized in French classes?

In French classes, young adolescents learn to communicate with one another in a second language. They are introduced to the richness and variety of the multi-cultural French-speaking world, thus increasing their own global awareness. In **Discovering French, Nouveau!** the focus is precisely on interactive learning. The daily-life lesson themes encourage students to learn about one another and appreciate their classmates' similarities and differences. As they progress through the program in manageable steps, they experience success in using the French language for communication and can assess their progress in realistic contexts.

What is the role of the textbook in a Middle School French class?

With the emphasis on process, rather than content, many teachers at the middle level prefer to focus on non-textbook materials for much of the class work, using the textbook more as a reference tool and source of reading materials. An important role of the effective French textbook, however, is to present the new language in meaningful, yet manageable, increments, and allow for continuous recycling and regular reentry of new phrases and vocabulary. In this way, the textbook provides a carefully constructed framework around which each teacher can personalize his or her lesson plans.

What should be the place of technology in the Middle School French program?

For young adolescents, technology in the classroom should encourage interaction and collaboration, rather than having students work alone or be passive spectators. Moreover, media should be used to enhance students' learning and to encourage self-expression in purposeful contexts.

In **Discovering French, Nouveau!** the media support has been designed specifically to meet the above goals. The *Video Program* not only has interactive segments that elicit students' responses, but the *Video Activities* encourage multiple viewings and provide communicative practice. Similarly, the *Audio Program* lets students listen to authentic speech, and encourages them to work together in guided listening activities.

How do French classes interrelate with other Middle School subject matter areas?

Many of the themes and topics which are explored in the French class parallel and reinforce concepts students are learning in other areas of study: friendship, family life, the home, the local community, and, of course, the global community. Students build skills that can be equally well used in social studies, language arts, or math classes. Creative Middle School teachers have found that the opportunities for contact between French classes and other curriculum areas are numerous.

> Young adolescents need to discover that French is a living language.

Implementing Discovering French, *Nouveau!* at the Middle Level

French classes in Middle School differ somewhat from those at the secondary level because young adolescents perform best within an age-appropriate curriculum designed for their needs. Middle School teachers have found that there are many effective ways of implementing the **Discovering French, *Nouveau!*** materials in the classroom.

Here are a few specific suggestions:

Plan daily lessons so that they incorporate non-textbook materials and techniques which respond to the needs of different learners.

In Middle School classes, the textbook is used primarily as a reference and a source of specific readings and small group activities. With **Discovering French, *Nouveau!*** teachers have a variety of non-textbook means of presenting and practicing the new material.

- **Video** The *Video Program* is made up of 28 modules. Each include conversations, candid interviews, listening practice, speaking practice, and a cultural vignette. These videos are carefully integrated with each lesson of the student text, and they lend themselves exceptionally well to a Middle School program. Many segments were filmed in a *collège,* the French equivalent of a middle school.
- **Overhead Transparencies** Colorful overhead visuals allow the teacher to present the new vocabulary and speech patterns for visual learners. Many of these visuals also allow for student interaction.
- **Interpersonal Communication** The *Communipak* activities, especially the *Échanges* (information gathering) and *Tête à Tête* (information gap activities) encourage students to use French in meaningful conversation and interpersonal communication.
- **Middle School Copymasters** offer additional age-appropriate activities, games, and puzzles

Within the classroom, set up several different "learning stations."

At the middle level, the emphasis is on the language learning process: developing communication skills. Young adolescents learn more effectively in small groups where each person is actively involved in a given activity. There are many possibilities:

- **Video/DVD Station:** Place several desks around a monitor, and have students do the *Video Activities* in groups, checking comprehension together.
- **Listening Practice Station:** This station is furnished with CD players, preferably each with two headsets. Students, in pairs, do the *Listening activities,* replaying the audio as needed.

- **Conversation Station:** Copy the *Answer Key* pages which correspond to the *Communipak* activities for the lesson, especially those entitled *Interviews, Tu as la parole* and *Conversations.* In each triad, two students engage in the conversations while the third student acts as a coach.
- **Writing Practice Station:** Students work in pairs or small groups to check their Workbook writing activities. If they disagree as to the correct answer, they can consult the appropriate pages of the Workbook TE in the Unit Resource Book.
- **Assessment Station:** Students can be invited individually to take the brief teacher-administered *Speaking Proficiency Tests* or take make-up quizzes. (Since the *Lesson Quizzes* all have a listening portion, the Assessment Station would need a CD player and headset.) Students can also come to this station to work on material for their portfolios.

Encourage students to use French outside the classroom.

Young adolescents need to discover that French is a living language. They should be encouraged to use French in reaching out to their families, to others in the school community, and to those in the community at large.

- **At home:** Since each lesson of **Discovering French, *Nouveau!*–Bleu Première partie** focuses on common conversational themes, students can be encouraged (perhaps for extra credit) to teach a few of their newly-learned phrases to siblings and other family members.
- **Within the school:** As an assignment, have students take the *Communipak Interview* and *Échange* sheets and interview students in the school who are now in more advanced French classes. You might also be able to identify some colleagues and administrators who (with a bit of advanced warning, e.g., by giving them copies of the *Communipak* sheets) would be willing to be interviewed in French.
- **Within the community:** Students can be given the opportunity to be "teachers" at an elementary school and introduce the younger students to a bit of French (perhaps with the support of some **Discovering French, *Nouveau!*–Bleu** overhead transparencies). They can also be encouraged to identify adults who speak French and have brief conversations with them, perhaps by using modified forms of the *Communipak* sheets. (Some teachers have found that this is an excellent way of involving young adolescents with people across generations.)

Discovering French, *Nouveau!* provides tools for building the foundation for continued future success in the study of French. Students at the middle level are encouraged to develop positive attitudes toward linguistic and cultural diversity while expanding their own individual language skills.

Building Comprehension in the French Classroom

The Role of Listening Comprehension

Listening comprehension provides a very effective introduction to second-language learning. More specifically, listening activities in which students respond physically in some way (moving around, pointing, handling objects, etc.) are not only excellent ways of establishing comprehension of new phrases, but material learned in this manner is remembered longer. This explains why students learn the parts of the body more quickly by playing "Simon Says" than by repeating the same vocabulary words after the teacher.

How is an effective comprehension activity structured?

In a typical comprehension activity, the teacher gives commands to the students, either as a full class, a small group, or individually. The activity often consists of four steps:

STEP 1 Group performance with a teacher model

The teacher gives a command and then performs the action. The students listen, watch and imitate the teacher. Three to five new commands are presented in this way.

STEP 2 Group performance without a teacher model

When the teacher feels the students understand the new phrases, he or she gives the command without moving. It is the students who demonstrate their comprehension by performing the desired action. If the students seem unsure about what to do, the teacher will model the action again.

STEP 3 Individual performance without a teacher model

Once the group can perform the new commands easily, the teacher gives these commands to individual students. If an individual student does not remember a given command, the teacher calls on the group to perform the command. It is important to maintain a relaxing atmosphere where all students feel comfortable.

STEP 4 Individual performance of a series of commands

When the class is comfortable with the new commands, the teacher gives an individual student a series of two or more commands. This type of activity builds retention and encourages more careful listening.

These four steps are repeated each time new commands are introduced. As the activities progress, the new commands are intermingled with those learned previously.

How many new commands are introduced at any one time?

Generally three to five new commands are introduced and then practiced. It is important not to bring in new items until all the students are comfortable with the current material. Practice can be made more challenging by giving the commands more rapidly.

There are essentially two kinds of comprehension activities:

• **TEXT-RELATED ACTIVITIES** These activities introduce material which will be immediately activated in the corresponding lesson of the book. The comprehension activity helps students build their listening comprehension before being asked to produce this new material in speaking and writing. Then, when students are presented with this material formally, they can concentrate on details such as pronunciation and spelling because they will already know what all the new words mean.

• **COMPREHENSION-EXPANSION ACTIVITIES** These activities are designed to expand the students' listening proficiency and introduce vocabulary and structures which will not be formally presented until later in the program. Since this approach is fun, and since the material presented is not formally "tested," comprehension activities can be effectively used for vocabulary expansion and for introduction of new material.

Sample classroom commands

Here is a listing of some sample commands in both the "tu" and the "vous" forms. As a teacher, you have two options:
- You can use the formal "vous" form for both group and individual commands.
- You can address the class and small groups with the plural "vous" form and then address individual students as "tu."

Movements			
	Stand up.	**Lève-toi.**	**Levez-vous.**
		Debout.	**Debout.**
	Sit down.	**Assieds-toi.**	**Asseyez-vous.**
	Walk.	**Marche.**	**Marchez.**
	Jump.	**Saute.**	**Sautez.**
	Stop.	**Arrête.**	**Arrêtez.**
	Turn around.	**Tourne-toi.**	**Tournez-vous.**
	Turn right / left.	**Tourne à droite/à gauche.**	**Tournez à droite/à gauche.**
	Go …	**Va** (au tableau).	**Allez** (à la fenêtre).
	Come …	**Viens** (au bureau).	**Venez** (au tableau).
	Raise …	**Lève** (la main).	**Levez** (le bras).
	Lower …	**Baisse** (la tête).	**Baissez** (les yeux).
Pointing out and manipulating objects	Point out …	**Montre** (le cahier).	**Montrez** (le livre).
	Touch …	**Touche** (la porte).	**Touchez** (la fenêtre).
	Pick up / Take …	**Prends** (le crayon).	**Prenez** (le stylo).
	Put …	**Mets** (le livre sur la table).	**Mettez** (le cahier sous la chaise).
	Take away …	**Enlève** (le livre).	**Enlevez** (le cahier).
	Empty …	**Vide** (le sac).	**Videz** (la corbeille).
	Give …	**Donne** (la cassette à Anne).	**Donnez** (le CD à Paul).
	Give back …	**Rends** (la cassette à Marie).	**Rendez** (le CD à Michel).
	Pass …	**Passe** (le stylo à Denise).	**Passez** (le crayon à Marc).
	Keep …	**Garde** (la cassette).	**Gardez** (la cassette).
	Open …	**Ouvre** (la porte).	**Ouvrez** (le livre).
	Close …	**Ferme** (la fenêtre).	**Fermez** (le cahier).
	Throw …	**Lance** (la balle à Jean).	**Lancez** (le ballon à Claire).
	Bring me …	**Apporte-moi** (la balle).	**Apportez-moi** (le ballon).
Activities with pictures and visuals	Look at …	**Regarde** (la carte).	**Regardez** (le plan de Paris).
	Look for / Find …	**Cherche** (la Suisse).	**Cherchez** (la tour Eiffel).
	Show me …	**Montre-moi** (Genève).	**Montrez-moi** (Notre-Dame).
Paper or chalkboard activities	Draw …	**Dessine** (une maison).	**Dessinez** (un arbre).
	Write …	**Écris** (ton nom).	**Écrivez** (votre nom).
	Erase …	**Efface** (le dessin).	**Effacez** (la carte).
	Color …	**Colorie** (le chat en noir).	**Coloriez** (le chien en jaune).
	Put an "x" on …	**Mets un "x" sur** (le garçon).	**Mettez un "x" sur** (la fille).
	Circle …	**Trace un cercle autour de** (la chemise rouge).	**Tracez un cercle autour de** (la jupe blanche).
	Cut out …	**Découpe** (un coeur).	**Découpez** (un cercle).

Professional Language Organizations

American Association of Teachers of French (AATF)

Mailcode 4510
Southern Illinois University
Carbondale, IL 62901-4510

Phone: (618) 453-5731

www.frenchteachers.org

As an AATF member:

• you will receive subscriptions to the French Review and the AATF National Bulletin.

• you will be able to attend local, regional, and national AATF meetings where you can share ideas and meet new colleagues.

• you have the opportunity to apply for one of the many summer scholarships to France and Quebec offered to AATF members.

• you may sponsor a chapter of the *Société Honoraire de Français* at your school so that your students will then be eligible to compete for study abroad travel grants and participate in the SHF creative writing contest.

• you can have your students participate in the National French Contest and be considered for local, regional, and national awards.

• you can obtain pen pals for your students through the *Bureau de Correspondance Scolaire.*

American Council on the Teaching of Foreign Languages (ACTFL)

6 Executive Plaza
Yonkers, NY 10701

Phone: (914) 963-8830

headquarters@actfl.org

www.actfl.org

Governmental Organizations

Alliance Française

The *Alliance Française* is a French organization dedicated to the promotion of French language and culture.

To obtain the address of the Alliance Française nearest you, write:

Délégation Générale de l'Alliance Française, Inc.
1900 L Street NW, Suite 314
Washington, DC 20036-5027

Phone: 800-6-FRANCE (800-637-2623)

federation@afusa.org

www.afusa.org

French Cultural Services

The French Cultural Services are very supportive of French teaching in the United States. For more information, contact the French Cultural Officer at the French Consulate nearest you or write the New York office.

To obtain information about available French cultural materials, write:

Services Culturels de France
934 Fifth Avenue
New York, NY 10021-2603

Phone: (212) 606-3688

www.consulfrance-newyork.org

info@consulfrance-newyork.org

Other Useful Addresses

Sister Cities International

If your town has a Sister City in a French-speaking country, you might want to explore the possibility of initiating a youth or education exchange program. If your town does not yet have a French-speaking Sister City, you might want to encourage your community to set up such an affiliation.

For information on both youth exchanges and the establishment of a sister-city association, contact:

Sister Cities International
120 South Payne St.
Alexandria, VA 22314-2939

Phone: (703) 836-3535

www.sister-cities.org

info@sister-cities.org

Nacel Open Door

Nacel Open Door is a nonprofit organization sponsoring cultural exchanges between American and foreign families and students. If you have students who would like to host a French-speaking student for a month during the summer, or who would themselves like to stay with a family in France or Senegal, have them contact the non-profit organization Nacel Open Door.

Nacel Open Door
3410 Federal Drive, Suite 101
St. Paul, MN 55122-1337

Phone: 800-NACELLE (800-622-3553)

info@nacelopendoor.org

www.nacelopendoor.org

BLEU

1a

Première
partie

Discovering
FRENCH
Nouveau!

Jean-Paul Valette
Rebecca M. Valette

McDougal Littell
A HOUGHTON MIFFLIN COMPANY
Evanston, Illinois • Boston • Dallas

Cover photography

Background: Marseille, France; Inset: French Quarter, New Orleans; Credits appear on page R38

McDougal Littell wishes to express its heartfelt appreciation to **Gail Smith,** Supervising Editor for DISCOVERING FRENCH. Her creativity, organizational skills, determination, and sheer hard work have been invaluable in all aspects of the program.

Bienvenue ... and welcome!

Chers amis,

Welcome to *Discovering French-Nouveau!* and congratulations on your choice of French as a foreign language! Perhaps someone in your family speaks French. Maybe you know people who are of French-speaking origin — from France or Canada or Louisiana or Haiti or western Africa — and you want to better appreciate their heritage. Or perhaps you are hoping to travel to Quebec or Martinique or Paris, and want to be able to get around easily on your own. Perhaps simply you were influenced by the fact that French is a beautiful language. Or maybe you have studied ballet and already know quite a few French expressions. Or you like to bicycle and enjoy watching the **Tour de France.** Or you love the Internet and want to explore the many exciting French sites. Or perhaps your friends have told you that French class is fun and opens doors to a whole new world. Whatever the reason or reasons, welcome and **bienvenue!**

By learning French, you will get to know and communicate with people who use French in their daily lives. These millions of French speakers or **francophones** come from a wide variety of ethnic and cultural backgrounds. As you will see, they live not only in France and other parts of Europe, but also in Africa, in North and South America, in Asia . . . in fact, on all continents.

By studying French, you will also develop a better understanding of your own language and how it works. And by exploring cultural similarities and differences, you will grow to appreciate your own culture and value the culture of others.

On the pages of this book and in the accompanying video, you will meet many young people who speak French. Listen carefully to what they say and how they express themselves. They will help you understand not only their language but also the way they live.

Bonne chance!

Jean-Paul Valette   *Rebecca M. Valette*

UNITÉ 1 Invitation au français

To Make Knowledge

Faisons connaissance 12

Thème Getting acquainted
Introduction culturelle Salutations 13

LEÇON 1 Bonjour!

VIDÉO-SCÈNE A: La rentrée 14

- **Notes culturelles**
  1. La rentrée 2. Les prénoms français 15
- **Pour communiquer**
  Bonjour! Je m'appelle ..., Comment t'appelles-tu? 15
- **Petit commentaire** Astérix 16
- **L'alphabet** 17
- **Les signes orthographiques** 17
- **Les nombres de 0 à 10** 17

VIDÉO-SCÈNE B: Tu es français? 18

- **Note culturelle** En Bref: La Martinique 19
- **Pour communiquer**
  Tu es de ...?, Je suis de ...; Les nationalités 19
- **Petit commentaire**
  La statue de la Liberté et la tour Eiffel 20
- **Français, française** 20
- **Les nombres de 10 à 20** 21
- **Prononciation** Les lettres muettes 21

VIDÉO-SCÈNE C: Salut! Ça va? 22

- **Note culturelle** Bonjour ou Salut? 23
- **Pour communiquer**
  Bonjour! Comment vas-tu? 23, 24
- **Les nombres de 20 à 60** 25
- **Prononciation** Les consonnes finales 25

LEÇON 2 Famille et copains

VIDÉO-SCÈNE A: Copain ou copine?   26

• **Note culturelle** Amis et copains **27**

• **Pour communiquer** Qui est-ce; les personnes **27**

• **Petit commentaire** *Cycling* **28**

• Un garçon, une fille **28**

• Les nombres de 60 à 79 . . . .**29**

• **Prononciation** La liaison **29**

VIDÉO-SCÈNE B: Une coïncidence   30

• **Note culturelle** En Bref: La province de Québec **31**

• **Pour communiquer**
     Tu connais …?, Comment s'appelle …? **31**

• **Petit commentaire** *The French and the U.S.* **32**

• Le garçon, la fille **32**

• Les nombres de 80 à 1 000 . . . .**33**

• **Prononciation** La voyelle nasale /ɛ̃/ **33**

VIDÉO-SCÈNE C: Les photos d'Isabelle   34

• **Note culturelle** La famille française **35**

• **Pour communiquer** La famille **35**

• **Petit commentaire** *Pets* **36**

• Mon cousin, ma cousine **36**

• **Pour communiquer** Quel âge as-tu? **37**

• **Prononciation** Les voyelles nasales /ã/ et /ɔ̃/ **37**

À VOTRE TOUR Communication/révision **38**

ENTRACTE 1 Lecture et culture **40**

UNITÉ 2 Invitation au français
In Everyday life

La vie courante 42

Thème Everyday life in Paris
Introduction culturelle Bon appétit! 43

LEÇON 3 Bon appétit!

VIDÉO-SCÈNE A: Tu as faim? **44**

• **Note culturelle** Les jeunes et la nourriture **45**
• **Pour communiquer**
Tu as faim? Tu veux …?; les nourritures **45**
• **Petit commentaire** *Sandwichs* **46**
• Un sandwich, une pizza **46**
• Prononciation: L'intonation **47**

VIDÉO-SCÈNE B: Au café **48**

• **Note culturelle** Le café **49**
• **Pour communiquer**
Tu as soif? S'il vous plaît …; les boissons **49**
• **Petit commentaire** *Favorite beverages* **50**
• **Prononciation** L'accent final **51**

VIDÉO-SCÈNE C: Ça fait combien? **52**

• **Note culturelle** L'argent européen **52**
• **Pour communiquer**
C'est combien? Il/elle coûte …; Prête moi **53**
• **Petit commentaire** Restaurants **54**
• **Prononciation** La consonne «r» **55**

LEÇON 4 *De jour en jour*

VIDÉO-SCÈNE A: L'heure   **56**

• **Pour communiquer A** Les heures **56**

• **Pour communiquer B**
   Les quarts d'heure, les minutes **58**

VIDÉO-SCÈNE B: Le jour et la date   **60**

• **Pour communiquer A** Les jours de la semaine **61**

• **Pour communiquer B** Les mois de l'année; la date **62**

VIDÉO-SCÈNE C: Le temps   **64**

• **Pour communiquer** Le temps; les saisons **65**

À VOTRE TOUR Communication/révision **66**

ENTRACTE 2 Lecture et culture **68**

Qu'est-ce qu'on fait? 70

Thème Daily activities

LEÇON 5 LE FRANÇAIS PRATIQUE

Mes activités 72

• Accent sur … Les activités de la semaine 72

• **Vocabulaire**

   A. Préférences 74

   B. Souhaits 77

   C. Invitations 78

• **Note culturelle** Le téléphone 79

À votre tour Communication/révision 80

LEÇON 6

Une invitation 82

• **Note culturelle** Le mercredi après-midi 83

• **A.** Le verbe **être** et les pronoms sujets 84

• **Vocabulaire** Où? 85

• **B.** Les questions à réponse affirmative ou négative 86

• Expressions pour la conversation:
   How to answer a yes/no question 87

• **C.** La négation 88

• **Vocabulaire** Mots utiles (**à, de**, etc.) 89

• **Prononciation** La voyelle /**a**/ 89

À votre tour Communication/révision 90

LEÇON 7

Une boum 92

- **Note culturelle** Une boum 93
- **A.** Les verbes en **-er**: le singulier 94
- **Vocabulaire** Les verbes en **-er** 95
- **B.** Les verbes en **-er**: le pluriel 96
- **C.** Le présent des verbes en **-er**: affirmatif, négatif 98
- **Vocabulaire** Mots utiles (**bien, mal,** etc.) 100
- Expressions pour la conversation:
  How to express approval or regret 100
- **D.** La construction: verbe + infinitif 101
- **Prononciation** Les voyelles /i/ et /u/ 101
- **À votre tour** Communication/révision 102

LEÇON 8

Un concert de musique africaine 104

- **Note culturelle** En Bref: Le Sénégal 105
- **A.** Les questions d'information 106
- **Vocabulaire** Expressions interrogatives 106
- Expressions pour la conversation:
  How to express surprise or mild doubt 107
- **B.** Les expressions interrogatives avec **qui** 108
- **C.** Qu'est-ce que? 109
- **D.** Le verbe **faire** 110
- **Vocabulaire** Expressions avec **faire** 110
- **E.** L'interrogation avec inversion 111
- **Prononciation** La voyelle /y/ 111
- **À votre tour** Communication/révision 112

TESTS DE CONTRÔLE 114
VOCABULAIRE 116
ENTRACTE 3 Lecture et culture 118

IMAGES À l'école en France 124

UNITÉ 4

Le monde personnel et familier 134

Thème People and possessions

LEÇON 9 LE FRANÇAIS PRATIQUE

Les personnes et les objets **136**

• Accent sur … Les jeunes Français **136**
• **Vocabulaire**
   A. La description des personnes **138**
   B. Les objets **140**
   C. Les affaires personnelles **142**
   D. Ma chambre **144**
   E. Mon ordinateur (Vocabulaire supplémentaire) **147**
À votre tour Communication/révision **148**

LEÇON 10

Vive la différence! **150**

• **Note culturelle** En Bref: Haïti **151**
• **A.** Le verbe **avoir** **152**
• **Vocabulaire** Expressions avec **avoir** **152**
• **B.** Les noms et les articles: masculin et féminin **153**
• **C.** Les noms et les articles: le pluriel **154**
• **D.** L'article indéfini dans les phrases négatives **156**
• Expressions pour la conversation:
   How to contradict a negative statement or question **157**
• **E.** L'usage de l'article défini dans le sens général **158**
• **F.** L'usage de l'article défini avec les jours de la semaine **159**
• **Prononciation** Les articles «**le**» et «**les**» **159**
À votre tour Communication/révision **160**

Reference Section

Appendix 1 Maps **R1**
Appendix 2 Sound/Spelling Correspondences **R4**
Appendix 3 Numbers **R6**
Appendix 4 Verbs **R7**

LEÇON 11

Le copain de Mireille 162

- **Note culturelle** L'amitié et la bande de copains 163
- **A.** Les adjectifs: masculin et féminin 164
- **Vocabulaire** La description 165
- **B.** Les adjectifs: le pluriel 166
- **Vocabulaire** Les adjectifs de nationalité 167
- Expressions pour la conversation:
  How to introduce a conclusion 167
- **C.** La place des adjectifs 168
- **Prononciation** Les consonnes finales 169

À votre tour Communication/révision 170

LEÇON 12

La voiture de Roger 172

- **Note culturelle** Les Français et la voiture 173
- **A.** Les couleurs 174
- **Vocabulaire** Les couleurs 174
- **B.** La place des adjectifs avant le nom 175
- **Vocabulaire** Les adjectifs qui précèdent le nom 175
- Expressions pour la conversation:
  How to get someone's attention 176
- **C.** Il est ou c'est 177
- **D.** Les expressions impersonnelles avec c'est 178
- **Vocabulaire** Opinions 178
- **Prononciation** Les lettres «ch» 179

À votre tour Communication/révision 180

TESTS DE CONTRÔLE 182
VOCABULAIRE 184
ENTRACTE 4 Lecture et culture 186

French-English Vocabulary R12
English-French Vocabulary R28
Index R36
Credits R38

Pourquoi parler français?

WHY SPEAK FRENCH?

Here are ten good reasons.

1. **French is an international language.**
   French is the first or second language in about fifty countries or regions in Europe, Africa, North and South America, Asia, and Oceania. It is spoken by over 100 million people around the world.

2. **French is an important diplomatic language.**
   French is one of the five official languages of the United Nations and one of the two main languages of the European Union.

3. **French is the second language on the Internet.**
   With French, you have immediate access to Internet sites in France and Quebec, as well as sites in Belgium, Switzerland, and French-speaking countries of Africa.

4. **France is a technologically advanced country.**
   Historically, French inventors have contributed significantly to the advancement of science. Today, France is a leader in areas such as aero-space technology, high-speed transportation, automotive design, and medical research.

5. **France is a leader in the world of art and literature.**
   Over the past 400 years, Paris has been an important cultural center, attracting artists and writers from around the world. France has won more Nobel Prizes in literature than any other country.

▲ un cybercafé à Paris

▲ l'Opéra National de Paris

le musée du Louvre ▶

2 deux

le TGV (train à grand vitesse) ▶
high-speed train

6. ***France is a prime tourist destination.***
If you like to travel, it will not surprise you to learn that millions of tourists visit France every year — and speaking French makes their vacations much more meaningful and more enjoyable.

7. ***For many people, France evokes style and elegance.***
When people think of high fashion, beauty products, perfumes, or gourmet cuisine, they think of France . . . and rightly so.

8. ***Knowing French will enrich your English.***
In 1066, William the Conqueror, a French nobleman, invaded England and became king, bringing with him his court and his language: French. Today over one-third of all English words are derived from French. As you study French, you will increase your English vocabulary.

9. ***Knowing French will help you with your university studies.***
University admissions officers look for candidates who have foreign language skills. In addition, research by the College Board shows that the longer students study a foreign language, the higher their math and verbal SAT scores.

10. ***Knowing French will be useful for your career.***
Many jobs require the knowledge of another language. France and Canada are major trading partners of the United States. In addition, about 1,000 French companies have subsidiaries in this country.

▲ l'Université Paris-Sorbonne

Et vous? *(And you?)*

Which three reasons for speaking French are most important to you? Take a class poll comparing your answers with those of your classmates. Which are the most popular reasons?

Photo cultural notes
- The top photo of the **TGV** was taken at the **Gare de Lyon** in Paris.
- The bottom photo is of the **Église de la Sorbonne.** The Sorbonne was founded in 1257 by Robert de Sorbon, but today the Église is the oldest part of the university. It was built by Lemercier between 1635 and 1642. The Sorbonne is located in the **Quartier latin,** which is full of cafés, bookstores, and shops that cater to the student population.

Teaching Resource Options

PRINT

Unit 1 Resource Book
  Videoscript, pp. 193–194

AUDIO & VISUAL
Overhead Transparencies
1 Map of France

VIDEO PROGRAM

VIDÉO   DVD
 IMAGES

A.2 La France
  (0:49–2:34 min.)

Cultural notes France

- **Les Alpes et Chamonix**
  Chamonix is located in a valley in the Alps at the foot of the **Massif du Mont Blanc.** (**Mont Blanc** is the highest mountain in Europe.) Chamonix is a famous ski resort. The first Winter Olympics were held there in 1924.

- **La Côte d'Azur**
  The French Riviera, or **la Côte d'Azur,** stretches about 100 miles along the Mediterranean, from the Toulon area to the Italian border. For the French, the Côte d'Azur is their favorite summer vacation place.

- **Les Pyrénées**
  The **Pyrénées** are a high mountain chain which separates France from Spain (**l'Espagne**).

- **Les Châteaux de la Loire**
  There are many castles located in the Loire Valley. **Les Châteaux de la Loire,** such as the Château de Chenonceau, were built by the French kings nearly 500 years ago.

Bonjour, la France!

CONNAISSEZ-VOUS LA FRANCE? *(Do you know France?)*

- In area, France is the second-largest country in Western Europe. It is smaller than Texas, but bigger than California.

- Geographically, France is a very diversified country, with the highest mountains in Europe (**les Alpes** and **les Pyrénées**) and an extensive coastline along the Atlantic (**l'océan Atlantique**) and the Mediterranean (**la Méditerranée**).

- France consists of many different regions which have maintained their traditions, their culture, and — in some cases — their own language. Some of the traditional provinces are Normandy and Brittany (**la Normandie** and **la Bretagne**) in the west, Alsace (**l'Alsace**) in the east, Touraine (**la Touraine**) in the center, and Provence (**la Provence**) in the south.

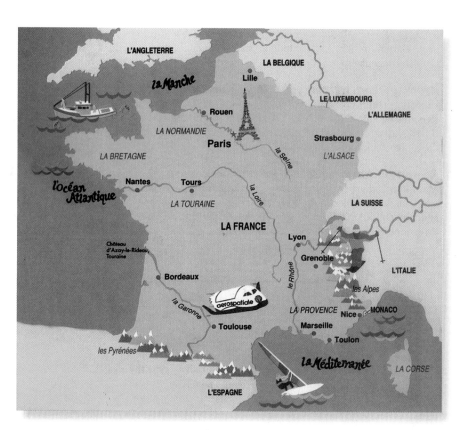

CLASSROOM PROJECT

You might have students prepare a bulletin board display about France using maps, postcards, travel brochures, etc.

Paris: Montmartre
Paris, the capital of France, is also its economic, intellectual, and artistic center. For many people, Paris is the most beautiful city in the world.

Snowboarding in the Alps
During winter vacation, many French young people enjoy snowboarding or skiing. The most popular destinations are the Alps and the Pyrenees.

Château de Chenonceau
The long history of France is evident in its many castles and monuments. This chateau, built in the 16th century, attracts nearly one million visitors a year.

Home in Provence
The French love flowers and take pride in making their homes beautiful. This house is built in the traditional style of Provence, a region in southern France.

Cultural notes

- **Size:** In area, one can compare France to:

  (a) 4/5 of Texas, or

  (b) Wyoming plus Oregon, or

  (c) New England plus New York, Pennsylvania and Ohio.

- **Technology:** The French Ariane rockets are launched from French Guiana (**la Guyane française**) in South America.

- **French cultural tradition:**

  –Philosophers: Voltaire, Montesquieu, Rousseau, Jean-Paul Sartre

  –Writers: Victor Hugo, Albert Camus, Colette, Baudelaire

  –Musicians: composers Debussy and Ravel, flutist Jean-Pierre Rampal

  –Artists: Gauguin, Renoir, Matisse

- **Pre-history:** the Cro-Magnon caveman and the caves of Lascaux

- **Roman times:** Julius Caesar conquered France (Gaul) in 43 B.C.; one can still visit the Roman ruins in Provence: Nîmes, Orange, Pont du Gard.

Bonjour, les Français!

Here are some facts about France and the French people.

LA FRANCE

Capitale: Paris

Population: 60 (soixante) millions d'habitants

Drapeau: bleu, blanc, rouge

Devise: Liberté, Égalité, Fraternité

Monnaie: l'euro

BLEU   BLANC   ROUGE

LE DRAPEAU FRANÇAIS

L'EURO

LA MONNAIE FRANÇAISE

LES FRANÇAIS

Origine de la population: multi-ethnique

- européenne (majorité)
- nord-africaine
- africaine
- asiatique

Principales religions pratiquées:

- catholique (majorité)
- musulmane
- juive
- protestante

STRATEGY Comparing Cultures

How does France compare to the United States or to your country of origin? Make a chart like the one above. Include the capital, the population, the flag, the motto, and the currency.

These are some of the young French people you will meet in the video.

Jean-Paul âge: 14 ans

Céline âge: 15 ans

Léa âge: 15 ans

François âge: 14 ans

Isabelle âge: 14 ans

Stéphanie âge: 14 ans

Philippe âge: 15 ans

Trinh âge: 14 ans

Antoine âge: 14 ans

Teaching Resource Options

PRINT

Unit 1 Resource Book
  Videoscript, pp. 193–194

AUDIO & VISUAL

Overhead Transparencies
2b Map of the French-speaking world
(page R2)
2c Map of the French-speaking world
(page R3)

VIDEO PROGRAM

VIDÉO   DVD
  IMAGES

A.3 Le monde francophone
   (2:35-4:42 min.)

A.4 Des francophones aux
   États-Unis (4:43-6:42 min.)

Cultural note There are also two
small French islands in the Atlantic, off
the Canadian coast: Saint Pierre and
Miquelon. Since 1985, Saint Pierre and
Miquelon (**Saint-Pierre-et-Miquelon**)
are considered as a "collectivité
territoriale" and not as a
"département".

Bonjour, le monde francophone!

CANADA
About one-third of the population speaks
French. These French speakers live mainly in
the province of Quebec (**le Québec**). They
are descendants of French settlers who came
to Canada in the 17th and 18th centuries.

HAÏTI
Haïti is the first Black Republic. Its
people speak Creole and French.

MARTINIQUE AND GUADELOUPE
These two Caribbean islands (**la Martinique**
and **la Guadeloupe**) are part of France.
Their inhabitants, primarily of African
ancestry, are French citizens.

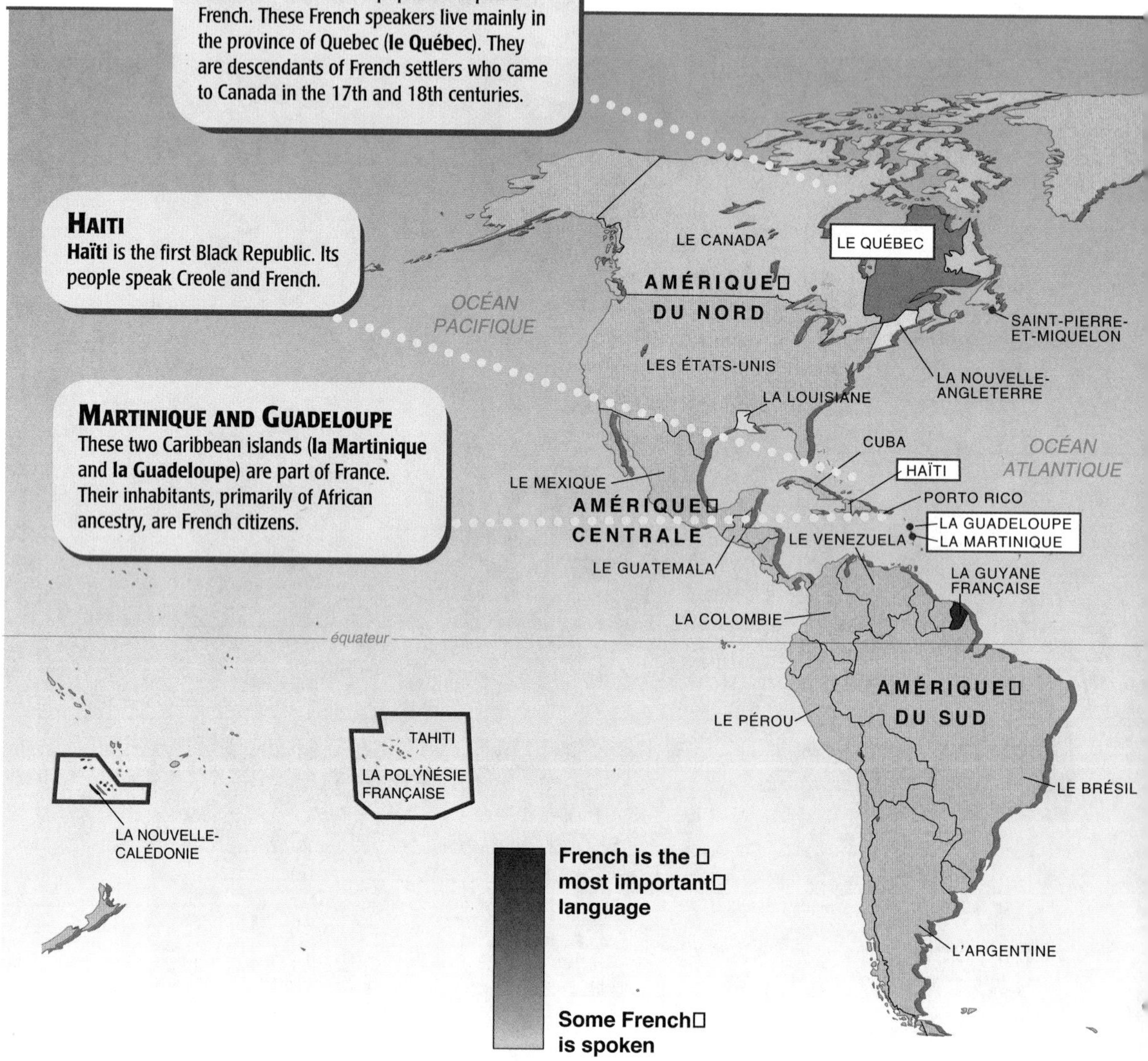

LE CANADA

LE QUÉBEC

AMÉRIQUE☐
DU NORD

SAINT-PIERRE-
ET-MIQUELON

OCÉAN
PACIFIQUE

LES ÉTATS-UNIS

LA NOUVELLE-
ANGLETERRE

LA LOUISIANE

CUBA

OCÉAN
ATLANTIQUE

LE MEXIQUE

HAÏTI

AMÉRIQUE☐
CENTRALE

PORTO RICO

LA GUADELOUPE
LA MARTINIQUE

LE VENEZUELA

LE GUATEMALA

LA GUYANE
FRANÇAISE

LA COLOMBIE

équateur

AMÉRIQUE☐
DU SUD

LE PÉROU

TAHITI

LA POLYNÉSIE
FRANÇAISE

LE BRÉSIL

LA NOUVELLE-
CALÉDONIE

French is the ☐
most important☐
language

L'ARGENTINE

Some French☐
is spoken

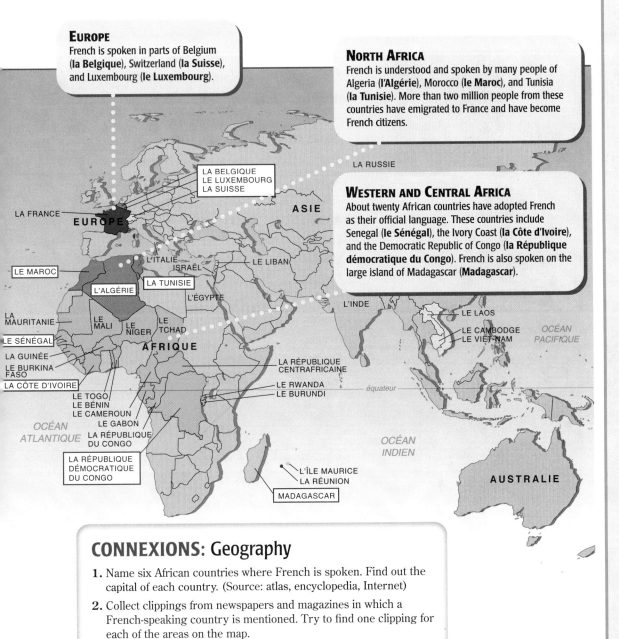

EUROPE
French is spoken in parts of Belgium (**la Belgique**), Switzerland (**la Suisse**), and Luxembourg (**le Luxembourg**).

NORTH AFRICA
French is understood and spoken by many people of Algeria (**l'Algérie**), Morocco (**le Maroc**), and Tunisia (**la Tunisie**). More than two million people from these countries have emigrated to France and have become French citizens.

WESTERN AND CENTRAL AFRICA
About twenty African countries have adopted French as their official language. These countries include Senegal (**le Sénégal**), the Ivory Coast (**la Côte d'Ivoire**), and the Democratic Republic of Congo (**la République démocratique du Congo**). French is also spoken on the large island of Madagascar (**Madagascar**).

LA BELGIQUE
LE LUXEMBOURG
LA SUISSE

LA RUSSIE

ASIE

LA FRANCE

EUROPE

L'ITALIE

LE MAROC

ISRAËL

LE LIBAN

L'ALGÉRIE

LA TUNISIE

L'ÉGYPTE

L'INDE

LA MAURITANIE

LE MALI

LE NIGER

LE TCHAD

LE SÉNÉGAL

AFRIQUE

LE LAOS

LE CAMBODGE
LE VIÊT-NAM

OCÉAN PACIFIQUE

LA GUINÉE

LE BURKINA FASO

LA CÔTE D'IVOIRE

LA RÉPUBLIQUE CENTRAFRICAINE

LE TOGO
LE BÉNIN
LE CAMEROUN

LE GABON

LE RWANDA
LE BURUNDI

équateur

OCÉAN ATLANTIQUE

LA RÉPUBLIQUE DU CONGO

OCÉAN INDIEN

LA RÉPUBLIQUE DÉMOCRATIQUE DU CONGO

L'ÎLE MAURICE
LA RÉUNION

AUSTRALIE

MADAGASCAR

CONNEXIONS: Geography

1. Name six African countries where French is spoken. Find out the capital of each country. (Source: atlas, encyclopedia, Internet)

2. Collect clippings from newspapers and magazines in which a French-speaking country is mentioned. Try to find one clipping for each of the areas on the map.

Cultural note Two African countries are named after the Congo river, one of the longest rivers in the world. In size, **la République démocratique du Congo** is the largest French-speaking country of Africa. It was known as **le Congo belge** before its independence in 1960, and as **le Zaïre** until 1997. Its eastern neighbor, **la République du Congo,** is a former French colony.

Cultural expansion

Names of African countries where French is an important language (capitals are given in parentheses):
   Algérie (Alger)
   Bénin (Porto-Novo)
   Burkina Faso (Ougadougou)
   Burundi (Bujumbura)
   Cameroun (Yaoundé)
   Côte d'Ivoire (Yamoussoukro)
   Djibouti (Djibouti)
   Gabon (Libreville)
   Guinée (Conakry)
   Madagascar (Antananarivo)
   Mali (Bamako)
   Maroc (Rabat)
   Mauritanie (Nouakchott)
   Niger (Niamey)
   République Centrafricaine (Bangui)
   République Démocratique du
      Congo (Kinshasa)
   République du Congo (Brazzaville)
   Ruanda [Rwanda] (Kigali)
   Sénégal (Dakar)
   Tchad (N'Djamena)
   Togo (Lomé)
   Tunisie (Tunis)

Middle School Copymasters

Class Starter: The French-Speaking World, p. 1

English equivalents of French boys' names

Alain (Alan)
André (Andrew)
Antoine (Anthony)
Christophe (Christopher)
Édouard (Edward)
Étienne (Steven)
François (Francis, Frank)
Frédéric (Frederick)
Geoffroy (Jeffrey)
Guillaume (William)
Henri (Henry)
Jacques (James)
Jean (John)
Julien (Julian)
Laurent (Lawrence)
Marc (Mark)
Mathieu (Matthew)
Michel (Michael)
Olivier (Oliver)
Philippe (Phillip)
Pierre (Peter)
Raoul (Ralph)

Bonjour, je m'appelle . . .

Antoine

Jérôme

As you begin your study of French, you may want to "adopt" a French identity. Here is a list of some common French names.

Noms traditionnels (garçons):

Alain	Henri	Nicolas
André	Jacques	Olivier
Antoine	Jean	Patrick
Bernard	Jean-Louis	Paul
Christophe	Jean-Paul	Philippe
Clément	Jérôme	Pierre
Édouard	Joseph	Robert
Éric	Julien	Stéphane
François	Laurent	Thomas
Frédéric	Marc	Vincent
Georges	Mathieu	
Guillaume	Michel	

Fatima

Some French people of North African or African descent have names that reflect their origin.

Noms d'origine nord-africaine

GARÇONS		FILLES	
Ali	Latif	Aïcha	Leila
Ahmed	Mustapha	Fatima	Yasmina
Habib	Youcef	Jamila	Zaïna

TEACHING NOTE Choosing French names

Let students adopt a new French identity. Some may want to find a French version of their English name. Others may want to pick a completely original name.

If some students do not want to choose a French name, teach them how to pronounce their own name with a French accent.

Aurélie

Léa

Noms traditionnels (filles):

Anne	Florence	Michèle
Anne-Marie	Françoise	Monique
Aurélie	Hélène	Nathalie
Béatrice	Isabelle	Nicole
Caroline	Jeanne	Pauline
Cécile	Julie	Sophie
Céline	Laure	Stéphanie
Charlotte	Léa	Suzanne
Christine	Louise	Sylvie
Claire	Marie	Thérèse
Élisabeth	Marie-Christine	Véronique
Élodie	Mathilde	Virginie
Émilie	Mélanie	

Mélanie

Noms d'origine africaine

GARÇONS		FILLES	
Abdou	Kouamé	Adjoua	Latifah
Amadou	Moussa	Asta	Malika
Koffi	Ousmane	Aya	Mariama

Ousmane

English equivalents of French girls' names

Andrée (Andrea)
Cécile (Cecilia)
Diane (Diana)
Éléonore (Eleanor)
Émilie (Emily)
Françoise (Frances)
Hélène (Helen)
Jeanne (Jean)
Laure (Laura)
Lise (Lisa)
Lucie (Lucy)
Marguerite (Margaret)
Marie (Mary)
Marthe (Martha)
Michèle (Michelle)
Monique (Monica)
Nathalie (Natalie)
Suzanne (Susan)
Sylvie (Sylvia)
Thérèse (Teresa)
Virginie (Virginia)

onze **11**

TEACHING NOTE Pronunciation

Read the above lists aloud and have students repeat the names after you. Be sure they always let the accent fall on the last syllable of each name.

Expansion activities PLANNING AHEAD

Games

• À la pêche! *Go Fish!*

Divide students into groups of four. Give each group two decks of cards. Have students remove the face cards and shuffle the remaining cards of the two decks together. One student deals five cards to each player. Players remove any pairs they have in their hand. The dealer then asks another player for a specific card. If the player has that card, he or she passes it to the dealer, and the dealer's turn continues. If the player does not have that card, he or she tells the dealer «*À la pêche!*» The dealer draws a card from the pile, and the turn passes to the next player. The game is over when there are no more cards left to draw from the stack. The player with the most pairs wins.

Pacing Suggestion: Upon completion of Leçon 1.

• Dix *Ah Zut! start à zero.*

Have students stand up at their desks. Begin in one corner of the room. The first student starts with the number «**Un**» and has the option to name up to three numbers in sequence. (For example, the student who begins has the option to say «**Un,**» «**Un, Deux,**» or «**Un, Deux, Trois.**») The next student continues, and again may name up to three sequential numbers, following from where the first student left off. The student who arrives at the point where he or she must say «**Dix**» is automatically out and has to sit down. The game then starts again at «**Un**» and continues as long as there are players left standing.

Pacing Suggestion: Upon completion of Leçon 1.

Projects

• Allons au Québec

Students will plan a vacation to Quebec. Divide the class into groups. Each group should choose a place in Quebec to visit. Suggest to students that they might consult travel agents or use the Internet. (You might suggest a specific search engine.) They should plan the following:

• the best way to get there (plane, train, car)
• historic and cultural sites they wish to visit
• where they will stay
• what activities they will try while they are there

Ask students to provide visuals—such as maps and travel posters—with the information they accumulate to give oral presentations of their itinerary to the rest of the class.

Pacing Suggestion: Upon completion of Leçon 2.

Bulletin Boards

• L'alphabet

Assign a letter of the alphabet to each student in the class and have students work together to create an alphabet bulletin board. Have each student write a French word that begins with his or her assigned letter on the bulletin board. Encourage students to use words they've already learned and the glossary at the back of the book to find cognates for the rest. Students may wish to design the bulletin board with a theme in mind, such as French first names or city names. The bulletin board should be colorful and visually appealing.

Pacing Suggestion: Upon completion of Leçon 1.

• Couleurs

List the names of the colors at the end of Unité 1 in French at the top of the board. Have students create a poster of francophone flags with labels for the colors and the countries.

Pacing Suggestion: Upon completion of Leçon 2.

Music

• *Frère Jacques*

Distribute the lyrics of the traditional French folk song *Frère Jacques* to students. Have them look up any unfamiliar words, and then discuss the general meaning. You may want to use the song lyrics for pronunciation practice.

> Frère Jacques,
> Frère Jacques,
> Dormez-vous?
> Dormez-vous?
> Sonnez les matines,
> Sonnez les matines,
> Ding, ding, dong!
> Ding, ding, dong!

Pacing Suggestion: Upon completion of Leçon 2.

Storytelling

• La famille

Make up a story about a fictional family. In the story, list the members of the family, their ages, their nationalities, and where they're from. Give students a script to read along, and have comprehension questions prepared in English to discuss with the students. Then, have students write a short story about their family to present to a partner. Once pair work has ended, select a few students to present their stories to the class.

Pacing Suggestion: Upon completion of Leçon 2.

Recipe

• Les tartines

Tartines are slices of bread or toast with a topping commonly served at breakfast or as an after-school snack. Encourage students to try toppings they've never had before. You may wish to include beverages that are typically served at a French breakfast: hot chocolate and café au lait.

Pacing Suggestion: Upon completion of Leçon 2.

Hands-on Crafts

• Une boite mosaïque

Have students use cardboard to fold into a cube. Then, on each side, have students create mosaic images of six of the flags found on pages 40–41. They can do this by tearing colored construction paper into very small pieces and pasting them onto the outer surface of the box. Each side should have a different flag representing one of the various francophone countries. Ask for volunteers to talk about their boxes to the class. Students can say which countries their box represents, where the countries are located, and what colors were chosen for their flags. Teachers may wish to make a small hole in one corner of each box and tie string or fishing line on them in order to hang the boxes from the ceiling.

Pacing Suggestion: Upon completion of Leçon 2.

End of Unit

• Une famille

Students will use what they've learned in Unité 1 to introduce either their real families or an invented "famous family" to the class. First assign a medium for students to use: videotape, a photo album and an audio recording, a booklet and audio recording, etc. Each presentation should include an audio and a visual component. Ask students to introduce each family member, give each person's name and age, and relation to the student. Have students introduce themselves as well. You may want to suggest supplementary vocabulary, such as **beau-père** and **belle-mère.**

Rubric   **A** = 13–15 pts. **B** = 10–12 pts. **C** = 7–9 pts. **D** = 4–6 pts. **F** = < 4 pts.

Criteria	Scale
Vocabulary Use	1 2 3 4 5
Grammar/Spelling Accuracy	1 2 3 4 5
Creativity	1 2 3 4 5

Les tartines

Ingrédients
- 2–3 baguettes
- confiture (de fraises, de framboises, d'abricots, d'oranges)
- pâte de noisettes et cacao
- beurre

Préparation
1. Coupez une baguette en tranches.
2. Sur chaque tranche de pain, étalez de la confiture, du beurre ou de la pâte de noisettes et cacao.

Ingredients
- 2–3 loaves of French bread
- jam (strawberry, raspberry, apricot, orange)
- chocolate-hazelnut spread
- butter

Directions
1. Cut a loaf of French bread into several slices.
2. Top each slice of bread with the spread of your choice.

UNITÉ 1

Planning Guide CLASSROOM MANAGEMENT

OBJECTIVES

Communication
- Say hello and good-bye *pp. 15, 23*
- Introduce yourself and say where you are from *pp. 15, 19*
- Introduce friends, family, and relatives *pp. 27, 35*
- Count to 100 *pp. 17, 21, 25, 29, 33*
- Say how old you are and find out someone's age *p. 37*

Pronunciation
- Les signes orthographiques *p. 17*
- Les lettres muettes *p. 21*
- Les consonnes finales *p. 25*
- La liaison *p. 29*
- La voyelle nasale /ɛ̃/ *p. 33*
- Les voyelles nasales /ã/ and /ɔ̃/ *p. 37*

Culture
- Salutations *p. 13*
- La rentrée *p. 15*
- Les prénoms français *p. 15*
- La Martinique *p. 19*
- Bonjour ou Salut? *p. 23*
- Amis et copains *p. 27*
- La province de Québec *p. 31*
- La famille française *p. 35*

PROGRAM RESOURCES

 Print
- Workbook PE, *pp. 1–28*
- *Activités pour tous* PE, *pp. 1–15*
- Block Scheduling Copymasters, *pp. 1–16*
- Teacher to Teacher Copymasters
- Unit 1 Resource Book
  - Lessons 1–2 Resources
    - Workbook TE
    - *Activités pour tous* TE
    - Lesson Plans
    - Block Scheduling Lesson Plans
    - Family Letter
    - Absent Student Copymasters
    - Family Involvement
    - Video Activities
    - Videoscripts
    - Audioscripts
    - Assessment Program
  - Unit 1 Resources
    - Communipak
    - *Activités pour tous* TE Reading
    - Workbook TE Reading and Culture Activities
    - Assessment Program
    - Answer Keys

 Audiovisual
- Audio Program PE CD 1 Tracks 1–27
- Audio Program Workbook CD 5 Tracks 1–34
- *Chansons* Audio CD
- Video Program Modules 1A, 1B, 1C, 2A, 2B, 2C
- Overhead Transparencies
  - 4 U.S., Canada, England, France *Les nationalités;*
  - 5 Expressions with *ça va;*
  - 7 People *Les personnes;*
  - 8 Family Tree *La famille*

 Technology
- Online Workbook
- ClassZone.com
- eTest Plus Online/Test Generator CD-ROM
- EasyPlanner Plus Online/EasyPlanner CD-ROM
- Power Presentations on CD-ROM

✓ **Assessment Program Options**
- Lesson Quizzes
- Portfolio Assessment
- Unit Test Form A
- Unit Test Form B
- Unit Test Part III Cultural Awareness
- Listening Comprehension Performance Test
- Speaking Performance Test
- Reading Comprehension Performance Test
- Writing Performance Test
- Multiple Choice Test Items
- Test Scoring Tools
- Audio Program CD 13 Tracks 1–11
- Answer Keys
- eTest Plus Online/Test Generator CD-ROM

Pacing Guide SAMPLE LESSON PLAN

DAY	DAY	DAY	DAY	DAY
1 Unité 1 Opener Introduction culturelle– Salutations **Leçon 1A** • Vidéo-scène–La rentrée • Pour communiquer • Notes culturelles– La rentrée, Les prénoms français	**2** **Leçon 1A** • L'alphabet • Prononciation–Les signes orthographiques • Les nombres de 0 à 10	**3** **Leçon 1B** • Vidéo-scène– Tu es français? • Pour communiquer • Note culturelle– La Martinique • Français, française	**4** **Leçon 1B** • Les nombres de 10 à 20 • Prononciation– Les lettres muettes **Leçon 1C** • Vidéo-scène–Salut! Ça va? • Pour communiquer • Note culturelle– Bonjour ou Salut?	**5** **Leçon 1C** • Pour communiquer • Les nombres de 20 à 60 • Prononciation– Les consonnes finales **Leçon 2A** • Vidéo-scène– Copain ou copine? • Un garçon, une fille
6 **Leçon 2A** • Pour communiquer • Note culturelle– Amis et copains • Les nombres de 60 à 79 • Prononciation–La liaison	**7** **Leçon 2B** • Vidéo-scène– Une coïncidence • Pour communiquer • Note culturelle– La province de Québec • Le garçon, la fille	**8** **Leçon 2B** • Les nombres de 80 à 100 et 1000 • Prononciation– La voyelle nasale /ɛ̃/ **Leçon 2C** • Vidéo-scène– Les photos d'Isabelle • Pour communiquer	**9** **Leçon 2C** • Note culturelle– La famille française • Mon cousin, ma cousine • Pour communiquer • Prononciation– Les voyelles nasales /ã/ and /ɔ̃/	**10** • À votre tour!
11 • Unit 1 Test	**12** • Entracte–Lecture et Culture	**13**	**14**	**15**
16	**17**	**18**	**19**	**20**

UNITÉ 1

Student Text Listening Activity Scripts
AUDIO PROGRAM

▶ **LEÇON 1** Bonjour!

• **Vidéo-scène A: La rentrée** *p. 14*

A. Compréhension orale CD 1, TRACK 1

This is the first day of school. Students are greeting their friends and meeting new classmates. Écoutez.

Trinh: Bonjour! Je m'appelle Trinh.
Céline: Et moi, je m'appelle Céline.
Marc: Je m'appelle Marc. Et toi?
Isabelle: Moi, je m'appelle Isabelle.
Jean-Paul: Comment t'appelles-tu?
Nathalie: Je m'appelle Nathalie.
Jean-Paul: Bonjour.
Nathalie: Bonjour.

B. Écoutez et répétez. CD 1, TRACK 2

You will now hear a paused version of the dialog. Listen to the speaker and repeat right after he or she has completed the sentence.

• **L'alphabet** *p. 17* CD 1, TRACK 3

Écoutez et répétez.

A # B # C # D # E # F # G # H # I # J # K # L # M #
N # O # P # Q # R # S # T # U # V # W # X # Y # Z #

• **Prononciation** *p. 17* CD 1, TRACK 4

Les signes orthographiques

French uses accents and spelling marks that do not exist in English. These marks are part of the spelling and cannot be left out.

In French, there are four accents that may appear on vowels.

l'accent aigu #   Cécile # Stéphanie #
l'accent grave #   Michèle # Hélène #
l'accent circonflexe #   Jérôme #
le tréma #   Noël # Joëlle #

There is only one spelling mark used with a consonant. It occurs under the letter "**c**."

la cédille #   François #

• **Les nombres de 0 à 10** *p. 17* CD 1, TRACK 5

Écoutez et répétez.

zéro # un # deux # trois # quatre # cinq # six # sept # huit # neuf # dix #

• **Vidéo-scène B: Tu es français?** *p. 18*

A. Compréhension orale CD 1, TRACK 6

It is the opening day of school and several of the students meet in the cafeteria (**la cafétéria** or **la cantine**) at lunchtime. Marc discovers that not everyone is French.

Marc: Tu es français?
Jean-Paul: Oui, je suis français.
Marc: Et toi, Patrick, tu es français aussi?
Patrick: Non! Je suis américain. Je suis de Boston.
Marc: Et toi, Stéphanie, tu es française ou américaine?
Stéphanie: Je suis française.
Marc: Tu es de Paris?
Stéphanie: Non, je suis de Fort-de-France.
Marc: Tu as de la chance!

B. Écoutez et répétez. CD 1, TRACK 7

You will now hear a paused version of the dialog. Listen to the speaker and repeat right after he or she has completed the sentence.

• **Les nombres de 10 à 20** *p. 21* CD 1, TRACK 8

Écoutez et répétez.

dix # onze # douze # treize # quatorze # quinze #
seize # dix-sept # dix-huit # dix-neuf # vingt #

• **Prononciation** *p. 21* CD 1, TRACK 9

Les lettres muettes

Écoutez: Pari**s̷**

In French, the last letter of a word is often not pronounced.

• Final "**e**" is always silent.
  Répétez: Célin**e̷** # Philipp**e̷** # Stéphani**e̷** # anglais**e̷** # français**e̷** #
  onz**e̷** # douz**e̷** # treiz**e̷** # quatorz**e̷** # quinz**e̷** # seiz**e̷** #
• Final "**s**" is almost always silent.
  Répétez: Pari**s̷** # Nicola**s̷** # Jacque**s̷** # anglai**s̷** # françai**s̷** # troi**s̷** #
• The letter "**h**" is always silent.
  Répétez: **H̷**élène # **H̷**enri # T**h̷**omas # Nat**h̷**alie # Cat**h̷**erine # T**h̷**érèse #

• **Vidéo-scène C: Salut! Ça va?** *p. 22*

A. Compréhension orale CD 1, TRACK 10

Please turn to page 22 for complete *vidéo-scène* text.

B. Écoutez et répétez. CD 1, TRACK 11

You will now hear a paused version of the dialog. Listen to the speaker and repeat right after he or she has completed the sentence.

• **Les nombres de 20 à 60** *p. 25* CD 1, TRACK 12

Écoutez et répétez.

20 # 21 # 22 # 23 # ... 29 #   30 # 31 # 32 # 33 # ... 39 #
40 # 41 # 42 # 43 # ... 49 #   50 # 51 # 52 # 53 # ... 59 # 60 #

• **Prononciation** *p. 25* CD 1, TRACK 13

Les consonnes finales

Écoutez: un̷ deux̷ troi**s̷**

In French, the last consonant of a word is often not pronounced.

• Remember: Final "**s**" is usually silent.
  Répétez: troi**s̷** # françai**s̷** # anglai**s̷**
• Most other final consonants are usually silent.
  Répétez: Richar**d̷** # Alber**t̷** # Rober**t̷** # salu**t̷** # américai**n̷** # canadie**n̷** # bie**n̷** # deu**x̷** #
  EXCEPTION: The following final consonants are usually pronounced: "**c**," "**f**," "**l**," and sometimes "**r**."
Répétez: Éri**c** # Danie**l** Lebeu**f** # Pasca**l** # Victo**r** #
However, the ending **-er** is usually pronounced /e/.
Répétez: Roge**r̷** # Olivie**r̷** #

▶ **LEÇON 2** Famille et copains

• **Vidéo-scène A: Copain ou copine?** *p. 26*

A. Compréhension orale CD 1, TRACK 14

In French there are certain girls' and boys' names that sound the same. Occasionally this can be confusing.

SCÈNE 1 Philippe et Jean-Paul
Philippe is at home with his friend Jean-Paul. He seems to be expecting someone. Who could it be . . . ? The doorbell rings.

Philippe: Tiens! Voilà Dominique!
Jean-Paul: Dominique? Qui est-ce? Un copain ou une copine?
Philippe: C'est une copine.

Scène 2 **Philippe, Jean-Paul, Dominique**
Philippe: Salut, Dominique! Ça va?
Dominique: Oui, ça va! Et toi?
Jean-Paul: *(thinking)* C'est vrai! C'est une copine!

B. Écoutez et répétez.   CD 1, TRACK 15

You will now hear a paused version of the dialog. Listen to the speaker and repeat right after he or she has completed the sentence.

• Les nombres de 60 à 79   *p. 29*   CD 1, TRACK 16

Écoutez et répétez.

60 # 61 # 62 # 63 # 64 # 65 # 66 # 67 # 68 # 69 #
70 # 71 # 72 # 73 # 74 # 75 # 76 # 77 # 78 # 79 #

• Prononciation   *p. 29*   CD 1, TRACK 17

La liaison

Écoutez: un ami

un ami # un Américain # un Anglais # un artiste #

In general, the "**n**" of **un** is silent. However, in the above words, the "**n**" of **un** is pronounced as if it were the *first* letter of the next word. This is called LIAISON.

Liaison occurs between two words when the second one begins with a VOWEL SOUND, that is, with "**a**," "**e**," "**i**," "**o**," "**u**," and sometimes "**h**" and "**y**."

Contrastez et répétez:

LIAISON: un ami # un Américain # un Italien # un artiste #
NO LIAISON: un copain # un Français # un Canadien # un prof #

• Vidéo-scène B: Une coïncidence   *p. 30*

A. Compréhension orale   CD 1, TRACK 18

Isabelle is at a party with her new Canadian friend Marc. She wants him to meet some of the other guests.

Isabelle: Tu connais la fille là-bas?
Marc: Non. Qui est-ce?
Isabelle: C'est une copine. Elle s'appelle Juliette Savard.
Marc: Elle est française?
Isabelle: Non, elle est canadienne. Elle est de Montréal.
Marc: Moi aussi!
Isabelle: Quelle coïncidence!

B. Écoutez et répétez.   CD 1, TRACK 19

You will now hear a paused version of the dialog. Listen to the speaker and repeat right after he or she has completed the sentence.

• Les nombres de 80 à 1000   *p. 33*   CD 1, TRACK 20

Écoutez et répétez.

80 # 81 # 82 # 83 # 84 # 85 # 86 # 87 # 88 # 89 #
90 # 91 # 92 # 93 # 94 # 95 # 96 # 97 # 98 # 99 #
100 # 1000 #

• Prononciation   *p. 33*   CD 1, TRACK 21

La voyelle nasale /ɛ̃/

In French, there are three nasal vowel sounds:

Écoutez: /ɛ̃/ **cinq** (5)   /ɔ̃/ **onze** (11)   /ã/ **trente** (30)

Practice the sound /ɛ̃/ in the following words.

Be sure not to pronounce an "**n**" or "**m**" after the nasal vowel.

Répétez: "in" #   cinq # quinze # vingt # vingt-cinq # quatre-vingt-quinze #
        "ain" #   américain # Alain # copain #
        "(i)en" #   bien # canadien # tiens! #
        "un" #   un #
        Tiens! Voilà Alain. Il est américain. Et Julien? Il est canadien. #

• Vidéo-scène C: Les photos d'Isabelle   *p. 34*

A. Compréhension orale   CD 1, TRACK 22

Isabelle is showing her family photo album to her friend Jean-Paul.

Isabelle: Voici ma mère.
Jean-Paul: Et le monsieur, c'est ton père?
Isabelle: Non, c'est mon oncle Thomas.

Jean-Paul: Et la fille, c'est ta cousine?
Isabelle: Oui, c'est ma cousine Béatrice. Elle a seize ans.
Jean-Paul: Et le garçon, c'est ton cousin?
Isabelle: Non, c'est un copain.
Jean-Paul: Un copain ou ton copain?
Isabelle: Dis donc, Jean-Paul, tu es vraiment trop curieux!

B. Écoutez et répétez.   CD 1, TRACK 23

You will now hear a paused version of the dialog. Listen to the speaker and repeat right after he or she has completed the sentence.

• Prononciation   *p. 37*   CD 1, TRACK 24

Les voyelles nasales /ã/ et /ɔ̃/

Écoutez: tante   oncle

The letters "**an**" and "**en**" usually represent the nasal vowel /ã/. Be sure not to pronounce an "**n**" after the nasal vowel.

Répétez: ans # tante # français # quarante # trente # comment # Henri Laurent #

The letters "**on**" represent the nasal vowel /ɔ̃/. Be sure not to pronounce an "**n**" after the nasal vowel.

Répétez: non # bonjour # oncle # garçon #

Contrastez: an–on # tante–ton # onze ans # Mon oncle François a trente ans. #

À votre tour!

• Écoutez bien!   *p. 38*   CD 1, TRACK 25

Loto is a French version of Bingo. You will hear a series of numbers. If the number is on Card A, raise your left hand. If it is on Card B, raise your right hand.

19, 19 # 67, 67 # 15, 15 # 8, 8 # 72, 72 # 12, 12 # 42, 42 # 93, 93 # 5, 5 # 82, 82 #
33, 33 # 48, 48 # 25, 25 # 3, 3 # 17, 17 # 61, 61 # 98, 98 # 89, 89 # 70, 70 # 55, 55 #

• Et toi?   *p. 38*   CD 1, TRACK 26

You and Nathalie meet at a sidewalk café. Respond to her greetings and questions. Répondez aux questions de Nathalie.

1. Salut! Ça va? #
2. Comment t'appelles-tu? #
3. Tu es canadien (canadienne)? #
4. Quel âge as-tu? #
5. Comment s'appelle ton copain (ta copine)? #
6. Quel âge a ton copain (ta copine)?

• Conversation dirigée   *p. 38*   CD 1, TRACK 27

Two students, Jean-Pierre and Janet, have met on the Paris-Lyon train. Écoutez leur conversation.

Jean-Pierre: Bonjour.
Janet: Bonjour. Ça va?
Jean-Pierre: Oui, ça va.
Janet: Comment t'appelles-tu?
Jean-Pierre: Je m'appelle Jean-Pierre. Et toi?
Janet: Je m'appelle Janet.
Jean-Pierre: Tu es anglaise?
Janet: Non, je suis américaine.
Jean-Pierre: Tu es de New York?
Janet: Non, je suis de San Francisco.

> Complete videoscripts, plus Workbook and Assessment audioscripts, are available in the Unit Resource Books.

Main Theme
• Getting acquainted

COMMUNICATION
• Saying hello and good-bye
• Introducing yourself
• Saying where you're from
• Introducing friends, family, and relatives
• Counting to 100
• Saying how old you are and finding out someone else's age

CULTURES
• Learning about French salutations
• Learning about going back to school in France
• Learning about French names
• Learning about Astérix
• Learning about Martinique
• Learning about French friendships
• Learning about Quebec
• Learning about the French family

CONNECTIONS
• Connecting to Math: Counting in French
• Connecting to History: The history of the Statue of Liberty and the Eiffel Tower
• Connecting to Geography: Learning about Martinique and the province of Quebec
• Connecting to Geography: Studying the flags, populations, and capitals of some French-speaking countries

COMPARISONS
• Comparing French and American salutations
• Comparing the French and American ideas of friends and family

COMMUNITIES
• Using French for personal enjoyment

UNITÉ
1 Invitation au français

Faisons connaissance

LEÇON 1 Bonjour!
VIDÉO-SCÈNES
A La rentrée
B Tu es français?
C Salut! Ça va?

LEÇON 2 Famille et copains
VIDÉO-SCÈNES
A Copain ou copine?
B Une coïncidence
C Les photos d'Isabelle

THÈME ET OBJECTIFS

Getting acquainted
In this unit, you will be meeting French people.
You will learn ...
• to say hello and good-bye
• to introduce yourself and say where you are from
• to introduce friends, family, and relatives

You will also learn ...
• to count to 100
• to say how old you are and find out someone's age

WEBQUEST
CLASSZONE.COM

OVERVIEW OF Invitation au français

Invitation au français begins **Discovering French, Nouveau!–Bleu** with a focus on oral communication, both listening comprehension and speaking. Basic conversational skills are introduced without a formal presentation of structure.

▶ New conversational patterns are grouped by function in the **Pour communiquer** sections.

▶ Students will learn how to greet people, introduce themselves, talk about their friends and family, and even order in a café.

▶ Telling time, talking about the days of the week, months and dates, the weather and seasons, and the numbers from 0–100 are introduced.

Introduction culturelle

Salutations *(Greetings)*

How do you greet people in the United States? You may nod or smile. With adults, you may shake hands when you are introduced for the first time.

In France, people shake hands with friends and acquaintances each time they see one another, and not only to say hello but also when they say good-bye. Among teenagers, boys shake hands with boys. Girls kiss each other on the cheeks two or three times. (This is called **une bise**). Boys and girls who are close friends also greet each other with **une bise.**

UNIT OVERVIEW

▶ **Communication Goals:** Students will learn greetings and basic phrases. They will also learn how to count and tell time.

▶ **Linguistic Goals:** Students will begin to recognize what French sounds like and learn how French words are pronounced.

▶ **Critical Thinking Goals:** Students will encounter the concept of linguistic differences. They will discover that often there is no word-for-word correspondence between French and English.

▶ **Cultural Goals:** Students will discover that in France people greet one another and interact differently than in the U.S.

Teaching Resource Options

PRINT
Unit 1 Resource Book
    Family Letter, p. 31

AUDIO & VISUAL
Audio Program
Chansons CD

TECHNOLOGY
EasyPlanner CD-ROM/EasyPlanner
    Plus Online

Cultural Note

French children kiss their parents good morning and good night.

Cross-cultural observation

Have students study the pictures carefully, looking at the young people, their dress, and their way of greeting one another.

• Which elements in the pictures seem to be definitely French?

• Which elements could also be American?

Middle School Copymasters

Unité 1: Additional projects, games, puzzles, worksheets, conversations, drills, map activities, pp. T1–T7

Pacing

Try to move through this unit rather quickly, concentrating on listening and speaking.

In the units following **Invitation au français,** students will encounter the same vocabulary again. At that time they will be expected to master the material in writing.

Leçon 1A

Main Topic Greeting and meeting friends

Teaching Resource Options

PRINT

Workbook PE, pp. 1–4
Activités pour tous PE, pp. 1–2
Block Scheduling Copymasters, pp. 1–8
Unit 1 Resource Book
   Activités pour tous TE, pp. 13–14
   Audioscript, pp. 54, 56–58
   Communipak, pp. 128–146
   Lesson Plans, pp. 19–20
   Block Scheduling Lesson Plans, pp. 25–26
   Absent Student Copymasters, p. 32
   Video Activities, pp. 38–41
   Videoscript, p. 50
   Workbook TE, pp. 1–4

AUDIO & VISUAL

Audio Program
CD 1 Tracks 1, 2
CD 5 Tracks 1–9

TECHNOLOGY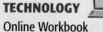
Online Workbook

VIDEO PROGRAM

VIDÉO   DVD

MODULE 1A
La rentrée

TOTAL TIME: 3:46 min.
  DVD Disk 1
  Videotape 1 (COUNTER: 6:53 min.)

1A.1 Dialogue: La rentrée
(6:53–7:54 min.)

1A.2 Mini-scenes: Meeting people
(7:55–9:14 min.)

1A.3 Vignette culturelle: Bonjour!
(9:15–10:39 min.)

Comprehension practice Play the entire module through as an introduction to the lesson.

Cultural Note

Trinh is a Vietnamese first name. Many people of Vietnamese and Cambodian origin live in France.

Some common Vietnamese names:

boys		girls	
Trinh	Chau	Kim	Hoa
Minh	Tam	Mai	Anh
My	Tan		

14 • **Culture et Communication**
  Unité 1 LEÇON 1A

LEÇON 1

Bonjour!
A La rentrée

This is the first day of school. Students are greeting their friends and meeting new classmates.

Trinh: Bonjour! Je m'appelle Trinh.
Céline: Et moi, je m'appelle Céline.

Marc: Je m'appelle Marc. Et toi?
Isabelle: Moi, je m'appelle Isabelle.

Jean-Paul: Comment t'appelles-tu?
Nathalie: Je m'appelle Nathalie.
Jean-Paul: Bonjour.
Nathalie: Bonjour.

USING THE VIDEO AND THE AUDIO PROGRAM

For each vidéo-scène of **Invitation au français,** the opening text corresponds to part 1 of the video.

First play the entire video module through as an introduction to the lesson. Have students observe how young people greet one another in France.

Then play the opening scene several more times and have students practice repeating the new phrases.

Write

Bonjour!

POUR COMMUNIQUER

▶ **How to say hello:**

Bonjour!	*Hello!*	—**Bonjour**, Nathalie!
		—**Bonjour**, Jean-Paul!

▶ **How to ask a classmate's name:**

Comment t'appelles-tu?	*What's your name?*	—**Comment t'appelles-tu?**
Je m'appelle …	*My name is …*	—**Je m'appelle** Céline.

Other Expressions

moi	*me*	**Moi**, je m'appelle Marc.
et toi?	*and you?*	**Et toi**, comment t'appelles-tu?

POUR COMMUNIQUER

Language note Literally, **bonjour** means *good day* and corresponds to *good morning* or *good afternoon*.

In the evening, **bonjour** may be replaced by **bonsoir** (*good evening*).

Bonne nuit (*good night*) is used when someone is going to bed.

Also: **Comment est-ce que tu t'appelles?**

Language note When speaking among themselves, French people often use casual speech. Since these forms are spoken (and not written), they are not formally presented in the students' textbook. If you wish, you may introduce them orally in class for recognition. For example, to ask someone's name in casual French one may say:

Tu t'appelles comment? or **Comment tu t'appelles?**

NOTES **culturelles**

1 La rentrée *(Back to school)*

French and American students have about the same number of days of summer vacation. In France, summer vacation usually begins at the end of June and classes resume in early September. The first day back to school in fall is called **la rentrée.**

2 Les prénoms français *(French first names)*

Many traditional French names have corresponding equivalents in English.

For boys:	For girls:
Jean *(John)*	**Marie** *(Mary)*
Pierre *(Peter)*	**Monique** *(Monica)*
Marc *(Mark)*	**Cécile** *(Cecilia)*
Philippe *(Philip)*	**Véronique** *(Veronica)*
Nicolas *(Nicholas)*	**Virginie** *(Virginia)*

Often the names **Jean** and **Marie** are combined in double names such as **Jean-Paul** and **Marie-Christine.** In recent years, names of foreign origin, like **Kevin** and **Laura**, have become quite popular.

Notes culturelles

There are four grades in a French **collège:**

- **sixième** (sixth grade),
- **cinquième** (seventh grade),
- **quatrième** (eighth grade) and
- **troisième** (ninth grade).

CHOOSING NAMES

Assign students French names or let them choose names for themselves from the list on pp. 10-11. Have students introduce themselves to the class. First practice the pronunciation of **je m'appelle** and then model the correct pronunciation of their French names. If you do not wish to use French names, help students pronounce their own names with a French accent.

Teaching Resource Options

PRINT

Workbook PE, pp. 1–4
Unit 1 Resource Book
  Audioscript, p. 54
  Communipak, pp. 128–146
  Video Activities, pp. 39–40
  Videoscript, p. 50
  Workbook TE, pp. 1–4

AUDIO & VISUAL

Audio Program
CD 1 Tracks 3, 4, 5

VIDEO PROGRAM

 VIDÉO   DVD

MODULE 1A

1A.2 Mini-scenes: Meeting people
(7:55–9:14 min.)

Petit commentaire
• Julius Caesar invaded Gaul around 50 B.C.
• The title of the book *Le tour de Gaule d'Astérix* is a take-off on the Tour de France bicycle race (see p. 28).

1 EXCHANGES greetings

– Bonjour!
– Bonjour!

2 COMMUNICATION identifying oneself

– Je m'appelle (Robert).
– Je m'appelle (Anne).

3 COMMUNICATION asking someone's name

– Comment t'appelles-tu?
– Je m'appelle (Daniel).

4 PRACTICE greetings

1. Bonjour, Céline!	5. Bonjour, Stéphanie!
2. Bonjour, Jean-Paul!	6. Bonjour, Nathalie!
3. Bonjour, Isabelle!	7. Bonjour, Trinh!
4. Bonjour, François!	

16 • Communication
Unité 1 LEÇON 1A

PETIT COMMENTAIRE
Astérix le Gaulois is one of the best-loved cartoon characters in France. Small in size but extremely clever and courageous, he represents the "little man" defending his country Gaul (the ancient name of France) against the invading Roman legions led by Julius Caesar.

1 **Bonjour!**

PARLER Say hello to the student nearest to you.

2 **Je m'appelle …**

PARLER Introduce yourself to your classmates.

▶ Je m'appelle (Paul).
▶ Je m'appelle (Denise).

3 **Et toi?**

PARLER Ask a classmate his or her name.

▶ —Comment t'appelles-tu?
  —Je m'appelle (Christine).

4 **Bonjour, les amis!** *(Hello everyone!)*

PARLER Say hello to the following students.

▶ Bonjour, Marc!

 **Marc**
 1. **Céline**
 2. **Jean-Paul**
 3. **Isabelle**
 4. **François**
 5. **Stéphanie**
 6. **Nathalie**
 7. **Trinh**

CHAIN ACTIVITY IN SMALL GROUPS

Student 1 asks Student 2 his/her name. Then Student 2 asks the name of Student 3, and so on. **Je m'appelle [Stéphanie]. Et toi? Moi, je m'appelle [David]. Et toi?** etc.

TEACHING THE ALPHABET

Say each letter of the alphabet and have students repeat as you write it on the board. Then, have a volunteer come and point to the letters as you say them in random order. The others can point to the corresponding letters in their textbook.

L'alphabet

A	B	C	D	E	F	G	H	I	J	K	L	M
a	bé	cé	dé	e	effe	gé	hache	i	ji	ka	elle	emme

N	O	P	Q	R	S	T	U	V	W	X	Y	Z
enne	o	pé	ku	erre	esse	té	u	vé	double vé	ixe	i grec	zède

Write

PRONONCIATION

Les signes orthographiques *(Spelling marks)*

French uses accents and spelling marks that do not exist in English. These marks are part of the spelling and cannot be left out.

In French, there are four accents that may appear on vowels.

´	**l'accent aigu** *(acute accent)*	Cécile, Stéphanie
`	**l'accent grave** *(grave accent)*	Michèle, Hélène
^	**l'accent circonflexe** *(circumflex)*	Jérôme
¨	**le tréma** *(diaeresis)*	Noël, Joëlle

There is only one spelling mark used with a consonant. It occurs under the letter "**c.**"

¸	**la cédille** *(cedilla)*	François

Write

5 **La rentrée**

PARLER It is the first day of class. The following students are introducing themselves. Act out the dialogues with your classmates.

▶ Hélène et Philippe   —Je m'appelle Hélène. Et toi?
                                  —Moi, je m'appelle Philippe.

1. Stéphanie et Marc
2. Cécile et Frédéric
3. Michèle et François
4. Anaïs et Clément
5. Céline et Jérôme
6. Mélanie et Noël

Les nombres de 0 à 10

Write

0	**1**	**2**	**3**
zéro	un	deux	trois

4	**5**	**6**	**7**
quatre	cinq	six	sept

8	**9**	**10**	
huit	neuf	dix	

6 **Numéros de téléphone**

PARLER Imagine you are visiting a family in Quebec. Give them your American phone number in French.

617-963-4028   six, un, sept —

                       neuf, six, trois —

                       quatre, zéro, deux, huit

PRONUNCIATION

Language notes

- The acute accent ´ occurs only on **e** to show it is pronounced /e/.
- The grave accent ` occurs mainly on **e** to show it is pronounced /ɛ/, and in the words **à, là,** and **où.**
- The circumflex ^ can occur on all vowels; often the corresponding English word has an "s": **forêt, hôpital, mât.**
- The diaeresis ¨ is placed on the second of two vowels to show that they are pronounced separately: **naïf.**
- The c-cedilla **ç** is used before **a, o, u** to show it is pronounced /s/: **ça, garçon, reçu.** Otherwise, **c** before **a, o, u** is pronounced /k/: **café, collège, culturel.**
- Note Accent marks are often not placed on capital letters. In this book, however, we will show accents on capital letters to make it easier for students.

5 **EXCHANGES** making introductions

– Moi, je m'appelle ... Et toi?
– Je m'appelle...

1. Stéphanie/Marc.
2. Cécile/Frédéric.
3. Michèle/François.
4. Anaïs/Clément.
5. Céline/Jérôme.
6. Mélanie/Noël.

Speaking activity To practice the numbers 0-10, knock loudly on your desk. Have the students identify the number of knocks in French. For example: (toc! toc!) **Deux!**, etc.

If students ask
un nombre = number or numeral, in the mathematical sense
un numéro = number, in a series; e.g., phone number, house number

6 **COMMUNICATION** giving one's telephone number

617-963-4028 (six, un, sept - neuf, six, trois - quatre, zéro, deux, huit)

Cultural note In Quebec, as in the United States, phone numbers are given digit by digit.

COMPREHENSION Numbers 0 to 10

With your right hand, demonstrate the numbers 0 to 5 as you say them:

Voici 0. [closed fist]

Voici 1. [thumb extended]

Voici 2. [thumb and index finger] ...

Have students respond to commands with the same gestures:

     Montrez-moi 0, 1, 2 ...

Practice the numbers in random order:

     Montrez-moi 3, 5, 2, ...

Continue with numbers 6 through 10, using both hands.

Leçon 1B

Main Topic Stating one's nationality and where one is from

Teaching Resource Options

PRINT

Workbook PE, pp. 5–8
Activités pour tous PE, pp. 3–4
Unit 1 Resource Book
  Activités pour tous TE, pp. 15–16
  Audioscript, pp. 55, 58–59
  Communipak, pp. 128–146
  Lesson Plans, pp. 21–22
  Block Scheduling Lesson Plans, pp. 27–28
  Absent Student Copymasters, pp. 33–34
  Video Activities, pp. 42–45
  Videoscript, pp. 51–52
  Workbook TE, pp. 5–8

AUDIO & VISUAL

Audio Program
CD 1 Tracks 6, 7
CD 5 Tracks 10–14

Overhead Transparencies
4 U.S., Canada, England, France
  Les nationalités

TECHNOLOGY
Online Workbook

VIDEO PROGRAM

MODULE 1B
Tu es français?

TOTAL TIME: 7:09 min.
  DVD Disk 1
  Videotape 1 (COUNTER: 10:49 min.)

1B.1 Dialogue: Tu es français?
(10:49–12:15 min.)

1B.2 Mini-scenes: Finding out where people are from
(12:16–13:48 min.)

1B.3 Vignette culturelle: Qui est français?
(13:49–17:58 min.)

Comprehension practice Play the entire module through as an introduction to the lesson.

Cultural note Marc tells Stéphanie **Tu as de la chance!** because he thinks she is lucky to live in Martinique, a tropical island with beautiful beaches and exotic flowers. For French people, Martinique evokes the kinds of images that "Hawaii" evokes for Americans.

18 • Culture et Communication
  Unité 1 LEÇON 1B

VIDÉO-SCÈNE   VIDÉO DVD AUDIO

B Tu es français?

It is the opening day of school and several of the students meet in the cafeteria (**la cafétéria** or **la cantine**) at lunchtime. Marc discovers that not everyone is French.

Marc: Tu es français?
Jean-Paul: Oui, je suis français.

Marc: Et toi, Patrick, tu es français aussi?
Patrick: Non! Je suis américain. Je suis de Boston.

Marc: Et toi, Stéphanie, tu es française ou américaine?
Stéphanie: Je suis française.
Marc: Tu es de Paris?
Stéphanie: Non, je suis de Fort-de-France.
Marc: Tu as de la chance!   *You're lucky!*

CLASSROOM MANAGEMENT Groups

Play the entire video module as an introduction to the lesson.

Divide the class into groups and name one person in each group as **secrétaire** *(recorder)*. Play Part 1 of the video again.

Have the groups list things they observed in the French school that are similar to their own school, as well as things that are different.

Have the recorders come forward to read their lists. The team with the most complete list is the winner. For confirmation, play the video once more.

Copy out for Nationality Quiz

POUR COMMUNIQUER

▶ *How to talk about where people are from:*

Tu es de …? *Are you from …?* —**Tu es de** Nice?
Je suis de … *I'm from …* —Non, **je suis de** Paris.

Tu es de Nice?

▶ *How to talk about one's nationality:*

Tu es …? *Are you …?* —Pierre, **tu es** français?
Je suis … *I am …* —Oui, **je suis** français.

#4 Nos. 11–20

Les nationalités

🇫🇷	**français**	**française**
🇬🇧	**anglais**	**anglaise**
🇺🇸	**américain**	**américaine**
🍁	**canadien**	**canadienne**

Other Expressions

oui	*yes*	Tu es français? **Oui**, je suis français.
non	*no*	Tu es canadien? **Non**, je suis américain.
et	*and*	Je suis de Paris. **Et** toi?
ou	*or*	Tu es français **ou** canadien?
aussi	*also, too*	Moi **aussi**, je suis française.

NOTE culturelle

La Martinique

★ Fort-de-France

EN BREF
Capitale: Fort-de-France
Population: 400 000
Langues: créole, français

La Martinique

Martinique is a small French island located in the Caribbean, southeast of Puerto Rico. Because Martinique is part of the French national territory, its inhabitants are French citizens. Most of them are of African origin. They speak French as well as a dialect called **créole.**

Teaching note This is the students' first introduction to adjective agreement, and should be kept as simple as possible. The key objective is that students hear the sound differences and pronounce the masculine and feminine forms correctly.

Notes from the authors Please note that students are now being introduced to the verb **être**. This is also the first time they encounter subject-verb agreement and adjective agreement. These concepts will be explored in depth in later units. Here, they are to be used conversationally.

Pronunciation Be sure students notice that the final consonant sound (/z/, /n/) is pronounced in the feminine forms but is silent in the masculine forms.

Cultural note As students have learned in **Bonjour, le monde francophone!** (pp. 8-9), the French national territory extends beyond continental France (**la France métropolitaine**).

Martinique is one of the five French overseas departments (**Départements d'Outre-Mer**).

LISTENING COMPREHENSION ACTIVITY

Read the following eight sentences.
Have students raise their hands (or stand) if the sentence refers to a girl.

Tu es français?	**Tu es américaine?**
Tu es canadienne?	**Tu es anglaise?**
Tu es anglais?	**Tu es américain?**
Tu es française?	**Tu es canadien?**

Teaching Resource Options

PRINT

Workbook PE, pp. 5–8
Unit 1 Resource Book
   Audioscript, p. 55
   Communipak, pp. 128–146
   Workbook TE, pp. 5–8

AUDIO & VISUAL

Audio Program
CD 1 Tracks 8, 9

TECHNOLOGY

Power Presentations

Petit commentaire
The Statue of Liberty was sculpted by Auguste Bartholdi, who called upon Gustave Eiffel to design the interior metal framework. Although the arm and torch were exhibited at the World's Fair in Philadelphia in 1876, the statue itself was not inaugurated until ten years later. Gustave Eiffel built the Eiffel Tower for the Paris World's Fair in 1889.

---

1 **COMMUNICATION** identifying oneself

- Bonjour! Je m'appelle (Karen Babcock). Je suis (américaine). Je suis de (Cleveland).
- Bonjour! Je m'appelle (Randy Bergholz). Je suis (américain). Je suis de (Palo Alto).

Pronunciation If your students are from a city that begins with a vowel sound, have them use **d'**: **Je suis d'(Atlanta).** (The concept of elision is presented formally in Lesson 6.)

---

2 **ROLE PLAY** discussing where people are from

– (x), tu es français(e)?
– Oui, je suis français(e). Je suis de …
1. Pierre/français/Paris
2. Paul/français/Bordeaux
3. Éric/français/Lyon
4. Marie/française/Marseille
5. Nicole/française/Nice

Extra speaking activity Ask students to pretend they are a famous English, French, Canadian, or American person. Have them introduce themselves to the class, say where they are from, and give their nationalities.

PETIT COMMENTAIRE
The Statue of Liberty (**la statue de la Liberté**) was a gift to the United States from the French people on the occasion of the 100th anniversary of American independence. The Eiffel Tower (**la tour Eiffel**) was built to celebrate the 100th anniversary of the French Revolution.

---

français, française

Names of nationalities may have two different forms, depending on whom they refer to:

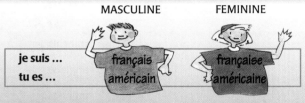

	MASCULINE	FEMININE
je suis …	français / américain	française / américaine
tu es …		

Note In written French the feminine forms always end in **-e**.

---

1 **Et toi?**

PARLER Give your name, your nationality, and your city of origin.

▼

Bonjour!
Je m'appelle Bob Jones.
Je suis américain.
Je suis de Providence.

Bonjour!
Je m'appelle Linda Carlson.
Je suis américaine.
Je suis de Boston.

---

2 **Français ou française?**

PARLER You meet the following young people. Ask them if they are French. A classmate will answer you, as in the model. (Be sure to use **français** with boys and **française** with girls.)

▶ —Sophie, tu es française?
   —Oui, je suis française. Je suis de Strasbourg.

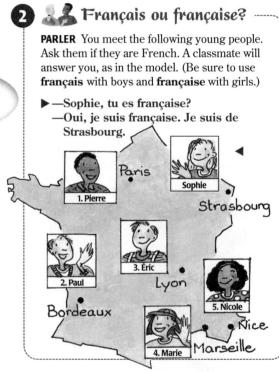

1. Pierre — Paris
2. Paul — Bordeaux
3. Éric — Lyon
4. Marie — Marseille
5. Nicole — Nice
Sophie — Strasbourg

CLASSROOM MANAGEMENT Pair Practice

In pair practice, students do activities together with a partner. Introduce the class to pair practice with Act. 2 and 3. Be sure each student has a partner.

First do the exercise with the entire class, having half the group give the first cue, and the other half the response.

Then let the students do the same activity again in pairs. For the odd numbered cues, Student A asks the question and Student B responds. For the even-numbered cues, the roles are reversed.

3 **Quelle nationalité?** *(Which nationality?)*

PARLER Greet the following young people and find out each one's nationality. A classmate will answer you, according to the model.

▸ —Bonjour, Marc. Tu es canadien?
—Oui, je suis canadien.
  Je suis de Montréal.

Marc
Montréal

1. Claire Québec
2. Patrick Boston

3. Denise Liverpool
4. Donna Memphis
5. Paul Cambridge

Les nombres de 10 à 20

10 dix	11 onze	12 douze	13 treize	14 quatorze	15 quinze
16 seize	17 dix-sept	18 dix-huit	19 dix-neuf	20 vingt	

4 **La fusée Ariane** *(The Ariane rocket)*

PARLER Give the countdown for the liftoff of the French rocket Ariane, from 20 to 0.

"Décoller!"

PRONONCIATION

Les lettres muettes *(Silent letters)*

In French, the last letter of a word is often not pronounced.

- Final "**e**" is always silent.
  Répétez: **Céline Philippe Stéphanie anglaise française onze douze treize quatorze quinze seize**

- Final "**s**" is almost always silent.
  Répétez: **Paris Nicolas Jacques anglais français trois**

- The letter "**h**" is always silent.
  Répétez: **Hélène Henri Thomas Nathalie Catherine Thérèse**

Paris

3 **ROLE PLAY** discussing one's nationality

1. – Bonjour, Claire. Tu es canadienne?
   – Oui, je suis canadienne. Je suis de Québec.
2. – Bonjour, Patrick. Tu es américain?
   – Oui, je suis américain. Je suis de Boston.
3. – Bonjour, Denise. Tu es anglaise?
   – Oui, je suis anglaise. Je suis de Liverpool.
4. – Bonjour, Donna. Tu es américaine?
   – Oui, je suis américaine. Je suis de Memphis.
5. – Bonjour, Paul. Tu es anglais?
   – Oui, je suis anglais. Je suis de Cambridge.

Language note People from the province of Quebec will often say: **Je suis québécois(e).**

Middle School Copymasters
Number Circle, p. T1; Crossword Puzzle: Numbers, p. 5

Pronunciation Note the pronunciation of **vingt** /vɛ̃/.

4 **PRACTICE** numbers 0 to 20

Vingt, dix-neuf, dix-huit, dix-sept, seize, quinze, quatorze, treize, douze, onze, dix, neuf, huit, sept, six, cinq, quatre, trois, deux, un, zéro!

Language note In French, a countdown is **un compte à rebours.**

Cultural note All the French Ariane rockets are launched from Kourou in French Guiana (South America). France is the only country in Europe with an on-going space program.

PRONUNCIATION

- Have students pronounce the French /r/ in Paris as if they were clearing their throats.
- In later lessons, students will encounter a few common words where the final "s" is pronounced: **un fils, mars, tennis**
- The letters "ph" represent the sound /f/, as in English: **Philippe, Stéphanie.**
- The letters "ch" usually represent the sound /ʃ/, as in: **Chicago, Michèle.**
- The letters "chr" represent the sound /kr/ as in: **Christophe, Christine.**

COMPREHENSION Numbers 11 to 20

PROPS: index cards with numbers 11 to 20

Place the first five index cards on the chalkboard tray. Point to the numbers as you name them: 11, 12, 13, 14, 15.

Have students come forward to point out and touch the numbers as you name them.
X, montre le 12. Touche le 15.

Present the second five cards.

Place all cards randomly on the tray. Ask students to pass numbers to their classmates.
Y, prends le 20 et donne-le à Z.

C Salut! Ça va?

On the way to school, François meets his friends.

Copy out!

Salut, Isabelle!

Salut! Ça va?

Ça va! Merci!

Salut, Nathalie! Ça va?

Ça va bien! Et toi?

Moi aussi!

Ça va, Philippe?

Ah non! Zut! Ça va mal.

François also meets his teachers.

Bonjour, monsieur.

Bonjour, François.

Monsieur Masson

Bonjour, madame.

Bonjour, François.

Madame Chollet

Bonjour, mademoiselle.

Bonjour, François.

Mademoiselle Lacour

After class, François says good-bye to his teacher and his friends.

Au revoir, mademoiselle.

Au revoir, François.

Au revoir, Nathalie!

Au revoir, François.

22 | vingt-deux
Unité 1 — *Invitation au français*

SETTING THE SCENE

Ask students how they greet their teachers when they meet them before school or in the hall.

Have them watch the video to see if French students greet their teachers with the same formality or informality.

Leçon 1C

Main Topic Saying hello and good-bye

Teaching Resource Options

PRINT

Workbook PE, pp. 9–12
Activités pour tous PE, pp. 5–6
Unit 1 Resource Book
  Activités pour tous TE, pp. 17–18
  Audioscript, pp. 55–56, 59–60
  Communipak, pp. 126–148
  Lesson Plans, pp. 23–24
  Block Scheduling Lesson Plans, pp. 29–30
  Absent Student Copymasters, p. 35
  Video Activities, pp. 46–49
  Videoscript, pp. 52–53
  Workbook TE, pp. 9–12

AUDIO & VISUAL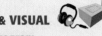

Audio Program
CD 1 Tracks 10, 11   *Text p22, 23*
CD 5 Tracks 15–20   *WB p. 9, 10*
                     Do A, B, C
TECHNOLOGY   *D, E, F.*
Online Workbook

VIDEO PROGRAM

VIDÉO   DVD

MODULE 1C
Salut! Ça va?

TOTAL TIME: 4:38 min.
  DVD Disk 1
  Videotape 1 (COUNTER: 18:08 min.)

1C.1 Dialogue: Salut! Ça va?
  (18:31–18:50 min.)

1C.2 Mini-scenes: Greeting people
  (18:51–21:26 min.)

1C.3 Vignette culturelle: Bonjour ou Salut?
  (21:27–22:46 min.)

Comprehension practice Play the entire module through as an introduction to the lesson.

22 · **Culture et Communication**
Unité 1 LEÇON 1C

Quiz #1 lesson #1 and #8

POUR COMMUNIQUER

▶ *How to greet a friend or classmate:*

Salut!   *Hi!*

▶ *How to greet a teacher or another adult:*

Bonjour!   *Hello!*   **Bonjour, monsieur.**
                              Bonjour, madame.
                              Bonjour, mademoiselle.

Salut!

▶ *How to say good-bye:*

Au revoir!   *Good-bye!*   **Au revoir, Philippe.**
                                   Au revoir, monsieur.

➜ In written French, the following abbreviations are commonly used:

M. Masson	Monsieur Masson
Mme Chollet	Madame Chollet
Mlle Lacour	Mademoiselle Lacour

➜ Young people often use **Salut!** to say good-bye to each other.

NOTE *culturelle*

Bonjour ou Salut?

French young people may greet one another with **Bonjour**, but they often prefer the less formal **Salut.** When they meet their teachers, however, they always use **Bonjour.** French young people are generally much more formal with adults than with their friends. This is especially true in their relationships with teachers, whom they treat with respect.

Have you noticed that in France adults are addressed as **monsieur, madame,** or **mademoiselle?** The last name is usually not used in greeting people.

POUR COMMUNIQUER

Language note When used alone, the titles **monsieur, madame,** and **mademoiselle** are not capitalized.

Casual speech Young people often use **salut** or the Italian **ciao** / tʃau / to say good-bye.

If students ask The French have no equivalent for "Ms." Instead they usually use **Madame.**

Abbreviations
• When an abbreviation includes only the first letter of a word, a period is used: **Monsieur = M.**

• When an abbreviation consists of the first and last letters of a word, no period is needed: **Madame = Mme, Mademoiselle = Mlle**

Note culturelle In France, young people almost never call adults by their first names.

TEACHING STRATEGY Greeting adults

To activate **Monsieur, Madame,** and **Mademoiselle,** give names of other teachers in your school. Ask students to imagine they see these people in the hall. Have them greet the teachers in French.

Mrs. Mills – **Bonjour, Madame!**
Mr. Tower – **Bonjour, Monsieur!**
Miss Swenson – **Bonjour, Mademoiselle!**

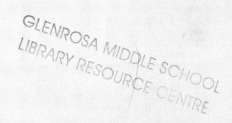

Teaching Resource Options

1 PRACTICE selecting an appropriate greeting

1. Salut, Céline!
2. Bonjour, monsieur!
3. Salut, Nathalie!
4. Salut, Marc!
5. Bonjour, madame!
6. Bonjour, mademoiselle!

Variation Say good-bye.
– **Au revoir, Valérie.**
– **Au revoir, mademoiselle.**

2 EXCHANGES greetings

Answers will vary.
– Salut, (Anne)! Ça va?
– Ça va (bien)! Et toi?
– Ça va (très bien). Merci.
– Salut, (Éric)! Ça va?
– (Non), ça va (mal). Et toi?
– Ça va (comme ci, comme ça). Merci.

---

1 Bonjour ou salut?

PARLER You are enrolled in a French school. Greet your friends and teachers.

▶ **Salut, Valérie!**   Valérie   ▶ **Bonjour, mademoiselle!**   Mademoiselle Pinot

1. Céline   2. Monsieur Masson   3. Nathalie   4. Marc   5. Madame Albert   6. Mademoiselle Boucher

POUR COMMUNIQUER

▶ *How to ask people how they feel:*

—**Ça va?**   *How are you? How are things going? How's everything?*
—**Ça va!**   *(I'm) fine. (I'm) okay. Everything's all right.*

Ça va …   **très bien**   **bien**   **comme ci, comme ça**   **mal**   **très mal**

▶ *How to express one's feelings of frustration and appreciation:*

Zut! *Darn!*   **Zut!** Ça va mal!   **Merci!** *Thanks!*   Ça va, **merci.**

→ **Ça va?** *(How are you?)* is an informal greeting that corresponds to the following expressions:

    Comment vas-tu? (when addressing a friend)
      Bonjour, Paul. Comment vas-tu?
    Comment allez-vous? (when addressing an adult)
      Bonjour, madame. Comment allez-vous?

2 **Dialogue**

PARLER Exchange greetings with your classmates and ask how they are doing.

▶—**Salut, (Thomas)! Ça va?**
  —**Ça va! Et toi?**
  —**Ça va bien. Merci.**

ÇA VA? / OUI, ÇA VA TRÈS BIEN! / ÇA VA? / AH NON! ÇA VA MAL!

TEACHING NOTE Spoken and written numbers

The emphasis in **Invitation au français** is on functional language use. In order to get around in a French-speaking country, it is very important to be able to understand and use numbers in communicative situations.

    At the basic level, students need a great deal of practice in order to understand and use numbers easily.

    As a challenge activity, some students may want to learn to spell the numbers, but spelling is not necessary at this level. Most French people use digits to write numbers, especially numbers over 20.

3 **Situations**

PARLER Sometimes we feel good and sometimes we don't. How would you respond in the following situations?

▶ You have the flu.
—Ça va?
—Ça va mal!

1. You just received an "A" in French.
2. You lost your wallet.
3. Your uncle gave you five dollars.
4. Your grandparents sent you a check for 100 dollars.
5. You bent the front wheel of your bicycle.
6. Your parents bought you a new video game.

7. Your little brother broke your cell phone.
8. It's your birthday.
9. You have a headache.
10. You just had an argument with your best friend.
11. Your French teacher has just canceled a quiz.

4 **Ça va?**

PARLER How would the following people answer the question **Ça va?**

Les nombres de 20 à 60

20 vingt	30 trente	40 quarante	50 cinquante	60 soixante
vingt et un	trente et un	quarante et un	cinquante et un	
vingt-deux	trente-deux	quarante-deux	cinquante-deux	
vingt-trois	trente-trois	quarante-trois	cinquante-trois	
…	…	…	…	
vingt-neuf	trente-neuf	quarante-neuf	cinquante-neuf	

Note Use **et** before **un: vingt et un.**

5 **Séries**

PARLER Read the following number series out loud.

13	21	37	42	55	60

16	20	29	31	48	56

PRONONCIATION

Les consonnes finales *(Final consonants)*

 un deux trois

In French, the last consonant of a word is often not pronounced.

• Remember: Final "**s**" is usually silent.
Répétez: **trois français anglais**

• Most other final consonants are usually silent.
Répétez: **Richard Albert Robert salut
américain canadien bien deux**

EXCEPTION: The following final consonants are usually pronounced: "**c**," "**f**," "**l**," and sometimes "**r**."
Répétez: **Éric Daniel Lebeuf Pascal Victor**

However, the ending **-er** is usually pronounced /e/.
Répétez: **Roger Olivier**

COMPREHENSION Numbers and prepositions

PROPS: Index cards for 10, 20, 30, 40, 50, 60

Spread out the index cards on a table. Place three cards in a row on the chalktray.
Je mets les nombres 10-20-30 en ligne droite.

Then have students perform similar actions.
X, mets les nombres 40-50-60 en ligne droite.

Introduce new numbers with **après** (*after*).
**Maintenant, je mets le 30 après le 20.
Y, mets le 10 après le 30. …**

Similarly introduce **avant** (*before*), **derrière** (*behind*), **devant** (*in front of*).
**Je mets le 40 avant le 10. …
Je mets le 50 derrière le 20. …
Je mets le 60 devant le 40. …**

---

3 ROLE PLAY expressing one's feelings

– Ça va?
– Ça va (très) …!

1. bien!
2. mal!
3. bien! (comme ci, comme ça.)
4. bien!
5. mal!
6. bien!
7. mal!
8. bien!
9. mal! (comme ci, comme ça.)
10. mal!
11. bien!

4 PRACTICE selecting an appropriate response

1. Ça va (très) bien!
2. Ça va (très) bien!
3. Ça va (très) bien!
4. Ça va (très) mal!
5. Ça va (très) mal!
6. Ça va (très) mal!

Les nombres de 20 à 60

Pronunciation Remind students that there is no liaison after **et**: 31 /trãteɛ̃/, etc.

Speaking activity Have the class say numbers in series.
• counting by 3s: 30 - 33 - 36 - 39 - 42 - 45 - 48 - 51 …
• by 4s: 28 - 32 - 36 - 40 - 44 …
• by 5s: 25 - 30 - 35 - 40 - 45 …

5 PRACTICE reading numbers up to 60

(top) treize, vingt et un, trente-sept, quarante-deux, cinquante-cinq, soixante
(bottom) seize, vingt, vingt-neuf, trente et un, quarante-huit, cinquante-six

Listening comprehension Read a number from one of the tickets and have students indicate whether the number appears on the top or bottom ticket.

PRONUNCIATION

Exceptions
• The final consonant is pronounced in **zut!** and numbers used in counting like **six, sept, huit, dix.**
• The "r" in **monsieur** is silent.

Memory aid These final consonants are found in the word: CaReFuL.

Leçon 2A

Main Topics Pointing out people and finding out who they are

Teaching Resource Options

PRINT

Workbook PE, pp. 13–16
Activités pour tous PE, pp. 7–8
Block Scheduling Copymasters,
  pp. 9–16
Unit 1 Resource Book
  Activités pour tous TE, pp. 77–78
  Audioscript, pp. 118, 120–121
  Communipak, pp. 128–146
  Lesson Plans, pp. 83–84
  Block Scheduling Lesson Plans,
    pp. 89–90
  Absent Student Copymasters, p. 95
  Video Activities, pp. 102–105
  Videoscript, p. 114
  Workbook TE, pp. 65–68

AUDIO & VISUAL

Audio Program
CD 1 Tracks 14, 15 ✓
CD 5 Tracks 21–25 — *Workbook*
                        p13,14
                        15,16
Overhead Transparencies
7 People *Les personnes*

TECHNOLOGY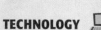
Online Workbook

VIDEO PROGRAM

 MODULE 2A
Copain ou copine?

TOTAL TIME: 3:34 min.
  DVD Disk 1
  Videotape 1 (COUNTER: 22:57 min.)

2A.1 Dialogue: Copain ou copine?
  (23:42–24:18 min.)

2A.2 Mini-scenes: Listening
  – Pointing out people
  (24:19–25:17 min.)

**2A.3 Vignette culturelle: La bande
  de copains**
  (25:18–26:31 min.)

Comprehension practice Play the entire module through as an introduction to the lesson.

LEÇON 2

Famille et copains
A Copain ou copine?

In French, there are certain girls' and boys' names that sound the same. Occasionally this can be confusing.

Dominique? Qui est-ce? Un copain ou une copine?

SCÈNE 1 **Philippe et Jean-Paul**
Philippe is at home with his friend Jean-Paul. He seems to be expecting someone. Who could it be … ? The doorbell rings.

Philippe: Tiens! Voilà Dominique!
Jean-Paul: Dominique? Qui est-ce?
  Un copain ou une copine?
Philippe: C'est une copine.

Salut, Dominique! Ça va?

SCÈNE 2 **Philippe, Jean-Paul, Dominique**

Philippe: Salut, Dominique! Ça va?
Dominique: Oui, ça va! Et toi?
Jean-Paul: *(thinking)* C'est vrai!   *It's true!*
  C'est une copine!

SETTING THE STAGE

Ask students to think of names for boys and girls that sound the same.

For example: Kim, Lynn, Marty, Bobby/Bobbie, Gene/Jean.

In French, also, there are many boy's and girl's names that are pronounced alike.

Names spelled the same:
  Dominique, Claude.

Names spelled differently:
  René/Renée, André/Andrée, Joël/Joëlle, Noël/Noëlle, Michel/Michèle, Daniel/Danielle, Gabriel/Gabrielle, Frédéric/Frédérique.

Tiens! Voilà Caroline! C'est une copine!

POUR COMMUNIQUER

▶ *How to introduce or point out someone:*

Voici …	*This is …, Here come(s) …*	**Voici** Jean-Paul.
		Voici Nathalie et François.
Voilà …	*This (That) is …, There's …*	**Voilà** Isabelle.
		Voilà Philippe et Dominique.

▶ *How to find out who someone is:*

| **Qui est-ce?** | *Who's that? Who is it?* | —**Qui est-ce?** |
| **C'est …** | *It's …, That's …, He's …, She's …* | —**C'est** Patrick. **C'est** un copain. |

▶ *How to get someone's attention or to express surprise:*

| **Tiens!** | *Look! Hey!* | **Tiens,** voilà Dominique! |

Les personnes

un garçon	*boy*
un ami	*friend (male)*
un copain	*friend (male)*
un monsieur	*gentleman*
un prof	*teacher*

une fille	*girl*
une amie	*friend (female)*
une copine	*friend (female)*
une dame	*lady*
une prof	*teacher*

NOTE *culturelle*

Amis et copains

French young people, like their American counterparts, enjoy spending time with their friends. They refer to their friends as **un ami** (for a boy) and **une amie** (for a girl) or — more commonly — as **un copain** or **une copine.** Note that the words **copain, copine** can also have special meanings. When a boy talks about **une copine,** he is referring to a friend who is a girl. However, when he says **ma** (*my*) **copine,** he may be referring to his girlfriend. Similarly, a girl would call her boyfriend **mon copain.**

Language notes
- The expression **voilà** may also mean *That is, There is, There are.*
- One can say: **C'est qui? Qui c'est?**

Cultural note There are several ways of referring to one's boyfriend or girlfriend:
- **mon petit ami, ma petite amie** (though these terms are not as commonly used as several years ago)
- **mon petit copain, ma petite copine**
- **mon ami, mon amie**

The possessive is used to signal a more personal relationship.

Language note

Un prof/une prof. In casual speech, both teachers and students in France use the terms **un prof** and **une prof.** These expressions are easier for beginners and are therefore introduced here in **Invitation au français.** The more formal term **un professeur,** which refers to both men and women, is introduced in Lesson 19.

COMPREHENSION Nouns with un/une

PROPS: Transparency 7: People *Les personnes*
Red and blue index cards
Model new words on the transparency.
   Voici un garçon. Voici une fille. …

Have students come point out the words.
   X, viens ici. Montre-nous une fille.

Distribute two cards to each student.

Voici "un". [Hold up the blue card.]
Voici "une". [Hold up the red card.]

As you make statements using the new words, have students hold up their cards.
   C'est un copain. Levez la carte bleue.
   C'est une amie. Levez la carte rouge.
   C'est un ami. [blue cards.]

Petit commentaire
• The **Tour de France,** which was created in 1904, is a month-long bicycle race that takes cyclists around France, with particularly grueling stages (**étapes**) in the Alps and the Pyrenees. Every year the route is somewhat different, but the finish line is always in Paris at the bottom of the Champs-Élysées.
• The **Tour de France féminin** began in 1984. From 1987 to 1989, it was dominated by the French cyclist Jeannie Longo.

Teaching note This is the first time students see indefinite articles. They are introduced to the concept of gender in that they discover that articles agree with the nouns they introduce.

1 **PRACTICE** identifying male and female friends

1. Alice est une copine. 4. Robert est un copain.
2. Cécile est une copine. 5. Céline est une copine.
3. Trinh est un copain.

Pronunciation
• Insist that students do not pronounce the "n" in **un** or **copain.**
• Note that liaison is common after **est:** Christine est‿une copine.

2 **ROLE PLAY** meeting and identifying friends

–Tiens, voilà ... !   1. Alice/une amie.
–Qui est-ce?   2. Cécile/une amie.
–C'est ...   3. Trinh/un ami.
                        4. Robert/un ami.
                        5. Céline/une amie.

3 **PRACTICE** choosing genders

1. une 2. un 3. une 4. une 5. un
6. un 7. une 8. une 9. un 10. une

PETIT COMMENTAIRE
Cycling is a popular competitive sport throughout France. The most popular races are the **Tour de France** for men and the **Grande Boucle Féminine Internationale** for women. French women cyclists have won many titles.

un garçon, une fille

In French, all NOUNS are either MASCULINE or FEMININE.
Nouns referring to boys or men are almost always MASCULINE.
    They are introduced by **un** *(a, an)*.
Nouns referring to girls or women are almost always FEMININE.
    They are introduced by **une** *(a, an)*.

	MASCULINE			FEMININE	
UN	**un** garçon	*a boy*	UNE	**une** fille	*a girl*
	un ami	*a friend (male)*		**une** amie	*a friend (female)*

1 ***Copain ou copine?***

PARLER Say that the following people are your friends. Use **un copain** or **une copine,** as appropriate.

▶ **Élodie est une copine.**

Élodie

1. Alice

2. Cécile

3. Trinh

4. Robert

5. Céline

2 ***Les amis***

PARLER The same young people are visiting your school. Point them out to your classmates, using **un ami** or **une amie,** as appropriate.

▶ —**Tiens, voilà Élodie!**
  —**Qui est-ce?**
  —**C'est une amie.**

3 ***Un ou une?***

PARLER Identify the people below by completing the sentences with **un** or **une.**

1. Voici … fille.
2. Voilà … garçon.
3. Voici … dame.
4. C'est … amie.
5. Nicolas est … ami.
6. Jean-Paul est … copain.
7. Cécile est … copine.
8. Voici Mlle Lacour. C'est … prof.
9. Voici M. Masson. C'est … prof.
10. Voici Mme Chollet. C'est … prof.

TEACHING NOTES un/une

The concept of gender is presented formally in Lesson 10. The focus in this lesson is on sound discrimination between **un** and **une.**
▶ Saying **un:** Be sure that students pronounce **un** without a final /n/ – except in liaison.
▶ Saying **une:** Have students think of **une** as "een" (and not "oon"). Then ask them to round their lips

as they say "een." (This way students will begin to acquire the French pronunciation.)

4 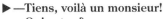 **À la fenêtre** (At the window)

PARLER You and a friend are walking down the street and you see the following people at their windows. Identify them in short dialogues.

▶ —Tiens, voilà un monsieur!
—Qui est-ce?
—C'est Monsieur Mercier.

Monsieur Mercier

 1. Nicole

 2. Mademoiselle Lasalle

 3. Éric

 4. Madame Albert

 5. Monsieur Lavie

 6. Alain

Les nombres de 60 à 79

60 soixante

61 soixante et un	66 soixante-six
62 soixante-deux	67 soixante-sept
63 soixante-trois	68 soixante-huit
64 soixante-quatre	69 soixante-neuf
65 soixante-cinq	

70 soixante-dix

71 soixante et onze	76 soixante-seize
72 soixante-douze	77 soixante-dix-sept
73 soixante-treize	78 soixante-dix-huit
74 soixante-quatorze	79 soixante-dix-neuf
75 soixante-quinze	

5 Numéros de téléphone

PARLER Read aloud the phone numbers of Jean-Paul's friends in Paris.

▶ Philippe   zéro un,
quarante-deux,
soixante et un,
dix-neuf,
soixante-quinze

▶ Philippe   01.42.61.19.75
Martine   01.41.33.64.79
Michèle   01.42.56.76.62
Stéphanie   01.45.68.77.35
François   01.49.78.13.62

PRONONCIATION

La liaison

un ami

Pronounce the following words:

un ami   un Américain   un Anglais   un artiste

In general, the "**n**" of **un** is silent. However, in the above words, the "**n**" of **un** is pronounced as if it were the *first* letter of the next word. This is called LIAISON.

Liaison occurs between two words when the second one begins with a VOWEL SOUND, that is, with "**a**", "**e**", "**i**", "**o**", "**u**", and sometimes "**h**" and "**y**".

→ Although liaison is not marked in written French, it will be indicated in your book by the symbol ‿ where appropriate.

Contrastez et répétez:

LIAISON: un ami   un Américain
un Italien   un artiste

NO LIAISON: un copain   un Français
un Canadien   un prof

---

4 **ROLE PLAY** discussing the identity of people

– Tiens, voilà ... !
– Qui est-ce?
– C'est ...

1. une fille (une copine, une amie)/Nicole.
2. une dame/Mademoiselle Lasalle.
3. un garçon (un ami, un copain)/Éric.
4. une dame (une prof)/Madame Albert.
5. un monsieur (un prof)/Monsieur Lavie.
6. un garçon (un copain, un ami)/Alain.

Encourage varied responses.

If students ask From 1 to 60, French uses the Roman system of counting by 10s. However, from 60 to 100, the French count by scores (or 20s). This system was brought to England and Normandy in the tenth century by the Vikings or Norsemen.

Pronunciation Remind students that there is no liaison after **et**: soixante et un, soixante et onze.

Note that in counting from 70-79, the French continue adding numbers to 60:

70 = 60 + 10
71 = 60 + 11
72 = 60 + 12

5 **PRACTICE** reading numbers up to 79

• Martine: zéro un, quarante et un, trente-trois, soixante-quatre, soixante-dix-neuf
• Michèle: zéro un, quarante-deux, cinquante-six, soixante-seize, soixante-deux
• Stéphanie: zéro un, quarante-cinq, soixante-huit, soixante-dix-sept, trente-cinq
• François: zéro un, quarante-neuf, soixante-dix-huit, treize, soixante-deux

Cultural note Paris phone numbers consist of 10 digits read in groups of two. The first digit for Paris is always 01.

Listening comprehension Have students close their books. Slowly dictate the numbers from the phone list. Then have students open their books to correct their work as you read the numbers once more.

GAME Mini-loto (Numbers 60-79)

PREPARATION: Write the numbers from 60-79 on slips of paper (or use commercial bingo numbers).

Have students draw a tic-tac-toe grid and fill the nine squares with numbers of their choice between 60 and 79.

Call out the numbers as you draw the slips in random order. When a student has three numbers in a row in any direction, have him/her call out "Loto."

PRONUNCIATION

You may want to point out that similar linking occurs in English after *an: an apple, an uncle, an hour.*

If students ask Adjectives of nationality are capitalized when they are used as nouns referring to people.

Teaching Resource Options

PRINT

Workbook PE, pp. 17–20
Activités pour tous PE, pp. 9–10
Unit 1 Resource Book
    Activités pour tous TE, pp. 79–80
    Audioscript, pp. 118–119, 121–122
    Communipak, pp. 128–146
    Lesson Plans, pp. 85–86
    Block Scheduling Lesson Plans,
      pp. 91–92
    Absent Student Copymasters,
      pp. 96–97
    Video Activities, pp. 106–109
    Videoscript, pp. 115–116
    Workbook TE, pp. 69–72

AUDIO & VISUAL

Audio Program
CD 1 Tracks 18, 19
CD 5 Tracks 26–30

Overhead Transparencies
4 U.S., Canada, England, France
  Les nationalités

TECHNOLOGY

Online Workbook

VIDEO PROGRAM

 MODULE 2B
  Une coïncidence

TOTAL TIME: 4:50 min.
  DVD Disk 1
  Videotape 1 (COUNTER: 26:42 min.)

2B.1 Dialogue: Une coïncidence
  (27:11–27:40 min.)

2B.2 Mini-scenes: Listening
  – Describing people
  (27:41–29:19 min.)

2B.3 Vignette culturelle: Le Québec
  (29:20–31:32 min.)

Comprehension practice Play the entire module through as an introduction to the lesson.

B Une coïncidence

Isabelle is at a party with her new Canadian friend Marc. She wants him to meet some of the other guests.

Isabelle:	Tu connais la fille <u>là-bas</u>?	*over there*
Marc:	Non. Qui est-ce?	
Isabelle:	C'est une copine. Elle s'appelle Juliette Savard.	
Marc:	Elle est française?	
Isabelle:	Non, elle est canadienne. Elle est de Montréal.	
Marc:	Moi aussi!	
Isabelle:	<u>Quelle coïncidence!</u>	*What a coincidence!*

30   trente
Unité 1   *Invitation au français*

WARM-UP AND REVIEW Nationalities

PROP: Transparency 4: U.S., Canada, England, France, *Les nationalités*

Ask students to give names to the 8 people, and write these names on the transparency next to each of the figures.

Pointing to the figures, have the students identify them.
   Qui est-ce? [C'est Marie.]

Then, having the students take the role of the figure, ask their nationalities.
   Marie, tu es française?
   [Oui, je suis française.]
   Marie, tu es anglaise?
   [Non, je suis française.]

POUR COMMUNIQUER

Tu connais la dame?

Oui, elle s'appelle Madame Leblanc.

▶ **How to inquire about people:**

Tu connais …?	*Do you know …?*	**Tu connais** Jean-Paul?

▶ **How to describe people and give their nationalities:**

Il est …	*He is …*	**Il est** canadien.
Elle est …	*She is …*	**Elle est** canadienne.

▶ **How to find out another person's name:**

Comment s'appelle …?	*What's the name of …?*	**Comment s'appelle** le garçon?
		Comment s'appelle la fille?
Il s'appelle …	*His name is …*	**Il s'appelle** Marc.
Elle s'appelle …	*Her name is …*	**Elle s'appelle** Juliette.

NOTE culturelle

La province de Québec

Québec (City)

Montréal

EN BREF

Capitale: Québec *(Quebec City)*
Population: 7 500 000
Langues: français, anglais

La province de Québec

The province of **Québec** is located in the eastern part of Canada. French speakers represent about 75% of its population. Most of them are descendants of French settlers who came to Canada in the 17th and 18th centuries. There are also a large number of Haitian immigrants who are of African origin.

Montréal (population 2 million) is the largest city in the province of Quebec. In population, it is the second-largest French-speaking city in the world after Paris.

Language note Current usage often replaces **la dame/le monsieur** with **la/cette femme, le/ce/homme.**

If students ask The largest city in Canada is Toronto.

Photo culture note

Le Vieux Montréal Place Jacques Cartier in the heart of Old Montreal. The building in the background with the green roof is the Hôtel de Ville. It is here that Charles de Gaulle made his famous proclamation, "Vive le Québec! Vive le Québec libre!"

Teaching Resource Options

PRINT

Workbook PE, pp. 17–20
Unit 1 Resource Book
   Audioscript, p. 119
   Communipak, pp. 128–146
   Workbook TE, pp. 69–72

AUDIO & VISUAL

Audio Program
CD 1 Tracks 20, 21

Overhead Transparencies
7 People *Les personnes*

TECHNOLOGY

Power Presentations

Petit commentaire
Cross-cultural understanding If students want to host a French student, they may contact Nacel (a non-profit organization that arranges student exchanges).

---

1 **PRACTICE** asking about people, using definite article

Qui est ... ?
1. le monsieur   4. le garçon   7. l'amie
2. la dame   5. le prof   8. la copine
3. la fille   6. l'ami

---

2 **EXCHANGES** identifying people

– Tu connais ... ?
– Oui, c'est ...
1. le prof/M. Simon   4. la dame/Mlle Lenoir
2. le garçon/Christophe   5. la prof/Mme Boucher
3. la fille/Charlotte   6. le monsieur/M. Duval

Expansion Have each student bring in a picture of a known personality:
– **Tu connais ce monsieur?** (holding up picture of a man)
– **Oui, c'est Jay Leno.** (Non, qui est-ce?)

---

3 **EXCHANGES** discussing people's names

– Comment s'appelle ... ?
1. le garçon/Il s'appelle Marc.
2. la fille/Elle s'appelle Céline.
3. le garçon/Il s'appelle François.
4. le garçon/Il s'appelle Jean-Paul.
5. la fille/Elle s'appelle Nathalie.
6. le garçon/Il s'appelle Trinh.
7. la fille/Elle s'appelle Isabelle.

If students ask
• The dropping of a final "e" (or "a," in the case of **la**) is called elision.
• A word that begins with **a, e, i, o,** or **u** is said to begin with a vowel sound.

PETIT COMMENTAIRE
Most French teenagers study English in school. They are generally very much interested in the United States. They love American music, American movies, and American fashions.

le garçon, la fille

The French equivalent of *the* has two basic forms: **le** and **la.**

	MASCULINE				FEMININE	
LE	**le** garçon	*the boy*		**LA**	**la** fille	*the girl*
	le copain	*the friend*			**la** copine	*the friend*

Note Both **le** and **la** become **l'** before a vowel sound.

un copain	→	le copain	une copine	→	la copine
un ami	→	l'ami	une amie	→	l'amie

---

1 **Qui est-ce?**

PARLER Ask who the following people are, using **le, la,** or **l'.**

▶ une prof
  Qui est la prof?

1. un monsieur   3. une fille   5. un prof   7. une amie
2. une dame   4. un garçon   6. un ami   8. une copine

---

2 **Tu connais ... ?**

PARLER Ask your classmates if they know the following people. They will answer that they do.

▶ une dame / Madame Vallée

1. un prof / Monsieur Simon
2. un garçon / Christophe
3. une fille / Charlotte
4. une dame / Mademoiselle Lenoir
5. une prof / Madame Boucher
6. un monsieur / Monsieur Duval

---

3 **Comment s'appelle ... ?**

PARLER Ask the names of the following people, using the words **le garçon, la fille.** A classmate will respond.

▶ —Comment s'appelle la fille?
  —Elle s'appelle Stéphanie.

 Stéphanie   1. Marc   2. Céline   3. François

 4. Jean-Paul   5. Nathalie   6. Trinh   7. Isabelle

---

32   trente-deux
     Unité 1   *Invitation au français*

COMPREHENSION Nouns with le/la

PROPS: Cards with people of Transparency 7: People *Les personnes;* Optional: red and blue index cards

Place the picture cards on the chalkboard tray. To review, have students point out people.
  X, viens ici. Montre-nous un garçon.
  Montre-nous une dame ....

Hand out the pictures to the class.
  Voici le prof. Je donne le prof à Y.
  Qui a le prof? [answer: Y]

Have students pass around the cards.
  Y, prends le garçon et donne-le à Z.

OPTIONAL: Describe classroom objects; have students raise blue (**le**) or red (**la**) cards:
  Voici le bureau. [blue] **Voici la porte.** [red]

4 Français, anglais, canadien ou américain?

PARLER Give the nationalities of the following people.

▶ Julia Roberts?
Elle est américaine.

1. le prince Charles?
2. Céline Dion?
3. Juliette Binoche?
4. Catherine Deneuve?
5. Pierre Cardin?
6. Matt Damon?
7. Oprah Winfrey?
8. Brad Pitt?
9. Elton John?

Les nombres de 80 à 1000

80 quatre-vingts
81 quatre-vingt-un
82 quatre-vingt-deux
83 quatre-vingt-trois
84 quatre-vingt-quatre
85 quatre-vingt-cinq

86 quatre-vingt-six
87 quatre-vingt-sept
88 quatre-vingt-huit
89 quatre-vingt-neuf

90 quatre-vingt-dix
91 quatre-vingt-onze
92 quatre-vingt-douze
93 quatre-vingt-treize
94 quatre-vingt-quatorze
95 quatre-vingt-quinze

96 quatre-vingt-seize
97 quatre-vingt-dix-sept
98 quatre-vingt-dix-huit
99 quatre-vingt-dix-neuf

100 cent   **1000** mille

➔ Note that in counting from 80 to 99, the French add numbers to the base of **quatre-vingts** *(fourscore)*:

$80 = 4 \times 20$ $90 = 4 \times 20 + 10$
$85 = 4 \times 20 + 5$ $99 = 4 \times 20 + 19$

5 Au téléphone

PARLER In France, the telephone area code (**l'indicatif**) is always a four-digit number. Your teacher will name a city (**une ville**) from the chart. Give the area code.

▶ Nice? C'est le zéro quatre quatre-vingt-treize.

VILLE 📞	INDICATIF
Albi	05-63
Avignon	04-90
Dijon	03-80
Marseille	04-91
Montpellier	04-67
Nancy	03-83
Nice	04-93
Nîmes	04-66
Rennes	02-99
Saint-Tropez	04-94
Strasbourg	03-88
Vichy	04-70

PRONONCIATION /ɛ̃/

La voyelle nasale /ɛ̃/

In French, there are three nasal vowel sounds:

/ɛ̃/ **cinq** (5)   /ɔ̃/ **onze** (11)   /ɑ̃/ **trente** (30)

Practice the sound /ɛ̃/ in the following words.

➔ Be sure not to pronounce an "n" or "m" after the nasal vowel.

Répétez: "in"   cin̦q quin̦ze vin̦gt vin̦gt-cin̦q quatre-vin̦gt-quin̦ze

"ain"   américain̦ Alain̦ copain̦

"(i)en"   bien̦ canadien̦ tien̦s!

"un"   un̦

Tien̦s! Voilà Alain̦. Il est américain̦. Et Julien̦? Il est canadien̦.

5 cinq

4 DESCRIPTION discussing people's nationalities

1. Il est anglais.
2. Elle est canadienne.
3. Elle est française.
4. Elle est française.
5. Il est français.
6. Il est américain.
7. Elle est américaine.
8. Il est américain.
9. Il est anglais.

Pronunciation There is no liaison between **quatre-vingt** and the numbers **un, huit, onze**.

Language notes
- Compare: quatre-vingt-sept = "Fourscore and seven years ago..." (opening words of the Gettysburg address)
- **Mille** is presented for recognition. Numbers between 100 and 1,000 are not activated. If students ask:

101 **cent un**   102 **cent deux**
111 **cent onze**   120 **cent vingt**

Teaching note Students should learn to understand the numbers and pronounce them correctly. They should not be expected to spell the numbers. (See notes and activities on page 25.)

5 COMPREHENSION identifying telephone area codes

- (Albi?) C'est le zéro cinq soixante-trois.
- (Avignon?) C'est le zéro quatre quatre-vingt-dix.
- (Dijon?) C'est le zéro trois quatre-vingts.
- (Marseille?) C'est le zéro quatre quatre-vingt-onze.
- (Montpellier?) C'est le zéro quatre soixante-sept.
- (Nancy?) C'est le zéro trois quatre-vingt-trois.
- (Nice?) C'est le zéro quatre quatre-vingt-treize.
- (Nîmes?) C'est le zéro quatre soixante-six.
- (Rennes?) C'est le zéro deux quatre-vingt-dix-neuf.
- (Saint-Tropez?) C'est le zéro quatre quatre-vingt-quatorze.
- (Strasbourg?) C'est le zéro trois quatre-vingt-huit.
- (Vichy?) C'est le zéro quatre soixante-dix.

Variation Quel est l'indicatif de Nice?

Cultural notes
- Outside of Paris, the **indicatif** is now part of the local phone number. (All numbers have 10 digits.)
- For the Paris area, the **indicatif** is "01" and is used only for long distance calls.

PRONUNCIATION

Some French people still distinguish between /ɛ̃/ (**in**) and /œ̃/ (**un**). However, most French speakers use only the nasal vowel /ɛ̃/. For simplicity, we are not introducing the nasal /œ̃/ at this level.

Point out to students that the nasal vowel /ɛ̃/ can have several different spellings.

GAME Numbers 11 to 99

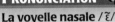

PROPS: Four sets of the numbers 0–9 on index cards Divide the class into two teams. Have two students from each team come to the front, stand side by side, and face the class. Give each student a set of the numbers 0–9.

Say a number in French: e.g., **vingt-cinq!** The first pair to hold up the correct cards [2 and 5] wins a point for its team.

You may wish to teach your students the expressions **Bravo!** *(Great!)*, **Allez-y!** *(Go for it!)*, and **C'est dommage!** *(That's too bad!).*

Leçon 2C

Main Topics Introducing one's family and talking about how old people are

Teaching Resource Options

PRINT

Workbook PE, pp. 21–24
Activités pour tous PE, pp. 11–12
Unit 1 Resource Book
  Activités pour tous TE, pp. 81–82
  Audioscript, pp. 119, 122–123
  Communipak, pp. 128–146
  Lesson Plans, pp. 87–88
  Block Scheduling Lesson Plans,
    pp. 93–94
  Absent Student Copymasters,
    pp. 98–99
  Video Activities, pp. 110–113
  Videoscript, pp. 116–117
  Workbook TE, pp. 73–76

AUDIO & VISUAL

Audio Program
CD 1 Tracks 22, 23
CD 5 Tracks 31–34

Overhead Transparencies
8 Family tree *La famille*

VIDEO PROGRAM

VIDÉO   DVD

MODULE 2C
Les photos d'Isabelle

TOTAL TIME: 0:00 min.
  DVD Disk 1
  Videotape 1 (COUNTER: 31:34 min.)

2C.1 Dialogue: Les photos d'Isabelle
  (32:02–32:32 min.)

2C.2 Monologue: La famille d'Isabelle
  (32:33–33:50 min.)

2C.3 Mini-scenes: How old are you?
  (33:51–35:27 min.)

2C.4 Vignette culturelle: La famille française: un mariage
  (35:28–38:20 min.)

Comprehension practice Play the entire module through as an introduction to the lesson.

34 · **Culture et Communication**
  Unité 1 LEÇON 2C

LEÇON 2

C Les photos d'Isabelle

Isabelle is showing her family photo album to her friend Jean-Paul.

Isabelle:	Voici ma mère.	
Jean-Paul:	Et <u>le monsieur</u>, c'est <u>ton</u> père?	*the man / your*
Isabelle:	Non, c'est mon oncle Thomas.	
Jean-Paul:	Et la fille, c'est <u>ta</u> cousine?	*your*
Isabelle:	Oui, c'est ma cousine Béatrice. <u>Elle a seize ans.</u>	*She's sixteen.*
Jean-Paul:	Et le garçon, c'est ton cousin?	
Isabelle:	Non, c'est un copain.	
Jean-Paul:	Un copain ou ton copain?	
Isabelle:	<u>Dis donc, Jean-Paul, tu es vraiment trop curieux!</u>	*Hey there, Jean-Paul, you are really too curious!*

ma mère

mon oncle Thomas

ma cousine Béatrice

? ?

WARM-UP AND REVIEW Copains et copines

Ask questions about students in the class:

[Point to a girl] **Qui est-ce?** [C'est Anne.]
  Est-ce que c'est un garçon ou une fille?
  [C'est une fille.]

  C'est un copain ou une copine?
  [C'est une copine.]

Address a boy in the class:
  Et toi, est-ce qu'Anne est une copine ou ta copine?
  [C'est une copine. or: C'est ma copine.]

Ask similar questions about other students.

Voici mon chien Malice.

POUR COMMUNIQUER

▶ *How to introduce your family:*

| Voici mon père. | *This is my father.* |
| Et voici ma mère. | *And this is my mother.* |

La famille (*Family*)

un frère	*brother*		une soeur	*sister*
un cousin	*cousin*		une cousine	*cousin*
un père	*father*		une mère	*mother*
un oncle	*uncle*		une tante	*aunt*
un grand-père	*grandfather*		une grand-mère	*grandmother*

Les animaux domestiques (*Pets*)

 un chat

 un chien

NOTE culturelle

La famille française

When you and your friends talk about your families, you usually are referring to your brothers, sisters, and parents. In French, however, **la famille** refers not only to parents and children but also to grandparents, aunts, uncles, cousins, as well as a whole array of more distant relatives related by blood and marriage.

Since the various members of a family often live in the same region, French teenagers see their grandparents and cousins fairly frequently. Even when relatives do not live close by, the family finds many occasions to get together: for weekend visits, during school and summer vacations, on holidays, as well as on special occasions such as weddings and anniversaries.

Supplementary vocabulary

FAMILY
un beau-père *stepfather*
une belle-mère *stepmother*
un beau-frère *stepbrother*
une belle-soeur *stepsister*
un demi-frère *halfbrother*
une demi-soeur *halfsister*

PETS
un hamster /ɛamster/, no liaison
un cochon d'Inde *Guinea pig*
un poisson rouge *goldfish*
une souris blanche *white mouse*
un oiseau *bird*
une perruche *parakeet*
un serpent *snake*

Cross-cultural observation

Ask students if they have ever attended a wedding. Discuss the similarities and differences between French and American weddings, pointing out especially the dual ceremony (church/**mairie**) in France.

COMPREHENSION The family

PROP: Transparency 8: Family tree, *La famille*
Describe the various family relationships, pointing to the transparency.
    François Mallet est le père de Véronique.
    M. Mallet est aussi le père de Frédéric. ...

Ask students to point out family members.
    X, viens à l'écran. Montre-nous la cousine de Catherine. ...
Follow-up: Ask the names of people.
    Comment s'appelle le frère de Véronique?
    [Il s'appelle Frédéric Mallet.]

Teaching Resource Options

PRINT

Workbook PE, pp. 21–24
Unit 1 Resource Book
  Audioscript, p. 119
  Communipak, pp. 128–146
  Family Involvement, pp. 100–101
  Video Activities, p. 112
  Videoscript, p. 117
  Workbook TE, pp. 73–76

Assessment
Lesson 2 Quiz, pp. 125–126
Audioscript for Quiz 2, p. 124
Answer Keys, pp. 195–197

AUDIO & VISUAL

Audio Program
CD 1 Track 24
CD 13 Track 3

Overhead Transparencies
8 Family tree *La famille*

TECHNOLOGY

Power Presentations

VIDEO PROGRAM

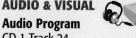

VIDÉO   DVD

MODULE 2C

2C.3 Mini-scenes: How old are you?
(33:51–35:27 min.)

 ① PRACTICE talking about friends, relatives, and pets

Voici ...
1. mon frère.
2. ma soeur.
3. ma tante Monique.
4. mon oncle Pierre.
5. mon père.
6. ma mère.
7. mon copain Nicolas.
8. mon ami Jérôme.
9. ma copine Pauline.
10. mon amie Florence.
11. ma grand-mère Michèle.
12. mon grand-père Robert.
13. mon chien Toto.
14. mon chat Minou.
15. ma cousine Émilie.
16. mon cousin Marc.

Pronunciation album /albɔm/

② COMMUNICATION discussing the names of relatives, friends, and pets

– Comment s'appelle ... ?
– ... s'appelle ...
1. ton oncle/Mon oncle
2. ta tante/Ma tante
3. ton cousin/Mon cousin
4. ta cousine/Ma cousine
5. ta copine/Ma copine
6. ton ami/Mon ami
7. ton grand-père/Mon grand-père
8. ta grand-mère/Ma grand-mère
9. ton chien/Mon chien
10. ton chat/Mon chat

Middle School Copymasters

Worksheet 2: *Ma famille*, pp. 7–8;
Game: Bingo, pp. 9–10

36 • **Communication**
Unité 1 LEÇON 2C

PETIT COMMENTAIRE
The French people love pets, especially cats and dogs. What is important is the animal's personality and friendliness rather than its pedigree. Some common names given to animals are:
Minou, Pompon, Fifi (cats)
Titus, Milou, Azor (dogs)

mon cousin, ma cousine

The French equivalents of *my* and *your* have the following forms:

MASCULINE	
mon cousin	*my cousin (male)*
mon frère	*my brother*
ton cousin	*your cousin (male)*
ton frère	*your brother*

FEMININE	
ma cousine	*my cousin (female)*
ma soeur	*my sister*
ta cousine	*your cousin (female)*
ta soeur	*your sister*

→ Note that the feminine **ma** becomes **mon** and the feminine **ta** becomes **ton** before a vowel sound. Liaison is required.

une amie → **mon** amie **ton** amie

① L'album de photos

PARLER You are showing a friend your photo album. Identify the following people, using **mon** and **ma,** as appropriate.

▶ cousine Jacqueline   **Voici ma cousine Jacqueline.**

1. frère
2. soeur
3. tante Monique
4. oncle Pierre
5. père
6. mère
7. copain Nicolas
8. ami Jérôme
9. copine Pauline
10. amie Florence
11. grand-mère Michèle
12. grand-père Robert
13. chien Toto
14. chat Minou
15. cousine Émilie
16. cousin Marc

② **Comment s'appelle ... ?**

PARLER Ask your classmates to name some of their friends, relatives, and pets. They can invent names if they wish.

▶ le copain   —Comment s'appelle ton copain?
        —Mon copain s'appelle Bob.

1. l'oncle
2. la tante
3. le cousin
4. la cousine
5. la copine
6. l'ami
7. le grand-père
8. la grand-mère
9. le chien
10. le chat

WARM-UP AND REVIEW

Numbers practice

Divide the class in half: side A and side B.

Point to side A and say a number. Then point to side B and say another number. Students on the side with the higher number raise their hands.

A – 22. B – 35. [Students on Side B raise their hands.]
A – 89. B – 64. [Students on Side A raise their hands.]

TEACHING NOTES

- This lesson provides an initial introduction to adjective agreement with the singular forms **mon/ma** and **ton/ta.**
- It is important that students learn to differentiate clearly between the pronunciation of **mon** and **ma, ton** and **ta.** They should pronounce the "n" of **mon** and **ton** only in liaison.
- In Lesson 16, students will encounter all the forms of the possessive adjectives.

POUR COMMUNIQUER

▶ **How to find out how old a friend is:**

Quel âge as-tu?	*How old are you?*	—Quel âge as-tu?
J'ai … ans.	*I'm … (years old).*	—J'ai quinze ans.

▶ **How to ask about how old others are:**

—**Quel âge a ton père?**	*How old is your father?*
—**Il a quarante-deux ans.**	*He is 42 (years old).*
—**Quel âge a ta mère?**	*How old is your mother?*
—**Elle a trente-neuf ans.**	*She is 39 (years old).*

> *Quel âge as-tu?*

> *J'ai quinze ans.*

→ Although *years old* may be left out in English, the word **ans** must be used in French when talking about someone's age.

Il a vingt ans. *He's twenty. (He's twenty years old.)*

3 *Quel âge as-tu?*

PARLER Ask your classmates how old they are.

▶ —Quel âge as-tu?
—J'ai (treize) ans.

4   *Joyeux anniversaire!*
(Happy birthday!)

PARLER Ask your classmates how old the following people are.

▶ —Quel âge a Stéphanie?
—Elle a quatorze ans.

Stéphanie

1. **Éric** 2. **Mademoiselle Doucette** 3. **Monsieur Boucher**

4. **Madame Dupont** 5. **Monsieur Camus** 6. **Madame Simon**

5 *Curiosité*

PARLER Find out the ages of your classmates' friends and relatives. If they are not sure, they can guess or invent an answer.

▶ la copine —Quel âge a ta copine?
—Ma copine a (treize) ans.

1. le père	4. la tante	7. le grand-père
2. la mère	5. le cousin	8. la grand-mère
3. l'oncle	6. la cousine	

PRONONCIATION /ɑ̃/ /ɔ̃/

Les voyelles nasales
/ɑ̃/ **et** /ɔ̃/

tante   **oncle**

The letters "**an**" and "**en**" usually represent the nasal vowel /ɑ̃/. Be sure not to pronounce an "**n**" after the nasal vowel.

Répétez: ans tante français quarante
trente comment Henri Laurent

The letters "**on**" represent the nasal vowel /ɔ̃/. Be sure not to pronounce an "n" after the nasal vowel.

Répétez: non bonjour oncle garçon

Contrastez: an–on tante–ton onze–ans
Mon oncle François a trente ans.

POUR COMMUNIQUER

Common colloquial alternatives Tu as quel âge? Quel âge as-tu?

If students ask Literally, these sentences mean: What age do you have? I have thirteen years.

3 **COMMUNICATION** asking how old someone is

– Quel âge as-tu?
– J'ai (quatorze) ans.

4 **PRACTICE** discussing people's ages

– Quel âge a … ?
– … ans.
1. Éric/dix-huit
2. Mademoiselle Doucette/vingt-cinq
3. Monsieur Boucher/trente-deux
4. Madame Dupont/soixante-quatre
5. Monsieur Camus/soixante-quinze
6. Madame Simon/quatre-vingt-trois

Listening comprehension Ask the ages of these people in random order. Students write down the number of the corresponding birthday cake.

Qui a soixante-quatre ans? (4)
Qui a trente-deux ans? (3)
Qui a dix-huit ans? (1)
Qui a quatre-vingt-trois ans? (6)
Qui a vingt-cinq ans? (2)
Qui a soixante-quinze ans? (5)

5 **COMMUNICATION** discussing friends' and relatives' ages

– Quel âge a … ?
– … a (X) ans.
1. ton père/Mon père
2. ta mère/Ma mère
3. ton oncle/Mon oncle
4. ta tante/Ma tante
5. ton cousin/Mon cousin
6. ta cousine/Ma cousine
7. ton grand-père/Mon grand-père
8. ta grand-mère/Ma grand-mère

If students have trouble guessing ages, put sample ages on the board.

E.g. 1. le père: 42   2. la mère: 39, etc.

PRONUNCIATION

- The combination **ien** is pronounced /jɛ̃/: **bien**
- Remind students that they should not pronounce an "n" after the nasal vowel.

TEACHING STRATEGY Ages

PROP: Transparency 8: Family tree, *La famille*

Ask students to determine the ages of the people on the transparency.

– **Quel âge a Frédéric?**
– [Student X]: Il a quinze ans.
– **Vous êtes d'accord?** Do you agree?

Write "15" in the box next to Frédéric.

Have students assign ages to the other members of the family. Then ask questions about the transparency.

Qui a quarante ans?
Quel âge a la sœur de Frédéric?

À VOTRE TOUR

Main Topic
• Recapitulation and review

Teaching Resource Options

PRINT

Workbook PE, pp. 1–24
Unit 1 Resource Book
   Audioscript, pp. 119–120
   Communipak, pp. 128–146
   Workbook TE, pp. 151–154

Assessment
Unit 1 Test, pp. 165–172
Portfolio Assessment, pp. 155–164
Multiple Choice Test Items, pp. 184–188
Listening Comprehension
   Performance Test, pp. 173–174
Reading Performance Test, pp. 179–181
Speaking Performance Test, pp. 175–178
Writing Performance Test, pp. 182–183
Test Scoring Tools, p. 189
Audioscripr for Tests, pp. 190–192
Answer Keys, pp. 195–197

AUDIO & VISUAL

Audio Program
CD 1 Tracks 25, 26, 27
CD 13 Tracks 4–11

TECHNOLOGY

Test Generator CD-ROM/eTest Plus
Online

❶ COMPREHENSION

19–B, 67–B, 15–B, 8–A, 72–A, 12–A, 42–A,
93–A, 5–B, 82–A, 33–B, 48–B, 25–A, 3–A,
17–A, 61–A, 98–B, 89–B, 70–B, 55–B,

❷ GUIDED ORAL EXPRESSION

1. Oui, ça va (très) bien. (Non, ça va [très] mal.)
   (Ça va comme ci, comme ça.)
2. Je m'appelle (Tom Banks / Lora Andrews).
3. Oui, je suis canadien (canadienne).
   (Non, je suis américain[e].)
4. J'ai (dix-sept) ans.
5. Mon copain s'appelle Pierre.
6. Il a (dix-huit) ans.

Speaking practice

• Play the audio, stopping after each
  question to elicit various student answers.
• Play the audio activity straight
  through, having students whisper
  their answers quickly in the pauses.
• Play the audio again, pointing to
  individual students to give their
  answers in the pauses.

À votre tour!

OBJECTIFS

Now you can...
• greet people and say where you are from
• introduce friends and relatives
• give your age and ask how old people are
• understand and use numbers up to 100

❶ 🎧 Écoutez bien!

STRATEGY Listening

Numbers As you hear
each number, repeat it
over and over in your
head until you find the
corresponding number
on the card.

ÉCOUTER Loto is a French version of Bingo. You will hear
a series of numbers. If the number is on Card A, raise your
left hand. If it is on Card B, raise your right hand.

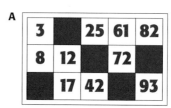

❷ 🎧 Et toi?

ÉCOUTER ET PARLER You and Nathalie meet at a sidewalk café. Respond to her
greetings and questions.

1. Salut! Ça va?
2. Comment t'appelles-tu?
3. Tu es canadien (canadienne)?
4. Quel âge as-tu?
5. Comment s'appelle ton copain (ta copine)?
6. Quel âge a ton copain (ta copine)?

❸ 🎧 Conversation dirigée

ÉCOUTER ET PARLER Two students, Jean-Pierre and Janet, meet on the Paris-Lyon
train. With a partner, compose and act out their dialogue according to the
suggested script.

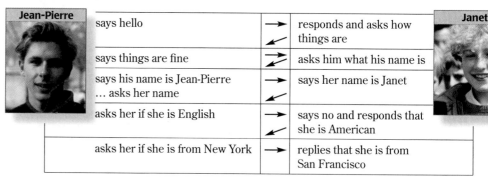

Jean-Pierre		Janet
says hello	→ ←	responds and asks how things are
says things are fine	⇄	asks him what his name is
says his name is Jean-Pierre … asks her name	→ ←	says her name is Janet
asks her if she is English	→ ←	says no and responds that she is American
asks her if she is from New York	→	replies that she is from San Francisco

À VOTRE TOUR

The communicative activities in this section move
from closely structured (Act. 1) to more open-ended
(Act. 5).

   Select those activities which are most appropriate
for your students. You may or may not wish to do
them all.

PAIR AND GROUP PRACTICE

PAIR WORK: Students do the activities in pairs. For
Act. 2, 3, and 4, they can check their work by listening
to the audio.

TRIOS: Students work in groups of 3. Two students
perform a dialogue. The third acts as monitor.

4 Ma famille *(My family)*

PARLER You are showing your friends pictures of your family. Introduce everyone, giving their ages. If you prefer, show your classmates a picture of your own family and give each person's age.

▶ **Voici ma soeur. Elle a douze ans.**

5 En scène

PARLER With a classmate, act out the following scene.

CHARACTERS:

You and a French guest

SITUATION:

You are in France. Your French friends have invited you to a picnic. You meet one of the guests and have a conversation.

- Greet the guest.
- Ask how things are.
- Tell the guest that you are American and ask the guest if he/she is French.
- Tell the guest how old you are and ask his/her age.
- *(The guest waves to a friend.)* Ask the guest the name of his/her friend.
- *(It is the end of the picnic.)* Say good-bye.

6 Les nombres

PARLER

1. Select any number between 0 and 15 and give the next five numbers in sequence.
2. Select a number between 1 and 9. Use that number as a starting point and count by tens to 100.

▶ **deux...**
douze, vingt-deux, trente-deux, etc.

 **LESSON REVIEW**
CLASSZONE.COM

ORAL PORTFOLIOS

For an introduction to oral portfolio assessment, see the **Unit 1 Resource Book** for a complete description.

Divide the class into pairs. Either assign all students the same activity, or let each pair select an activity at the appropriate level of challenge.

Have the pairs prepare their dialogues and make an audio (or video) recording. (Be sure they introduce themselves on the recording: **Je m'appelle X. Moi, je m'appelle Y.**)

If time allows, play all the recordings for the entire class. Store the audio as part of each student's oral portfolio.

---

3 GUIDED ORAL EXPRESSION

Jean-Pierre: Bonjour.
Janet: Bonjour. Ça va?
Jean-Pierre: Oui, ça va.
Janet: Comment t'appelles-tu?
Jean-Pierre: Je m'appelle Jean-Pierre. Et toi?
Janet: Je m'appelle Janet.
Jean-Pierre: Tu es anglaise?
Janet: Non, je suis américaine.
Jean-Pierre: Tu es de New York?
Janet: Non, je suis de San Francisco.

4 GUIDED ORAL EXPRESSION

1. Voici mon frère. Il a dix-sept ans.
2. Voici ma soeur. Elle a neuf ans.
3. Voici mon copain. Il a quinze ans.
4. Voici mon oncle. Il a quarante-deux ans.
5. Voici ma mère. Elle a quarante et un ans.
6. Voici mon grand-père. Il a soixante-six ans.

Listening practice Play the sample exchanges.

Pair Practice Have students in pairs prepare their own exchanges.

5 GUIDED ORAL EXPRESSION

Answers will vary.
élève 1: Salut! (Bonjour!)
élève 2: Salut! (Bonjour!)
élève 1: Ça va?
élève 2: Oui, ça va (très) bien, (merci).
élève 1: Je suis américain(e). Tu es français(e)?
élève 2: Oui, je suis français(e).
élève 1: J'ai dix-sept ans. Et toi?
élève 2: J'ai dix-huit ans.
élève 1: Comment s'appelle ton amie?
élève 2: Elle s'appelle Cécile.
élève 1: Au revoir!
élève 2: Au revoir!

6 GUIDED ORAL EXPRESSION

Answers will vary.
1. sept: huit, neuf, dix, onze, douze
2. trois: treize, vingt-trois, trente-trois, quarante-trois, cinquante-trois, soixante-trois, soixante-treize, quatre-vingt-trois, quatre-vingt-treize

Middle School Copymasters

Class Starter: *Qui est-ce?*, p. T1;
Conversations 1–3, pp. 2–4;
Worksheet 1: *Salut! Ça va?*, p. 6;
Notes culturelles, p. 11;
Projects 1–3, pp. 12–15;
Drills, pp. T2–T4

UNITÉ 1

ENTRACTE

• Increasing students' awareness of the francophone world
• Introducing colors

Teaching Resource Options

PRINT

Workbook PE, pp. 25–28
Activités pour tous PE, pp. 13–15
Unit 1 Resource Book
   Activités pour tous TE, pp. 147–149
   Workbook TE, pp. 151–154

Le drapeau des pays francophones

Answers

Le Luxembourg: Le drapeau est rouge, blanc et bleu.

La Suisse: Le drapeau est rouge et blanc.

Le Canada: Le drapeau est rouge et blanc.

Haïti: Le drapeau est bleu, rouge, blanc, vert et jaune.

Le Cameroun: Le drapeau est vert, rouge et jaune.

La Côte d'Ivoire: Le drapeau est orange, blanc et vert.

Le Maroc: Le drapeau est rouge et vert.

Le Mali: Le drapeau est vert, jaune et rouge.

La République démocratique du Congo: Le drapeau est bleu et jaune.

Le Sénégal: Le drapeau est vert, jaune et rouge.

Les Couleurs

rouge   orange   jaune   vert   bleu   violet   blanc   noir

Le drapeau des pays francophones

In the following countries, many people use French in their daily lives. Locate each country on the map on pages 8–9 and then describe the colors of its flag.

▶ La Belgique: Le drapeau est noir, jaune et rouge.

Europe

LA BELGIQUE
Population: 10 millions
Capitale: Bruxelles

LE LUXEMBOURG
Population: 0,5 million
Capitale: Luxembourg

LA SUISSE
Population: 7 millions
Capitale: Berne

Amérique

LE CANADA
Population: 31 millions
Capitale: Ottawa

HAÏTI
Population: 8 millions
Capitale: Port-au-Prince

rouge orange jaune vert bleu violet blanc noir

Afrique

LE CAMEROUN
Population: 15 millions
Capitale: Yaoundé

LA CÔTE D'IVOIRE
Population: 16 millions
Capitale: Yamoussoukro

LE MAROC
Population: 28 millions
Capitale: Rabat

LE MALI
Population: 10 millions
Capitale: Bamako

LA RÉPUBLIQUE DÉMOCRATIQUE DU CONGO
Population: 42 millions
Capitale: Kinshasa

LE SÉNÉGAL
Population: 9 millions
Capitale: Dakar

CONNEXIONS World Geography

Increase your awareness of the francophone world. Select one of the countries mentioned and make a poster which includes the flag and a map showing the capital city. Complete the poster with pictures or other information of interest (sources: atlas, encyclopedia, Internet, travel ads, newspapers, and magazines).

quarante et un **41**
Lecture et Culture

Language Learning Benchmarks

FUNCTION
- Greet and respond to greetings pp. 16, 24
- Engage in conversations pp. 16, 24
- Obtain information pp. 20, 28, 32
- Begin to provide information pp. 37

CONTEXT
- Converse in face-to-face social interactions pp. 16, 17, 24
- Listen to audio and video texts pp. 14, 17, 18, 22, 26, 30, 34
- Use authentic materials when reading: charts p. 33

TEXT TYPE
- Use short sentences when speaking pp. 17, 20, 25, 29
- Use learned words and phrases when speaking pp. 16, 28
- Use simple questions when speaking pp. 16, 24, 32, 36, 37
- Understand some ideas and familiar details presented in clear, uncomplicated speech when listening pp. 14, 18, 22, 26, 30, 34

CONTENT
- Understand and convey information about family pp. 36, 37
- Understand and convey information about friends pp. 28, 36, 37
- Understand and convey information about health p. 25
- Understand and convey information about numbers pp. 21, 25, 29, 33

ASSESSMENT
- Demonstrate culturally acceptable behavior for greeting and responding to greetings p. 38
- Demonstrate culturally acceptable behavior for engaging in conversations p. 38
- Demonstrate culturally acceptable behavior for obtaining information p. 39
- Demonstrate culturally acceptable behavior for providing information p. 39

Expansion activities PLANNING AHEAD

Games

• Chassez l'intrus

Ask each student to select three words related to a specific category (colors, numbers, family members, foods, beverages, days, months, and so on). Then have each student add a fourth word that does not belong to the category. Ask students to write the words in random order on a sheet of paper and collect them. Divide the class into two teams. Give one of the sheets of paper to the first member of Team A, who will read the words aloud. If the first player on Team B correctly identifies **l'intrus,** he or she wins a point for the team. Set a ten-second time limit and have teams take turns reading the lists for their opponents.

Pacing Suggestion: Upon completion of Leçon 4.

Projects

• Mon café

Have each student create a café menu complete with a restaurant name, food and beverages served there, and prices. Be sure they use only familiar vocabulary. Students may use colored pencils, cardboard, construction paper, photos, and illustrations to make their menus appealing. As an alternative, you may give students the option of creating menus on a computer.

Pacing Suggestion: Upon completion of Leçon 3.

• L'euro

Have students work in small groups to investigate the images found on euro coins. Explain to students that euro notes are the same for all the countries that use them. While the coins have one common face, each country selected individual images to use on the reverse. Each group will research the images selected by one of the countries using the euro. Have the groups give class presentations in which they show what the coins look like and explain what they have learned about the images. As an alternative, have students draw or download copies of the coins and put them on a map of the Euro-zone countries.

Pacing Suggestion: Upon completion of Leçon 3.

Bulletin Boards

• Le temps

Have students research current weather conditions in France. Assign groups different French cities and have students make a bulletin board with illustrations of a five-day forecast. Students might also include a five-day forecast of their own city or town. As a way of extending this exercise, you could change the city weekly and have groups alternate being responsible for the week's weather report. Post the best, funniest, clearest drawings on the bulletin board.

Pacing Suggestion: Upon completion of Leçon 4.

Music

• L'hymne national

Teach your students *O Canada,* the national anthem of Canada. The lyrics are provided below in French. You may also want to give students a list of vocabulary words from the song in English. You can download the music from the Internet.

The music for *O Canada* was composed in the 1880s by Calixa Lavallée to accompany a French poem written by Sir Adolphe-Basile Routhier. In 1968 an official English version was adopted. *O Canada* became the Canadian national anthem in 1980.

> *O Canada*
>
> O Canada! Terre de nos aïeux,
> Ton front est ceint de fleurons glorieux.
> Car ton bras sait porter l'épée,
> Il sait porter la croix.
> Ton histoire est une épopée,
> Des plus brillants exploits.
> Et ta valeur, de foi trempée,
> Protégera nos foyers et nos droits.

Pacing Suggestion: Upon completion of Leçon 4.

Storytelling

• Tu as faim?

Use two puppets to portray a client and a server at a café. Develop a dialogue and act it out for the students. Make sure to include an entertaining twist in the dialogue, such as someone ordering strange combinations, a conflict between the server and customer, or someone ordering too much food. Then, have students work in pairs to recreate a similar dialogue to act out in small groups or for the class.

Pacing Suggestion: Upon completion of Leçon 3.

Hands-on Crafts

• Mon calendrier

Have students make calendars or twelve-month agendas using one sheet of paper for each month of the year. Students should label the days and months in French. Have each student work with a partner to choose important events to add to their calendars, such as holidays and birthdays, school activities, games, and proms. Have students complete the project by making colorful covers for their calendars/agendas.

Pacing Suggestion: Upon completion of Leçon 4.

End of Unit

• Au café

Have students work in pairs or small groups to write and perform a café scene. In each scene, students will greet one another, order and pay for their food, and make small talk. (For example, they can discuss how they are, the weather, what they want to eat, places they would like to go, and times for appointments.) Students may wish to create menus and use other props to make their scenes more realistic. Have students present their scenes to the class live or on videotape.

Rubric   **A** = 13–15 pts. **B** = 10–12 pts. **C** = 7–9 pts. **D** = 4–6 pts. **F** = < 4 pts.

Criteria	Scale
Vocabulary Use	1 2 3 4 5
Grammar/Spelling Accuracy	1 2 3 4 5
Creativity	1 2 3 4 5

Recipe

• Croque-monsieur

Croque-monsieur, a toasted ham and cheese sandwich, has become a staple in French cafés. There are several variations: the sandwich may be served with a béchamel sauce or a slice of tomato. One variation is the **croque-madame,** a croque-monsieur topped with an egg.

Pacing Suggestion: Upon completion of Leçon 3.

Croque-monsieur

Ingrédients
- 2 tranches de pain de mie
- 1 tranche de jambon
- 25 grammes de Gruyère râpé
- du beurre

Préparation
1. Beurrez une tranche de pain.
2. Ajoutez le jambon et le Gruyère.
3. Beurrez l'autre tranche de pain et mettez-la sur le dessus du sandwich.
4. Faites cuire au four jusqu'à ce que le pain soit bien grillé.

Ingredients
- 2 slices of bread
- 1 slice of ham
- approx. 1 oz. of grated Gruyère (Swiss cheese)
- butter

Directions
1. Butter one slice of bread.
2. Add the ham and cheese.
3. Butter the second slice of bread and use it to top the sandwich.
4. Cook under the broiler or in a toaster oven until bread is browned.

UNITÉ 2

Planning Guide CLASSROOM MANAGEMENT

OBJECTIVES

Communication
- Order snacks and beverages in a café *p. 49*
- Ask about prices and pay for your food/drink *p. 53*
- Use French money *pp. 52–53*
- Tell time *pp. 56–58*
- Give the date and the day of the week *pp. 61–63*
- Talk about the weather *p. 65*

Pronunciation
- L'intonation *p. 47*
- L'accent final *p. 51*
- La consonne «r» *p. 55*

Culture
- Bon appétit! *p. 43*
- Les jeunes et la nourriture *p. 45*
- Le café *p. 49*
- L'argent européen *pp. 52–53*

PROGRAM RESOURCES

 Print

- Workbook PE, *pp. 29–58*
- *Activités pour tous* PE, *pp. 17–31*
- Block Scheduling Copymasters, *pp. 17–32*
- Teacher to Teacher Copymasters
- Unit 2 Resource Book
  - Lessons 3–4 Resources
    - Workbook TE
    - *Activités pour tous* TE
    - Lesson Plans
    - Block Scheduling Lesson Plans
    - Family Letter
    - Absent Student Copymasters
    - Family Involvement
    - Video Activities
    - Videoscripts
    - Audioscripts
    - Assessment Program
  - Unit 2 Resources
    - Communipak
    - *Activités pour tous* TE Reading
    - Workbook TE Reading and Culture Activities
    - Assessment Program
    - Answer Keys

 Audiovisual

- Audio Program PE CD 1 Tracks 28–49
- Audio Program Workbook CD 6 Tracks 1–31
- *Chansons* Audio CD
- Video Program Modules 3A, 3B, 3C, 4A, 4B, 4C
- Overhead Transparencies
  10 Foods;
  11 Beverages;
  12 Menu from "Le Select";
  6 Clock face;
  9 Calendar;
  13 Weather

 Technology

- Online Workbook
- ClassZone.com
- eTest Plus Online/Test Generator CD-ROM
- EasyPlanner Plus Online/EasyPlanner CD-ROM
- Power Presentations on CD-ROM

✓ Assessment Program Options

Lesson Quizzes
Portfolio Assessment
Unit Test Form A
Unit Test Form B
Unit Test Part III
  Cultural Awareness
Listening Comprehension
  Performance Test
Speaking Performance Test
Reading Comprehension
  Performance Test
Writing Performance Test
Multiple Choice Test Items
Test Scoring Tools
Audio Program CD 13 Tracks 12–22
Answer Keys
eTest Plus Online/Test Generator
  CD-ROM

Pacing Guide SAMPLE LESSON PLAN

DAY	DAY	DAY	DAY	DAY
1 **Unité 2 Opener Introduction culturelle– Bon appétit!** **Leçon 3A** • Vidéo-scène–Tu as faim? • Pour communiquer • Note culturelle–Les jeunes et la nourriture	**2** **Leçon 3A** • Un sandwich, une pizza • Prononciation–L'intonation **Leçon 3B** • Vidéo-scène–Au café	**3** **Leçon 3B** • Pour communiquer • Note culturelle–Le café • Prononciation– L'accent final	**4** **Leçon 3C** • Vidéo-scène– Ça fait combien? • Note culturelle– L'argent européen	**5** **Leçon 3C** • Pour communiquer • Prononciation– La consonne «r» **Leçon 4A** • Vidéo-scène–L'heure
6 **Leçon 4A** • Pour communiquer • Vidéo-scène–À quelle heure est le film?	**7** **Leçon 4B** • Pour communiquer • Vidéo-scène– Le jour et la date • Pour communiquer	**8** **Leçon 4B** • Vidéo-scène–Anniversaire • Pour communiquer • La date	**9** **Leçon 4C** • Vidéo-scène–Le temps • Pour communiquer	**10** • À votre tour!
11 • Unit 2 Test	**12** • Entracte: Lecture et Culture	**13**	**14**	**15**
16	**17**	**18**	**19**	**20**

UNITÉ 2 Student Text Listening Activity Scripts
AUDIO PROGRAM

▶ **LEÇON 3** Bon appétit!

• **Vidéo-scène A: Tu as faim?** *p. 44*

A. Compréhension orale CD 1, TRACK 28

Pierre, Philippe, and Nathalie are on their way home from school. They stop by a street vendor who sells sandwiches and pizza. Today it is Pierre's turn to treat his friends.

SCÈNE 1 Pierre et Nathalie
Pierre: Tu as faim?
Nathalie: Oui, j'ai faim.
Pierre: Tu veux un sandwich ou une pizza?
Nathalie: Donne-moi une pizza, s'il te plaît.
Pierre: Voilà.
Nathalie: Merci.

SCÈNE 2 Pierre et Philippe
Pierre: Et toi, Philippe, tu as faim?
Philippe: Oh là, là, oui, j'ai faim.
Pierre: Qu'est-ce que tu veux? Un sandwich ou une pizza?
Philippe: Je voudrais un sandwich . . . euh . . . et donne-moi aussi une pizza.
Pierre: C'est vrai! Tu as vraiment faim!

B. Écoutez et répétez. CD 1, TRACK 29

You will now hear a paused version of the dialog. Listen to the speaker and repeat right after he or she has completed the sentence.

• **Prononciation** *p. 47* CD 1, TRACK 30

L'intonation
Écoutez: Voici un steak . . . et une salade.

When you speak, your voice rises and falls. This is called INTONATION. In French, as in English, your voice goes down at the end of a statement. However, in French, your voice rises after each group of words in the middle of a sentence. (This is the opposite of English, where your voice drops a little when you pause in the middle of a sentence.)
Répétez: Je voudrais une pizza. #
Je voudrais une pizza et un sandwich. #
Je voudrais une pizza, un sandwich et un hamburger. #
Voici un steak. #
Voici un steak et une salade. #
Voici un steak, une salade et une glace. #

• **Vidéo-scène B: Au café** *p. 48*

A. Compréhension orale CD 1, TRACK 31

This afternoon Trinh and Céline went shopping. They are now tired and thirsty. Trinh invites Céline to a café.

SCÈNE 1 Trinh, Céline
Trinh: Tu as soif?
Céline: Oui, j'ai soif.
Trinh: On va dans un café? Je t'invite.
Céline: D'accord!

SCÈNE 2 Le garçon, Céline, Trinh
Le garçon: Vous désirez, mademoiselle?
Céline: Un jus d'orange, s'il vous plaît.
Le garçon: Et pour vous, monsieur?
Trinh: Donnez-moi une limonade, s'il vous plaît.

SCÈNE 3 Le garçon, Céline, Trinh
Le garçon: *(à Céline)* La limonade, c'est pour vous, mademoiselle?
Trinh: Non, c'est pour moi.
Le garçon: Ah, excusez-moi. Voici le jus d'orange, mademoiselle.
Céline: Merci.

B. Écoutez et répétez. CD 1, TRACK 32

You will now hear a paused version of the dialog. Listen to the speaker and repeat right after he or she has completed the sentence.

• **Prononciation** *p. 51* CD 1, TRACK 33

L'accent final
Écoutez: un chocolat

In French, the rhythm is very even and the accent always falls on the *last* syllable of a word or a group of words.
Répétez: Philippe # Thomas # Alice # Sophie # Dominique #
un café # Je voudrais un café. #
une salade # Donnez-moi une salade. #
un chocolat # Donne-moi un chocolat. #

• **Vidéo-scène C: Ça fait combien?** *p. 52*

A. Compréhension orale CD 1, TRACK 34

At the café, Trinh and Céline have talked about many things. It is now time to go. Trinh calls the waiter so he can pay the check.

Trinh: S'il vous plaît?
Le garçon: Oui, monsieur.
Trinh: Ça fait combien?
Le garçon: Voyons, un jus d'orange, 2 euros 50, et une limonade, 1 euro 50. Ça fait 4 euros.
Trinh: 4 euros . . . Très bien . . . Mais, euh . . . Zut! Où est mon porte-monnaie . . . ? Dis, Céline, prête-moi 5 euros, s'il te plaît.

B. Écoutez et répétez. CD 1, TRACK 35

You will now hear a paused version of the dialog. Listen to the speaker and repeat right after he or she has completed the sentence.

• **Prononciation** *p. 55* CD 1, TRACK 36

La consonne «r»
Écoutez: Marie

The French consonant "**r**" is not at all like the English "**r**." It is pronounced at the back of the throat. In fact, it is similar to the Spanish "jota" sound of José.
Répétez: Marie # Paris # orange # Henri #
franc # très # croissant # fromage #
bonjour # pour # Pierre # quart #
Robert # Richard # Renée # Raoul #
Marie, prête-moi trente euros. #

▶ **LEÇON 4** De jour en jour

• **Vidéo-scène A: L'heure** *p. 56*

1. Un rendez-vous

A. Compréhension orale CD 1, TRACK 37

Jean-Paul and Stéphanie are sitting in a café. Stéphanie seems to be in a hurry to leave.

Stéphanie: Quelle heure est-il?
Jean-Paul: Il est trois heures.
Stéphanie: Trois heures?
Jean-Paul: Oui, trois heures.
Stéphanie: Oh là là. J'ai un rendez-vous avec David dans vingt minutes. Au revoir, Jean-Paul.
Jean-Paul: Au revoir, Stéphanie. À bientôt!

B. Écoutez et répétez. CD 1, TRACK 38

You will now hear a paused version of the dialog. Listen to the speaker and repeat right after he or she has completed the sentence.

• Écoutez bien! *p. 57* CD 1, TRACK 39

Listen as people talk about the time. For each dialog, indicate which of the watches below corresponds to the time you hear.

1. —Quelle heure est-il?
   —Il est sept heures. #
2. —Quelle heure est-il?
   —Il est deux heures. #
3. —Quelle heure est-il?
   —Il est huit heures. #
4. —Quelle heure est-il?
   —Il est midi. # *noon*
5. —Quelle heure est-il?
   —Il est dix heures. #
6. —Quelle heure est-il?
   —Il est cinq heures. #

2. À quelle heure est le film? *p. 58*
A. Compréhension orale CD 1, TRACK 40

Stéphanie and David have decided to go to a movie.

Stéphanie: Quelle heure est-il?
David: Il est trois heures et demie.
Stéphanie: Et à quelle heure est le film?
David: À quatre heures et quart.
Stéphanie: Ça va. Nous avons le temps. *time*

B. Écoutez et répétez. CD 1, TRACK 41

You will now hear a paused version of the dialog. Listen to the speaker and repeat right after he or she has completed the sentence.

• Vidéo-scène B: Le jour et la date *p. 60*

1. Quel jour est-ce?
A. Compréhension orale CD 1, TRACK 42

For many people, the days of the week are not all alike.

DIALOGUE 1 Vendredi
Philippe: Quel jour est-ce?
Stéphanie: C'est vendredi.
Philippe: Super! Demain, c'est samedi!

DIALOGUE 2 Mercredi
Nathalie: Ça va?
Marc: Pas très bien.
Nathalie: Pourquoi?
Marc: Aujourd'hui, c'est mercredi.
Nathalie: Et alors?
Marc: Demain, c'est jeudi! Le jour de l'examen.
Nathalie: Zut! C'est vrai! Au revoir, Marc.
Marc: Au revoir, Nathalie. À demain!

B. Écoutez et répétez. CD 1, TRACK 43

You will now hear a paused version of the dialog. Listen to the speaker and repeat right after he or she has completed the sentence.

2. Anniversaire *p. 62*
A. Compréhension orale CD 1, TRACK 44

François and Isabelle are on their way to Nathalie's birthday party. As they are talking, François wants to know when Isabelle's birthday is.

François: C'est quand, ton anniversaire?
Isabelle: C'est le 18 mars!
François: Le 18 mars? Pas possible!
Isabelle: Si! Pourquoi?
François: C'est aussi mon anniversaire.
Isabelle: Quelle coïncidence!

B. Écoutez et répétez. CD 1, TRACK 45

You will now hear a paused version of the dialog. Listen to the speaker and repeat right after he or she has completed the sentence.

• Vidéo-scène C: Le temps *p. 64*
A. Compréhension orale CD 1, TRACK 46

It is nine o'clock Sunday morning. Cécile and her brother Philippe have planned a picnic for the whole family. Cécile is asking about the weather.

Cécile: Quel temps fait-il?
Philippe: Il fait mauvais!
Cécile: Il fait mauvais?
Philippe: Oui, il fait mauvais! Regarde! Il pleut!
Cécile: Zut, zut et zut!
Philippe: !!!??
Cécile: Et le pique-nique?
Philippe: Le pique-nique? Ah, oui, le pique-nique! . . . Écoute, ça n'a pas d'importance.
Cécile: Pourquoi?
Philippe: Pourquoi? Parce que Papa va nous inviter au restaurant.
Cécile: Super!

B. Écoutez et répétez. CD 1, TRACK 47

You will now hear a paused version of the dialog. Listen to the speaker and repeat right after he or she has completed the sentence.

À votre tour!
• Ecoutez bien! *p. 66* CD 1, TRACK 48

Isabelle is in a café talking to Jean-Paul. You will hear Isabelle asking questions. For each of Isabelle's questions, select Jean-Paul's response from the suggested answers. She will repeat each question. Écoutez.

1. Quel temps fait-il? #
2. Tu veux un sandwich? #
3. Tu veux un jus d'orange? #
4. Quelle heure est-il? #
5. C'est quand, ton anniversaire? #
6. Combien coûte le sandwich? # *cost*

• Conversation dirigée *p. 66* CD 1, TRACK 49

Stéphanie is in a café called Le Select. The waiter is taking her order. Écoutez leur conversation.

Le garçon: Bonjour, mademoiselle! Vous désirez?
Stéphanie: Je voudrais un croissant, s'il vous plaît. Combien coûte un jus d'orange?
Le garçon: 2 euros.
Stéphanie: Donnez-moi un jus d'orange, s'il vous plaît! . . . Monsieur, s'il vous plaît! Ça fait combien?
Le garçon: Ça fait 4 euros cinquante.
Stéphanie: Voici 5 euros.
Le garçon: Merci, mademoiselle.

Complete videoscripts, plus Workbook and Assessment audioscripts, are available in the Unit Resource Books.

UNITÉ 2

Main Theme
• Daily Activities

COMMUNICATION
• Ordering snacks and beverages in a café
• Asking about prices and paying for food/drink
• Using French money
• Telling time
• Giving the date and day of the week
• Talking about the weather

CULTURES
• Learning about the euro
• Learning where French teens eat with their friends
• Learning about the cafe

CONNECTIONS
• Connecting to Math: Tallying a restaurant check
• Connecting to Science: Learning about the weather
• Connecting to Music: Singing "Alouette"

COMPARISONS
• Comparing where teens in France and the U.S. go for a snack
• Comparing what teens in France and the U.S. eat

COMMUNITIES
• Using French to order in a restaurant
• Using French to perform for people in the community

UNITÉ 2 Invitation au français

Everyday Life

La vie courante

LEÇON 3 Bon appétit!
VIDÉO-SCÈNES
A Tu as faim?
B Au café
C Ça fait combien?

LEÇON 4 De jour en jour
VIDÉO-SCÈNES
A L'heure
B Le jour et la date
C Le temps

THÈME ET OBJECTIFS

Everyday life in France

In this unit, you will learn how to get along in France. In particular, you may want to know how to buy something to eat or drink.

You will learn ...
• to order snacks and beverages in a café
• to ask about prices and pay for your food/drink
• to use French money

You will also learn ...
• to tell time
• to give the date and the day of the week
• to talk about the weather

 WEBQUEST
CLASSZONE.COM

UNIT OVERVIEW

▶ **Communication Goals:** Students will learn to order something to eat or drink in a café or fast food restaurant. They will also learn to talk about weather.

▶ **Linguistic Goals:** Students will begin to acquire features of the French sound system, particularly rhythm, stress, intonation, and the French / r /.

▶ **Critical Thinking Goals:** Students will discover that all nouns — even those referring to things — have gender. They will observe that in French it is expressed as either **il** or **elle.**

▶ **Cultural Goals:** Students will become aware of types of eating establishments and the French monetary system.

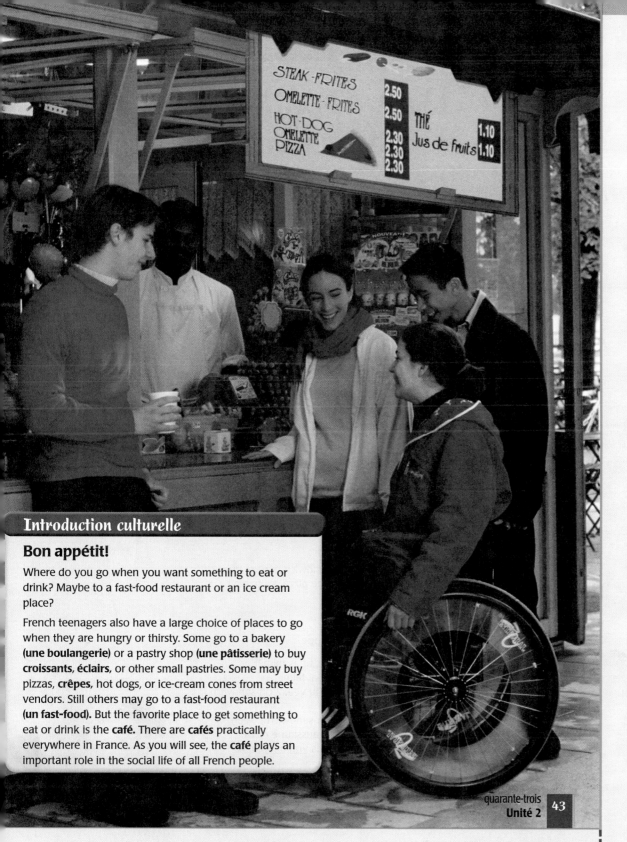

STEAK - FRITES   2.50

OMELETTE - FRITES   2.50

HOT - DOG   2.30

OMELETTE   2.30

PIZZA   2.30

THÉ   1.10

Jus de fruits   1.10

Introduction culturelle

Bon appétit!

Where do you go when you want something to eat or drink? Maybe to a fast-food restaurant or an ice cream place?

French teenagers also have a large choice of places to go when they are hungry or thirsty. Some go to a bakery (**une boulangerie**) or a pastry shop (**une pâtisserie**) to buy **croissants**, **éclairs**, or other small pastries. Some may buy pizzas, **crêpes**, hot dogs, or ice-cream cones from street vendors. Still others may go to a fast-food restaurant (**un fast-food**). But the favorite place to get something to eat or drink is the **café**. There are **cafés** practically everywhere in France. As you will see, the **café** plays an important role in the social life of all French people.

PRINT

Unit 2 Resource Book
  Family Letter, p. 31

AUDIO & VISUAL

Audio Program
Chansons CD

TECHNOLOGY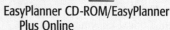

EasyPlanner CD-ROM/EasyPlanner
  Plus Online

Language note The expression **Bon appétit!** is used as people sit down to eat. It means *Enjoy the meal!*

Cultural note
Les fast-foods

Fast-food restaurants (**les fast-foods**, or technically, **les restaurants de restauration rapide**) have multiplied in France in recent years and are now very popular with French teenagers. One can order:
- hamburgers (**des hamburgers**)
- hot dogs (**des saucisses, des hot dogs**)
- French fries (**des frites**)
- salads (**des salades**), and sometimes
- pastries (**des pâtisseries**)

A typical meal at a fast-food restaurant costs about 6 euros. In addition to familiar American chains, there are also other chains, like *Quick, Free Time, Le Duff,* and *La Croissanterie.*

Language note The term for "drive-up" at fast-food restaurants is **service au volant** (*service at the steering wheel*).

Middle School Copymasters

Unité 2: Weather project, word puzzles, vocabulary game, conversations, nature project, pp. T9–T13

Pacing

Try to move through this unit rather quickly, focusing on listening and speaking.

In later lessons, students will encounter the same vocabulary again. At that time they will be expected to master the material in writing.

Leçon 3A

Main Topics Offering and asking for food

Teaching Resource Options

PRINT

Workbook PE, pp. 29–32
Activités pour tous PE, pp. 17–18
Block Scheduling Copymasters,
  pp. 17–24
Absent Student Copymasters
Unit 2 Resource Book
  Activités pour tous TE, pp. 13–14
  Audioscript, pp. 56, 57–59
  Communipak, pp. 132–156
  Lesson Plans, pp. 19–20
  Block Scheduling Copymasters,
    pp. 25–26
  Absent Student Copymasters,
    pp. 32–33
  Video Activities, pp. 38–41
  Videoscript, pp. 50–51
  Workbook TE, pp. 1–4

AUDIO & VISUAL

Audio Program
CD 1 Tracks 28, 29
CD 6 Tracks 1–5
Overhead Transparencies
10 Foods

TECHNOLOGY

Online Workbook

VIDEO PROGRAM

VIDÉO   DVD

MODULE 3A
Tu as faim?

TOTAL TIME: 5:51 min.
  DVD Disk 1
  Videotape 1 (COUNTER: 38:31 min.)

3A.1 Dialogue: Tu as faim?
  (38:40–39:35 min.)

3A.2 Mini-scenes: Ordering food
  (39:36–41:29 min.)

3A.3 Vignette culturelle: Qu'est-ce qu'on mange?
  (41:30–44:22 min.)

Comprehension practice Play the entire module through as an introduction to the lesson.

Bon appétit!
A Tu as faim?

Pierre, Philippe, and Nathalie are on their way home from school. They stop by a street vendor who sells sandwiches and pizza. Today it is Pierre's turn to treat his friends.

SCÈNE 1   **Pierre et Nathalie**

Pierre: Tu as faim?
Nathalie: Oui, j'ai faim.
Pierre: Tu veux un sandwich ou une pizza?
Nathalie: Donne-moi une pizza, s'il te plaît.
Pierre: Voilà.
Nathalie: Merci.

SCÈNE 2   **Pierre et Philippe**

Pierre: Et toi, Philippe, tu as faim?
Philippe: Oh là là, oui, j'ai faim.
Pierre: Qu'est-ce que tu veux? Un sandwich ou une pizza?
Philippe: Je voudrais un sandwich … <u>euh</u> …   *er …*
  et donne-moi aussi une pizza.
Pierre: C'est vrai! Tu as <u>vraiment</u> faim!   *really*

CROSS-CULTURAL OBSERVATION

Have students look at the foods pictured in **Pour communiquer.**

The only word that may be unfamiliar to them is **frites** *(French fries).*

Model the words and have students repeat them with a French accent.

Observation questions:
• Which of the food names are originally American words?
• Which of the food names are French?
• Which food name is Italian?

J'ai faim!
Tu as faim?

POUR COMMUNIQUER

write out! Conversation Practice

▶ *How to say that you are hungry:*

J'ai faim. *fai*	*I'm hungry.*
Tu as faim?	*Are you hungry?*

▶ *How to offer a friend something:*

Tu veux … ?	*Do you want …?*	**Tu veux** un sandwich?
Qu'est-ce que tu veux?	*What do you want?*	**Qu'est-ce que tu veux?**
		Un sandwich ou une pizza?

▶ *How to ask a friend for something:*

Je voudrais …	*I would like …*	**Je voudrais** un sandwich.
Donne-moi …	*Give me …*	**Donne-moi** une pizza.
S'il te plaît …	*Please …*	**S'il te plaît**, François, donne-moi une pizza.

Les nourritures *(Foods)*

 un croissant   un sandwich   un steak   un steak-frites   un hamburger   un hot dog

 une salade   une pizza   une omelette   une crêpe   une glace *sa*

NOTE *culturelle*

Les jeunes et la nourriture

In general, French teenagers eat their main meals at home with their families. On weekends or after school, however, when they are with friends, they often stop at a fast-food restaurant or a café for something to eat.

At fast-food restaurants, French teenagers order pretty much the same types of foods as Americans: hamburgers, hot dogs, and pizza.

At a café, teenagers may order a croissant, a sandwich, or a dish of ice cream. Some favorite sandwiches are ham (**un sandwich au jambon**), Swiss cheese (**un sandwich au fromage**), or salami (**un sandwich au saucisson**). And, of course, they are made with French bread, which has a crunchy crust. Another traditional quick café meal is a small steak with French fries (**un steak-frites).**

COMPREHENSION **Foods**

PROPS: Pictures of the foods (above)

Present the French names of the foods.
[Hold up "croissant."] **Voici un croissant.**
[Hold up "sandwich."] **Voici un sandwich.**
Est-ce que c'est un croissant? [Non.]
Est-ce que c'est un sandwich? [Oui.]

Have students distribute the "foods."
  X, prends le croissant et donne-le à Y.
  Qui a le croissant? [Y.]

You may give more complex commands.
  X, prends une pizza et un steak.
  Donne la pizza à Y et le steak à Z.

Photo culture note

Les pizzas In France, pizzas are sold:
• at pizzerias (**une pizzéria**)
• at certain bakeries (**une boulangerie**)
• at deli shops (**une charcuterie**).
One can buy individual mini-pizzas about 5 inches in diameter. (These are sometimes served at home as an **hors-d'oeuvre**.)
Pizzas may have the following ingredients as toppings:
• cheese (**du fromage**)
• anchovies (**des anchois**)
• pepperoni (**du chorizo**)
• green peppers (**des poivrons**)
• mushrooms (**des champignons**)
Note the sign for take-out pizza (**pizza à emporter**).

POUR COMMUNIQUER

If students ask Literally, **j'ai faim** means *I have hunger.*

Pronunciation Be sure the students say the American words with a French accent: nasal "a" and no "n" or "m" in **sandwich**, **hamburger**; no liaison and a silent "h" in **un hot dog**.

Les nourritures Another traditional sandwich is **un croque-monsieur** which is a toasted ham and cheese sandwich.

Supplementary vocabulary
FOODS
une salade verte
une salade de tomates
une tarte *pie*
un gâteau *cake*
un éclair
une glace à la vanille
une glace au chocolat

Cross-cultural observation
Have students note similarities and differences in where French young people stop for food and what they eat.

Cultural note In France, **les fast-foods** are not drive-ins, but are located in downtown areas and shopping malls. They often have only stand-up counters and are not designed for simply sitting and talking with friends.

J'AI FAIM! JE VOUDRAIS UN SANDWICH.

 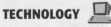
PETIT COMMENTAIRE

In France, sandwiches are traditionally very simple: a piece of French bread with a slice of ham or cheese. However, nowadays one can buy fancier sandwiches made with different breads, such as "panini", and a variety of ingredients.

Petit commentaire

Two popular sandwiches sold in cafés are **le croque-monsieur** and **le croque-madame**.
• The **croque-monsieur** is a grilled ham and cheese sandwich made with American-style bread.
• The **croque-madame** is similar, but with a fried egg on top.

un sandwich, une pizza

You may have noted that the names of some foods are masculine and others are feminine. In French, ALL NOUNS, whether they designate people or things, are either MASCULINE or FEMININE.

MASCULINE NOUNS		FEMININE NOUNS	
un sandwich	**le** sandwich	**une** pizza	**la** pizza
un croissant	**le** croissant	**une** salade	**la** salade

1 EXCHANGES offering food and making a selection

– Qu'est-ce que tu veux? ...?
– Donne-moi ... s'il te plaît.

1. Un hamburger ou un steak?/un hamburger (un steak)
2. Un hot dog ou un sandwich?/un hot dog (un sandwich)
3. Une salade ou une omelette?/ une salade (une omelette)
4. Un steak-frites ou une pizza?/un steak-frites (une pizza)
5. Une crêpe ou un croissant?/une crêpe (un croissant)
6. Une glace à la vanille ou une glace au chocolat?/une glace à la vanille (une glace au chocolat)

Variation To simplify this activity, have students choose one of the two foods in each item.
– **Donne-moi une pizza, s'il te plaît.**
– **Voilà.**
– **Merci.**

Challenge (dialogue format)
– **Tu as faim?**
– **Oui, j'ai faim.**
– **Tu veux un hamburger?**
– **Oui, donne-moi un hamburger, s'il te plaît.**

1 **Au choix** *(Your choice)*

PARLER Offer your classmates a choice between the following items. They will decide which one they would like.

▶ une pizza ou un sandwich?

1. un hamburger ou un steak?
2. un hot dog ou un sandwich?
3. une salade ou une omelette?
4. un steak-frites ou une pizza?
5. une crêpe ou un croissant?
6. une glace à la vanille ou une glace au chocolat?

Qu'est-ce que tu veux? Une pizza ou un sandwich?

Donne-moi un sandwich s'il te plaît.

2 Au café

PARLER You are in a French café. Ask for the following dishes.

▶

 1
 2
3

4
5
 6

▶ Je voudrais un croissant.

LISTENING PRACTICE Gender identification

PROPS: Red and blue index cards for each student

Quickly read aloud sentences containing masculine and feminine nouns. Have the students hold up the blue card for masculine nouns and the red card for feminine nouns.

1. **Voici une salade.** [R]
2. **Voici le sandwich.** [B]
3. **Voici la glace.** [R]
4. **Voici une crêpe.** [R]
5. **Voici un steak.** [B]
6. **Voici le croissant.** [B]
7. **Voici la pizza.** [R]
8. **Voici un hot dog.** [B]

Choose 3/6
Write out and circulate.

3 Tu as faim?

PARLER You have invited French friends to your home. Ask if they are hungry and offer them the following foods.

▶ —Tu as faim?
—Oui, j'ai faim.
—Tu veux un hamburger?
—Oui, merci.

▶

 1
 2
 3
 4
 5   6

Present!

4 Qu'est-ce que tu veux?

PARLER Say which foods you would like to have in the following circumstances.

▶ You are very hungry.

Je voudrais un steak-frites.

1. You are at an Italian restaurant.
2. You are on a diet.
3. You are a vegetarian.
4. You are having breakfast.
5. You would like a dessert.
6. You want to eat something light for supper.

PRONONCIATION

L'intonation

When you speak, your voice rises and falls. This is called INTONATION. In French, as in English, your voice goes down at the end of a statement. However, in French, your voice rises after each group of words in the middle of a sentence. (This is the opposite of English, where your voice drops a little when you pause in the middle of a sentence.)

Voici un steak . . . et une salade.

Répétez: **Je voudrais une pizza.**

Je voudrais une pizza et un sandwich.

Je voudrais une pizza, un sandwich et un hamburger.

Voici un steak.

Voici un steak et une salade.

Voici un steak, une salade et une glace.

---

2 COMMUNICATION ordering food

Je voudrais...
1. un sandwich.
2. une salade.
3. une pizza.
4. une glace.
5. une omelette.
6. un steak-frites.

3 ROLE PLAY offering food and accepting it

1. – Tu as faim?
   – Oui, j'ai faim.
   – Tu veux une pizza?
   – Oui, merci.
2. – Tu as faim?
   – Oui, j'ai faim.
   – Tu veux un steak?
   – Oui, merci.
3. – Tu as faim?
   – Oui, j'ai faim.
   – Tu veux un sandwich?
   – Oui, merci.
4. – Tu as faim?
   – Oui, j'ai faim.
   – Tu veux un hot dog?
   – Oui, merci.
5. – Tu as faim?
   – Oui, j'ai faim.
   – Tu veux une glace?
   – Oui, merci.
6. – Tu as faim?
   – Oui, j'ai faim
   – Tu veux une crêpe?
   – Oui, merci.

4 COMPREHENSION selecting food according to specific circumstances

Answers will vary.
1. Je voudrais une pizza.
2. Je voudrais une salade.
3. Je voudrais une salade (un sandwich, un croissant, une crêpe).
4. Je voudrais un croissant (une omelette).
5. Je voudrais une crêpe (une glace).
6. Je voudrais un sandwich (une salade, un hot dog, une omelette, un croissant).

SOUNDING FRENCH

A key outcome of **Invitation au français** is that students begin to "sound French" so that they can be easily understood by French speakers.

One of the most important parts of "sounding French" is to acquire the intonation patterns of the language.

An effective technique is to have students say English sentences using French intonation. Use English equivalents of the above sentences to practice. For example:

I would like a pizza.

I would like a pizza and a sandwich.

I would like a pizza, a sandwich, and a hamburger.

Leçon 3B

Main Topic Ordering something to drink

Teaching Resource Options

PRINT

Workbook PE, pp. 33–36
Activités pour tous PE, pp. 19–20
Unit 2 Resource Book
  Activités pour tous TE, pp. 15–16
  Audioscript, pp. 56–57, 59–60
  Communipak, pp. 132–156
  Lesson Plans, pp. 21–22
  Block Scheduling Lesson Plans,
    pp. 27–28
  Absent Student Copymasters, p. 34
  Video Activities, pp. 42–45
  Videoscript, pp. 52–53
  Workbook TE, pp. 5–8

AUDIO & VISUAL

Audio Program
CD 1 Tracks 31, 32
CD 6 Tracks 6–10
Overhead Transparencies
11 Beverages

TECHNOLOGY

Online Workbook

VIDEO PROGRAM

VIDÉO DVD
 MODULE 3B
Au café

TOTAL TIME: 4:34 min.
  DVD Disk 1
  Videotape 1 (COUNTER: 44:33 min.)

3B.1 Dialogue: Au café
  (14:41–45:38 min.)

3B.2 Mini-scenes: Saying please
  (45:39–47:27 min.)

3B.3 Vignette culturelle: Qu'est-ce qu'on boit?
  (47:28–49:07 min.)

Comprehension practice Play the entire module through as an introduction to the lesson.

Photo culture note Le garçon de café French waiters (un garçon de café) are usually dressed formally: black pants, white shirt and bow tie, vest or jacket.

B Au café

This afternoon Trinh and Céline went shopping. They are now tired and thirsty. Trinh invites Céline to a café.

SCÈNE 1   Trinh, Céline

Trinh: Tu as soif?
Céline: Oui, j'ai soif.
Trinh: <u>On va dans un café?</u>   *Shall we go to a café?*
  <u>Je t'invite.</u>   *I'm treating (inviting).*
Céline: <u>D'accord!</u>   *Okay!*

SCÈNE 2   Le garçon, Céline, Trinh

Le garçon: Vous désirez, mademoiselle?
Céline: Un jus d'orange, s'il vous plaît.
Le garçon: Et <u>pour</u> vous, monsieur?   *for*
Trinh: Donnez-moi une limonade,* s'il vous plaît.

SCÈNE 3   Le garçon, Céline, Trinh

Le garçon: *(à Céline)* La limonade, c'est pour vous, mademoiselle?
Trinh: Non, c'est pour moi.
Le garçon: <u>Ah, excusez-moi.</u>   *Oh, excuse me.*
  Voici le jus d'orange, mademoiselle.
Céline: Merci.

*****Une limonade** *is a popular inexpensive soft drink with a slight lemon flavor.*

WARM-UP AND REVIEW Forms of address

PROPS: Magazine pictures of individual men, women, and teenagers.

Have students greet one another saying:

– **Salut, X! Comment vas-tu?**

– **Ça va très bien (comme ci, comme ça).**

Hold up the magazine pictures; point out that students do not know these people.

Ask them to greet each person in the picture formally:

Bonjour, madame (monsieur, mademoiselle). Comment allez-vous?

Then have them observe how people address one another in the café scene from the video.

POUR COMMUNIQUER

Write out

#3 Garçon   Practise/Present

Donnez-moi une limonade, s'il vous plaît!

▶ How to say that you are thirsty:

J'ai soif.	*I'm thirsty.*
Tu as soif?	*Are you thirsty?*

▶ How to order in a café:

Vous désirez?	*May I help you?*	**—Vous désirez?**
Je voudrais …	*I would like …*	**—Je voudrais** un jus d'orange.

▶ How to request something …

from a friend:	*from an adult:*	
S'il te plaît, donne-moi …	**S'il vous plaît, donnez-moi …**	*Please, give me …*

→ Note that French people have two ways of saying please. They use
s'il te plaît with friends, and
s'il vous plaît with adults.
As we will see later, young people address their friends as **tu** and
adults that they do not know very well as **vous**.

Les boissons *(Beverages)*

| un soda | un jus d'orange | un jus de pomme | un jus de tomate | un jus de raisin* | une limonade | un café | un thé | un chocolat |

NOTE *culturelle*

Le café

The café is a favorite gathering place for French young
people. They go there not only when they are hungry or
thirsty but also to meet their friends. They can sit at a
table and talk for hours over a cup of coffee or a glass
of juice. French young people also enjoy mineral water
and soft drinks. In a French café, a 15% service charge is
included in the check. However, most people also leave
some small change as an added tip.

Jus de raisin is a golden-colored juice made from grapes.

Language notes
• When calling a waiter, one may also
say **"Garçon!"** It is becoming
common, however, to use the more
polite **"Monsieur!"**
• The traditional term **un garçon** is
slowly being replaced by **un serveur**.
• A waitress is **une serveuse**.

POUR COMMUNIQUER

Language note Literally, **tu as soif**
means *you have thirst.*

Supplementary vocabulary
BEVERAGES

un café crème *coffee with cream*
un jus d'ananas *pineapple juice*
un jus de pamplemousse *grapefruit
juice*
un citron pressé *freshly squeezed
lemon juice, served with water and
sugar on the side*
une orange pressée *freshly squeezed
orange juice, served with water and
sugar on the side*

Cross-cultural observation
Have students note similarities and
differences in where French young
people like to eat and drink.

COMPREHENSION Beverages

PROPS: Transparency 11: Beverages
red and blue transparency markers

Point out beverages on the transparency.
> **Voici un café. Voici un soda.** etc.

Have students point out beverages.
> **X, viens ici. Montre-nous un café.**

Hold up the blue and the red markers.
> **Voici un stylo bleu et un stylo rouge. Si vous
> entendez un, prenez le stylo bleu. Si vous
> entendez une, prenez le rouge.**

> **Dessinez un cercle autour de la boisson.**

> **Écoutez. «Je voudrais un thé.»**

[Draw a blue circle around the tea.]

Teaching Resource Options

PRINT

Workbook PE, pp. 33–36
Unit 2 Resource Book
  Audioscript, p. 57
  Communipak, pp. 132–156
  Workbook TE, pp. 5–8

AUDIO & VISUAL

CD 1 Track 33

Petit commentaire

French young people often order mineral water mixed with a **sirop** or flavored concentrate, such as **menthe** (mint), **orange, citron, grenadine** (pomegranate), or **fraise** (strawberry). These drinks are named according to the mineral water used.

1 EXCHANGES offering and selecting beverages

– Tu veux ...
– Donne-moi ..., s'il te plaît.
1. un thé ou un café?/un thé (un café)
2. une limonade ou un soda?/une limonade (un soda)
3. un jus de pomme ou un jus d'orange?/ un jus de pomme (un jus d'orange)
4. un jus de raisin ou un jus de tomate?/ un jus de raisin (un jus de tomate)

2 ROLE PLAY placing an order at a café

– Monsieur (Mademoiselle), s'il vous plaît!
– Vous désirez?
– ..., s'il vous plaît!
1. Un chocolat
2. Une limonade
3. Un jus de pomme
4. Un thé
5. Un café
6. Un jus de tomate

Variation (more basic): You may want to do the exercise quickly with the whole class, having students give just a one-sentence response: **Un jus d'orange, s'il vous plaît.** Then have students in pairs practice the dialogue format as indicated in the text.

PETIT COMMENTAIRE

At a café, French young people often order carbonated soft drinks. They also enjoy natural beverages, such as flavored mineral water or juice. In the larger cities, one can find inviting juice bars that offer a wide selection of freshly blended fruit drinks.

1 Tu as soif?

PARLER You have invited a French friend to your house. You offer a choice of beverages and your friend (played by a classmate) responds.

▶ un thé ou un chocolat?
  —Tu veux un thé ou un chocolat?
  —Donne-moi un chocolat, s'il te plaît.

1. un thé ou un café?
2. une limonade ou un soda?
3. un jus de pomme ou un jus d'orange?
4. un jus de raisin ou un jus de tomate?

2 Au café

PARLER You are in a French café. Get the attention of the waiter (**Monsieur**) or the waitress (**Mademoiselle**) and place your order. Act out the dialogue with a classmate.

GAME C'est logique?

PREPARATION: Prepare 2 bags of cards:
- (Bag A: 10 cards) On 5 cards, write **J'ai faim.** On the other 5, write **J'ai soif.**
- (Bag B: 21 cards) Begin each card with **Je voudrais, Donne-moi,** or **Donnez-moi** and add a food or beverage from pages 45 and 49.

Divide the class into two teams: **logique** and **illogique.**

A player from each team comes up. One reads a card from Bag A, the other reads one from Bag B. If the sentences fit logically, the **logique** team earns a point. If not, a point goes to the **illogique** team. For example:

J'ai soif. Donne-moi une pizza. = illogique

3 Que choisir? *(What to choose?)*

PARLER You are in a French café. Decide what beverage you are going to order in each of the following circumstances.

▶ You are very thirsty.
  S'il vous plaît, une limonade (un jus de pomme) …

1. It is very cold outside.
2. You do not want to spend much money.
3. You like juice but are allergic to citrus fruits.
4. It is breakfast time.
5. You have a sore throat.

4  **La faim et la soif** *(Hungry and thirsty)*

PARLER You are having a meal in a French café. Order the food suggested in the picture. Then order something to drink with that dish. A classmate will play the part of the waiter.

Note: **Et avec ça?** means *And with that?*

1
2
3
4

Vous désirez?

Je voudrais un steak-frites.

Et avec ça?

Un jus de tomate, s'il vous plaît!

PRONONCIATION 🎧

L'accent final

In French, the rhythm is very even and the accent always falls on the *last* syllable of a word or group of words.

Répétez: **Philippe   Thomas   Alice   Sophie   Dominique**

un café	**Je voudrais un café.**
une salade	**Donnez-moi une salade.**
un chocolat	**Donne-moi un chocolat.**

un chocolat

SOUNDING FRENCH

Along with intonation, one of the most important parts of "sounding French" is to acquire the rhythm and stress patterns of the language.

An effective technique is to let students mimic a French accent in English. Have them speak in a staccato rhythm, ending each group of words with a longer syllable, and using rising intonation at the end of phrases in the middle of a sentence.

In-the-French-lan-guage/
all-syl-la-bles-are-e-ven/
ex-cept-the-last-one/
which-gets-the-ac-cent.

---

un soda

3 COMPREHENSION selecting an appropriate beverage

Answers will vary.
1. S'il vous plaît, un thé (un chocolat, un café).
2. S'il vous plaît, une limonade (un café).
3. S'il vous plaît, un jus de raisin (de tomate, de pomme).
4. S'il vous plaît, un thé (un café, un chocolat).
5. S'il vous plaît, un jus d'orange (un thé).

Variation
Donnez-moi une limonade (un jus de pomme), s'il vous plaît.

4 ROLE PLAY ordering food and a beverage

1. – Vous désirez?
   – Je voudrais une omelette.
   – Et avec ça?
   – (Un thé), s'il vous plaît.
2. – Vous désirez?
   – Je voudrais une glace.
   – Et avec ça?
   – (Un chocolat), s'il vous plaît.
3. – Vous désirez?
   – Je voudrais un hot dog.
   – Et avec ça?
   – (Un jus de pomme), s'il vous plaît.
4. – Vous désirez?
   – Je voudrais une salade.
   – Et avec ça?
   – (Un jus de raisin), s'il vous plaît.

PRONUNCIATION 🎧

For the sample sentences, you may want to tap out the syllables evenly making the last one somewhat longer than the rest.

Middle School Copymasters

Drill: *Au café*, pp. T11–T12; Puzzle 1: *Bon appétit!*, p. 18; Game: Round the Room, p. 27

Language note Since the French terms for milk and water are generally used with the partitive, they have not been included in this lesson.

Optional expansion You may want to teach:
du lait
de l'eau
de l'eau minérale

Communication
Unité 2 LEÇON 3B **· 51**

Leçon 3C

Main Topic Asking about prices

Teaching Resource Options

PRINT

Workbook PE, pp. 37–40
Activités pour tous PE, pp. 21–22
Unit 2 Resource Book
   Activités pour tous TE, pp. 17–18
   Audioscript, pp. 57, 60–62
   Communipak, pp. 132–156
   Lesson Plans, pp. 23–24
   Block Scheduling Lesson Plans,
    pp. 29–30
   Absent Student Copymasters, p. 35
   Video Activities, pp. 46–49
   Videoscript, pp. 54–55
   Workbook TE, pp. 9–12

AUDIO & VISUAL

Audio Program
CD 1 Tracks 34, 35
CD 6 Tracks 11–15

TECHNOLOGY

Online Workbook

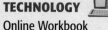

VIDEO PROGRAM

MODULE 3C
Ça fait combien?

TOTAL TIME: 7:10 min.
   DVD Disk 1
   Videotape 1 (COUNTER: 49:19 min.)

3C.1 Dialogue: Ça fait combien?
   (49:38–50:15 min.)

3C.2 Mini-scenes: Asking what one owes
   (50:16–52:15 min.)

3C.3 Vignette culturelle: L'argent français
   (52:16–56:29 min.)

Comprehension practice Play the entire module through as an introduction to the lesson.

C Ça fait combien?

At the café, Trinh and Céline have talked about many things.
It is now time to go. Trinh calls the waiter so he can pay the check.

Dis, Céline, prête-moi 5 euros, s'il te plaît.

Trinh:	S'il vous plaît?
Le garçon:	Oui, monsieur.
Trinh:	Ça fait combien?
Le garçon:	Voyons, un jus d'orange, 2 euros 50, et une limonade, 1 euro 50. Ça fait 4 euros.
Trinh:	4 euros … Très bien … Mais, <u>euh</u> … *uh …*
	Zut! <u>Où est mon porte-monnaie …?</u> *Where is my wallet?*
	<u>Dis</u>, Céline, prête-moi 5 euros, s'il te plaît. *Hey*

NOTE *culturelle*

L'argent européen *(European money)*

Since 2002, twelve European countries have been using a new currency: the euro (**l'euro**). These countries include France, as well as Germany, Ireland, Austria, Italy, Spain, Portugal, Greece, Finland, Belgium, Luxembourg, and the Netherlands. The euro has the same value in all of these countries. It is also very convenient since you do not need to change money when you travel from one country to another.

The euro is divided into 100 cents or **centimes**. The euro currency consists of 7 different bills and 8 different coins. The euro bills are of different colors and different sizes. The largest is worth 500 euros and the smallest 5 euros.

WARM-UP Numbers

Teach the students the following phrase:
   Combien font deux plus deux?
   (Note that the "s" on **plus** is pronounced /plys/.)
Have the class solve arithmetic problems.
   Combien font quatorze plus seize?
   [Trente] or
   [Quatorze plus seize font trente.]

POUR COMMUNIQUER

[handwritten: Write out!]

> C'est combien?

[handwritten: er/o]

▶ **How to ask how much something costs:**

C'est combien?	*How much is it?*	—**C'est combien?**
Ça fait combien?	*How much does that come to (make)?*	—**Ça fait combien?**
Ça fait …	*That's …, That comes to …*	—**Ça fait** 10 euros.
Combien coûte …?	*How much does … cost?*	—**Combien coûte** le sandwich?
Il/Elle coûte …	*It costs …*	—**Il coûte** 5 euros.

▶ **How to ask a friend to lend you something:**

Prête-moi …	*Lend me …, Loan me …*	**Prête-moi** 30 euros, s'il te plaît.

→ Note that masculine nouns can be replaced by **il** and feminine nouns can be replaced by **elle**.

Voici **une glace.**	**Elle** coûte 2 euros.	*It costs 2 euros.*
Voici **un sandwich.**	**Il** coûte 5 euros.	*It costs 5 euros.*

[handwritten: er/o peu peux veux]

STRATEGY Speaking

Linking words When counting in euros, be sure to use the proper liaisons and elisions.

un euro	trois euros	cinq euros	sept euros	neuf euros
(n)	*(z)*	*(k)*	*(t)*	
deux euros	quatre euros	six euros	huit euros	dix euros
(z)		*(z)*	*(t)*	*(z)*

GAME

Divide the class into teams A and B. Two players come forward.

Player A asks a math question.

If player B answers correctly, both teams get a point.

If player B is wrong, and player A can answer his/her own question correctly, team A gets a point.

Then the next two players have their turn. This time player B asks the question. Etc.

POUR COMMUNIQUER

Language note In asking for prices, the casual speech forms given are much more common than **Combien est-ce que c'est?** or **Combien est-ce que ça fait?**

Cultural note The exchange rate between the dollar and the euro fluctuates daily. For the purposes of the activities, an exchange rate of 1 dollar = 1 euro can be used, unless there is a substantial variation in that parity.

Note culturelle

The denominations of the euro bills are: 5, 10, 20, 50, 100, 200 and 500 euros. The face of a euro bill shows an archway, door or window to symbolize opportunity and opening to new ideas. The bridge on the back of each bill emphasizes the strong links among the various European countries shown in the map underneath the bridge.

The eight euro coins are issued in the following values: 1, 2, 5, 10, 20 and 50 cents, and 1 and 2 euros.

If students ask

French-speaking countries each have their own currency:

Quebec: le dollar canadien

Switzerland: le franc suisse

Algeria and Tunisia: le dinar

Morocco: le dirham

Senegal, Ivory Coast, etc.: le franc CFA (de la Communauté financière africaine)

Teaching Resource Options

PRINT
Workbook PE, pp. 37–40
Unit 2 Resource Book
    Audioscript, p. 57
    Communipak, pp. 132–156
    Family Involvement, pp. 36–37
    Workbook TE, pp. 9–12

Assessment
Lesson 3 Quiz, pp. 63–64
Audioscript for Quiz 3, p. 62
Answer Keys, pp. 195–198

AUDIO & VISUAL
Audio Program
CD 1 Track 36
CD 13 Track 12
Overhead Transparencies
12 Menu from "Le Select"

TECHNOLOGY
Test Generator CD-ROM/eTest Plus
Online

Petit commentaire
The **Guide Michelin,** the classic guide to restaurants in France, annually grants "stars" for outstanding cuisine. About 575 restaurants are given one star, 85 restaurants receive two stars, and about 20 truly outstanding restaurants are awarded the coveted three stars.

---

1 PRACTICE asking someone for a loan

1. S'il te plaît, prête-moi deux euros.
2. S'il te plaît, prête-moi trois euros.
3. S'il te plaît, prête-moi dix euros.
4. S'il te plaît, prête-moi vingt euros.
5. S'il te plaît, prête-moi trente euros.
6. S'il te plaît, prête-moi quarante euros.
7. S'il te plaît, prête-moi vingt-cinq euros.
8. S'il te plaît, prête-moi quinze euros.
9. S'il te plaît, prête-moi cinquante euros.

Realia note Ask the students:
Comment s'appelle le café/restaurant? [Le Select]

Middle School Copymasters
Conversations 1: *Allons dans un café!* p. 17; Worksheet 2: *Petites scènes,* pp. 22–23

ÇA FAIT COMBIEN?

PETIT COMMENTAIRE
French people of all ages love to eat out, and French restaurants have the reputation of offering the best cuisine in the world. Of course, there are all kinds of restaurants for all kinds of budgets, ranging from the simple country inn **(l'auberge de campagne)** with its hearty regional food to the elegant three-star restaurant **(restaurant trois étoiles)** with its exquisite—and expensive—menu.

1 S'il te plaît …

PARLER You have been shopping in Paris and discover that you did not exchange enough money. Ask a friend to loan you the following sums.

▶ 5 euros
    S'il te plaît, prête-moi cinq euros.

1. 2 euros
2. 3 euros
3. 10 euros
4. 20 euros
5. 30 euros
6. 40 euros
7. 25 euros
8. 15 euros
9. 50 euros

2 Décision

PARLER Before ordering at a café, Charlotte and Fatima are checking the prices. Act out the dialogues.

▶ le chocolat

Combien coûte le chocolat?

Il coûte deux euros cinquante.

1. le thé
2. le jus d'orange
3. la salade de tomates
4. la glace à la vanille
5. le café
6. le steak-frites
7. le hot dog
8. l'omelette
9. la salade mixte
10. le jus de raisin

LE SÉLECT
CAFÉ RESTAURANT

BOISSONS
café.............................1€50
chocolat.........................2€50
thé ....2€
limonade.........................2€50
jus d'orange.....................2€70
jus de raisin ....2€70

GLACES
glace au chocolat ....2€50
glace à la vanille............2€50

SANDWICHS
sandwich au jambon .....3€50
sandwich au fromage ....3€50

ET AUSSI …
steak-frites.......................8€
salade mixte....................3€50
salade de tomates.............4€
omelette..........................4€25
hot dog ....4€
croissant ....1€40
pizza ....8€

PROJECT Un menu

Using the "Le Select" menu as a model, have the students prepare menus in French. They should include the name, address, and telephone number of the café/restaurant and illustrate with original drawings or cut-out pictures. Display the finished products on the bulletin board and/or around the room. If you choose to have your students do the Challenge activity on p. 67, they can use the menus in their café conversations.

3 🗣️ **Ça fait combien?**

PARLER You have gone to Le Select with your friends and have ordered the following items. Now you are ready to leave the café, and each one wants to pay. Check the prices on the menu for Le Select, and act out the dialogue.

1
2
3
4
5

▶ —Ça fait combien,
   s'il vous plaît?
—Ça fait deux euros cinquante.
—Voici deux euros cinquante.
—Merci.

Write out ① Act out ~ partner!

4 🗣️ **Au «Select»**

PARLER You are at Le Select. Order something to eat and drink. Since you are in a hurry, ask for the check right away. Act out the dialogue with a classmate who will play the part of the waiter/waitress.

Vous désirez?

Monsieur, s'il vous plaît!

Je voudrais un sandwich au jambon et un café. Ça fait combien?

 # costs! *(total)*

Ça fait 5 euros.

---

1. – Combien coûte le thé?
   – Il coûte deux euros.
2. – Combien coûte le jus d'orange?
   – Il coûte deux euros soixante-dix.
3. – Combien coûte la salade de tomates?
   – Elle coûte quatre euros.
4. – Combien coûte la glace à la vanille?
   – Elle coûte deux euros cinquante.
5. – Combien coûte le café?
   – Il coûte un euro cinquante.
6. – Combien coûte le steak-frites?
   – Il coûte huit euros.
7. – Combien coûte le hot dog?
   – Il coûte quatre euros.
8. – Combien coûte l'omelette?
   – Elle coûte quatre euros vingt-cinq.
9. – Combien coûte la salade mixte?
   – Elle coûte trois euros cinquante.
10. – Combien coûte le jus de raisin?
   – Il coûte deux euros soixante-dix.

3 **EXCHANGES** asking the price of something and paying for it

1. – Ça fait combien, s'il vous plaît?
   – Ça fait un euro quarante.
   – Voici un euro quarante.
   – Merci.
2. – Ça fait combien, s'il vous plaît?
   – Ça fait huit euros.
   – Voici huit euros.
   – Merci.
3. – Ça fait combien, s'il vous plaît?
   – Ça fait trois euros cinquante.
   – Voici trois euros cinquante.
   – Merci.
4. – Ça fait combien, s'il vous plaît?
   – Ça fait deux euros soixante-dix.
   – Voici deux euros soixante-dix.
   – Merci.
5. – Ça fait combien, s'il vous plaît?
   – Ça fait deux euros.
   – Voici deux euros.
   – Merci.

4 **ROLE PLAY** ordering something to eat and drink

Answers will vary.
– Monsieur (Mademoiselle), s'il vous plaît!
– Vous désirez?
– Je voudrais (une omelette et un jus de raisin). Ça fait combien?
– Ça fait (6 euros 95).

PRONONCIATION 🎧   /r/

La consonne «r»

The French consonant "r" is not at all like the English "r." It is pronounced at the back of the throat. In fact, it is similar to the Spanish "jota" sound of José.

silly

Répétez: **Marie   Paris   orange   Henri
franc   très   croissant   fromage
bonjour   pour   Pierre   quart
Robert   Richard   Renée   Raoul**

Marie, prête-moi trente euros.

Marie

name person (s)/place

PRONUNCIATION 🎧

If students have trouble producing the sound, it is better for them to identify the French "r" with an American "h" sound than with an American "r."

Teaching Resource Options

PRINT

Workbook PE, pp. 41–44
Activités pour tous PE, pp. 23–24
Block Scheduling Copymasters, pp. 25–32
Unit 2 Resource Book
   Activités pour tous TE, pp. 79–80
   Audioscript, pp. 121, 123–124
   Communipak, pp. 132–156
   Lesson Plans, pp. 85–86
   Absent Student Copymasters, pp. 97–98
   Block Scheduling Lesson Plans, pp. 91–92
   Video Activities, pp. 103–106
   Videoscript, pp. 115–116
   Workbook TE, pp. 65–68

AUDIO & VISUAL

Audio Program
CD 1 Tracks 37–39
CD 6 Tracks 16–21

TECHNOLOGY

Online Workbook

VIDEO PROGRAM

VIDÉO   DVD

MODULE 4A
Le français pratique
L'heure

TOTAL TIME: 7:30 min.
DVD Disk 1
Videotape 1 (COUNTER: 56:39 min.)

4A.1 Dialogue: Un rendez-vous
(56:47–57:13 min.)

4A.2 Mini-scenes: Telling time
(57:17–1:01:40 min.)

4A.3 À quelle heure est le film?
(1:01:41–1:02:00 min.)

4A.4 Mini-scenes: Indicating at what time an event occurs
(1:02:01–1:02:37 min.)

4A.5 Vignette culturelle: L'heure officielle
(1:02:38–1:05:09 min.)

Comprehension practice Play the entire module of the video through as an introduction to the lesson.

Day after Day

De jour en jour

A L'heure

1. Un rendez-vous

Jean-Paul and Stéphanie are sitting in a café. Stéphanie seems to be in a hurry to leave.

Stéphanie: Quelle heure est-il?
Jean-Paul: Il est trois heures.
Stéphanie: Trois heures?
Jean-Paul: Oui, trois heures.
Stéphanie: Oh là là. J'ai un rendez-vous avec David dans vingt minutes. Au revoir, Jean-Paul.   *I have a date with*
Jean-Paul: Au revoir, Stéphanie. À bientôt!   *See you soon!*

Il est huit heures!

POUR COMMUNIQUER

▶ *How to talk about the time:*

Quelle heure est-il?	*What time is it?*
Il est …	*It's …*

une heure	deux heures	trois heures	quatre heures	cinq heures	six heures

sept heures	huit heures	neuf heures	dix heures	onze heures	midi	minuit

WARM-UP Reviewing numbers

Have the students each write their phone numbers on a slip of paper and place them in a box.

Draw the first number and read it out loud (Quebec style: digit by digit).

The student whose number is read stands up and recites his/her phone number back. Then that student comes forward, draws a new number, and reads it aloud. The game continues until no numbers are left in the box.

1 🎧 Écoutez bien!

Never say 12 o'clock.

ÉCOUTER Listen as people talk about the time. For each dialog, indicate which of the watches below corresponds to the time you hear.

A 7:00   B 5:00   C 10:00   D 8:00   E 2:00   F 12:00

2 👥 Quelle heure est-il?

PARLER Ask your classmates what time it is.

Quelle heure est-il?
Il est quatre heures.

1   2   3   4   5   6   7

→ Although *o'clock* may be left out in English, the expression **heure(s)** must be used in French when giving the time.

It's ten. (It's ten o'clock.)   **Il est dix heures.**

→ To distinguish between A.M. and P.M., the French use the following expressions:

du matin	*in the morning*	Il est dix heures **du matin.**
de l'après-midi	*in the afternoon*	Il est deux heures **de l'après-midi.**
du soir	*in the evening*	Il est huit heures **du soir.**

NOTE DE PRONONCIATION: In telling time, the NUMBER and the word **heure(s)** are linked together. Remember, in French the letter "h" is always silent.

une heure   deux heures   trois heures   quatre heures   cinq heures   six heures

sept heures   huit heures   neuf heures   dix heures   onze heures

---

1 PRACTICE understanding the spoken time

1. A	4. F
2. E	5. C
3. D	6. B

2 PRACTICE asking and telling the time

1. – Quelle heure est-il?
   – Il est trois heures.
2. – Quelle heure est-il?
   – Il est six heures.
3. – Quelle heure est-il?
   – Il est une heure.
4. – Quelle heure est-il?
   – Il est neuf heures.
5. – Quelle heure est-il?
   – Il est onze heures.
6. – Quelle heure est-il?
   – Il est midi.
7. – Quelle heure est-il?
   – Il est minuit.

Cross-cultural observation

As is described in the video, the French use a 24-hour clock on timetables and TV schedules:

1 p.m. = **13h (treize heures)**

8 p.m. = **20h (vingt heures)**

- To go from p.m. to the 24-hour clock, add 12 hours:
  1 p.m. = 1 + 12 = **13 heures**
- To go from the 24-hour clock to p.m., simply subtract 12 hours:
  20 heures = 20 − 12 = 8 p.m.

COMPREHENSION Telling time

PROP: Clock with movable hands
Move the hands of the clock to show the hours and give the corresponding times.

> **Quelle heure est-il? Il est une heure.**
> **Il est deux heures.** etc.

Call on individual students to move the hands of the clock as you give the time.

> **Il est cinq heures.**
> **X, viens ici. Montre-nous cinq heures.**

VIDEO PROGRAM

 MODULE 4A

4A.3 À quelle heure est le film?
(1:01:41–1:02:00 min.)

4A.4 Mini-scenes: Indicating at what time an event occurs
(1:02:01–1:02:37 min.)

4A.5 Vignette culturelle: L'heure officielle
(1:02:38–1:05:09 min.)

If students ask To refer to clock time, the French use the word **heure**:
 Quelle heure est-il?
To talk about time in the general sense, they use the word **temps**:
 Nous avons le temps.

POUR COMMUNIQUER

Language notes

• It is correct to use either **avoir un rendez-vous** or **avoir rendez-vous** to discuss dates and appointments. **Avoir un rendez-vous** is used in this program since it parallels English usage (have **a** date, **an** appointment).

• Since people use digits when writing out times, students at the basic level do not need to spell these phrases out. (Therefore, the spelling **demi** as in **midi et demi**, is not shown.)

• **Expansion** You may want to introduce **moins** + minutes, as in **deux heures moins dix**. At the basic level, students can simply say **une heure cinquante**. This is more and more common with the increased use of digital clocks in France.

---

avoir = conjugate.

2. À quelle heure est le film?

Stéphanie and David have decided to go to a movie.

Stéphanie: Quelle heure est-il?
David: Il est trois heures et demie.
Stéphanie: Et à quelle heure est le film?
David: À quatre heures et quart.
Stéphanie: Ça va. Nous avons le temps.   *That's okay. / We have time.*

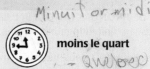
À quelle heure est le dîner?

POUR COMMUNIQUER

▶ *How to ask at what time something is scheduled:*

À quelle heure est …?	At what time is …?
—À quelle heure est le concert?	At what time is the concert?
—Le concert est à huit heures.	The concert is at eight.

▶ *How to say that you have an appointment or a date:*

J'ai un rendez-vous à …	I have an appointment (a date) at …	J'ai un rendez-vous à deux heures.

▶ *How to indicate the minutes:*

Il est … dix heures dix | six heures vingt-cinq | sept heures trente-cinq | deux heures cinquante-deux

▶ *How to indicate the half hour and the quarter hours:*

Minuit or midi

 et quart | et demie | moins le quart

par | | *Quebec*

 Il est une heure **et quart.** | Il est deux heures **et demie.** | Il est trois heures **moins le quart.**

COMPREHENSION Quarter hours and minutes practice

PROP: clock with movable hands

Model the quarter hours and minutes, moving the hands on the clock.
 Il est trois heures et quart. etc.
Have students show the times on the clock.
 X, montre-nous cinq heures dix.

Send two students to the board to write the times as you say them.
 Y et Z, venez au tableau.
 Il est dix heures vingt. Écrivez l'heure. [Students write: "10h20".]
Students at their desks can also write down the times.

3 L'heure

PARLER Give the times according to the clocks.

▶ Il est une heure et quart.

le quart

▶

4 À quelle heure?

conjugate être

PARLER Ask your classmates at what time certain activities are scheduled. They will answer according to the information below.

▶ 8h 50   le film
—À quelle heure est le film?
—Le film est à huit heures cinquante.

1. 7h 15   le concert
2. 2h 30   le match de football *(soccer)*
3. 3h 45   le match de tennis   *or*
4. 5h 10   le récital   *si*   *or* =
5. 7h 45   le dîner   *or*

5 Rendez-vous

Write out first - do c partner

PARLER Isabelle has appointments with various classmates and teachers. Look at her notebook and act out her dialogues with Philippe.

▶ ISABELLE: **J'ai un rendez-vous avec Marc.**
    PHILIPPE: **À quelle heure?**
    ISABELLE: **À onze heures et demie.**

11h30 Marc
2h10 Mme Chollet
3h20 M. Masson
4h35 Mlle Lacour
6h50 Jean-Paul
9h40 Nathalie
new

copy

6 À la gare *(At the train station)*

PARLER You are at the information desk of a French train station. Travelers ask you the departure times for the following trains. Answer them according to the posted schedule.

▶ le train pour Nice

À quelle heure est le train pour Nice?

Le train pour Nice est à six heures dix.

DÉPARTS			
NICE	♦ 6h 10	TOULON	♦ 9h 35
LYON	♦ 7h 15	COLMAR	♦ 10h 40
CANNES	♦ 7h 30	TOULOUSE	♦ 10h 45
TOURS	♦ 8h 12	MARSEILLE	♦ 10h 50
DIJON	♦ 8h 25	BORDEAUX	♦ 10h 55

---

3 PRACTICE telling time

1. Il est deux heures et demie (deux heures trente).
2. Il est quatre heures moins le quart (trois heures quarante-cinq).
3. Il est quatre heures et quart (quatre heures quinze).
4. Il est six heures et demie (six heures trente).
5. Il est onze heures moins le quart (dix heures quarante-cinq).

4 EXCHANGES asking and answering questions about time of events

– À quelle heure est ...?
– ... est à ...
1. le concert?/sept heures (et quart/quinze).
2. le match de football?/deux heures (et demie/trente).
3. le match de tennis?/quatre heures moins le quart (trois heures quarante-cinq).
4. le récital?/cinq heures dix.
5. le dîner?/huit heures moins le quart (sept heures quarante-cinq).

If students ask
• The "h" dividing the hours from the minutes in French stands for **heures** and corresponds to the colon used in English.
• U.S. football is **le football américain**.

5 EXCHANGES discussing appointment times

Isabelle: J'ai un rendez-vous avec ...
Philippe: À quelle heure?
Isabelle: À ...
• Mme Chollet./deux heures dix.
• M. Masson./trois heures vingt.
• Mlle Lacour./quatre heures trente-cinq.
• Jean-Paul./six heures cinquante.
• Nathalie./neuf heures quarante.

6 ROLE PLAY asking and answering questions about train schedules

– À quelle heure est le train pour ... ?
– Le train pour ... est à ...
• Lyon/sept heures (et quart/quinze)
• Cannes/sept heures (et demie/trente)
• Tours/huit heures douze
• Dijon/huit heures vingt-cinq
• Toulon/neuf heures trente-cinq
• Colmar/dix heures quarante
• Toulouse/onze heures moins le quart (dix heures quarante-cinq)
• Marseille/dix heures cinquante
• Bordeaux/dix heures cinquante-cinq.

Variation (easier format):

– **À quelle heure est le train pour Nice?**
– **À six heures dix.**

Leçon 4B

Main Topics Talking about days of the week and dates

Teaching Resource Options

PRINT

Workbook PE, pp. 45–49
Activités pour tous PE, pp. 25–26
Unit 2 Resource Book
   Activités pour tous TE, pp. 81–82
   Audioscript, pp. 121–122, 124–126
   Communipak, pp. 132–156
   Lesson Plans, pp. 87–88
   Block Scheduling Lesson Plans,
     pp. 93–94
   Absent Student Copymasters, p. 99
   Video Activities, pp. 107–110
   Videoscript, pp. 117–118
   Workbook TE, pp. 69–73

AUDIO & VISUAL

Audio Program
CD 1 Tracks 42, 43
CD 6 Tracks 22–27

TECHNOLOGY

Online Workbook

VIDEO PROGRAM

VIDÉO   DVD

MODULE 4B
Le français pratique
Le jour et la date

TOTAL TIME: 5:48 min.
   DVD Disk 1
   Videotape 1 (COUNTER: 1:05:21 min.)

4B.1 Dialogues:
   1. Quel jour est-ce?
   (1:05:28–1:06:23 min.)
   2. Anniversaire
   (1:06:24–1:06:41 min.)

**4B.2 Mini-scenes: Dates and
birthdays**
   (1:06:42–1:09:20 min.)

**4B.3 Vignette culturelle: Joyeux
anniversaire!**
   (1:09:21–1:11:09 min.)

Comprehension practice Play the entire module of the video through as an introduction to the lesson.

LEÇON 4

VIDÉO-SCÈNE VIDÉO DVD AUDIO

B Le jour et la date

1. Quel jour est-ce?

For many people, the days of the week are not all alike.

DIALOGUE 1   **Vendredi**

  Philippe: Quel jour est-ce?
  Stéphanie: C'est vendredi.
  Philippe: Super! Demain, c'est samedi!

> Super! Demain, c'est samedi!

DIALOGUE 2   **Mercredi**

  Nathalie: Ça va?
    Marc: Pas très bien.
  Nathalie: <u>Pourquoi?</u>   *Why?*
    Marc: Aujourd'hui, c'est
         mercredi.
  Nathalie: <u>Et alors?</u>   *So?*
    Marc: Demain, c'est jeudi!
         Le jour de l'examen.
  Nathalie: <u>Zut!</u> <u>C'est vrai!</u>   *Darn! /That's right!*
         Au revoir, Marc.
    Marc: Au revoir, Nathalie.
         À demain!

> Demain, c'est jeudi!
> Le jour de l'examen.

WARM-UP AND REVIEW Ça va?

Ask students how they are feeling, reviewing the expressions from Lesson 3. For example:
  Bonjour, X. Ça va?
  [Oui, ça va très bien.]
  Et toi, Y, ça va bien ou ça va mal?
  [Ça va mal.]

Z, demande à W si ça va.
[–Bonjour W, ça va?
–Ça va comme ci, comme ça.]

POUR COMMUNIQUER

▶ **How to talk about days of the week:**

Quel jour est-ce?	*What day is it?*
Aujourd'hui, c'est mercredi.	*Today is Wednesday.*
Demain, c'est jeudi.	*Tomorrow is Thursday.*

▶ **How to tell people when you will see them again:**

À samedi!	*See you Saturday!*
À demain!	*See you tomorrow!*

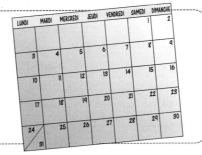

À samedi!

Les jours de la semaine *(Days of the week)*

lundi	*Monday*	**vendredi**	*Friday*	**aujourd'hui**	*today*
mardi	*Tuesday*	**samedi**	*Saturday*	**demain**	*tomorrow*
mercredi	*Wednesday*	**dimanche**	*Sunday*		
jeudi	*Thursday*				

1 Questions

PARLER

1. Quel jour est-ce aujourd'hui?
2. Et demain, quel jour est-ce?

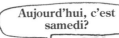

Aujourd'hui, c'est samedi?

Non, aujourd'hui, c'est dimanche!

2 Un jour de retard *(One day behind)*

PARLER Georges has trouble keeping track of the date. He is always one day behind. Monique corrects him.

▶ samedi

1.	lundi	3.	jeudi	5.	dimanche
2.	mardi	4.	vendredi	6.	mercredi

3 Au revoir!

write out first!

PARLER You are on the phone with the following friends. Say good-bye and tell them when you will see them.

▶ Christine/lundi
Au revoir, Christine. À lundi.

1.	David/dimanche	4.	Julie/vendredi
2.	Nicolas/samedi	5.	Thomas/mardi
3.	Céline/mercredi	6.	Pierre/jeudi

LUNDI	MARDI	MERCREDI	JEUDI	VENDREDI	SAMEDI	DIMANCHE
					1	2
3	4	5	6	7	8	9
10	11	12	13	14	15	16
17	18	19	20	21	22	23
24	25	26	27	28	29	30
31						

LANGUAGE NOTE Days of the week

You may wish to tell your students that the days are named for the Roman gods. The suffix **di** comes from the Latin **dies** *(day)*.

lun-di	(moon-day)
mar-di	(Mars-day)
mercre-di	(Mercury-day)

jeu-di	(Jupiter-day)
vendre-di	(Venus-day)
same-di	(Saturn-day)

Dimanche comes from the Latin **Dominus** *(the Lord)*.

POUR COMMUNIQUER

Language note Also: **Quel jour sommes-nous? Quel jour est-on?**

Casual speech One can say: **C'est quel jour? On est quel jour?**

Supplementary vocabulary
À bientôt! *See you soon!*

Cultural note On French calendars, the week traditionally begins with **lundi**. On Canadian calendars, however, the week begins with **dimanche**.

If students ask The days of the week are usually not capitalized in French.

1 COMMUNICATION stating today's and tomorrow's dates

Answers will vary
1. Aujourd'hui, c'est (lundi).
2. Demain, c'est (mardi).

2 EXCHANGES getting the date right

1. – Aujourd'hui, c'est lundi?
   – Non, aujourd'hui, c'est mardi!
2. – Aujourd'hui, c'est mardi?
   – Non, aujourd'hui, c'est mercredi!
3. – Aujourd'hui, c'est jeudi?
   – Non, aujourd'hui, c'est vendredi!
4. – Aujourd'hui, c'est vendredi?
   – Non, aujourd'hui, c'est samedi!
5. – Aujourd'hui, c'est dimanche?
   – Non, aujourd'hui, c'est lundi!
6. – Aujourd'hui, c'est mercredi?
   – Non, aujourd'hui, c'est jeudi!

Variation Philippe is one day ahead.

– **Aujourd'hui, c'est samedi?**
– **Non, aujourd'hui, c'est vendredi.**

3 ROLE PLAY telling people good-bye and when you will see them again

1. Au revoir, David. À dimanche!
2. Au revoir, Nicolas. À samedi!
3. Au revoir, Céline. À mercredi!
4. Au revoir, Julie. À vendredi!
5. Au revoir, Thomas. À mardi!
6. Au revoir, Pierre. À jeudi!

Challenge (dialogue format)

– **Au revoir, Christine.**
– **Au revoir. À lundi.**

Conversation

2. Anniversaire

François and Isabelle are on their way to Nathalie's birthday party. As they are talking, François wants to know when Isabelle's birthday is.

François:	C'est quand, ton anniversaire?
Isabelle:	C'est le 18 mars!
François:	Le 18 mars? <u>Pas possible!</u> *That's not possible!*
Isabelle:	<u>Si! Pourquoi?</u> *Yes, it is! Why?*
François:	C'est aussi mon anniversaire.
Isabelle:	<u>Quelle coïncidence!</u> *What a coincidence!*

POUR COMMUNIQUER

▶ *How to talk about the date:*

Quelle est la date?	*What's the date?*
C'est le 12 (douze) octobre.	*It's October 12.*
C'est le premier juin.	*It's June first.*

▶ *How to talk about birthdays:*

—C'est quand, ton anniversaire?	*When is your birthday?*
—Mon anniversaire est le 2 (deux) mars.	*My birthday is March 2.*

Les mois de l'année *(Months of the year)*

janvier	avril	juillet	octobre
février	mai	août	novembre
mars	juin	septembre	décembre

Quelle est la date?

Teaching Resource Options

PRINT

Workbook PE, pp. 45–49
Unit 2 Resource Book
   Audioscript, p. 122
   Communipak, pp. 132–156
   Video Activities, pp. 107–109
   Videoscript, pp. 117–118
   Workbook TE, pp. 69–73

AUDIO & VISUAL

Audio Program
CD 1 Tracks 44, 45
Overhead Transparencies
9 Calendar

TECHNOLOGY

Power Presentations

VIDEO PROGRAM

 MODULE 4B

4B.1 Dialogue: Anniversaire
(1:06:24–1:06:41 min.)

4B.2 Mini-scenes: Dates and birthdays (1:06:42–1:09:20 min.)

Middle School Copymasters

Conversations 2: *Bon anniversaire*, p. 17; Puzzle 3: *Les jours et les mois*, p. 20

If students ask Explain that **si** *(yes)* is used to respond to a negative statement or question.

POUR COMMUNIQUER

Language note To ask for the date, one can also say:

Quel jour est-ce?

Quel jour est-on? or

Quel jour sommes-nous?

Common colloquial alternative

On est quelle date?

If students ask The months are usually not capitalized in French.

CASUAL SPEECH PRACTICE

In French, casual speech is often heard, but rarely written. (This is like English, where people often say: *You coming?* and write: *Are you coming?*)

In this textbook, students are introduced to standard written French.

Some forms of casual speech are so common that they have been accepted into general usage. Two examples of this are **un prof** and **jouer au foot.**

In this lesson, students learn the casual **C'est quand, ton anniversaire?** which is simpler than **Quand est-ce, ton anniversaire?**

[handwritten notes at top:] La fête des Mères Mother's Day / le Jour de la reine Victoria / le vingt-deuxième du mois de mai

La date

To express a date in French, the pattern is:

le	+	NUMBER	+	MONTH
le		11 (onze)		novembre
le		20 (vingt)		mai

L'ÉVÉNEMENT MUSICAL DE L'ANNÉE
LE 19 JANVIER

EXCEPTION: The first of the month is **le premier.**

➜ In front of numbers, the French use **le** (and never **l'**): **le onze, le huit.**

➜ Note that when dates are abbreviated in French, the day always comes first.

2/8 **le deux août** 1/11 **le premier novembre**

---

4  *Anniversaires*

PARLER Ask your classmates when their birthdays are.

▶ C'est quand, ton anniversaire?

Mon anniversaire est le 3 février.

---

5 *Quelle est la date?*

PARLER Ask what the date is.

▶ —Quelle est la date?
—C'est le douze septembre.

1 30 JUIN   2 8 MAI   3 4 MARS   4 21 NOVEMBRE   5 1 AVRIL   6 25 AOÛT

---

6 *Dates importantes*

PARLER Give the following dates in French.

▶ Noël *(Christmas)*: 25/12   **C'est le vingt-cinq décembre.**

1. le jour de l'An *(New Year's Day)*: 1/1
2. la fête *(holiday)* de Martin Luther King: 15/1
3. la Saint-Valentin: 14/2
4. la Saint-Patrick: 17/3
5. la fête nationale américaine: 4/7
6. la fête nationale française: 14/7
7. la fête de Christophe Colomb: 12/10

PROJECT Calendars

You may wish to have your students prepare a calendar of the month of their next birthday. Have them label the month, the days of the week, and their birthday in French. Ask them to illustrate the top of the calendar with an original drawing.

This activity is particularly appropriate for younger learners.

Language notes

• You may wish to introduce the year:
2004 deux mille quatre
2006 deux mille six, etc.
Aujourd'hui, nous sommes le vingt septembre deux mille cinq.

• Also: **le un** (when **un** is a number and not a pronoun).

• Abbreviations of dates may also be punctuated with hyphens or periods.
  – The months are sometimes expressed in roman numerals: **le 2.VIII.**
  – Note: **le premier** may be abbreviated as **le 1ᵉʳ.**

---

4 **COMMUNICATION** discussing birthdays

Answers will vary
– C'est quand, ton anniversaire?
– Mon anniversaire est le (8 mai).

Variation
Have students walk around the room grouping themselves according to the month of their birth.
– **C'est quand, ton anniversaire?**
– **Mon anniversaire est le 1ᵉʳ mai. Et toi?**
As a follow-up, begin with January, and have students in each group give their birthdays before sitting back down.

---

5 **EXCHANGES** asking today's date

1. – Quelle est la date?
   – C'est le trente juin.
2. – Quelle est la date?
   – C'est le huit mai.
3. – Quelle est la date?
   – C'est le quatre mars.
4. – Quelle est la date?
   – C'est le vingt et un novembre.
5. – Quelle est la date?
   – C'est le premier avril.
6. – Quelle est la date?
   – C'est le vingt-cinq août.

---

6 **PRACTICE** telling the date of certain events

1. C'est le premier janvier.
2. C'est le quinze janvier.
3. C'est le quatorze février.
4. C'est le dix-sept mars.
5. C'est le quatre juillet.
6. C'est le quatorze juillet.
7. C'est le douze octobre.

Teaching Resource Options

PRINT

Workbook PE, pp. 51–54
Activités pour tous PE, pp. 27–28
Unit 2 Resource Book
   Activités pour tous TE, pp. 83–84
   Audioscript, pp. 122, 126–128
   Communipak, pp. 132–156
   Lesson Plans, pp. 89–90
   Block Scheduling Lesson Plans, pp. 95–96
   Absent Student Copymasters, p. 100
   Family Involvement, pp. 101–102
   Video Activities, pp. 111–114
   Videoscript, pp. 119–120
   Workbook TE, pp. 75–78

Assessment
   Lesson 4 Quiz, pp. 129–130
   Audioscript for Quiz 4, p. 120
   Answer Keys, pp. 195–198

AUDIO & VISUAL

Audio Program
CD 1 Tracks 46, 47
CD 6 Tracks 28–31
CD 13 Tracks 13, 14
Overhead Transparencies
13 Weather

TECHNOLOGY

Online Workbook
Test Generator CD-ROM/eTest Plus
Online

VIDEO PROGRAM

MODULE 4C
Le français pratique
Le temps

TOTAL TIME: 5:29 min.
   DVD Disk 1
   Videotape 1 (COUNTER: 1:11:21 min.)

4C.1 Dialogue: Le temps
   (1:11:30–1:12:10 min.)

4C.2 Mini-scenes: Talking about weather
   (1:12:11–1:13:53 min.)

4C.3 Vignette culturelle: La géographie de la France
   (1:13:54–1:16:50 min.)

Comprehension practice Play the entire module through as an introduction to the lesson.

C Le temps

It is nine o'clock Sunday morning. Cécile and her brother Philippe have planned a picnic for the whole family. Cécile is asking about the weather.

Quel temps fait-il?

Il fait mauvais.

Zut, zut et zut!

Papa va nous inviter au restaurant.

Cécile:	Quel temps fait-il?	
Philippe:	Il fait mauvais!	
Cécile:	Il fait mauvais?	
Philippe:	Oui, il fait mauvais! <u>Regarde!</u> Il pleut!	*Look!*
Cécile:	Zut, zut et zut!	
Philippe:	!!!???	
Cécile:	Et le <u>pique-nique?</u>	*picnic*
Philippe:	Le pique-nique? Ah oui, le pique-nique! … <u>Écoute, ça n'a pas d'importance.</u>	*Listen, it doesn't matter. (It's not important.)*
Cécile:	<u>Pourquoi?</u>	*Why?*
Philippe:	Pourquoi? <u>Parce que Papa va nous inviter au restaurant.</u>	*Because Dad is going to take us out (invite us) to a restaurant.*
Cécile:	Super!	

WARM-UP AND REVIEW Months and dates

Have the class name the months of the year as you write their abbreviations across the top of the chalkboard.

Then go around the class asking all the students to give their birthdays.
   Sue, c'est quand, ton anniversaire?
   [Sue: C'est le 21 août.]

Write the student's name and abbreviated birthdate under the appropriate month.
   [août] Sue: le 21/8.

Have students read the dates. Ask:
   C'est quand, l'anniversaire de Sue?

Note: In a class of 25 the odds are 50/50 that two people will share the same birthday.

POUR COMMUNIQUER

Quel temps fait-il?

▶ **How to talk about the weather:**

Quel temps fait-il?   *How's the weather?*

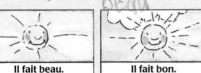

Il fait beau.	Il fait bon.	Il fait chaud.	Il fait frais.

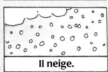

Il fait froid.	Il fait mauvais.	Il pleut.	Il neige.

Les saisons *(Seasons)*

le printemps	*spring*	**au printemps**	*in (the) spring*
l'été	*summer*	**en été**	*in (the) summer*
l'automne	*fall, autumn*	**en automne**	*in (the) fall*
l'hiver	*winter*	**en hiver**	*in (the) winter*

---

1 **Ta région**

PARLER Say what the weather is like in your part of the country.

▶ en juillet

En juillet, il fait chaud.

1. en août
2. en septembre
3. en novembre
4. en janvier
5. en mars
6. en mai

2 **Les quatre saisons**

PARLER Describe what the weather is like in each of the four seasons in the following cities.

▶ à Miami

En été, il fait chaud. En automne, il fait chaud aussi. En hiver, il fait frais. Au printemps, il fait bon.

Miami

1. à Chicago
2. à San Francisco
3. à Denver
4. à Boston
5. à Seattle
6. à Dallas

COMPREHENSION Weather

PROPS: Transparency 13: Weather, *Quel temps fait-il?* Teach the weather expressions by pointing to the pictures on the overhead.

Quel temps fait-il? Il fait beau.
Et maintenant, quel temps fait-il?
Il pleut.
Est-ce qu'il fait beau? [Non.]

Have students point out the weather.
X, viens ici. Montre-nous le temps.
Il pleut. [points to rain]
Il neige. [points to snow] etc.

POUR COMMUNIQUER

Language note Contrast:

Il fait beau. *It's beautiful weather, the sun is out.*
Il fait bon. *It's nice weather, comfortable, warm.*

Expansion **Il fait très beau, très froid,** etc.

Pronunciation notes
• Be sure students do not pronounce the silent letters in **temps** and **printemps**.
• Be sure students make the following liaisons: **en hiver, en été, en automne**.

1 **COMMUNICATION** talking about the weather

Answers will vary.
1. En août, il fait beau (chaud).
2. En septembre, il fait bon (beau).
3. En novembre, il fait mauvais (il fait froid, il pleut).
4. En janvier, il neige (il fait froid).
5. En mars, il pleut (il fait frais, il neige).
6. En mai, il fait frais (bon, beau).

Variation (dialogue format)
– Quel temps fait-il en juillet?
– Il fait chaud.

2 **DESCRIPTION** giving details about the weather

Answers will vary.
1. (à Chicago) En été, il fait chaud. En automne, il fait bon (beau). En hiver, il fait froid (il fait mauvais, il neige). Au printemps, il fait frais (beau).
2. (à San Francisco) En été, il fait beau (chaud, bon). En automne, il fait bon (frais, beau). En hiver, il fait beau (il fait frais, il pleut). Au printemps, il fait beau (il fait bon, il pleut).
3. (à Denver) En été, il fait chaud. En automne, il fait beau (frais). En hiver, il fait froid (et il neige). Au printemps, il fait bon (beau, frais).
4. (à Boston) En été, il fait chaud. En automne, il fait beau (frais). En hiver, il fait froid (il fait mauvais, il neige). Au printemps, il fait frais (il fait beau, il fait bon, il pleut).
5. (à Seattle) En été, il fait chaud (beau, bon). En automne, il fait beau (il fait frais, il pleut). En hiver, il fait froid (il pleut, il neige). Au printemps, il fait beau (il fait bon, il fait frais, il pleut).
6. (à Dallas) En été, il fait (très) chaud. En automne, il fait chaud. En hiver, il fait beau (bon). Au printemps, il fait chaud (il fait beau, il pleut).

Geography activity/Pre-viewing activity In preparation for the **Vignette culturelle**, have students turn to page 4 and locate the following provinces on the map of France: Touraine, Alsace, Provence.

UNITÉ 2

À VOTRE TOUR

Main Focus
• Recapitulation and review

Teaching Resource Options

PRINT

Workbook PE, pp. 55–58
Unit 2 Resource Book
   Audioscript, p. 122
   Communipak, pp. 132–156
   Workbook TE, pp. 161–164

Assessment
Unit 2 Test, pp. 165–170
Portfolio Assessment, Unit 1 URB,
   pp. 155–164
Multiple Choice Test Items, pp. 185–190
Listening Comprehension
   Performance Test, pp. 171–172
Reading Performance Test, pp. 177–180
Speaking Performance Test, pp. 173–176
Writing Performance Test, pp. 181–184
Test Scoring Tools, p. 191
Audioscript for Tests, pp. 192–194
Answer Keys, pp. 195–198

AUDIO & VISUAL

Audio Program
CD 1 Tracks 48, 49
CD 13 Tracks 15–22

TECHNOLOGY

Test Generator CD-ROM/eTest Plus
   Online

❶ COMPREHENSION

1. Quel temps fait-il? [f]
2. Tu veux un sandwich? [e]
3. Tu veux un jus d'orange? [c]
4. Quelle heure est-il? [b]
5. C'est quand, ton anniversaire? [d]
6. Combien coûte le sandwich? [a]

❷ ORAL EXPRESSION

Answers will vary.
1. Il est deux heures.
2. Il est trois heures (quinze/et quart).
3. Il est onze heures (et demie/trente).
4. Il est midi.
5. Il est quatre heures quarante-cinq (cinq heures moins le quart).
6. Il est huit heures cinq.

66 • À votre tour!
Unité 2

À votre tour!

❶ 🎧 Écoutez bien!

ÉCOUTER Isabelle is in a café talking to Jean-Paul. You will hear Isabelle asking questions. For each of Isabelle's questions, select Jean-Paul's response from the suggested answers.

a. Deux euros cinquante.
b. Quatre heures et demie.
c. Oui, j'ai soif.
d. C'est le 3 novembre.
e. Oui, j'ai faim.
f. Il fait beau.

❷ 👥 Quelle heure est-il?

PARLER Give the times indicated on the following clocks.

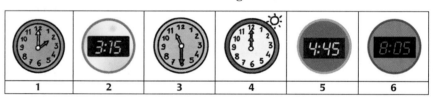

1	2	3	4	5	6

❸ 🎧👥 Conversation dirigée

ÉCOUTER ET PARLER Stéphanie is in a café called Le Select. The waiter is taking her order. With a partner, compose and act out a dialogue according to the script suggested below.

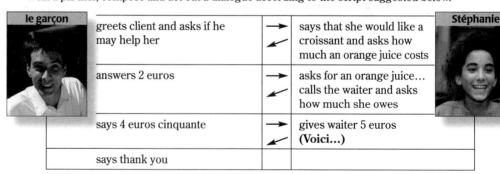

le garçon		Stéphanie
greets client and asks if he may help her	→ ↙	says that she would like a croissant and asks how much an orange juice costs
answers 2 euros	→ ↙	asks for an orange juice… calls the waiter and asks how much she owes
says 4 euros cinquante	→ ↙	gives waiter 5 euros **(Voici…)**
says thank you		

66 soixante-six
Unité 2   *Invitation au français*

À VOTRE TOUR

For specific teaching suggestions, see the **Teacher Notes** in Unit 1, page 38.

You will want to select those activities which are most appropriate for your students. Encourage them to work in pairs and in trios (where one acts as monitor).

The first and third activities are on CD.

Act. 1: Play Track 48 of CD 1 so that students can check their answers.
Act. 3: Play Track 49 of CD 1 as a model. Then have students act out their own dialogues.

4  **Au café** --

PARLER You are in a French café. Call the waiter/waitress and order the following items. A classmate will play the part of the waiter/waitress.

▶ —Monsieur (Mademoiselle), s'il vous plaît!
 —Vous désirez?
 —Un croissant, s'il vous plaît!
 (Donnez-moi un croissant, s'il vous plaît!)
 (Je voudrais un croissant, s'il vous plaît!)

5  **En scène** --

STRATEGY Speaking

Sounding French If you want French people to understand you, the most important thing is to speak with an even rhythm and to stress the last syllable in each group of words. (Try speaking English this way: people will think you have a French accent!)

PARLER With two other classmates, act out the following scene.

CHARACTERS:
You, a French friend, and the waiter in the café

SITUATION:
A French friend has been showing you around Paris. You invite your friend to a café and discover too late that you have not changed enough money. Your friend will respond to your questions.

- Ask your friend if he/she is thirsty.
- Ask if he/she wants a soft drink.
- Ask if he/she is hungry.
- Ask if he/she wants a sandwich.

- When the waiter comes, your friend orders and you ask for a croissant and a cup of hot chocolate.
- Ask the waiter how much everything is.
- Ask your friend to please lend you 20 euros.

6 **La date, la saison et le temps** --

PARLER Look at the calendar days. For each one, give the day and the date, the season, and the weather.

▶ C'est mardi, le dix avril.
 C'est le printemps.
 Il pleut.

1   2   3   4   5

LESSON REVIEW
CLASSZONE.COM

PORTFOLIO ASSESSMENT

For more specific guidelines, see the Teacher Notes in Unit 1, page 39.

The café conversations of the **Challenge** activity on the right could be recorded for the oral portfolio.

CHALLENGE ACTIVITY

Students in groups of 3 or 4 prepare original café conversations. One person is the waiter, and the others are teenage customers who are talking to one another. Encourage them to use expressions they learned in Units 1 and 2: greetings, introductions, time, etc.

---

3 **GUIDED ORAL EXPRESSION**

G: Bonjour, mademoiselle! Vous désirez?
S: (Donnez-moi, Je voudrais) un croissant, s'il vous plaît. Combien coûte un jus d'orange?
G: (Un jus d'orange coûte) 2 euros.
S: (Donnez-moi, Je voudrais) un jus d'orange, s'il vous plaît! . . . Monsieur, s'il vous plaît! Ça fait combien?
G: (Ça fait) 4 euros 50.
S: Voici 5 euros.
G: Merci, mademoiselle.

4 **GUIDED ORAL EXPRESSION**

– Monsieur (Mademoiselle), s'il vous plaît!
– Vous désirez?
– (Je voudrais/Donnez-moi) ..., s'il vous plaît!

1. une glace
2. une pizza
3. un chocolat
4. un jus de raisin
5. un steak-frites

Challenge You are leaving the café and want to know what you owe. Your classmate will invent a reasonable price.
– **Monsieur/Mademoiselle, s'il vous plaît! Ça fait combien?**
– **Ça fait huit euros cinquante.**

5 **GUIDED ORAL EXPRESSION**

Answers will vary.
1: Tu as soif, (Paul / Nicole)?
2: Oui, j'ai soif!
1: Tu veux un soda?
2: Oui, je voudrais un soda, s'il te plaît.
1: Tu as faim?
2: Oui, j'ai faim!
1: Tu veux un sandwich?
2: Oui, je voudrais un sandwich au jambon. (The waiter [waitress] comes.)
2: Donnez-moi un soda et un sandwich au jambon, s'il vous plaît!
1: Je voudrais un croissant et un chocolat . . . Ça fait combien?
3: Ça fait 20 euros.
1: Prête-moi 20 euros, s'il te plaît!
2: Voila.
1: Merci, (Paul / Nicole).

6 **GUIDED ORAL EXPRESSION**

1. C'est vendredi, le quatre janvier. C'est l'hiver. Il neige.
2. C'est jeudi, le cinq juillet. C'est l'été. Il fait chaud.
3. C'est mercredi, le vingt-six septembre. C'est l'automne. Il fait mauvais (froid, frais).
4. C'est samedi, le dix-neuf mai. C'est le printemps. Il fait beau (bon).
5. C'est lundi, le premier octobre. C'est l'automne. Il fait frais.

Middle School Copymasters

Quel temps fait-il?, p. 19;
Class Starter: *La météo*, p. T9;
Project 1: *La météo*, p. 29; Worksheet 2: *Petites scènes*, pp. 22–23; Project 2: Nature calendar, pp. 30–31

UNITÉ 2

ENTRACTE 2

Objectives
- Development of cross-cultural awareness
- Vocabulary expansion

Teaching Resource Options

PRINT

Workbook PE, pp. 55–58
Activités pour tous PE, pp. 29–31
Unit 2 Resource Book
   Activités pour tous TE, pp. 157–159
   Workbook PE, pp. 161–164

Les parties du corps

Objective
- Learning parts of the body

Game Vrai ou faux? When the teacher mentions a part of the body and points to it correctly, students respond by saying **vrai**. When the teacher points to the wrong part of the body, students respond by saying **faux**. E.g.,
Voici ma jambe. (point to leg) **vrai**
Voici mon pied. (point to arm) **faux**

Jacques a dit
Expansion
Les mains sur les épaules
   (shoulders).
Les mains sur la taille *(waist)*.
Les mains sur les genoux *(knees)*.

Une chanson: Alouette

Objectives
- Introducing a popular French-Canadian folksong
- Introducing parts of the body

Cultural note
- **In Canada,** the lark was formerly hunted as a game bird. In this song, the cook is plucking the bird's feathers before preparing to roast it.
- **English equivalent**
   Lark, sweet lark, I will pluck you
   I will pluck your head …, your beak
   …, your neck …, your wings …, your back …, your legs …, your tail …

Les parties du corps

(Parts of the body)

la tête
les cheveux
l'oeil (les yeux)
l'oreille
le nez
la bouche
le cou
la main
le bras
le ventre
le dos
la jambe
le pied

Un jeu: Jacques a dit

The French sometimes play a game called **Jacques a dit** *(Jim said)*. The rules are the same as the English game of *Simon Says*. Everyone stands up to play.

The game leader says: **Jacques a dit: Les mains sur la tête!** placing her hands on her head. The other players also place their hands on their heads.

Then the game leader may say: **Les mains sur le dos!** placing her hands on her back. This time, however, the other players should not move, because the game leader did not first say **Jacques a dit**. Any player that did move must sit down, but may continue playing.

The game continues until only one player is left standing.

COMPREHENSION Parts of the body

PROP: Halloween skeleton
Introduce the class to the skeleton, to whom you have given a name.
   Qui est-ce? C'est mon ami Victor.
Shake hands with the skeleton.
   Je donne la main à Victor.

Call on individual students to come up.
   X, viens ici et donne la main à Victor.
   Touche-lui l'épaule.
   Montre-nous sa bouche. …

Optional: Have students contort Victor.
   Y, viens et mets-lui le pied sur la tête.
   Mets-lui la main gauche sur le cou.

Une chanson: Alouette

ALOUETTE *(The Lark)* is a popular folk song of French-Canadian origin. As the song leader names the various parts of the bird's anatomy, he points to his own body. The chorus repeats the refrain with enthusiasm.

Alouette

A - lou-et - te, gen - tille a - lou-et - te,
a - lou-et - te, Je te plu-me-rai.
Je te plu-me-rai la tête, Je te plu-me-rai la tête.
Et la tête, et la tête, a - lou-ett', a - lou-ett', oh!

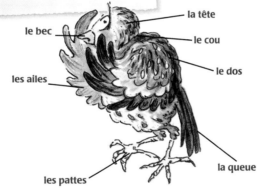

la tête
le bec
le cou
le dos
les ailes
les pattes
la queue

1. Alouette, gentille alouette,
   Alouette, je te plumerai.

   Je te plumerai la tête,
   Je te plumerai la tête.

   Et la tête—et la tête
   Alouette—Alouette
   Oh oh oh oh

2. Alouette, gentille alouette
   Alouette, je te plumerai.

   Je te plumerai le bec,
   Je te plumerai le bec.

   Et le bec—et le bec
   Et la tête—et la tête
   Alouette—Alouette
   Oh oh oh oh

3. Je te plumerai le cou ...

4. Je te plumerai les ailes ...

5. Je te plumerai le dos ...

6. Je te plumerai les pattes ...

7. Je te plumerai la queue ...

COMMUNAUTÉS: French song

As a class project, you might want to memorize *Alouette* and perform it at a senior center or teach the song to a local grade school class.

CLASSROOM MANAGEMENT

Pre-reading activity

Ask how many students know the song "Alouette."
  • What country is the song from? [Canada]
  • What kind of bird is an **alouette**? [lark]
  • What is the song all about? [telling a lark what parts of its body the singer is going to pluck]

Post-reading activity

Ask students if they know other French songs. Perhaps they can sing "Frère Jacques."
Frère Jacques / Dormez-vous? /
Sonnez les matines. / Din din don. /
(Are you sleeping / Brother John? / Morning bells are ringing / Ding dang dong)

Language Learning Benchmarks

FUNCTION
• Engage in conversations p. 59
• Make requests pp. 50, 51, 55
• Obtain information pp. 57, 59, 63
• Begin to provide information pp. 54, 65

CONTEXT
• Converse in face-to-face social interactions pp. 47, 51, 54, 55, 59, 61, 63
• Listen during social interactions p. 63
• Listen to audio and video texts pp. 44, 47, 48, 51, 52, 55, 56, 60, 64
• Use authentic materials when reading:
  – menus pp. 54, 55
  – posters p. 63
  – schedules p. 59

TEXT TYPE
• Use short sentences when speaking p. 55
• Use learned words and phrases when speaking pp. 46, 54
• Use simple questions when speaking pp. 47, 55, 57
• Use commands when speaking p. 50
• Understand some ideas and familiar details presented in clear, uncomplicated speech when listening p, 57

CONTENT
• Understand and convey information about
  – schedules p. 59
  – prices pp. 54, 55
  – weather and seasons p. 65
  – days p. 61
  – dates p, 63
  – months p. 63
  – time p. 57, 58
  – food and customs pp. 46, 47, 50, 51

ASSESSMENT
• Communicate effectively with some hesitation and errors, which do not hinder comprehension p. 66
• Demonstrate culturally acceptable behavior for
  – engaging in conversations p. 67
  – making requests pp. 66, 67
  – providing information pp. 66, 67

Expansion activities PLANNING AHEAD

Games

• Charades

Divide the class into two or three teams. Choose one of the vocabulary words from pages 74–75, and tell one member from each team the word for that round. These team members alternate acting out clues until one team guesses the correct word. The first team to guess the word gets a point and starts the next round with a new member from each team as performer. Set a 1-minute time limit for each round. The team with the most points is the winner.

Pacing Suggestion: Upon completion of Leçon 5.

• Mais non!

First, have each student draw a quick illustration of a person in one of the places taught in **Vocabulaire** on page 85. Ask students to write a true or false caption for their illustration. For example, if a student draws a boy near the Eiffel Tower, the caption might read either **Jean est à Paris** (true), or **Jean est à la maison** (false). Then divide the class into two teams. Have a student from one team show his or her illustration to the class and read the caption aloud. The first student to raise his or her hand gets the opportunity to respond **«Oui, c'est vrai»** or **«Mais non!»** If they respond **«Mais non!»** they must correct the sentence using **ne . . . pas** and name the place the illustration really portrays to earn a point. Have teams alternate presenting their drawings.

Pacing Suggestion: Upon completion of Leçon 6.

Projects

• Invitation à une boum

Have students create a party invitation. The invitations should tell when and where the party will be and who is throwing the party. Using vocabulary they have learned, students may wish to list the refreshments that will be served. The invitations should be decorated with markers, stickers, glitter, beads, etc. As a variation, you may want to have students create invitations online.

Pacing Suggestion: Upon completion of Leçon 7.

• Le Sénégal

Divide the class into small groups. Have each group find information about Senegal. Groups may:

• create a map that shows where Senegal is located
• find information about activities that are common among young people in Senegal
• find or create illustrations that show what Senegal looks like
• find information about the weather, people, politics, industry, etc., of Senegal

Each group should create a colorful booklet or pamphlet they can use to present the information they obtained to the rest of the class. Students can create these by hand or on the computer.

Pacing Suggestion: Upon completion of Leçon 8.

Bulletin Boards

• La musique francophone

Have students search the Internet to find out what singers, musical groups, and songs are currently popular in France or in francophone countries. (You could assign a different country to pairs or groups of students and suggest specific Web sites for their search.) Ask students to find photos of some of these artists and create a bulletin board about francophone music. You can expand the activity by having students draw comparisons between their findings and some of their favorite popular music groups and performers in the United States.

Pacing Suggestion: Upon completion of Leçon 5.

Storytelling

• Une mini-histoire

Model a brief conversation in which you call a friend. Invite your friend to do something you both enjoy, acting out the conversation with stuffed animals or puppets. Pass out copies of your conversation and say it aloud with pauses, allowing students to repeat after you, or fill in the words. Then have them work in pairs to expand on their versions. Ask students to write out their conversations, practice them for intonation, and perform them for the class.

Pacing Suggestion: Upon completion of Leçon 6.

• Écrire un poème

Explain to students that French is rich in rhyme. (You can point out, for example, that the infinitive form of all verbs ending in *-er* rhyme.) Have students brainstorm some rhyming words they have learned in French. Then have them use their lists of words to create a short poem. You may wish to ask for volunteers to share their poems with the class.

MODEL: Je n'aime pas nager, je préfère danser.
Mais je veux bien parler français.
Maintenant je ne peux pas nager,
Je ne peux pas danser.
Je dois étudier le français!

Pacing Suggestion: Upon completion of Leçon 7.

Recipe

• Fondue au chocolat

Fondue, which originated in Switzerland, is a typical French party food. Fondue can be made of melted cheese, chocolate, caramel, etc. You may wish to tell students that fondue is traditionally served in a fondue pot and that guests dip their foods using fondue forks.

Pacing Suggestion: Upon completion of Leçon 7.

Hands-on Crafts

• Le tama

Have pairs of students make a collage inspired by the **tama,** a traditional Senegalese drum, like the one pictured on this page. Suggest that students begin with colored or construction paper as a base. Ask them to bring in twine, rope, and other decorative materials to build up their two-dimensional drum designs into layers. When they have finished, have students set up a display of their drums.

Pacing Suggestion: Upon completion of Leçon 8.

End of Unit

• C'est moi!

Each student will create a poster to tell about his or her activities. First, have students write several sentences with their name, age, and several activities in which they participate. Then ask them to exchange papers with a classmate. Once they have corrected any errors, have students write their sentences on a poster, and use magazine photos or drawings to illustrate each sentence. You may want to have students give oral presentations to the class using their posters. As an alternative, have students act out and videotape their self-portraits.

Rubric   **A** = 13–15 pts. **B** = 10–12 pts. **C** = 7–9 pts. **D** = 4–6 pts. **F** = < 4 pts.

Criteria	Scale				
Vocabulary Use	1	2	3	4	5
Grammar/Spelling Accuracy	1	2	3	4	5
Creativity	1	2	3	4	5

Fondue au chocolat

Ingrédients
• 250 grammes de chocolat ou chocolat au lait
• 40 cl lait concentré sucré
• 10 cl lait
• des morceaux de gâteau et de fruits

Préparation
1. Cassez le chocolat en morceaux et mettez-le dans une casserole.
2. Ajoutez le lait et le lait concentré sucré.
3. Mélangez bien.
4. Ajoutez plus de lait si la fondue devient trop épaisse.
5. Piquez le fruit et le gâteau avec une fourchette et trempez-les dans le chocolat.

Pour huit personnes.

Ingredients
• approx. 8 oz. dark or milk chocolate
• approx. 1 cup sweetened condensed milk
• approx. 1/4 cup milk
• squares of cake and chunks of assorted fruit for dipping

Directions
1. Break the chocolate into pieces and melt it in a Crock-Pot.
2. Add regular milk and condensed milk.
3. Stir well.
4. Add extra milk if the mixture becomes too thick.
5. Use forks or skewers to dip cake or fruit into the chocolate.

Serves eight.

UNITÉ 3

Planning Guide CLASSROOM MANAGEMENT

OBJECTIVES

Communication
- Describe some of your daily activities *pp. 72–73, 95*
- Say what you like and do not like to do *pp. 74–75, 77*
- Ask and answer questions about where others are and what they are doing *pp. 85–86, 89*
- Invite friends to do things with you *p. 78*
- Politely accept or turn down an invitation *p. 78*

Grammar
- Le verbe *être* et les pronoms sujets *pp. 84–85*
- Les questions à réponse affirmative ou négative *pp. 86–87*
- La négation *p. 88*
- Les verbes en *-er:* le singulier *p. 94*
- Les verbes en *-er:* le pluriel *p. 96*
- Le présent des verbes en *-er:* forme affirmative et forme négative *p. 98*
- La construction: verbe + infinitif *p. 101*
- Les questions d'information *p. 106*
- Les expressions interrogatives avec *qui p. 108*
- *Qu'est-ce que? p. 109*
- Le verbe *faire p. 110*
- L'interrogation avec inversion *p. 111*

Vocabulary
- Préférences *pp. 74–75*
- Souhaits *p. 77*
- Invitations *p. 78*
- Où? *p. 85*
- Expressions pour la conversation *pp. 87, 100, 107*
- Mots utiles *pp. 89, 100*
- Les verbes en *-er p. 95*
- Expressions interrogatives *p. 106*
- Expressions avec *faire p. 110*

Pronunciation
- La voyelle /a/ *p. 89*
- Les voyelles /i/ et /u/ *p. 101*
- La voyelle /y/ *p. 111*

Culture
- Le téléphone *p. 79*
- Le mercredi après-midi *p. 83*
- Une boum *p. 93*
- Le Sénégal *p. 105*
- Les jeunes Français et l'Internet *p. 121*
- Les Vietnamiens en France *p. 123*

PROGRAM RESOURCES

Print
- Workbook PE, *pp. 59–84*
- *Activités pour tous* PE, *pp. 33–49*
- Block Scheduling Copymasters, *pp. 33–64*
- Teacher to Teacher Copymasters
- Unit 3 Resource Book
  - Lessons 5–8 Resources
    - Workbook TE
    - *Activités pour tous* TE
    - Lesson Plans
    - Block Scheduling Lesson Plans
    - Family Letter
    - Absent Student Copymasters
    - Family Involvement
    - Video Activities
    - Videoscripts
    - Audioscripts
    - Assessment Program
  - Unit 3 Resources
    - Communipak
    - *Activités pour tous* TE Reading
    - Workbook TE Reading and Culture Activities
    - Assessment Program
    - Answer Keys

Audiovisual
- Audio Program PE CD 2 Tracks 1–23
- Audio Program Workbook CD 7 Tracks 1–21
- *Chansons* Audio CD
- Video Program Modules 5, 6, 7, 8
- Overhead Transparencies
  - 15 *Où sont-ils?*;
  - 12 Menu from "Le Select";
  - 16 Subject Pronouns;
  - 14a, 14b, 17 *-er* Verbs;
  - 16 Subject Pronouns;
  - 6 Clock face *Quelle heure est-il?*;
  - 8 Expressions with *faire*

Technology
- Online Workbook
- ClassZone.com
- eTest Plus Online/Test Generator CD-ROM
- EasyPlanner Plus Online/EasyPlanner CD-ROM
- Power Presentations on CD-ROM

✓ Assessment Program Options

Lesson Quizzes
Portfolio Assessment
Unit Test Form A
Unit Test Form B
Unit Test Part III (Alternate) Cultural Awareness
Listening Comprehension Performance Test
Speaking Performance Test
Reading Comprehension Performance Test
Writing Performance Test
Multiple Choice Test Items
Test Scoring Tools
Audio Program CD 14 Tracks 1–16
Answer Keys
eTest Plus Online/Test Generator CD-ROM

Pacing Guide SAMPLE LESSON PLAN

DAY	DAY	DAY	DAY	DAY
1 Unité 3 Opener Leçon 5 • Vocabulaire et Culture– Mes activités • Vocabulaire–Préférences	**2** Leçon 5 • Vocabulaire–Préférences (continued) • Vocabulaire–Souhaits	**3** Leçon 5 • Vocabulaire–Invitations • Note culturelle– Le téléphone	**4** Leçon 5 • À votre tour!	**5** Leçon 6 • Une invitation • Note culturelle– Le mercredi après-midi • Le verbe être et les pronoms sujets
6 Leçon 6 • Vocabulaire–Où? • Les questions à réponse affirmative ou négative	**7** Leçon 6 • Vocabulaire–Expressions pour la conversation • La négation	**8** Leçon 6 • La négation (continued) • Vocabulaire–Mots utiles • Prononciation– Le voyelle /a/	**9** Leçon 6 • À votre tour!	**10** Leçon 7 • Une boum • Note culturelle–Une boum • Les verbes en -er: le singulier • Vocabulaire–Les verbes en -er
11 Leçon 7 • Vocabulaire–Les verbes en -er (continued) • Les verbes en -er: le pluriel	**12** Leçon 7 • Le présent des verbes en -er: forme affirmative et forme négative	**13** Leçon 7 • Vocabulaire–Mots utiles • Vocabulaire–Expressions pour la conversation • La construction: verbe + infinitif	**14** Leçon 7 • Prononciation– Les voyelles /i/ et /u/ • À votre tour!	**15** Leçon 8 • Un concert de musique africaine • Note culturelle– Le Sénégal • Les questions d'information
16 Leçon 8 • Vocabulaire–Expressions interrogatives • Vocabulaire–Expressions pour la conversation	**17** Leçon 8 • Les expressions interrogatives avec qui • Qu'est-ce que?	**18** Leçon 8 • Le verbe faire • Vocabulaire– Expressions avec faire • L'interrogation avec inversion	**19** Leçon 8 • Prononciation– La voyelle /y/ • À votre tour!	**20** • Tests de contrôle
21 • Unit 3 Test	**22** • Entracte: Lecture et culture			

Student Text Listening Activity Scripts
AUDIO PROGRAM

▶ **LEÇON 5 LE FRANÇAIS PRATIQUE** Mes activités

• **Préférences** *p. 74* CD 2, TRACK 1

How to talk about what you like and don't like to do. Écoutez et répétez.

Est-ce que tu aimes . . . ? #	Est-ce que tu aimes parler français? #
J'aime . . . #	Oui, j'aime parler français. #
Je n'aime pas . . . #	Non, je n'aime pas parler français. #
Je préfère . . . #	Je préfère parler anglais. #

Now practice the names of the activities.

téléphoner #	J'aime téléphoner. #
parler français #	J'aime parler français. #
parler anglais #	J'aime parler anglais. #
parler espagnol #	J'aime parler espagnol. #
manger #	J'aime manger. #
chanter #	J'aime chanter. #
danser #	J'aime danser. #
nager #	J'aime nager. #
jouer au tennis #	J'aime aussi jouer au tennis. #
jouer au basket #	J'aime aussi jouer au basket. #
jouer au foot #	J'aime aussi jouer au foot. #
jouer aux jeux vidéo #	J'aime aussi jouer aux jeux vidéo. #
regarder la télé #	Mais je préfère regarder la télé. #
écouter la radio #	Mais je préfère écouter la radio. #
dîner au restaurant #	Mais je préfère dîner au restaurant. #
voyager #	Mais je préfère voyager. #
étudier #	Je n'aime pas toujours étudier. #
travailler #	Je n'aime pas toujours travailler. #

À votre tour!

• **Écoutez bien!** *p. 80* CD 2, TRACK 2

You will hear French young people telling you what they like to do. Listen carefully to each activity. If it is illustrated in the picture on the left, mark A. If it is illustrated in the picture on the right, mark B.

1. J'aime écouter la radio.
2. J'aime téléphoner.
3. J'aime manger.
4. J'aime jouer au tennis.
5. J'aime nager.
6. J'aime regarder la télé.
7. J'aime étudier.
8. J'aime voyager.
9. J'aime jouer aux jeux vidéo.
10. J'aime jouer au foot.

• **Communication** *p. 80* CD 2, TRACK 3

Listen to the following conversation.

1. —Est-ce que tu aimes regarder la télé?
   —Oui, j'aime regarder la télé.
2. —Est-ce que tu veux jouer aux jeux vidéo?
   —Oui, je veux jouer aux jeux vidéo. (Non, je ne veux pas jouer aux jeux vidéo.)
3. —Est-ce que tu aimes écouter la radio?
   —Oui, j'aime écouter la radio. (Non, je n'aime pas écouter la radio.)
4. —Est-ce que tu veux manger une pizza?
   —Oui, je veux manger un pizza. (Non, je ne veux pas manger de pizza.)

• **Conversation dirigée** *p. 80* CD 2, TRACK 4

Écoutez la conversation entre Trinh et Céline.

Trinh: Salut, Céline. Ça va?
Céline: Oui, ça va, merci.
Trinh: Tu veux dîner au restaurant?
Céline: À quelle heure?
Trinh: À huit heures.
Céline: Je regrette, mais je dois étudier.
Trinh: Dommage!

• **Créa-dialogue** *p. 81* CD 2, TRACK 5

Listen to the following sample *Créa-dialogue*. Ecoútez les conversations.

Modèle: —Est-ce que tu veux jouer au tennis avec moi?
                —Non, je ne peux pas. Je dois travailler.

Here are some sample dialogues.

1. —Est-ce que tu veux jouer au basket avec moi?
   —Non, je ne peux pas. Je dois téléphoner à une copine. #
2. —Est-ce que tu veux manger une pizza?
   —Non, je ne peux pas. Je dois dîner avec ma cousine. #
3. —Est-ce que tu veux regarder la télé?
   —Non, je ne peux pas. Je dois parler avec ma mère. #
4. —Est-ce que tu veux jouer au ping-pong?
   —Non, je ne peux pas. Je dois étudier. #
5. —Est-ce que tu veux dîner au restaurant?
   —Non, je ne peux pas. Je dois chanter avec la chorale. #
6. —Est-ce que tu veux jouer aux jeux vidéo?
   —Non, je ne peux pas. Je dois étudier. #

▶ **LEÇON 6** Une invitation

• **Une invitation** *p. 82*

A. Compréhension orale CD 2, TRACK 6

Please turn to page 82 for complete *Compréhension orale* text.

B. Écoutez et répétez. CD 2, TRACK 7

You will now hear a paused version of the dialog. Listen to the speaker and repeat right after he or she has completed the sentence.

• **Prononciation** *p. 89* CD 2, TRACK 8

La voyelle /a/

Écoutez: chat

The letter "**a**" alone always represents the sound /a/ as in the English word *ah*. It never has the sound of "*a*" as in English words like *class, date,* or *cinema*.

Répétez: chat # ça va # à # la # là-bas # avec # ami # voilà #
              classe # café # salade # dame # date # Madame # Canada #
              Anne est au Canada avec Madame Laval. #

À votre tour!

• **Allô!** *p. 90* CD 2, TRACK 9

Jacques is phoning some friends. Match his questions on the left with his friends' answers on the right.

1. Où es-tu?	Je suis à la maison.
2. Où est ta soeur?	Elle est en classe.
3. Est-ce que ton frère est à la maison?	Non, il est au cinéma.
4. Tes parents sont en vacances, n'est-ce pas?	Oui! Ils sont à Paris.
5. Ta soeur est avec une copine?	Oui, elles sont au restaurant.

• **Créa-dialogue** *p. 91* CD 2, TRACK 10

Listen to some sample *Créa-dialogues.* Écoutez les conversations.

Modèle: —Bonjour. Vous êtes anglaise?
                —Oui, je suis anglaise.
                —Est-ce que vous êtes de Londres?
                —Mais non, je ne suis pas de Londres. Je suis de Liverpool.

Maintenant, écoutez le dialogue numéro 1.

—Bonjour. Vous êtes américaine?
—Oui, je suis américaine.
—Est-ce que vous êtes de New York?
—Mais non, je ne suis pas de New York. Je suis de Washington.

▶ LEÇON 7 Une boum

• Une boum *p. 92*

A. Compréhension orale   CD 2, TRACK 11

Please turn to page 92 for complete *Compréhension orale* text.

B. Écoutez et répétez.   CD 2, TRACK 12

You will now hear a paused version of the dialog. Listen to the speaker and repeat right after he or she has completed the sentence.

• Écoutez bien! *p. 99*   CD 2, TRACK 13

You will hear French young people tell you what they do and do not do. Listen carefully to what they each say and determine if they do the following activities.

Modèle: Je ne joue pas au foot. Je joue au basket. #

Let's begin.

1. Je parle anglais. Je ne parle pas espagnol. #
2. Je n'habite pas à Tours. J'habite à Paris. #
3. Je dîne à la maison. Je ne dîne pas au restaurant. #
4. Je téléphone à un copain. Je ne téléphone pas à une copine. #
5. Je ne mange pas une pizza. Je mange un sandwich. #
6. J'étudie l'espagnol. Je n'étudie pas l'anglais. #
7. Je n'écoute pas la radio. J'écoute un CD. #

• Prononciation *p. 101*   CD 2, TRACK 14

Les voyelles /i/ et /u/

Écoutez: /u/ où?   /i/ ici!

Be sure to pronounce the French "**i**" as in **Mimi.**

Répétez: /i/ # ici # Philippe # il # Mimi # Sylvie # visite #
Alice visite Paris avec Sylvie. #
/u/ # où # nous # vous # écoute # joue # toujours #
Vous jouez au foot avec nous? #

À votre tour!

• Allô! *p. 102*   CD 2, TRACK 15

Sophie is phoning some friends. Match her questions on the left with her friends' answers on the right.

1. Est-ce que Marc est canadien?   Oui, il habite à Montréal.
2. Est-ce que tu joues au tennis?   Oui, mais pas très bien.
3. Ton frère est à la maison?   Non, il dîne au restaurant avec un copain.
4. Ta mère est en vacances?   Non, elle travaille.
5. Tu invites Christine et   Bien sûr! Elles aiment
   Juliette à la boum?   beaucoup danser.

• Créa-dialogue *p. 102*   CD 2, TRACK 16

Listen to some sample *Créa-dialogues.* Écoutez les conversations.

Modèle: –Robert, est-ce que tu joues au tennis? –Non, je ne joue pas au tennis.
   –Est-ce que tu écoutes la radio?   –Oui, j'écoute souvent la radio.

Maintenant, écoutez un autre dialogue.

–Louise, est-ce que tu nages?   –Non, je ne nage pas.
–Est-ce que tu chantes?   –Oui, je chante un peu.

▶ LEÇON 8 Un concert de musique africaine

• Un concert de musique africaine *p. 104*

A. Compréhension orale   CD 2, TRACK 17

Please turn to page 104 for complete *Compréhension orale* text.

B. Écoutez et répétez.   CD 2, TRACK 18

You will now hear a paused version of the dialog. Listen to the speaker and repeat right after he or she has completed the sentence.

• Écoutez bien! *p. 107*   CD 2, TRACK 19

The questions that you will hear can be logically answered by only one of the following options. Listen carefully to each question and select the logical answer. You will hear each question twice. Let's begin.

1. Où est-ce que tu habites? #
2. À quelle heure est-ce que vous dînez? #
3. Comment est-ce que vous parlez français? #
4. Quand est-ce que vous visitez Dakar? #
5. Où est-ce que ton oncle travaille? #
6. Quand est-ce que ton copain voyage en France? #
7. À quelle heure est-ce que vous regardez la télé? #
8. Comment est-ce que tu chantes? #

• Prononciation *p. 111*   CD 2, TRACK 20

La voyelle /y/

Écoutez: Super!

The vowel sound /y/—represented by the letter "**u**"—does not exist in English. To say **super,** first say the French word **si.** Then round your lips as if to whistle and say **si** with rounded lips: /sy/. Now say **si-per.** Then round your lips as you say the first syllable: **super!**

Répétez: /y/ # super # tu # étudie # bien sûr # Lucie # Luc # Tu étudies avec Lucie. #

À votre tour!

• Allô! *p. 112*   CD 2, TRACK 21

Fatou is phoning some friends. Match her questions on the left with her friends' answers on the right.

1. Qu'est-ce que tu fais?   J'étudie.
2. Qu'est-ce que vous faites samedi?   Nous faisons un match de tennis.
3. Où est ton père?   Il fait une promenade.
4. Quand est-ce que tu veux jouer   Dimanche. D'accord?
   au tennis avec moi?
5. Qui est-ce que tu invites au cinéma?   Ma cousine Alice.
6. Pourquoi est-ce que tu étudies l'anglais? Parce que je voudrais habiter à New York.

• Créa-dialogue *p. 113*   CD 2, TRACK 22

Listen to some sample *Créa-dialogues.* Écoutez les conversations.

Modèle: –Qu'est-ce que tu fais lundi?   –Je joue au tennis.
   –Ah bon? À quelle heure est-ce que tu joues? –À deux heures.
   –Et avec qui?   –Avec Anne-Marie.

Maintenant, écoutez un autre dialogue.

–Qu'est-ce que tu fais mardi?   –J'étudie.
–Ah bon? À quelle heure est-ce que tu étudies? –À six heures.
–Et avec qui?   –Avec un copain.

• Écoutez bien! *p. 133*   CD 2, TRACK 23

Imagine you are in a school in France. Listen carefully to what different French teachers ask you to do and carry out their instructions. If you have trouble understanding the commands, your teacher will mime the actions for you.

1. Prends ton crayon.
2. Prends ton livre.
3. Ouvre ton livre.
4. Ouvre ton cahier.
5. Montre-moi ton cahier.
6. Montre-moi ton stylo.
7. Montre-moi ton sac.
8. Lève-toi.
9. Va au tableau.
10. Montre-moi un morceau de craie.
11. Va à la porte.
12. Va à la fenêtre.
13. Assieds-toi.
14. Prends une feuille de papier.
15. Écris avec ton crayon.

Très bien!

Complete videoscripts, plus Workbook and Assessment audioscripts, are available in the Unit Resource Books.

UNITÉ 3

Main Theme
- Daily Activities

COMMUNICATION
- Describing daily activities
- Saying what you like and don't like to do
- Asking and answering questions about where others are and what they're doing
- Inviting friends to do things
- Accepting and turning down invitations

CULTURES
- Learning how French teens spend their leisure time
- Learning about what French young people do at parties
- Learning about Senegal and African music
- Learning how the French use the Internet
- Learning about the Vietnamese in France

CONNECTIONS
- Connecting to English: Learning grammar terms
- Connecting to Math: Understanding the 24-hour clock
- Connecting to English: Recognizing cognates

COMPARISONS
- Comparing French and American attitudes toward cell phones
- Comparing the school schedule in France and the U.S.
- Comparing parties in France and the U.S.
- Comparing t.v. schedules in France and the U.S.
- Comparing Internet use of teens in France and the U.S.

COMMUNITIES
- Using French when making a phone call
- Using French when writing e-mail

UNITÉ 3

Qu'est-ce qu'on fait?

LEÇON 5 **LE FRANÇAIS PRATIQUE:** Mes activités

LEÇON 6 **Une invitation**

LEÇON 7 **Une boum**

LEÇON 8 **Un concert de musique africaine**

THÈME ET OBJECTIFS

Daily activities

In this unit, you will be talking about the things you do every day, such as working and studying, as well as watching TV or playing sports.

You will learn ...

- to describe some of your daily activities
- to say what you like and do not like to do
- to ask and answer questions about where others are and what they are doing

You will also learn ...

- to invite friends to do things with you
- to politely accept or turn down an invitation

 WEBQUEST
CLASSZONE.COM

UNIT OVERVIEW

▶ **Communication Goals:** Students will learn to talk about their daily activities and how to extend and respond to invitations.

▶ **Linguistic Goals:** The primary focus is on the present tense (affirmative, negative) and question formation.

▶ **Critical Thinking Goals:** Students are introduced to the concept of subject-verb agreement and the importance of verb endings in French.

▶ **Cultural Goals:** This unit focuses on the daily activities of French young people: school and homework, as well as sports and leisure activities.

PRINT

Unit 3 Resource Book
  Family Letter, p.14

AUDIO & VISUAL

Audio Program
Chansons CD

TECHNOLOGY 🖥️

EasyPlanner CD-ROM/EasyPlanner
  Plus Online

Cross-cultural observation

This picture was taken in France.

As usual, have students look at the photo and answer the following questions:

• Could this photo have been taken in the United States?

• Why or why not?

• Which elements in the picture seem to be definitely French?

Middle School Copymasters

Unité 3: Internet Pen Pals and Student Exchange projects, charades, drills, *mots croisés*, worksheets, pp. T15–T18

Pacing

Beginning with Unit 3, the lessons are longer and there is a dual emphasis on both oral and written skills.

For specific suggestions on pacing, turn to page 69D.

Leçon 5

Main Topics
- Describing daily activities
- Offering and receiving invitations

Teaching Resource Options

PRINT

Workbook PE, pp. 59–63
Activités pour tous PE, pp. 33–35
Block Scheduling Copymasters, pp. 33–40
Unit 3 Resource Book
  Activités pour tous TE, pp. 7–9
  Audioscript, pp. 28–30
  Communipak, pp. 128–143
  Lesson Plans, pp. 10–11
  Block Scheduling Lesson Plans, pp. 12–13
  Absent Student Copymasters, pp. 15–18
  Video Activities, pp. 21–24
  Videoscript, pp. 25–26
  Workbook TE, pp. 1–5

AUDIO & VISUAL

Audio Program
CD 7, Tracks 1–5

TECHNOLOGY

Online Workbook

VIDEO PROGRAM

 MODULE 5
Le français pratique
Mes activités

TOTAL TIME: 5:59 min.
  DVD Disk 1
  Videotape 2 (COUNTER: 5:50 min.)

5.1 Mini-scenes: Listening
  – J'aime téléphoner
  (6:44–7:28 min.)

5.2 Mini-scenes: Speaking
  – Tu aimes écouter la radio?
  (7:29–8:30 min.)

5.3 Mini-scenes: Listening
  – Invitations
  (8:31–8:52 min.)

5.4 Dialogue: Tennis
  (8:53–10:00 min.)

5.5 Vignette culturelle:
  Le téléphone
  (10:01–11:49 min.)

Comprehension practice Play the entire module through as an introduction to the lesson.

LEÇON 5

Mes activités

LE FRANÇAIS PRATIQUE
VIDÉO DVD AUDIO

Accent sur ... Les activités de la semaine

French teenagers spend a great deal of time on their studies since they and their families consider it important to do well in school. They have a longer class day than American students and are given more homework.

However, French teenagers do not study all the time. They also enjoy listening to music, watching TV, and playing computer games. Many participate in various sports activities, but to a lesser extent than American students. On weekends, they like to go out with their friends to shop or see a movie. They also go to parties and love dancing.

Mélanie est à la maison. Elle écoute un CD.
Mélanie: J'aime le rock anglais.

Marc, Élodie et David sont au stade. Ils jouent au foot.
  Marc: Nous jouons au foot.
  Élodie: Nous jouons aussi au basket.
  David: Nous aimons les sports.

72 soixante-douze
Unité 3

USING THE VIDEO

Beginning with this lesson, there is more variety in the sequencing of the video modules.

Play the entire module through as an introduction to the cultural themes and new linguistic material of the lesson.

The various parts of the video are closely correlated to specific sections in the lesson. Notes in the Teacher's Edition (prefaced with the video logo) indicate points at which you may want to use certain video segments.

Olivier est en ville. Il téléphone.

Olivier: J'aime téléphoner.
Je téléphone à une copine.

Zaïna joue aux jeux vidéo.

Zaïna: J'aime jouer aux jeux vidéo.
J'aime aussi regarder la télé.

soixante-treize **73**
Leçon 5

TEACHING STRATEGY Le français pratique

Beginning with Unit 3, the first lesson of each unit introduces the communication theme and the related vocabulary. All of these new words and phrases are then re-entered in a variety of situations in the remainder of the unit.

Try to move rather quickly through **Le français pratique** because students will have ample opportunity to master the new material as they do the many activities in the next three lessons.

SECTION A

Communicative function
Expressing likes and dislikes

Teaching Resource Options

PRINT

Workbook PE, pp. 59–63
Unit 3 Resource Book
   Audioscript, p. 27
   Communipak, pp. 128–143
   Video Activities, pp. 21–22
   Videoscript, p. 25
   Workbook TE, pp. 1–5

AUDIO & VISUAL

Audio Program
CD 2 Track 1

Overhead Transparencies
14a, 14b, 17 *-er* verbs

VIDEO PROGRAM

  MODULE 5

5.1 Mini-scenes: J'aime téléphoner
(6:44–7:28 min.)

5.2 Mini-scenes: Tu aimes écouter la radio? (7:29–8:30 min.)

Pronunciation practice This audio activity models the new vocabulary in sentence context.

Looking ahead In this lesson, students will become familiar with the meaning of these verbs in the infinitive form. In Lesson 7, they will learn how to use them in the present tense.

A VOCABULAIRE Préférences

Est-ce que tu aimes parler français?

▶ **How to talk about what you like and don't like to do:**

Est-ce que tu aimes …?	*Do you like …?*	**Est-ce que tu aimes** parler *(to speak)* français?
J'aime …	*I like …*	Oui, **j'aime** parler français.
Je n'aime pas …	*I don't like …*	Non, **je n'aime pas** parler français.
Je préfère …	*I prefer …*	**Je préfère** parler anglais.

 J'aime …

téléphoner	**parler français**	**parler anglais**	**parler espagnol**
to phone	*to talk, speak French*	*to speak English*	*to speak Spanish*

manger	**chanter**	**danser**	**nager**
to eat	*to sing*	*to dance*	*to swim*

1 **Et toi?**

PARLER/ÉCRIRE Indicate what you like to do in the following situations by completing each sentence with two of the suggested activities.

1 En classe, j'aime … mais je préfère …
   étudier • écouter le professeur • parler avec *(with)* **un copain • parler avec une copine**

2. En été, j'aime … mais je préfère …
   travailler • nager • voyager • jouer au volley *(volleyball)*

74 soixante-quatorze
Unité 3

COMPREHENSION Everyday activities

PROPS: Transparencies 14a, 14b, 17: Verbs, *-er* verbs
   Develop a gesture for each verb.

Model the sentences in the verb charts and have the class mimic the action with you.
   J'aime téléphoner. [Gesture "dialing"]
   J'aime manger. [Gesture "eating"]
   J'aime jouer au foot. [Gesture "kicking"]

Say sentences with students acting out verbs. Have students point out the actions on the transparency:
   X, montre-nous l'action: J'aime chanter., etc.

Have students repeat each sentence with you as they gesture the action. Do the action and have the class say the sentence.

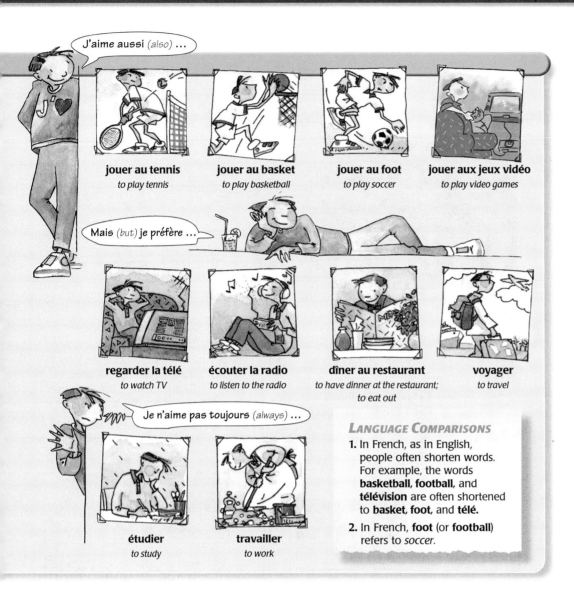

J'aime aussi *(also)* …

jouer au tennis
to play tennis

jouer au basket
to play basketball

jouer au foot
to play soccer

jouer aux jeux vidéo
to play video games

Mais *(but)* je préfère …

regarder la télé
to watch TV

écouter la radio
to listen to the radio

dîner au restaurant
*to have dinner at the restaurant;
to eat out*

voyager
to travel

Je n'aime pas toujours *(always)* …

étudier
to study

travailler
to work

Supplementary vocabulary

jouer aux jeux d'ordinateur *to play computer games*

Middle School Copymasters

Charades, p. 33; Crossword: *Quelques activités*, pp. 35–36; Worksheet 3: *Curiosité*, pp. 39–40

> ### LANGUAGE COMPARISONS
>
> 1. In French, as in English, people often shorten words. For example, the words **basketball**, **football**, and **télévision** are often shortened to **basket**, **foot**, and **télé**.
> 2. In French, **foot** (or **football**) refers to *soccer*.

1 **COMMUNICATION** indicating preferences

Answers will vary.
1. En classe, j'aime (écouter le professeur), mais je préfère (parler avec un copain).
2. En été, j'aime (nager), mais je préfère (jouer au volley).
3. Avec mes copains, j'aime (écouter la radio), mais je préfère (jouer au basket).
4. Avec ma famille, j'aime (dîner au restaurant), mais je préfère (voyager).
5. À la maison, j'aime (étudier), mais je préfère (écouter mes CD).

Oral introduction

- Model the options in each question for listening comprehension, asking for a show of hands.

  En classe, qui aime étudier?
  Qui aime écouter le professeur?
  Qui préfère parler avec un copain?
  Qui préfère parler avec une copine?

- Ask individual students who have raised their hands to respond orally:

  X, en classe, est-ce que tu aimes étudier?
  X: Oui, j'aime étudier.

---

3. Avec mes *(my)* copains, j'aime … mais je préfère …
   chanter • manger • écouter la radio • jouer au basket

4. Avec ma famille, j'aime … mais je préfère …
   voyager • regarder la télé • jouer aux jeux vidéo • dîner au restaurant

5. À la maison *(At home)*, j'aime … mais je préfère …
   étudier • téléphoner • manger • écouter mes CD

CLASSROOM MANAGEMENT Group Practice

As a preparation for group work, first introduce Activity 1 orally. (See side note.)

Then divide the class into groups, each with a recorder (**un/une secrétaire**).

Individual group members take turns indicating their preferences (Act. 1).
En classe, je préfère étudier.

The **secrétaire** tallies the group's responses.
#1. La majorité préfère étudier.
(La majorité préfère écouter le professeur.)

The results can be reported back to the class, or handed in to the teacher.

Teaching Resource Options

PRINT

Workbook PE, pp. 59–63
Unit 3 Resource Book
  Communipak, pp. 128–143
  Workbook TE, pp. 1–5

2 COMMUNICATION expressing likes and dislikes

Answers will vary.
1. J'aime manger. (Je n'aime pas manger.)
2. J'aime étudier. (Je n'aime pas étudier.)
3. J'aime danser. (Je n'aime pas danser.)
4. J'aime téléphoner. (Je n'aime pas téléphoner.)
5. J'aime voyager. (Je n'aime pas voyager.)
6. J'aime travailler. (Je n'aime pas travailler.)
7. J'aime regarder la télé. (Je n'aime pas regarder la télé.)
8. J'aime dîner au restaurant. (Je n'aime pas dîner au restaurant.)
9. J'aime jouer au basket. (Je n'aime pas jouer au basket.)
10. J'aime jouer aux jeux vidéo. (Je n'aime pas jouer aux jeux vidéo.)
11. J'aime écouter la radio. (Je n'aime pas écouter la radio.)
12. J'aime parler français. (Je n'aime pas parler français.)

3 EXCHANGES asking friends what they like to do

–Est-ce que tu aimes ...?
–Oui, j'aime ... (Non, je n'aime pas ...)

1. jouer au tennis
2. écouter la radio
3. jouer au foot
4. voyager
5. étudier
6. nager
7. chanter
8. dîner au restaurant
9. travailler

4 ROLE PLAY discussing preferred activities

Mark: Est-ce que tu aimes ...?
Léa: Oui, mais je préfère ...

1. jouer au basket/jouer au foot
2. parler anglais/parler espagnol
3. chanter/danser
4. écouter la radio/regarder la télé
5. étudier/(voyager, téléphoner)

Variation Have "Léa" ask the question using the activity in the bottom row. Philippe answers, using the activity in the top row.

L: Est-ce que tu aimes jouer au tennis?
M: Oui, mais je préfère nager.

---

2 Tu aimes ou tu n'aimes pas?

PARLER/ÉCRIRE Say whether or not you like to do the following things.

▶ chanter?

J'aime chanter.

Je n'aime pas chanter.

1. manger?
2. étudier?
3. danser?
4. téléphoner?
5. voyager?
6. travailler?
7. regarder la télé?
8. dîner au restaurant?
9. jouer au basket?
10. jouer aux jeux vidéo?
11. écouter la radio?
12. parler français?

3 Préférences

PARLER Ask your classmates if they like to do the following things.

▶ —Est-ce que tu aimes téléphoner?
—Oui, j'aime téléphoner. (Non, je n'aime pas téléphoner.)

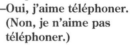 ◄

1 2 3

4 5 6

7 8 9

4 Dialogue

PARLER Marc is asking Léa if she likes to do certain things. She replies that she prefers to do other things. Play both roles. Note: "??" means you can invent an answer.

▶ MARC: Est-ce que tu aimes nager?
  LÉA: Oui, mais je préfère jouer au tennis.

▶
1

2 3

HELLO!
¡BUENOS DÍAS!

4 5
??

TEACHING NOTE Writing activities

Beginning with Unit 3, students will be developing both their writing and speaking skills. Activities which lend themselves to written (as well as oral) practice will be signaled in the Pupil Edition with the skill indicator **PARLER/ÉCRIRE**.

The Student Workbook provides a wide variety of additional writing activities.

B VOCABULAIRE Souhaits *(Wishes)*

Je voudrais voyager en France.

▶ **How to talk about what you want, would like, and do not want to do:**

Je veux …	*I want …*	**Je veux** parler français.
Je voudrais …	*I would like …*	**Je voudrais** voyager en France.
Je ne veux pas …	*I don't want …*	**Je ne veux pas** étudier aujourd'hui.

---

5 *Ce soir* *(Tonight)*

PARLER/ÉCRIRE Say whether or not you want to do the following things tonight.

▶ étudier?
  Oui, je veux étudier.
  (Non, je ne veux pas étudier.)

1. parler français?
2. travailler?
3. jouer aux jeux vidéo?
4. chanter?
5. danser?
6. regarder la télé?
7. écouter la radio?
8. dîner avec une copine?
9. manger une pizza?
10. téléphoner à mon cousin?

6 *Week-end*

PARLER/ÉCRIRE Léa and her friends are discussing their weekend plans. What do they say they would like to do?

▶ LÉA: **Je voudrais jouer au tennis.**

Léa 1. Jérôme 2. Monique
3. Jean-Louis 4. Caroline 5. Patrick

---

7 *Trois souhaits* *(Three wishes)*

ÉCRIRE Read the list of suggested activities and select the three that you would like to do most.

parler français
parler espagnol
parler avec *(with)* Oprah Winfrey
dîner avec le Président
dîner avec Matt Damon

voyager avec ma cousine
voyager en France
chanter comme *(like)* Britney Spears
jouer au tennis comme Venus Williams
jouer au basket comme Shaquille O'Neal

▶ Je voudrais parler espagnol.
  Je voudrais chanter comme Britney Spears.
  Je voudrais voyager en France.

SECTION B

Communicative function
Expressing wishes

5 **COMMUNICATION** indicating what you want/don't want to do

Oui, je veux … (Non, je ne veux pas …)

1. parler français
2. travailler
3. jouer aux jeux vidéo
4. chanter
5. danser
6. regarder la télé
7. écouter la radio
8. dîner avec une copine
9. manger une pizza
10. téléphoner à mon cousin

Language note In French, one must say **téléphoner à,** *to phone "to" someone.*

6 **DESCRIPTION** indicating what people would like to do

1. Jérôme: Je voudrais nager.
2. Monique: Je voudrais dîner au restaurant.
3. Jean-Louis: Je voudrais danser.
4. Caroline: Je voudrais jouer au basket.
5. Patrick: Je voudrais écouter la radio.

Challenge Add **Et toi?** The next student replies with an alternative activity.
Léa: **Je voudrais jouer au tennis. Et toi?**
Élève A: **Je voudrais jouer au foot (chanter, etc.).**

7 **COMMUNICATION** indicating what you would like to do

Answers will vary.
• Je voudrais parler français.
  Je voudrais dîner avec le Président.
  Je voudrais jouer au tennis comme Venus Williams.
• Je voudrais dîner avec Matt Damon.
  Je voudrais voyager avec ma cousine.
  Je voudrais parler espagnol.
• Je voudrais parler avec Oprah Winfrey.
  Je voudrais jouer au basket comme Shaquille O'Neal.
  Je voudrais chanter comme Britney Spears.

Variation Have students substitute other names in their responses.
  Je voudrais parler avec Chris Rock.

Variation Have the students select the three activities they would like to do least. Then have them compare their responses with a partner.
  Je ne voudrais pas voyager avec ma cousine., etc.

SECTION C

Communicative function
Extending invitations

Teaching Resource Options

PRINT

Workbook PE, pp. 59–63
Unit 3 Resource Book
  Communipak, pp. 128–143
  Video Activities, pp. 23–24
  Videoscript, pp. 25–26
  Workbook TE, pp. 1–5

VIDEO PROGRAM

VIDÉO   DVD

MODULE 5

5.3 Mini-scenes: Invitations
(8:31–8:52 min.)

5.4 Dialogue: Tennis?
(8:53–10:00 min.)

5.5 Vignette culturelle: Le téléphone
(10:01–11:49 min.)

⑧ ROLE PLAY extending and accepting invitations

1. –Thomas, est-ce que tu veux parler français avec moi?
  –Oui, d'accord, je veux bien parler français avec toi.
2. –Simon, est-ce que tu veux étudier avec moi?
  –Oui, d'accord, je veux bien étudier avec toi.
3. –Céline, est-ce que tu veux jouer au tennis avec moi?
  –Oui, d'accord, je veux bien jouer au tennis avec toi.
4. –Anne, est-ce que tu veux manger une pizza avec moi?
  –Oui, d'accord, je veux bien manger une pizza avec toi.
5. –Jean-Claude, est-ce que tu veux chanter avec moi?
  –Oui, d'accord, je veux bien chanter avec toi.
6. –Caroline, est-ce que tu veux danser avec moi?
  –Oui, d'accord, je veux bien danser avec toi.

Challenge Students can use other phrases as they accept the invitations: e.g., **D'accord / Oui, merci / Oui, bien sûr.**

C VOCABULAIRE Invitations

Est-ce que tu veux jouer au tennis?

▶ *How to invite a friend:*

Est-ce que tu veux …?	*Do you want to …?*	**Est-ce que tu veux** jouer au tennis?
Est-ce que tu peux …?	*Can you …?*	**Est-ce que tu peux** parler à mon copain?
avec moi/toi	*with me/you*	Est-ce que tu veux dîner **avec moi?**

▶ *How to accept an invitation:*

Oui, bien sûr …	*Yes, of course …*	
Oui, merci …	*Yes, thanks …*	
Oui, d'accord …	*Yes, all right, okay …*	
je veux bien.	*I'd love to.*	**Oui, bien sûr, je veux bien.**
je veux bien …	*I'd love to …*	**Oui, merci, je veux bien** dîner avec toi.

▶ *How to turn down an invitation:*

Je regrette, mais	*I'm sorry, but*	**Je regrette, mais je ne peux pas**
je ne peux pas …	*I can't …*	dîner avec toi.
Je dois …	*I have to, I must …*	**Je dois** étudier.

⑧ 😊 Oui, d'accord

PARLER Invite the following French students (played by your classmates) to do things with you. They will accept.

▶ Monique / dîner

Monique, est-ce que tu veux dîner avec moi?

Oui, d'accord, je veux bien dîner avec toi.

1. Thomas / parler français
2. Simon / étudier
3. Céline / jouer au tennis
4. Anne / manger une pizza
5. Jean-Claude / chanter
6. Caroline / danser

⑨ 😊 Conversation

PARLER Ask your classmates if they want to do the following things. They will answer that they cannot and explain why.

▶ jouer au basket?
  (étudier)
  — **Est-ce que tu veux jouer au basket?**
  — **Non, je ne peux pas. Je dois étudier.**

1. jouer aux jeux vidéo?
  (travailler)
2. jouer au ping-pong?
  (téléphoner à ma cousine)
3. étudier avec moi?
  (étudier avec ma copine)
4. dîner avec moi?
  (dîner avec ma famille)
5. nager?
  (jouer au foot à deux heures)

TEACHING THE VIDEO DIALOGUE

For Lesson 5, the video (part 5.4) contains a series of conversations.

Step 1: Set the scene. Tell students: In this scene Jean-Claude is looking for a tennis partner. **Regardez. (Écoutez.)**

Step 2: Play the video segment.

Step 3: Have students in small groups try to recall the scenes.

Écrivez l'invitation de Jean-Claude et les réponses de ses amis.

Step 4: Play the segment again to let groups check their work.

Step 5: Compare the group answers.

NOTE *culturelle*

Le téléphone

French teenagers, like their American counterparts, love to talk with their friends on the phone. At home, they can use the family phone, but now more and more young people also have a cell phone which is called **un téléphone portable** or simply **un portable** for short. (**Portable** comes from the French verb **porter**, which means *to carry*.)

Europeans have been ahead of Americans in the use of mobile phones. In France, for instance, almost half of the people own a cell phone. This proportion is higher with teenagers and college students. Cell phones have many advantages. You can call your friends from wherever you are and whenever you want, and if you are going to be late for dinner, you can call and let your parents know. Cell phones, however, can be annoying and even distracting. In France, it is illegal to make cell phone calls while driving a car. Moreover, students are not allowed to bring cell phones to class. It is also considered impolite to use them in restaurants, cinemas, and concert halls.

COMPARAISONS CULTURELLES

Compare the French and American attitudes toward the use of cell phones.

How do you feel about people using cell phones in the following circumstances? Indicate whether you think it is appropriate or not by saying: **C'est acceptable.** or **Ce n'est pas acceptable.**

- au café
- au cinéma
- au restaurant
- pendant *(during)* la classe de français
- pendant un concert de rock
- en conduisant *(while driving)*

L'étiquette téléphonique

- to introduce yourself when phoning a friend, you say:
  Allô … Ici Thomas. Bonjour. Ça va?

- if your friend is not home and if a parent answers, you say:
  Allô … Ici Thomas Rémi. Bonjour, monsieur (madame).
  Est-ce que je pourrais (May I) parler à Mélanie?

- if you would like to leave a message, you ask:
  Est-ce que je peux (Can I) laisser un message?

- before hanging up, you say:
  Merci, monsieur (madame). Au revoir.

10 **Allô!**

PARLER Céline is phoning Trinh to ask him if he wants to go to a movie. Trinh's mother says that he is not home. Céline asks her to take a message. Act out the conversation between Céline and Trinh's mother.

9 **EXCHANGES** extending and refusing invitations

1. – Est-ce que tu veux jouer aux jeux vidéo?
   – Non, je ne peux pas. Je dois travailler.
2. – Est-ce que tu veux jouer au ping-pong?
   – Non, je ne peux pas. Je dois téléphoner à ma cousine.
3. – Est-ce que tu veux étudier avec moi?
   – Non, je ne peux pas. Je dois étudier avec ma copine.
4. – Est-ce que tu veux dîner avec moi?
   – Non, je ne peux pas. Je dois dîner avec ma famille.
5. – Est-ce que tu veux nager?
   – Non, je ne peux pas. Je dois jouer au foot à deux heures.

Teaching Note

These phone phrases are presented only for guided role play, and are not considered active vocabulary.

10 **ROLE PLAY** engaging in a phone conversation

– Allô . . . Ici Céline (Renoir). Bonjour, madame. Est-ce que je pourrais parler à Trinh?
– Trinh n'est pas à la maison. Il est en ville.
– Est-ce que je peux laisser un message?
– Oui, bien sûr.
– Je vais aller au cinéma ce soir, et je veux inviter Trinh.
– D'accord, Céline.
– Merci, madame. Au revoir.

À votre tour!

1 Écoutez bien!

ÉCOUTER You will hear French young people telling you what they like to do. Listen carefully to each activity. If it is illustrated in the picture on the left, mark A. If it is illustrated in the picture on the right, mark B.

A

B

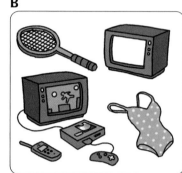

	A	B
1.		
2.		
3.		
4.		
5.		
6.		

2 Communication

ÉCOUTER You have invited a French friend to spend the weekend at your house. Ask your friend …

• if he/she likes to watch TV
• if he/she wants to play video games
• if he/she likes to listen to the radio
• if he/she wants to eat a pizza

A classmate will play the role of your French friend and answer your questions.

3 Conversation dirigée

PARLER Trinh is phoning Céline. Write out their conversation according to the directions. You may want to act out the dialogue with a classmate.

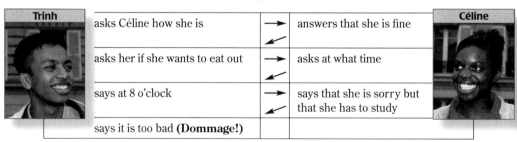

Trinh				Céline
	asks Céline how she is	→ ←	answers that she is fine	
	asks her if she wants to eat out	→ ←	asks at what time	
	says at 8 o'clock	→ ←	says that she is sorry but that she has to study	
	says it is too bad (**Dommage!**)			

À VOTRE TOUR

Beginning with this lesson, the **À votre tour** sections have both oral and written communication activities. Depending on your goals and objectives, you may or may not wish to assign all of the activities in the **À votre tour** section.

4 🎧 👥 *Créa-dialogue*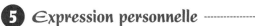

PARLER Ask your classmates if they want to do the following things with you. They will answer that they cannot and will give one of the excuses below.

> jouer au tennis

1. jouer au basket
2. manger une pizza
3. regarder la télé
4. jouer au ping-pong
5. dîner au restaurant
6. jouer aux jeux vidéo

EXCUSES:

téléphoner à une copine

étudier   travailler   parler avec ma mère

dîner avec ma cousine   chanter avec la chorale (choir)

Speech bubble (left): Est-ce que tu veux jouer au tennis avec moi?

Speech bubble (right): Non, je ne peux pas. Je dois travailler.

---

5 *Expression personnelle*

PARLER/ÉCRIRE What we like to do often depends on the circumstances. Complete the sentences below saying what you like and don't like to do in the following situations.

> En hiver …
> **En hiver, j'aime regarder la télé.**
> **J'aime aussi jouer au basket.**
> **Je n'aime pas nager.**

1. En été …
2. En automne …
3. Le samedi *(On Saturdays)* …
4. Le dimanche …
5. Le soir *(In the evening)* …
6. En classe …
7. Avec mes *(my)* amis …
8. Avec ma famille …

---

 6 *Correspondance*

ÉCRIRE This summer you are going to spend two weeks in France. Your e-mail correspondent Vincent has written asking what you like and don't like to do on vacation **(en vacances).** Respond with a short e-mail, answering his questions.

STRATEGY Writing

1. Make a list of activities you like and do not like. Use only vocabulary that you know.

2. Write your e-mail. *Cher Vincent,*
   En vacances, j'aime …

3. Read over your letter to be sure you have used the right verb forms.

LESSON REVIEW
CLASSZONE.COM

PORTFOLIO ASSESSMENT

Beginning with Unit 3, students may start a Written Portfolio.

You will perhaps want to do only one oral portfolio recording and one written composition per unit. In this lesson, a good written portfolio topic is Act. 6.

---

4 **WRITTEN SELF-EXPRESSION**

1. –Est-ce que tu veux jouer au basket avec moi?
   –Non, je ne peux pas. Je dois (téléphoner à une copine).
2. –Est-ce que tu veux manger une pizza avec moi?
   –Non, je ne peux pas. Je dois (dîner avec ma cousine).
3. –Est-ce que tu veux regarder la télé avec moi?
   –Non, je ne peux pas. Je dois (parler avec ma mère).
4. –Est-ce que tu veux jouer au ping-pong avec moi?
   –Non, je ne peux pas. Je dois (étudier).
5. –Est-ce que tu veux dîner au restaurant avec moi?
   –Non, je ne peux pas. Je dois (chanter avec la chorale).
6. –Est-ce que tu veux jouer aux jeux vidéo avec moi?
   –Non, je ne peux pas. Je dois (étudier).

Variation Using the audio, have students match numbers 1–6 with the excuses given by the speakers.

---

5 **WRITTEN SELF-EXPRESSION**

Answers will vary.
1. En été, j'aime (nager). J'aime aussi (voyager). Je n'aime pas (travailler).
2. En automne, j'aime (jouer au basket). J'aime aussi (chanter). Je n'aime pas (nager).
3. Le samedi, j'aime (danser). J'aime aussi (téléphoner). Je n'aime pas (travailler).
4. Le dimanche, j'aime (jouer au volley). J'aime aussi chanter. Je n'aime pas (regarder la télé).
5. Le soir, j'aime (écouter la radio). J'aime aussi (téléphoner). Je n'aime pas (étudier).
6. En classe, j'aime (parler français). J'aime aussi (étudier). Je n'aime pas (danser).
7. Avec mes amis, j'aime (aller au restaurant). J'aime aussi (danser). Je n'aime pas (étudier).
8. Avec ma famille, j'aime (aller au restaurant). J'aime aussi voyager. Je n'aime pas (jouer au basket).

---

6 **WRITTEN SELF-EXPRESSION**

Answers will vary.
1. **J'aime** — **Je n'aime pas**

J'aime	Je n'aime pas
• voyager	• étudier
• danser	• regarder la télé
• nager	• parler anglais

2. Cher Vincent,
   En vacances, j'aime voyager, danser, nager, jouer au volley et parler français. Je n'aime pas étudier, regarder la télé, parler anglais et jouer au basket.
   Paul (Carole)

Group Reading Practice Have students prepare a writing activity for homework. Then, in class, divide students into small groups and let them read one another's compositions.

Leçon 6

Main Topic Finding out where people are

Teaching Resource Options

PRINT

Workbook PE, pp. 65–68
Activités pour tous PE, pp. 37–39
Block Scheduling Copymasters,
  pp. 41–48
Unit 3 Resource Book
  Activités pour tous TE, pp. 37–38
  Audioscript, pp. 55, 56–57
  Communipak, pp. 128–143
  Lesson Plans, pp. 39–40
  Block Scheduling Lesson Plans,
    pp. 41–42
  Absent Student Copymasters,
    pp. 43–46
  Video Activities, pp. 49–52
  Videoscript, pp. 53–54
  Workbook TE, pp. 33–36

AUDIO & VISUAL

Audio Program
CD 2 Tracks 6, 7
CD 7 Tracks 6–11

TECHNOLOGY

Online Workbook

VIDEO PROGRAM

MODULE 6
Une invitation

TOTAL TIME: 4:43 min.
  DVD Disk 1
  Videotape 2 (COUNTER: 11:59 min.)

6.1 Dialogue: Une invitation
  (12:37–13:28 min.)

6.2 Mini-scenes: Listening
  – Je suis en classe (13:29–13:51 min.)

6.3 Mini-scenes: Speaking
  – Où sont-ils? (13:52–15:05 min.)

6.4 Vignette culturelle: Au café
  (15:06–16:42 min.)

Comprehension practice Play the entire module through as an introduction to the lesson.

Compréhension
Answers
1. Léa est à la maison.
2. Mathieu est en ville.
3. Julie et Stéphanie sont au restaurant.
4. Antoine et Céline sont au café.

LEÇON 6

Une invitation

VIDÉO   DVD   AUDIO

It is Wednesday afternoon. Antoine is looking for his friends but cannot find anyone. Finally he sees Céline at the Café Le Bercy and asks her where everyone is.

Antoine:	<u>Où</u> est Léa?	*Where*
Céline:	Elle est <u>à la maison</u>.	*at home*
Antoine:	Et Mathieu? Il est <u>là</u>?	*here*
Céline:	Non, il n'est pas là.	
Antoine:	Où est-il?	
Céline:	Il est <u>en ville</u> avec une copine.	*in town*
Antoine:	Et Julie et Stéphanie? Est-ce qu'elles sont <u>ici</u>?	*here*
Céline:	Non, elles sont au restaurant.	
Antoine:	<u>Alors</u>, qui est là?	*So*
Céline:	Moi, je suis ici.	
Antoine:	C'est <u>vrai</u>, tu es ici! Eh bien, <u>puisque</u> tu es là, <u>je t'invite au cinéma</u>. D'accord?	*true / since* *I'll invite you to the movies.*
Céline:	Super! Antoine, tu es un <u>vrai</u> copain!	*real*

Compréhension

Indicate where the following people are by selecting the appropriate completions.

1. Léa est …
2. Mathieu est …
3. Julie et Stéphanie sont …
4. Antoine et Céline sont …

en ville
au café
à la maison
au restaurant

SETTING THE STAGE

You may want to introduce the opening text by having students listen to the audio with their books closed. They will hear a conversation between Antoine et Céline. Antoine is looking for **Léa, Mathieu,** and **Julie et Stéphanie.**

    Draw three sets of stick figures (a girl, a boy, two girls) and identify them, as above.

Then label line drawings of three places: **en ville, au restaurant, à la maison.**
    Tell students they are to listen to the conversation carefully and determine who is where.

NOTE culturelle

Le mercredi après-midi

French middle school students do not usually have classes on Wednesday afternoons. Some young people use this free time to go out with their friends or to catch up on their homework. For other students, Wednesday afternoon is also the time for music and dance lessons as well as sports activities. Many students play soccer with their school team or with their local sports club. Other popular activities include tennis, skateboarding, and in-line skating.

COMPARAISONS CULTURELLES

• How does the school week in France compare to the school week in the United States?

• Do you see any differences in the ways French and American teenagers spend their free time? Explain.

• Do American and French teenagers like the same sports? Explain.

Oral comprehension Read each statement and have students indicate whether it is true **(vrai)** or false **(faux)**.
1. Léa est à la maison. (vrai)
2. Mathieu est à la maison. (faux)
3. Julie est au restaurant. (vrai)
4. Stéphanie est au cinéma. (faux)
5. Céline est au café. (vrai)

Note culturelle For more information about the French school system, turn to the photo essay on pp. 124–131, **À l'école en France.**

Cross-cultural observation After showing the video segment, have students in pairs make a list of similarities and differences between the French **café** and similar places where teens go in the United States.

Supplementary Vocabulary
le skate *skateboarding*
un skate(board) *skateboard*
faire du skate *to go skateboarding*
le roller *in-line skating*
des rollers *in-line skates*
faire du roller *to go in-line skating*

quatre-vingt-trois
Leçon 6 83

SECTION A

Communicative function
Identifying people and where they are

Teaching Resource Options

PRINT

Workbook PE, pp. 65–68
Unit 3 Resource Book
　　Communipak, pp. 128–143
　　Video Activities, pp. 50–51
　　Videoscript, p. 53
　　Workbook TE, pp. 33–36

AUDIO & VISUAL

Overhead Transparencies
15 *Où sont-ils?*

TECHNOLOGY

Power Presentations

VIDEO PROGRAM

VIDÉO　DVD
MODULE 6

6.2 Mini-scenes: Je suis en classe
(13:29–13:51 min.)

6.3 Mini-scenes: Où sont-ils?
(13:52–15:05 min.)

Teaching notes
Why begin with être?

The conjugation of the verb **être** is presented in Leçon 6, ahead of the **–er** verbs for the following reasons:
• **Être** is the most frequently used verb in the French language.
• Students are introduced to the concept of conjugation (in the affirmative, negative and interrogative) with a single verb.
In Leçon 7, students will learn about infinitives, stems and endings.

Re-entry and review

Remind students that they have already been using the singular forms of **être:**
　　Je suis américain.
　　Tu es français.
　　Il est canadien.

Pronunciation note There is usually liaison after **est**: Elle **est** ici. Liaison is optional after other forms of **être**: Ils **sont** ici. or Ils **sont** ici.

A Le verbe *être* et les pronoms sujets

Être *(to be)* is the most frequently used verb in French. Note the forms of **être** in the chart below.

	être	to be	
SINGULAR	je **suis**	*I am*	Je **suis** américain.
	tu **es**	*you are*	Tu **es** canadienne.
	il/elle **est**	*he/she is*	Il **est** anglais.
PLURAL	nous **sommes**	*we are*	Nous **sommes** à Paris.
	vous **êtes**	*you are*	Vous **êtes** à San Francisco.
	ils/elles **sont**	*they are*	Ils **sont** à Genève.

→ Note the liaison in the **vous** form:
　　Vous êtes français?
　　　　　z

→ Note the expression **être d'accord** *(to agree):*
　—Tu **es d'accord**　　　*Do you agree*
　　avec moi?　　　　　　*with me?*
　—Oui, je **suis d'accord!**　*Yes, I agree!*

TU or VOUS?

When talking to ONE person, the French have two ways of saying *you:*

• **tu** ("familiar *you*") is used to talk to someone your own age (or younger) or to a member of your family

• **vous** ("formal *you*") is used when talking to anyone else

When talking to TWO or more people, the French use **vous.**

 RAPPEL You should use …
• **vous** to address your teacher
• **tu** to address a classmate

LEARNING ABOUT LANGUAGE

• The words **je** *(I)*, **tu** *(you)*, **il** *(he)*, **elle** *(she)*, etc. are called SUBJECT PRONOUNS.
　• SINGULAR pronouns refer to one person (or object).
　• PLURAL pronouns refer to two or more people (or objects).
• The VERB **être** *(to be)* is IRREGULAR because its forms do not follow a predictable pattern.
• A chart showing the subject pronouns and their corresponding verb forms is called a CONJUGATION.

Tu es français?

Vous êtes français?

Vous êtes français?

TEACHING NOTE　Adapting instruction

To meet the needs of different learners, **Discovering French, *Nouveau!*** presents French structures in several ways:

▶ Structures in context (in dialogues)—for those who learn best by hearing and repeating.

▶ Charts and brief explanations—for those who need to understand a pattern before practicing it.

▶ Cartoon drawings (where appropriate)—for those who find it helpful to visualize a concept in picture form.

ILS or ELLES?

The French have two ways of saying *they*:

- **ils** refers to two or more males or to a mixed group of males and females
- **elles** refers to two or more females

Ils sont à Paris.   Ils sont à Bordeaux.

Ils sont à Lyon.   Elles sont à Nice.

1 En France

PARLER/ÉCRIRE The following students are on vacation in France. Which cities are they in?

▶ Sophie … à Nice.   **Sophie est à Nice.**

1. Antoine … à Tours.
2. Nous … à Toulouse.
3. Vous … à Marseille.
4. Je … à Strasbourg.
5. Julie et Marie … à Lille.
6. Éric et Vincent … à Lyon.
7. Ma cousine … à Paris.
8. Tu … à Bordeaux.

VOCABULAIRE Où?

Où est Cécile?	*Where is Cécile?*		
Elle est …	**ici** *(here)*	**là** *(here, there)*	**là-bas** *(over there)*
	à Paris *(in Paris)*	**à** Boston	**à** Québec
	en classe *(in class)*	**en ville** *(in town)*	
	en vacances *(on vacation)*	**en** France *(in France)*	
	au café *(at the café)*	**au restaurant**	**au cinéma** *(at the movies)*
	à la maison *(at home)*		

2 À Tours

PARLER/ÉCRIRE You are spending your summer vacation in Tours at the home of your friend Léa. Ask the following people questions using **Tu es** or **Vous êtes** as appropriate.

▶ *(the mailman)* … français?   <u>Vous êtes</u> français?

1. *(Léa's mother)* … de Tours?
2. *(Léa's best friend)* … française?
3. *(Léa's brother)* … en vacances?
4. *(a lady in the park)* … française?
5. *(Léa's cousin)* … de Paris?
6. *(a little girl)* … avec ta mère?
7. *(Léa's teacher)* … strict?
8. *(a tourist)* … américain?

COMPREHENSION In France

PROPS: signs: Paris, Bordeaux, Lyon, Nice
Place signs dividing class into 4 "cities."

> **Voici Paris. Voici Bordeaux.** etc.

Ask in which city students are.

> **Où est X?** [À Bordeaux.]
> **Où sont Y et Z?** [À Paris.]

Then have students move around.

> **X, où es-tu?** [À Bordeaux.]
> **Lève-toi et va à Nice.**
> **Où es-tu maintenant?** [À Nice.] …
> **Y et Z, levez-vous et allez à Lyon.**
> **Où êtes-vous?** [À Lyon.] …

Optional, with full answers:

> **[Je suis à Nice.]**

If students ask The pronouns **il** and **elle** may also mean *it*.
Remind them that in **Invitation au français** they used sentences like:

> [le sandwich] **Il coûte 5 euros.**

Learning aid Always use **vous** with people you address as **Monsieur**, **Madame**, or **Mademoiselle**.

Teaching tip Use **Transparency 16** (Subject pronouns) as a visual aid to present and practice verb forms throughout this program.

1 PRACTICE saying where people are

1. Antoine <u>est</u> à Tours.
2. Nous <u>sommes</u> à Toulouse.
3. Vous <u>êtes</u> à Marseille.
4. Je <u>suis</u> à Strasbourg.
5. Julie et Marie <u>sont</u> à Lille.
6. Éric et Vincent <u>sont</u> à Lyon.
7. Ma cousine <u>est</u> à Paris.
8. Tu <u>es</u> à Bordeaux.

Middle School Copymasters

Worksheet 1: *Où?*, p. 37

2 COMPREHENSION using tu and vous

1. Vous êtes de Tours?
2. Tu es française?
3. Tu es en vacances?
4. Vous êtes française?
5. Tu es de Paris?
6. Tu es avec ta mère?
7. Vous êtes strict?
8. Vous êtes américain?

If students ask In French, the word for vacation (**les vacances**) is always plural.

Comprehension Variation Use places from the **Vocabulaire** section: en classe, au café, au cinéma, à la maison …

Teaching Resource Options

PRINT

Workbook PE, pp. 65–68
Unit 3 Resource Book
  Communipak, pp. 128–143
  Video Activities, p. 51
  Videoscript, p. 53
  Workbook TE, pp. 33–36

VIDEO PROGRAM

VIDÉO   DVD

MODULE 6

6.3 Mini-scenes: Où sont-ils?
(13:52–15:05 min.)

3 PRACTICE saying where people are

1. Oui, elle est à Lyon.
2. Oui, il est à San Francisco.
3. Oui, elles sont à la maison.
4. Oui, elles sont au café.
5. Oui, elle est en ville.
6. Oui, il est en vacances.
7. Oui, ils sont au cinéma.
8. Oui, ils sont à Montréal.

Variation Respond in the negative, naming another location of your choice.

– **Ta cousine est à Chicago?**
– **Non, elle est à Saint Louis (à Boston, etc.).**

4 EXCHANGES finding out where people are

– Où est ... ?

1. Daniel/Il est à Paris.
2. Caroline/Elle est au cinéma.
3. Jean-Louis/Il est au café.
4. Robert/Il est en classe (à l'école).
5. Florence/Elle est en vacances.
6. Hélène/Elle est au restaurant.
7. Julien/Il est en ville.

Challenge Have students imagine that they are with the people in Act. 4.
a) Statement: **Je suis avec Céline. Nous sommes à New York.**
b) Dialogue format: First teach the question **Où êtes-vous?**
  – **Je suis avec Céline.**
  – **Où êtes-vous?**
  – **Nous sommes à New York.**

---

3 *Où sont-ils?*

PARLER Corinne is wondering if some of the people she knows are in certain places. Tell her she is right, using **il, elle, ils,** or **elles** in your answers.

▶ Ta cousine est à Chicago?   **Oui, elle est à Chicago.**

1. Stéphanie est à Lyon?
2. Monsieur Thomas est à San Francisco?
3. Léa et Céline sont à la maison?
4. Cécile et Charlotte sont au café?
5. Ta soeur est en ville?
6. Ton cousin est en vacances?
7. Claire, Alice et Éric sont au cinéma?
8. Monsieur et Madame Joli sont à Montréal?

4  *Où?*

PARLER You want to know where certain people are. A classmate will answer you.

▶ —Où est Céline?
—Elle est à New York.

▶ Céline

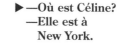
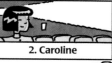

1. Daniel   2. Caroline   3. Jean-Louis

4. Robert   5. Florence   6. Hélène   7. Julien

B Les questions à réponse affirmative ou négative

The sentences on the left are statements. The sentences on the right are questions. These questions are called YES/NO QUESTIONS because they can be answered by *yes* or *no*. Note how the French questions begin with **est-ce que.**

STATEMENTS	YES/NO QUESTIONS	
Stéphanie est ici.	**Est-ce que** Stéphanie est ici?	*Is Stéphanie here?*
Tu es français.	**Est-ce que** tu es français?	*Are you French?*
Paul et Marc sont au café.	**Est-ce qu'**ils sont au café?	*Are they at the café?*
Tu veux jouer au foot.	**Est-ce que** tu veux jouer au foot?	*Do you want to play soccer?*

Yes/no questions can be formed according to the pattern:

est-ce que + STATEMENT?	**Est-ce que** Pierre est ici?
est-ce qu' (+ VOWEL SOUND)	**Est-ce qu'**il est en ville?

TEACHING NOTE Elision

The dropping of the final letter (usually "e") of a one-syllable word, as in **que → qu'**, is called ELISION.

Students have seen examples of elision already with **le, la → l'**. In this lesson they will also encounter **ne → n'** and **de → d'**. The term "elision" is not used in the student text. Note, however, that words which have an elision form will be pointed out in the appropriate grammar sections.

→ In yes/no questions, the voice goes up at the end of the sentence.

Est-ce que Paul et Florence sont au café?

→ In casual conversation, yes/no questions can be formed without **est-ce que** simply by letting your voice rise at the end of the sentence.

Tu es français?   Cécile est en ville?

Observation When you expect someone to agree with you, another way to form a yes/no question is to add the tag **n'est-ce pas** at the end of the sentence.

Tu es américain, **n'est-ce pas?**	*You are American, **aren't you?***
Tu aimes parler français, **n'est-ce pas?**	*You like to speak French, **don't you?***
Vous êtes d'accord, **n'est-ce pas?**	*You agree, **don't you?***

5 *Nationalités*

PARLER/ÉCRIRE You are attending an international music camp. Ask about other people's nationalities.

▶ Marc/canadien?   **Est-ce que Marc est canadien?**

1. Jim / américain?   **3.** Paul et Philippe / français?   **5.** vous / anglais?   **7.** Ellen et Carol / américaines?
2. Luisa / mexicaine?   **4.** tu / canadien?   **6.** Anne / française?

VOCABULAIRE **Expressions pour la conversation**

How to answer a yes/no question:

Oui!	*Yes!*	**Peut-être …**	*Maybe …*	**Non!**	*No!*
Mais oui!	*Sure!*			**Mais non!**	*Of course not!*
Bien sûr!	*Of course!*				

6 *Conversation*

PARLER Ask your classmates the following questions. They will answer, using an expression from **Expressions pour la conversation.**

▶ Ton cousin est français?

1. Ta mère est à la maison?
2. Ta cousine est en France?
3. Ton copain est en classe?
4. Tu veux manger une pizza avec moi?
5. Tu veux jouer aux jeux vidéo avec moi?

Alice, est-ce que ton cousin est français?

Mais oui! (Mais non!)

LANGUAGE COMPARISON

You may want to draw the students' attention to the fact that French uses only one tag question (**n'est-ce pas?**) whereas English has a very complex system of tags. Let students generate the following tags, and then reflect on how difficult it must be to learn tags in English.

you can	can't you?
he works	doesn't he?
she will	won't she?
they won't come	will they?
you understood	didn't you?

Communicative function
Asking questions

Language note Point out that **est-ce que** literally means *is it that?*

Pronunciation As in English, your voice goes up at the end of the tag.

5 **PRACTICE** asking questions about nationality

1. Est-ce que Jim est américain?
2. Est-ce que Luisa est mexicaine?
3. Est-ce que Paul et Philippe sont français?
4. Est-ce que tu es canadien (canadienne)?
5. Est-ce que vous êtes anglais(e/es)?
6. Est-ce qu'Anne est française?
7. Est-ce qu'Ellen et Carol sont américaines?

 Re-entry and review
Nationalities from Unit 1, Leçon 1B.

Challenge Answer each question affirmatively.
    – **Est-ce que Marc est canadien?**
    – **Oui, il est canadien.**

Note Help students differentiate between singular and plural in items 4 and 5:
    4. Oui, je suis …
    5. Oui, nous sommes …

Variation Formulate tag questions with **n'est-ce pas.**
    Marc est canadien, n'est-ce pas?

Supplementary vocabulary
Bien sûr que oui! *Why, of course!*
Bien sûr que non! *Why, of course not!*

6 **COMMUNICATION** asking personal questions

1. – (Diane), est-ce que ta mère est à la maison?
    – Mais oui! (Bien sûr! / Peut-être … / Mais non!)
2. – (Paul), est-ce que ta cousine est en France?
    – Mais oui! (Bien sûr! / Peut-être … / Mais non!)
3. – (Anne), est-ce que ton copain est en classe?
    – Mais oui! (Bien sûr! / Peut-être … / Mais non!)
4. – (Philippe), est-ce que tu veux manger une pizza avec moi?
    – Mais oui! (Bien sûr! / Peut-être … / Mais non!)
5. – (Marie), est-ce que tu veux jouer aux jeux vidéo avec moi?
    – Mais oui! (Bien sûr! / Peut-être … / Mais non!)

7 DESCRIPTION answering questions in the negative

1. Non, je ne suis pas canadien (canadienne).
2. Non, je ne suis pas à Québec.
3. Non, je ne suis pas à la maison.
4. Non, je ne suis pas au café.
5. Non, je ne suis pas en vacances.
6. Non, je ne suis pas au cinéma.

Expansion Continue your answer with a positive statement.
– Est-ce que tu es français?
– Non, je ne suis pas français(e).
  Je suis américain(e).

8 PRACTICE saying who does/doesn't agree

1. Nous sommes d'accord.
2. Je suis d'accord.
3. Tu n'es pas d'accord.
4. Vous n'êtes pas d'accord.
5. Patrick et Marc sont d'accord.
6. Claire et Stéphanie ne sont pas d'accord.
7. Ma copine est d'accord.
8. Mon frère n'est pas d'accord.

C La négation

Compare the affirmative and negative sentences below:

AFFIRMATIVE	NEGATIVE	
Je **suis** américain.	Je **ne suis pas** français.	*I'm not French.*
Nous **sommes** en classe.	Nous **ne sommes pas** en vacances.	*We are not on vacation.*
Claire **est** là-bas.	Elle **n'est pas** ici.	*She is not here.*
Tu **es** d'accord avec moi.	Tu **n'es pas** d'accord avec Marc.	*You do not agree with Marc.*

Negative sentences are formed as follows:

SUBJECT + **ne** + VERB + **pas**	Éric et Anne **ne** sont **pas** là.
n' (+ VOWEL SOUND)	Michèle **n'**est **pas** avec moi.

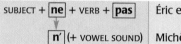

Nous sommes en ville.
Nous **ne** sommes **pas** à la maison.

7 Non!

PARLER Answer the following questions negatively.

▶ —Est-ce que tu es français (française)?
  —Non, je ne suis pas français (française).

1. Est-ce que tu es canadien (canadienne)?
2. Est-ce que tu es à Québec?
3. Est-ce que tu es à la maison?
4. Est-ce que tu es au café?
5. Est-ce que tu es en vacances?
6. Est-ce que tu es au cinéma?

8 D'accord

PARLER It is raining. François suggests to his friends that they go to the movies. Say who agrees and who does not, using the expression **être d'accord.**

▶ Philippe Philippe n'est pas d'accord.

▶ Hélène Hélène est d'accord.

1. nous
2. je
3. tu
4. vous
5. Patrick et Marc
6. Claire et Stéphanie
7. ma copine
8. mon frère

SPEAKING PRACTICE

PROP: Transparency 15: *Où sont-ils?* with names written in the boxes below each picture.

Point to the picture of the café.
  Qui est-ce? [C'est Sophie.]
  Est-ce que Sophie est au café?
  [Mais oui, elle est au café.]
Similarly introduce each picture.

Then practice negatives. Point to Sophie.
  Qui est-ce? C'est Marc?
  [Non, ce n'est pas Marc. C'est Sophie.]
  Est-ce que Sophie est en classe?
  [Non, elle n'est pas en classe.]
  Est-ce que Sophie est à la maison?
  [Mais non, elle n'est pas à la maison.]
  Où est Sophie? [Elle est au café.]

Language note You may wish to point out the spelling difference between **ou** *(or)* and **où** *(where)*:

Où est Juliette?
Au café <u>ou</u> au cinéma?

Cultural realia Ask your students:

– What event is taking place in Paris? [the national holiday]
– What is the date of this event? [Tuesday, July 14]
– **Quelle est la date de la Fête Nationale? [le mardi 14 juillet]**
– **À quelle heure est la fête? [À 22h.]**

VOCABULAIRE Mots utiles *(Useful words)*

à	*at*	Je suis **à** la maison **à** dix heures.
	in	Nous sommes **à** Paris.
de	*from*	Vous êtes **de** San Francisco.
	of	Voici une photo **de** Paris.
et	*and*	Anne **et** Sophie sont en vacances.
ou	*or*	Qui est-ce? Juliette **ou** Sophie?
avec	*with*	Philippe est **avec** Pauline.
pour	*for*	Je veux travailler **pour** Monsieur Martin.
mais	*but*	Je ne suis pas français, **mais** j'aime parler français.

→ **De** becomes **d'** before a vowel sound:
   Patrick est **de** Lyon.   François est **d'**Annecy.

Fête Nationale
mardi 14 juillet
à 22h

P A R I S

---

9 **Le mot juste** *(The right word)*

PARLER/ÉCRIRE Complete each sentence with the word in parentheses that fits logically.

1. Monsieur Moreau est en France. Aujourd'hui, il est … Lyon. (à/de)
2. Martine est canadienne. Elle est … Montréal. (de/et)
3. Florence n'est pas ici. Elle est … Jean-Claude. (et/avec)
4. Léa … Paul sont en ville. (avec/et)
5. Jean-Pierre n'est pas à la maison. Il est au café … au cinéma. (ou/et)
6. J'aime jouer au tennis … je ne veux pas jouer avec toi. (ou/mais)
7. Je travaille … mon père. (pour/à)

10 **Être ou ne pas être**

PARLER/ÉCRIRE We cannot be in different places at the same time. Express this according to the model.

▶ Aline est en ville. (ici)
  Aline n'est pas ici.

1. Frédéric est là-bas. (à la maison)
2. Nous sommes en classe. (au restaurant)
3. Tu es à Nice. (à Tours)
4. Vous êtes au café. (au cinéma)
5. Jean est avec Sylvie. (avec Julie)
6. Juliette et Sophie sont avec Éric. (avec Marc)

9 **COMPREHENSION** choosing prepositions and conjunctions

1. Monsieur Moreau est en France. Aujourd'hui, il est <u>à</u> Lyon.
2. Martine est canadienne. Elle est <u>de</u> Montréal.
3. Florence n'est pas ici. Elle est <u>avec</u> Jean-Claude.
4. Léa <u>et</u> Paul sont en ville.
5. Jean-Pierre n'est pas à la maison. Il est au café <u>ou</u> au cinéma.
6. J'aime jouer au tennis <u>mais</u> je ne veux pas jouer avec toi.
7. Je travaille <u>pour</u> mon père.

10 **DESCRIPTION** saying where people are not

1. Frédéric n'est pas à la maison.
2. Nous ne sommes pas au restaurant.
3. Tu n'es pas à Tours.
4. Vous n'êtes pas au cinéma.
5. Jean n'est pas avec Julie.
6. Juliette et Sophie ne sont pas avec Marc.

PRONONCIATION   /a/

La voyelle /a/

The letter "**a**" alone always represents the sound /a/ as in the English word *ah*. It never has the sound of "*a*" as in English words like *cl<u>a</u>ss, d<u>a</u>te,* or *cinem<u>a</u>.*

Répétez: ch<u>a</u>t   <u>ç</u><u>a</u> v<u>a</u>   <u>à</u> l<u>a</u>   l<u>à</u>-b<u>a</u>s   <u>a</u>vec   <u>a</u>mi   voil<u>à</u>
          cl<u>a</u>sse   café   s<u>a</u>l<u>a</u>de   d<u>a</u>me   d<u>a</u>te   M<u>a</u>d<u>a</u>me   C<u>a</u>n<u>a</u>d<u>a</u>

<u>A</u>nne est au C<u>a</u>n<u>a</u>d<u>a</u> <u>a</u>vec M<u>a</u>d<u>a</u>me L<u>a</u>v<u>a</u>l.

chat

LISTENING GAME Une invitation

Prepare a cloze version of the video script of **Une invitation** with selected words deleted.

Play the video dialogue.

Divide the class into teams of three and distribute one script to each team.

The teams all try to fill in as many missing words as they can remember.

Replay the video, pausing after each sentence so that the teams can try to complete their texts.

Have teams exchange and correct their scripts. The team with the most correct completions is the winner.

À votre tour!

① 🎧 👥 Allô!

PARLER Jacques is phoning some friends. Match his questions on the left with his friends' answers on the right.

1. Où es-tu?
2. Où est ta soeur?
3. Est-ce que ton frère est à la maison?
4. Tes parents sont en vacances, n'est-ce pas?
5. Ta soeur est avec une copine?

a. Non, il est au cinéma.
b. Oui, elles sont au restaurant.
c. Je suis à la maison.
d. Elle est en classe.
e. Oui! Ils sont à Paris.

② Où sont-ils?

LIRE Read what the following people are saying and decide where they are.

▶ Anne et Éric sont au café.

Une limonade, s'il vous plaît.
▶ Anne et Éric

Le film est génial (great).
1. nous

Où est le musée (museum)?
2. les touristes

Une pizza, s'il vous plaît.
3. vous

Bonjour, maman.
4. tu

Aujourd'hui, c'est le jour de l'examen!
5. Valérie

3 *Créa-dialogue*

PARLER You are working for a student magazine in France. Your assignment is to interview tourists who are visiting Paris. Ask them where they are from. (Make sure to address the people appropriately as **tu** or **vous**.) Remember: The symbol "??" means you may invent your own responses.

Nationalité	Villes *(Cities)*	
anglaise	Londres? *(London)* Liverpool	

▶ —Bonjour. <u>Vous êtes anglaise</u>?
—Oui, je suis <u>anglaise</u>.
—Est-ce que <u>vous êtes</u> de <u>Londres</u>?
—Mais non, je ne suis pas de <u>Londres</u>. Je suis de <u>Liverpool</u>.

Nationalité	Villes	
1 américaine	New York? Washington	
2 canadien	Québec? Montréal	
3 française	Paris? Nice	
4 mexicain	Mexico? Puebla	
5 ??	?? ??	
6 ??	?? ??	

4 *Composition: Personnellement*

ÉCRIRE On a separate piece of paper, or on a computer, write where you are and where you are not at each of the following times. Use only words you know.

▶ à 9 heures du matin

- à 4 heures
- à 7 heures du soir
- samedi
- dimanche
- en juillet

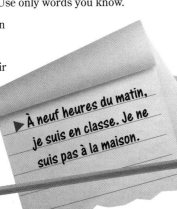

À neuf heures du matin, je suis en classe. Je ne suis pas à la maison.

À neuf heures du matin, je suis en classe. Je ne suis pas à la maison.

LESSON REVIEW
CLASSZONE.COM

Leçon 6 91

---

3 **GUIDED ORAL EXPRESSION**

1. – Bonjour. Vous êtes américaine?
   – Oui, je suis américaine.
   – Est-ce que vous êtes de New York?
   – Mais non, je ne suis pas de New York. Je suis de Washington.
2. – Bonjour. (Salut!) Tu es canadien?
   – Oui, je suis canadien.
   – Est-ce que tu es de Québec?
   – Mais non, je ne suis pas de Québec. Je suis de Montréal.
3. – Bonjour. (Salut!) Tu es française?
   – Oui, je suis française.
   – Est-ce que tu es de Paris?
   – Mais non, je ne suis pas de Paris. Je suis de Nice.
4. – Bonjour. Vous êtes mexicain?
   – Oui, je suis mexicain.
   – Est-ce que vous êtes de Mexico?
   – Mais non, je ne suis pas de Mexico. Je suis de Puebla.
5. – Bonjour. (Salut!) Tu es (française)?
   – Oui, je suis (française).
   – Est-ce que tu es de (Bordeaux)?
   – Mais non, je ne suis pas de (Bordeaux). Je suis de (Marseille).
6. – Bonjour. Vous êtes (anglais)?
   – Oui, je suis (anglais).
   – Est-ce que vous êtes de (Manchester)?
   – Mais non, je ne suis pas de (Manchester). Je suis de (Londres).

4 **WRITTEN SELF-EXPRESSION**

Answers will vary.
- À 4 heures, je suis (au café). Je ne suis pas (au restaurant).
- À 7 heures du soir, je suis (au cinéma). Je ne suis pas (au café).
- Samedi, je suis (à Paris). Je ne suis pas (à Nice).
- Dimanche, je suis (à la maison). Je ne suis pas (en ville).
- En juillet, je suis (en vacances). Je ne suis pas (en classe).

> **Middle School Copymasters**
>
> Conversation 1: *Un examen? Oh zut!;* Conversation 2: *Andrée n'aime pas étudier.,* p. 34

PORTFOLIO ASSESSMENT

You will probably select only one speaking activity and one writing activity to go into the students' portfolios for Unit 3.

In this lesson, Act. 3 lends itself well to an oral portfolio recording. Act. 4 is a good writing portfolio topic. (Encourage your students to invent their own responses as in items 5 and 6 in Act. 3.)

Unité 3 Leçon 6 • **91**

Leçon 7

Main Topic Talking about one's activities

Teaching Resource Options

PRINT

Workbook PE, pp. 69–74
Activités pour tous PE, pp. 39–41
Block Scheduling Copymasters, pp. 49–55
Unit 3 Resource Book
  Activités pour tous TE, pp. 67–69
  Audioscript, pp. 87, 88–89
  Communipak, pp. 128–143
  Lesson Plans, pp. 70–71
  Block Scheduling Lesson Plans, pp. 72–73
  Absent Student Copymasters, pp. 74–78
  Video Activities, pp. 81–84
  Videoscript, pp. 85–86
  Workbook TE, pp. 61–66

AUDIO & VISUAL

Audio Program
CD 2 Tracks 11, 12
CD 7 Tracks 12–17

TECHNOLOGY

Online Workbook

VIDEO PROGRAM

VIDÉO   DVD

 MODULE 7
Une boum

TOTAL TIME: 4:38 min.
  DVD Disk 1
  Videotape 2 (COUNTER: 16:53 min.)

7.1 Mini-scenes: Listening
  – J'étudie (17:15–18:06 min.)

7.2 Mini-scenes: Listening
  – Tu téléphones? (18:07–18:41 min.)

7.3 Mini-scenes: Speaking
  – Est-ce qu'il travaille?
  (18:42–19:45 min.)

7.4 Dialogue: Jean-Paul à la boum
  (19:46–20:38 min.)

7.5 Vignette culturelle: Une boum
  (20:39–21:31 min.)

Compréhension: Vrai ou faux Answers
1. C'est vrai!
2. C'est vrai!
3. C'est faux! (Elle ne danse pas très bien.)
4. C'est faux! (Il ne sait pas danser.)
5. C'est vrai!
6. C'est vrai!

92 • **Conversation et Culture**
Unité 3 LEÇON 7

LEÇON 7

Conversation et Culture

Une boum AUDIO

Jean-Marc has been invited to a party. He is trying to decide whether to bring Béatrice or Valérie.

Jean-Marc:	<u>Dis</u>, Béatrice, tu aimes danser?	*Hey*
Béatrice:	Oui, j'adore danser. Je danse très, <u>très bien</u>.	*very well*
Jean-Marc:	Et toi, Valérie, tu danses bien?	
Valérie:	Non, je ne danse pas très bien.	
Jean-Marc:	Est-ce que tu veux <u>aller</u> à une boum avec moi samedi?	*to go*
Valérie:	Oui, d'accord, mais <u>pourquoi</u> est-ce que tu n'invites pas Béatrice? Elle adore danser …	*why*
Jean-Marc:	Oui, mais moi, <u>je ne sais pas</u> danser et je ne veux pas être <u>ridicule</u> …	*don't know how* *ridiculous*
Béatrice:	Écoute. <u>Entre</u> copains, <u>on n'est jamais</u> ridicule.	*Among / one is never*
Jean-Marc:	C'est vrai! <u>Alors</u>, je <u>vous invite toutes les deux</u>!	*Then / invite both of you*
Béatrice:	Super!	

Compréhension: Vrai ou faux?

Say whether the following statements are true **(C'est vrai!)** or false **(C'est faux!).**

1. Béatrice aime danser.
2. Elle danse bien.
3. Valérie danse très bien.
4. Jean-Marc adore danser.
5. Jean-Marc ne veut pas être ridicule.
6. Jean-Marc invite Béatrice et Valérie.

92 quatre-vingt-douze
Unité 3

SETTING THE STAGE

Ask students if they organize informal parties at home for their friends.

  What do they serve to eat and drink?

  What do they do? Talk? Dance? Sing?

Tell them that in this lesson they will learn about French parties.

Comprehension practice Play the entire module through as an introduction to the lesson.

NOTE culturelle

Une boum

On weekends, French teenagers like to go to parties that are organized at a friend's home. These informal parties have different names according to the age group of the participants. For students at a **collège** (middle school), a party is sometimes known as **une boum** or **une fête.** For older students at a **lycée** (high school), it is called **une soirée.**

At a **boum**, parents are usually around to help out and set up a buffet which often features items contributed by the guests. Pizza and chips are very popular. There may also be homemade sandwiches or Chinese food. Preferred beverages are sodas and mineral waters.

Most of the young people like to dance and listen to their favorite music. Some may get drawn into the latest video games. Others simply enjoy getting together to talk about the week's events. For everyone, it is a way to spend a relaxing evening with friends.

COMPARAISONS CULTURELLES

How do French parties compare to parties that you and your friends organize? Explain.

quatre-vingt-treize
Leçon 7 93

CROSS-CULTURAL UNDERSTANDING

Have students watch the video (or look at the above photographs).

What kinds of similarities and differences do they notice between parties in France and parties that they go to?

A Les verbes en *-er:* le singulier

The basic form of a verb is called the infinitive. Many French infinitives end in **-er**. Most of these verbs are conjugated like **parler** *(to speak)* and **habiter** *(to live)*. Note the forms of the present tense of these verbs in the singular. Pay attention to their endings.

INFINITIVE	parler	habiter	ENDINGS
STEM	parl-	habit-	
PRESENT TENSE (SINGULAR)	Je **parle** français. Tu **parles** anglais. Il/Elle **parle** espagnol.	J' **habite** à Paris. Tu **habites** à Boston. Il/Elle **habite** à Madrid.	-e -es -e

The present tense forms of **-er** verbs consist of two parts:

> STEM + ENDING

• The STEM does not change. It is the infinitive minus **-er**:

  parler **parl-** habiter **habit-**

• The ENDINGS change with the subject:

  je → **-e** tu → **-es** il/elle → **-e**

→ The above endings are silent.
→ **Je** becomes **j'** before a vowel sound.

  je parle **j'**habite

1   Curiosité

PARLER At the party, Olivier wants to learn more about Isabelle. She answers his questions affirmatively. Play both roles.

Tu parles anglais?

Oui, je parle anglais.

▶ parler anglais?

1. parler espagnol?
2. habiter à Paris?
3. danser bien?
4. jouer aux jeux vidéo?
5. jouer au basket?
6. chanter?
7. téléphoner à ton copain?
8. travailler en été?

CRITICAL THINKING ABOUT LANGUAGE

In this lesson, students are encouraged to think about how verbs work in French.

In Section A, they will learn the singular forms, which sound the same, but which are not all spelled the same.

In Section B, they will learn the plural forms with their endings, and notice how liaison helps link subject and verb together.

Finally in Section C, they will see the complete verb charts with both affirmative and negative forms. They will learn what a paradigm for regular verbs looks like, and how it can serve as a model.

VOCABULAIRE Les verbes en *-er*

▶ **Verbs you already know:**

chanter	*to sing*	nager	*to swim*
danser	*to dance*	parler	*to speak, talk*
dîner	*to have dinner*	regarder	*to watch, look at*
écouter	*to listen (to)*	téléphoner (à)	*to phone, call*
étudier	*to study*	travailler	*to work*
jouer	*to play*	voyager	*to travel*
manger	*to eat*		

▶ **New verbs:**

aimer	*to like*	Tu **aimes** Paris?
habiter (à)	*to live (in + city)*	Philippe **habite** à Toulouse?
inviter	*to invite*	J'**invite** un copain.
organiser	*to organize*	Sophie **organise** une **boum**/ une **soirée**/une **fête** *(party)*.
visiter	*to visit (places)*	Céline **visite** Québec.

➜ **Regarder** has two meanings:

to look (at)	Paul **regarde** Cécile.
to watch	Cécile **regarde** la télé.

➜ Note the construction **téléphoner à:**

Céline **téléphone**	**à**	Marc.
Céline calls	...	*Marc.*

Danser

➜ Note the constructions with **regarder** *(to look at)* and **écouter** *(to listen to)*:

Philippe **regarde**	...	Alice.
Philippe looks	*at*	*Alice.*

Alice **écoute**	...	le professeur.
Alice listens	*to*	*the teacher.*

2 Quelle activité?

PARLER/ÉCRIRE Describe what the following people are doing by completing the sentences with one of the verbs below. Be logical.

chanter écouter travailler voyager inviter
parler manger regarder habiter

1. Je ... un sandwich. Tu ... une pizza.
2. Tu ... anglais. Je ... français.
3. Éric ... la radio. Claire ... un CD.
4. Jean-Paul ... la télé. Tu ... un match de tennis.
5. M. Simon ... en *(by)* bus. Mme Dupont ... en train.
6. Nicolas ... Marie à la boum. Tu ... Alain.
7. Mlle Thomas ... dans *(in)* un hôpital. Je ... dans un supermarché *(supermarket)*.
8. La chorale *(choir)* ... bien. Est-ce que tu ... bien?
9. Tu ... en France. Aya ... en Afrique.

quatre-vingt-quinze **Leçon 7** 95

Teaching Tip You may point out that in French dictionaries, verbs are listed in the infinitive form.

Pronunciation You may want to point out that the singular forms of **-er** verbs all sound the same. There is a difference in spelling in the **tu-** form.

Language comparison English has many two-word verbs. Usually these two-word verbs are expressed in one word in French.

to look at	**regarder**
to look for	**chercher**
to listen to	**écouter**

Have students try to think of other English two-word verbs. (E.g., to look after, to look into, to look up; to go after, to go over, etc.)

1 ROLE PLAY getting acquainted

1. – Tu parles espagnol?
   – Oui, je parle espagnol.
2. – Tu habites à Paris?
   – Oui, j'habite à Paris.
3. – Tu danses bien?
   – Oui, je danse bien.
4. – Tu joues aux jeux vidéo?
   – Oui, je joue aux jeux vidéo.
5. – Tu joues au basket?
   – Oui, je joue au basket.
6. – Tu chantes?
   – Oui, je chante.
7. – Tu téléphones à ton copain?
   – Oui, je téléphone à mon copain.
8. – Tu travailles en été?
   – Oui, je travaille en été.

2 COMPREHENSION saying what people are doing

1. Je mange un sandwich. Tu manges une pizza.
2. Tu parles anglais. Je parle français.
3. Éric écoute la radio. Claire écoute un CD.
4. Jean-Paul regarde la télé. Tu regardes un match de tennis.
5. M. Simon voyage en bus. Mme Dupont voyage en train.
6. Nicolas invite Marie à la boum. Tu invites Alain.
7. Mlle Thomas travaille dans un hôpital. Je travaille dans un supermarché.
8. La chorale chante bien. Est-ce que tu chantes bien?
9. Tu habites en France. Aya habite en Afrique.

3 **DESCRIPTION** describing what people are doing

1. Monsieur Dupin regarde la télé.
2. Madame Ménard écoute la radio.
3. Patrick étudie.
4. Florence chante.
5. Coco parle.

4 **EXCHANGES** discussing where people are

1. – Où est Pauline?
  – Elle est au restaurant. Elle dîne.
2. – Où est Véronique?
  – Elle est à la maison. Elle téléphone.
3. – Où est Madame Dupont?
  – Elle est en ville. Elle travaille.
4. – Où est Monsieur Lemaire?
  – Il est en France. Il voyage.
5. – Où est Léa?
  – Elle est à Paris. Elle visite la tour Eiffel.
6. – Où est André?
  – Il est au stade. Il joue au foot.
7. – Où est Alice?
  – Elle est à l'Olympic Club. Elle nage.

Variation Divide the class into three sections: A, B, C. Elicit part-choral or individual responses from the students in each section.
A: Où est Jacques?
B: Il est en classe.
C: Il étudie.

Pronunciation Note that **il parle** and **ils parlent** sound the same.

Language notes

• The "e" is inserted to keep the soft "g" sound.
• This spelling change is presented mainly for recognition.

---

3 **Les voisins** *(The neighbors)*

PARLER/ÉCRIRE Simon is explaining what his neighbors are doing. Describe each person's activity.

▶ **Madame Dumas téléphone.**

| Mme Dumas | 1 M. Dupin | 2 Mme Ménard |
| 3 Patrick | 4 Florence | 5 Coco |

4   **Où sont-ils?**

PARLER You want to know where the following people are. A classmate tells you and says what they are doing.

▶ Jacques? (en classe/étudier)

Où est Jacques?

Il est en classe. Il étudie.

1. Pauline? (au restaurant/dîner)
2. Véronique? (à la maison/téléphoner)
3. Mme Dupont? (en ville/travailler)
4. M. Lemaire? (en France/voyager)
5. Léa? (à Paris/visiter la tour Eiffel)
6. André? (au stade/jouer au foot)
7. Alice? (à l'Olympic Club/nager)

B **Les verbes en -*er*: le pluriel**

Note the plural forms of **parler** and **habiter**, paying attention to the endings.

INFINITIVE	parler	habiter	ENDINGS
STEM	parl-	habit-	
PRESENT TENSE (PLURAL)	Nous **parlons** français. Vous **parlez** anglais. Ils/Elles **parlent** espagnol.	Nous **habitons** à Québec. Vous **habitez** à Chicago. Ils/Elles **habitent** à Caracas.	-ons -ez -ent

→ In the present tense, the plural endings of **-er** verbs are:

  nous → **-ons**   vous → **-ez**   ils / elles → **-ent**

→ The **-ent** ending is silent.

→ Note the liaison when the verb begins with a vowel sound:

  Nous étudions.   Vous invitez Thomas.   Ils habitent en France.   Elles aiment Paris.

Observation When the infinitive of the verb ends in **-ger**, the **nous** form ends in **-geons**.

  nager: nous na**geons**   **manger:** nous man**geons**   **voyager:** nous voya**geons**

COMPREHENSION Subject pronouns

Teach students gestures for each pronoun.
  Montrez-moi "je". [point to self]
  Montrez-moi "tu". [point straight ahead, somewhat down, as if to a child]
  Montrez-moi "il" ou "elle" [stretch one arm out to the side, hand open]
Add: **"nous"** [both hands point to self]

  "vous" [both hands point straight ahead]
  "ils/elles" [both arms stretched to side]
Have students identify subjects.
  Nous organisons une boum. ["nous"]
The subjects **il(s)/elle(s)** may be ambiguous.
  Il(s) joue(nt) au tennis. ["il" or "ils"]
Clarify: **Pierre joue au tennis. ["il"]**

5 Qui?

PARLER/ÉCRIRE Élodie is speaking to or about her friends. Complete her sentences with **tu, elle, vous,** or **ils.**

▶ … étudient à Toulouse.
   Ils étudient à Toulouse.

1. … habitez à Tours.
2. … joue aux jeux vidéo.
3. … étudiez à Bordeaux.
4. … aiment danser.
5. … organisent une boum.
6. … parlez espagnol.
7. … téléphone à Jean-Pierre.
8. … invites un copain.
9. … dîne avec Cécile.
10. … invitent Monique.

6 À la boum

PARLER At a party, Olivier is talking to two Canadian students, Monique and her friend. Monique answers yes to his questions.

▶ parler français?

Vous parlez français, n'est-ce pas?

Oui, nous parlons français.

1. parler anglais?
2. habiter à Québec?
3. étudier à Montréal?
4. voyager en France?
5. voyager en train?
6. visiter Paris?
7. aimer Paris?
8. aimer la France?

7 En colonie de vacances (At summer camp)

PARLER/ÉCRIRE Describe the activities of the following campers by completing the sentences.

▶ À cinq heures, Alice et Marc …   **À cinq heures, Alice et Marc jouent au foot.**

▶

1. À neuf heures, nous …
2. À quatre heures, vous …
3. À huit heures, Véronique et Pierre …
4. À sept heures, nous …
5. À trois heures, Thomas et François …
6. À six heures, vous …

8 Un voyage à Paris

PARLER/ÉCRIRE A group of American students is visiting Paris. During their stay, they do all of the following things:

voyager en bus	téléphoner à un copain	inviter une copine
visiter la tour Eiffel	dîner au restaurant	parler français

Describe the trips of the following people.

▶ Jim   **Il voyage en bus, il visite la tour Eiffel …**

1. Linda   2. Paul et Louise   3. nous   4. vous   5. Jen et Sarah

quatre-vingt-dix-sept
Leçon 7 97

---

5 PRACTICE selecting subject pronouns

1. Vous   5. Ils   9. Elle
2. Elle   6. Vous   10. Ils
3. Vous   7. Elle
4. Ils   8. Tu

Be sure students make the liaison in 1, 3, 4, 5, and 10.

6 ROLE PLAY getting to know people

– Vous …, n'est-ce pas?
– Oui, nous …

1. – parlez/parlons anglais
2. – habitez/habitons à Québec
3. – étudiez/étudions à Montréal
4. – voyagez/voyageons en France
5. – voyagez/voyageons en train
6. – visitez/visitons Paris
7. – aimez/aimons Paris
8. – aimez/aimons la France

Variation Ask questions with **est-ce que**; respond with **bien sûr.**
– **Est-ce que vous parlez français?**
– **Bien sûr, nous parlons français.**

7 COMPREHENSION describing what people do at various times of day

1. téléphonons   4. dînons
2. jouez au tennis   5. jouent au basket
3. regardent la télé   6. nagez

♻ **Re-entry and review**
Before doing this exercise you may want to review telling time (Unit 2, Leçon 4A).

8 PRACTICE describing activities on a trip

1. Elle voyage en bus. Elle visite la tour Eiffel. Elle téléphone à un copain. Elle dîne au restaurant. Elle invite une copine. Elle parle français.
2. Ils voyagent en bus. Ils visitent la tour Eiffel. Ils téléphonent à un copain. Ils dînent au restaurant. Ils invitent une copine. Ils parlent français.
3. Nous voyageons en bus. Nous visitons la tour Eiffel. Nous téléphonons à un copain. Nous dînons au restaurant. Nous invitons une copine. Nous parlons français.
4. Vous voyagez en bus. Vous visitez la tour Eiffel. Vous téléphonez à un copain. Vous dînez au restaurant. Vous invitez une copine. Vous parlez français.
5. Elles voyagent en bus. Elles visitent la tour Eiffel. Elles téléphonent à un copain. Elles dînent au restaurant. Elles invitent une copine. Elles parlent français.

CLASSROOM MANAGEMENT Writing Practice

Act. 8 lends itself to pair and group writing practice. First go through the entire model paragraph with the whole class.

Then group students in pairs and assign each pair a number (1, 2, 3, or 4). Each pair then writes out the paragraph corresponding to its number. When all are done, have each pair pass its paper to the next pair.

The pairs then read and check the new paragraph they have received. (For example, pair 2 passes its paper to pair 3 and reads the paper it receives from pair 1.)

Pronunciation bus /bys/

SECTION C

Communicative function
Describing what people do and don't do

Teaching Resource Options

PRINT

Workbook PE, pp. 69–74
Unit 3 Resource Book
   Audioscript, p. 87
   Communipak, pp. 128–143
   Video Activities, p. 82
   Videoscript, p. 85
   Workbook TE, pp. 61–66

AUDIO & VISUAL

Audio Program
CD 2 Track 13

Overhead Transparencies
16 Subject Pronouns

TECHNOLOGY

Power Presentations

VIDEO PROGRAM

VIDÉO   DVD
 MODULE 7

7.3 Mini-scenes: Est-ce qu'il travaille? (18:42–19:45 min.)

Teaching tip You can make large subject pronoun flashcards by projecting the drawings from the transparency onto heavy paper and tracing the outlines with markers. If desired, you can label each drawing with the corresponding pronoun. Use these cards throughout the program to practice verb forms.

Language note Be sure students notice that the one word **parle** in French may correspond to two words in English:

is speaking, does speak.

Point out that **is** corresponds to **est** only when it represents the main verb.

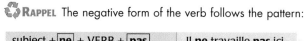

C Le présent des verbes en -er: forme affirmative et forme négative

Compare the affirmative and negative forms of **parler.**

AFFIRMATIVE	NEGATIVE
Je **parle**	je **ne parle pas**
tu **parles**	tu **ne parles pas**
il/elle **parle**	il/elle **ne parle pas**
nous **parlons**	nous **ne parlons pas**
vous **parlez**	vous **ne parlez pas**
ils/elles **parlent**	ils/elles **ne parlent pas**

 **RAPPEL** The negative form of the verb follows the pattern:

subject + **ne** + VERB + **pas**	Il **ne** travaille **pas** ici.
n' (+ VOWEL SOUND)	Je **n'**invite **pas** Pierre.

Il **ne** travaille **pas**.

Ils **n'**écoutent **pas**.

Elle **ne** chante **pas** bien.

LANGUAGE COMPARISONS

English has several verb forms for expressing actions in the present.
In French there is only one form. Compare:

Je **joue** au tennis.
{ *I play* tennis.
{ *I do play* tennis.
{ *I am playing* tennis.

Je **ne joue pas** au tennis.
{ *I do not play* tennis. (*I don't play* tennis.)
{ *I am not playing* tennis. (*I'm not playing* tennis.)

TEACHING NOTE Verb endings

Use Transparency 16: Subject pronouns to help students learn to spell the verb endings and say the forms. First have the students identify the pronoun cartoons (**je, tu, ...**).

With a washable transparency marker, write the forms of **dîner** below each picture.

With a second color, box the endings.

Have students read the verbs aloud, first in sequence (**je dîne, tu dînes, ...**) and then randomly as you point to them (**nous dînons, elle dîne, ...**).

Erase the forms of **dîner.** Have volunteers come write the forms of other verbs.

9 Non!

PARLER One cannot do everything. From the following list of activities, select at least three that you do *not* do.

▶ **Je ne joue pas au bridge.**

parler espagnol

parler italien

danser le tango

jouer au hockey

jouer au water-polo

jouer au bridge

étudier à Paris

habiter à Québec

étudier le japonais

nager en hiver

dîner avec le prof

travailler dans un restaurant

10 Écoutez bien!

STRATEGY Listening

Negative sentences To know if a sentence is negative, listen for the word **pas** immediately after the verb.

ÉCOUTER You will hear French young people tell you what they do and do not do. Listen carefully to what they each say and determine if they do the following activities.

▶ Marc: jouer au foot?
Non. Marc ne joue pas au foot.

1. Sophie: parler espagnol?
2. Vincent: habiter à Tours?
3. Mélanie: dîner à la maison?
4. Nicolas: téléphoner à un copain?
5. Julie: manger une pizza?
6. Jean: étudier l'anglais?
7. Marie: écouter un CD?

11 Un jeu: Week-end!

PARLER/ÉCRIRE On weekends, people like to do different things. For each person, pick an activity and say what that person does. Select another activity and say what that person does not do.

▶ Antoine et Isabelle
**Antoine et Isabelle dansent.
Ils ne regardent pas la télé.**

1. je
2. tu
3. ma cousine
4. nous
5. Nicolas et Élodie
6. Madame Jolivet
7. vous
8. le professeur

GAME Week-end!

You can treat Act. 11 as a game. Divide the class into teams of three. Each team picks a person from the list and decides what that subject is doing and not doing. All three team members must write the same two sentences correctly.

Then the team chooses another subject plus two other activities. All three write down the next two sentences.

The game is played against the clock. For example, you may set a 5-minute time limit. The team whose three members have written the greatest number of correct sentences in that time is the winner.

9 COMMUNICATION stating activities that one does not do

Answers will vary.
Je ne parle pas (espagnol, italien).
Je ne danse pas le tango.
Je ne joue pas au (hockey, water-polo, bridge).
Je n'étudie pas (à Paris, le japonais).
Je n'habite pas à Québec.
Je ne nage pas en hiver.
Je ne dîne pas avec le prof.
Je ne travaille pas dans un restaurant.

Pair Practice
• Use the cues as the basis of a poll.
• Divide the class into pairs, and have students interview one another to discover what their partners do and do not do.
  – Tu joues au bridge?
  – Oui, je joue au bridge.
    (Non, je ne joue pas au bridge.)

Variation Use other subjects: **nous, tu, mon copain, ma copine.**

10 PRACTICE saying what people are not doing today

1. Non. Sophie ne parle pas espagnol.
2. Non. Vincent n'habite pas à Tours.
3. Oui. Mélanie dîne à la maison.
4. Oui. Nicolas téléphone à un copain.
5. Non. Julie ne mange pas de pizza.
6. Non. Jean n'étudie pas l'anglais.
7. Oui. Marie écoute un CD.

Teaching Suggestion First play the recording for this activity and have students respond with "**oui**" or "**non**". Then, play the recording again, pausing after each cue so that students can reply with a full sentence.

Teaching Note Number 5 requires "pas de," which the students have not yet learned. You may want to mention it in passing.

11 COMPREHENSION stating what people do and don't do

Answers will vary.
1. Je danse. Je ne dîne pas au restaurant.
2. Tu écoutes la radio. Tu ne regardes pas la télé.
3. Ma cousine joue aux jeux vidéo. Elle ne danse pas.
4. Nous étudions. Nous ne nageons pas.
5. Nicolas et Élodie regardent la télé. Ils ne jouent pas au basket.
6. Madame Jolivet travaille. Elle n'écoute pas la radio.
7. Vous jouez au basket. Vous ne nagez pas.
8. Le professeur nage. Il (Elle) ne travaille pas.

Teaching Resource Options

PRINT

Workbook PE, pp 69–74
Unit 3 Resource Book
  Audioscript, p. 87
  Communipak, pp. 128–143
  Video Activities, p. 83
  Videoscript, pp. 85–86
  Workbook TE, pp. 61–66

AUDIO & VISUAL

Audio Program
CD 2 Track 14

TECHNOLOGY

Power Presentations

VIDEO PROGRAM

VIDÉO DVD **MODULE 7**

7.4 Mini-scenes: Jean-Paul à la boum (19:46–20:38 min)

12 COMMUNICATION describing how well or often one does things

Answers will vary.
1. mal (bien, très bien, souvent, toujours, rarement, un peu, beaucoup)
2. bien (mal, très bien, souvent, toujours, rarement, un peu, beaucoup)
3. souvent (toujours, rarement, un peu, beaucoup)
4. beaucoup (bien, mal, très bien, souvent, toujours, rarement, un peu)
5. rarement (souvent, toujours, beaucoup)
6. très bien (bien, souvent, toujours, rarement)
7. un peu (toujours, souvent, rarement)
8. un peu (toujours, souvent, rarement)
9. bien (très bien, toujours, beaucoup)

13 COMMUNICATION expressing approval or regret

– Est-ce que tu … ?
– Oui, je … (Non, je ne … pas …)
– Super! (Dommage!)

1. parles/parle/ne parle pas (espagnol)
2. joues/joue/ne joue pas (au basket)
3. chantes/chante/ne chante pas (bien)
4. voyages/voyage/ne voyage pas (beaucoup)
5. dînes/dîne/ne dîne pas (au restaurant)
6. invites souvent ton copain/invite mon copain/n'invite pas mon copain

Variation Address two or more students.
– **Est-ce que vous chantez?**
– **Oui, nous aimons chanter.**
  (Non, nous n'aimons pas chanter.)

100 · Langue et Communication
Unité 3 LEÇON 7

VOCABULAIRE Mots utiles

bien	well	Je joue **bien** au tennis.
très bien	very well	Je ne chante pas **très bien**.
mal	badly, poorly	Tu joues **mal** au volley.
beaucoup	a lot, much, very much	Paul aime **beaucoup** voyager.
un peu	a little, a little bit	Nous parlons **un peu** français.
souvent	often	Thomas joue **souvent** aux jeux vidéo.
toujours	always	Charlotte travaille **toujours** en été.
aussi	also, too	Je téléphone à Marc. Je téléphone **aussi** à Véronique.
maintenant	now	J'étudie **maintenant**.
rarement	rarely, seldom	Vous voyagez **rarement**.

→ In French, the above expressions *never* come *between* the subject and the verb. They usually come *after* the verb. Compare their positions in French and English.

Nous parlons **toujours** français.   We *always* speak French.
Tu joues **bien** au tennis.   You play tennis *well*.

12 Expression personnelle

PARLER/ÉCRIRE Complete the following sentences with one of the suggested expressions.

bien   mal   très bien   toujours   souvent   rarement   un peu   beaucoup

1. Je chante …
2. Je nage …
3. Je regarde … la télé.
4. Je mange …
5. Je voyage … en bus.
6. Le prof parle … français.
7. Mes copains surfent … sur l'Internet.
8. Mon ami joue … aux jeux vidéo.
9. Les Yankees jouent … au baseball.

VOCABULAIRE Expressions pour la conversation

How to express approval or regret:

| **Super!** | *Terrific!* | Tu parles français? **Super!** |
| **Dommage!** | *Too bad!* | Tu ne joues pas au tennis? **Dommage!** |

13 Conversation

PARLER Ask your classmates if they do the following things. Then express approval or regret.

▶ parler français?

1. parler espagnol?
2. jouer au basket?
3. chanter bien?
4. voyager beaucoup?
5. dîner souvent au restaurant?
6. inviter souvent ton copain?

Est-ce que tu parles français?
Oui, je parle français.
(Non, je ne parle pas français.)
Super! (Dommage!)

 100 cent Unité 3

TEACHING TIP

Have students notice the two-column (French-English) format in the **Vocabulaire** sections. Encourage them to practice the vocabulary by covering one of the two columns with a slip of paper and then saying or writing the corresponding expression in the other language. They can verify their responses by sliding the paper down the page as they go through the list.

Section D

Communicative function
Talking about what people like and don't like to do

D La construction: verbe + infinitif

Note the use of the infinitive in the following French sentences.

J'aime **parler** français.	*I like to speak French. I like speaking French.*
Ils n'aiment pas **danser.**	*They don't like to dance. They don't like dancing.*

To express what they like and don't like to do, the French use these constructions:

SUBJECT + PRESENT TENSE + INFINITIVE … of **aimer**			SUBJECT + **n'** + PRESENT TENSE + **pas** + INFINITIVE … of **aimer**		
Nous	**aimons**	**voyager.**	Nous	**n'aimons pas**	**voyager.**

Note that in this construction, the verb **aimer** may be affirmative or negative:

AFFIRMATIVE: Jacques **aime** voyager.   NEGATIVE: Philippe **n'aime pas** voyager.

→ The infinitive is also used after the following expressions:

Je préfère …	*I prefer …*	**Je préfère travailler.**
Je voudrais …	*I would like …*	**Je voudrais voyager.**
Je (ne) veux (pas) …	*I (don't) want …*	**Je veux jouer** au foot.
Est-ce que tu veux …	*Do you want …*	**Est-ce que tu veux danser?**
Je (ne) peux (pas) …	*I can (I can't) …*	**Je ne peux pas dîner** avec toi.
Je dois …	*I have to …*	**Je dois étudier.**

14 **Dialogue**

PARLER Ask your friends if they like to do these things.

▶ nager?
—Est-ce que tu aimes nager?
—Oui, j'aime nager. (Non, je n'aime pas nager.)

1. étudier?	**4.** téléphoner?	**7.** jouer au foot?
2. voyager?	**5.** manger?	**8.** jouer au basket?
3. chanter?	**6.** danser?	**9.** travailler en été?

15 **Une excellente raison** *(An excellent reason)*

PARLER/ÉCRIRE The following people are doing certain things. Say that they like these activities.

▶ Thomas joue au tennis.   **Il aime jouer au tennis.**

1. Alice chante.	**6.** Julie et Paul dansent.
2. Pierre voyage.	**7.** Nous jouons au frisbee.
3. Céline joue au foot.	**8.** Éric et Lise nagent.
4. Tu téléphones.	**9.** Vous surfez sur l'Internet.
5. Nous travaillons.	**10.** Léa organise la boum.

PRONONCIATION

Les voyelles /i/ et /u/

/u/ **où?**   /i/ **ici!**

Be sure to pronounce the French "**i**" as in **Mimi.**

Répétez:

/i/   **ici Philippe il
      Mimi Sylvie visite**
Alice visite Paris avec Sylvie.

/u/   **où nous vous
      écoute joue toujours**
Vous jouez au foot avec nous?

14 **COMMUNICATION** discussing likes and dislikes

1. –Est-ce que tu aimes étudier?
   –Oui, j'aime étudier. (Non, je n'aime pas étudier.)
2. –Est-ce que tu aimes voyager?
   –Oui, j'aime voyager. (Non, je n'aime pas voyager.)
3. –Est-ce que tu aimes chanter?
   –Oui, j'aime chanter. (Non, je n'aime pas chanter.)
4. –Est-ce que tu aimes téléphoner?
   –Oui, j'aime téléphoner. (Non, je n'aime pas téléphoner.)
5. –Est-ce que tu aimes manger?
   –Oui, j'aime manger. (Non, je n'aime pas manger.)
6. –Est-ce que tu aimes danser?
   –Oui, j'aime danser. (Non, je n'aime pas danser.)
7. –Est-ce que tu aimes jouer au foot?
   –Oui, j'aime jouer au foot. (Non, je n'aime pas jouer au foot.)
8. –Est-ce que tu aimes jouer au basket?
   –Oui, j'aime jouer au basket. (Non, je n'aime pas jouer au basket.)
9. –Est-ce que tu aimes travailler en été?
   –Oui, j'aime travailler en été. (Non, je n'aime pas travailler en été.)

Expansion In the event of an affirmative answer, a follow-up question could be asked with **bien** or **souvent.**
   Est-ce que tu chantes bien?

15 **PRACTICE** saying what people like to do

1. Elle aime chanter.
2. Il aime voyager.
3. Elle aime jouer au foot.
4. Tu aimes téléphoner.
5. Nous aimons travailler.
6. Ils aiment danser.
7. Nous aimons jouer au frisbee.
8. Ils aiment nager.
9. Vous aimez surfer sur l'Internet.
10. Elle aime organiser la boum.

Challenge Continue the response by inventing an activity that the person does not like to do.
Il aime voyager mais il n'aime pas parler anglais.

PRONUNCIATION

/i/ Spelled **i, y.**
Be sure students pronounce /i/ like "ee" of *beet* and not the "i" of *bit.*
/u/ Spelled **ou, où.**

JEAN-PAUL À LA BOUM

▶ Divide the class into teams of four.
▶ Play the video segment **Jean-Paul à la boum.**
▶ Replay the first scene and pause so that each team can write as many phrases from the conversation as they can remember. Do the same for the second scene.

▶ Then play both scenes once more so the teams can try to complete their texts.
▶ Distribute a copy of the video script to each team so that they can circle all the phrases they listed correctly. Play the scenes a final time for confirmation.

À votre tour!

1  **Allô!**

PARLER Sophie is phoning some friends. Match her questions on the left
with her friends' answers on the right.

1. Est-ce que Marc est canadien?
   a. Non, elle travaille.

2. Est-ce que tu joues au tennis?
   b. Oui, mais pas très bien.

3. Ton frère est à la maison?
   c. Bien sûr! Elles aiment beaucoup danser.

4. Ta mère est en vacances?
   d. Oui, il habite à Montréal.

5. Tu invites Christine et Juliette à la boum?
   e. Non, il dîne au restaurant avec un copain.

2  **Créa-dialogue**

PARLER Find out how frequently your classmates do the following activities.
They will respond using one of the expressions on the scale.

NON	OUI			
	rarement →	un peu →	souvent →	beaucoup

▶ —**Robert**, est-ce que tu
joues au tennis?
—Non, je ne joue pas
au tennis.
—Est-ce que tu écoutes
la radio?
—Oui, j'écoute souvent
la radio.

 cent deux
Unité 3

À VOTRE TOUR

Depending on your goals and objectives, you may
or may not wish to assign all of the activities in the
À votre tour section.

PAIR AND GROUP PRACTICE

In Act. 1 and 2, you may want to have students work
together in trios, with two performing and one acting
as monitor.

3 Qu'est-ce qu'ils font?
(What do they do?)

PARLER/ÉCRIRE Look at what the following students have put in their lockers and say what they like to do.

Éric aime jouer au tennis.
Il aime aussi ...

ÉRIC — HÉLÈNE & ANNE — NOUS — VOUS

4 Message illustré

ÉCRIRE Marc wrote about certain activities, using pictures. On a separate sheet, write out his description replacing these pictures with the missing words.

À la maison, ma soeur Catherine ☎ à une copine. Mon frère Éric 📻 ♪. En général, nous 🐾 à sept heures et demie. Après° le dîner, mes° parents 📺. Moi, j'📖 pour la classe de français. En vacances, nous ❌. Je 🏊. Éric et Catherine 🎾. Parfois° mes parents 🍷 au restaurant.

Après *After*   **mes** *my*   **Parfois** *Sometimes*

5 Point de vue personnel

ÉCRIRE Write a short composition in which you describe some of the activities you do and don't do in different situations: at home, in class, on vacation, with your friends, and with your family. If appropriate, you may indicate how frequently you engage in certain activities.

STRATEGY Writing

- First list the activities you want to mention, using infinitives.
- Write out your paragraph describing your activities and those that you do not do.
- Check your composition to be sure all verb forms are correct.

	😊	😞
• à la maison	_____	_____
• en classe	_____	_____
• en vacances	_____	_____
• avec mes copains	_____	_____
• avec ma famille	_____	_____

LESSON REVIEW
CLASSZONE.COM

PORTFOLIO ASSESSMENT

You will probably only select one speaking activity and one writing activity to go into the students' portfolios for Unit 3.

In this lesson, Act. 2 can be the basis of an oral portfolio recording. (You may want to use the Challenge version of Act. 4 for the written portfolio.)

---

3 COMPREHENSION

Éric aime jouer au tennis. Il aime aussi parler (étudier le) français.
Hélène et Anne aiment danser. Elles aiment aussi écouter la radio.
Nous aimons jouer au basket. Nous aimons aussi parler (étudier l') espagnol.
Vous aimez nager. Vous aimez aussi jouer au foot.

4 COMPREHENSION

À la maison, ma soeur Catherine <u>téléphone</u> à une copine. Mon frère Éric <u>écoute la radio</u>. En général, nous <u>dînons</u> à sept heures et demie. Après le dîner, mes parents <u>regardent la télé</u>. Moi, j'<u>étudie</u> pour la classe de français. En vacances, nous <u>n'étudions pas</u>. Je <u>nage</u>. Éric et Catherine <u>jouent au tennis</u>. Parfois mes parents <u>dînent</u> au restaurant.

Challenge De nouveaux messages
Have students, alone or in pairs, prepare their own **messages illustrés** (complete with an answer key on the back). Let them exchange their messages with each other. On a separate sheet of paper, have them replace the pictures with the missing words and check their answers using the answer key provided.

5 WRITTEN SELF-EXPRESSION

Answers will vary.
- écouter le prof
- étudier
- regarder la télé
- dîner
- parler avec mon ami
- écouter la radio
- jouer au volley
- jouer au tennis

À la maison, je regarde la télé et je dîne. Je n'écoute pas la radio.

En classe, j'écoute le prof et j'étudie. Je ne parle pas avec mon ami.

En vacances, je nage et je parle au téléphone. Je n'étudie pas.

Avec mes copains, je joue au basket et je joue au foot. Je ne joue pas au volley.

Avec ma famille, je dîne au restaurant et je voyage. Je ne joue pas au tennis.

Middle School Copymasters

Worksheets 2: *À Rome, je parle italien!*, p. 38

Leçon 8

Main Topic Finding out information

Teaching Resource Options

PRINT

Workbook PE, pp. 75–79
Activités pour tous PE, pp. 43–45
Block Scheduling Copymasters,
  pp. 57–64
Unit 3 Resource Book
  Activités pour tous TE, 99–101
  Audioscript, pp. 120, 121–122
  Communipak, pp. 128–143
  Lesson Plans, pp. 102–103
  Block Scheduling Lesson Plans,
    pp. 104–106
  Absent Student Copymasters,
    pp. 107–111
  Video Activities, pp. 114–117
  Videoscript, pp. 118–119
  Workbook TE, pp. 93–97

AUDIO & VISUAL

Audio Program
CD 2 Tracks 17, 18
CD 7 Tracks 18–21

TECHNOLOGY
Online Workbook

VIDEO PROGRAM

VIDÉO   DVD

MODULE 8
  Un concert de musique
  africaine

TOTAL TIME: 6:14 min.
  DVD Disk 1
  Videotape 2 (COUNTER: 21:45 min.)

8.1 Mini-scenes: Listening
  – Où est-ce qu'il va?
  (22:39–24:04 min.)

8.2 Mini-scenes: Listening
  – Qu'est-ce que tu fais?
  (24:05–24:53 min.)

8.3 Mini-scenes: Speaking
  – Questions
  (24:54–25:35 min.)

**8.4 Dialogue: Un concert de
  musique africaine**
  (25:36–26:26 min.)

8.5 Vignette culturelle: Le Sénégal
  (26:27–27:59 min.)

104 · **Conversation et Culture**
  Unité 3 LEÇON 8

Un concert de musique africaine

VIDÉO   DVD   AUDIO

Nicolas is at a café with his new friend Fatou. He is interviewing her for an article in his school newspaper.

Nicolas:	Bonjour, Fatou. Ça va?	
Fatou:	Oui, ça va.	
Nicolas:	Tu es <u>sénégalaise</u>, n'est-ce pas?	*from Senegal*
Fatou:	Oui, je suis sénégalaise.	
Nicolas:	Où est-ce que tu habites?	
Fatou:	Je suis de Dakar, mais maintenant j'habite à Paris avec ma famille.	
Nicolas:	Est-ce que tu aimes Paris?	
Fatou:	J'adore Paris.	
Nicolas:	Qu'est-ce que tu fais le week-end?	
Fatou:	<u>Ça</u> dépend. En général, je regarde la télé ou je <u>sors</u> avec mes copains. Dis, Nicolas! Est-ce que je peux <u>te poser</u> une question?	*That / go out* / *ask you*
Nicolas:	Oui, bien sûr!	
Fatou:	Qu'est-ce que tu fais <u>ce</u> week-end?	*this*
Nicolas:	Euh, … <u>je ne sais pas</u>.	*I don't know*
Fatou:	Est-ce que tu veux aller avec nous à un concert de Youssou N'Dour, le musicien sénégalais?	
Nicolas:	Oui, bien sûr! <u>Où</u>? <u>Quand</u>? Et à quelle heure?	*Where? / When?*

Compréhension:

1. Est-ce que Fatou est française?
2. Où est-ce qu'elle habite maintenant?
3. Qu'est-ce que *(What)* Fatou aime faire *(to do)* le week-end?
4. Qui est-ce qu'elle invite au concert de musique africaine?

104 cent quatre
Unité 3

SETTING THE SCENE

Ask students how many African countries they can name. Write these on the board. Do they remember which of these countries use French as an official language? Circle these countries. (If necessary, have them turn back to the photo essay on pages 8–9.)

Locate these French-speaking countries on the map. In particular, have students locate Senegal and its capital city Dakar. Tell them that in this chapter they will meet a student from Dakar.

NOTE *culturelle*

Le Sénégal
★ Dakar

EN BREF: Le Sénégal
Capitale: Dakar
Population: 10 000 000
Langue officielle: français

A former French colony, Senegal became an independent republic in 1960. Its population is divided into about a dozen ethnic groups, each with its own language, the most important being **wolof** and **pulaar.**

Youssou N'Dour

Youssou N'Dour is an internationally known musician from Senegal who combines traditional African music with pop, rock, and jazz. He sings in French and English, as well as in three Senegalese dialects. His lyrics promote African unity and human dignity. In many of his songs, he also plays the **tama**, a traditional Senegalese drum covered with reptile skins.

Le tama

Dakar, Sénégal

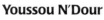

Des jeunes Sénégalais

CONNEXIONS Senegal and African Music

- As a class project, make a display board on Senegal, using information and pictures from travel brochures or from the Internet.
- Obtain a CD of Youssou N'Dour or of music from another French-African country and play your favorite selection for the class.

cent cinq
Leçon 8 105

USING THE VIDEO

In this lesson, the opening text corresponds to the video interview. However, the printed text is somewhat different from the video version.

First, have students follow in their books as you read the text aloud.

Tell the class that the recorded version will not be exactly the same, and play it for them.

Then play the video a second time. Have students find those sentences which are different from those in the recorded dialogue.

Communicative function
• Asking for information
• The video/audio sequence
  includes questions with **qui.**

Teaching Resource Options

PRINT

Workbook PE, pp. 75–79
Unit 3 Resource Book
   Audioscript, p. 120
   Communipak, pp. 128–143
   Video Activities, p. 114
   Videoscript, p. 118
   Workbook TE, pp. 93–97

AUDIO & VISUAL

Audio Program
CD 2 Track 19

Overhead Transparencies
6 Clock face *Quelle heure est-il?*

TECHNOLOGY
Power Presentations

VIDEO PROGRAM

VIDÉO   DVD
  MODULE 8

8.1 Mini-scenes: Où est-ce qu'il va?
(22:39–24:04 min.)

1 LISTENING COMPREHENSION

1. b   2. a   3. d   4. c
5. b   6. c   7. a   8. d

Pronunciation Note that the "t" is
not pronounced in **Montréal** since it is
considered as the final consonant of a
word: **Mont Réal** *(Mount Royal).*

A Les questions d'information

The questions below ask for specific information and are called INFORMATION QUESTIONS.
The INTERROGATIVE EXPRESSIONS in heavy print indicate what kind of information is requested.

—**Où** est-ce que tu habites?	**Where** do you live?
—J'habite **à Nice.**	I live **in Nice.**
—**À quelle heure** est-ce que vous dînez?	**At what time** do you eat dinner?
—Nous dînons **à sept heures.**	We eat **at seven.**

→ In French, information questions may be formed according to the pattern:

INTERROGATIVE EXPRESSION + **est-ce que** + SUBJECT + VERB ... ?
À quelle heure   **est-ce que**   vous   travaillez?

→ **Est-ce que** becomes **est-ce qu'** before a vowel sound.

   Quand **est-ce qu'**Alice et Roger dînent?

→ In information questions, your voice rises on the interrogative expression
and then falls until the last syllable.

Quand est-ce que tu travailles?   **À quelle heure** est-ce que vous dînez?

Observation In casual conversation, French speakers frequently form information
questions by placing the interrogative expression at the end of the sentence.
The voice rises on the interrogative expression.

Vous habitez **où?**   Vous dînez **à quelle heure?**

VOCABULAIRE Expressions interrogatives

où	*where?*	**Où** est-ce que vous travaillez?
quand?	*when?*	**Quand** est-ce que ton copain organise une boum?
à quelle heure?	*at what time?*	**À quelle heure** est-ce que tu regardes la télé?
comment?	*how?*	**Comment** est-ce que tu chantes? Bien ou mal?
pourquoi?	*why?*	—**Pourquoi** est-ce que tu étudies le français?
parce que	*because*	—**Parce que** je veux voyager en France.

→ **Parce que** becomes **parce qu'** before a vowel sound.
   Juliette invite Olivier **parce qu'**il danse bien.

WARM-UP AND REVIEW

PROP: Transparency 6: Clock face, *Quelle heure est-il?* or clock with hands

Review times by asking students at what time they do
certain things. Then ask a classmate to show the
corresponding time on the clock face.
  Dis-moi, W, à quelle heure est-ce que tu dînes?
[Je dîne à six heures et quart.]

X, viens ici et montre-nous six heures et quart.

Y, à quelle heure est-ce que tu étudies? ...

**Z, à quelle heure est-ce que tu écoutes
la radio? ...**

1  Écoutez bien!

STRATEGY Listening

Understanding questions Pay attention to the interrogative expression. It tells what type of information is asked for.

ÉCOUTER The questions that you will hear can be logically answered by only one of the following options. Listen carefully to each question and select the logical answer.

a. à sept heures   **c.** en octobre
b. à Paris   **d.** assez bien

2 Curiosité

PARLER At a party in Paris, Nicolas meets Béatrice, a Canadian student. He wants to know more about her. Play both roles.

▶ où / habiter? (à Québec)

   NICOLAS: **Où est-ce que tu habites?**
   BÉATRICE: **J'habite à Québec.**

1. où/étudier? (à Montréal)
2. où/travailler? (dans [in] une pharmacie)
3. quand/parler français? (toujours)
4. quand/parler anglais? (souvent)
5. comment/jouer au tennis? (bien)
6. comment/danser? (très bien)
7. pourquoi/être en France? (parce que j'aime voyager)
8. pourquoi/être à Paris? (parce que j'étudie ici)

VOCABULAIRE Expressions pour la conversation

How to express surprise or mild doubt:

Ah bon?   *Oh? Really?*   —Stéphanie organise une soirée.
                                —**Ah bon?** Quand?

3 Au téléphone

PARLER Jacques calls Élodie to tell her about his plans.

▶ organiser une soirée (quand? samedi)

J'organise une soirée.

Samedi.

Ah bon? Quand est-ce que tu organises une soirée?

1. organiser un pique-nique (quand? dimanche)
2. dîner avec Pauline (quand? lundi)
3. dîner avec Caroline (où? au restaurant Belcour)
4. regarder «Batman» (à quelle heure? à 9 heures)
5. inviter Brigitte (où? à un concert)
6. parler espagnol (comment? assez bien)
7. étudier l'italien (pourquoi? je veux voyager en Italie)

4 Questions personnelles   PARLER/ÉCRIRE

1. Où est-ce que tu habites? *(name of your city)*
2. Où est-ce que tu étudies? *(name of your school)*
3. À quelle heure est-ce que tu dînes?
4. À quelle heure est-ce que tu regardes la télé?
5. Quand est-ce que tu nages? (en été? en hiver?)
6. Quand est-ce que tu joues au volley? (en mai? en juillet?)
7. Comment est-ce que tu chantes? (bien? très bien? mal?)
8. Comment est-ce que tu nages?

VARIATION Written self-expression

Have students describe themselves by answering the questions from Activity 4 in writing. They may vary the sequence of their answers and add additional information for extra credit.

2 ROLE PLAY finding out information about someone

1. **N:** Où est-ce que tu étudies?
   B: J'étudie à Montréal.
2. **N:** Où est-ce que tu travailles?
   B: Je travaille dans une pharmacie.
3. **N:** Quand est-ce que tu parles français?
   B: Je parle toujours français.
4. **N:** Quand est-ce que tu parles anglais?
   B: Je parle souvent anglais.
5. **N:** Comment est-ce que tu joues au tennis?
   B: Je joue bien au tennis.
6. **N:** Comment est-ce que tu danses?
   B: Je danse très bien.
7. **N:** Pourquoi est-ce que tu es en France?
   B: Je suis en France parce que j'aime voyager.
8. **N:** Pourquoi est-ce que tu es à Paris?
   B: Je suis à Paris parce que j'étudie ici.

3 ROLE PLAY asking for information

1. – J'organise un pique-nique.
   – Ah bon? Quand est-ce que tu organises un pique-nique?
   – Dimanche.
2. – Je dîne avec Pauline.
   – Ah bon? Quand est-ce que tu dînes avec Pauline?
   – Lundi.
3. – Je dîne avec Caroline.
   – Ah bon? Où est-ce que tu dînes avec Caroline?
   – Au restaurant Belcour.
4. – Je regarde «Batman».
   – Ah bon? À quelle heure est-ce que tu regardes «Batman»?
   – À 9 heures.
5. – J'invite Brigitte.
   – Ah bon? Où est-ce que tu invites Brigitte?
   – À un concert.
6. – Je parle espagnol.
   – Ah bon? Comment est-ce que tu parles espagnol?
   – Assez bien.
7. – J'étudie l'italien.
   – Ah bon? Pourquoi est-ce que tu étudies l'italien?
   – Je veux voyager en Italie.

4 COMMUNICATION answering personal questions

Answers will vary.
1. J'habite à (Boston).
2. J'étudie à (Jefferson High School).
3. Je dîne à (6 h 30).
4. Je regarde la télé à (8h).
5. Je nage (en été).
6. Je joue au volley en mai (en juillet).
7. Je chante très bien (bien, mal).
8. Je nage mal (bien, très bien).

Middle School Copymasters

Worksheet 3: *Curiosité*, pp. 39–40;
Game: *C'est normal, non?*, p. 43

Teaching Resource Options

PRINT

Workbook PE, pp. 75–79
Unit 3 Resource Book
  Communipak, pp. 128–143
  Video Activities, pp. 114–115
  Videoscript, pp. 118–119
  Workbook TE, pp. 93–97

TECHNOLOGY

Power Presentations

VIDEO PROGRAM

VIDÉO   DVD
    MODULE 8

8.2 Mini-scenes: Qu'est-ce que tu fais? (24:05–24:53 min.)

8.3 Mini-scenes: Questions (24:54–25:35 min.)

5 **ROLE PLAY** finding out information about others

1. – Jean-Pierre téléphone.
   – Ah bon? À qui est-ce qu'il téléphone?
   – Il téléphone à Sylvie.
2. – Frédéric étudie.
   – Ah bon? Avec qui est-ce qu'il étudie?
   – Il étudie avec un copain.
3. – Madame Masson parle.
   – Ah bon? À qui est-ce qu'elle parle?
   – Elle parle à Madame Bonnot.
4. – Monsieur Lambert travaille.
   – Ah bon? Avec qui est-ce qu'il travaille?
   – Il travaille avec Monsieur Dumont.
5. – Juliette danse.
   – Ah bon? Avec qui est-ce qu'elle danse?
   – Elle danse avec Georges.
6. – François parle à Michèle.
   – Ah bon? De qui est-ce qu'il parle à Michèle? (De qui est-ce qu'ils parlent?)
   – Il parle (Ils parlent) de toi.

Language note Unlike their English equivalents, the two words in expressions like **à qui** and **avec qui** cannot be separated.
  Avec qui est-ce que tu travailles?
  Who(m) do you work with?

Language note In French as in English, the verb in **qui** questions is singular even if the expected answer is plural.
  – **Qui joue au tennis?** *(Who is playing tennis?)*
  – **Paul et Monique.**

108 · **Langue et Communication**
Unité 3 LEÇON 8

B Les expressions interrogatives avec *qui*

To ask about PEOPLE, French speakers use the following interrogative expressions:

qui?	*who(m)?*	**Qui** est-ce que tu invites au concert?
à qui?	*to who(m)?*	**À qui** est-ce que tu téléphones?
de qui?	*about who(m)?*	**De qui** est-ce que vous parlez?
avec qui?	*with who(m)?*	**Avec qui** est-ce que Pierre étudie?
pour qui?	*for who(m)?*	**Pour qui** est-ce que Laure organise la boum?

To ask *who is doing something*, French speakers use the construction:

qui + VERB … ?	
Qui habite ici?	*Who lives here?*
Qui organise la boum?	*Who is organizing the party?*

5 *Curiosité*

PARLER Anne is telling Élodie what certain people are doing. Élodie asks for more details. Play both roles.

▶ Alice dîne. (avec qui? avec une copine)

1. Jean-Pierre téléphone. (à qui? à Sylvie)
2. Frédéric étudie. (avec qui? avec un copain)
3. Madame Masson parle. (à qui? à Madame Bonnot)
4. Monsieur Lambert travaille. (avec qui? avec Monsieur Dumont)
5. Juliette danse. (avec qui? avec Georges)
6. François parle à Michèle. (de qui? de toi)

Alice dîne.
Elle dîne avec une copine.
Ah bon? Avec qui est-ce qu'elle dîne?

6 *Un sondage* (A poll)

PARLER Take a survey to find out how your classmates spend their free time. Ask who does the following things.

▶ écouter la radio
   Qui écoute la radio?

La radio   LA MUSIQUE

1. voyager souvent
2. aimer chanter
3. nager
4. aimer danser
5. regarder la télé
6. jouer au tennis
7. parler italien
8. travailler
9. regarder les clips *(music videos)*
10. jouer aux jeux vidéo
11. étudier beaucoup
12. visiter souvent New York

GAME Getting acquainted

On a separate sheet of paper, have each student copy the model and 12 cues of Act. 6.

Students then move around asking classmates one by one if they do an activity on the list.
  Annie: **Marc, est-ce que tu nages?**
  Marc: **Oui, je nage.**

Annie writes Marc's name next to **nager**. If Marc says no, Annie asks someone else.

The first person to complete his/her sheet with 13 different names is the winner.

7 Questions

PARLER/ÉCRIRE For each illustration, prepare a short dialogue with a classmate using the suggested cues.

où?
à la maison

▶ —Où est-ce que tu dînes?
—Je dîne à la maison.

1. à quelle heure?

à 8 heures

2. quand?

en septembre

3. comment?

BONJOUR!
très bien

4. avec qui?

avec Denise

5. à qui?

à mon cousin

6. de qui?

BLA BLA BLA...
de toi

7. pour qui?

pour M. Lambert

C *Qu'est-ce que?*

Note the use of the interrogative expression **qu'est-ce que** *(what)* in the questions below.

Qu'est-ce que tu regardes?   Je regarde un match de tennis.

Qu'est-ce qu'Alice mange?   Elle mange une pizza.

To ask *what people are doing,* the French use the following construction:

qu'est-ce que + SUBJECT + VERB + …?	**Qu'est-ce que** tu regardes?
qu'est-ce qu' (+ VOWEL SOUND)	**Qu'est-ce qu'**elle mange?

8 À la FNAC

PARLER People in Column A are at the FNAC, a store that sells books and recordings. Use a verb from Column B to ask what they are listening to or looking at. A classmate will answer you, using an item from Column C.

A	**B**	**C**
tu	écouter?	un livre de photos
vous	regarder?	un poster
Alice		un CD de rock
Éric		un CD de jazz
Antoine et Claire		un album de Youssou N'Dour

Qu'est-ce qu'Éric écoute?

Il écoute un album de Youssou N'Dour.

VARIATION Un jeu

Using the cues from Activitiy 8, have teams of students see how many correct dialogues they can write in five minutes.

Casual speech In casual conversation, the entire interrogative expression may go to the end of the sentence: **Tu travailles avec qui?**

6 COMMUNICATION taking a survey

1. Qui voyage souvent?
2. Qui aime chanter?
3. Qui nage?
4. Qui aime danser?
5. Qui regarde la télé?
6. Qui joue au tennis?
7. Qui parle italien?
8. Qui travaille?
9. Qui regarde les clips?
10. Qui joue aux jeux vidéo?
11. Qui étudie beaucoup?
12. Qui visite souvent New York?

Pronunciation **clips** /klips/
Note **un clip** is a music video.

7 EXCHANGES asking and answering questions

1. – À quelle heure est-ce que tu regardes la télé?
   – Je regarde la télé à 8 (huit) heures.
2. – Quand est-ce que tu visites Paris?
   – Je visite Paris en septembre.
3. – Comment est-ce que tu parles français?
   – Je parle très bien français.
4. – Avec qui est-ce que tu joues au tennis?
   – Je joue au tennis avec Denise.
5. – À qui est-ce que tu téléphones?
   – Je téléphone à mon cousin.
6. – De qui est-ce que tu parles (vous parlez)?
   – Je parle (Nous parlons) de toi.
7. – Pour qui est-ce que tu travailles?
   – Je travaille pour Monsieur Lambert.

Expansion Have students make up their own answers to the questions.
– **Où est-ce que tu dînes?**
– **Je dîne au restaurant. (etc.)**

SECTION C

Communicative function
Asking what people are doing

Casual speech Note how **quoi** is used instead of **qu'est-ce que** in casual questions.
Tu regardes quoi?
Alice mange quoi?

8 EXCHANGES asking and answering questions

Answers will vary.
• – Qu'est-ce que tu écoutes?
  – J'écoute (un CD de rock).
• – Qu'est-ce que vous regardez?
  – Nous regardons (Je regarde) (un poster).
• – Qu'est-ce qu'Alice (écoute)?
  – Alice écoute (un CD de jazz).
• – Qu'est-ce qu'Éric (regarde)?
  – Éric regarde (un livre de photos).
• – Qu'est-ce qu'Antoine et Claire (écoutent)?
  – Antoine et Claire écoutent (un album de Youssou N'Dour).

Section D

Communicative function
Describing what people are doing

Teaching Resource Options

PRINT

Workbook PE, pp. 75–79
Unit 3 Resource Book
  Audioscript, p. 120
  Communipak, pp. 128–143
  Workbook TE, pp. 93–97

AUDIO & VISUAL

Audio Program
CD 2 Track 20

Overhead Transparencies
18 Expressions with *faire*

TECHNOLOGY

Power Presentations

Teaching strategy Ask students what other irregular verb they have learned (**être**). Have them point out the similarities between **être** and **faire**: singular forms end in **-s, -s, -t**; **vous**-form ends in **-tes**; **ils**-form ends in **-ont**.

Practice drill Have students practice sentences with **faire**.
  Je fais une pizza.
  (Tu) Tu fais une pizza., etc.
  Qu'est-ce que je fais?
  (Vous) Qu'est-ce que vous faites?, etc.

Supplementary vocabulary
faire un pique-nique *to have a picnic*
faire un tour *to go for a short walk or ride*
Note: **faire une promenade** may also mean *to go for a ride*: **faire une promenade à vélo, en voiture.** (This is re-entered in Lesson 14.)

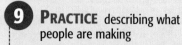 **Review** Remind students that **faire** is used in many weather expressions: **Il fait beau. Il fait bon.**

9 PRACTICE describing what people are making

1. faisons	**2.** fais	**3.** faites	**4.** font
5. fait	**6.** fait	**7.** font	**8.** font

D Le verbe *faire*

Faire *(to do, make)* is an IRREGULAR verb. It is used in many French expressions. Note the forms of **faire** in the present tense.

faire *(to do, make)*	
je **fais**	Je **fais** un sandwich.
tu **fais**	Qu'est-ce que tu **fais** maintenant?
il/elle **fait**	Qu'est-ce que ton copain **fait** samedi?
nous **faisons**	Nous **faisons** une pizza.
vous **faites**	Qu'est-ce que vous **faites** ici?
ils/elles **font**	Qu'est-ce qu'elles **font** pour la boum?

VOCABULAIRE Expressions avec *faire*

faire un match	*to play a game (match)*	Mes cousins **font un match** de tennis.
faire une promenade	*to go for a walk*	Caroline **fait une promenade** avec Olivier.
faire un voyage	*to take a trip*	Ma copine **fait un voyage** en France.
faire attention	*to pay attention*	Je **fais attention** quand le prof parle.

9 La boum de Léa

PARLER/ÉCRIRE Léa's friends are helping her prepare food for a party. Use the verb **faire** to say what everyone is doing.

▶ Je … une crêpe.

Je fais une crêpe.

1. Nous … une salade.
2. Tu … une salade de fruits.
3. Vous … une tarte *(pie)*.
4. Cécile et Marina … un gâteau *(cake)*.
5. Christine … une pizza.
6. Marc … un sandwich.
7. Patrick et Thomas … une omelette.
8. Pierre et Karine … une quiche.

10 Qu'est-ce qu'ils font?

PARLER/LIRE Read the descriptions below and say what the people are doing. Use the verb **faire** and an expression from the list.

un voyage
une promenade
une pizza
un match
attention

▶ Madame Dumont est en Chine.
  Elle fait un voyage.

1. Léa travaille dans *(in)* un restaurant.
2. Nous sommes en ville.
3. Céline et Jean-Paul jouent au tennis.
4. Je suis dans la cuisine *(kitchen)*.
5. Marc est dans le train Paris-Nice.
6. Vous jouez au volley.
7. Je suis dans le parc.
8. Monsieur Lambert visite Tokyo.
9. Nous écoutons le prof.

E L'interrogation avec inversion

LEARNING ABOUT LANGUAGE

In conversational French, questions are usually formed with **est-ce que.** However, when the subject of the sentence is a pronoun, French speakers often use inversion, that is, they invert or reverse the order of the subject pronoun and the verb.

REGULAR ORDER: **Vous parlez** français.
SUBJECT VERB

INVERSION: **Parlez-vous** anglais?
VERB SUBJECT

The pairs of questions below ask the same thing. Compare the position of the subject pronouns.

Est-ce que **tu** parles anglais?	Parles-**tu** anglais?	*Do you speak English?*
Est-ce que **vous** habitez ici?	Habitez-**vous** ici?	*Do you live here?*
Où est-ce que **nous** dînons?	Où dînons-**nous**?	*Where are we having dinner?*
Où est-ce qu'**il** est?	Où est-**il**?	*Where is he?*

Inverted questions are formed according to the patterns:

YES/NO QUESTION	VERB / SUBJECT PRONOUN ...?	
	Voyagez-vous	souvent?

INFORMATION QUESTION	INTERROGATIVE EXPRESSION + VERB / SUBJECT PRONOUN ...?	
	Avec qui **travaillez-vous**	demain?

→ In inversion, the verb and the subject pronoun are connected by a hyphen.

Observation In inversion, liaison is required before **il/elle** and **ils/elles**. If a verb in the singular ends on a vowel, the letter **"t"** is inserted after the verb so that liaison can occur:

Où travaille-**t**-il?   Où travaille-**t**-elle?   Avec qui dîne-**t**-il?   Avec qui dîne-**t**-elle?

  11 *Conversation*

PARLER Ask your classmates a few questions, using inversion.

▶ où / habiter? —**Où habites-tu?**
—**J'habite à (Boston).**

1. à quelle heure / dîner?
2. à quelle heure / regarder la télé?
3. avec qui / parler français?
4. à qui / téléphoner souvent?
5. comment / nager?
6. avec qui / étudier?
7. où / jouer aux jeux vidéo?
8. comment / chanter?

 PRONONCIATION /y/

La voyelle /y/

The vowel sound /y/ — represented by the letter "u" — does not exist in English.

Super!

To say **super**, first say the French word **si**. Then round your lips as if to whistle and say **si** with rounded lips: /sy/. Now say **si-per.** Then round your lips as you say the first syllable: **super!**

Répétez: /y/   **super   tu   étudie   bien sûr
Lucie   Luc
Tu étudies avec Lucie.**

TEACHING STRATEGY

If students have trouble producing /y/, have them pronounce the sound as /i/. They should not pronounce it as /u/.

---

10 COMPREHENSION describing what people are doing

1. Elle fait une pizza.
2. Nous faisons une promenade.
3. Ils font un match.
4. Je fais une pizza.
5. Il fait un voyage.
6. Vous faites un match.
7. Je fais une promenade.
8. Il fait un voyage.
9. Nous faisons attention.

SECTION E

Communicative function
Asking questions

Teaching note Inversion is taught mainly for recognition here. It is not emphasized in Book One.

11 COMMUNICATION getting acquainted

Answers will vary.
1. – À quelle heure dînes-tu?
   – Je dîne à (6 [six]) heures.
2. – À quelle heure regardes-tu la télé?
   – Je regarde la télé à (8 [huit]) heures.
3. – Avec qui parles-tu français?
   – Je parle français avec (mon copain).
4. – À qui téléphones-tu souvent?
   – Je téléphone souvent à (ma cousine).
5. – Comment nages-tu?
   – Je nage (très bien).
6. – Avec qui étudies-tu?
   – J'étudie avec (ma copine).
7. – Où joues-tu aux jeux vidéo?
   – Je joue aux jeux vidéo (à la maison).
8. – Comment chantes-tu?
   – Je chante (bien).

For additional practice, use the cues of this activity to practice other subject pronouns.
a) Address your questions to several students:
–Où habitez-vous?
–Nous habitons à (San Francisco).
b) Ask questions about Mélanie:
–Où habite-t-elle?
–Elle habite à (Lille).
c) Ask questions about Pierre:
–Où habite-t-il?
–Il habite à (Fort-de-France).
d) Ask questions about Trinh and Céline:
–Où habitent-ils?
–Ils habitent à (Paris).

Additional practice To practice inversion with **il/elle**, have the students redo Act. 5, p. 108 using inversion instead of **est-ce que.**
– Alice dîne.
– Ah bon? Avec qui dîne-t-elle?
– Elle dîne avec une copine.

Middle School Copymasters

Drill: *Changements*, pp. T16–T17

À votre tour!

1 🎧 👥 Allô!

PARLER Fatou is phoning some friends. Match her questions on the left with her friends' answers on the right.

1 Qu'est-ce que tu fais?

2 Qu'est-ce que vous faites samedi?

3 Où est ton père?

4 Quand est-ce que tu veux jouer au tennis avec moi?

5 Qui est-ce que tu invites au cinéma?

6 Pourquoi est-ce que tu étudies l'anglais?

a Il fait une promenade.

b Ma cousine Alice.

c Dimanche. D'accord?

d J'étudie.

e Nous faisons un match de tennis.

f Parce que je voudrais habiter à New York.

2 Les questions

LIRE/PARLER The following people are answering questions. Read what they say and figure out what questions they were asked.

Je chante très mal.

▶ **Comment est-ce que tu chantes?**

Nous dînons à l'Hippopotame.

1 J'habite à Québec.

2 Je dîne à sept heures.

3

4 Je mange une pizza.

5 Je regarde un film.

6 J'invite Catherine.

À VOTRE TOUR

Depending on your goals and objectives, you may or may not wish to assign all of the activities in the **À votre tour** section.

PAIR PRACTICE

Act. 1–4 lend themselves to pair practice.

③ 🎧 Créa-dialogue

PARLER Ask your classmates what they do on different days of the week. Carry out conversations similar to the model. Note: "??" means you can invent your own answers.

▶ —Qu'est-ce que tu fais <u>lundi</u>?
—Je <u>joue au tennis</u>.
—Ah bon? À quelle heure est-ce que tu <u>joues</u>?
—<u>À deux heures</u>.
—Et avec qui?
—Avec <u>Anne-Marie</u>.

	lundi	mardi	mercredi	jeudi	vendredi	samedi	dimanche
ACTIVITÉ						??	??
À QUELLE HEURE?	2 heures	6 heures	??	??	??	??	??
AVEC QUI?	avec Anne-Marie	avec un copain	??	??	??	??	??

④ Faisons connaissance! *(Let's get acquainted!)*

PARLER/ÉCRIRE Get better acquainted with a classmate. Ask five or six questions in French. Then write a summary of your conversation and give it to the friend you have interviewed.

▶ Mon ami(e) s'appelle ...
Il/elle habite ...

You might ask questions like:

- Where does he/she live?
- Does he/she speak French at home? With whom?
- Does he/she watch TV? When? What programs (**quelles émissions**)?
- Does he/she play video games? When? With whom?
- Does he/she play soccer (or another sport)? Where? When?
- Does he/she like to swim? When? Where?
- What does he/she like to do on weekends? When? Where? With whom?

⑤ Curiosité

ÉCRIRE Imagine that a French friend has just made the following statements. For each one, write down three or four related questions you could ask him or her.

Je joue au foot demain.

- Avec qui est-ce que tu joues?
- Où est-ce que vous jouez?
- À quelle heure est-ce que vous jouez?
- Pourquoi est-ce que vous jouez au foot?

Je joue au tennis. 1
2 Je dîne avec un copain.
3 Je fais une promenade.
4 J'organise une soirée.

LESSON REVIEW
CLASSZONE.COM

cent treize **Leçon 8** 113

PORTFOLIO ASSESSMENT

You will probably only select one speaking activity and one writing activity to go into the students' portfolios for Unit 3.

In this lesson, Act. 3 and 4 are good oral portfolio conversation topics.

TESTS DE CONTRÔLE

Teaching Resource Options

PRINT

Unit 3 Resource Book
Communipak, pp. 128–143

Assessment
Unit 3 Test, pp. 157–165
Portfolio Assessment, Unit 1 URB,
pp. 155–164
Multiple Choice Test Items, pp. 177–184
Listening Comprehension
Performance Test, pp. 166–167
Reading Performance Test, pp. 172–174
Speaking Performance Test, pp. 168–171
Writing Performance Test, pp. 175–176
Comprehensive Test 1, Units 1–3,
pp. 185–204
Test Scoring Tools, pp. 205–207
Audioscript for Tests, pp. 208–213
Answer Keys, pp. 216–219

AUDIO & VISUAL
Audio Program
CD 14 Tracks 5–16

TECHNOLOGY
Test Generator CD-ROM/eTest Plus
Online

1 COMPREHENSION

1. Jean-Paul <u>mange</u> une pizza.
2. Vous <u>jouez</u> aux jeux vidéo.
3. Isabelle <u>écoute</u> un CD de rock.
4. Monsieur Mercier <u>travaille</u> pour une banque.
5. Mon cousin <u>habite</u> à Chicago.
6. Ils <u>chantent</u> dans une chorale.
7. Nous <u>regardons</u> une comédie à la télé.
8. Est-ce que tu <u>parles</u> français ou anglais?

2 COMPREHENSION

1. Je <u>suis</u> en classe. Je <u>fais</u> attention.
2. Léa <u>est</u> dans la cuisine. Elle <u>fait</u> un sandwich.
3. Nous <u>sommes</u> en ville. Nous <u>faisons</u> une promenade.
4. Les touristes <u>sont</u> en France. Ils <u>font</u> un voyage.
5. Vous <u>êtes</u> au stade. Vous <u>faites</u> un match de foot.

114 • Tests de contrôle
Unité 3

Tests de contrôle

By taking the following tests, you can check your progress in French and also prepare for the unit test. Write your answers on a separate sheet of paper.

① The right activity

Review ...
• the uses and forms of -er verbs:
pp. 94, 95, 96, and 98

Complete each of the following sentences by filling in the blank with the appropriate form of one of the verbs in the box. Be logical in your choice of verbs.

chanter	manger	écouter	habiter
jouer	parler	regarder	travailler

1. Jean-Paul — une pizza.
2. Vous — aux jeux vidéo.
3. Isabelle — un CD de rock.
4. Monsieur Mercier — pour une banque (*bank*).
5. Mon cousin — à Chicago.
6. Ils — dans une chorale (*choir*).
7. Nous — une comédie à la télé.
8. Est-ce que tu — français ou anglais?

② Être and faire

Review ...
• être and faire:
pp. 84 and 110

For each item, fill in the first blank with the appropriate form of **être** and the second blank with the appropriate form of **faire.**

1. Je — en classe. Je — attention.
2. Léa — dans la cuisine (*kitchen*). Elle — un sandwich.
3. Nous — en ville. Nous — une promenade.
4. Les touristes — en France. Ils — un voyage.
5. Vous — au stade *(stadium)*. Vous — un match de foot.

③ Non!

Review ...
• negative sentences:
pp. 88 and 98

Rewrite the following sentences in the negative, replacing the underlined words with the words in parentheses.

▶ Thomas parle <u>français</u>. **(anglais)**   **Thomas ne parle pas anglais.**

1. Léa est <u>française</u>. **(américaine)**
2. Nous jouons <u>au foot</u>. **(au basket)**
3. Vous dînez <u>au restaurant</u>. **(à la maison)**
4. Tu invites <u>Céline</u>. **(Isabelle)**
5. Ils habitent <u>à Québec</u>. **(à Montréal)**

4 The right question

Write out the questions that correspond to the answers below. Make sure to begin your sentences with the question words that correspond to the underlined information. Use **tu** in your questions.

▶ J'habite <u>à Paris.</u>   **Où est-ce que tu habites?**

1. Je téléphone <u>à Marc.</u>

2. Je dîne <u>à sept heures.</u>

3. Je mange <u>une pizza.</u>

4. Je voyage <u>en juillet.</u>

5. J'écoute <u>un CD.</u>

6. Je joue <u>très bien</u> au foot.

Review ...
• information questions: pp. 106 and 108

5 The right choice

Choose the word or expression in parentheses which logically completes each of the following sentences.

1. François habite — France. **(à, au, en)**

2. Isabelle est au café — Céline. **(et, avec, pour)**

3. Nicolas parle français, — il ne parle pas espagnol. **(pourquoi, mal, mais)**

4. Pierre écoute — radio. **(à, la, à la)**

5. Je n'habite pas ici. J'habite —. **(où, aussi, là-bas)**

6. Tu ne chantes pas bien. Tu chantes —. **(mal, souvent, beaucoup)**

7. Philippe aime beaucoup jouer au foot. Il joue —. **(pour, mais non, souvent)**

8. Je ne peux pas dîner avec toi. Je — étudier pour l'examen. **(dois, veux, n'aime pas)**

9. J'étudie l'espagnol — je voudrais visiter Madrid. **(où, comment, parce que)**

10. Qui est-ce? Jérôme — Patrick? **(pour, ou, aussi)**

Review ...
• vocabulary: pp. 77, 78, 85, 89, 95, 100, 106

6 Composition: Les vacances

Write a short paragraph of five or six sentences saying what you and your friends do and don't do during summer vacation. Use only vocabulary and expressions that you know in French.

STRATEGY Writing

a Make a list of activities that you do and a second list of things that you don't do. Use infinitives.

b Organize your ideas and write your paragraph, using **je** or **nous**.

c Check each sentence to be sure that the verb endings agree with the subject.

	oui	non
• *nager*	•	
•	•	
•	•	
•	•	
•	•	

3 COMPREHENSION

1. Léa n'est pas américaine.
2. Nous ne jouons pas au basket.
3. Vous ne dînez pas à la maison.
4. Tu n'invites pas Isabelle.
5. Ils n'habitent pas à Montréal.

4 COMPREHENSION

1. À qui est-ce que tu téléphones?
2. À quelle heure est-ce que tu dînes?
3. Qu'est-ce que tu manges?
4. Quand est-ce que tu voyages?
5. Qu'est-ce que tu écoutes?
6. Comment est-ce que tu joues au foot?

5 COMPREHENSION

1. François habite <u>en</u> France.
2. Isabelle est au café <u>avec</u> Céline.
3. Nicolas parle français, <u>mais</u> il ne parle pas espagnol.
4. Pierre écoute <u>la</u> radio.
5. Je n'habite pas ici. J'habite <u>là-bas.</u>
6. Tu ne chantes pas bien. Tu chantes <u>mal.</u>
7. Philippe aime beaucoup jouer au foot. Il joue <u>souvent.</u>
8. Je ne peux pas dîner avec toi. Je <u>dois</u> étudier pour l'examen.
9. J'étudie l'espagnol <u>parce que</u> je voudrais visiter Madrid.
10. Qui est-ce? Jérôme <u>ou</u> Patrick?

6 WRITTEN SELF-EXPRESSION

Answers will vary.

oui	non
a. nager	étudier
regarder la télé	dîner avec la famille
écouter la radio	parler anglais
jouer au tennis	jouer au foot
jouer au volley	manger au restaurant

b. En été, j'aime regarder la télé avec mes copains. Nous jouons au tennis mais nous ne jouons pas au foot. Je n'étudie pas quand je suis en vacances et je nage avec mes copains. Nous jouons au volley souvent et nous écoutons la radio.

UNITÉ 3

VOCABULAIRE

Language Learning Benchmarks

FUNCTION
- Engage in conversations pp. 87, 107
- Express likes and dislikes p. 76
- Obtain information pp. 88, 97, 100
- Begin to provide information p. 88

CONTEXT
- Converse in face-to-face social interactions pp. 88, 96, 101
- Listen during social interactions p. 108
- Listen to audio and video texts pp. 72-73, 89, 99, 101, 107, 111, 124
- Use authentic materials when reading: schedules pp. 118, 131
- Use authentic materials when reading: short narratives p. 121
- Write lists pp. 103, 115, 121
- Write short letters p. 123

TEXT TYPE
- Use short sentences when speaking p. 76
- Use short sentences when writing pp. 74, 97
- Use learned words and phrases when speaking p. 76
- Use learned words and phrases when writing pp. 77, 99
- Use simple questions when speaking pp. 78, 86, 95, 111
- Use simple questions when writing pp. 87, 109
- Understand some ideas and familiar details presented in clear, uncomplicated speech when listening p. 107

Vocabulaire

POUR COMMUNIQUER

Talking about likes and preferences

Est-ce que tu aimes	parler anglais?	Do you like	to speak English?
J'aime		I like	
Je n'aime pas		I don't like	
Je préfère	parler français.	I prefer	to speak French.
Je veux		I want	
Je voudrais		I would like	
Je ne veux pas		I don't want	

Inviting a friend

Est-ce que tu veux [jouer au tennis]?	Do you want to [play tennis]?
Est-ce que tu peux [jouer au foot] avec moi?	Can you [play soccer] with me?

Accepting or declining an invitation

Oui, bien sûr.	Yes, of course.	Je regrette, mais je ne peux pas.	I'm sorry, but I can't.
Oui, merci.	Yes, thanks.	Je dois [travailler].	I have to, I must [work].
Oui, d'accord.	Yes, all right, okay.		
Oui, je veux bien.	Yes, I'd love to.		

Expressing approval, regret, or surprise

Super!	Terrific!
Dommage!	Too bad!
Ah bon?	Oh? Really?

Answering a yes/no question

Oui!	Yes!	Non!	No!
Mais oui!	Sure!	Mais non!	Of course not!
Bien sûr!	Of course!	Peut-être …	Maybe …

Asking for information

où?	where?	qu'est-ce que …?	what?
quand?	when?	qui?	who, whom?
à quelle heure?	at what time?	à qui?	to who(m)?
comment?	how?	de qui?	about who(m)?
pourquoi?	why?	avec qui?	with who(m)?
parce que …	because	pour qui?	for who(m)?

Saying where people are

Pierre est …

ici	here	à la maison	at home	en classe	in class
là	here, there	au café	at the café	en France	in France
là-bas	over there	au cinéma	at the movies	en vacances	on vacation
à [Paris]	in [Paris]	au restaurant	at the restaurant	en ville	in town

Saying how well, how often, and when

bien	well	beaucoup	a lot, much, very much	maintenant	now
très bien	very well	un peu	a little, a little bit	souvent	often
mal	badly, poorly	rarement	rarely, seldom	toujours	always

MOTS ET EXPRESSIONS

Verbes réguliers en -er

aimer	to like	jouer aux jeux vidéo	to play video games
chanter	to sing	manger	to eat
danser	to dance	nager	to swim
dîner	to have dinner	organiser une boum	to organize a party
dîner au restaurant	to eat out	parler anglais	to speak English
écouter	to listen, to listen to	parler espagnol	to speak Spanish
écouter la radio	to listen to the radio	parler français	to speak French
étudier	to study	regarder	to watch, to look at
habiter (à Paris)	to live (in Paris)	regarder la télé	to watch TV
inviter	to invite	téléphoner (à Céline)	to phone (Céline)
jouer au basket	to play basketball	travailler	to work
jouer au foot	to play soccer	visiter (Paris)	to visit (Paris)
jouer au tennis	to play tennis	voyager	to travel

Verbes irréguliers

être	to be	faire	to do, make
être d'accord	to agree	faire un match	to play a game (match)
		faire une promenade	to go for a walk
		faire un voyage	to take a trip
		faire attention	to pay attention

Mots utiles

à	at, in	et	and
aussi	also	mais	but
avec	with	ou	or
de	from, of	pour	for

TEST PREP
CLASSZONE.COM

FLASHCARDS
AND MORE!

CONTENT
- Understand and convey information about leisure activities pp. 74, 76, 77
- Understand and convey information about campus life pp. 127, 131
- Understand and convey information about likes and dislikes p. 76

ASSESSMENT
- Communicate effectively with some hesitation and errors, which do not hinder comprehension pp. 91, 103
- Demonstrate culturally acceptable behavior for greeting and responding to greetings p. 80
- Demonstrate culturally acceptable behavior for engaging in conversations pp. 80, 103, 113
- Demonstrate culturally acceptable behavior for expressing likes and dislikes p. 81
- Demonstrate culturally acceptable behavior for obtaining information pp. 80, 91, 113, 115
- Demonstrate culturally acceptable behavior for providing information p. 91

UNITÉ 3

ENTRACTE 3

Objectives
- Reading skill development
- Re-entry of materials in the unit
- Development of cultural awareness
- Vocabulary expansion

À la télé

Objectives
- Reading for information
- Selecting programs from a French TV guide

Teaching Resource Options

PRINT

Workbook PE, pp. 81–84
Activités pour tous PE, pp. 47–49
Unit 3 Resource Book
    Activités pour tous TE, pp. 145–147
    Workbook TE, pp. 149–152

Sélection de la semaine

émission *TV show*
hôtel de police *police department*
bossu *hunchback*

Ce week-end, à la télé

Le week-end, les jeunes Français regardent souvent la télé. Ils aiment regarder les films et le sport. Ils regardent aussi les jeux et les séries américaines et françaises. Les principales chaînes° sont TF1, France 2, France 3, Cinquième Arte, M6 et Canal Plus. Voici le programme de télévision pour ce week-end.

chaînes *channels*

Note In French TV listings, times are expressed using a 24-hour clock. In this system, 8 p.m. is 20.00 **(vingt heures)**, 9 p.m. is 21.00 **(vingt et une heures)**, 10 p.m. is 22 heures **(vingt-deux heures)**, etc.

SÉLECTION DE LA SEMAINE	VENDREDI	SAMEDI
TF1	**20.50** Magazine **SUCCÈS** Émission présentée par Julien Courbet et Anne Magnien **23.15** MAGAZINE • Célébrités	**20.50** Jeu **QUI VEUT GAGNER DES MILLIONS?** avec Jean-Pierre Foucault **21.50** SÉRIE • Les Soprano
2 France	**20.55** Série **HÔTEL DE POLICE** **Le gentil Monsieur** de Claude Barrois avec Cécile Magnet **23.20** DOCUMENTAIRE • Histoires Naturelles	**21.00** Variétés **CHAMPS-ÉLYSÉES** Invités: Ricky Martin, Juliette Binoche, Ben Affleck **22.35** SÉRIE • Buffy contre les Vampires
france 3	**21.00** Film **LE CINQUIÈME ÉLÉMENT** de Luc Besson avec Bruce Willis et Milla Jovovich **22.15** CONCERT • Viva Latino	**20.40** Série **INSPECTEUR BARNABY** avec Daniel Casey **22.50** SPORT • Grand Prix d'Italie Motocyclisme
france 5 arte	**20.45** Documentaire **CATHÉDRALES** de Jean-François Delassus **22.20** FILM • Quasimodo, le bossu de Notre Dame	**20.50** Documentaire **ARCHITECTURES** La Tour Eiffel **20.05** CONCERT • Le Philharmonique de Vienne
M6	**20.50** Variétés **GRAINES DE STAR** émission présentée par Laurent Boyer **22.20** THÉÂTRE • Rhinocéros	**20.35** Film **LE MARIAGE DE MON MEILLEUR AMI** avec Julia Roberts **22.15** SÉRIE • Police District
CANAL+	**20.50** Football **MARSEILLE-NICE** Championnat de France **22.50** FILM • Air Force One avec Harrison Ford	**20.45** Film **MON PÈRE, CE HÉROS** avec Gérard Depardieu **23.15** RUGBY • Toulouse-Biarritz

CLASSROOM MANAGEMENT

Pre-reading

Ask pairs of students to name their favorite TV programs.

    Quelle est votre émission favorite?
    Nous aimons [les matchs de football].

Group reading activity

Divide the class into groups of 4 or 5. Each group must decide on which early and which late show they will watch each night. Then they report their decision to the class.

    Vendredi nous allons regarder ... et ...
    Samedi nous allons regarder ... et ...

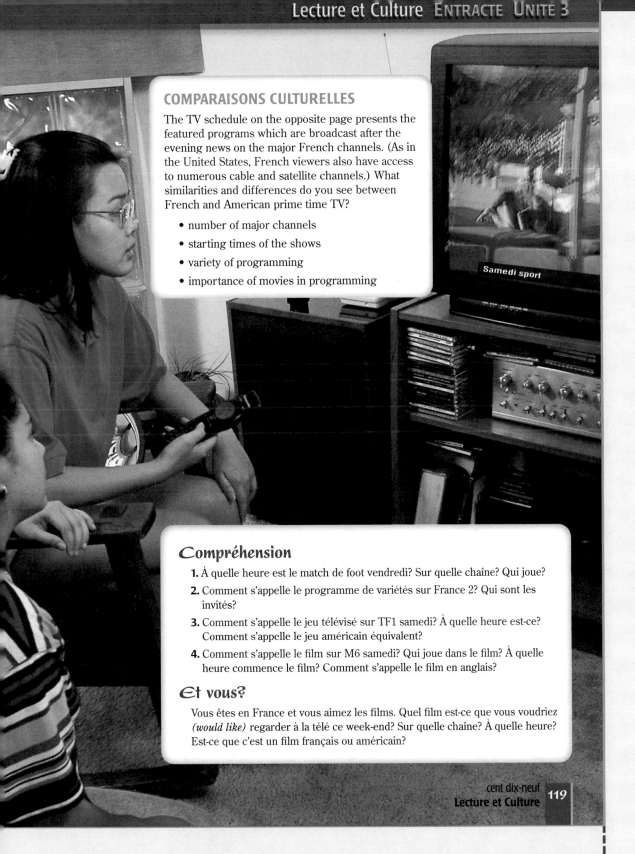

Samedi sport

COMPARAISONS CULTURELLES

The TV schedule on the opposite page presents the featured programs which are broadcast after the evening news on the major French channels. (As in the United States, French viewers also have access to numerous cable and satellite channels.) What similarities and differences do you see between French and American prime time TV?

- number of major channels
- starting times of the shows
- variety of programming
- importance of movies in programming

Compréhension

1. À quelle heure est le match de foot vendredi? Sur quelle chaîne? Qui joue?

2. Comment s'appelle le programme de variétés sur France 2? Qui sont les invités?

3. Comment s'appelle le jeu télévisé sur TF1 samedi? À quelle heure est-ce? Comment s'appelle le jeu américain équivalent?

4. Comment s'appelle le film sur M6 samedi? Qui joue dans le film? À quelle heure commence le film? Comment s'appelle le film en anglais?

Et vous?

Vous êtes en France et vous aimez les films. Quel film est-ce que vous voudriez *(would like)* regarder à la télé ce week-end? Sur quelle chaîne? À quelle heure? Est-ce que c'est un film français ou américain?

Compréhension

Answers.
1. Le match de foot est à 20.50 (à 8 h 50) sur Canal Plus. Marseille et Nice jouent.
2. Le programme de variétés s'appelle «Champs-Élysées». Les invités sont Ricky Martin, Juliette Binoche et Ben Affleck.
3. Le jeu télévisé sur TF1 samedi s'appelle «Qui veut gagner des millions?» Il est à 20.50. Le jeu américain équivalent s'appelle «Who Wants to Be a Millionaire?»
4. Le film sur M6 samedi s'appelle «Le mariage de mon meilleur ami». Julia Roberts joue dans le film. Le film commence à 20.35. En anglais, le film s'appelle «My Best Friend's Wedding».

Et vous?
Answers will vary.
Je voudrais regarder «Mon père, ce héros» sur Canal Plus à 20.45. C'est un film français.

L'internet, c'est cool!

Objectives

• Reading a longer text
• Develop logical thinking

Teaching Resource Options

PRINT

Workbook PE, pp. 81–84
Activités pour tous PE, pp. 47–49
Unit 3 Resource Book
   Activités pour tous TE, pp. 145–147
   Workbook TE, pp. 149–152

Teaching strategy

Do not have students read aloud since they will have difficulty pronouncing the new words and cognates. Have them follow along silently as you read the text.

Cultural note

Êtes vous branché(e)?

In France, people who like to "surf the Net," **surfer sur le Net,** are called **les cybernautes** or **les internautes.** With the Web, we can make a reservation in a Parisian hotel . . . or visit Mont-Saint-Michel . . . or take an African safari . . . **tout est possible avec l'Internet!** Young French people love to play computer games or **les jeux d'ordinateur.** Some games are on CD-ROM and are interactive. One game even allows students to visit the Louvre, with photos of paintings, and commentary (**les récits**). Also included may be sound clips (**les citations sonores**), animations (**les animations**), text, and illustrations.

L'INTERNET, c'est cool!

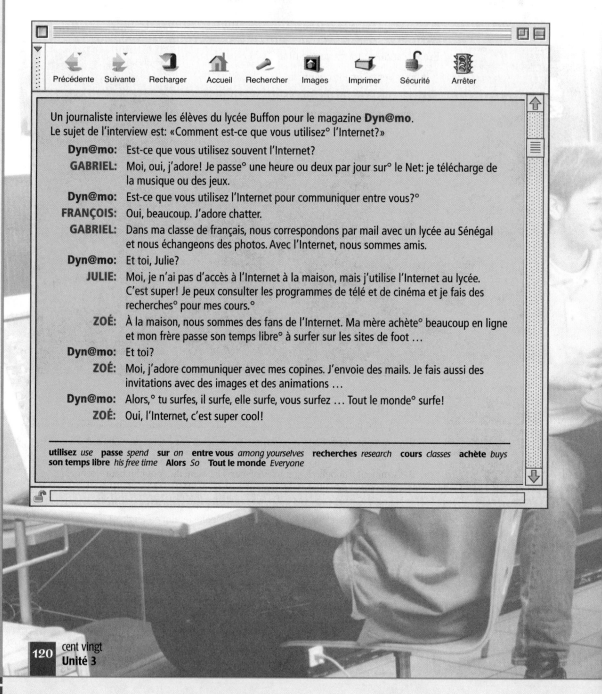

Un journaliste interviewe les élèves du lycée Buffon pour le magazine **Dyn@mo**.
Le sujet de l'interview est: «Comment est-ce que vous utilisez° l'Internet?»

Dyn@mo: Est-ce que vous utilisez souvent l'Internet?

GABRIEL: Moi, oui, j'adore! Je passe° une heure ou deux par jour sur° le Net: je télécharge de la musique ou des jeux.

Dyn@mo: Est-ce que vous utilisez l'Internet pour communiquer entre vous?°

FRANÇOIS: Oui, beaucoup. J'adore chatter.

GABRIEL: Dans ma classe de français, nous correspondons par mail avec un lycée au Sénégal et nous échangeons des photos. Avec l'Internet, nous sommes amis.

Dyn@mo: Et toi, Julie?

JULIE: Moi, je n'ai pas d'accès à l'Internet à la maison, mais j'utilise l'Internet au lycée. C'est super! Je peux consulter les programmes de télé et de cinéma et je fais des recherches° pour mes cours.°

ZOÉ: À la maison, nous sommes des fans de l'Internet. Ma mère achète° beaucoup en ligne et mon frère passe son temps libre° à surfer sur les sites de foot …

Dyn@mo: Et toi?

ZOÉ: Moi, j'adore communiquer avec mes copines. J'envoie des mails. Je fais aussi des invitations avec des images et des animations …

Dyn@mo: Alors,° tu surfes, il surfe, elle surfe, vous surfez … Tout le monde° surfe!

ZOÉ: Oui, l'Internet, c'est super cool!

---

utilisez *use* passe *spend* sur *on* entre vous *among yourselves* recherches *research* cours *classes* achète *buys*
son temps libre *his free time* Alors *So* Tout le monde *Everyone*

120 cent vingt
Unité 3

NOTE *culturelle*

Les jeunes Français et l'Internet

French people are technologically very sophisticated. They developed the **Minitel,** a precursor of the Internet, many years before this newer system of transmitting information became universally adopted.

At school, French students learn how to use the Internet in their computer science classes (**les cours d'informatique**). Many have Internet connections at home. Those who do not can go to a **cybercafé** where they can surf the Net while having a sandwich or a soda.

PETIT DICTIONNAIRE DE L'INTERNET

Télérama
le site internet

- **chatter** = *to chat*
- **envoyer un mail (un mél)** = *to send an e-mail*
- **surfer sur l'Internet (le Net)** = *to surf the Internet*
- **télécharger** = *to download*
- **être en ligne** = *to be online*

COMPARAISONS CULTURELLES

Read the **Dyn@mo** interview again and make a list of the different ways students at the lycée Buffon use the Internet. Then list the ways in which you use the Internet. Do you engage in some of the same activities as the French teenagers?

les jeunes Français
-
-
-

moi
-
-
-

cent vingt et un
Lecture et Culture 121

Comparaisons culturelles

Answers.
les jeunes Français
(Ils utilisent l'Internet pour ...)
- télécharger de la musique
- télécharger des jeux
- chatter
- correspondre par mail avec un lycée au Sénégal
- échanger des photos
- consulter les programmes de télé et de cinéma
- faire des recherches
- (acheter des choses en ligne)
- surfer
- envoyer des mails (communiquer avec des amis)
- faire des invitations

Bonjour, Trinh!
Objective
• Reading at the paragraph level

Teaching Resource Options

PRINT

Workbook PE, pp. 81–84
Activités pour tous PE, pp. 47–49
Unit 3 Resource Book
  Activités pour tous TE, pp. 145–147
  Workbook TE, pp. 149–152

Language notes
• Trinh writes in a casual style.
  Point out the shortened words:
  un prof (professeur)
  sympa (sympathique)

Teaching note
If your school has computer
capabilities, you may want to
explore the possibility of using the
Internet to facilitate instruction. You
may also consider linking your class
with an English class in France
through e-mail correspondance.
Contact the American Association of
Teachers of French (AATF) for
more information and ideas.

Questions sur le texte

1. Pourquoi est-ce que Trinh aime les boums? [Il adore danser.]

2. Quelle sorte de musique est-ce qu'il aime? [le rock, le rap, le reggae]

3. Quels sports est-ce qu'il pratique en hiver? Et en été? [En hiver, il fait du snowboard. En été, il nage et il joue au tennis.]

4. Comment est-ce qu'il joue au tennis? [assez bien]

5. Pourquoi est-ce qu'il aime l'anglais? [Le prof est sympa.]

6. Qu'est-ce qu'il aime regarder à la télé? [le sport et les films d'aventures]

7. À qui est-ce qu'il téléphone? [à sa copine]

8. Pourquoi est-ce qu'il ne téléphone pas souvent? [Son père n'aime pas ça.]

Bonjour, Trinh!

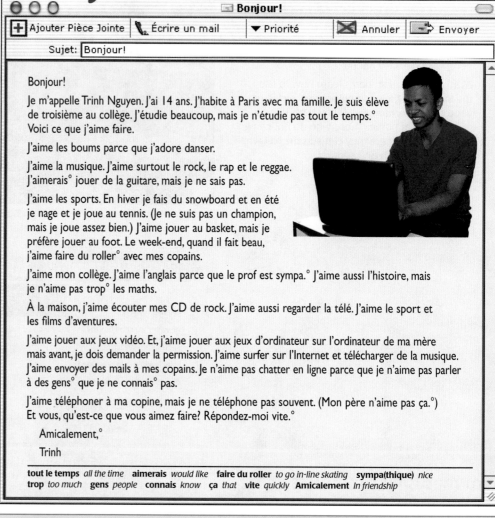

🔲 Bonjour!

➕ Ajouter Pièce Jointe   ✎ Écrire un mail   ▼ Priorité   ✉ Annuler   ➡ Envoyer

Sujet: [Bonjour!]

Bonjour!

Je m'appelle Trinh Nguyen. J'ai 14 ans. J'habite à Paris avec ma famille. Je suis élève de troisième au collège. J'étudie beaucoup, mais je n'étudie pas tout le temps.° Voici ce que j'aime faire.

J'aime les boums parce que j'adore danser.

J'aime la musique. J'aime surtout le rock, le rap et le reggae. J'aimerais° jouer de la guitare, mais je ne sais pas.

J'aime les sports. En hiver je fais du snowboard et en été je nage et je joue au tennis. (Je ne suis pas un champion, mais je joue assez bien.) J'aime jouer au basket, mais je préfère jouer au foot. Le week-end, quand il fait beau, j'aime faire du roller° avec mes copains.

J'aime mon collège. J'aime l'anglais parce que le prof est sympa.° J'aime aussi l'histoire, mais je n'aime pas trop° les maths.

À la maison, j'aime écouter mes CD de rock. J'aime aussi regarder la télé. J'aime le sport et les films d'aventures.

J'aime jouer aux jeux vidéo. Et, j'aime jouer aux jeux d'ordinateur sur l'ordinateur de ma mère mais avant, je dois demander la permission. J'aime surfer sur l'Internet et télécharger de la musique. J'aime envoyer des mails à mes copains. Je n'aime pas chatter en ligne parce que je n'aime pas parler à des gens° que je ne connais° pas.

J'aime téléphoner à ma copine, mais je ne téléphone pas souvent. (Mon père n'aime pas ça.°) Et vous, qu'est-ce que vous aimez faire? Répondez-moi vite.°

  Amicalement,°

  Trinh

---

tout le temps *all the time* **aimerais** *would like* **faire du roller** *to go in-line skating* **sympa(thique)** *nice*
trop *too much* **gens** *people* **connais** *know* **ça** *that* **vite** *quickly* **Amicalement** *In friendship*

STRATEGY Reading

Cognates You have already discovered that there are many words in French that look like English words and have similar meanings. These are called cognates. Cognates let you increase your reading comprehension effortlessly. Be sure to pronounce them the French way!

• Sometimes the spelling is the same, or almost the same:

un champion	*champion*
la permission	*permission*

• Sometimes the spelling is a little different:

les maths	*math*

122 cent vingt-deux
Unité 3

PRE-READING

Ask if any of the students in the class have pen pals.
  Est-ce que vous avez un correspondant ou une correspondante?
  Où habite votre correspondant(e)?
Tell them this is an e-mail from a French pen pal.

Activité écrite: Une lettre à Trinh

You are writing an e-mail to Trinh in which you introduce yourself and explain what you like to do. Be sure to use only vocabulary that you know in French. You may tell him:

- if you like music (and what kind)
- what sports you like to do in fall or winter
- what sports you like to do in spring or summer
- which school subjects you like and which you do not like
- what you like to do at home
- which programs you like to watch on TV
- what you like to do on the Internet and what you do not like to do

Writing Hint Use Trinh's letter as a model.

NOTE culturelle

Les Vietnamiens en France

Vietnam and other Southeast Asian countries like Laos and Cambodia have a long civilization. For a period of about eighty years until the mid-1950s, these countries were occupied and administered by France which established schools and promoted the use of the French language among their populations.

In recent years, many Vietnamese people like Trinh's family have emigrated to France. Vietnamese restaurants are very popular with French students because of their fine yet inexpensive cuisine.

cent vingt-trois
Lecture et Culture 123

Questions personnelles

1. Est-ce que tu aimes la musique? Quelle sorte de musique est-ce que tu aimes écouter? [Oui, j'aime la musique. (Non, je n'aime pas la musique.) J'aime écouter le rap.]

2. Est-ce que tu joues d'un instrument? [Oui, je joue (de la guitare). (Non, je ne joue pas d'un instrument.)]

3. Quels sports est-ce que tu pratiques en hiver? en été? [En été, je (nage). En hiver, je (joue au basketball).]

4. Est-ce que tu aimes ton école? Quelles matières est-ce que tu aimes? Quelles matières est-ce que tu n'aimes pas? [Oui, j'aime mon école. (Non, je n'aime pas mon école.) J'aime (le français et les maths). Je n'aime pas (l'anglais et l'histoire).]

5. Est-ce que tu aimes étudier le français? (Pourquoi ou pourquoi pas?) [J'aime étudier le français parce que (j'aime parler avec les Français). Je n'aime pas étudier le français parce que (mes copains ne sont pas dans la classe).]

6. Est-ce que tu téléphones souvent? À qui? Est-ce que tu aimes téléphoner? [Oui, je téléphone souvent. (Non, je ne téléphone pas souvent.) Je téléphone à (des copains). Oui, j'aime téléphoner. (Non, je n'aime pas téléphoner.)]

Additional cognates

adore
la musique
le rock
la guitare
les sports
le tennis
le week-end
mes CD
les maths ...

Teaching note

Have students use a French search engine (**un portail**) to find and set up free "French" e-mail accounts and have their own French e-mail boxes (**boîtes aux lettres**). They can even use instant messaging (**la messagerie instantanée**) to talk to their new French friends.

À l'école en France

Teaching Resource Options

PRINT

Workbook PE, pp. 81–84
Activités pour tous PE, pp. 47–49
Unit 3 Resource Book
   Activités pour tous TE, pp. 145–147
   Lesson Plans, pp. 153–154
   Block Scheduling Lesson Plans,
    pp. 155–156
   Videoscript, p. 215
   Workbook TE, pp. 149–152

VIDEO PROGRAM

VIDÉO   DVD

 IMAGES
À l'école en France

TOTAL TIME: 5:36 min.
   DVD Disk 1
   Videotape 2 (COUNTER: 00:00 min.)

B.1 Visite avec Nathalie Aubin
    (0:00-1:00 min.)

B.2 Le lycée Jean-Baptiste Corot
    (1:01-3:31 min.)

**B.3 Mini-scenes: Quel est ton sujet
    favori?**
    (3:32-4:04 min.)

B.4 Conclusion de la visite
    (4:05-5:36 min.)

À l'école en France

Bonjour, Nathalie!

Bonjour!
Je m'appelle Nathalie Aubin.
J'ai 15 ans et j'habite à Savigny-sur-Orge
avec ma famille. (Savigny est
une petite° ville à 20 kilomètres
au sud° de Paris.)
J'ai un frère, Christophe, 17 ans,
et deux soeurs, Céline, 13 ans,
et Florence, 7 ans.
Mon père est programmeur.
(Il travaille à Paris.)
Ma mère est dentiste.
(Elle travaille à Savigny.)
Je vais au lycée Jean-Baptiste
Corot.
Je suis élève° de seconde.°
Et vous?

              Nathalie

---

petite *small* **sud** *south* **élève** *student* **seconde** *tenth grade*

124 cent vingt-quatre
Unité 3

USING THE VIDEO

This **Images, À l'école en France,** was filmed at the
Lycée Jean-Baptiste Corot in Savigny-sur-Orge, near
Paris. Play the entire module as an introduction to the
photo essay.

Les photos de Nathalie

ma mère *ma soeur Céline*

Voici ma famille.

moi

mon père

mon frère Christophe et ma soeur Florence

Voici ma maison. (C'est une maison confortable, mais ce n'est pas un château!)

Voici mon école.°
Le lycée Jean-Baptiste Corot
est dans° un château!°

école *school* **dans** *in* **château** *castle*

cent vingt-cinq `125`
Lecture et Culture

CLASSROOM MANAGEMENT Groups

After showing the video, have students in groups discuss the similarities and differences between their school and the Lycée Corot. Let each group name a recorder (**secrétaire**) who will list their findings.

As a follow-up, you may want to play the video a second time.

As a full class activity, ask the recorders to read their lists and compare the findings. Which group was most observant?

Le lycée Jean-Baptiste Corot

Le lycée Jean-Baptiste Corot

Teaching Resource Options

PRINT

Workbook PE, pp. 81–84
Activités pour tous PE, pp. 47–49
Unit 3 Resource Book
    Activités pour tous TE, pp. 145–147
    Videoscript, p. 215
    Workbook TE, pp. 149–152

VIDEO PROGRAM

VIDÉO   DVD
  IMAGES

B.2 Le lycée Jean-Baptiste Corot
    (1:01-3:31 min.)

**B.3 Mini-scenes: Quel est ton
sujet favori?**
    (3:32-4:04 min.)

Teaching suggestion You may
want to play these two segments
again, having students focus on the
school itself rather than on Nathalie.

Cultural notes

• **Savigny-sur-Orge** The
construction of the **R.E.R. (Réseau
Express Régional)**, a fast commuter
train, has brought Savigny-sur-Orge
within easy commuting distance of
Paris. It takes only half an hour to
get from Savigny to the center of the
capital.

• Paintings
  –The top painting is a self-portrait of
    Jean-Baptiste Corot.
  –The bottom painting by Corot is a
    view of Chatelaine, Geneva.

Le lycée Jean-Baptiste Corot

Jean-Baptiste Corot

The lycée Jean-Baptiste Corot is located in Savigny-sur-Orge, a small town about 12 miles south of Paris. Like many French schools, it is named after a famous French person. Jean-Baptiste Corot was a 19th century painter, remembered especially for his landscapes.

The lycée Jean-Baptiste Corot is both old and modern. It was created in the 1950s on the grounds of a historical castle dating from the 12th century. The castle, which serves as the administrative center, is still surrounded by a moat. The lycée itself has many modern facilities which include:

    • **les salles de classe** *(classrooms)*
    • **la cantine** *(cafeteria)*
    • **le stade** *(stadium)* **et**
      le terrain de sport *(playing field)*

un pastel de Corot

Supplementary vocabulary
réfectoires élèves   *student cafeteria*
réfectoire professeurs   *teachers' cafeteria*

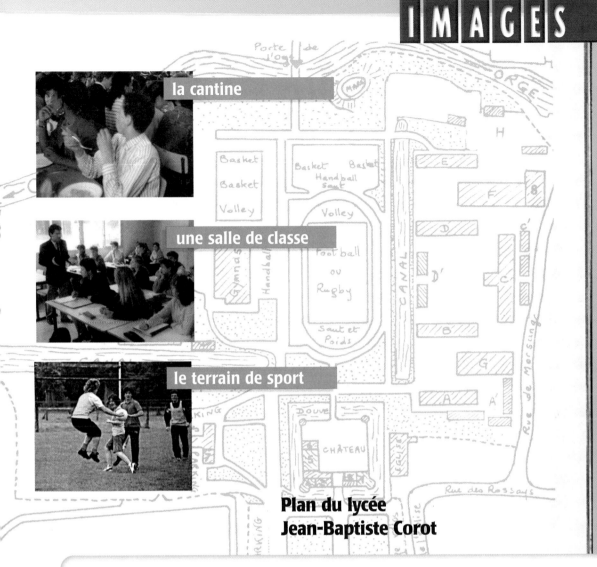

la cantine

une salle de classe

le terrain de sport

Plan du lycée Jean-Baptiste Corot

Comparaisons Culturelles

1. Compare your school to the lycée Jean-Baptiste Corot.

- Is your school named after somebody? If so, why is this person famous?

- Is your school older or more modern than the lycée Jean-Baptiste Corot? When was it built (approximately)?

- Does your school have the same facilities as the lycée Jean-Baptiste Corot? Does it have other facilities?

2. Make a map of your school, giving French names to its facilities. (Ask for your teacher's help for words you do not know.)

Teaching Resource Options

PRINT

Workbook PE, pp. 81–84
Activités pour tous PE, pp. 47–49
Unit 3 Resource Book
  Activités pour tous TE, pp. 145–147
  Workbook TE, pp. 149–152

Supplementary Vocabulary

le proviseur *principal*
le proviseur adjoint *vice principal*
le conseiller principal d'éducation
  guidance counselor
le professeur principal *homeroom
  teacher*

L'école secondaire en France

There are two types of secondary schools in France:

- **le collège,** which corresponds to the U.S. middle school (grades 6 to 9)
- **le lycée,** which corresponds to the U.S. high school (grades 10 to 12)

On the following chart, you will notice that each grade **(une classe)** is designated by a number (as in the United States): **sixième (6ᵉ), cinquième (5ᵉ), quatrième (4ᵉ),** etc. However, the progression from grade to grade is the opposite in France. The secondary school begins in France with **sixième** and ends with **terminale.**

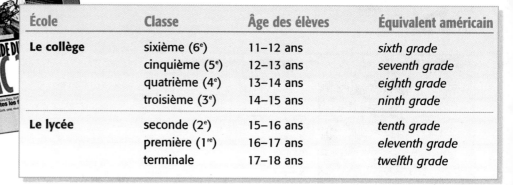

École	Classe	Âge des élèves	Équivalent américain
Le collège	sixième (6ᵉ)	11–12 ans	*sixth grade*
	cinquième (5ᵉ)	12–13 ans	*seventh grade*
	quatrième (4ᵉ)	13–14 ans	*eighth grade*
	troisième (3ᵉ)	14–15 ans	*ninth grade*
Le lycée	seconde (2ᵉ)	15–16 ans	*tenth grade*
	première (1ʳᵉ)	16–17 ans	*eleventh grade*
	terminale	17–18 ans	*twelfth grade*

A student **(un/une élève)** who does not do well in a given grade has to repeat that grade the next year. This is called **redoubler.** About 50% of the French students are kept back at least once during their secondary school studies.

At the end of high school, French students take a two-part national examination called **le baccalauréat,** or **le bac** for short, which they have to pass in order to enter the university.

- The first part, which focuses on the French language, is administered at the end of **première.**
- The second part, which is given at the end of **terminale,** offers students over twenty options reflecting their area of specialization.

Only 75% of the students who take the **bac** in a given year pass the exam. Of those who are successful, about 85% continue their studies either at the university or at a specialized professional school. Since education in France is considered a responsibility of the government, tuition is free at all public universities.

Des élèves vous parlent

David Souliac, 14 ans

J'habite à Bergerac, une petite ville
dans le sud-ouest° de la France.   *southwest*
Je suis élève de 4ᵉ au collège Jacques Prévert.
Là, j'étudie l'anglais et l'espagnol.

Antoine Restaut, 14 ans

J'habite à Paris.
Je suis élève au collège Jeannine Manuel.
C'est un collège international.
J'aime les maths et les sciences.
Je voudrais être pilote comme° mon père.   *like*

Pauline Lescure, 16 ans

Je suis élève de première au lycée Schoelcher
à Fort-de-France en Martinique.
J'étudie les sciences.
Je veux être médecin.°   *doctor*
Je voudrais aller° à l'université à Paris.   *to go*
Mais d'abord,° je dois être reçue° au bac.   *first/pass*

Le programme scolaire

Teaching Resource Options

PRINT

Workbook PE, pp. 81–84
Activités pour tous PE, pp. 47–49
Unit 3 Resource Book
   Activités pour tous TE, pp. 145–147
   Workbook TE, pp. 149–152

Le programme scolaire *(School curriculum)*

At the middle school **(au collège)**, all French students take certain required subjects **(des matières obligatoires)**. In **quatrième,** for instance, these subjects include French, math, one foreign language, history and geography, science **(sciences de la vie et de la terre** – life and earth sciences), and art. Depending on their preferences and career plans, they can also choose among a certain number of electives **(des matières facultatives).** Many opt for a second foreign language **(une langue).**

Here is a list of subjects taught in French middle schools. (Note that no school offers all the languages listed, but most schools offer three or four.) How many of the subjects can you identify?

Matières obligatoires	Matières facultatives	Langues modernes
français	latin	allemand
maths	grec	anglais
1ère langue moderne	2ème langue moderne	arabe
histoire		espagnol
géographie		hébreu
physique-chimie		italien
sciences de la vie et de la terre		portugais
technologie		russe
éducation civique		
éducation physique et sportive		
arts plastiques		
éducation musicale		

Comparaisons Culturelles

Compare the curriculum of an eighth grader in the United States with that of a French teenager in the equivalent grade **(quatrième).** You may first want to list the subjects offered in your school system for grades six through nine.

    a) Matières obligatoires
    b) Matières facultatives
    c) Langues modernes

Do you prefer the French or the American curriculum? Explain.

L'emploi du temps de Nathalie

Nathalie Aubin est en seconde au lycée Jean-Baptiste Corot. Voici son emploi du temps.

LYCÉE JEAN-BAPTISTE COROT

Étudiante: AUBIN, Nathalie

	LUNDI	MARDI	MERCREDI	JEUDI	VENDREDI	SAMEDI
8h30 à 9h30	Histoire	Allemand		Informatique°		Français
9h30 à 10h30	Anglais	Français	Anglais	Physique	Allemand	Français
10h30 à 11h30	Sport	Français	Informatique	Maths	Latin	Latin
11h30 à 12h30	Français	Latin	Maths		Sciences vie et terre	Histoire ou civilisation
13h00 à 14h00						
14h00 à 15h00	Sciences vie et terre	Maths				
15h00 à 16h00	Géographie	Maths		Allemand		
16h00 à 17h00	Physique	Anglais		Sport		

informatique *computer science*

Comparaisons Culturelles

Compare Nathalie's schedule with that of an American student in the same grade (tenth grade). You may want to make a chart:

	France	United States
number of classes per week		
number of foreign languages		
number of hours per week for sports		
other differences		

On the basis of your comparisons, do you prefer the French system or the American system? Explain.

Mon emploi du temps
Write out your own school schedule in French.

L'emploi du temps de Nathalie

Comparaisons Culturelles
Answers
Number of classes per week: 12
(Allemand, Anglais, Français, Latin, Physique, Sciences vie et terre, Informatique, Maths, Civilisation Géographie, Histoire, Sport)

Number of foreign languages: 3
(Anglais, Allemand, Latin)

Number of hours per week for sports: 2

Expressions pour la classe

Expressions pour la classe

Teaching Resource Options

PRINT

Workbook PE, pp. 81–84
Activités pour tous PE, pp. 47–49
Unit 3 Resource Book
   Activités pour tous TE, pp. 145–147
   Audioscript, p. 214
   Workbook TE, pp. 149–152

AUDIO & VISUAL

Audio Program
CD 2 Track 23

Overhead Transparencies
50 Classroom Objects
51 *La technologie*
52 *Une classe branchée*

Expressions pour la classe

Le professeur dit …

Écoutez!

à une élève   à un élève   à la classe

Regarde! *(Look!)*	**Regardez!**
Regarde la vidéo.	Regardez la vidéo.
Écoute! *(Listen!)*	**Écoutez!**
Écoute la cassette *(tape)*.	Écoutez la cassette.
Parle! *(Speak!)*	**Parlez!**
Parle plus fort *(louder)*.	Parlez plus fort.
Réponds! *(Answer!)*	**Répondez!**
Réponds à la question.	Répondez à la question.
Répète! *(Repeat!)*	**Répétez!**
Répète la phrase *(sentence)*.	Répétez la phrase.
Lis! *(Read!)*	**Lisez!**
Lis l'exercice.	Lisez l'exercice.
Écris! *(Write!)*	**Écrivez!**
Écris dans ton cahier.	Écrivez dans vos cahiers.

Prends *(Take)*	une feuille de papier.	**Prenez**	une feuille de papier.
	un crayon		un crayon
Ouvre *(Open)*	ton livre.	**Ouvrez**	vos livres.
	la porte		la porte
Ferme *(Close)*	ton cahier.	**Fermez**	vos cahiers.
	la fenêtre		la fenêtre

Viens! *(Come!)*	**Venez!**
Viens ici.	Venez ici.
Va! *(Go!)*	**Allez!**
Va au tableau.	Allez au tableau.
Lève-toi! *(Stand up!)*	**Levez-vous!**
Assieds-toi! *(Sit down!)*	**Asseyez-vous!**

Apporte-moi *(Bring me)*		**Apportez-moi**	
Donne-moi *(Give me)*	ton devoir.	**Donnez-moi**	vos devoirs.
Montre-moi *(Show me)*		**Montrez-moi**	

132 cent trente-deux
Unité 3

TEACHING NOTE

Le professeur dit

These phrases are primarily for listening comprehension. Try to use these regularly in class so that students can internalize them and acquire a feeling for French rhythm and intonation patterns.

Quelques objets; Tu dis

These words and phrases are active. Students will be using them to express themselves in class and ask questions.

Quelques objets

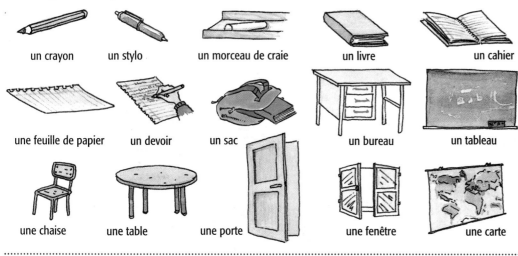

un crayon   un stylo   un morceau de craie   un livre   un cahier

une feuille de papier   un devoir   un sac   un bureau   un tableau

une chaise   une table   une porte   une fenêtre   une carte

Tu dis ...

Je sais.   *I know.*

Je ne sais pas.   *I don't know.*

Je ne comprends pas.   *I don't understand.*

Que veut dire ... ?   *What does ... mean?*

Comment dit-on ... en français?   *How does one say ... in French?*

Écoutez bien!

Imagine you are in a school in France. Listen carefully to what different French teachers ask you to do and carry out their instructions. If you have trouble understanding the commands, your teacher will mime the actions for you.

Supplementary vocabulary

l'adresse f. électronique   *e-mail address*
l'autoroute f. de l'information, l'Inforoute   *the information highway*
un casque   *headphones*
le clavier   *keyboard*
le disque dur   *hard drive (computer)*
un écran   *screen (computer)*
envoyer quelque chose par e-mail (courrier électronique), par messagerie vocale   *send an e-mail message, send a voice mail message*
un fax-modem   *the machine that sends* **un fax**
faxer (envoyer un fax)   *to fax*
une imprimante   *printer*
un lecteur de CD   *CD player*
un mail (un mél)   *e-mail*
la messagerie vocale   *voice mail*
le répondeur   *answering machine*
le tapis souris   *mouse pad*

COMPREHENSION   Classroom objects

You may want to introduce these words with gestures.
    Montrez-moi une feuille de papier. etc.
    Mettez un stylo sur la feuille de papier.
    Mettez un livre sur le stylo.
    Mettez un morceau de craie sur le bureau.

Expansion activities PLANNING AHEAD

Games

• Vous rappelez-vous? *(Do you remember?)*

Place a covered transparency of the items presented on pages 140, 142, or 147 on an overhead projector. Uncover the transparency for 30 seconds and have students look at it. Then, recover the items and have students write down, in French, all of the items they can remember seeing. The student who remembers the most objects on the transparency, and spells them correctly, is the winner. You can expand the activity by having students practice prepositions of location and write down the positions of the objects in relation to each other.

Pacing Suggestion: Upon completion of Leçon 9.

• La course aux verbes

After reviewing the conjugation of *-er* verbs, *être, faire,* and *avoir,* divide the class into two or three teams. Announce an infinitive and a subject pronoun. The first member of each team should hurry to the board, write the conjugation, and then use the verb form in a simple sentence (i.e., subject/verb/object.) The first player to finish writing the correct form in a correct sentence wins a point for his or her team.

Pacing Suggestion: Upon completion of Leçon 10.

• Qui est-ce?

Select one person in the class to be the mystery person and don't tell the other students whom you have chosen. Students will try to guess who the mystery person is by asking you *oui/non* questions. You may want to give students some sample questions to get them started. The first student to correctly guess the mystery person gets to select someone else. His or her classmates then try to guess the new mystery student.

MODEL: —C'est un garçon?
—Non.

—C'est une fille?
—Oui!

—Elle est grande?
—Oui.

—Elle aime jouer au tennis?
—Oui.

—C'est Lucie?
—Oui.

Pacing Suggestion: Upon completion of Leçon 11.

Projects

• Mon site Internet

Have students visit several French Web sites. You may want to give them clues for an effective search using a French word such as *musée* as the basis of their search. Ask them to find the French words for the buttons normally found on a Web page, such as "Home," "Help," and "Back." (You may also have students refer to the Web page found on page 120.) Then have students use these words to create their own French Web page layout. Select a topic for the Web page or have students make a personal Web page telling who they are and what they do. Then have them create a visual model of what the Web page would look like. Students may create their layouts by hand or on the computer.

Pacing Suggestion: Upon completion of Leçon 12.

Bulletin Boards

• Favorite Celebrities

Suggest that students create posters profiling their favorite celebrities. Divide the class into small groups. Have the students in each group compile a list of their favorite celebrities with descriptions of each. Groups may:

• look for information about the backgrounds of their chosen celebrities
• find out what they like to do and where they like to go
• bring photos from magazines or the internet to illustrate their posters
• use adjectives and the verb *avoir* in their descriptions

Each group should create a colorful poster they can use to present the information to the rest of the class. As an alternative, you may want to have students create personal profiles and posters illustrating **Notre Classe** or **Notre École.**

Pacing Suggestion: Upon completion of Leçon 10.

Storytelling

• Mini-histoire

Ask students to use the vocabulary on page 144 to create a description of their real bedrooms or of their "dream" bedrooms. First, have students draw a simple picture of their rooms and have them write out a description of the objects in it. Then have them elaborate on their image, adding details and changing the sentences.

Pacing Suggestion: Upon completion of Leçon 9.

Recipe

• Gratin de pommes de terre

This tasty side dish combines the flavors of potatoes, onions, and cheese. Serve with a main dish of fish, meat, or chicken.

Since *crème fraîche* is not widely available in the United States, it is possible to create your own using any of the following combinations.

• half sour cream and half heavy cream
• heavy cream with some lemon juice or buttermilk added to it
• skim of the heavy cream layer of a large container of organic plain whole milk yogurt

Pacing Suggestion: Upon completion of Leçon 11.

Hands-on Crafts

• Les voitures françaises

Have students investigate what French cars look like. They may want to visit the Web sites of Renault, Peugeot-Citroën, and other car manufacturers. Then have each student create a model of one of the French cars using clay. Display the finished models and have students vote on the car they would most like to buy.

Pacing Suggestion: Upon completion of Leçon 12.

End of Unit

• Mobile

First, have students brainstorm a list of words to describe themselves. Students may wish to include information about their families, favorite colors, favorite activities, etc. (Encourage students to provide positive information.) Next, have them cut out photos or create illustrations to represent each of their descriptive words and mount the photos or illustrations on pieces of construction paper or cardboard. Have students write a sentence caption for each image. For example **«Je suis blonde.» «J'aime regarder la télé.»** Finally, have students use string and dowel rods or straws to connect their illustrated sentences and create a mobile. You may wish to display the mobiles by hanging them from the classroom ceiling.

Rubric   **A** = 13–15 pts. **B** = 10–12 pts. **C** = 7–9 pts. **D** = 4–6 pts. **F** = < 4 pts.

Criteria	Scale				
Vocabulary Use	1	2	3	4	5
Grammar/Spelling Accuracy	1	2	3	4	5
Creativity	1	2	3	4	5

Gratin de pommes de terre

Ingrédients
• 120 g de Gruyère râpé
• 1 oeuf
• 15 cl de crème fraîche
• 30 g de beurre
• 1 oignon, coupé finement
• 700 g de pommes de terres moyennes, épluchées et coupées en tranches

Préparation
1. Préchauffez le four à 180° C et beurrez un plat à four.
2. Mettez les tranches de pommes de terres dans un bol d'eau.
3. Mettez le beurre et l'oignon dans une casserole, et cuisez à feu doux jusqu'à ce que l'oignon soit mou.
4. Mettez une couche de pommes de terres dans la casserole. Ajoutez une cuillère d'oignon dessus.
5. Saupoudrez de fromage. Continuez à ajouter des couches de pommes de terre, d'oignons et de fromage.
6. Battez l'œuf dans la crème. Versez sur les pommes de terre. Saupoudrez de fromage.
7. Mettez une heure et demie au four.

Ingredients
• approx. 1/2 cup grated Gruyère (Swiss) cheese
• 1 egg
• approx. 3 tsp. crème fraîche (1/2 sour cream, 1/2 heavy cream)
• approx. 2 tbsp. butter
• 1 onion, cut in thin slices
• approx. 3 cups medium-sized potatoes, peeled and cut in slices

Directions
1. Preheat the oven to 356° F. Butter a baking dish.
2. Put the potato slices in a bowl of water.
3. Cook the onions in butter on low heat until they soften.
4. Put a layer of potatoes in the baking dish. Top with a spoonful of onion.
5. Sprinkle with cheese. Continue to add layers of potatoes, onions, and cheese.
6. Beat the egg with the crème fraîche. Pour over the potatoes and add more cheese.
7. Bake for an hour and a half.

Planning Guide CLASSROOM MANAGEMENT

OBJECTIVES

Communication
- Talk about yourself: your personality and what you look like *pp. 138–139, 165, 167*
- Describe your friends and how old they are *pp. 138–139*
- Describe your room *p. 144*
- Talk about everyday objects that you own or use *pp. 140, 142, 147*
- Describe these objects: their color and size *pp. 174, 175*

Grammar
- Le verbe *avoir p. 152*
- Les noms et les articles: masculin et féminin *p. 153*
- Les noms et les articles: le pluriel *pp. 154–155*
- L'article indéfini dans les phrases négatives *p. 156*
- L'usage de l'article défini dans le sens général *p. 158*
- L'usage de l'article défini avec les jours de la semaine *p. 159*
- Les adjectifs: masculin et féminin *p. 164*
- Les adjectifs: le pluriel *p. 166*
- La place des adjectifs *p. 168*
- Les couleurs *p. 174*
- La place des adjectifs avant le nom *p. 175*
- *Il est* ou *c'est*? *p. 177*
- Les expressions impersonnelles avec *c'est p. 178*

Vocabulary
- La description des personnes *pp. 138–139*
- Les objets *p. 140*
- Les affaires personnelles *p. 142*
- Ma chambre *p. 144*
- Mon ordinateur *p. 147*
- Expressions pour la conversation *pp. 157, 167, 176*
- La description *p. 165*
- Les adjectifs de nationalité *p. 167*
- Les couleurs *p. 174*
- Les adjectifs qui précèdent le nom *p. 175*
- Opinions *p. 178*

Pronunciation
- Les articles *le* et *les p. 159*
- Les consonnes finales *p. 169*
- Les lettres «ch» *p. 179*

Culture
- Haïti *p. 151*
- L'amitié et la bande de copains *p. 163*
- Les Français et la voiture *p. 173*
- La mobylette et le scooter *p. 189*
- Toulouse *p. 191*

PROGRAM RESOURCES

 Print
- Workbook PE, *pp. 85–116*
- *Activités pour tous* PE, *pp. 51–69*
- Block Scheduling Copymasters, *pp. 65–96*
- Teacher to Teacher Copymasters
- Unit 4 Resource Book
  - Lessons 9–12 Resources
    - Workbook TE
    - *Activités pour tous* TE
    - Lesson Plans
    - Block Scheduling Lesson Plans
    - Family Letter
    - Absent Student Copymasters
    - Family Involvement
    - Video Activities
    - Videoscripts
    - Audioscripts
    - Assessment Program
  - Unit 4 Resources
    - Communipak
    - *Activités pour tous* TE Reading
    - Workbook TE Reading and Culture Activities
    - Assessment Program
    - Answer Keys

 Audiovisual
- Audio Program PE CD 2 Tracks 24–45
- Audio Program Workbook CD 8 Tracks 1–24
- *Chansons* Audio CD
- Video Program Modules 9, 10, 11, 12
- Overhead Transparencies
  - 2a Map of the French-Speaking World;
  - 19 *La description physique;*
  - 20 *Quelques objets (a);*
  - 21 *Quelques objets (b);*
  - 22 *Dans ma chambre;*
  - 23 *Les prépositions;*
  - 24 *Le grenier;*
  - 25 Class schedule;
  - 26 *La description;*
  - 27 *Les adjectifs de nationalité;*
  - 28 *Les couleurs;*

 Technology
- Online Workbook
- ClassZone.com
- eTest Plus Online/Test Generator CD-ROM
- EasyPlanner Plus Online/EasyPlanner CD-ROM
- Power Presentations on CD-ROM

 Assessment Program Options

Lesson Quizzes
Portfolio Assessment
Unit Test Form A
Unit Test Form B
Unit Test Part III (Alternate) Cultural Awareness
Listening Comprehension Performance Test
Speaking Performance Test
Reading Comprehension Performance Test
Writing Performance Test
Multiple Choice Test Items
Test Scoring Tools
Audio Program CD 14 Tracks 17–24
Answer Keys
eTest Plus Online/Test Generator CD-ROM

Pacing Guide SAMPLE LESSON PLAN

DAY	DAY	DAY	DAY	DAY
1 **Unité 4 Opener** **Leçon 9** • Vocabulaire et Culture– Les personnes et les objets • Vocabulaire–La description des personnes	**2** **Leçon 9** • Vocabulaire–La description des personnes *(continued)* • Vocabulaire–Les objets	**3** **Leçon 9** • Vocabulaire–Les affaires personnelles • Vocabulaire–Ma chambre	**4** **Leçon 9** • Vocabulaire–Ma chambre *(continued)* • Vocabulaire– Mon ordinateur	**5** **Leçon 9** • À votre tour!
6 **Leçon 10** • Vive la différence! • Note culturelle–Haïti • Le verbe *avoir* • Vocabulaire– Expressions avec *avoir*	**7** **Leçon 10** • Les noms et les articles: masculin et féminin • Les noms et les articles: le pluriel	**8** **Leçon 10** • L'article indéfini dans les phrases négatives	**9** **Leçon 10** • Vocabulaire–Expressions pour la conversation • L'usage de l'article défini dans le sens général	**10** **Leçon 10** • L'usage de l'article défini avec les jours de la semaine • Prononciation– Les articles *le* et *les*
11 **Leçon 10** • À votre tour!	**12** **Leçon 11** • Le copain de Mireille • Note culturelle–L'amitié et la bande de copains • Les adjectifs: masculin et féminin	**13** **Leçon 11** • Vocabulaire– La description • Les adjectifs: le pluriel	**14** **Leçon 11** • Vocabulaire–Les adjectifs de nationalité • Vocabulaire–Expressions pour la conversation • La place des adjectifs • Prononciation– Les consonnes finales	**15** **Leçon 11** • À votre tour!
16 **Leçon 12** • La voiture de Roger • Note culturelle– Les Français et la voiture • Les couleurs • Vocabulaire–Les couleurs	**17** **Leçon 12** • La place des adjectifs avant le nom • Vocabulaire–Les adjectifs qui précèdent le nom • Vocabulaire–Expressions pour la conversation	**18** **Leçon 12** • *Il est* ou *c'est*? • Les expressions impersonnelles avec *c'est* • Vocabulaire–Opinions • Prononciation– Les lettres «ch»	**19** **Leçon 12** • À votre tour!	**20** • Tests de contrôle
21 • Unit 4 Test	**22** • Entracte–Lecture et culture			

Student Text Listening Activity Scripts
AUDIO PROGRAM

▶ **LEÇON 9 LE FRANÇAIS PRATIQUE** Les personnes et les objets

• **La description des personnes** *p. 138* CD 2, TRACK 24

How to describe someone. Écoutez et répétez.

Qui est-ce? #   C'est un copain. #
Qui est-ce? #   C'est une copine. #
Comment s'appelle-t-il? #   Il s'appelle Marc. #
Comment s'appelle-t-elle? #   Elle s'appelle Sophie. #
Quel âge a-t-il? #   Il a seize ans. #
Quel âge a-t-elle? #   Elle a quinze ans. #
Comment est-il? #   Il est petit. # Il est blond. #
Comment est-elle? #   Elle est grande. # Elle est brune. #

Les personnes

une personne #
un étudiant #   une étudiante #
un élève #   une élève #
un camarade #   une camarade #
un homme #   une femme #
un professeur, un prof #   un professeur, une prof #
un voisin #   une voisine #

La description physique

Il est grand. #   Elle est grande. #
Il est petit. #   Elle est petite. #
Il est brun. #   Elle est brune. #
Il est blond. #   Elle est blonde. #
Il est beau. #   Elle est belle. # Elle est jolie. #
Il est jeune. #   Elle est jeune. #

À votre tour!

• **Écoutez bien!** *p. 148* CD 2, TRACK 25

You will hear a series of sentences. In each one an object is mentioned. If you see the object only in Léa's room, mark A. If you see the object only in Pierre's room, mark B. If you see the object in the two rooms, mark both A and B. You will hear each sentence twice. Listen carefully. Écoutez bien.

1. Tu as un ordinateur. #
2. Regarde l'affiche. #
3. La fenêtre est grande. #
4. Montre-moi ton baladeur, s'il te plaît. #
5. Où est la radiocassette? #
6. Qu'est-ce qu'il y a sur le lit? #
7. C'est derrière la porte. #
8. Tu joues de la guitare? #
9. La table n'est pas très grande. #
10. Est-ce que l'appareil-photo marche bien? #
11. Est-ce que je peux utiliser le téléphone? #
12. Où est ton livre de français? #
13. Est-ce que tu as un portable? #
14. La chaise est assez confortable. #
15. J'écoute souvent la chaîne hi-fi. #
16. Le bureau est assez petit. #
17. C'est une raquette anglaise. #
18. Zut! La lampe ne marche pas. #

• **Conversation dirigée** *p. 148* CD 2, TRACK 26

Écoutez la conversation entre André et Marie.

André: Est-ce que tu as un ordinateur?
Marie: Oui.
André: Est-ce qu'il marche bien?

Marie: Oui, il marche très bien. Pourquoi?
André: Je voudrais envoyer un mail à un copain.
Marie: L'ordinateur est sur le bureau dans ma chambre.

• **Créa-dialogue** *p. 149* CD 2, TRACK 27

Listen to the sample *Créa-dialogues.* Écoutez les conversations.
Modèle: –Qui est-ce?   –C'est un copain.
          –Comment s'appelle-t-il?   –Il s'appelle Éric.
          –Quel âge a-t-il?   –Il a quatorze ans.

Maintenant, écoutez le dialogue numéro 1.

–Qui est-ce?   –C'est une cousine.
–Comment s'appelle-t-elle?   –Elle s'appelle Valérie.
–Quel âge a-t-elle?   –Elle a vingt ans.

▶ **LEÇON 10** Vive la différence!

• **Vive la différence!** *p. 150*

A. Compréhension orale CD 2, TRACK 28

Please turn to page 150 for complete *Compréhension orale* text.

B. Écoutez et répétez. CD 2, TRACK 29

You will now hear a paused version of the dialog. Listen to the speaker and repeat right after he or she has completed the sentence.

• **Prononciation** *p. 159* CD 2, TRACK 30

Les articles *le* et *les*

Écoutez: le sac   les sacs

Be sure to distinguish between the pronunciation of **le** and **les.** In spoken French, that is often the only way to tell the difference between a singular and a plural noun.

Répétez: /lə/   le # le sac # le vélo # le portable # le copain # le voisin #
           /le/   le$ # le$ sac$ # le$ vélo$ # le$ portable$ # le$ copain$ # le$ voisin$ #

À votre tour!

• **Allô!** *p. 160* CD 2, TRACK 31

Jean-Marc is phoning some friends. Match his questions on the left with his friends' answers on the right.

1. Quel âge a ton copain?   Quatorze ans.
2. Est-ce qu'Éric a un scooter?   Non, mais il a une moto.
3. Où est l'appareil-photo?   Il est sur la table.
4. Tu as un baladeur?   Oui, mais je n'ai pas de chaîne hi-fi.
5. Est-ce que tu aimes étudier l'anglais? Oui, mais je préfère l'espagnol.
6. Tu as soif?   Oui, je voudrais une limonade.

• **Créa-dialogue** *p. 161* CD 2, TRACK 32

Listen to some sample *Créa-dialogues.* Écoutez les conversations.
Modèle: –Tu aimes le tennis?   –Oui, j'aime le tennis.
          –Tu as une raquette?   –Oui, j'ai une raquette.

          –Tu aimes le tennis?   –Non, je n'aime pas le tennis.
          –Tu as une raquette?   –Non, je n'ai pas de raquette.

Maintenant, écoutez le dialogue numéro 1.

–Tu aimes la musique?   –Oui, j'aime la musique.
–Tu as une radiocassette?   –Non, je n'ai pas de radiocassette.

▶ **LEÇON 11** Le copain de Mireille

• **Le copain de Mireille** *p. 162*

A. Compréhension orale CD 2, TRACK 33

Please turn to page 162 for complete *Compréhension orale* text.

B. Écoutez et répétez. CD 2, TRACK 34

You will now hear a paused version of the dialog. Listen to the speaker and repeat right after he or she has completed the sentence.

• Vocabulaire p. 165 CD 2, TRACK 35

La description

Listen and repeat the descriptions after the speaker. Écoutez et répétez.

Il est **amusant**. #	Elle est **amusante**. #
Il est **intelligent**. #	Elle est **intelligente**. #
Il est **intéressant**. #	Elle est **intéressante**. #
Il n'est pas **méchant**. #	Elle n'est pas **méchante**. #
Il n'est pas **bête**. #	Elle n'est pas **bête**. #
Il est **sympathique**. #	Elle est **sympathique**. #
Il est **timide**. #	Elle n'est pas **timide**. #
Il est **gentil**. #	Elle est **gentille**. #
Il est **mignon**. #	Elle est **mignonne**. #
Il est **sportif**. #	Elle est **sportive**. #
assez #	Nous sommes **assez** intelligents. #
très #	Vous n'êtes pas **très** sportifs! #

• Prononciation p. 169 CD 2, TRACK 36

Les consonnes finales

Écoutez: blond   blonde

As you know, when the last letter of a word is a consonant, that consonant is often silent. But when a word ends in "**e**," the consonant before it is pronounced. As you practice the following adjectives, be sure to distinguish between the masculine and the feminine forms.

Répétez: blond #	blonde #
grand #	grande #
petit #	petite #
amusant #	amusante #
français #	française #
anglais #	anglaise #
américain #	américaine #
canadien #	canadienne #

À votre tour!

• Allô! p. 170 CD 2, TRACK 37

Listen to the phone conversations. Écoutez les conversations.

1. Ton frère aime jouer au foot?   Oui, il est très sportif.
2. Cécile et Sophie sont mignonnes, n'est-ce pas?   Oui, et intelligentes aussi!
3. Pourquoi est-ce que tu invites Olivier?   Parce qu'il est amusant et sympathique.
4. Tu aimes la classe?   Oui, j'ai un professeur très intéressant.
5. Tu as des cousins?   Oui, mais ils ne sont pas très sympathiques.

• Créa-dialogue p. 170 CD 2, TRACK 38

Listen to some sample *Créa-dialogues*. Écoutez les conversations.

Modèle: –J'ai des cousins mexicains.
　　　　　–Ils sont mignons?
　　　　　–Oui, ils sont très mignons.

Maintenant, écoutez le dialogue numéro 1.

–J'ai une voisine anglaise.
–Elle est blonde?
–Non, elle est brune.

▶ LEÇON 12 La voiture de Roger

• Dialogue p. 172

A. Compréhension orale CD 2, TRACK 39

Please turn to page 172 for complete *Compréhension orale* text.

B. Écoutez et répétez. CD 2, TRACK 40

You will now hear a paused version of the dialog. Listen to the speaker and repeat right after he or she has completed the sentence.

• Vocabulaire p. 174 CD 2, TRACK 41

Les couleurs

Écoutez et répétez.

blanc #	blanche #
noir #	noire #
bleu #	bleue #
rouge #	rouge #
jaune #	jaune #
vert #	verte #
gris #	grise #
marron #	marron #
orange #	orange #
rose #	rose #

• Vocabulaire p. 175 CD 2, TRACK 42

Les adjectifs qui précèdent le nom

Écoutez et répétez.

beau # **belle** #	Regarde la **belle** voiture!
joli #	Qui est la **jolie** fille avec André?
grand #	Nous habitons dans un **grand** appartement.
petit #	Ma soeur a un **petit** ordinateur.
bon # **bonne** #	Tu es un **bon** copain.
mauvais #	Patrick est un **mauvais** élève.

• Prononciation p. 179 CD 2, TRACK 43

Les lettres «ch»

Écoutez: chien

The letters "**ch**" are usually pronounced like the English "*sh.*"

Répétez: chien # chat # chose # marche #
　　　　　chouette # chocolat # affiche #
　　　　　Michèle a un chat et deux chiens. #

À votre tour

• Allô! p. 180 CD 2, TRACK 44

Listen to the phone conversations. Écoutez les conversations.

1. De quelle couleur est ton vélo?   Il est vert.
2. Ta raquette est bleue?   Non, elle est blanche.
3. Tu aimes regarder la télé?   Oui, c'est amusant.
4. C'est un magazine français?   Non, il est canadien.
5. Philippe n'aime pas parler en public?   C'est vrai! Il est très timide.

• Créa-dialogue p. 180 CD 2, TRACK 45

Listen to some sample *Créa-dialogues*. Écoutez les conversations.

Modèle: **Détective 1:** Qu'est-ce qu'il y a devant le café?
　　　　　Détective 2: Il y a une voiture.
　　　　　Détective 1: Elle est grande ou petite?
　　　　　Détective 2: C'est une petite voiture.

Maintenant, écoutez le dialogue numéro 1.

Détective 1: Qu'est-ce qu'il y a devant la phamarcie?
Détective 2: Il y a une moto.
Détective 1: Elle est rouge ou bleue?
Détective 2: C'est une moto rouge.

Complete videoscripts, plus Workbook and Assessment audioscripts, are available in the Unit Resource Books.

UNITÉ 4

Main Theme
• People and possessions

COMMUNICATION
• Telling others about yourself
• Describing friends
• Giving people's ages
• Describing a bedroom
• Talking about and describing everyday objects

CULTURES
• Learning about how French teens spend their free time
• Learning about Haiti
• Learning how to get a driver's license in France
• Learning how French teenagers use scooters or mopeds.

CONNECTIONS
• Connecting to Art: Learning about Haitian art
• Connecting to Music: Learning about Haitian music styles
• Connecting to English: Learning grammar terms

COMPARISONS
• Comparing attitudes toward friendship in France and the U.S.
• Comparing animal expressions in French and English

COMMUNITIES
• Using French for personal enjoyment
• Using French to write a letter

UNITÉ 4
Le monde personnel et familier

LEÇON 9 LE FRANÇAIS PRATIQUE: Les personnes et les objets

LEÇON 10 Vive la différence!

LEÇON 11 Le copain de Mireille

LEÇON 12 La voiture de Roger

THÈME ET OBJECTIFS

People and possessions

When you meet French teenagers, you will want to share information about yourself, your friends, and your possessions.

In this unit, you will learn …

• to talk about yourself: your personality and what you look like
• to describe your friends and how old they are
• to describe your room
• to talk about everyday objects that you own or use
• to describe these objects: their size and color

WEBQUEST
CLASSZONE.COM

UNIT OVERVIEW

▶ **Communication Goals:** Students will learn to describe themselves and their family, friends, and personal possessions.

▶ **Linguistic Goals:** The focus is on the noun group: articles, nouns, and adjectives. The passé composé is introduced informally.

▶ **Critical Thinking Goals:** Students are introduced to the concepts of gender and noun-adjective agreement. They learn to observe and apply these patterns in French.

▶ **Cultural Goals:** This unit presents the multi-cultural reality of contemporary France, while highlighting the common interests of French and American youth.

cent trente-cinq
Unité 4 135

Teaching Resource Options

PRINT

Unit 4 Resource Book
    Family Letter, p. 17

AUDIO & VISUAL

Audio Program
Chansons CD

TECHNOLOGY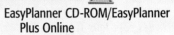

EasyPlanner CD-ROM/EasyPlanner
    Plus Online

Middle School Copymasters

Unité 5: Conversations, worksheets, vocabulary games and drills, word-search puzzle, practice teaching project, pp. T25–T29

Pacing

Unit 4 reviews and expands considerably on Unit 1 of **Invitation au français**. As in Unit 3, there is a dual emphasis on both oral and written skills.

For specific suggestions on pacing, turn to page 133D.

Leçon 9

Main Topic Describing people and things

Teaching Resource Options

PRINT

Workbook PE, pp. 85–92
Activités pour tous PE, pp. 51–53
Block Scheduling Copymasters,
pp. 65–72
Unit 4 Resource Book
Activités pour tous TE, pp. 9–11
Audioscript, pp. 32–34
Communipak, pp. 140–160
Lesson Plans, pp. 12–13
Block Scheduling Lesson Plans, pp. 14–16
Absent Student Copymasters, pp. 18–22
Video Activities, pp. 25–28
Videoscript, pp. 29–30
Workbook TE, pp. 1–8

AUDIO & VISUAL

Audio Program
CD 8 Tracks 1–6

Overhead Tranparencies
2a Map of the French-Speaking World

TECHNOLOGY
Online Workbook

VIDEO PROGRAM

VIDÉO   DVD

MODULE 9
Le français pratique
Les personnes et les objets

TOTAL TIME: 7:28 min.
DVD Disk 1
Videotape 2 (COUNTER: 28:10 min.)

9.1 Mini-scenes: Listening
– J'ai une guitare (29:20–30:31 min.)

9.2 Mini-scenes: Speaking
– Qu'est-ce que c'est?
(30:32–31:39 min.)

9.3 Dialogue: Tu as un portable?
(31:40–32:57 min.)

9.4 Mini-scenes: Speaking
– Où est-il? (32:58–34:13 min.)

9.5 Vignette culturelle: La chambre de Catherine (34:14–35:38 min.)

Comprehension practice Play the entire module through as an introduction to the lesson.

LEÇON

9

LE FRANÇAIS
PRATIQUE
VIDÉO · DVD · AUDIO

Les personnes et les objets

Accent sur … les jeunes Français

France is a young country. One quarter of the population is under the age of twenty. In their daily lives outside school, young people in France are not that different from their counterparts in the United States. They enjoy listening to music and going to the movies. On weekends, they go to the mall or into the city to check out the newest teen fashions and the latest in video games and sound equipment. As computers become more and more widespread, French young people often spend their free time surfing the Internet and participating in chat rooms and forums.

Since almost everyone studies English in school, French teenagers are very much aware of the American way of life. They have a generally positive attitude towards the United States and many would like to visit our country.

Thomas a un vélo. C'est un vélo anglais. Michèle n'a pas de vélo. Elle a un scooter.

Élodie et Paul font une promenade en ville. Paul a un baladeur. Il écoute un CD. Élodie a un portable. Elle téléphone à une copine.

136 cent trente-six
Unité 4

SETTING THE SCENE

Ask students what kinds of things they buy, other than food and clothes: school supplies, books, posters, CDs, audio equipment, etc.

Ask what other possessions they have: a watch, a camera, a bicycle, etc.

As they watch **Video Module 9,** they will meet many French young people who will talk about their own possessions.

In the last segment, Olivier invites them to his room and points out some of his favorite things.

Cultural notes

• The U.S. population is about 290 million. Less than 20% percent of the U.S. population is under 20.

• North Africa, French-speaking West Africa, Vietnam, Laos, and Cambodia are all former French colonies.

Photo cultural note

• **Le baladeur** Like their American counterparts, French teenagers love to listen to music through headphones (**des écouteurs**) on their portable players (**un baladeur**).

Jean-Marc et Valérie sont devant un magasin d'équipement hi-fi. Ils regardent des mini-chaînes.

Zaïna a un ordinateur. Elle surfe sur l'Internet. Elle aime aussi jouer aux jeux d'ordinateur avec Ousmane.

cent trente-sept
Leçon 9 137

MULTICULTURALISM IN FRANCE

PROP: Transparency 2a: Map of the French-Speaking World

French society is becoming increasingly multicultural as the country attracts immigrants representing many different traditions and backgrounds.

On the world map on pp. R2–R3, have students find the main countries of origin of these French immigrant groups:

Les Arabes et les Musulmans: l'Algérie, la Tunisie, le Maroc

Les Noirs: l'Afrique occidentale – la Côte d'Ivoire, le Sénégal, le Mali ...

Les Orientaux: le Viêt-Nam, le Cambodge

138 · Vocabulaire et Communication
Unité 4 LEÇON 9

SECTION A

Communicative function
Describing people

Teaching Resource Options

PRINT

Workbook PE, pp. 85–92
Unit 4 Resource Book
  Audioscript, p. 31
  Communipak, pp. 140–160
  Workbook TE, pp. 1–8

AUDIO & VISUAL

Audio Program
CD 2 Track 24
Overhead Transparencies
19 *La description physique*

 Review and expansion

Phrases from **Invitation au français.**

Casual speech Questions can be formed using a rising intonation:

C'est qui?
Il/Elle s'appelle comment?
Il/Elle a quel âge?

Language note The term **un étudiant (une étudiante)** refers to college students, although it is now sometimes used in talking about high school students, especially older ones. The traditional term for high school students is **un lycéen (une lycéenne)**.

Teaching strategy To help students differentiate between the sound of **un** and **une**, point to various students and ask:

Est-ce que c'est un élève ou une élève?

Est-ce que c'est un camarade ou une camarade?

A VOCABULAIRE La description des personnes

▶ *How to describe someone:*

Qui est-ce?
C'est un copain.

Qui est-ce?
C'est un copain.

Qui est-ce?
C'est une copine.

Comment s'appelle-t-il?
Il s'appelle Marc.

Comment s'appelle-t-elle?
Elle s'appelle Sophie.

Quel âge a-t-il?
Il a seize ans.

Quel âge a-t-elle?
Elle a quinze ans.

Comment est-il?
Il est petit.
Il est blond.

Comment est-elle?
Elle est grande.
Elle est brune.

Les personnes

une **personne**		une **personne**	
un **étudiant**	student	une **étudiante**	
un **élève**	pupil	une **élève**	
un **camarade**	classmate	une **camarade**	
un **homme**	man	une **femme**	woman
un **professeur**, un **prof**	teacher	un **professeur**, une **prof**	
un **voisin**	neighbor	une **voisine**	

→ **Une personne** is always feminine whether it refers to a male or female person.

→ **Un professeur** is always masculine whether it refers to a male or female teacher. However, in casual French, one distinguishes between **un prof** (male) and **une prof** (female).

COMPREHENSION
Descriptive adjectives

PROPS: Blue and red index cards

Give each student a blue and a red card.

On the board, draw a stick figure of a boy (labeled Michel) and a girl (labeled Michelle).

Voici Michel. C'est un copain.
Et voilà Michelle. C'est une copine.

Hold a blue card next to Michel, and a red card next to Michelle.

La carte bleue est pour Michel.
La carte rouge est pour Michelle.

Read descriptions using new vocabulary and have students hold up the right card.

Michel est grand. [blue card]
Michelle est belle. [red card]
Michel(le) est jeune. [either: both cards]

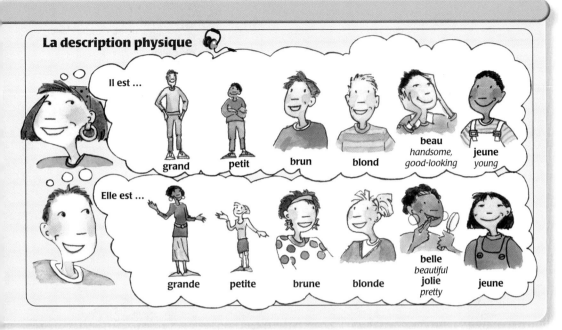

La description physique

Il est ...

grand petit brun blond **beau** *handsome, good-looking* **jeune** *young*

Elle est ...

grande petite brune blonde **belle** *beautiful* **jolie** *pretty* jeune

La description physique

Looking ahead
- Noun-adjective agreement is formally presented in Lesson 11.
- The masculine form **joli** is introduced in Lesson 12. Note that **joli** is not used to describe men and boys.

Extra practice Have students describe similar-looking twins: **Marc et Sophie.**
Marc est grand. Sophie est grande.
Sophie est belle. Marc est beau., etc.

Supplementary vocabulary

roux (rousse) *red-head*
fort (forte) *strong*
faible *weak*
laid (laide) *ugly*
moche *plain*
âgé (âgée) *old*
vieux (vieille) *old*

---

1 Oui ou non?

PARLER Describe the people below in affirmative or negative sentences.

▶ Frankenstein / beau?
Frankenstein n'est pas beau.

1. Shaquille O'Neal / grand?
2. Brad Pitt / brun?
3. Dracula / beau?
4. mon copain / blond?
5. mon père / petit?
6. mon voisin / jeune?
7. Britney Spears / belle?
8. le président / jeune?
9. Oprah Winfrey / grande?
10. ma copine / petite?
11. ma mère / brune?
12. ma voisine / jolie?

2 Vacances à Québec

PARLER/ÉCRIRE You spent last summer in Quebec and have just had your photographs developed. Describe each of the people, giving name, approximate age, and two or three characteristics.

Alain

blond(e)   petit(e)
brun(e)   beau (belle)
grand(e)   jeune

▶ Il s'appelle Alain.
Il est blond.
Il a seize ans.
Il n'est pas grand.
Il est petit.

1. Anne-Marie

2. Jean-Pierre

3. Claire

4. Mademoiselle Lévêque

5. Madame Paquette

6. Monsieur Beliveau

cent trente-neuf
Leçon 9 139

1 DESCRIPTION describing people

1. Shaquille O'Neal (est/n'est pas) grand.
2. Brad Pitt (est/n'est pas) brun.
3. Dracula (est/n'est pas) beau.
4. Mon copain (est/n'est pas) blond.
5. Mon père (est/n'est pas) petit.
6. Mon voisin (est/n'est pas) jeune.
7. Britney Spears (est/n'est pas) belle.
8. Le président (est/n'est pas) jeune.
9. Oprah Winfrey (est/n'est pas) grande.
10. Ma copine (est/n'est pas) petite.
11. Ma mère (est/n'est pas) brune.
12. Ma voisine (est/n'est pas) jolie.

2 COMMUNICATION describing appearance and age

Answers will vary.
1. Elle s'appelle Anne-Marie. Elle est brune. Elle a (seize) ans. Elle n'est pas petite. Elle est grande.
2. Il s'appelle Jean-Pierre. Il est brun. Il a (six) ans. Il est petit. Il est jeune. Il n'est pas grand.
3. Elle s'appelle Claire. Elle a (onze) ans. Elle est blonde. Elle n'est pas grande. Elle est petite.
4. Elle s'appelle Mlle Lévêque. Elle a (trente-cinq) ans. Elle est jeune. Elle est grande. Elle n'est pas petite. Elle est belle.
5. Elle s'appelle Mme Paquette. Elle a (soixante-cinq) ans. Elle n'est pas jeune. Elle est petite.
6. Il s'appelle M. Beliveau. Il a (soixante) ans. Il est grand. Il n'est pas beau.

Teaching strategy If you do not introduce **âgé** (old) at this point, students can describe an older person by saying:

Il/Elle n'est pas jeune.

GAME Qui est-ce?

PROPS: Magazine pictures showing a variety of individuals with different looks

Tape the pictures across the chalkboard. Have the class identify each one. Write the names.
Voici une femme. Comment s'appelle-t-elle?
[Elle s'appelle Mme Duroc.] ...

Each student stands and describes one of the people without mentioning his/her name. The others try to guess who it is.
C'est une femme. Elle est blonde. Elle est grande. Elle n'est pas jeune. Qui est-ce? [C'est Madame Duroc.]

Variation Use well-known personalities.

B VOCABULAIRE Les objets

Qu'est-ce que c'est?

▶ *How to identify something:*

Qu'est-ce que c'est?	*What is it? What's that?*	—Qu'est-ce que c'est?
C'est …	*It's …, That's …*	—C'est un livre.

▶ *How to say that you know or do not know:*

Je sais.	*I know.*
Je ne sais pas.	*I don't know.*

▶ *How to point out something:*

—Regarde ça.	*Look at that.*
—Quoi?	*What?*
—Ça, là-bas.	*That, over there.*

Quelques objets *(A few objects)*

un objet   un stylo   un crayon   un téléphone

un livre   un cahier   un sac

une chose *(thing)*   une montre   une raquette   une guitare

une affiche *(un poster)*   une calculatrice

♻ **RAPPEL**

In French, the names of objects are
MASCULINE or FEMININE.

Masculine objects can be introduced by **un**
or **le (l')**: **un stylo, le stylo, l'objet.**

Feminine objects can be introduced by **une**
or **la (l')**: **une montre, la montre, l'affiche.**

COMPREHENSION Everyday objects

PROPS: Objects from the above vocabulary

Hold up the objects (or corresponding pictures),
identifying them one by one.
   Voici un stylo.
   Voici un cahier. ...

Go over the objects, misidentifying some.
   Voici un stylo. [holding a pencil]

Ah non, ce n'est pas un stylo.
Est-ce que c'est un livre? [non]
Est-ce que c'est un crayon? [oui]

Have students manipulate the objects.
   X, viens ici. Montre-nous le sac.
   Y, prends la raquette et donne-la à Z.

—QU'EST-CE QUE
C'EST QUE ÇA?
—QUOI?
—ÇA, LÀ-BAS!
—C'EST UNE TÉLÉ.

—OH LÀ LÀ, NON!
REGARDE! C'EST
UN EXTRA-
TERRESTRE!

3 ⟡ **Qu'est-ce que c'est?**

PARLER Ask a classmate to identify the
following objects.

▶ Qu'est-ce que c'est?
  C'est un stylo.

▶

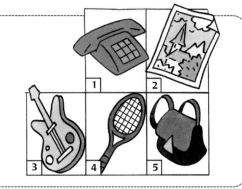

4 ⟡ **S'il te plaît**

PARLER Ask a classmate to give you the
following objects.

▶ —S'il te plaît, donne-moi le livre.
  —Voilà le livre.
  —Merci.

▶

Teaching strategy Have students
note the use of **ça** and **quoi** in the
cartoon at left.

3 DESCRIPTION identifying
   objects

1. – Qu'est-ce que c'est?
   – C'est un téléphone.
2. – Qu'est-ce que c'est?
   – C'est une affiche.
3. – Qu'est-ce que c'est?
   – C'est une guitare.
4. – Qu'est-ce que c'est?
   – C'est une raquette.
5. – Qu'est-ce que c'est?
   – C'est un sac.

Variation Go around the classroom
holding up or pointing to objects
students can identify.

– **Regardez ça. Qu'est-ce que c'est?**
– **C'est [un crayon].**
– **Et ça? Qu'est-ce que c'est?**
– **C'est [un stylo].**

4 EXCHANGES asking for things

1. – S'il te plaît, donne-moi le crayon.
   – Voilà le crayon.
   – Merci.
2. – S'il te plaît, donne-moi l'affiche.
   – Voilà l'affiche.
   – Merci.
3. – S'il te plaît, donne-moi la montre.
   – Voilà la montre.
   – Merci.
4. – S'il te plaît, donne-moi la calculatrice.
   – Voilà la calculatrice.
   – Merci.
5. – S'il te plaît, donne-moi le cahier.
   – Voilà le cahier.
   – Merci.

cent quarante et un **141**
Leçon 9

Communicative function
Discussing possessions

Teaching Resource Options

PRINT

Workbook PE, pp. 85–92
Unit 4 Resource Book
  Communipak, pp. 140–160
  Video Activities, pp. 25–26
  Videoscript, p. 29
  Workbook TE, pp. 1–8

AUDIO & VISUAL
Overhead Transparencies
21 *Quelques objets (b)*

VIDEO PROGRAM

VIDÉO   DVD   **MODULE 9**

9.1 Mini-scenes: J'ai une guitare
  (29:20–30:31 min.)

**9.2 Mini-scenes: Qu'est-ce que
  c'est?** (30:32–31:39 min.)

Looking ahead The negative **pas
de** (je n'ai pas de guitare) is taught
in Lesson 10.

Supplementary vocabulary

un appareil-photo numérique
  digital camera
une caméra *movie camera*
un caméscope *camcorder*
un radio-réveil *clock radio*
une radiocassette/CD *boombox with
  CD player*
une chaîne stéréo, une stéréo
  stereo set
une micro-chaîne *mini stereo*
un casque *head set*
un lecteur de CD *CD player*
un lecteur de DVD *DVD player*
un lecteur de MP3 *MP3 player*
un magnétoscope *VCR*
un téléviseur *TV set*
une console de jeux vidéo *video
  game console*
un cédérom *CD-ROM*
un VTT *mountain bike*
un skate *skateboard*
des rollers *in-line skates*
une trottinette *scooter*

C   VOCABULAIRE Les affaires personnelles *(personal belongings)*

Est-ce que
tu as une moto?

Oui, j'ai une moto.

▶ *How to talk about things you have:*

Est-ce que tu as … ? *Do you have … ?*   —**Est-ce que tu as** une moto?
Oui, j'ai … *Yes, I have …*   —**Oui, j'ai** une moto.

Quelques objets

un portable   un appareil-photo   un baladeur   un CD

une télé   un DVD   une cassette vidéo   un ordinateur

une radio   une radiocassette   une chaîne hi-fi
(une mini-chaîne)   une voiture
(une auto)

un vélo   une mobylette   un scooter   une moto
(une bicyclette)

▶ *How to ask if an object works:*

—Est-ce que la radio **marche?**   *Does the radio work?*
—Oui, elle **marche.**   *Yes, it works.*

→ The verb **marcher** has two meanings:

for people: *to walk*   Nous **marchons.**

for things: *to work, to run*   Le scooter ne **marche** pas bien.

RAPPEL
Masculine nouns can be
replaced by **il.**
  Le vélo marche.
  Il marche bien.
Feminine nouns can be
replaced by **elle.**
  La voiture marche.
  Elle marche bien.

SPEAKING PRACTICE

Have students bring in a picture of one of the
above vocabulary items. Ask each one to describe
his/her object and say if it works.
  **Voici un baladeur. Il est petit.
  Il marche bien.**

LANGUAGE NOTES

- You might want to mention that **VTT** stands for
  vélo tout terrain.
- Remind students that *to work* in the sense of *doing
  work* is **travailler.** You may want to point out that
  in English something "runs" well, whereas in French
  it "walks."
- **Casual speech** Common shortened forms: **un
  appareil, un magnéto, une mob, une chaîne**

5 Et toi?

PARLER

1. J'ai … *(Name 3 objects you own.)*
2. Je voudrais … *(Name 3 things you would like to have.)*
3. Pour Noël / Hanoukka, je voudrais … *(Name 2 gifts you would like to receive.)*

6 Joyeux anniversaire *(Happy birthday)*

PARLER/ÉCRIRE For your birthday, a rich aunt is giving you the choice between different possible gifts. Indicate your preferences.

▶ vélo ou scooter?

1. mobylette ou moto?
2. portable ou baladeur?
3. appareil-photo ou radio?
4. radiocassette ou chaîne hi-fi?
5. télé ou ordinateur?
6. DVD ou cassette vidéo?

> Je préfère le vélo.

> Je préfère le scooter.

7 Qu'est-ce que tu as?

PARLER Éric asks Léa if she has the following objects. She says that she does. Play both roles.

▶ ÉRIC: **Est-ce que tu as une guitare?**
LÉA: **Oui, j'ai une guitare.**

▶

8 Est-ce qu'il marche bien?

PARLER Tell your classmates that you own the following objects. They will ask you if the objects are working. Answer according to the illustrations.

▶ —J'ai un vélo.
—Est-ce qu'il marche bien?
—Non, il ne marche pas bien.

▶ —J'ai une télé.
—Est-ce qu'elle marche bien?
—Oui, elle marche très bien.

cent quarante-trois
Leçon 9 143

LANGUAGE NOTE

The word **mobylette** was originally a brand name. The word has become the generic term for *motorbike* in French, replacing **vélomoteur**. Other common examples of brand names that have become generic terms are:

un frigidaire or **un frigo** (replacing **un réfrigérateur**)
un bic (replacing **un stylo à bille**)

---

5 COMMUNICATION talking about what one has and what one wants

Answers will vary.
1. J'ai (un baladeur, une affiche et une montre).
2. Je voudrais (un vélo, un stylo et une télé).
3. Pour Noël / Hanoukka, je voudrais (un téléphone et une calculatrice).

Expansion Ask students if the objects they mentioned in number 1 of Act. 5 work well.
– J'ai une chaîne hi-fi.
– Est-ce qu'elle marche bien?
– Non, elle ne marche pas bien.

6 COMMUNICATION indicating preferences

1. Je préfère la mobylette. (la moto)
2. Je préfère le portable. (le baladeur)
3. Je préfère l'appareil-photo. (la radio)
4. Je préfère la radiocassette. (la chaîne hi-fi)
5. Je préfère la télé. (l'ordinateur)
6. Je préfère le DVD. (la cassette vidéo)

Photo cultural note Scooters are an increasingly popular mode of transportation among French young people. To drive a scooter you must be 14 years old, carry a license (**un permis**), and wear a helmet (**un casque**). However, **le vélo, la mobylette** and **la moto** are most popular.

7 ROLE PLAY discussing what one has

Éric: Est-ce que tu as … ?
Léa: Oui, j'ai …
1. une mobylette
2. un portable
3. un vélo (une bicyclette)
4. un ordinateur
5. un appareil-photo
6. une chaîne hi-fi

8 EXCHANGES talking about whether things work

1. – J'ai un appareil-photo.
 – Est-ce qu'il marche bien?
 – Non, il ne marche pas bien.
2. – J'ai un scooter.
 – Est-ce qu'il marche bien?
 – Oui, il marche très bien.
3. – J'ai une chaîne hi-fi.
 – Est-ce qu'elle marche bien?
 – Oui, elle marche très bien.
4. – J'ai une mobylette.
 – Est-ce qu'elle marche bien?
 – Non, elle ne marche pas bien.
5. – J'ai une radio.
 – Est-ce qu'elle marche bien?
 – Oui, elle marche très bien.
6. – J'ai une montre.
 – Est-ce qu'elle marche bien?
 – Non, elle ne marche pas bien.

D VOCABULAIRE **Ma chambre** *(My room)*

Dans ma chambre il y a une télé.

▶ *How to talk about what there is in a place:*

il y a	*there is* *there are*	Dans *(In)* ma chambre, **il y a** une télé. Dans le garage, **il y a** deux voitures.
est-ce qu'il y a … ?	*is/are there … ?*	**Est-ce qu'il y a** un ordinateur dans la classe?
qu'est-ce qu'il y a … ?	*what is there … ?*	**Qu'est-ce qu'il y a** dans le garage?

Dans ma chambre

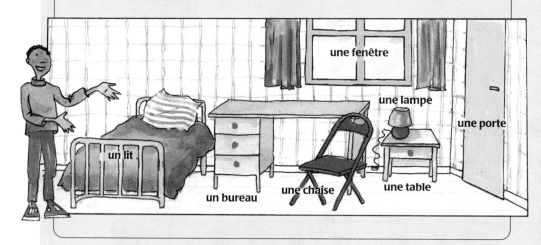

▶ *How to say where something or someone is:*

COMPREHENSION Location

PROPS: Objects from the lesson

Demonstrate prepositions of place:
    Je mets le CD dans le sac.
    Je mets la raquette sur la chaise.
    Je mets la guitare sous la table.
    Je mets le stylo derrière le livre. …

Have students move the objects around.
    X, viens ici. Mets le CD dans le sac.
    Y, viens et mets le crayon devant le sac.
    Z, prends le livre et mets-le derrière le sac.

Optional give more complex commands.
    X, mets le crayon dans le sac.
    Et puis mets le sac sous la chaise de Y.

9 *Qu'est-ce qu'il y a?*

PARLER Describe the various objects that are in the pictures.

1. Sur la table, il y a …   **2.** Sous le lit, il y a …   **3.** Dans le garage, il y a …

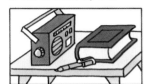 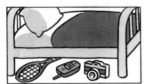 

10 *Ma chambre*

PARLER/ÉCRIRE Describe the various objects (pieces of furniture and personal belongings) that are in your room.

▶ **Dans ma chambre, il y a une radio, …**
Il y a aussi …

11 *Où est le téléphone?*

PARLER Michèle is looking for the telephone. Jean-Claude tells her where it is.

▶ MICHÈLE: **Où est le téléphone?**
JEAN-CLAUDE: **Il est sur la table.**

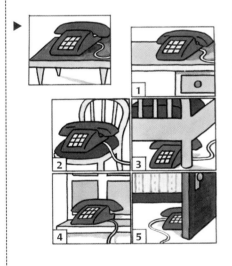

12 *C'est étrange!* *(It's strange!)*

PARLER/ÉCRIRE Funny things sometimes happen. Describe these curious happenings by selecting an item from Column A and putting it in one of the places listed in Column B.

Il y a un éléphant sous le lit!

▶ Il y a …

A	B
un rhinocéros	dans la classe
un éléphant	sur le bureau
une girafe	sous la table
un crabe	sous le lit
une souris *(mouse)*	derrière la porte
un ami de King Kong	sur la tour Eiffel
un extra-terrestre	dans le jardin *(garden)*
	devant le restaurant

---

9 **DESCRIPTION** saying where things are

1. Sur la table, il y a une radio, un stylo et un livre.
2. Sous le lit, il y a une raquette, un portable et un appareil-photo.
3. Dans le garage, il y a un scooter, une voiture (une auto) et un vélo (une bicyclette).

10 **COMMUNICATION** describing one's room

Answers will vary.
Dans ma chambre, il y a un lit et une chaise. Il y a aussi un bureau, une table, un téléphone, un livre et un sac.

11 **ROLE PLAY** saying where something is

1. **M:** Où est le téléphone?
    JC: Il est sur le bureau.
2. **M:** Où est le téléphone?
    JC: Il est sur la chaise.
3. **M:** Où est le téléphone?
    JC: Il est sous le lit.
4. **M:** Où est le téléphone?
    JC: Il est devant la fenêtre.
5. **M:** Où est le téléphone?
    JC: Il est derrière la porte.

12 **COMMUNICATION** describing improbable locations

Answers will vary.
Il y a un rhinocéros (derrière la porte)!
Il y a un éléphant (dans le jardin)!
Il y a une girafe (sur le bureau)!
Il y a un crabe (sous la table)!
Il y a une souris (sous le lit)!
Il y a un ami de King Kong (sur la tour Eiffel)!
Il y a un extra-terrestre (devant le restaurant)!

Expansion Have students invent other improbable statements using known vocabulary.

Teaching Resource Options

PRINT

Workbook PE, pp. 85–92
Unit 4 Resource Book
  Communipak, pp. 140–160
  Video Activities, p. 28
  Videoscript, p. 30
  Workbook TE, pp. 1–8

VIDEO PROGRAM

 MODULE 9

**9.5 Vignette culturelle:
La chambre de Catherine**
(34:14–35:38 min.)

13 ROLE PLAY asking where
things are

1. **F:** Où est la raquette?
   N: Elle est sous le lit.
2. **F:** Où est la guitare?
   N: Elle est derrière la chaise.
3. **F:** Où est le livre?
   N: Il est dans le sac.
4. **F:** Où est le vélo?
   N: Il est devant la fenêtre.
5. **F:** Où est l'ordinateur?
   N: Il est sur le bureau.
6. **F:** Où est le sac?
   N: Il est devant la télé (sur la table).
7. **F:** Où est la radio?
   N: Elle est sur le bureau.
8. **F:** Où est le CD?
   N: Il est sur la table.
9. **F:** Où est le portable?
   N: Il est sur la chaise.

14 COMPREHENSION describing
where someone is

1. M. Vénard est <u>dans</u> la voiture.
2. M. Vénard est <u>sous</u> la voiture.
3. M. Vénard est <u>derrière</u> la voiture.
4. La contractuelle est <u>devant</u> la voiture.

Cultural note **La contractuelle** is
an auxiliary police officer who is
authorized to write tickets (**une
contravention**) for illegally parked
vehicles. The traffic sign in the cartoon
signals a no parking zone
(**stationnement interdit**).

---

13 **La chambre de Nicole**

PARLER Florence wants to borrow a few things from Nicole's room.
Nicole tells her where each object is.

▶ la télé
  FLORENCE: **Où est la télé?**
  NICOLE: **Elle est sur la table.**

1. la raquette
2. la guitare
3. le livre
4. le vélo
5. l'ordinateur
6. le sac
7. la radio
8. le CD
9. le portable

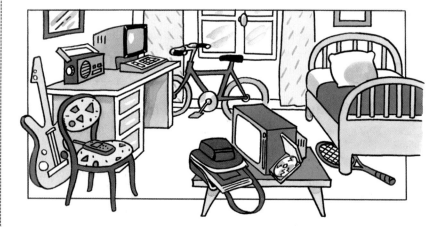

14 Pauvre Monsieur Vénard *(Poor Mr. Vénard)*

PARLER/ÉCRIRE Today Monsieur Vénard left on vacation, but he soon ran out
of luck. Describe the four cartoons by completing the sentences below.

Le voyage de Monsieur Vénard

1. M. Vénard est ____ la voiture.
2. M. Vénard est ____ la voiture.
3. M. Vénard est ____ la voiture.
4. La contractuelle° est ____ la voiture.

la contractuelle *meter maid*

SECTION E

The vocabulary in this section "Mon ordinateur" is presented primarily for recognition. Students should not be expected to memorize and/or produce these expressions independently.

E VOCABULAIRE Mon ordinateur

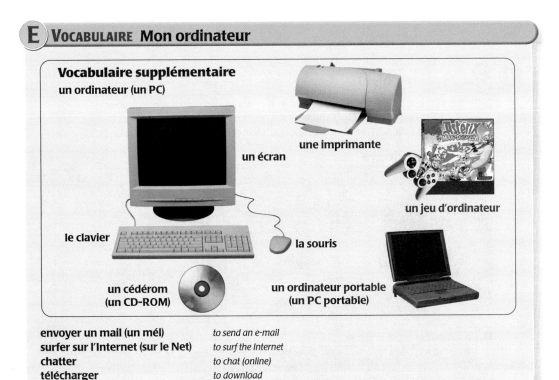

Vocabulaire supplémentaire
un ordinateur (un PC)

une imprimante

un écran

un jeu d'ordinateur

le clavier

la souris

un cédérom (un CD-ROM)

un ordinateur portable (un PC portable)

envoyer un mail (un mél)	to send an e-mail
surfer sur l'Internet (sur le Net)	to surf the Internet
chatter	to chat (online)
télécharger	to download

Teaching note Envoyer is presented for recognition. If appropriate, you may introduce the present tense forms:

j'**envoie**	nous **envoyons**
tu **envoies**	vous **envoyez**
il/elle **envoie**	ils/elles **envoient**

Supplementary vocabulary

graver un CD *to burn a CD*
un graveur de CD *CD burner*
le disque dur *hard drive*
le logiciel *software*
le modem *modem*
un scanner *scanner*

COMPARAISONS INTERPERSONNELLES

Here is a list of various activities that you can do with a computer. List the four activities you like to do best, ranking them in order of preference. Compare your lists with your classmates.

- chatter
- faire mes devoirs *(homework)*
- écouter de la musique
- envoyer un mail à un copain / une copine
- surfer sur le Net

- regarder les nouvelles *(news)*
- télécharger de la musique
- faire des recherches *(research)* pour la classe de français
- jouer aux jeux d'ordinateur

UN SONDAGE

Conduct a poll in your class to determine which two of the above computer activities students like the best and which two they like the least.

À VOTRE TOUR

Main Topic
• Recapitulation and review

Teaching Resource Options

PRINT
Workbook PE, pp. 85–92
Unit 4 Resource Book
    Audioscript, pp. 31–32
    Communipak, pp. 140–160
    Family Involvement, pp. 23–24
    Workbook TE, pp. 1–8

Assessment
Lesson 9 Quiz, pp. 35–36
Portfolio Assessment, Unit 1 URB,
    pp. 155–164
Audioscript for Quiz 9, p. 34
Answer Keys, pp. 201–205

AUDIO & VISUAL
Audio Program
CD 2 Tracks 25, 26, 27
CD 14 Track 17

TECHNOLOGY
Test Generator CD-ROM/eTest Plus
Online

① LISTENING COMPREHENSION

1. A	7. B	13. A
2. B	8. B	14. A
3. A	9. B	15. B
4. A	10. A	16. A
5. B	11. B	17. A
6. A, B	12. B	18. A, B

Middle School Copymasters
Class Starter: Ten-second categories
to practice descriptions, p. T19

② GUIDED ORAL EXPRESSION

A: Est-ce que tu as (As-tu) un ordinateur?
M: Oui.
A: Est-ce qu'il marche bien?
M: Oui, il marche très bien. Pourquoi?
A: Je voudrais envoyer un mail à un copain.
M: L'ordinateur est sur le bureau dans ma chambre.

148 • À votre tour!
Unité 4 LEÇON 9

À votre tour!

OBJECTIFS
Now you can …
• describe your belongings
• talk about people and give their ages

① Écoutez bien!

ÉCOUTER You will hear a series of sentences. In each one an object is mentioned. If you see the object only in Léa's room, mark A. If you see the object only in Pierre's room, mark B. If you see the object in the two rooms, mark both A and B.

A. La chambre de Léa

B. La chambre de Pierre

	A Léa	B Pierre
1.		
2.		
3.		
4.		
5.		
6.		
7.		
8.		
9.		
10.		
11.		
12.		
13.		
14.		
15.		
16.		
17.		
18.		

② Conversation dirigée

PARLER André is visiting his cousin Marie. Act out the dialogue according to the instructions.

André

		Marie
asks Marie if she has a computer	→ ←	answers affirmatively
asks her if it works well	→ ←	says that it works very well and asks why
says he would like to send an e-mail to a friend	→	says that the computer is on the desk in her room

Marie

148 cent quarante-huit
Unité 4

À VOTRE TOUR
Select those activities which are most appropriate for your students.

GROUP PRACTICE
In Act. 2 and 3, you may want to have students work in trios, with two performing and one acting as monitor.

③ Créa-dialogue

PARLER Daniel is showing Nathalie his recent photographs, and she is asking questions about the various people. Create similar dialogues and act them out in class.

un copain

Éric/14

▶ —Qui est-ce?
—C'est **un copain**.
—Comment s'appelle-t-**il**?
—**Il** s'appelle <u>Éric</u>.
—Quel âge a-t-**il**?
—**Il** a <u>quatorze</u> ans.

1. une cousine	2. un camarade	3. une camarade	4. un voisin	5. une voisine	6. un professeur
Valérie/20	Philippe Boucher/13	Nathalie Masson/15	Monsieur Dumas/70	Madame Smith/51	Monsieur Laval/35

④ Mes affaires

ÉCRIRE Imagine that your family is going to move to another city. Prepare for the move by making a checklist of your things. Write out your list by hand or on a computer.

```
Mes affaires:
• un lit
•
•
•
```

⑤ Ma chambre

ÉCRIRE A French student is going to spend two weeks at your house. Write him/her a short e-mail describing your room. In your note, mention …

- at least 3 pieces of furniture
- at least 3 school-related objects
- 4 personal belongings

If you wish, you can add some descriptive comments.

⑥ Un ordinateur

ÉCRIRE Imagine that you have just won a brand new computer in a contest at your school. Write a short paragraph in which you …

- describe its various components
- mention 3 ways in which you want to use it

LESSON REVIEW
CLASSZONE.COM

cent quarante-neuf
Leçon 9 149

PORTFOLIO ASSESSMENT

You will probably select only one speaking activity and one writing activity to go into the students' portfolios for Unit 4.

In this lesson, Activities 5 and 6 are appropriate writing portfolio topics.

---

③ GUIDED ORAL EXPRESSION

1. – Qui est-ce?
 – C'est une cousine.
 – Comment s'appelle-t-elle?
 – Elle s'appelle Valérie.
 – Quel âge a-t-elle?
 – Elle a vingt ans.
2. – Qui est-ce?
 – C'est un camarade.
 – Comment s'appelle-t-il?
 – Il s'appelle Philippe Boucher.
 – Quel âge a-t-il?
 – Il a treize ans.
3. – Qui est-ce?
 – C'est une camarade.
 – Comment s'appelle-t-elle?
 – Elle s'appelle Nathalie Masson.
 – Quel âge a-t-elle?
 – Elle a quinze ans.
4. – Qui est-ce?
 – C'est un voisin.
 – Comment s'appelle-t-il?
 – Il s'appelle Monsieur Dumas.
 – Quel âge a-t-il?
 – Il a soixante-dix ans.
5. – Qui est-ce?
 – C'est une voisine.
 – Comment s'appelle-t-elle?
 – Elle s'appelle Madame Smith.
 – Quel âge a-t-elle?
 – Elle a cinquante et un ans.
6. – Qui est-ce?
 – C'est un professeur.
 – Comment s'appelle-t-il?
 – Il s'appelle Monsieur Laval.
 – Quel âge a-t-il?
 – Il a trente-cinq ans.

④ WRITTEN SELF-EXPRESSION

Answers will vary.
Mes affaires:
- un lit
- un bureau
- un vélo
- une chaise
- une guitare
- un CD

⑤ WRITTEN SELF-EXPRESSION

Chère Carole,
Dans ma chambre, il y a un lit, un petit bureau et une chaise. En général, sur le bureau, il y a un cahier, un stylo et des crayons. Il y a aussi une chaîne hi-fi, un ordinateur et beaucoup de CD dans ma chambre.
–Julie

⑥ WRITTEN SELF-EXPRESSION

Answers will vary.
L'ordinateur est génial! C'est un ordinateur portable. Il a une souris, un modem et un graveur de CD! Je voudrais télécharger de la musique (française, bien sûr!), chatter avec mes copains et surfer sur le Net.

Leçon 10

Main Topic Talking about possessions and preferences

Teaching Resource Options

PRINT

Workbook PE, pp. 93–100
Activités pour tous PE, pp. 55–57
Block Scheduling Copymasters,
  pp. 73–79
Unit 4 Resource Book
  Activités pour tous TE, pp. 45–47
  Audioscript, pp. 66, 67–68
  Communipak, pp. 140–160
  Lesson Plans, pp. 48–49
  Block Scheduling Lesson Plans, pp. 50–51
  Absent Student Copymasters, pp. 52–57
  Video Activities, pp. 60–63
  Videoscript, pp. 64–65
  Workbook TE, pp. 37–44

AUDIO & VISUAL

Audio Program
CD 2 Tracks 28, 29
CD 8 Tracks 7–13

TECHNOLOGY

Online Workbook

VIDEO PROGRAM

VIDÉO   DVD

MODULE 10
Tu as un vélo?

TOTAL TIME: 5:15 min.
  DVD Disk 1
  Videotape 2 (COUNTER: 35:48 min.)

10.1 Mini-scenes: Listening
  —Tu as un vélo? (36:21–37:02 min.)

10.2 Mini-scenes: Listening
  — Qu'est-ce que tu as?
  (37:03–38:06 min.)

10.3 Mini-scenes: Speaking
  —Est-ce que tu as un vélo?
  (38:07–39:08 min.)

10.4 Dialogue: J'organise une boum (39:09–39:42 min.)

10.5 Vignette culturelle: La mobylette (39:43–41:03 min.)

Language note In French, **pas de** is often followed by a singular noun.

Il n'a pas de frère. = *He doesn't have a brother. (He has no brothers.)*

150 · Conversation et Culture
  Unité 4 LEÇON 10

LEÇON 10

Vive la différence! AUDIO

We are not necessarily like our friends. Léa describes herself and her best friend Céline. Both of them live in Paris and are quite different.

Léa

Céline

Je m'appelle Léa.

Je suis française.

J'ai des frères, mais je n'ai pas de soeur.

J'ai un chien.

J'ai un scooter.

J'aime la musique classique.

J'aime le basket et le tennis.

Elle s'appelle Céline.

Elle est haïtienne.

Elle n'a pas de frère, mais elle a deux soeurs.

Elle n'a pas de chien, mais elle a un chat très mignon.

Elle a un vélo.

Elle préfère le compas.

Elle préfère le foot.

Céline et moi, nous sommes très différentes … mais nous sommes copines. C'est l'essentiel, non?

Compréhension

Answer the questions below with the appropriate names: **Léa, Céline,** or **Léa et Céline.**

1. Qui habite en France?
2. Qui a deux soeurs?
3. Qui n'a pas de frère?

4. Qui a un vélo?
5. Qui aime la musique classique?
6. Qui aime les sports?

cent cinquante
Unité 4

SETTING THE SCENE

The theme of this opening text is that friends do not always have identical tastes and backgrounds.

NOTE culturelle

Haïti
★
Port-au-Prince

EN BREF: Haïti

Capitale: Port-au-Prince
Population: 8 millions d'habitants
Langues: créole, français

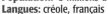

Une peinture haïtienne

Un marché à Pétionville (près de Port-au-Prince)

Haïti occupies the western part of the large Caribbean island on which the Dominican Republic is also located. Its inhabitants are of African origin. Their enslaved ancestors revolted against their French masters in 1805 and established the first independent Black nation in modern history. Today many Haitians have emigrated to France, Canada, and especially to the United States. There are sizable Haitian communities in Florida and in cities along the northeastern seaboard.

Haitians are friendly, industrious, and artistic people. In the twentieth century, Haitian painters developed their own widely appreciated folk art style and Haitian paintings are now in collections around the world. The Haitians also love music, especially **compas** or **kompas** which highlights a variety of instruments including conga drums, guitar, and keyboard. Its creole lyrics are expressed against a background of African, Caribbean, reggae, and rock rhythms.

Haitian creole cuisine, which features rice dishes, pork, and shellfish, is often quite spicy. Typical Haitian dishes include **griots** (fried pork), **riz djon-djon** (rice with mushrooms), and **pain patate** (sweet potato cake).

CONNEXIONS Haïti

Learn more about Haiti. Divide the class into several groups, each with a different assignment. For example:

• Create a bulletin board display with pictures, maps, and newspaper clippings about Haiti.

• Find books on Haitian paintings and Haitian artists and make a presentation to the class.

• Find examples of **compas** music and play a selection for the class.

cent cinquante et un 151
Leçon 10

USING THE VIDEO

Video Module 10 prepares students to talk about various things they own. They will meet a wide variety of French people who will describe their possessions. The **Vignette culturelle** is about the moped.

COMPOSITION

Have students use the **Vive la différence** dialogue as a point of departure for writing a composition about themselves and one of their friends. Suggest that they write their descriptions in two columns, using as a model Léa's and Céline's text on p. 148.

Communicative function
Talking about what one has

Teaching Resource Options

PRINT

Workbook PE, pp. 93–100
Unit 4 Resource Book
    Communipak, pp. 140–160
    Workbook TE, pp. 37–44

TECHNOLOGY
Power Presentations

 Review and expansion

Students learned the singular forms of
avoir in **Invitation au français.** Point
out that the plural form **ont** is similar
to **sont** and **font.**

Teaching note Use flashcards for
subject pronouns and known objects
to practice the forms of **avoir.**

On the chalkledge place 2 cards, e.g.,
card [**nous**] + card [*tennis racket*]

Response: **Nous avons une raquette.**

1 PRACTICE saying what
people have

1. Tu as une
   raquette.
2. Il a un baladeur.
3. Tu as une télé.
4. Vous avez un
   portable.
5. Nous avons un
   baladeur.
6. Vous avez un
   ordinateur.
7. Elles ont une raquette.
8. Ils ont un ordinateur.

2 COMMUNICATION giving
people's ages

1. J'ai (quinze) ans.
2. Tu as (seize) ans.
3. Vous avez (trente-huit) ans.
4. Mon copain a (seize) ans.
5. Ma copine a (quinze) ans.
6. La voisine a (soixante-huit) ans.

Expansion Have students guess the
ages of well-known sports and TV
figures.

Language note The French always
use **ans** after the number when giving
someone's age.

A Le verbe *avoir*

The verb **avoir** *(to have, to own)* is irregular. Note the forms of this verb in the present tense.

avoir	to have	
j' **ai**	*I have*	J'**ai** une copine à Québec.
tu **as**	*you have*	Est-ce que tu **as** un frère?
il/elle **a**	*he/she has*	Philippe **a** une cousine à Paris.
nous **avons**	*we have*	Nous **avons** un ordinateur.
vous **avez**	*you have*	Est-ce que vous **avez** une moto?
ils/elles **ont**	*they have*	Ils n'**ont** pas ton appareil-photo.

→ There is liaison in the forms: **nous avons, vous avez, ils ont, elles ont.**

VOCABULAIRE Expressions avec *avoir*

avoir faim	*to be hungry*	J'**ai faim.** Et toi, est-ce que tu **as faim?**
avoir soif	*to be thirsty*	Paul **a soif.** Sylvie n'**a** pas **soif.**
avoir ... ans	*to be ... (years old)*	J'**ai** 14 **ans.** Le prof **a** 35 **ans.**

1 Qu'est-ce qu'ils ont?

PARLER From what the people
are doing, say which object in
the box they have.

un baladeur
un ordinateur
un portable
une raquette
une télé

▶ Léa regarde un film.
   Elle a une télé.

1. Tu joues au tennis.
2. Éric écoute du rock.
3. Je regarde un film.
4. Vous téléphonez.
5. Nous écoutons un CD.
6. Vous envoyez un mail.
7. Elles jouent au tennis.
8. Ils surfent sur le Net.

2 Expression personnelle

PARLER/ÉCRIRE How old are the
following people? Complete the
sentences below. If you don't
know their ages, guess.

1. J'ai ...
2. *(A classmate)* Tu as ...
3. *(The teacher)* Vous ...
4. Mon copain ...
5. Ma copine ...
6. La voisine ...

3 **Faim ou soif?**

PARLER You are at a party with your classmates. Offer
them the following foods and beverages. They will accept
or refuse by saying whether they are hungry or thirsty.

Tu veux un
sandwich?

Oui, merci! J'ai faim.
(Non, merci! Je n'ai pas faim.)

▶ un sandwich

1. une crêpe
2. un soda
3. un hamburger
4. un jus d'orange
5. un croissant
6. un jus de raisin
7. une pizza
8. une limonade

TEACHING NOTE Introducing the past tense

Once students learn the present tense forms of **avoir,**
you may want to introduce the PASSÉ COMPOSÉ for
conversation practice. (The tense is presented
formally in Unit 7.)

Beginning with this lesson, you will find optional oral
questions about past events.

To talk about what happened yesterday (**hier**), the
French use the PASSÉ COMPOSÉ:

    present of **avoir** + past participle

For **-er** verbs, the past participle ends in **-é.** (You
may want to use the chart on p. 321.)

B Les noms et les articles: masculin et féminin

NOUNS

- Nouns designating PEOPLE

Nouns that designate male persons are almost always *masculine:*

un garçon   **un ami**

Nouns that designate female persons are almost always *feminine:*

une fille   **une amie**

→ EXCEPTIONS:

une personne is always feminine (even when it refers to a male)

un professeur is always masculine (even when it refers to a woman)

- Nouns designating ANIMALS, OBJECTS, and THINGS

There is no systematic way to determine whether these nouns are masculine or feminine. Therefore, it is very important to learn these nouns with their articles.

MASCULINE: **un** portable   **un** vélo   **un** ordinateur

FEMININE: **une** chaîne hi-fi   **une** moto   **une** affiche

> **LEARNING ABOUT LANGUAGE**
>
> NOUNS are words that designate people, animals, objects, and things.
>
> In French, all nouns have GENDER: they are either MASCULINE or FEMININE.

ARTICLES

Note the forms of the articles in the chart below.

	MASCULINE		FEMININE			
INDEFINITE ARTICLE	**un**	*a, an*	**une**	*a, an*	**un** garçon	**une** fille
DEFINITE ARTICLE	**le**	*the*	**la**	*the*	**le** garçon	**la** fille

> **LEARNING ABOUT LANGUAGE**
>
> Nouns are often introduced by ARTICLES. In French, ARTICLES have the *same* gender as the nouns they introduce.

→ Both **le** and **la** become **l'** before a vowel sound:

le garçon   **l'ami**

la fille   **l'amie**

PRONOUNS

Note the forms of the pronouns in the chart below.

MASCULINE	**il**	*he*	Où est **le** garçon?	**Il** est en classe.
		it	Où est **le** portable?	**Il** est sur la table.
FEMININE	**elle**	*she*	Où est **la** fille?	**Elle** est en ville.
		it	Où est **la** voiture?	**Elle** est là-bas.

> **LEARNING ABOUT LANGUAGE**
>
> Nouns may be replaced by PRONOUNS. In French, PRONOUNS have the *same* gender as the nouns they replace.

 EXCHANGES offering, accepting, and refusing food

– Tu veux ... ?
– Oui, merci! J'ai ... / (Non, merci! Je n'ai pas ...)

1. une crêpe/faim	5. un croissant/faim
2. un soda/soif	6. un jus de raisin/soif
3. un hamburger/faim	7. une pizza/faim
4. un jus d'orange/soif	8. une limonade/soif

Re-entry and review Foods and **avoir faim/soif** from Unit 2, Lessons 3A and 3B.

Language note French people say **merci** both to accept and refuse something.

SECTION B

Communicative function Designating people and things

Language notes
- For the more common farm animals, the gender of the noun does correspond to the sex of the animal: **un taureau, une vache.**
- Be sure students understand that gender is linked to the NOUN and <u>not</u> to the object itself. For example, a *bicycle* can be referred to as <u>**une bicyclette**</u> or <u>**un vélo.**</u>

Re-entry and review

Definite and indefinite articles from Unit 1, Lessons 2A and 2B; pronouns from Unit 2, Lesson 3C and Unit 3, Lesson 6.

Critical thinking: Pronouns
Have students look at the sentences in the pronoun chart. How can they tell if **il** means *he* or *it*?

Il est en classe. *He is in class.*

Il est sur la table. *It is on the table.*

[They look at the context to see what **il** is referring to: **le garçon? le CD?**]

Similarly, how can they tell if **elle** means *she* or *it*?

TALKING ABOUT PAST EVENTS

▶ Let's talk about what you did yesterday.

Est-ce que tu as étudié hier? Oui, j'ai étudié hier. (Non, je n'ai pas étudié hier.)

- **Est-ce que tu as étudié hier?**
- **Est-ce que tu as travaillé hier?**
- **Est-ce que tu as regardé la télé hier?**
- **Est-ce que tu as écouté la radio?**

- **Est-ce que tu as parlé français?**
- **Est-ce que tu as joué au tennis?**
- **Est-ce que tu as dîné au restaurant?**
- **Est-ce que tu as mangé un steak?** (Reminder: use **pas de** in the negative.)
- **Est-ce que tu as mangé une omelette?**

Teaching Resource Options

PRINT

Workbook PE, pp. 93–100
Unit 4 Resource Book
   Communipak, pp. 140–160
   Workbook TE, pp. 37–44

TECHNOLOGY

Power Presentations

SECTION C

Communicative function
Identifying people and things

Language note Note the following plural: **des appareils-photo**

There is no "s" on **photo** since this is a shortened form of **photographique(s)**.

Vocabulary note **gens** is masculine.

Realia note The **Galeries Lafayette** is a well-known Parisian department store.

---

4 **EXCHANGES** identifying celebrities

– Tiens, voilà ... !
– Qui est-ce?
– Un(e) ...

1. Dan Rather/Un journaliste.
2. Julia Roberts/Une actrice.
3. Brad Pitt/Un acteur.
4. Will Smith/Un chanteur.
5. Britney Spears/Une chanteuse.
6. Tiger Woods/Un athlète.
7. Venus Williams/Une athlète.
8. Whoopi Goldberg/Une comédienne.

Expansion Have students suggest other names for each of the categories in Act. 4: e.g., **Leslie Stahl est une journaliste.**

---

5 **ROLE PLAY** describing location

Caroline: Où est ... ?
Cécile: (Le/La) ... ? (Il/Elle) est (sur/sous) la table.

1. (l'ordinateur) Il est sur la table.
2. (le sac) Il est sur la table.
3. (l'affiche) Elle est sur la table.
4. (la calculatrice) Elle est sous la table.
5. (la raquette) Elle est sous la table.
6. (l'appareil-photo) Il est sous la table.
7. (la radiocassette) Elle est sous la table.
8. (la télé) Elle est sous la table.

Expansion Use classroom objects.
– Où est le livre?
– Il est sur le bureau.

---

4 **Les célébrités**

PARLER You and Jean-Pierre have been invited to a benefit attended by many American celebrities. Jean-Pierre asks you who each person is. Answer him using **un** or **une**, as appropriate.

▶ Katie Couric/journaliste
—**Tiens, voilà Katie Couric!**
—**Qui est-ce?**
—**Une journaliste.**

1. Dan Rather/journaliste
2. Julia Roberts/actrice
3. Brad Pitt/acteur
4. Will Smith/chanteur *(singer)*
5. Britney Spears/chanteuse
6. Tiger Woods/athlète
7. Venus Williams/athlète
8. Whoopi Goldberg/comédienne

---

5   **Sur la table ou sous la table?**

PARLER Caroline is looking for the following objects. Cécile tells her where each one is: on or under the table.

▶ baladeur
CAROLINE: **Où est le baladeur?**
CÉCILE: **Le baladeur?**
     Il est sur la table.

1. ordinateur
2. sac
3. affiche
4. calculatrice
5. raquette
6. appareil-photo
7. radiocassette
8. télé

C **Les noms et les articles: le pluriel**

Compare the singular and plural forms of the articles and nouns in the sentences below.

SINGULAR	PLURAL
Tu as **le livre**?	Tu as **les livres**?
Qui est **la fille** là-bas?	Qui sont **les filles** là-bas?
Voici **un sac.**	Voici **des sacs.**
J'invite **une copine.**	J'invite **des copines.**

PLURAL NOUNS

In written French, the plural of most nouns is formed as follows:

> SINGULAR NOUN + **s** = PLURAL NOUN

→ If the noun ends in **-s** in the singular, the singular and plural forms are the same.

    Voici **un Français.**   Voici **des Français.**

→ In spoken French, the final **-s** of the plural is always silent.

→ NOTE: **des gens** *(people)* is always plural. Compare:

| **une personne** | *person* | Qui est **la personne** là-bas? |
| **des gens** | *people* | Qui sont **les gens** là-bas? |

Les sacs

COMPREHENSION Singular and plural forms

PROPS: Classroom objects

Point out either one or two common objects.
  Voici un crayon.
  Voici des crayons.
  Voilà une fenêtre.
  Voilà des fenêtres.
  Où sont les livres? Où est le livre?

Then have individual students point out one or several objects.
  X, montre-nous un stylo.
  Maintenant, montre-nous des stylos.
  Y, montre-nous le livre de français.
  Où sont les livres de français?
  Z, montre-nous des élèves.
  Maintenant, montre-nous une élève.

SINGULAR AND PLURAL ARTICLES

The forms of the articles are summarized in the chart below.

	SINGULAR		PLURAL			
DEFINITE ARTICLE	le (l') la (l')	*the*	les	*the*	les garçons les filles	les ordinateurs les affiches
INDEFINITE ARTICLE	un une	*a, an*	des	*some*	des garçons des filles	des ordinateurs des affiches

→ There is liaison after **les** and **des** when the next word begins with a vowel sound.

→ **Des** corresponds to the English article *some*. While *some* is often omitted in English, **des** MUST be expressed in French. Contrast:

Il y a	des	livres sur la table.
There are	*some*	*books on the table.*

Je dîne avec	des	amis.
I'm having dinner with	*…*	*friends.*

6 Pluriel, s'il vous plaît

PARLER/ÉCRIRE Give the plurals of the following nouns.

▶ une copine
des copines

▶ l'ami
les amis

1. un copain
2. une amie
3. un homme
4. une femme
5. un euro
6. une affiche
7. le voisin
8. l'élève
9. la cousine
10. le livre
11. l'ordinateur
12. la voiture

7 Shopping

PARLER You are in a department store looking for the following items. Ask the salesperson if he or she has these items. The salesperson will answer affirmatively.

▶ —Pardon, monsieur (madame).
Est-ce que vous avez des sacs?
—Bien sûr, nous avons des sacs.

8 Qu'est-ce qu'il y a?

PARLER/ÉCRIRE Explain what there is in the following places. Complete the sentences with **il y a** and at least two nouns of your choice. Be sure to use the appropriate articles: **un, une, des.**

Dans le garage, il y a une moto (des voitures …).

▶ Dans le garage, …

1. Sur le bureau, …
2. À la boum, …
3. Dans la classe, …
4. Au café, sur la table, …
5. Dans ma chambre, …
6. Dans mon sac, …

cent cinquante-cinq
Leçon 10 155

---

1. des copains
2. des amies
3. des hommes
4. des femmes
5. des euros
6. des affiches
7. les voisins
8. les élèves
9. les cousines
10. les livres
11. les ordinateurs
12. les voitures

Teaching Tip Do this activity rapidly, focusing on student pronunciation.

7 ROLE PLAY asking for items in a store

1. – Pardon, monsieur (madame). Est-ce que vous avez des télés?
   – Bien sûr, nous avons des télés.
2. – Pardon, monsieur (madame). Est-ce que vous avez des radios?
   – Bien sûr, nous avons des radios.
3. – Pardon, monsieur (madame). Est-ce que vous avez des ordinateurs?
   – Bien sûr, nous avons des ordinateurs.
4. – Pardon, monsieur (madame). Est-ce que vous avez des portables?
   – Bien sûr, nous avons des portables.
5. – Pardon, monsieur (madame). Est-ce que vous avez des raquettes?
   – Bien sûr, nous avons des raquettes.
6. – Pardon, monsieur (madame). Est-ce que vous avez des cahiers?
   – Bien sûr, nous avons des cahiers.
7. – Pardon, monsieur (madame). Est-ce que vous avez des montres?
   – Bien sûr, nous avons des montres.
8. – Pardon, monsieur (madame). Est-ce que vous avez des affiches?
   – Bien sûr, nous avons des affiches.
9. – Pardon, monsieur (madame). Est-ce que vous avez des calculatrices?
   – Bien sûr, nous avons des calculatrices.

Teaching note Be sure students make the required liaisons in items 3 and 8.
Listening activity Read the following sentences aloud and have students mark whether the nouns are singular or plural.
   Voici le professeur. [singular]
   Voici les élèves. [plural], etc.

8 COMPREHENSION saying where things are

1. Sur le bureau, il y a (un stylo, des livres, un ordinateur).
2. À la boum, il y a (des filles et des garçons).
3. Dans la classe, il y a (des livres, un professeur, des stylos, des élèves, une table).
4. Au café, sur la table, il y a (une limonade et des croissants).
5. Dans ma chambre, il y a (un stylo, des livres, des affiches, un lit, un ordinateur, une table).
6. Dans mon sac, il y a (des stylos, des livres, des cahiers, un portable, une calculatrice).

LISTENING ACTIVITY

Quickly read off sentences containing singular or plural articles. Have students raise one finger if they hear a singular article. Have them extend all fingers if they hear a plural article.

1. **Voici des copines.** [P]
2. **Voici le vélo.** [S]
3. **Voici une affiche.** [S]

4. **Voici les professeurs.** [P]
5. **Voici des ordinateurs.** [P]
6. **Voici un camarade.** [S]
7. **Voici les amis.** [P]
8. **Voici l'appareil-photo.** [S]

SECTION D

Communicative function
Expressing negation

Teaching Resource Options

PRINT

Workbook PE, pp. 93–100
Unit 4 Resource Book
  Communipak, pp. 140–160
  Video Activities, pp. 60–63
  Videoscript, pp. 64–65
  Workbook TE, pp. 37–44

AUDIO & VISUAL

Overhead Transparencies
21 Objects *Quelques objets* (b)
24 *Le grenier*

TECHNOLOGY
Power Presentations

VIDEO PROGRAM

VIDÉO   DVD
 MODULE 10

10.1 Mini-scenes: Tu as un vélo?
(36:21–37:02 min.)

10.2 Mini-scenes: Qu'est-ce que tu as? (37:03–38:06 min.)

10.3 Mini-scenes: Est-ce que tu as un vélo? (38:07–39:08 min.)

10.4 Dialogue: J'organise une boum
(39:09–39:42 min.)

10.5 Vignette culturelle: La mobylette (39:43–41:03 min.)

9 EXCHANGES discussing possessions

Answers will vary.
– Est-ce que tu as … ?
– Oui, j'ai un(e) … (Non, je n'ai pas de (d') …)
  1. un appareil-photo (pas d'appareil-photo)
  2. (une/pas de) moto
  3. (une/pas de) mobylette
  4. (une/pas de) clarinette
  5. (des/pas de) jeux vidéo
  6. des affiches (pas d'affiches)
  7. (un/pas de) boa
  8. un alligator (pas d'alligator)
  9. des hamsters (pas de hamsters)
  10. (un/pas de) portable

Expansion Ask a third person to report the answer.
X a un ordinateur. (X n'a pas d'ordinateur.)

Variation (with people)
1. un ami à Paris   4. des cousins à Lille
2. une amie à Québec   5. des cousines à Dijon
3. un oncle riche

 L'article indéfini dans les phrases négatives

Compare the forms of the indefinite article in affirmative and negative sentences.

AFFIRMATIVE	NEGATIVE	
Tu as **un** vélo?	Non, je n'ai **pas de** vélo.	*No, I don't have a bike.*
Est-ce que Paul a **une** radio?	Non, il n'a **pas de** radio.	*No, he doesn't have a radio.*
Vous invitez **des** copains demain?	Non, nous n'invitons **pas de** copains.	*No, we are not inviting any friends.*

After a NEGATIVE verb:

> **pas + un, une, des** becomes **pas de**

→ Note that **pas de** becomes **pas d'** before a vowel sound.
  Alice a un ordinateur.   Paul n'a **pas d'**ordinateur.
  J'ai des amis à Québec.   Je n'ai **pas d'**amis à Montréal.

→ The negative form of **il y a** is **il n'y a pas:**
  Dans ma chambre,
    il y a une radio.   **Il n'y a pas de** télé.   *There is no TV.*
    il y a des affiches.   **Il n'y a pas de** photos.   *There are no photographs.*

→ After **être**, the articles **un, une,** and **des** do NOT change.
  Philippe est un voisin.   Éric n'est **pas un** voisin.
  Ce sont des vélos.   Ce ne sont **pas des** mobylettes.

9  **Possessions**

PARLER Ask your classmates if they own the following.

▶ un ordinateur

Est-ce que tu as un ordinateur?

Oui, j'ai un ordinateur.
(Non, je n'ai pas d'ordinateur.)

1. un appareil-photo	6. des affiches
2. une moto	7. un boa
3. une mobylette	8. un alligator
4. une clarinette	9. des hamsters
5. des jeux vidéo	10. un portable

10 *Oui et non*

PARLER/ÉCRIRE One cannot have everything. Say that the following people do not have what is indicated in parentheses.

▶ Paul a un vélo. (un scooter)
  Il n'a pas de scooter.

1. Julien a un scooter. (une voiture)
2. J'ai une radio. (une télé)
3. Vous avez un baladeur. (une chaîne hi-fi)
4. Léa a une calculatrice. (un ordinateur)
5. Vous avez des frères. (une soeur)
6. Nous avons un chien. (des chats)
7. Tu as des copains à Bordeaux.
   (des copains à Lyon)
8. Marc a un oncle à Québec.
   (un oncle à Montréal)
9. Nathalie a des cousins à Paris.
   (des cousins à Lille)

TEACHING STRATEGY Il y a with objects

PROP: Transparency 21: Objects, *Quelques objets* (b)

Using a transparency marker, draw an "X" through eight of the objects shown. Describe what is and is not in the picture.
  Point to the bicycle, saying: **Il y a un vélo.**
  Cross out the scooter: **Il n'y a pas de scooter.**
  Continue, having students repeat after you.

When eight items have been crossed out, ask questions about the transparency.
Est-ce qu'il y a une voiture?
  [Oui, il y a une voiture.]
Est-ce qu'il y a un ordinateur?
  [Non, il n'y a pas d'ordinateur.]

11 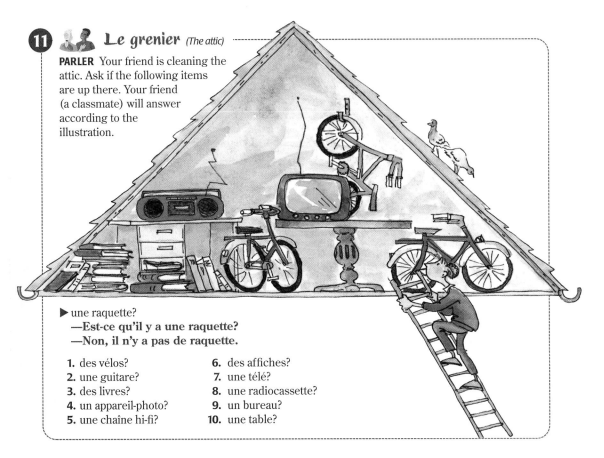 👥 *Le grenier* (The attic)

PARLER Your friend is cleaning the attic. Ask if the following items are up there. Your friend (a classmate) will answer according to the illustration.

▶ une raquette?
—**Est-ce qu'il y a une raquette?**
—**Non, il n'y a pas de raquette.**

1. des vélos?
2. une guitare?
3. des livres?
4. un appareil-photo?
5. une chaîne hi-fi?
6. des affiches?
7. une télé?
8. une radiocassette?
9. un bureau?
10. une table?

Vocabulaire **Expression pour la conversation**

Tu n'as pas de chaîne hi-fi?

Si! J'ai une chaîne hi-fi.

▶ *How to contradict a negative statement or question:*

Si! *Yes!* —Tu n'as pas de chaîne hi-fi?
—**Si!** J'ai une chaîne hi-fi.

12 *Contradictions!*

PARLER/ÉCRIRE Contradict all of the following negative statements.

▶ Tu ne parles pas anglais!   **Si, je parle anglais!**

1. Tu ne parles pas français!
2. Tu n'étudies pas!
3. Tu ne joues pas au basket!
4. Tu n'aimes pas les sports!
5. Tu n'aimes pas la musique!
6. Tu n'écoutes pas le professeur!

cent cinquante-sept
Leçon 10 157

---

10 **PRACTICE** saying what people don't have

1. Il n'a pas de voiture.
2. Je n'ai pas de télé.
3. Vous n'avez pas de chaîne hi-fi.
4. Elle n'a pas d'ordinateur.
5. Vous n'avez pas de soeur.
6. Nous n'avons pas de chats.
7. Tu n'as pas de copains à Lyon.
8. Il n'a pas d'oncle à Montréal.
9. Elle n'a pas de cousins à Lille.

Language note Remind students that in French, the noun after **pas de** may be in the singular.
Je n'ai pas de copain à Lyon.
or: **Je n'ai pas de copains à Lyon.**

11 **EXCHANGES** locating objects

1. – Est-ce qu'il y a des vélos?
   – Oui, il y a des vélos.
2. – Est-ce qu'il y a une guitare?
   – Non, il n'y a pas de guitare.
3. – Est-ce qu'il y a des livres?
   – Oui, il y a des livres.
4. – Est-ce qu'il y a un appareil-photo?
   – Non, il n'y a pas d'appareil-photo.
5. – Est-ce qu'il y a une chaîne hi-fi?
   – Non, il n'y a pas de chaîne hi-fi.
6. – Est-ce qu'il y a des affiches?
   – Non, il n'y a pas d'affiches.
7. – Est-ce qu'il y a une télé?
   – Oui, il y a une télé.
8. – Est-ce qu'il y a une radiocassette?
   – Oui, il y a une radiocassette.
9. – Est-ce qu'il y a un bureau?
   – Oui, il y a un bureau.
10. – Est-ce qu'il y a une table?
    – Oui, il y a une table.

12 **PRACTICE** contradicting negative statements

1. Si, je parle français!
2. Si, j'étudie!
3. Si, je joue au basket!
4. Si, j'aime les sports!
5. Si, j'aime la musique!
6. Si, j'écoute le professeur!

♻️ **Re-entry and review**
Verbs from Unit 3.

Teaching strategy Have students contrast the negative question and response in the example with the following affirmative question and response:
– Tu as une chaîne hi-fi?
– Oui, j'ai une chaîne hi-fi.

SECTION E

Communicative function
Making generalizations

Teaching Resource Options

PRINT

Workbook PE, pp. 93–100
Unit 4 Resource Book
  Audioscript, p. 66
  Communipak, pp. 140–160
  Workbook TE, pp. 37–44

AUDIO & VISUAL

Audio Program
CD 2 Track 30

Overhead Transparencies
25 Class schedule

TECHNOLOGY

Power Presentations

Language note Usually, English does not use articles to introduce abstract nouns or nouns used in a general sense.

Realia note Have students read the sign: **J'aime le français.** (They may want to make similar signs of their own.)

13 COMMUNICATION expressing likes and dislikes

Answers will vary.
(J'aime beaucoup) la musique.
(J'aime un peu) la nature.
(Je n'aime pas) les sports.
(J'aime un peu) le camping.
(J'aime beaucoup) le français.
(J'aime un peu) les maths.
(J'aime un peu / Je n'aime pas) les sciences.
(Je n'aime pas) la violence.
(Je n'aime pas) l'injustice.
(J'aime beaucoup) la liberté.
(J'aime un peu) le théâtre.
(J'aime beaucoup) le cinéma.
(J'aime un peu) la danse.
(J'aime beaucoup) la photo.

Teaching hint Model the new words and cognates, being sure that students pronounce them the French way.

14 COMPREHENSION describing what people like

1. Jean-Claude aime le tennis.
2. Léa aime la nature.
3. Vouz aimez l'art.
4. J'aime le cinéma.
5. Nous aimons le français.
6. Véronique et Roger aiment la danse.

E L'usage de l'article défini dans le sens général

In French, the definite article **(le, la, les)** is used more often than in English. Note its use in the following sentences.

J'aime **la musique.**	*(In general) I like* **music.**
Tu préfères **le tennis** ou **le golf?**	*(Generally) do you prefer* **tennis** *or* **golf?**
Julie aime **les jeux vidéo.**	*(In general) Julie likes* **video games.**
Nous aimons **la liberté.**	*(In general) we love* **liberty.**

> **LANGUAGE COMPARISONS**
> In contrast with English, French uses the definite article **(le, la, les)** to introduce ABSTRACT nouns, or nouns used in a GENERAL or COLLECTIVE sense.

J'♥ le français

13 Expression personnelle

PARLER/ÉCRIRE Say how you feel about the following things, using one of the suggested expressions.

Je n'aime pas …
J'aime un peu …
J'aime beaucoup …

▶ **Je n'aime pas la violence.**

la musique	le français	la violence	le théâtre
la nature	les maths	l'injustice	le cinéma
les sports	les sciences	la liberté	la danse
le camping			la photo
			(photography)

Elle m'aime …
Il m'aime …
passionnément
à la folie
beaucoup
pas du tout
un peu

14 C'est évident! *(It's obvious!)*

PARLER Read about the following people and say what they like. Choose the appropriate item from the list. (Masculine nouns are in blue. Feminine nouns are in red.)

▶ Sophie écoute des CD.
  Sophie aime la musique.

art	cinéma	**danse**	français
	musique	nature	tennis

1. Jean-Claude a une raquette.
2. Léa fait une promenade dans la forêt.
3. Nous visitons un musée *(museum)*.
4. Tu regardes un film.
5. Vous étudiez en classe de français.
6. Véronique et Roger sont dans une discothèque.

158 cent cinquante-huit
Unité 4

TEACHING HINT

Have students memorize the **comptine** that accompanies the daisy petals. (It begins: **Elle m'aime un peu...** and continues clockwise.) Point out that the odds of being "loved" are much greater in the French than in the English version (*he/she loves me, he/she loves me not ...*).

F **L'usage de l'article défini avec les jours de la semaine**

Compare the following sentences.

REPEATED EVENTS
Le samedi, je dîne avec des copains.
*(On) Saturdays (in general), I have
   dinner with friends.*

SINGLE EVENT
Samedi, je dîne avec mon cousin.
*(On) Saturday (that is, this Saturday),
   I am having dinner with my cousin.*

To indicate a repeated or habitual event, French uses the construction:

> **le** + DAY OF THE WEEK

→ When an event happens only once, no article is used.

 15 *Questions personnelles* **PARLER**

1. Est-ce que tu étudies le samedi?
2. Est-ce que tu dînes au restaurant le dimanche? Si *(If)* oui, avec qui?
3. Est-ce que tu as une classe de français le lundi? le mercredi?
4. Est-ce que tu regardes les matchs de football américain le samedi? le dimanche?
5. Est-ce que tu travailles? Où? *(Name of place or store)* Quand?

16 *L'emploi du temps*

PARLER/ÉCRIRE

	LUNDI	MARDI	MERCREDI	JEUDI	VENDREDI
9 h	français	physique	sciences	biologie	
10 h		histoire		maths	anglais
11 h	maths	sciences	anglais		français

The following students all have the same morning schedule. Complete the sentences accordingly.

▶ **Nous avons une classe de français
le lundi …**

1. J'ai une classe de maths _____.
2. Tu as une classe de sciences _____.
3. Jacques a une classe de physique _____.
4. Thérèse a une classe d'histoire _____.
5. Vous avez une classe de biologie _____.
6. Les élèves ont une classe d'anglais _____.

PRONONCIATION le/lə/ les/le/

Les articles *le* et *les*

Be sure to distinguish between the pronunciation of **le** and **les**. In spoken French, that is often the only way to tell the difference between a singular and a plural noun.

le sac   **les sacs**

Répétez: /lə/ **le**   **le sac**   **le vélo**   **le portable**   **le copain**   **le voisin**
          /le/ **les** **les sacs** **les vélos** **les portables** **les copains** **les voisins**

TALKING ABOUT PAST EVENTS

Let's talk about what you did last Saturday.

Est-ce que tu as étudié samedi dernier? Oui, j'ai étudié samedi dernier. (Non, je n'ai pas étudié samedi dernier.)

- **Est-ce que tu as travaillé?**
- **Est-ce que tu as regardé la télé?**
- **Est-ce que tu as joué au basket?**

- **Est-ce que tu as organisé une boum?**
- **Est-ce que tu as dansé?**
- **Est-ce que tu as dîné au restaurant?**
- **Est-ce que tu as mangé un hot dog?**
  (Reminder: use **pas de** in the negative.)
- **Est-ce que tu as mangé une pizza?**

Communicative function
Discussing repeated events

 Re-entry and review
Days of the week from Lesson 4B.

Language note In French, the word **sur** *(on)* is never used with days of the week.

 15 **COMMUNICATION** answering personal questions

Answers will vary.
1. Oui, j'étudie le samedi.
   (Non, je n'étudie pas le samedi.)
2. Oui, je dîne au restaurant le dimanche. Je dîne avec (mes parents). (Non, je ne dîne pas au restaurant le dimanche.)
3. Oui, j'ai une classe de français le lundi et le mercredi. (Non, je n'ai pas de classe de français le lundi. J'ai une classe de français le mercredi.) (Non, je n'ai pas de classe de français le lundi et le mercredi.)
4. Oui, je regarde les matchs de football américain le samedi et le dimanche. (Non, je ne regarde pas les matchs de football américain le samedi et le dimanche.)
5. Oui, je travaille. Je travaille (à la maison / à Mini Mart…). Je travaille (le samedi).

Language note Point out that in French, **si** has two meanings:
- *if* (as in **s'il vous plaît:** literally, *if it pleases you*)
- *yes* (to contradict a negative statement)

---

16 **COMPREHENSION** describing school schedules

1. J'ai une classe de maths le lundi et le jeudi.
2. Tu as une classe de sciences le mardi et le mercredi.
3. Jacques a une classe de physique le mardi.
4. Thérèse a une classe d'histoire le mardi.
5. Vous avez une classe de biologie le jeudi.
6. Les élèves ont une classe d'anglais le mercredi et le vendredi.

Additional practice Show Transparency 25: Class schedule or have students turn to the **emploi du temps** on p. 131. Let them imagine that they have the same schedule and ask them questions:
–**Quel jour avez-vous une classe de français?**
–**Nous avons une classe de français le lundi, le mardi,** etc.

COMPREHENSION

1. Quel âge a ton copain?
   (c) Quatorze ans.
2. Est-ce qu'Éric a un scooter?
   (f) Non, mais il a une moto.
3. Où est l'appareil-photo?
   (b) Il est sur la table.
4. Tu as un baladeur?
   (a) Oui, mais je n'ai pas de chaîne hi-fi.
5. Est-ce que tu aimes étudier l'anglais?
   (e) Oui, mais je préfère l'espagnol.
6. Tu as soif?
   (d) Oui, je voudrais une limonade.

 ORAL EXPRESSION

• Qui a une montre?
  (Dix-sept) élèves ont une montre.
• Qui a un vélo?
  (Treize) élèves ont un vélo.
• Qui a une radio?
  (Douze) élèves ont une radio.
• Qui a un baladeur?
  (Seize) élèves ont un baladeur.
• Qui a des affiches?
  (Dix) élèves ont des affiches.
• Qui a un ordinateur?
  (Huit) élèves ont un ordinateur.
• Qui a des CD?
  (Neuf) élèves ont des CD.

160 • À votre tour!
Unité 4 LEÇON 10

À votre tour!

OBJECTIFS

Now you can …
• talk about what you have and do not have
• describe in general what you like and do not like

1 🎧 Allô!

PARLER Jean-Marc is phoning some friends. Match his questions on the left with his friends' answers on the right.

1 Quel âge a ton copain?

2 Est-ce qu'Éric a un scooter?

3 Où est l'appareil-photo?

4 Tu as un baladeur?

5 Est-ce que tu aimes étudier l'anglais?

6 Tu as soif?

a Oui, mais je n'ai pas de chaîne hi-fi.

b Il est sur la table.

c Quatorze ans.

d Oui, je voudrais une limonade.

e Oui, mais je préfère l'espagnol.

f Non, mais il a une moto.

2 Un sondage

PARLER/ÉCRIRE A French consumer research group wants to know what things American teenagers own. Conduct a survey in your class asking who has the objects on the list. Count the number of students who raise their hands for each object, and report your findings on a separate piece of paper.

Qui a un portable? … Quinze élèves ont des portables.

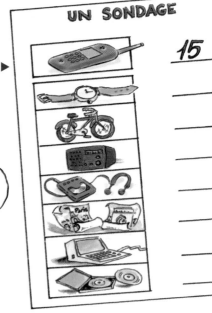

UN SONDAGE

15

160 cent soixante
Unité 4

À VOTRE TOUR

Depending on your goals and objectives, you may or may not wish to assign all of the activities in the **À votre tour** section.

PAIR AND GROUP PRACTICE

Act. 1 lends itself to pair practice. It can also be done in trios, with two students performing and the third acting as monitor.

3  Créa-dialogue

PARLER Ask your classmates if they like the following things. Then ask if they own the corresponding object.

le tennis

1. la musique	2. le jogging	3. les maths	4. la photo	5. les matchs de baseball	6. l'exercice

▶ —Tu aimes <u>le tennis</u>?　　　—Tu as <u>une raquette</u>?
　—Oui, j'aime <u>le tennis</u>.　　—Oui, j'ai <u>une raquette</u>.
　　(Non, je n'aime pas <u>le tennis</u>.)　　(Non, je n'ai pas <u>de raquette</u>.)

4 Quelle est la différence?

PARLER/ÉCRIRE Sophie went away with her family for the weekend and she took some of her belongings with her. Describe what is in her room on Friday and what is missing on Saturday.

VENDREDI

SAMEDI

▶ Il y a …

▶ Il n'y a pas de …

5 Composition: Ma semaine

ÉCRIRE In a short paragraph, describe what you do (or do not do) regularly on various days of the week. Select three days and two different activities for each day. Use only vocabulary that you know. Perhaps you might want to exchange paragraphs with a friend by e-mail.

Le lundi, j'ai une classe de français …

LESSON REVIEW
CLASSZONE.COM

PORTFOLIO ASSESSMENT

You will probably select only one speaking activity and one writing activity to go into the students' portfolios for Unit 4.

In this lesson, Act. 5 is a good written portfolio topic. You might also wish to use the composition suggested at the bottom of page 151 of the TE.

---

3 GUIDED ORAL EXPRESSION

1. – Tu aimes la musique?
   – Oui, j'aime la musique.
   (Non, je n'aime pas la musique.)
   – Tu as une radiocassette?
   (Non, je n'ai pas de radiocassette.)
2. – Tu aimes le jogging?
   – Oui, j'aime le jogging.
   (Non, je n'aime pas le jogging.)
   – Tu as un baladeur?
   – Oui, j'ai un baladeur.
   (Non, je n'ai pas de baladeur.)
3. – Tu aimes les maths.
   – Oui, j'aime les maths.
   (Non, je n'aime pas les maths.)
   – Tu as une calculatrice?
   – Oui, j'ai une calculatrice.
   (Non, je n'ai pas de calculatrice.)
4. – Tu aimes la photo.
   – Oui, j'aime la photo.
   (Non, je n'aime pas la photo.)
   – Tu as un appareil-photo?
   – Oui, j'ai un appareil-photo.
   (Non, je n'ai pas d'appareil-photo.)
5. – Tu aimes les matchs de baseball?
   – Oui, j'aime les matchs de baseball.
   (Non, je n'aime pas les matchs de baseball.)
   – Tu as une télé?
   – Oui, j'ai une télé.
   (Non, je n'ai pas de télé.)
6. – Tu aimes l'exercice?
   – Oui, j'aime l'exercice.
   (Non, je n'aime pas l'exercice.)
   – Tu as un vélo?
   – Oui, j'ai un vélo.
   (Non, je n'ai pas de vélo.)

Middle School Copymasters
Drill: *Au tableau*, pp. T22–T23

---

4 COMPREHENSION

• Vendredi, il y a une affiche, une raquette, une guitare, une télé, un lit, un sac, des CD, des livres, un portable, une radiocassette, une chaîne hi-fi, une chaise, un bureau, un appareil-photo, des crayons, des stylos, un baladeur et un chat.
• Samedi, il n'y a pas d'appareil-photo, de raquette, de radiocassette, de CD, de sac, de chat, de portable.

---

5 WRITTEN SELF-EXPRESSION

Answers will vary.
• Le mardi, j'ai une classe de sciences. Je dîne avec ma famille à sept heures.
• Le mercredi je joue au tennis à quatre heures avec ma copine. Après le dîner, j'étudie.
• Le dimanche, j'écoute la radio et je regarde un film à la télé.

Leçon 11

Main Topic Describing people

Teaching Resource Options

PRINT

Workbook PE, pp. 101–106
Activités pour tous PE, pp. 59–61
Block Scheduling Copymasters,
  pp. 81–88
Unit 4 Resource Book
  Activités pour tous TE, pp. 79–81
  Audioscript, pp. 100, 101–102
  Communipak, pp. 140–160
  Lesson Plans, pp. 82–83
  Block Scheduling Lesson Plans, pp. 84–85
  Absent Student Copymasters, pp. 86–89
  Video Activities, pp. 92–97
  Videoscript, pp. 98–99
  Workbook TE, pp. 73–78

AUDIO & VISUAL

Audio Program
CD 2 Tracks 33, 34
CD 8 Tracks 14–18

TECHNOLOGY

Online Workbook

VIDEO PROGRAM

 MODULE 11
Le copain de Mireille

TOTAL TIME: 4:56 min.
  DVD Disk 1
  Videotape 2 (COUNTER: 4:15 min.)

11.1 Introduction: Listening
  —Je suis américain
  (41:50–42:08 min.)

11.2 Mini-scenes: Listening
  —Qui est-ce? (42:09–43:01 min.)

11.3 Mini-scenes: Speaking
  — Comment sont-ils?
  (43:02–43:54 min.)

11.4 Dialogue: Le copain de Mireille
  (43:55–44:42 min.)

11.5 Vignette culturelle: La France et ses voisins (44:43–46:11 min.)

Compréhension
Answers
1. Nicolas regarde une fille.
2. Elle s'appelle Mireille Labé.
3. Oui, elle est jolie (elle est mignonne).
4. Oui! Elle est amusante, intelligente et sympathique.
5. Oui, elle a un copain.
6. C'est Jean-Claude.

162 · **Conversation et Culture**
Unité 4 LEÇON 11

LEÇON 11

Le copain de Mireille

VIDÉO DVD AUDIO

Nicolas and Jean-Claude are having lunch at the school cafeteria. Nicolas is looking at the students seated at the other end of their table.

Nicolas:	Regarde la fille là-bas!
Jean-Claude:	La fille blonde?
Nicolas:	Oui! Qui est-ce?
Jean-Claude:	C'est Mireille Labé.
Nicolas:	Elle est <u>mignonne</u>!
Jean-Claude:	Elle est aussi <u>amusante</u>, intelligente et <u>sympathique</u>.
Nicolas:	Est-ce qu'elle a un copain?
Jean-Claude:	Oui, elle a un copain.
Nicolas:	Il est sympathique?
Jean-Claude:	Oui … Très sympathique!
Nicolas:	Et intelligent?
Jean-Claude:	Aussi!
Nicolas:	Dommage! … Qui est-ce?
Jean-Claude:	C'est moi!
Nicolas:	Euh … oh … Excuse-moi et <u>félicitations</u>!

cute

fun/nice

congratulations

Compréhension

1. Qui est-ce que Nicolas regarde?
2. Comment s'appelle la fille?
3. Est-ce qu'elle est jolie?
4. Est-ce qu'elle a d'autres *(other)* qualités?
5. Est-ce qu'elle a un copain?
6. Qui est le copain de Mireille *(Mireille's boyfriend)*?

162 cent soixante-deux
Unité 4

SETTING THE SCENE

The opening text introduces several students having lunch at the Lycée Corot. Not untypically, they are engaged in people-watching. (For more background on this **lycée,** have students turn to pp. 124–127.)

To help students develop listening comprehension skills, have them keep their books closed as they watch the video. Then have them open their books and read the text.

NOTE *culturelle*

L'amitié et la bande de copains

French people believe in friendship (**l'amitié**) and family life and rank these values far above money, material comfort, and personal success. The friendships they establish at an early age tend to be durable. Since French people move much less frequently than Americans, and since distances are much smaller, they remain in close contact with their high school friends throughout their entire lives.

French teenagers, like their American counterparts, are very sociable. They have a close-knit group of friends, known as **la bande de copains**, with whom they share common interests. They go out together, especially to movies, concerts, and parties. This group may include classmates, cousins, other young people whom they have met during vacations, as well as the children of family friends. When young people invite their friends to the house, it is customary to introduce them to their parents.

COMPARAISONS CULTURELLES

What similarities and differences do you see between the French and American attitudes towards friendship?

- les similarités
- les différences

In your opinion, are these attitudes basically the same? Explain.

OPINION PERSONNELLE

Rank the following values mentioned in the text from 1 (the highest) to 5.

- l'amitié
- l'argent *(money)*
- le confort matériel
- la famille
- le succès personnel

Compare your rankings with your classmates.

MULTICULTURALISM IN FRANCE

The opening segments of **Video Module 11** focus on the diversity of the French population. The final **Vignette culturelle** presents the various national origins of the people of contemporary France.

Teaching Resource Options

PRINT

Workbook PE, pp. 101–106
Unit 4 Resource Book
 Audioscript, p. 100
 Communipak, pp. 140–160
 Workbook TE, pp. 73–78

AUDIO & VISUAL

Audio Program
CD 2 Track 35

Overhead Transparencies
26a *La description*
26b *La description* (overlay)

TECHNOLOGY
Power Presentations

Teaching hint Use **Transparencies
26a** and **26b,** *La description* and the
overlay, to present the descriptive
adjectives.

① PRACTICE adjective forms

1. Carole n'est pas blonde.
2. Mireille n'est pas petite.
3. Marthe n'est pas belle.
4. Louise n'est pas grande.
5. Émilie n'est pas riche.
6. Lisa n'est pas française.
7. Céline n'est pas espagnole.
8. Julie n'est pas américaine.

Language note Point out that
nationalities are adjectives.

Expansion (dialogue format)
Jean-Marc est blond. (Mélanie)
– Jean-Marc est blond.
– Et Mélanie? Elle est blonde?
– Mais non, elle n'est pas blonde.

② COMMUNICATION describing people

Answers will vary.
1. Il est sympathique. (Il n'est pas sympathique.)
2. Elle est sportive. (Elle n'est pas sportive.)
3. Elle est gentille. (Elle n'est pas gentille.)
4. Elle est mignonne. (Elle n'est pas mignonne.)
5. Elle est intelligente. (Elle n'est pas intelligente.)
6. Il n'est pas bête. (Il est bête.)
7. Il est amusant. (Il n'est pas amusant.)
8. Il n'est pas méchant. (Il est méchant.)

Variation (dialogue format)
– Est-ce que le prince Charles est intéressant?
– Oui, il est intéressant. (Non, il n'est pas intéressant.)

164 · Langue et Communication
Unité 4 LEÇON 11

A Les adjectifs: masculin et féminin

Compare the forms of the adjectives in heavy print as they
describe masculine and feminine nouns.

MASCULINE	FEMININE
Le scooter est **petit.**	La voiture est **petite.**
Patrick est **intelligent.**	Caroline est **intelligente.**
L'ordinateur est **moderne.**	La télé est **moderne.**

In written French, feminine adjectives are usually formed
as follows:

> MASCULINE ADJECTIVE + **-e** = FEMININE ADJECTIVE

→ If the masculine adjective ends in **-e,** there is no change in the feminine form.

 Jérôme est **timide.** Juliette est **timide.**

→ Adjectives that follow the above patterns are called REGULAR adjectives. Those
 that do not are called IRREGULAR adjectives. For example:

 Marc est **beau.** Sylvie est **belle.**
 Paul est **canadien.** Marie est **canadienne.**

NOTE French dictionaries list adjectives by their masculine forms. For irregular adjectives,
the feminine form is indicated in parentheses.

NOTES DE PRONONCIATION:

- If the masculine form of an adjective ends in a silent consonant, that consonant is
 pronounced in the feminine form.

- If the masculine form of an adjective ends in a vowel or a pronounced consonant,
 the masculine and feminine forms sound the same.

DIFFERENT PRONUNCIATION		SAME PRONUNCIATION	
petit	petite	timide	timide
blond	blonde	joli	jolie
français	française	espagnol	espagnole

LEARNING ABOUT LANGUAGE
ADJECTIVES are words that describe
people, places, and things.

In French, MASCULINE adjectives
are used with masculine nouns,
and FEMININE adjectives are used
with feminine nouns. This is
called NOUN-ADJECTIVE AGREEMENT.

① Vive la différence!

PARLER/ÉCRIRE People can be friends and yet be quite different.
Describe the girls named in parentheses, indicating that they are
not like their friends.

▶ Jean-Marc est blond. (Mélanie) **Mélanie n'est pas blonde.**

1. Jean-Louis est blond. (Carole)
2. Paul est petit. (Mireille)
3. Éric est beau. (Marthe)
4. Jérôme est grand. (Louise)
5. Michel est riche. (Émilie)
6. André est français. (Lisa)
7. Antonio est espagnol. (Céline)
8. Bill est américain. (Julie)

COMPREHENSION Descriptions

PROPS: Blue and red index cards

On the board, draw a stick figure of a boy (labeled
René) and a girl (labeled Renée).

 Voici René. C'est un voisin. [blue]
 Et ici Renée. C'est une voisine. [red]

Give each student a blue and a red card.

As you read descriptions using the new vocabulary,
they raise the appropriate card.

 René est amusant. [blue card]
 Renée est mignonne. [red card]
 René(e) est timide. [either: both cards]
 Renée est assez sportive. [red card]
 René est très intelligent. [blue card] ...

Vocabulaire La description

Voici Olivier.

Voici Sophie.

ADJECTIFS

amusant	amusing, fun	Il est **amusant**.	Elle est **amusante**.
intelligent	intelligent	Il est **intelligent**.	Elle est **intelligente**.
intéressant	interesting	Il est **intéressant**.	Elle est **intéressante**.
méchant	mean, nasty	Il n'est pas **méchant**.	Elle n'est pas **méchante**.
bête	silly, dumb	Il n'est pas **bête**.	Elle n'est pas **bête**.
sympathique	nice, pleasant	Il est **sympathique**.	Elle est **sympathique**.
timide	timid	Il est **timide**.	Elle n'est pas **timide**.
gentil (gentille)	nice, kind	Il est **gentil**.	Elle est **gentille**.
mignon (mignonne)	cute	Il est **mignon**.	Elle est **mignonne**.
sportif (sportive)	athletic	Il est **sportif**.	Elle est **sportive**.

ADVERBES

assez	rather	Nous sommes **assez** intelligents.
très	very	Vous n'êtes pas **très** sportifs!

---

2 **Oui ou non?**

PARLER In your opinion, do the following people have the suggested traits? (Note: These traits are given in the masculine form only.)

Il est intéressant.

Il n'est pas intéressant.

▶ le prince William / intéressant?

1. le Président / sympathique?
2. Venus Williams / sportif?
3. ma copine / gentil?
4. Britney Spears / mignon?
5. Oprah Winfrey / intelligent?
6. Einstein / bête?
7. Jay Leno / amusant?
8. le prof / méchant?

---

3 **Descriptions**

PARLER Select one of the following characters. Using words from the **Vocabulaire,** describe this character in two affirmative or negative sentences.

▶ Frankenstein
  Il est très méchant.
  Il n'est pas très mignon.

1. Tarzan
2. King Kong
3. Big Bird
4. Batman
5. Miss Piggy
6. Wonder Woman
7. Charlie Brown
8. Blanche-Neige (*Snow White*)
9. Garfield
10. Snoopy

---

4 **L'idéal**

PARLER/ÉCRIRE Now you have the chance to describe your ideal people. Use two adjectives for each one.

1. Le copain idéal est … et …
2. La copine idéale est … et …
3. Le professeur idéal est … et …
4. L'étudiant idéal est … et …
5. L'étudiante idéale est … et …

cent soixante-cinq
Leçon 11 165

Language notes
- In conversational speech, **sympathique** is often shortened to **sympa**. This shortened form is invariable and does not take adjective endings.
- Adverbs like **assez** and **très** often modify adjectives. Note that liaison is required after **très**. In conversation, there is usually no liaison after **assez**.

Pronunciation
gentil /ʒ ɑ̃tí/   **gentille** /ʒ ɑ̃tíj/

Supplementary vocabulary
content ≠ **triste** *happy ≠ sad*
fort ≠ **faible** *strong ≠ weak*
riche ≠ **pauvre** *rich ≠ poor*
fatigué ≠ **énergique** *tired ≠ energetic*
génial ≠ **stupide** *brilliant ≠ dumb*
poli ≠ **impoli** *polite ≠ impolite*
drôle ≠ **pénible** *funny ≠ "a pain"*
optimiste ≠ **pessimiste**
sincère   **athlétique**
indépendant   **dynamique**

3 **COMMUNICATION** describing people

Answers will vary.
1. Il est (très sportif). Il est (assez bête).
2. Il n'est pas (très mignon). Il est (assez timide).
3. Il est (grand). Il n'est pas (très intelligent).
4. Il n'est pas (timide). Il est (très intelligent).
5. Elle est (très bête). Elle est (assez amusante).
6. Elle est (très intelligente). Elle est (très sportive).
7. Il est (sympathique). Il n'est pas (très sportif).
8. Il est (belle). Elle est (assez timide).
9. Il est (amusant). Il n'est pas (très sportif)
10. Il est (sympathique). Il n'est pas (méchant).

4 **COMMUNICATION** describing ideal people

Answers will vary.
1. (amusant, intéressant)
2. (intelligente, amusante)
3. (sympathique, intéressant)
4. (intelligent, intéressant)
5. (intelligente, intéressante)

Variation (in the negative)
Le copain idéal n'est pas (méchant) …

Expansion le père idéal, la mère idéale, le frère idéal, la soeur idéale

---

GAME Descriptions

Have students in pairs pick one of the characters in Act. 3 and write a description in two identical copies.

Then ask each pair to give one copy of the description to the pair on their left, and the other to the pair on their right.

Each pair now has two new descriptions to read. They read the two descriptions and at the bottom of each they write down the name of the person they think is being described.

The descriptions are then returned to the "original authors." The winners are those pairs who had both copies of their descriptions identified correctly.

SECTION B

Communicative function
Describing people and objects

Teaching Resource Options

PRINT

Workbook PE, pp. 101–106
Unit 4 Resource Book
 Communipak pp. 140–160
 Video Activities, pp. 92–93
 Videoscript, p. 98
 Workbook TE, pp. 73–78

AUDIO & VISUAL

Overhead Transparencies
27 *Les adjectifs de nationalité*

TECHNOLOGY

Power Presentations

VIDEO PROGRAM

 MODULE 11

11.1 Introduction: Je suis américain
 (41:50–42:08 min.)

11.2 Mini-scenes: Qui est-ce?
 (42:09–43:01 min.)

11.3 Mini-scenes: Comment sont-ils?
 (43:02–43:54 min.)

Language note When a plural adjective describes two or more nouns, one of which is masculine, the masculine plural is used.
 Patrick et Anne sont français.
 Ils ne sont pas américains.

Looking ahead Irregular plural forms like **beau–beaux** are taught in Lesson 11.

 COMPREHENSION describing more than one person

1. Elles sont amusantes.
2. Ils sont timides.
3. Elles sont sportives.
4. Elles sont intelligentes.
5. Ils ne sont pas sportifs.
6. Ils ne sont pas sympathiques.

Langue et Communication
Unité 4 LEÇON 11

166 ·

B Les adjectifs: le pluriel

Compare the forms of the adjectives in heavy print as they describe singular and plural nouns.

SINGULAR	PLURAL
Paul est **intelligent** et **timide**.	Paul et Éric sont **intelligents** et **timides**.
Alice est **intelligente** et **timide**.	Alice et Claire sont **intelligentes** et **timides**.

In written French, plural adjectives are usually formed as follows:

> SINGULAR ADJECTIVE + **-s** = PLURAL ADJECTIVE

→ If the masculine singular adjective already ends in **-s**, there is no change in the plural form.

Patrick est **français**.	Patrick et Daniel sont **français**.
BUT: Anne est **française**.	Anne et Alice sont **françaises**.

NOTE DE PRONONCIATION: Because the final **-s** of plural adjectives is silent, singular and plural adjectives sound the same.

SUMMARY: Forms of regular adjectives

	MASCULINE	FEMININE	*also:*	
SINGULAR	**-** grand	**-e** grand**e**	timide	timide
PLURAL	**-s** grand**s**	**-es** grand**es**	français	français**es**

5 Une question de personnalité

PARLER/ÉCRIRE Indicate whether or not the following people exhibit the personality traits in parentheses. (These traits are given in the masculine singular form only. Make the necessary agreements.)

▶ Alice et Thérèse aiment parler en public. (timide?)

1. Claire et Valérie sont très populaires. (amusant?)
2. Robert et Jean-Luc n'aiment pas danser. (timide?)
3. Catherine et Martine aiment jouer au foot. (sportif?)
4. Laure et Léa ont un «A» en français. (intelligent?)
5. Thomas et Vincent n'aiment pas le jogging. (sportif?)
6. Les voisins n'aiment pas parler avec nous. (sympathique?)

Elles ne sont pas timides.

TALKING ABOUT PAST EVENTS

Let's talk about what you did last summer.

▶ **Est-ce que tu as voyagé l'été dernier?**
 Oui, j'ai voyagé l'été dernier.
 (Non, je n'ai pas voyagé l'été dernier.)

 • **Est-ce que tu as visité Paris l'été dernier?**
 • **Est-ce que tu as visité Québec?**

 • **Est-ce que tu as étudié?**
 • **Est-ce que tu as travaillé?**
 • **Est-ce que tu as joué au volley?**
 • **Est-ce que tu as joué au tennis?**
 • **Est-ce que tu as nagé?**
 • **Est-ce que tu as dîné au restaurant?**

VOCABULAIRE Les adjectifs de nationalité

américain	*American*	**italien (italienne)**	*Italian*
mexicain	*Mexican*	**canadien (canadienne)**	*Canadian*
français	*French*	**japonais**	*Japanese*
anglais	*English*	**chinois**	*Chinese*
espagnol	*Spanish*		
suisse	*Swiss*		

SiLC PASSEPORT POUR LE MONDE

➔ Words that describe nationality are adjectives and take adjective endings.

Monsieur Katagiri est **japonais.**

Kumi et Michiko sont **japonaises.**

VOCABULAIRE Expression pour la conversation

▶ *How to introduce a conclusion:*

alors *so, then* —J'habite à Québec.
—**Alors**, tu es canadien!

J'habite à Québec.

Alors, tu es canadien.

6 🧑‍🤝‍🧑 *Quelle nationalité?*

PARLER Ask where the following people live and what their nationalities are. A friend will answer you.

▶ —Où habitent Lois et Kim?
—Elles habitent à Miami.
—Alors, elles sont américaines?
—Mais oui, elles sont américaines.

Lois et Kim	1. Jim et Bob	2. Léa et Aline
Miami	Liverpool	Toulouse
américain	anglais	français
3. Clara et Tere	4. Luc et Paul	5. ??
Madrid	Montréal	??
espagnol	??	??

7 **Les nationalités**

PARLER/ÉCRIRE Give the nationalities of the following people.

▶ Silvia et Maria sont de Rome.
Elles sont italiennes.

1. Lise et Nathalie étudient à Québec.
2. Michael et Dennis sont de Liverpool.
3. Luis et Paco étudient à Madrid.
4. Isabel et Carmen travaillent à Acapulco.
5. Yoko et Kumi sont de Tokyo.
6. Monsieur et Madame Chen habitent à Beijing.
7. Jean-Pierre et Claude sont de Genève.
8. Françoise et Sylvie travaillent à Paris.

♻️ **Review and expansion**
Adjectives of nationality from Lesson 1B.

Language note Remind students that adjectives of nationality are not capitalized in French.

Supplementary vocabulary

allemand *German*
hollandais *Dutch*
portugais *Portuguese*
libanais *Lebanese*
russe *Russian*
grec (grecque) *Greek*
égyptien(ne) *Egyptian*
israëlien(ne) *Israeli*
brésilien(ne) *Brazilian*
péruvien(ne) *Peruvian*
coréen(ne) *Korean*
vietnamien(ne) *Vietnamese*

6 **EXCHANGES** discussing nationalities

1. – Où habitent Jim et Bob?
   – Ils habitent à Liverpool.
   – Alors, ils sont anglais?
   – Mais oui, ils sont anglais.
2. – Où habitent Léa et Aline?
   – Elles habitent à Toulouse.
   – Alors, elles sont françaises?
   – Mais oui, elles sont françaises.
3. – Où habitent Clara et Tere?
   – Elles habitent à Madrid.
   – Alors, elles sont espagnoles?
   – Mais oui, elles sont espagnoles.
4. – Où habitent Luc et Paul?
   – Ils habitent à Montréal.
   – Alors, ils sont canadiens?
   – Mais oui, ils sont canadiens.
5. – Où habitent (Kim et Ted)?
   – (Ils) habitent à (Seattle).
   – Alors, ils sont (américains)?
   – Mais oui, il sont (américains).

7 **COMPREHENSION** identifying nationality

1. Elles sont canadiennes.
2. Ils sont anglais.
3. Ils sont espagnols.
4. Elles sont mexicaines.
5. Elles sont japonaises.
6. Ils sont chinois.
7. Ils sont suisses.
8. Elles sont françaises.

Now you will learn to talk about what others did last summer. (First ask one student what he/she did. Then ask the class to reaffirm.)

▶ **X, est-ce que tu as voyagé l'été dernier?**
Oui, j'ai voyagé.

(to the class) **Est-ce que X a voyagé?**
Oui, il a voyagé.

Z, est-ce que tu as visité Paris?
Non, je n'ai pas visité Paris.
(to the class) **Est-ce que Z a visité Paris?**
Non, elle n'a pas visité Paris.

(Use the questions on the facing page.)

C La place des adjectifs

Note the position of the adjectives in the sentences on the right.

Philippe a une voiture.   Il a une voiture **anglaise.**
Denise invite des copains.   Elle invite des copains **américains.**
Voici un livre.   Voici un livre **intéressant.**
J'ai des amies.   J'ai des amies **sympathiques.**

In French, adjectives usually come AFTER the noun they modify,
according to the pattern:

ARTICLE	+	NOUN	+	ADJECTIVE
une		voiture		**française**
des		copains		**intéressants**

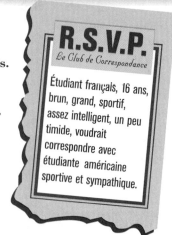

R.S.V.P.
Le Club de Correspondance

Étudiant français, 16 ans,
brun, grand, sportif,
assez intelligent, un peu
timide, voudrait
correspondre avec
étudiante américaine
sportive et sympathique.

8 Préférences personnelles

PARLER For each person or object below,
choose among the characteristics in
parentheses. Indicate your preference.

▶ avoir un copain (sympathique,
intelligent, sportif)
Je préfère avoir un copain intelligent.

1. avoir une copine (amusante,
mignonne, intelligente)
2. avoir un professeur (gentil, intelligent,
amusant)
3. avoir des voisins (sympathiques,
intéressants, riches)
4. avoir une voiture (moderne,
confortable, rapide)
5. avoir une calculatrice (japonaise,
américaine, française)
6. avoir une montre (suisse, japonaise,
française)
7. dîner dans un restaurant (italien,
chinois, français)
8. regarder un film (intéressant, amusant,
intelligent)
9. travailler avec des personnes
(gentilles, amusantes, sérieuses)
10. faire un voyage avec des gens
(amusants, riches, sympathiques)

9 Qui se ressemble ...

(Birds of a feather ...)

PARLER Say that the following people have
friends, relatives, or acquaintances with the
same personality or nationality.

▶ Claire est anglaise. (un copain)
Elle a un copain anglais.

1. Jean-Pierre est sympathique.
(des cousines)
2. La prof est intelligente. (des étudiants)
3. Madame Simon est intéressante.
(des voisines)
4. Alice est américaine. (des copines)
5. Véronique est amusante. (un frère)
6. Michel est sportif. (une soeur)
7. Pedro est espagnol. (des camarades)
8. Antonio est mexicain. (une copine)
9. Bernard est sportif. (un voisin)

Birds of a feather flock together.

 cent soixante-huit
Unité 4

TALKING ABOUT PAST EVENTS

Let's talk about what you and your friends did last
weekend.

**W et X, est-ce que vous avez étudié le week-end
dernier?
Oui, nous avons étudié.
(Non, nous n'avons pas étudié.)**

• **Est-ce que vous avez regardé la télé?**
• **Est-ce que vous avez joué au foot?**
• **Est-ce que vous avez joué au tennis?**
• **Est-ce que vous avez nagé?**
• **Est-ce que vous avez organisé une boum?**
• **Est-ce que vous avez invité des copains?**
• **Est-ce que vous avez dansé?**
• **Est-ce que vous avez chanté?**

10 Préférences internationales

PARLER/ÉCRIRE Choose an item from Column A and indicate your preference as to country of origin by choosing an adjective from Column B. Be sure to make the necessary agreement.

> Je préfère les voitures italiennes.

A	B
la musique	anglais
la cuisine	américain
les voitures	français
les ordinateurs	mexicain
les appareils-photo	chinois
les CD	japonais
les restaurants	italien

Je préfère …

PRONONCIATION

Les consonnes finales

/-/ /d/

As you know, when the last letter of a word is a consonant, that consonant is often silent. But when a word ends in "**e**," the consonant before it is pronounced. As you practice the following adjectives, be sure to distinguish between the masculine and the feminine forms.

blond   blonde

MASCULINE ADJECTIVE (no final consonant sound)		FEMININE ADJECTIVE (final consonant sound)
Répétez:	blond	/d/	blonde
	grand		grande
	petit	/t/	petite
	amusant		amusante
	français	/z/	française
	anglais		anglaise
	américain	/n/	américaine
	canadien		canadienne

---

cent soixante-neuf
Leçon 11 169

▶ Now you will learn to talk about what others did last weekend. (First ask one pair what they did. Then ask the class to reaffirm.)

W et X, est-ce que vous avez étudié le week-end dernier?

Oui, nous avons étudié. (Turn to class:)
Est-ce que W et X ont étudié?
Oui, ils/elles ont étudié.

Y et Z, est-ce que vous avez étudié?
Non, nous n'avons pas étudié.

(Then ask the class:)
Est-ce que Y et Z ont étudié?
Non, ils/elles n'ont pas étudié.

(Use the questions on the facing page.)

---

8 COMMUNICATION expressing preferences

Answers will vary.
1. Je préfère avoir une copine (intelligente).
2. Je préfère avoir un professeur (amusant).
3. Je préfère avoir des voisins (sympathiques).
4. Je préfère avoir une voiture (confortable).
5. Je préfère avoir une calculatrice (américaine).
6. Je préfère avoir une montre (suisse).
7. Je préfère dîner dans un restaurant (italien).
8. Je préfère regarder un film (amusant).
9. Je préfère travailler avec des personnes (sérieuses).
10. Je préfère faire un voyage avec des gens (amusants).

---

9 PRACTICE pointing out similarities

1. Il a des cousines sympathiques.
2. Elle a des étudiants intelligents.
3. Elle a des voisines intéressantes.
4. Elle a des copines américaines.
5. Elle a un frère amusant.
6. Il a une soeur sportive.
7. Il a des camarades espagnol(e)s.
8. Il a une copine mexicaine.
9. Il a un voisin sportif.

---

10 COMPREHENSION expressing preferences

Answers will vary.
• Je préfère la musique (mexicaine).
• Je préfère la cuisine (française).
• Je préfère les voitures (italiennes).
• Je préfère les ordinateurs (américains).
• Je préfère les appareils-photo (japonais).
• Je préfère les CD (anglais).
• Je préfère les restaurants (chinois).

Language note Remind students that the plural of **l'appareil-photo** is **les appareils-photo.**

Expansion (dialogue format)

– **Je préfère les voitures anglaises. Et toi?**
– **Moi, je préfère les voitures américaines.**

Teaching strategy Be sure students end the masculine adjectives on a vowel sound. In contrast, have them exaggerate the final consonants on the feminine adjectives.

À votre tour!

❶ 🎧 Allô!

PARLER Valérie is phoning some friends. Match her questions on the left with her friends' answers on the right.

1. Ton frère aime jouer au foot?
2. Cécile et Sophie sont mignonnes, n'est-ce pas?
3. Pourquoi est-ce que tu invites Olivier?
4. Tu aimes la classe?
5. Tu as des cousins?

a. Oui, et intelligentes aussi!
b. Parce qu'il est amusant et sympathique.
c. Oui, j'ai un professeur très intéressant.
d. Oui, il est très sportif.
e. Oui, mais ils ne sont pas très sympathiques.

❷ 🎧 Créa-dialogue

PARLER With your classmates, talk about the people of different nationalities you may know or objects you may own.

des cousins / mignon?

▶ —J'ai des <u>cousins mexicains</u>.
—Ils sont mignons?
—Oui, ils sont très mignons.

1. une voisine	2. un prof	3. des copines	4. un livre	5. une voiture
blond?	sympathique?	sportif?	intéressant?	grand?

③ *Avis de recherche* (Missing person's bulletin)

ÉCRIRE The two people in the pictures to the right have been reported missing. Describe each one as well as you can, using your imagination. Mention:

- the (approximate) age of the person
- the way he/she looks
- personality traits
- other features or characteristics

④ **Descriptions**

PARLER Give an oral presentation describing your favorite actor **(un acteur)** and actress **(une actrice).** In your descriptions, include:

- the person's name
- approximate age
- nationality
- physical appearance
- personality traits
- a film he/she plays in (Il/elle joue dans ...)

You may wish to show photos of the two actors you have chosen to talk about.

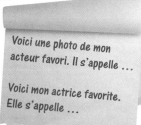

Voici une photo de mon acteur favori. Il s'appelle ...

Voici mon actrice favorite. Elle s'appelle ...

⑤ **Composition: Fête d'anniversaire**

ÉCRIRE You have invited Jean-Pierre, a French exchange student, to your upcoming birthday party. Write him an e-mail describing two of the guests that he will meet at the party: a boy and a girl. For each person (who may be real or imaginary), provide such information as name, age, nationality, physical appearance, and personality traits.

Il y a un garçon qui s'appelle ...

Il y a une fille qui s'appelle ...

LESSON REVIEW
CLASSZONE.COM

PORTFOLIO ASSESSMENT

You will probably select only one speaking activity and one writing activity to go into the students' portfolios for Unit 4.

In this lesson, Act. 2 and 4 are good oral portfolio topics.

Act. 3 and 5 lend themselves well to written portfolio compositions.

Leçon 12

Main Topic Describing objects by color and size

Teaching Resource Options

PRINT

Workbook PE, pp. 107–112
Activités pour tous PE, pp. 63–65
Block Scheduling Copymasters,
  pp. 89–96
Unit 4 Resource Book
  Activités pour tous TE, pp. 111–113
  Audioscript, pp. 132, 133–135
  Communipak, pp. 140–160
  Lesson Plans, pp. 114–115
  Block Scheduling Lesson Plans, pp. 116–118
  Absent Student Copymasters, pp. 119–123
  Video Activities, pp. 126–129
  Videoscript, pp. 130–131
  Workbook TE, pp. 105–110

AUDIO & VISUAL

Audio Program
CD 2 Tracks 39, 40
CD 8 Tracks 19–24

TECHNOLOGY

Online Workbook

VIDEO PROGRAM

VIDÉO   DVD

MODULE 12
La voiture de Roger

TOTAL TIME: 6:46 min.
  DVD Disk 1
  Videotape 2 (COUNTER: 46:26 min.)

12.1 Introduction: Listening
  – Les couleurs (46:39–48:35 min.)

12.2 Mini-scenes: Listening
  – De quelle couleur?
  (48:36–48:59 min.)

12.3 Mini-scenes: Speaking
  – Qu'est-ce que tu préfères?
  (49:00–50:23 min.)

12.4 Dialogue: La voiture de Roger
  (50:24–51:28 min.)

**12.5 Vignette culturelle: Les Français
  et l'auto** (51:29–53:12 min.)

Compréhension
Answers
1. Il y a une voiture dans la rue.
2. Non, elle n'est pas grande (elle est petite).
3. Il s'appelle Roger.
4. Il est dans le café.
5. Elle s'appelle Véronique.
6. La voiture est rouge.

172 · **Conversation et Culture**
Unité 4 LEÇON 12

LEÇON 12
La voiture de Roger

VIDÉO   DVD   AUDIO

Dans la <u>rue</u>, il y a une voiture <u>rouge</u>.   *street/red*
C'est une petite voiture. C'est une voiture de sport.
Dans la rue, il y a aussi un café. Au café, il y a un jeune homme.
Il s'appelle Roger.
C'est le <u>propriétaire</u> de la voiture rouge.   *owner*
Une jeune fille <u>entre dans</u> le café.   *enters*
Elle s'appelle Véronique.
C'est <u>l'amie de Roger</u>.   *Roger's friend*
Véronique parle à Roger.

Véronique: Tu as une <u>nouvelle</u> voiture, n'est-ce pas?   *new*
Roger: Oui, j'ai une nouvelle voiture.
Véronique: Est-ce qu'elle est grande ou petite?
Roger: C'est une petite voiture.
Véronique: De quelle couleur est-elle?
Roger: C'est une voiture rouge.
Véronique: Est-ce que c'est une voiture italienne?
Roger: Oui, c'est une voiture italienne. Mais <u>dis donc</u>,   *hey there*
  Véronique, tu es <u>vraiment</u> très curieuse!   *really*
Véronique: Et toi, tu n'es pas <u>assez curieux</u>!   *curious enough*
Roger: Ah bon? Pourquoi?
Véronique: Pourquoi?! … Regarde la <u>contractuelle</u> là-bas!   *meter maid*
Roger: Ah, zut alors!

Compréhension

1. Qu'est-ce qu'il y a dans la rue?
2. Est-ce que la voiture est grande?
3. Comment s'appelle le jeune homme?
4. Où est-il?
5. Comment s'appelle la jeune fille?
6. De quelle couleur est la voiture?

 cent soixante-douze
Unité 4

SETTING THE SCENE

Video Module 12 prepares students for the introductory dialogue by first teaching the colors.

  The scene with Roger and his car constitutes Segment 4 of the video.

  The *Vignette culturelle* develops the *Note culturelle* on the facing page about the French and their cars.

NOTE *culturelle*

Les Français et la voiture

France is one of the leading producers of automobiles in the world. The two automakers, **Renault** and **Peugeot-Citroën**, manufacture a variety of models ranging from sports cars to mini-vans and buses.

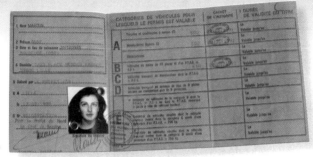

To obtain a driver's license (**un permis de conduire**) in France, you must be eighteen years old and pass a very difficult driving test. French teenagers can, however, begin to drive at the age of sixteen, as long as they take lessons at an accredited driving school (**auto-école**) and are accompanied by an adult. Lessons in these schools are expensive and it may cost you 300 euros before you pass the exam and get your official license.

The French driver's license is a **permis à points** (license with points). A new license carries with it 12 points. When a driver commits a traffic violation, such as speeding or not wearing a seat belt, a corresponding number of points is subtracted from the license. If a driver loses all 12 points, the license is revoked and that person can no longer drive.

OPINION PERSONNELLE

Do you think that the **permis à points** is a good idea? Explain your position.

Photo cultural note
Saint-Germain-des-Prés

The neighborhood around Saint-Germain-des-Prés (**le quartier Saint-Germain**) is one of the oldest areas of Paris. Because of its numerous shops and movie theaters, **le boulevard Saint-Germain** is a favorite strolling place for Parisians. There are also many cafés, including the famous **Café des Deux Magots.**

Cultural background

- Gasoline costs about 1 euro a liter, which comes to about 4 dollars a gallon.

- With a production of nearly 2 million vehicles per year, Renault is one of the leading European automobile manufacturers. It is owned by the French government (**régie nationale** = government enterprise).

Language note In Quebec, a driving school is **une école de conduite**.

Note culturelle

Cultural note Once a driver has reached 12 points, his or her license is revoked and he or she cannot drive for at least six months. In order to get his or her license back, the driver has to take a written test. If the driver has had his or her license for less than three years, he or she must also take a road test.

TALKING ABOUT PAST EVENTS

Let's talk about what you did last weekend.

Note that the past participle of **faire** is **fait.**

  Est-ce que tu as fait une promenade le week-end dernier?
  Oui, j'ai fait une promenade.
  (Non, je n'ai pas fait de promenade.)

- **Est-ce que tu as fait un match de tennis?**
- **Est-ce que tu as fait un match de basket?**
- **Est-ce que tu as fait un match de foot?**
- **Est-ce que tu as fait un pique-nique?**

(Remember to use **pas de** in the negative.)

Teaching Resource Options

PRINT

Workbook PE, pp. 107–112
Unit 4 Resource Book
  Audioscript, p. 132
  Communipak, pp. 140–160
  Video Activities, pp. 126–127
  Videoscript, p. 130
  Workbook TE, pp. 105–110

AUDIO & VISUAL

Audio Program
CD 2 Tracks 41, 42

Overhead Transparencies
28 *Les couleurs*
21 Objects (b) *Quelques objets*

TECHNOLOGY
Power Presentations

VIDEO PROGRAM

VIDÉO   DVD

MODULE 12

12.1 Introduction: Les couleurs
(46:39–48:35 min.)

12.2 Mini-scenes: De quelle couleur? (48:36–48:59 min.)

12.3 Mini-scenes: Qu'est-ce que tu préfères? (48:60–50:23 min.)

Language notes

• When colors are used as nouns they are always masculine. J'aime **le noir.** Je déteste **le rose.**
• Another word for *brown* is **brun(e),** which is used to describe hair and eyes.

Teaching strategy To activate colors, use names of articles of clothing, especially **tee-shirt** which is a cognate. **De quelle couleur est le tee-shirt de Jim? Il est bleu et jaune.**

Looking ahead In conjunction with colors, you may want to pre-teach selected items of clothing:

un pantalon	**une chemise**
un tee-shirt	**une robe**
un sweater	**une jupe**
un polo	**des chaussures**

(Clothes are taught in Lesson 17.)

A Les couleurs

Note the form and position of the color words in the following sentences:

Alice a un vélo **bleu.**	*Alice has a **blue** bicycle.*
Nous avons des chemises **bleues.**	*We have **blue** shirts.*

Names of colors are ADJECTIVES and take adjective ENDINGS. They come *after* the noun.

VOCABULAIRE Les couleurs

De quelle couleur … ?   *What color … ?*   —**De quelle couleur** est la moto?
—Elle est rouge.

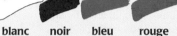

blanc	noir	bleu	rouge	jaune	vert	gris	marron	orange	rose
(blanche)	(noire)	(bleue)	(rouge)	(jaune)	(verte)	(grise)	(marron)	(orange)	(rose)

→ The colors **orange** and **marron** are INVARIABLE. They do not take any endings.
  un sac **orange**   des sacs **orange**
  un tee-shirt **marron**   une chemise **marron**

1 *De quelle couleur?*

PARLER Ask your classmates to name the colors of things they own. (They may invent answers.)

▶ ta chambre?

De quelle couleur est ta chambre?

Elle est blanche et bleue.

1. ta bicyclette?
2. ton tee-shirt?
3. ton appareil-photo?
4. ta montre?
5. ta raquette de tennis?
6. ton livre de français?
7. ton chien (chat)?

2 *Possessions*

PARLER Ask what objects or pets the following people own. A classmate will answer, giving the color.

▶ —Est-ce que Léa a un chat?
—Oui, elle a un chat jaune.

Léa

1. Mme Mercier

2. Marc

3. Delphine

4. Sophie

5. Éric

COMPREHENSION Colors

PROPS: For each student: scissors and colored paper (red, yellow, blue, green, orange, pink, brown, white, black, gray)

Have students cut out shapes.
  Découpez un cercle, un carré (square), **un triangle.**

(Or distribute precut colored paper shapes.)

Have students hold up a shape.
  Montrez-moi un cercle.

Take one student's circle and name its color.
  Voici un cercle vert.
  Si vous avez un cercle vert, levez la main.

Continue, teaching other colors and shapes.
  X a un carré noir. Qui a un carré blanc?
  Y a un triangle gris. Qui a un cercle gris?

③ L'arche de Noé

PARLER/ÉCRIRE Noah's ark has just landed.
Give the colors of the animals as they get off the ship.

▶ le chien   **Le chien est blanc.**

1. le chat
2. l'éléphant *(m.)*
3. la panthère
4. le zèbre
5. le flamant
6. le cardinal
7. le lion
8. le perroquet

B La place des adjectifs avant le nom

Compare the position of the adjectives in the following sentences.

Voici une voiture **française.**   Voici une **petite** voiture.
Paul est un garçon **intelligent.**   Pierre est un **beau** garçon.

A few adjectives like **petit** and **beau** come BEFORE the noun they modify.

→ The article **des** often becomes **de** before an adjective. Compare:

     des voitures → **de** petites voitures

VOCABULAIRE Les adjectifs qui précèdent le nom

beau (belle)	*beautiful, handsome*	Regarde la **belle** voiture!
joli	*pretty*	Qui est la **jolie** fille avec André?
grand	*big, large, tall*	Nous habitons dans un **grand** appartement.
petit	*little, small, short*	Ma soeur a un **petit** ordinateur.
bon (bonne)	*good*	Tu es un **bon** copain.
mauvais	*bad*	Patrick est un **mauvais** élève.

→ There is a LIAISON after the above adjectives when the noun which follows
begins with a vowel sound. Note that in liaison:
 • the "**d**" of **grand** is pronounced /t/: **un grand appartement**
 • **bon** is pronounced like **bonne: un bon élève**

---

① COMMUNICATION asking about colors

Answers will vary.
– De quelle couleur est ... ?
– (Il/Elle) est ...

1. (ta bicyclette) Elle est (noire).
2. (ton tee-shirt) Il est (vert).
3. (ton appareil-photo) Il est (noir).
4. (ta montre) Elle est (marron).
5. (ta raquette de tennis) Elle est (grise).
6. (ton livre de français) Il est (bleu).
7. (ton chien) Il est (blanc).

② EXCHANGES describing colors

1. – Est-ce que Mme Mercier a une voiture?
   – Oui, elle a une voiture rouge.
2. – Est-ce que Marc a un scooter?
   – Oui, il a un scooter jaune.
3. – Est-ce que Delphine a un vélo?
   – Oui, elle a un vélo noir (gris).
4. – Est-ce que Sophie a une guitare?
   – Oui, elle a une guitare orange.
5. – Est-ce qu'Éric a un chien?
   – Oui, il a un chien blanc.

Game One person describes what
one of the people in the picture has,
mentioning its color. The other
students identify the person.

③ DESCRIPTION describing colors of animals

1. Le chat est orange.
2. L'éléphant est gris.
3. La panthère est noire.
4. Le zèbre est noir et blanc.
5. Le flammant est rose.
6. Le cardinal est rouge.
7. Le lion est jaune.
8. Le perroquet est vert.

Teaching strategy Model the
pronunciation of the animal names
for students.

SECTION B

Communicative function
Describing objects

Language notes
• In current French, it is becoming
 more and more common to use **des**
 before the adjective. Therefore,
 students should be able to recognize
 the **de** construction when they
 encounter it, but should not be
 penalized for failing to produce it.
• **Jeune** comes before the noun in
 expressions like **un jeune homme**
 and **une jeune fille.**

Teaching Resource Options

PRINT

Workbook PE, pp. 107–112
Unit 4 Resource Book
    Communipak, pp. 140–160
    Workbook TE, pp. 105–110

TECHNOLOGY
Power Presentations

4 **COMMUNICATION** expressing opinions

1. *Titanic* est un bon (mauvais) film.
2. «60 Minutes» est un bon (mauvais) programme de télé.
3. Britney Spears est une bonne (mauvaise) chanteuse.
4. Matt Damon est un bon (mauvais) acteur.
5. Dracula est une bonne (mauvaise) personne.
6. Les Yankees sont une bonne (mauvaise) équipe de baseball.
7. Les Lakers sont une bonne (mauvaise) équipe de basket.
8. Je suis un bon (mauvais) élève/Je suis une bonne (mauvaise) élève.
9. *Discovering French* est un bon (mauvais) livre.

Language note If students ask, the **plural** forms are **Dites!** and **Dites donc!**

5 **ROLE PLAY** discussing and describing possessions

– Dis, Thomas, tu as ... ?
– Oui, j'ai ...

1. une télé/une petite télé.
2. une guitare/une guitare espagnole.
3. un vélo/un vélo rouge.
4. une calculatrice/une petite calculatrice.
5. un sac/ un grand sac.
6. des livres/des livres intéressants.
7. une copine/une copine amusante.
8. une mobylette/une mobylette bleue.
9. une montre/une belle montre.
10. un copain/un bon copain.
11. une cousine/une jolie cousine.
12. une radio/une radio japonaise.

Expansion Have students use adjectives and write three original sentences about their possessions and friends.

J'ai une bicyclette rouge.
J'ai un bon copain.
J'ai une montre suisse.

---

4 *Opinions personnelles*

PARLER/ÉCRIRE Give your opinion about the following people and things, using the adjectives **bon** or **mauvais.**

▶ Julia Roberts est (une) actrice *(actress)*.
   Julia Roberts est une bonne actrice (une mauvaise actrice).

1. *Titanic* est un film.
2. «60 Minutes» est un programme de télé.
3. Britney Spears est (une) chanteuse.
4. Matt Damon est (un) acteur.
5. Dracula est une personne.
6. Les Yankees sont une équipe *(team)* de baseball.
7. Les Lakers sont une équipe de basket.
8. Je suis un(e) élève.
9. *Discovering French* est un livre.

VOCABULAIRE Expressions pour la conversation

▶ *How to get someone's attention:*

Dis!	*Say! Hey!*	**Dis,** Éric, est-ce que tu as une voiture?
Dis donc!	*Hey there!*	**Dis donc,** est-ce que tu veux faire une promenade avec moi?

---

5 *Dialogue*

PARLER Christine asks her cousin Thomas if he has certain things. He responds affirmatively, describing each one. Play both roles.

▶ une chaîne hi-fi (petite)   ▶ un scooter (italien)

1. une télé (petite)
2. une guitare (espagnole)
3. un vélo (rouge)
4. une calculatrice (petite)
5. un sac (grand)
6. des livres (intéressants)
7. une copine (amusante)
8. une mobylette (bleue)
9. une montre (belle)
10. un copain (bon)
11. une cousine (jolie)
12. une radio (japonaise)

TEACHING STRATEGY Using chants

Certain grammatical constructions, such as the use of **c'est** vs. **il est,** can be internalized through the use of chants.

For example, the phrase **c'est un** can be chanted to the "Mexican Hat Dance" tune.

    C'est un, c'est un, c'est un...
    C'est un ami mexicain.

C'est une, c'est une, c'est une...
C'est une amie mexicaine.
C'est un, c'est un, c'est un...
C'est un vélo italien.
C'est une, c'est une, c'est une...
C'est une voiture italienne.

C Il est ou c'est?

When describing a person or thing, French speakers use two different constructions,
il est (elle est) and **c'est.**

		Il est + ADJECTIVE Elle est + ADJECTIVE	C'est + ARTICLE + NOUN (+ ADJECTIVE)
Roger	He is …	**Il est** amusant.	**C'est** un copain. **C'est** un copain amusant.
Véronique	She is …	**Elle est** sportive.	**C'est** une amie. **C'est** une bonne amie.
un scooter	It is …	**Il est** joli.	**C'est** un scooter français. **C'est** un bon scooter.
une voiture	It is …	**Elle est** petite.	**C'est** une voiture anglaise. **C'est** une petite voiture.

→ Note the corresponding plural forms:

(Pierre et Marc) *They are …* **Ils sont** amusants. **Ce sont** des copains.
(Claire et Anne) *They are …* **Elles sont** timides. **Ce sont** des copines.

→ In negative sentences, **c'est** becomes **ce n'est pas.**

Ce **n'est pas** un mauvais élève. *He's not a bad student.*
Ce **n'est pas** une Peugeot. *It's not a Peugeot.*

→ **C'est** is also used with names of people

C'est Véronique. C'est Madame Lamblet.

SCOOTERS PEUGEOT

6 Descriptions

PARLER/ÉCRIRE Complete the following descriptions with **Il est, Elle est,**
or **C'est,** as appropriate.

A. Roger
1. _____ grand.
2. _____ brun.
3. _____ un garçon sympathique.
4. _____ un mauvais élève.

B. Véronique
5. _____ une fille brune.
6. _____ une amie sympathique.
7. _____ très amusante.
8. _____ assez grande.

C. La voiture de Roger
9. _____ une voiture moderne.
10. _____ une petite voiture.
11. _____ rouge.
12. _____ très rapide.

D. Le scooter de Véronique
13. _____ bleu et blanc.
14. _____ très économique.
15. _____ un joli scooter.
16. _____ assez confortable.

Communicative function
Describing people and things

Language notes

- The adjective may either follow or precede the noun.
- **C'est** is also used when a possessive adjective introduces the noun:
C'est mon frère. *He's my brother.*
- In negative sentences with **être,** the articles **un, une,** and **des** remain unchanged. Compare:
Ce **n'est pas un** copain.
Je **n'ai pas de** copain.
Ce **ne sont pas des** motos japonaises.
Nous **n'avons pas de** motos japonaises.

6 DESCRIPTION pointing out people and things

A. Roger	C. La voiture de Roger
1. Il est	9. C'est
2. Il est	10. C'est
3. C'est	11. Elle est
4. C'est	12. Elle est

B. Véronique	D. Le scooter de Véronique
5. C'est	13. Il est
6. C'est	14. Il est
7. Elle est	15. C'est
8. Elle est	16. Il est

SPEAKING ACTIVITY Show and tell

Have students bring an object to class and describe it
using **il/elle est…, c'est…** and appropriate adjectives.

J'ai une montre.
C'est une montre suisse.
Elle est rouge et noire.
C'est une jolie montre; elle marche très bien.
J'aime beaucoup ma montre!

Variation This can also be done as a written activity
with students illustrating their objects.

Note This works particularly well after the holiday
season when students have gifts to talk about.

SECTION D

Communicative function
Expressing opinions

Teaching Resource Options

PRINT
Workbook PE, pp. 107–112
Unit 4 Resource Book
Audioscript, p. 132
Communipak, pp. 140–160
Workbook TE, pp. 105–110

AUDIO & VISUAL
Audio Program
CD 2 Track 43

TECHNOLOGY
Power Presentations

Language note This construction is not used to describe specific people and things.
Paul? Il est amusant.
Les livres? Ils sont intéressants.

Casual speech It is very common to drop the **ne** in negative expressions:
C'est pas amusant.
C'est pas vrai.

Language notes
- The French often tend to use negative constructions in a positive sense:
  Ce (n')est pas mal.
  That's not bad. = That's very good.
  Ce (n')est pas bête. *That's not stupid = That's a smart idea.*
- A current popular anglicism is:
  C'est cool.
- **Super** may be used in combination with other expressions:
  C'est super-chouette.
  C'est super-difficile.
- **Extra** is the short form of **extraordinaire.**

7 COMPREHENSION geographic locations

1. C'est faux! (Paris est en France.)
2. C'est vrai!
3. C'est faux! (Genève est en Suisse.)
4. C'est vrai!
5. C'est faux! (Fort-de-France est à la Martinique.)
6. C'est faux! (Québec est au Canada.)
7. C'est vrai!
8. C'est vrai!

Additional cues
Casablanca est en Afrique. (vrai)
Rome est en France. (faux: en Italie)
Vancouver est en France. (faux: au Canada)
Strasbourg est en France. (vrai)
Bordeaux est en Italie. (faux: en France)

D Les expressions impersonnelles avec *c'est*

Note the use of **c'est** in the following sentences.

J'aime parler français.	**C'est** intéressant.	*It's interesting.*
Je n'aime pas travailler le week-end.	**Ce n'est pas** amusant.	*It's no(t) fun.*

To express an opinion on a general topic, French speakers use the construction:

C'est / **Ce n'est pas** } + MASCULINE ADJECTIVE

VOCABULAIRE Opinions

C'est ... *It's ..., That's ...*
Ce n'est pas ... *It's not ..., That's not ...*

vrai	*true*	**chouette**	*neat*
faux	*false*	**super**	*great*
		génial	*terrific*
facile	*easy*	**pénible**	*a pain, annoying*
difficile	*hard, difficult*	**drôle**	*funny*

→ To express an opinion, French speakers also use adverbs like **bien** and **mal.**

C'est bien.	*That's good.*	Tu étudies? **C'est bien.**
C'est mal.	*That's bad.*	Alain n'étudie pas. **C'est mal.**

7 Vrai ou faux?

PARLER Imagine that your little sister is talking about where certain cities are located. Tell her whether her statements are right or wrong.

1. Paris est en Italie.
2. Los Angeles est en Californie.
3. Genève est en Italie.
4. Dakar est en Afrique.
5. Fort-de-France est au Canada.
6. Québec est en France.
7. Port-au-Prince est en Haïti.
8. Montréal est au Canada.

TALKING ABOUT PAST EVENTS

- **V, qu'est-ce que tu as fait hier soir?**
  J'ai étudié (regardé la télé, travaillé...).
- **W et X, qu'est-ce que vous avez fait?**
  Nous avons joué aux jeux vidéo (...).

Ask individuals what they did. Have others report back. Ask if they did the same thing.

- **V, qu'est-ce que tu as fait hier soir?**
- **Y, qu'est-ce que V a fait hier soir? Est-ce que tu as fait la même chose?**
- **W et X, qu'est-ce que vous avez fait?**
- **Z, qu'est-ce que W et X ont fait hier soir? Est-ce que tu as fait la même chose?**

8 🧑🧑🧑 *Opinion personnelle*

PARLER Ask your classmates if they like to do the following things.
They will answer, using an expression from the **Vocabulaire.**

▶ nager

1. téléphoner
2. parler en public
3. parler français
4. danser
5. voyager
6. dîner en ville
7. jouer aux jeux vidéo
8. étudier le week-end
9. écouter la musique classique
10. surfer sur l'Internet
11. télécharger de la musique

PRONONCIATION 🎧 ch /ʃ/

Les lettres «ch»

The letters "**ch**" are usually pronounced like the English "*sh.*"

Répétez: **chien   chat   chose   marche**
chouette   chocolat   affiche
Michèle a un chat et deux chiens.

chien

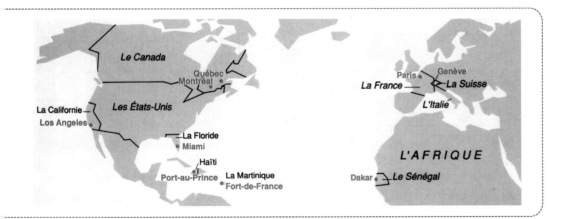

---

8 **COMMUNICATION** talking about what one likes to do

Answers will vary.
1. – Tu aimes téléphoner?
   – Oui, c'est (chouette)!
     (Non, c'est [pénible]!)
2. – Tu aimes parler en public?
   – Oui, c'est (facile)!
     (Non, c'est [difficile]!)
3. – Tu aimes parler français?
   – Oui, c'est (génial)!
     (Non, c'est [difficile]!)
4. – Tu aimes danser?
   – Oui, c'est (facile)!
     (Non, c'est [difficile]!)
5. – Tu aimes voyager?
   – Oui, c'est (super)!
     (Non, c'est [pénible]!)
6. – Tu aimes dîner en ville?
   – Oui, c'est (génial)!
     (Non, c'est [pénible]!)
7. – Tu aimes jouer aux jeux vidéo?
   – Oui, c'est (drôle)!
     (Non, c'est [pénible]!)
8. – Tu aimes étudier le week-end?
   – Oui, c'est (génial)!
     (Non, c'est [pénible]!)
9. – Tu aimes écouter la musique classique?
   – Oui, c'est (super)!
     (Non, c'est [pénible]!)
10. – Tu aimes surfer sur l'Internet?
    – Oui, c'est (génial)!
      (Non, c'est [pénible]!)

♻ **Re-entry and review**

Verbs from Unit 3.

Challenge The second student asks the same question of the first student, who must respond using another adjective.
– **Tu aimes nager?**
– **Oui, c'est génial! Et toi, tu aimes nager?**
– **Non, c'est difficile.**

PRONUNCIATION 🎧

- Although "ch" is usually pronounced /tʃ/ in English, as in *march* and *chocolate,* the letters do represent the sound /ʃ/ in words and names that came directly from French: **Chef, chauffeur, chic, touché,** etc.

- Sometimes the letters "ch" are pronounced /k/ in French, just as they are in the corresponding English cognates: **orchestre, Christine, écho.** Exception: **architecte,** which has the sound /ʃ/.

À votre tour!

1 🎧 👥 *Allô!*

PARLER Christophe is phoning some friends. Match his questions on the left with his friends' answers on the right.

2 🎧 👥 *Créa-dialogue*

PARLER There has been a burglary in the rue Saint-Pierre. By walkie-talkie, two detectives are describing what they see. Play both roles.

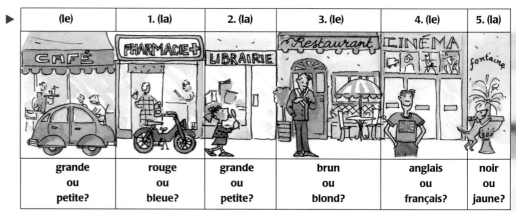

	(le)	1. (la)	2. (la)	3. (le)	4. (le)	5. (la)
	grande ou petite?	rouge ou bleue?	grande ou petite?	brun ou blond?	anglais ou français?	noir ou jaune?

▶ DÉTECTIVE 1: **Qu'est-ce qu'il y a devant** le café?   DÉTECTIVE 1: **Elle** est **grande** ou **petite**?
  DÉTECTIVE 2: **Il y a** une voiture.   DÉTECTIVE 2: **C'est** une petite voiture.

 cent quatre-vingts
Unité 4

À VOTRE TOUR

Depending on your goals and objectives, you may or may not wish to assign all of the activities in the **À votre tour** section.

PAIR PRACTICE

Act. 1, 2, 3, and 4 lend themselves to pair practice.

3 Faisons connaissance!

PARLER Try to find out which students have the same interests you do. Select two activities you enjoy from Column A and ask a classmate if he/she likes to do them. Your classmate will answer yes or no, using an appropriate expression from Column B.

A	B
téléphoner	chouette
envoyer des mails	super
surfer sur l'Internet	génial
jouer aux jeux vidéo	amusant
jouer au foot	intéressant
voyager	pénible
organiser des boums	drôle
parler avec les voisins	difficile
parler français en classe	facile
étudier pour l'examen	
travailler dans le jardin	

Tu aimes voyager?

Oui, c'est amusant.

Tu aimes étudier pour l'examen?

Non, c'est difficile.

4 Dialogue: Un chien!

PARLER Imagine that your classmate has just received a dog for his/her birthday. You want to know more about this new pet. Ask your classmate ...

- what the dog's name is
- how old he is
- what color he is
- if he is a small dog or a big dog
- if he is cute
- if he is a mean dog (un chien méchant)

5 Composition: Une voiture

ÉCRIRE Describe your parents' car or any other car you have seen recently. Provide the following information, writing a sentence for each of these points.

- make/model
- color
- age
- country of origin
- size (petit? grand?)
- other characteristics (confortable? rapide? économique?)

LESSON REVIEW
CLASSZONE.COM

cent quatre-vingt-un
Leçon 12 181

PORTFOLIO ASSESSMENT

You will probably select only one speaking activity and one writing activity to go into the students' portfolios for Unit 4.

In this lesson, Act. 5 is a good written portfolio topic.

---

2 GUIDED ORAL EXPRESSION
CONTINUED

4. **D1:** Qu'est-ce qu'il y a devant le cinéma?
   D2: Il y a un garçon.
   D1: Il est anglais ou français?
   D2: C'est un garçon anglais.
5. **D1:** Qu'est-ce qu'il y a devant la fontaine?
   D2: Il y a un chien.
   D1: Il est noir ou jaune?
   D2: C'est un chien jaune.

3 CONVERSATION

Answers will vary.
- – Tu aimes téléphoner?
  – Oui, c'est (amusant).
  (Non, c'est [pénible].)
- – Tu aimes envoyer des mails?
  – Oui, c'est (chouette).
  (Non, c'est [difficile].)
- – Tu aimes surfer sur l'Internet?
  – Oui, c'est (facile).
  (Non, c'est [difficile].)
- – Tu aimes jouer aux jeux vidéo?
  – Oui, c'est (amusant).
  (Non, c'est [pénible].)
- – Tu aimes jouer au foot?
  – Oui, c'est (super).
  (Non, c'est [difficile].)
- – Tu aimes voyager?
  – Oui, c'est (amusant).
  (Non, c'est [pénible].)
- – Tu aimes organiser des boums?
  – Oui, c'est (génial).
  (Non, c'est [difficile].)
- – Tu aimes parler avec les voisins?
  – Oui, c'est (intéressant).
  (Non, c'est [pénible].)
- – Tu aimes parler français en classe?
  – Oui, c'est (facile).
  (Non, c'est [difficile].)
- – Tu aimes étudier pour l'examen?
  – Oui, c'est (chouette).
  (Non, c'est [pénible].)
- – Tu aimes travailler dans le jardin?
  – Oui, c'est (chouette).
  (Non, c'est [pénible].)

4 ORAL SELF-EXPRESSION

Answers will vary.
– Comment s'appelle-t-il, ton chien?
– Il s'appelle Ernie.
– Est-ce que c'est un chien grand ou petit?
– Il est petit.
– Quel âge a ton chien?
– Il a trois ans.
– Est-ce qu'il est mignon?
– Oui, il est très mignon.
– De quelle couleur est-il?
– Il est noir.
– Est-ce que c'est un chien méchant?
– Non, il est très gentil.

5 WRITTEN SELF-EXPRESSION

Answers will vary.
Mes parents ont une Renault. Elle est verte. Elle a deux ans. Elle est française. Elle est assez grande. Elle est très confortable et assez rapide.

TESTS DE CONTRÔLE

Teaching Resource Options

PRINT

Unit 4 Resource Book
  Communipak, pp. 140–160
  Assessment
  Unit 4 Test, pp. 169–177
  Portfolio Assessment, Unit 1 URB,
    pp. 155–164
  Multiple Choice Test Items, pp. 190–197
  Listening Comprehension
    Performance Test, pp. 178–179
  Reading Performance Test, pp. 184–186
  Speaking Performance Test, pp. 180–183
  Writing Performance Test, pp. 187–189
  Test Scoring Tools, p. 198
  Audioscript for Tests, pp. 199–200
  Answer Keys, pp. 201–205

AUDIO & VISUAL
Audio Program
CD 14 Tracks 21–24

TECHNOLOGY
Test Generator CD-ROM/eTest Plus
  Online

1 COMPREHENSION

1. un stylo
2. une montre
3. un cahier
4. un ordinateur
5. un baladeur
6. une bicyclette
   (un vélo)
7. une voiture
   (une auto)
8. un appareil-photo
9. un lit
10. une fenêtre

2 COMPREHENSION

1. Tu <u>as</u> une chaîne hi-fi.
2. Tu <u>es</u> français.
3. Céline <u>a</u> quinze ans.
4. Nous <u>avons</u> soif.
5. Thomas <u>est</u> sympathique.
6. Mes copains <u>sont</u> amusants.
7. Vous <u>avez</u> un portable.
8. Est-ce que vous <u>avez</u> faim?

Tests de contrôle

By taking the following tests, you can check your progress in French and also prepare for the unit test. Write your answers on a separate sheet of paper.

1 The right object

Review...
• names of objects:
  pp. 140, 142, and 144

Name the following objects. Make sure to use the appropriate article: **un** or **une.**

1.　2.　3.　4.　5.

6.　7.　8.　9.　10.

2 Être and avoir

Review ...
• être and avoir:
  pp. 84 and 152

Complete the following sentences with the appropriate forms of **être** or **avoir.**

1. Tu — une chaîne hi-fi.
2. Tu — français.
3. Céline — quinze ans.
4. Nous — soif.
5. Thomas — sympathique.
6. Mes copains — amusants.
7. Vous — un portable.
8. Est-ce que vous — faim?

3 The right adjectives

Review ...
• adjectives:
  pp. 164-165,
  166-167

Complete the following descriptions with the appropriate forms of the adjectives in parentheses.

1. **(français)**   une amie …   des copains …
2. **(américain)**   des filles …   des garçons …
3. **(sympathique)**   une copine …   des personnes …
4. **(intelligent)**   une personne …   des amies …
5. **(sportif)**   une fille …   des copines …
6. **(gentil)**   des amies …   des copains …
7. **(rouge)**   une voiture …   un vélo …
8. **(blanc)**   une moto …   des bicyclettes …
9. **(japonais)**   une mini-chaîne … des ordinateurs …

④ The right choice

Complete the following sentences with the appropriate option suggested in parentheses.

(Note: ⁄ means that no word is needed.)

1. Qui est — fille là-bas? **(le, la, l')**
2. — ordinateur est sur la table. **(L', Le, La)**
3. Jean-Paul aime — musique classique. **(⁄, la, une)**
4. Léa a — copines canadiennes. **(⁄, une, des)**
5. Philippe n'a pas — portable. **(⁄, un, de)**

6. Ma mère a une voiture — . **(jaune, jolie, grande)**
7. Nous avons un — professeur. **(bon, sympathique, intéressant)**

8. Voici Catherine. — une amie sympathique. **(Il est, Elle est, C'est)**
9. Voici Marc. — canadien. **(Il est, Elle est, C'est)**

Review...
• definite and indefinite articles: pp. 153-156, 158

Review ...
• position of adjectives: pp. 168, 175

Review ...
• il est or c'est: p. 177

⑤ Composition: Mon cousin / Ma cousine

Write a paragraph of five or six sentences describing one of your cousins, real or imaginary. Give your cousin's name, nationality and age, plus a brief description. Say why your cousin is interesting (or not interesting). Use only vocabulary and expressions that you know in French.

STRATEGY Writing	
a) Make a list of the things you want to say about your cousin.	nom: _____
b) Organize your ideas and write your description.	nationalité: _____ âge: _____
c) Check that all the adjectives have the right endings.	description physique: _____ personnalité:_____ intéressant(e)? (pourquoi) _____

③ COMPREHENSION

1. une amie française
   des copains français
2. des filles américaines
   des garçons américains
3. une copine sympathique
   des personnes sympathiques
4. une personne intelligentes
   des amies intelligente
5. une fille sportive
   des copines sportives
6. des amies gentilles
   des copains gentils
7. une voiture rouge
   un vélo rouge
8. une moto blanche
   des bicyclettes blanches
9. une mini-chaîne japonaise
   des ordinateurs japonais

④ COMPREHENSION

1. Qui est <u>la</u> fille là-bas?
2. <u>L'</u>ordinateur est sur la table.
3. Jean-Paul aime <u>la</u> musique classique.
4. Léa a <u>des</u> copines canadiennes.
5. Philippe n'a pas <u>de</u> portable.
6. Ma mère a une voiture <u>jaune.</u>
7. Nous avons un <u>bon</u> professeur.
8. Voici Catherine. <u>C'est</u> une amie sympathique.
9. Voici Marc. <u>Il est</u> canadien.

⑤ WRITTEN SELF-EXPRESSION

Answers will vary.
nom: Christine
nationalité: américaine
âge: 12 ans
description physique: brune, petite
personnalité: amusante, gentille, intelligente
intéressante parce qu'elle voyage beaucoup et
parle français & espagnol

Ma cousine s'appelle Christine.
Elle est américaine. Elle a douze ans. Elle est
brune et petite. Elle est amusante, gentille, et
intelligente. C'est une personne intéressante.
Elle voyage beaucoup et elle parle français et
espagnol.

Vocabulaire

VOCABULAIRE

Language Learning Benchmarks

FUNCTION
- Engage in conversations pp. 157, 167
- Express likes and dislikes p. 158
- Make requests p. 141
- Obtain information p. 143
- Understand some ideas and familiar details p. 150

CONTEXT
- Converse in face-to-face social interactions pp. 143, 146, 157, 175, 176
- Listen during social interactions p. 156
- Listen to audio and video texts pp. 136-137, 150, 159, 162, 165, 169, 172, 174, 175, 179
- Use authentic materials when reading: schedules p. 159
- Use authentic materials when reading: short narratives p. 190
- Write lists p .149
- Write short letters pp. 149, 191

TEXT TYPE
- Use short sentences when speaking pp. 154, 168, 179
- Use short sentences when writing pp. 145, 155, 167, 175
- Use learned words and phrases when speaking pp. 145, 165
- Use learned words and phrases when writing pp. 139, 165
- Use simple questions when speaking pp. 152, 154, 167, 174
- Understand some ideas and familiar details presented in clear, uncomplicated speech when listening pp. 150, 162, 172

POUR COMMUNIQUER

Talking about people

Qui est-ce?	*Who is it?*
Comment est il/elle?	*What is he/she like?*
Quel âge a-t-il/elle?	*How old is he/she?*

Talking about things

Qu'est-ce que c'est?	*What is it? What's that?*	Il y a ...	*There is ..., There are ...*
C'est ...	*It's ...*	Est-ce qu'il y a ...?	*Is there ...? Are there ...?*
		Qu'est-ce qu'il y a ...?	*What is there ...?*
Est-ce que tu as ...?	*Do you have ...?*		
Oui, j'ai ...	*Yes, I have ...*	De quelle couleur ...?	*What color ...?*
Regarde ça.	*Look at that.*		
Quoi?	*What?*		
Ça, là-bas.	*That, over there.*		

Expressing opinions

C'est ...	*It's ...*						
bien	*good*	drôle	*funny*	génial	*terrific*	super	*great*
chouette	*neat*	facile	*easy*	mal	*bad*	vrai	*true*
difficile	*hard, difficult*	faux	*false*	pénible	*a pain, annoying*		

MOTS ET EXPRESSIONS

Les personnes

un camarade	*classmate*	une camarade	*classmate*	un prof	*teacher*	une prof	*teacher*
un élève	*pupil, student*	une élève	*pupil, student*	un professeur	*teacher*	une personne	*person*
un étudiant	*student*	une étudiante	*student*	un voisin	*neighbor*	une voisine	*neighbor*

Quelques possessions

un appareil-photo	*camera*	une affiche	*poster*
un baladeur	*portable CD player*	une auto	*car*
un cahier	*notebook*	une bicyclette	*bicycle*
un CD	*CD*	une calculatrice	*calculator*
un crayon	*pencil*	une cassette vidéo	*videotape*
un DVD	*DVD*	une chaîne hi-fi	*stereo set*
un livre	*book*	une chose	*thing*
un objet	*object*	une guitare	*guitar*
un ordinateur	*computer*	une mini-chaîne	*compact stereo*
un portable	*cell phone*	une mobylette	*motorbike, moped*
un sac	*bag*	une montre	*watch*
un scooter	*motor scooter*	une moto	*motorcycle*
un stylo	*pen*	une radio	*radio*
un téléphone	*phone*	une radiocassette	*boom box*
un vélo	*bicycle, bike*	une raquette	*tennis racket*
		une télé	*TV set*
		une voiture	*car*

La chambre

un bureau	desk	une chaise	chair	une porte	door
un lit	bed	une fenêtre	window	une table	table
		une lampe	lamp		

Où?

dans	in	devant	in front of	sur	on, on top of
derrière	behind, in back of	sous	under		

La description

amusant(e)	amusing, fun	jeune	young		
beau (belle)*	beautiful, handsome	joli(e)*	pretty		
bête	silly, dumb	mauvais(e)*	bad		
blond(e)	blonde	méchant(e)	mean, nasty		
bon (bonne)*	good	mignon (mignonne)	cute	assez	rather
brun(e)	brown, dark-haired	petit(e)*	small, little, short	très	very
gentil (gentille)	nice, kind	sportif (sportive)	athletic		
grand(e)*	big, large, tall	sympathique	nice, pleasant		
intelligent(e)	intelligent, smart	timide	timid, shy		
intéressant(e)	interesting				

* Adjectives that come before the noun

Les adjectifs de nationalité

américain(e)	American	espagnol(e)	Spanish	mexicain(e)	Mexican
anglais(e)	English	français(e)	French	suisse	Swiss
canadien (canadienne)	Canadian	italien (italienne)	Italian		
chinois(e)	Chinese	japonais(e)	Japanese		

Les couleurs

blanc (blanche)	white	jaune	yellow	orange*	orange	vert(e)	green
bleu(e)	blue	marron*	brown	rose	pink		
gris(e)	grey	noir(e)	black	rouge	red		

* Invariable adjectives

Verbes réguliers en -er

marcher	to work, to run (to function)
	to walk

Verbes irréguliers

avoir	to have
avoir faim	to be hungry
avoir soif	to be thirsty
avoir … ans	to be … (years old)

Expressions utiles

Dis!	Say! Hey!	Je sais.	I know.	lundi	on Monday
Dis donc!	Hey there!	Je ne sais pas.	I don't know.	le lundi	on Mondays
alors	so, then	Si!	Yes!	le week-end	on weekends

VOCABULAIRE SUPPLÉMENTAIRE: L'informatique

un CD-ROM (cédérom)	CD-ROM	une imprimante	printer	chatter	to chat (online)
un clavier	keyboard	une souris	mouse	envoyer un mail	to send an e-mail
un écran	screen			surfer sur l'Internet	to surf the Internet
un jeu d'ordinateur	computer game			télécharger	to download
un mail (un mél)	e-mail				
un ordinateur portable	laptop				
un PC	PC				

TEST PREP
CLASSZONE.COM

FLASHCARDS
AND MORE!

cent quatre-vingt-cinq
Vocabulaire 185

CONTENT
- Understand and convey information about friends p. 139
- Understand and convey information about rooms p. 145
- Understand and convey information about pets and animals p. 187
- Understand and convey information about geography p. 178
- Understand and convey information about colors p. 174, 175

ASSESSMENT
- Communicate effectively with some hesitation and errors, which do not hinder comprehension p. 181
- Demonstrate culturally acceptable behavior for engaging in conversations pp. 148, 181
- Demonstrate culturally acceptable behavior for expressing likes and dislikes p. 161
- Demonstrate culturally acceptable behavior for obtaining information pp. 160, 180, 181
- Demonstrate culturally acceptable behavior for understanding some ideas and familiar details pp. 170, 171
- Demonstrate culturally acceptable behavior for providing information pp. 149, 171, 183
- Understand most important information. pp. 160, 170, 180

ENTRACTE 4

Objectives
• Reading skills development
• Re-entry of materials in the unit
• Development of cultural awareness

Teaching Resource Options

PRINT

Workbook PE, pp. 113–116
Activités pour tous PE, pp. 67–69
Unit 4 Resource Book
   Activités pour tous TE, pp. 161–163
   Workbook TE, pp. 165–168

Le monde personnel

Objectives
• Reading for fun and vocabulary enrichment

Casual speech For **sensationnel(le)** one can also say **sensas** /sãsas/

LANGUAGE COMPARISONS

Over the centuries, French and English have influenced one another.

• Which of the compliments and insults did French borrow from English? Which word has English borrowed from French? Sometimes French and English express themselves in different ways.

• Which of the animal comparisons on the next page are the same in French and English? Which are different?

PRE-READING

Have students suggest English sayings about personality traits that mention animals. E.g.,
   Blind as a bat.
   Sly as a fox.
   An elephant never forgets.
   More fun than a barrel of monkeys.
   Stubborn as a mule.

POST-READING

Which of the French sayings are similar to American sayings? Which are different?

LES ANIMAUX et LE LANGAGE

Selon° toi, est-ce que les animaux ont une personnalité? Pour les Français,
les animaux ont des qualités et des défauts,° comme° nous. Devine° comment
on° complète les phrases suivantes° en français.

1 Philippe n'aime pas étudier. Il préfère dormir.° Il est paresseux° comme° …

 un tigre

 un chat

 un lézard

2 Charlotte adore parler. Elle est bavarde° comme …

 une poule

 une pie

 un lion

3 Isabelle est une excellente élève. Elle a une mémoire extraordinaire. Elle a une mémoire de (d') …

 éléphant

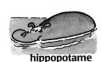 hippopotame

 kangourou

4 Le petit frère de Christine est jeune, mais il est très intelligent. Il est malin° comme …

 un cheval

 un singe

 une girafe

5 Où est Jacques? Il n'est pas prêt!° Oh là là! Il est lent° comme …

 une tortue

 un poisson

 un rhinocéros

6 Nicole a très, très faim. Elle a une faim de (d') …

 lion

 ours

 loup

Selon *According to* **défauts** *shortcomings* **comme** *like* **Devine** *Guess* **on** *one* **phrases suivantes** *following sentences* **dormir** *to sleep*
paresseux *lazy* **comme** *as* **bavarde** *talkative* **malin** *clever* **prêt** *ready* **lent** *slow*

Voici les réponses:
1. un lézard 2. une pie 3. éléphant 4. un singe 5. une tortue 6. loup

---

CLASSROOM MANAGEMENT GAME Pair Reading

Be sure all students cover the answers at the bottom of the page. (If you prefer, you can make a transparency of the questions and project it on the overhead.)

Divide the class into pairs. How many groups can complete the six expressions correctly?

Le scooter, c'est génial!

Le scooter, c'est génial!

Objectives
- Rapid reading at the sentence level
- Reading for cultural information about personal possessions and attitudes of French people

---

Teaching Resource Options

PRINT

Workbook PE, pp. 113–116
Activités pour tous PE, pp. 67–69
Unit 4 Resource Book
  Activités pour tous TE, pp. 161–163
  Videoscript, p. 65
  Workbook TE, pp. 165–168

VIDEO PROGRAM

VIDÉO   DVD

MODULE 10

**10.5 Vignette culturelle:
La mobylette**
(39:43–41:03 min.)

Language note

Whereas one can say **à moto** or **en moto**, **à vélo** or **en vélo**, the only correct preposition with **scooter** is **en** – because one's legs are inside the structure of the scooter, and do not straddle it the way one straddles a motorcycle.

Compréhension
Answers
1 vrai
2 faux
3 vrai
4 faux
5 vrai

Et vous?
Answers will vary.
1 Advantages: Wouldn't have to walk or ride a bike; faster; fun. Disadvantages: It's expensive to buy gas. It can be dangerous
2 I would ride to school instead of walking or taking the bus.

Je m'appelle Mélanie et j'ai 15 ans. J'ai un scooter. C'est un cadeau° d'anniversaire de ma grand-mère. Il est rouge et il est très confortable.

Ma copine Élodie a une mobylette. C'est une MBK. Nous allons° au collège ensemble.° Nous avons le BSR et nous sommes prudentes.° Nous portons° un casque° et nous respectons la limite de vitesse:° 45 kilomètres l'heure.

Le week-end, nous allons au centre-ville. Nous n'avons pas de problème de stationnement.° Quand il fait beau, nous allons à la campagne.° Quand nous sommes sur nos° petites machines, nous avons l'impression de liberté. Le scooter, c'est génial!

---

cadeau *gift* **allons** *go* **ensemble** *together* **prudentes** *careful* **portons** *wear* **casque** *helmet* **vitesse** *speed* **stationnement** *parking* **campagne** *country* **nos** *our*

Compréhension: vrai ou faux

1. Mélanie a un scooter.
2. Élodie a un scooter aussi.
3. Quand Mélanie est en scooter, elle porte un casque.
4. Avec un scooter, on a souvent un problème de stationnement.
5. En scooter, Mélanie a l'impression de liberté.

Et vous?

1. What are the advantages or disadvantages of owning a moped or a scooter?
2. What would you do if you had a motor scooter? How would this change your habits?

CONNEXIONS

Go to the Internet site of a French manufacturer of mopeds and scooters and make a poster showing some of the products you find.

 188 cent quatre-vingt-huit
Unité 4

PRE-READING

Ask students what kinds of two-wheelers they have.
   Qui a un vélo?
   Qui a un VTT (**vélo tout terrain:** *mountain bike*)?
   Qui a une mobylette?

Mobylette . . . ou scooter?

Modèle:	MBK Club
Couleurs:	noir, gris, bleu
Prix:	680 €

Modèle:	MBK Booster Spirit
Couleurs:	rouge, bleu, noir
Prix:	1 600 €

Et vous?

1. Which of the above would you choose? Use the following in your response:

   modèle   *couleur*   *prix en €*   *prix en $*

2. Is it expensive? *(cher, chère)*

3. Why did you choose it?

NOTE culturelle

La mobylette et le scooter

Mopeds and motor scooters are very popular among French teenagers. To drive one, you must be at least 14 years old. If you are under 16, you cannot go over 45 kilometers (about 30 miles) per hour. You must also have a license known as the **BSR** or **Brevet de Sécurité Routière** *(Certificate of Highway Safety)* which you get after a short course of driver's education. And, of course, whenever you are riding, you must wear a helmet!

The most popular makes of mopeds and scooters include Peugeot, Renault, and MBK, all manufactured in France. The term **mobylette** was originally a brand name which French students shortened to **mob.** It now is used to refer to any type of moped.

French teens love their mopeds and their scooters, and they take great care of them. During the week, many students ride them to school. On weekends, they use them to go into town, to get to their sports clubs, or to go for a ride in the country with their friends.

cent quatre-vingt-neuf
Lecture et Culture 189

Bonjour, Brigitte!

Objectives
- Reading a complete text
- Building reading skills

Teaching Resource Options

PRINT

Workbook PE, pp. 113–116
Activités pour tous PE, pp. 67–69
Unit 4 Resource Book
  Activités pour tous TE, pp. 161–163
  Workbook PE, pp. 165–168

Questions sur le texte

1. Quel âge a Brigitte? (Elle a quatorze ans.)

2. Comment est-elle physiquement? (Elle est de taille moyenne. Elle est brune et elle a les yeux verts.)

3. Quels sports est-ce qu'elle aime? (Elle aime le ski, le jogging et la danse moderne.)

4. Où est-ce qu'elle habite? (Elle habite à Toulouse.)

5. Où travaille son père? Qu'est-ce qu'il fait? (Son père travaille dans l'industrie aéronautique. Il est ingénieur.)

6. Où travaille sa mère? Qu'est-ce qu'elle fait? (Sa mère travaille dans une banque. Elle est directrice du personnel.)

7. Comment s'appelle la soeur de Brigitte? Quel âge a-t-elle? Comment est-elle? (Elle s'appelle Élodie. Elle a cinq ans. Elle est très mignonne.)

8. Comment s'appelle le frère de Brigitte? Quel âge a-t-il? Comment est-il? (Il s'appelle Mathieu. Il a treize ans. Il est pénible.)

9. Est-ce que Brigitte a des animaux? (Elle a un chien, Attila. Elle a aussi deux poissons rouges.)

10. Quelles choses est-ce qu'elle a? (Elle a un baladeur et des CD. Elle a un ordinateur et une mob.)

11. Est-ce qu'elle a un petit copain? (Non, elle n'a pas de petit copain.)

Bonjour, Brigitte!

Chers° copains américains,

Je m'appelle Brigitte Lavie. J'ai quatorze ans. Voici ma photo. Je ne suis pas très grande, mais je ne suis pas petite. Je suis de taille° moyenne.° Je suis brune, mais j'ai les yeux verts. Je suis sportive. J'aime le ski, le jogging et la danse moderne.

J'habite à Toulouse avec ma famille. Mon père travaille dans l'industrie aéronautique. Il est ingénieur.° Ma mère travaille dans une banque. Elle est directrice° du personnel.

J'ai une soeur et un frère. Ma petite soeur s'appelle Élodie. Elle a cinq ans. Elle est très mignonne. Mon frère s'appelle Mathieu. Il a treize ans. Il est pénible. J'ai un chien. Il s'appelle Attila mais il est très gentil (Il est plus gentil que° mon frère!) J'ai aussi deux poissons rouges.° Ils n'ont pas de nom.°

J'ai un baladeur et des quantités de CD. Je n'ai pas de mini-chaîne. J'ai un ordinateur. C'est un cadeau° de ma marraine.° Je surfe sur l'Internet et j'envoie des mails. Je n'ai pas de scooter mais j'ai une mob.

J'ai beaucoup de copains, mais je n'ai pas de «petit copain°». Ça n'a pas d'importance!° Je suis heureuse° comme ça.°

Amitiés,
Brigitte

Chers *Dear* **taille** *size* **moyenne** *average* **ingénieur** *engineer* **directrice** *director* **plus gentil que** *nicer than* **poissons rouges** *goldfish* **nom** *name* **cadeau** *gift* **marraine** *godmother* **petit copain** *boyfriend* **Ça n'a pas d'importance!** *It doesn't matter!* **heureuse** *happy* **comme ça** *like that*

TEACHING NOTE

Ask if students know in which American city NASA (National Aeronautic and Space Agency) is headquartered. [Houston]

Then ask if they know where the French space center is located. [Toulouse]

Tell them they will be reading a letter from Toulouse.

Questions personnelles
Answers will vary.

1. Quel âge as-tu? [J'ai (quinze) ans.]
2. Est-ce que tu es grand(e), petit(e) ou de taille moyenne? [Je suis (grand).]
3. Est-ce que tu as les yeux bleus ou marron *(brown)* ou noirs? [J'ai les yeux (bleus).]
4. Est-ce que tu as des frères ou des soeurs? [J'ai (une soeur).]
5. (Pour chaque frère ou chaque soeur): Comment est-ce qu'il/elle s'appelle? [Il/Elle s'appelle ...] Quel âge est-ce qu'il/elle a? [Il/Elle a ... ans.] Comment est-il/elle? [Il est (grand). /Elle est (petite).]
6. Est-ce que tu as un chien? un chat? un poisson rouge? Comment est-ce qu'il s'appelle? [J'ai (un chien). Il s'appelle (Spot).]
7. Est-ce que tu as un vélo? Est-ce que tu aimes faire des promenades à vélo? [Oui, j'ai un vélo. J'aime faire des promenades à vélo.]
8. Quels autres *(other)* objets est-ce que tu as? [J'ai (un baladeur et une guitare).]

STRATEGY Reading

Guessing from context As you read French, try to guess the meanings of unfamiliar words before you look at the English equivalents. Often the context provides good hints. For example, Brigitte writes:

> **Je ne suis pas très grande, mais je ne suis pas petite. Je suis de taille moyenne.**

She is neither tall nor short. She must be about average:

> **de taille moyenne** = *of medium height or size*

Sometimes you know what individual words in an expression mean, but the phrase does not seem to make sense. Then you have to guess at the real meaning. For example, Brigitte writes that she has:

> **deux poissons rouges** *?? red fish??*

If you guessed that these are most likely *goldfish*, you are right!

Activité écrite: Une lettre à Brigitte

Write a letter to Brigitte in which you describe yourself and your family. You may tell her:

- your name and how old you are
- if you are tall or short
- if you like sports, and which ones
- if you have brothers and sisters (and if so, their names and ages)
- if you have pets (and if so, give their names)
- a few things you own
- a few things you like to do

Writing Hint Use Brigitte's letter as a model.

Pour écrire une lettre

To write to a boy, begin with:	**Cher**	**Cher Patrick,**
To write to a girl, begin with:	**Chère**	**Chère Brigitte,**
End your letter with:	**Amicalement,** *(In friendship,)*	
	Amitiés, *(Best regards,)*	

NOTE culturelle

Toulouse

Toulouse, with a population of nearly one million people, is the center of the French aeronautic and space industry. It is in Toulouse that the Airbus planes and the Ariane rockets are being built in cooperation with other European countries.

POST-READING ACTIVITY

Maybe your class would like to exchange letters (or e-mail) with a French class in another school in your area. (The advantage of cross-city exchanges is that letters can be exchanged easily.)

Have your students each write letters introducing themselves.

Place these in a large envelope and exchange packets with a French teacher in another school. The first set of correspondence will be distributed randomly. From then on, however, students will have a specific pen pal to correspond with during the year.

Reference Section

CONTENTS

APPENDIX 1 Maps   **R1**

APPENDIX 2 Sound-Spelling Correspondences   **R4**

APPENDIX 3 Numbers   **R6**

APPENDIX 4 Verbs   **R7**

French-English Vocabulary   **R12**

English-French Vocabulary   **R28**

Index   **R36**

Credits   **R38**

APPENDIX 1

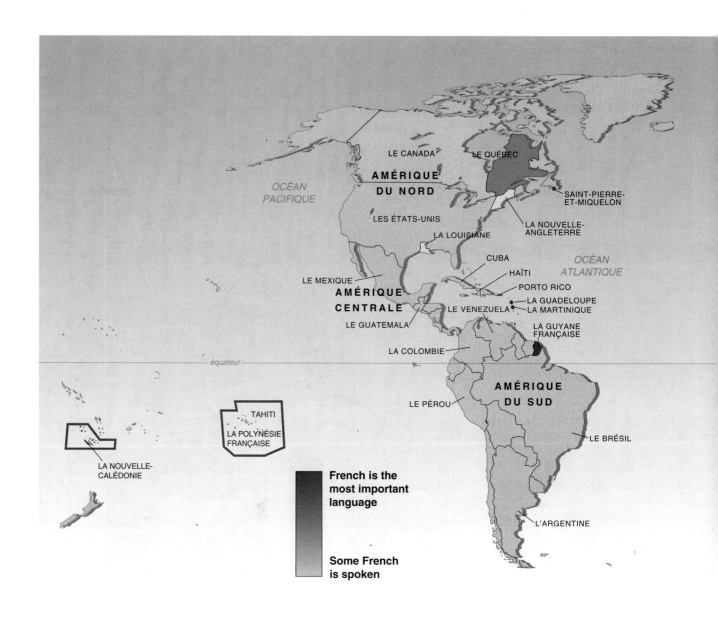

LE CANADA
LE QUÉBEC

AMÉRIQUE
DU NORD

OCÉAN
PACIFIQUE

SAINT-PIERRE-
ET-MIQUELON

LES ÉTATS-UNIS

LA NOUVELLE-
ANGLETERRE

LA LOUISIANE

CUBA

OCÉAN
ATLANTIQUE

HAÏTI

LE MEXIQUE

PORTO RICO

AMÉRIQUE
CENTRALE

LA GUADELOUPE
LA MARTINIQUE

LE VENEZUELA

LE GUATEMALA

LA GUYANE
FRANÇAISE

LA COLOMBIE

équateur

AMÉRIQUE
DU SUD

LE PÉROU

TAHITI

LA POLYNÉSIE
FRANÇAISE

LE BRÉSIL

LA NOUVELLE-
CALÉDONIE

French is the
most important
language

L'ARGENTINE

Some French
is spoken

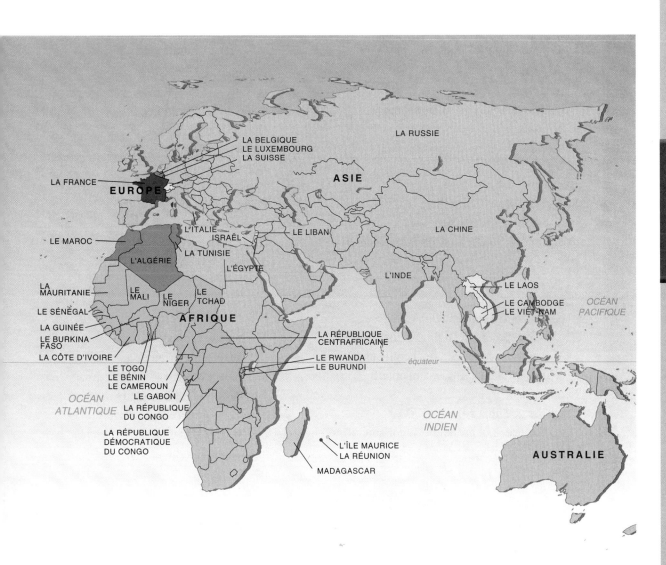

LA BELGIQUE
LE LUXEMBOURG
LA SUISSE

LA RUSSIE

LA FRANCE

EUROPE

ASIE

LE MAROC

L'ITALIE
ISRAËL

LE LIBAN

LA CHINE

L'ALGÉRIE

LA TUNISIE

L'ÉGYPTE

L'INDE

LA
MAURITANIE

LE
MALI

LE
NIGER

LE
TCHAD

LE LAOS

OCÉAN
PACIFIQUE

LE SÉNÉGAL

AFRIQUE

LE CAMBODGE
LE VIÊT-NAM

LA GUINÉE

LE BURKINA
FASO

LA CÔTE D'IVOIRE

LA RÉPUBLIQUE
CENTRAFRICAINE

LE TOGO
LE BÉNIN
LE CAMEROUN

LE RWANDA
LE BURUNDI

équateur

LE GABON

OCÉAN
ATLANTIQUE

LA RÉPUBLIQUE
DU CONGO

OCÉAN
INDIEN

LA RÉPUBLIQUE
DÉMOCRATIQUE
DU CONGO

L'ÎLE MAURICE
LA RÉUNION

AUSTRALIE

MADAGASCAR

APPENDIX 2

VOWELS

SOUND	SPELLING	EXAMPLES
/a/	a, à, â	Madame, là-bas, théâtre
/i/	i, î	visite, Nice, dîne
	y (initial, final, or between consonants)	Yves, Guy, style
/u/	ou, où, oû	Toulouse, où, août
/y/	u, û	tu, Luc, sûr
/o/	o (final or before silent consonant)	piano, idiot, Margot
	au, eau	jaune, Claude, beau
	ô	hôtel, drôle, Côte d'Ivoire
/ɔ/	o	Monique, Noël, jolie
	au	Paul, restaurant, Laure
/e/	é	Dédé, Québec, télé
	e (before silent final z, t, r)	chez, et, Roger
	ai (final or before final silent consonant)	j'ai, mai, japonais
/ɛ/	è	Michèle, Ève, père
	ei	seize, neige, tour Eiffel
	ê	tête, être, Viêt-nam
	e (before two consonants)	elle, Pierre, Annette
	e (before pronounced final consonant)	Michel, avec, cher
	ai (before pronounced final consonant)	française, aime, Maine
/ə/	e (final or before single consonant)	je, Denise, venir
/φ/	eu, oeu	deux, Mathieu, euro, oeufs
	eu (before final se)	nerveuse, généreuse, sérieuse
/œ/	eu (before final pronounced consonant except /z/)	heure, neuf, Lesieur
	oeu	soeur, coeur, oeuf
	oe	oeil

NASAL VOWELS

SOUND	SPELLING	EXAMPLES
/ã/	an, am	France, quand, lampe
	en, em	Henri, pendant, décembre
/ɔ̃/	on, om	non, Simon, bombe
/ɛ̃/	in, im	Martin, invite, impossible
	yn, ym	syndicat, sympathique, Olympique
	ain, aim	Alain, américain, faim
	(o) + in	loin, moins, point
	(i) + en	bien, Julien, viens
/œ̃/	un, um	un, Lebrun, parfum

Sound-Spelling Correspondences

SEMI-VOWELS

SOUND	SPELLING	EXAMPLES
/j/	i, y (before vowel sound)	bien, piano, Lyon
	-il, -ill (after vowel sound)	oeil, travaille, Marseille, fille
/ɥ/	u (before vowel sound)	lui, Suisse, juillet
/w/	ou (before vowel sound)	oui, Louis, jouer
/wa/	oi, oî	voici, Benoît
	oy (before vowel)	voyage

CONSONANTS

SOUND	SPELLING	EXAMPLES
/b/	b	Barbara, banane, Belgique
/k/	c (before a, o, u, or consonant)	casque, cuisine, classe
	ch(r)	Christine, Christian, Christophe
	qu, q (final)	Québec, qu'est-ce que, cinq
	k	kilo, Kiki, ketchup
/ʃ/	ch	Charles, blanche, chez
/d/	d	Didier, dans, médecin
/f/	f	Félix, franc, neuf
	ph	Philippe, téléphone, photo
/g/	g (before a, o, u, or consonant)	Gabriel, gorge, légumes, gris
	gu (before e, i, y)	vague, Guillaume, Guy
/ɲ/	gn	mignon, champagne, Allemagne
/ʒ/	j	je, Jérôme, jaune
	g (before e, i, y)	rouge, Gigi, gymnastique
	ge (before a, o, u)	orangeade, Georges, nageur
/l/	l, ll	Lise, elle, cheval
/m/	m	Maman, moi, tomate
/n/	n	banane, Nancy, nous
/p/	p	peu, Papa, Pierre
/r/	r, rr	arrive, rentre, Paris
/s/	c (before e, i, y)	ce, Cécile, Nancy
	ç (before a, o, u)	ça, garçon, déçu
	s (initial or before consonant)	sac, Sophie, reste
	ss (between vowels)	boisson, dessert, Suisse
	t (before i + vowel)	attention, Nations Unies, natation
	x	dix, six, soixante
/t/	t	trop, télé, Tours
	th	Thérèse, thé, Marthe
/v/	v	Viviane, vous, nouveau
/gz/	x	examen, exemple, exact
/ks/	x	Max, Mexique, excellent
/z/	s (between vowels)	désert, Louise, télévision
	z	Suzanne, zut, zéro

A. CARDINAL NUMBERS

0	zéro	18	dix-huit	82	quatre-vingt-deux
1	un (une)	19	dix-neuf	90	quatre-vingt-dix
2	deux	20	vingt	91	quatre-vingt-onze
3	trois	21	vingt et un (une)	100	cent
4	quatre	22	vingt-deux	101	cent un (une)
5	cinq	23	vingt-trois	102	cent deux
6	six	30	trente	200	deux cents
7	sept	31	trente et un (une)	201	deux cent un
8	huit	32	trente-deux	300	trois cents
9	neuf	40	quarante	400	quatre cents
10	dix	41	quarante et un (une)	500	cinq cents
11	onze	50	cinquante	600	six cents
12	douze	60	soixante	700	sept cents
13	treize	70	soixante-dix	800	huit cents
14	quatorze	71	soixante et onze	900	neuf cents
15	quinze	72	soixante-douze	1 000	mille
16	seize	80	quatre-vingts	2 000	deux mille
17	dix-sept	81	quatre-vingt-un (une)	1 000 000	un million

Notes:
1. The word **et** occurs only in the numbers 21, 31, 41, 51, 61, and 71:   **vingt et un**   **soixante et onze**
2. **Un** becomes **une** before a feminine noun: **trente et une filles**
3. **Quatre-vingts** becomes **quatre-vingt** before another number: **quatre-vingt-cinq**
4. **Cents** becomes **cent** before another number: **trois cent vingt**
5. **Mille** never adds an **-s**:   **quatre mille**

B. ORDINAL NUMBERS

1$^{er\ (ère)}$	**premier (première)**	5^e	**cinquième**	9^e	**neuvième**
2^e	**deuxième**	6^e	**sixième**	10^e	**dixième**
3^e	**troisième**	7^e	**septième**	11^e	**onzième**
4^e	**quatrième**	8^e	**huitième**	12^e	**douzième**

Note: **Premier** becomes **première** before a feminine noun: **la première histoire**

C. METRIC EQUIVALENTS

1 gramme	= 0.035 ounces		1 ounce	= **28,349 grammes**
1 kilogramme	= 2.205 pounds		1 pound	= **0,453 kilogrammes**
1 litre	= 1.057 quarts		1 quart	= **0,946 litres**
1 mètre	= 39.37 inches		1 foot	= **30,480 centimètres**
1 kilomètre	= 0.62 miles		1 mile	= **1,609 kilomètres**

A. REGULAR VERBS

INFINITIVE	PRESENT		PASSÉ COMPOSÉ	
parler	je **parle**	nous **parlons**	j'ai **parlé**	nous avons **parlé**
(to talk, speak)	tu **parles**	vous **parlez**	tu as **parlé**	vous avez **parlé**
	il **parle**	ils **parlent**	il a **parlé**	ils ont **parlé**

IMPERATIVE: **parle, parlons, parlez**

INFINITIVE	PRESENT		PASSÉ COMPOSÉ	
finir	je **finis**	nous **finissons**	j'ai **fini**	nous avons **fini**
(to finish)	tu **finis**	vous **finissez**	tu as **fini**	vous avez **fini**
	il **finit**	ils **finissent**	il a **fini**	ils ont **fini**

IMPERATIVE: **finis, finissons, finissez**

INFINITIVE	PRESENT		PASSÉ COMPOSÉ	
vendre	je **vends**	nous **vendons**	j'ai **vendu**	nous avons **vendu**
(to sell)	tu **vends**	vous **vendez**	tu as **vendu**	vous avez **vendu**
	il **vend**	ils **vendent**	il a **vendu**	ils ont **vendu**

IMPERATIVE: **vends, vendons, vendez**

B. -er VERBS WITH SPELLING CHANGES

INFINITIVE	PRESENT		PASSÉ COMPOSÉ
acheter	j'**achète**	nous **achetons**	j'ai **acheté**
(to buy)	tu **achètes**	vous **achetez**	
	il **achète**	ils **achètent**	

Verb like **acheter:** amener *(to bring, take along)*

INFINITIVE	PRESENT		PASSÉ COMPOSÉ
espérer	j'**espère**	nous **espérons**	j'ai **espéré**
(to hope)	tu **espères**	vous **espérez**	
	il **espère**	ils **espèrent**	

Verbs like **espérer:** célébrer *(to celebrate)*, préférer *(to prefer)*

INFINITIVE	PRESENT		PASSÉ COMPOSÉ
commencer	je **commence**	nous **commençons**	j'ai **commencé**
(to begin, start)	tu **commences**	vous **commencez**	
	il **commence**	ils **commencent**	

INFINITIVE	PRESENT		PASSÉ COMPOSÉ
manger	je **mange**	nous **mangeons**	j'ai **mangé**
(to eat)	tu **manges**	vous **mangez**	
	il **mange**	ils **mangent**	

Verbs like **manger:** nager *(to swim)*, voyager *(to travel)*

INFINITIVE	PRESENT		PASSÉ COMPOSÉ
payer	je **paie**	nous **payons**	j'ai **payé**
(to pay, pay for)	tu **paies**	vous **payez**	
	il **paie**	ils **paient**	

Verbs like **payer:** nettoyer *(to clean)*

APPENDIX 4

C. IRREGULAR VERBS

INFINITIVE	PRESENT		PASSÉ COMPOSÉ
avoir *(to have, own)*	j'ai tu as il a	nous avons vous avez ils ont	j'ai eu
	IMPERATIVE: aie, ayons, ayez		
être *(to be)*	je suis tu es il est	nous sommes vous êtes ils sont	j'ai été
	IMPERATIVE: sois, soyons, soyez		
aller *(to go)*	je vais tu vas il va	nous allons vous allez ils vont	je suis allé(e)
	IMPERATIVE: va, allons, allez		
boire *(to drink)*	je bois tu bois il boit	nous buvons vous buvez ils boivent	j'ai bu
connaître *(to know)*	je connais tu connais il connaît	nous connaissons vous connaissez ils connaissent	j'ai connu
devoir *(to have to, should, must)*	je dois tu dois il doit	nous devons vous devez ils doivent	j'ai dû
dire *(to say, tell)*	je dis tu dis il dit	nous disons vous dites ils disent	j'ai dit
dormir *(to sleep)*	je dors tu dors il dort	nous dormons vous dormez ils dorment	j'ai dormi
écrire *(to write)*	j'écris tu écris il écrit	nous écrivons vous écrivez ils écrivent	j'ai écrit
	Verb like écrire: décrire *(to describe)*		
faire *(to make, do)*	je fais tu fais il fait	nous faisons vous faites ils font	j'ai fait

C. IRREGULAR VERBS

INFINITIVE	PRESENT		PASSÉ COMPOSÉ
lire *(to read)*	je **lis** tu **lis** il **lit**	nous **lisons** vous **lisez** ils **lisent**	j'ai **lu**
mettre *(to put, place)*	je **mets** tu **mets** il **met**	nous **mettons** vous **mettez** ils **mettent**	j'ai **mis**

Verb like **mettre:** promettre *(to promise)*

ouvrir *(to open)*	j'**ouvre** tu **ouvres** il **ouvre**	nous **ouvrons** vous **ouvrez** ils **ouvrent**	j'ai **ouvert**

Verbs like **ouvrir:** découvrir *(to discover)*, offrir *(to offer)*

partir *(to leave)*	je **pars** tu **pars** il **part**	nous **partons** vous **partez** ils **partent**	je **suis parti(e)**
pouvoir *(to be able, can)*	je **peux** tu **peux** il **peut**	nous **pouvons** vous **pouvez** ils **peuvent**	j'ai **pu**
prendre *(to take)*	je **prends** tu **prends** il **prend**	nous **prenons** vous **prenez** ils **prennent**	j'ai **pris**

Verbs like **prendre:** apprendre *(to learn)*, comprendre *(to understand)*

savoir *(to know)*	je **sais** tu **sais** il **sait**	nous **savons** vous **savez** ils **savent**	j'ai **su**
sortir *(to go out, get out)*	je **sors** tu **sors** il **sort**	nous **sortons** vous **sortez** ils **sortent**	je **suis sorti(e)**
venir *(to come)*	je **viens** tu **viens** il **vient**	nous **venons** vous **venez** ils **viennent**	je **suis venu(e)**

Verb like **venir:** revenir *(to come back)*

voir *(to see)*	je **vois** tu **vois** il **voit**	nous **voyons** vous **voyez** ils **voient**	j'ai **vu**

APPENDIX 4

C. IRREGULAR VERBS *continued*

INFINITIVE	PRESENT		PASSÉ COMPOSÉ
vouloir *(to want)*	je **veux**	nous **voulons**	j'ai **voulu**
	tu **veux**	vous **voulez**	
	il **veut**	ils **veulent**	

D. VERBS WITH *ÊTRE* IN THE *PASSÉ COMPOSÉ*

aller *(to go)*	je **suis allé(e)**	**passer** *(to go by, through)*	je **suis passé(e)**
arriver *(to arrive, come)*	je **suis arrivé(e)**	**rentrer** *(to go home)*	je **suis rentré(e)**
descendre *(to go down)*	je **suis descendu(e)**	**rester** *(to stay)*	je **suis resté(e)**
entrer *(to enter, go in)*	je **suis entré(e)**	**revenir** *(to come back)*	je **suis revenu(e)**
monter *(to go up)*	je **suis monté(e)**	**sortir** *(to go out, get out)*	je **suis sorti(e)**
mourir *(to die)*	il/elle **est mort(e)**	**tomber** *(to fall)*	je **suis tombé(e)**
naître *(to be born)*	je **suis né(e)**	**venir** *(to come)*	je **suis venu(e)**
partir *(to leave)*	je **suis parti(e)**		

French-English Vocabulary

The French-English vocabulary contains active and passive words from the text, as well as the important words of the illustrations used within the units. Obvious passive cognates have not been listed.

The numbers following an entry indicate the lesson in which the word or phrase is activated. (**I** stands for the list of classroom expressions at the end of the first Images section; **E** stands for Entracte.)

Nouns: If the article of a noun does not indicate gender, the noun is followed by *m. (masculine)* or *f. (feminine)*. If the plural *(pl.)* is irregular, it is given in parentheses.

Adjectives: Adjectives are listed in the masculine form. If the feminine form is irregular, it is given in parentheses. Irregular plural forms *(pl.)* are also given in parentheses.

Verbs: Verbs are listed in the infinitive form. An asterisk (*) in front of an active verb means that it is irregular. (For forms, see the verb charts in Appendix 4C.) Irregular present tense forms are listed when they are used before the verb has been activated. Irregular past participle *(p.p.)* forms are listed separately.

Words beginning with an **h** are preceded by a bullet (•) if the **h** is aspirate; that is, if the word is treated as if it begins with a consonant sound.

A

a: il y a there is, there are **9**
à at, in, to **6**
  à côté next door; next to
  à partir de as of, beginning
  à samedi! see you Saturday! **4B**
abolir to abolish
abondant plentiful, copious, large
un **abricot** apricot
absolument absolutely
un **accent** accent mark, stress
accepter to accept
un **accord** agreement
d' **accord** okay, all right **5**
  être d'accord to agree **6**
un **achat** purchase
un **acteur, une actrice** actor, actress
une **activité** activity
l' **addition** *f.* check
adorer to love
adroit skilled, skillful
un(e) **adulte** adult
aéronautique aeronautic, aeronautical
un **aéroport** airport
affectueusement affectionately *(at the end of a letter)*
une **affiche** poster **9**
affirmativement affirmatively
l' **Afrique** *f.* Africa
l' **âge** *m.* age
  quel âge a-t-il/elle? how old is he/she? **9**
  quel âge as-tu? how old are you? **2C**

  quel âge a ton père/ta mère? how old is your father/your mother? **2C**
âgé old
une **agence** agency
une **agence de tourisme** tourist office
une **agence de voyages** travel agency
agiter to shake
agité agitated
ah! ah!, oh!
  ah bon? oh? really? **8**
  ah non! ah, no!
ai *(see* **avoir***)*: **j'ai** I have **9**
  j'ai… ans I'm … (years old) **2C**
une **aile** wing
aimer to like **7**
  est-ce que tu aimes…? do you like …? **5**
  j'aime… I like … **5**
  j'aimerais I would like
  je n'aime pas… I don't like … **5**
ainsi thus
aîné older
  un frère aîné older brother
  une soeur aînée older sister
ajouter to add
l' **Algérie** *f.* Algeria *(country in North Africa)*
  algérien (algérienne) Algerian
l' **Allemagne** *f.* Germany
allemand German
aller to go
  allez *(see* **aller***)*: **allez-vous en** go away!

  allez-y come on!, go ahead!, do it!
  comment allez-vous? how are you? **1C**
allô! hello! *(on the telephone)*
alors so, then **11**
une **alouette** lark
les **Alpes** *f.* (the) Alps
l' **alphabet** *m.* alphabet
l' **Alsace** *f.* Alsace *(province in eastern France)*
américain American **1B, 11**
  à l'américaine American-style
  un Américain, une Américaine American person
l' **Amérique** *f.* America
un **ami, une amie** *(close)* friend **2A**
amicalement love *(at the end of a letter)*
l' **amitié** *f.* friendship
amitiés best regards *(at the end of a letter)*
amusant funny, amusing **11**
amuser to amuse
  s'amuser to have fun
  on s'est bien amusé! we had a good time!
un **an** year
  avoir… ans to be … (years old) **10**
  il/elle a… ans he/she is … (years old) **2C**
  j'ai… ans I'm … (years old) **2C**
l' **an dernier** last year
  par an per year
un **ananas** pineapple

ancien (ancienne) former, old, ancient

un **âne** donkey

un **ange** angel

anglais English **1B, 11**
   un **Anglais, une Anglaise** English person

un **animal** (*pl.* **animaux**) animal

une **animation** live entertainment

animé animated, lively

une **année** year **4B**
   toute l'année all year long

un **anniversaire** birthday **4B**
   joyeux anniversaire! happy birthday!
   c'est quand, ton anniversaire? when is your birthday? **4B**
   mon anniversaire est le (2 mars) my birthday is (March 2nd) **4B**

un **annuaire** telephone directory

un **anorak** ski jacket

les **antiquités** *f.* antiquities, antiques

août *m.* August **4B**

un **appareil-photo** (*pl.* **appareils-photo**) (*still*) camera **9**

s' **appeller** to be named, called
   comment s'appelle…? what's …'s name? **2B**
   comment s'appelle-t-il/elle? what's his/her name? **9**
   comment t'appelles-tu? what's your name? **1A**
   il/elle s'appelle… his/her name is … **2B**
   je m'appelle… my name is … **1A**

apporter: apporte-moi (apportez-moi) bring me **I**

apprécier to appreciate

approprié appropriate

après after, afterwards
   d' après according to
   de l'après-midi in the afternoon, P.M. **4A**

l' **arabe** *m.* Arabic (*language*)

un **arbre** tree
   un arbre généalogique family tree

l' **arche** *f.* **de Noé** Noah's Ark

l' **argent** *m.* money
   l'argent de poche allowance, pocket money

arrêter to arrest; to stop

arriver to arrive, come

j' **arrive!** I'm coming!

une **arrivée** arrival

un **arrondissement** district

un **artifice: le feu d'artifice** fireworks

un **artiste, une artiste** artist

as (*see* **avoir**): **est-ce que tu as…?** do you have …? **9**

un **ascenseur** elevator

un **aspirateur** vacuum cleaner

s' **asseoir: asseyez-vous!** sit down! **I**

assez rather **11**; enough

assieds-toi! sit down! **I**

associer to associate

l' **Atlantique** *m.* Atlantic Ocean

attention *f.:* **faire attention** to be careful, pay attention **8**

attentivement carefully

au (**à + le**) to (the), at (the), in (the) **6**
   au revoir! good-bye! **1C**

une **auberge** inn

aucun: ne… aucun none, not any

aujourd'hui today **4B**
   aujourd'hui, c'est… today is … **4B**

aussi also, too **1B, 7**

une **auto** (**automobile**) car, automobile **9**

une **auto-école** driving school

un **autobus** bus

l' **automne** *m.* autumn, fall
   en automne in (the) autumn, fall **4C**

autre other
   d'autres others
   un(e) autre another

avant before
   avant hier the day before yesterday

en **avant** let's begin

avantageux (avantageuse) reasonable, advantageous

avec with **6**
   avec moi, avec toi with me, with you **5**
   avec qui? with who(m)? **8**

un **avis** opinion
   avis de recherche missing person's bulletin
   à votre avis in your opinion

* **avoir** to have **10**
   avoir… ans to be … (years old) **10**
   avoir faim to be hungry **10**
   avoir lieu to take place
   avoir soif to be thirsty **10**

avril *m.* April **4B**

B

le **babyfoot** tabletop soccer game

le **babysitting: faire du babysitting** to baby-sit

les **bagages** *m.* bags, baggage

un **baladeur** portable player **9**

une **bande dessinée** comic strip

des **bandes dessinées** comics

la **Bannière étoilée** Star-Spangled Banner

une **banque** bank

une **barbe: quelle barbe!** what a pain! (*colloq.*)

le **bas** the bottom
   au bas at the bottom
   basé based

le **basket** (**basketball**) basketball
   jouer au basket to play basketball **5**

un **bateau-mouche** sightseeing boat

battre to beat

bavard talkative

beau (**bel, belle; *m.pl.* beaux**) handsome, good-looking, beautiful **9, 12**
   il est beau he is good-looking, handsome **9**
   il fait beau it's beautiful (nice) out **4C**

un **beau-frère** stepbrother, brother-in-law

un **beau-père** stepfather, father-in-law
   beaucoup (de) much, very much, many, a lot **7**

la **beauté** beauty

un **bec** beak

la **Belgique** Belgium
   belle (*see* **beau**) beautiful **9, 12**
   elle est belle she is beautiful **9**

une **belle-mère** stepmother, mother-in-law

une **belle-soeur** stepsister, sister-in-law

les **Bermudes** *f.* Bermuda

le **besoin** need
   des besoins d'argent money needs
   bête dumb, silly **11**

une **bicyclette** bicycle **9**
   bien well, very well, carefully **7**
   bien sûr of course **5**
   ça va bien everything's fine (going well) **1C**

French-English Vocabulary   *continued*

ça va très bien I'm (everything's) very well **1C**

c'est bien that's good (fine) **12**

je veux bien (...) I'd love to (...), I do, I want to **5**

oui, bien sûr... yes, of course ... **5**

très bien very well **7**

bientôt: à bientôt! see you soon!

bienvenue welcome

le biffteck steak

un biffteck de tortue turtle steak

bilingue bilingual

la biologie biology

une biscotte dry toast

blaff de poisson *m.* fish stew

blanc (blanche) white **E1, 12**

Blanche-Neige Snow White

blanchir to blanch, turn white

bleu blue **E1, 12**

blond blonde **9**

il/elle est blond(e) he/she is blond **9**

une boisson drink, beverage **3B**

une boîte box

un bol deep bowl

bon (bonne) good **12**

ah bon? oh, really? **8**

de bonne humeur in a good mood

il fait bon the weather's good (pleasant) **4C**

le bonheur happiness

bonjour hello **1A, 1C**

une bouche mouth **E2**

une boucherie butcher shop

le boudin sausage

une boulangerie bakery

une boum party **5, 7**

boxe: un match de boxe boxing match

un bras arm **E2**

brésilien (brésilienne) Brazilian

la Bretagne Brittany *(province in northwestern France)*

bricoler to do things around the house

broche: à la broche on the spit

bronzé tan

un bruit noise

brun brown, dark-haired **9**

il/elle est brun(e) he/she has dark hair **9**

brunir to turn brown

Bruxelles Brussels

le bulletin de notes report card

un bureau desk **I, 9**; office

un bus bus

un but goal; end

C

ça that, it

ça fait combien? ça fait... how much is that (it)? that (it) is ... **3C**

ça, là-bas that (one), over there **9**

ça va? how's everything? how are you? **1C**

ça va everything's fine, I'm OK **1C**

ça va (très) bien, ça va bien everything's going very well, everything's fine (going well) **1C**

ça va comme ci, comme ça everything's (going) so-so **1C**

ça va (très) mal things are going (very) badly **1C**

regarde ça look at that **9**

une cabine d'essayage fitting room

les cabinets *m.* toilet

un cadeau (*pl.* **cadeaux)** gift, present

cadet (cadette) younger

un frère cadet (a) younger brother

une soeur cadette (a) younger sister

le café coffee **3B**

un café au lait coffee with hot milk

un café café *(French coffee shop)* **6**

au café to (at) the café **6**

un cahier notebook **I, 9**

une calculatrice calculator **9**

un calendrier calendar

un camarade, une camarade classmate **9**

le Cambodge Cambodia *(country in Asia)*

un cambriolage burglary

un cambrioleur burglar

une caméra movie camera

la campagne countryside

une auberge de campagne country inn

le Canada Canada

canadien (canadienne) Canadian **1B, 11**

un Canadien, une Canadienne Canadian person

un canard duck

un car scolaire school bus

une carotte carrot

des carottes râpées grated carrots

un carré square

le Vieux Carré *the French Quarter in New Orleans*

une carte map **I**; card

une carte postale postcard

un cas case

en cas de in case of

une cassette cassette tape

une cassette vidéo videotape **9**

le catch wrestling

une cathédrale cathedral

une cave cellar

un CD CD, compact disc **9**

ce (c') this, that, it

ce n'est pas that's/it's not **12**

ce que what

ce sont these are, those are, they are **12**

c'est it's, that's **2A, 9, 12**

c'est + *day of the week* it's ... **4B**

c'est + *name or noun* it's ... **2A**

c'est bien/mal that's good/bad **12**

c'est combien? how much is that/it? **3C**

c'est le (12 octobre) it's (October 12) **4B**

qu'est-ce que c'est? what is it? what's that? **9**

qui est-ce? who's that/this? **9**

ce n'est pas it's (that's) not **12**

un cédérom (un CD-ROM) CD-ROM

une cédille cedilla

cela that

célèbre famous

cent one hundred **2B**

une centaine about a hundred

un centime centime *(1/100 of a euro)*

un centre center

certain certain

certains some of them

c'est (*see* **ce**)

chacun each one, each person

une chaise chair **I, 9**

une chaîne (TV) channel

une **chaîne hi-fi** stereo set **9**
une **mini-chaîne** compact stereo
la **chaleur** heat, warmth
une **chambre** bedroom **9**
un **champion, une championne** champion
la **chance** luck
une **chanson** song
 chanter to sing **5, 7**
un **chanteur, une chanteuse** singer
 chaque each, every
 charmant charming
un **chat** cat **2C, E4**
un **château** (*pl.* **châteaux**) castle
 chatter to chat (online)
 chaud warm, hot
  il fait chaud it's warm (hot) (weather) **4C**
 chauffer to warm, heat up
un **chauffeur** driver
un **chef** boss; chef
un **cheval** (*pl.* **chevaux**) horse **E4**
les **cheveux** *m.* hair **E2**
 chic (*inv.*) nice; elegant, in style
  une chic fille a great girl
un **chien** dog **2C**
la **chimie** chemistry
 chinois Chinese **11**
le **chinois** Chinese (*language*)
le **chocolat** hot chocolate, cocoa **3B**
  une glace au chocolat chocolate ice cream
un **choix** choice
  au choix choose one, your choice
une **chorale** choir
une **chose** thing **9**
 chouette great, terrific **12**
le **cidre** cider
un **cinéaste, une cinéaste** film maker
le **cinéma** the movies
  au cinéma to (at) the movies, movie theater **6**
 cinq five **1A**
 cinquante fifty **1C**
une **circonstance** circumstance
 cité: la Cité Interdite Forbidden City
une **classe** class
  en classe in class **6**
 classique classical
un **client, une cliente** customer
un **clip** music video
un **cochon** pig

un **coiffeur, une coiffeuse** hairdresser
un **coin** spot
une **coïncidence** coincidence
le **Colisée** the Coliseum (*a large stadium built by the Romans*)
un **collège** junior high school
une **colonie** colony
une **colonne** column
 combien how much
  combien coûte…? how much does…cost? **3C**
  combien de temps? how long?
  combien d'heures? how many hours?
  ça fait combien? how much is this (it)? **3C**
  c'est combien? how much is this (it)? **3C**
 commander to order
 comme like, as, for
 comme ci, comme ça so-so
  ça va comme ci, comme ça everything's so-so **1C**
 commencer to begin, start
 comment? how? **8**; what?
  comment allez-vous? how are you? **1C**
  comment est-il/elle? what's he/she like? what does he/she look like? **9**
  comment dit-on… en français? how do you say … in French? **I**
  comment lire reading hints
  comment s'appelle…? what's…'s name? **2B**
  comment s'appelle-t-il/elle? what's his/her name? **9**
  comment t'appelles-tu? what's your name? **1A**
  comment vas-tu? how are you? **1C**
un **commentaire** comment, commentary
le **commérage** gossip
 communiquer to communicate
un **compact (disc), un CD** compact disc, CD **9**
 complément object
 compléter to complete
* **comprendre** to understand
  je (ne) comprends (pas) I (don't) understand **I**
 compter to count (on); to expect, intend
 concerne: en ce qui

 concerne as for
un **concombre** cucumber
une **connaissance** acquaintance
  faire connaissance (avec) to become acquainted (with)
* **connaître** to know, be acquainted with
  tu connais…? do you know…? are you acquainted with…? **2B**
un **conseil** piece of advice, counsel
  des conseils *m.* advice
un **conservatoire** conservatory
une **consonne** consonant
se **contenter** to limit oneself
le **contenu** contents
une **contradiction** disagreement
une **contravention** (*traffic*) ticket
 cool cool, neat
un **copain, une copine** friend, pal **2A**
  un petit copain, une petite copine boyfriend, girlfriend
 copier to copy
une **copine** friend **2A**
 coréen (coréenne) Korean
un **corps** body
 correspondant corresponding
 correspondre to correspond, agree
la **Corse** Corsica (*French island off the Italian coast*)
un **costume** man's suit
la **Côte d'Azur** Riviera (*southern coast of France on the Mediterranean*)
la **Côte d'Ivoire** Ivory Coast (*French-speaking country in West Africa*)
 côté: à côté (de) next door; next to
une **côtelette de porc** pork chop
le **cou** neck **E2**
une **couleur** color **12**
  de quelle couleur …? what color …? **12**
un **couloir** hall, corridor
 coup: dans le coup with it
 courageux (courageuse) courageous
le **courrier électronique** e-mail, electronic mail
une **course** race
un **cousin, une cousine** cousin **2C**
le **coût: le coût de la vie** cost of living
 coûter to cost

combien coûte...? how much does...cost? **3C**
    il (elle) coûte... it costs...**3C**
un **couturier, une couturière** fashion designer
un **crabe** crab
    des matoutou crabes stewed crabs with rice
la **craie** chalk
    un morceau de craie piece of chalk **I**
un **crayon** pencil **I, 9**
créer to create
un **crétin** idiot
une **crêpe** crepe *(pancake)* **3A**
une **crêperie** crepe restaurant
une **crevaison** flat tire
une **croisade** crusade
un **croissant** crescent *(roll)* **3A**
une **cuillère** spoon
    une cuillère à soupe soup spoon
cuit cooked
culturel (culturelle) cultural
curieux (curieuse) curious, strange
    la curiosité curiosity
le **cybercafé** internet café
un **cyclomoteur** moped

d'accord okay, all right
    être d'accord to agree **6**
    oui, d'accord yes, okay **5**
une **dame** lady, woman *(polite term)* **2A**
dangereux (dangereuse) dangerous
dans in **9**
danser to dance **5, 7**
la **date** date **4B**
    quelle est la date? what's the date? **4B**
de (d') of, from, about **6**
    de l'après-midi in the afternoon **4A**
    de quelle couleur...? what color ...? **12**
    de qui? of whom? **8**
    de quoi? about what?
    de temps en temps from time to time
    pas de not any, no **10**
débarquer to land
décembre *m.* December **4B**
décider (de) to decide (to)

une **déclaration** statement
décoré decorated
* **découvrir** to discover
* **décrire** to describe
    décrivez... describe...
un **défaut** shortcoming
un **défilé** parade
dehors outside
    en dehors de outside of
déjà already; ever
demain tomorrow **4B**
    à demain! see you tomorrow! **4B**
    demain, c'est... (jeudi) tomorrow is ... (Thursday) **4B**
un **demi-frère** half-brother
une **demi-soeur** half-sister
demi: ... heures et demie half past ... **4A**
    midi et demi half past noon **4A**
    minuit et demi half past midnight **4A**
un **démon** devil
une **dent** tooth
un **départ** departure
se **dépêcher: dépêchez-vous!** hurry up!
dépend: ça dépend that depends
une **dépense** expense
derrière behind, in back of **9**
des some, any **10**
le **désert** desert
désirer to wish, want
    vous désirez? what would you like? may I help you? **3B**
désolé sorry
le **dessin** art, drawing
    un dessin animé cartoon
détester to hate, detest **1C**
deux two **1A**
le **deuxième étage** third floor
devant in front of **9**
développer to develop
deviner to guess
un **devoir** homework assignment **I**
    les devoirs *m.* homework
d'habitude usually
différemment differently
différent different
difficile hard, difficult **12**
la **dignité** dignity
dimanche *m.* Sunday **4B**
dîner to have dinner **7**
    dîner au restaurant to have

dinner at a restaurant **5**
* **dire** to say, tell
    que veut dire...? what does...mean? **I**
directement straight
un **directeur, une directrice** director, principal
dirigé directed, guided
dis! *(see* **dire)** say!, hey! **12**
    dis donc! say there!, hey there! **12**
discuter to discuss
une **dispute** quarrel, dispute
dit *(p.p. of* **dire)** said
    dit *(see* **dire): comment dit-on... en français?** how do you say...in French? **I**
    dites... *(see* **dire)** say..., tell...
dix ten **1A, 1B**
dix-huit eighteen **1B**
dix-neuf nineteen **1B**
dix-sept seventeen **1B**
un **docteur** doctor
dois *(see* **devoir): je dois** I have to (must) **5**
domestique domestic
les **animaux** *m.* **domestiques** pets **2C**
dommage! too bad! **7**
donner to give
    donne-moi... give me... **3A, I**
    donnez-moi... give me **3B, I**
    s'il te plaît, donne-moi... please, give me... **3B**
doré golden brown
* **dormir** to sleep
le **dos** back **E2**
douze twelve **1B**
drôle funny **12**
du *(partitive)* of the
    du matin in the morning, A.M. **4A**
    du soir in the evening, P.M. **4A**
dur hard
    des oeufs *(m.)* **durs** hard-boiled eggs
durer to last
un **DVD** DVD **9**
dynamique dynamic

E

un **échange** exchange
les **échecs** *m.* chess
une **éclosion** hatching
économiser to save money
écouter to listen to **I, 7**
  écouter la radio to listen to
    the radio **5**
l' **écran** *m.* screen *(computer)*
l' **éducation** *f.* education
  l'éducation civique civics
  l'éducation physique
    physical education
égyptien (égyptienne)
  Egyptian
électronique: une guitare
  électrique electric guitar
un **éléphant** elephant **E4**
un **élève, une élève** pupil, student
  9
élevé high
elle she, it **3C, 6, 10**
elle coûte... it costs ... **3C**
  elle est (canadienne) she's
    (Canadian) **2B**
  elle s'appelle... her name is
    ... **2B**
embrasser: je t'embrasse love
  and kisses *(at the end of a
  letter)*
un **emploi du temps** time-table *(of
  work)*
emprunter á to borrow from
en in, on, to, by
  en ce qui concerne as for
  en face opposite, across
    (the street)
  en fait in fact
  en famille at home
  en plus in addition
  en scène on stage
  en solde on sale
un(e) **enfant** child
entier (entière) entire
l' **entracte** *m.* interlude
entre between
  une entrée entry *(of a house)*
un **entretien** discussion
envers toward
l' **envie** *f.* envy; feeling
envoyer to send
  envoyer un mail to send an
    e-mail
épicé hot (spicy)
une **épicerie** grocery store
les **épinards** *m.* spinach
une **équipe** team

une **erreur** error, mistake
es *(see* **être)**
  tu es + *nationality* you are ...
    1B
  tu es + *nationality?* are you
    ...? **1B**
  tu es de...? are you from ...?
    1B
un **escalier** staircase
un **escargot** snail
l' **Espagne** *f.* Spain
espagnol Spanish **11**
  parler espagnol to speak
    Spanish **5**
un **esprit** spirit
essayer to try on, to try
l' **essentiel** *m.* the important
    thing
est *(see* **être)**
  est-ce que (qu')...? *phrase
    used to introduce a question*
    6
  c'est... it's ..., that's ... **2A,
    2C, 12**
  c'est le + *date* it's ... **4B**
  il/elle est + *nationality*
    he/she is ... **2B**
  n'est-ce pas...? isn't it? **6**
  où est...? where is ...? **6**
  quel jour est-ce? what day is
    it? **4B**
  qui est-ce? who's that (this)?
    2A, 9
l' **est** *m.* east
et and **1B, 6**
  et demi(e), et quart half past,
    quarter past **4A**
  et toi? and you? **1A**
établir to establish
un **étage** floor of a building, story
les **États-Unis** *m.* United States
l' **été** *m.* summer
  en été in (the) summer **4C**
  l'heure d'été daylight
    savings time
étendre to spread
une **étoile** star
étrange strange
étranger (étrangère) foreign
* **être** to be **6**
  être à to belong to
  être d'accord to agree **6**
une **étude** study
un **étudiant, une étudiant(e)**
    (college) student **9**
étudier to study **5, 7**
eu *(p.p. of* **avoir)** **il y a eu** there
    was

euh... er ..., uh ...
euh non... well, no
un **euro** euro; monetary unit of
    Europe
européen (européenne)
  European
eux: eux-mêmes themselves
un **examen** exam, test
  réussir à un examen to pass
    an exam, a test
un **exemple** example
par **exemple** for instance
un **exercice** exercise
  faire des exercices to
    exercise
exiger to insist
expliquer to explain
  expliquez... explain ...
exprimer to express
extérieur: à l'extérieur outside
extraordinaire extraordinary
  **il a fait un temps
    extraordinaire!** the
    weather was great!

F

face: en face (de) opposite,
  across (the street) from
facile easy **12**
faible weak
la **faim** hunger
  j'ai faim I'm hungry **3A**
  tu as faim? are you hungry?
    3A
faire to do, make **8**
  faire attention to pay
    attention, be careful **8**
  faire les magasins to go
    shopping (browsing from
    store to store)
  faire partie de to be a
    member of
  faire sauter to flip
  faire un match to play a
    game (match) **8**
  faire un voyage to take
    a trip **8**
  faire une promenade to take
    a walk **8**
fait: en fait in fact
  fait *(see* **faire):** **ça fait
    combien?** how much is
    that (it)? **3C**
  ça fait... euros that's (it's) ...
    euros **3C**

FRENCH-ENGLISH VOCABULARY

French-English Vocabulary *continued*

il fait (**beau**, etc.) it's (beautiful, etc.) *(weather)* **4C**

quel temps fait-il? what (how) is the weather? **4C**

familial with the family

une **famille** family **2C**

en **famille** at home

un **fana, une fana** fan

un **fantôme** ghost

la **farine** flour

fatigué tired

faux (fausse) false **12**

favori (favorite) favorite

les **félicitations** *f.* congratulations

une **femme** woman **9**

une **fenêtre** window **I, 9**

fermer to close **I**

une **fête** party, holiday

le **feu d'artifice** fireworks

une **feuille** sheet, leaf **I**

une **feuille de papier** sheet of paper **I**

un **feuilleton** series, serial story *(in newspaper)*

février *m.* February **4B**

la **fièvre** fever

une **fille** girl **2A**

un **film policier** detective movie

la **fin** end

flamand Flemish

un **flamant** flamingo

une **fleur** flower

un **fleuve** river

un **flic** cop *(colloq.)*

une **fois** time

à la **fois** at the same time

la **folie: à la folie** madly

folklorique: une chanson folklorique folksong

fonctionner to work, function

fondé founded

le **foot (football)** soccer

le **football américain** football

jouer au foot to play soccer **5**

une **forêt** forest

formidable great!

fort strong

plus fort louder **I**

un **fouet** whisk

la **fourrure** fur

un **manteau de fourrure** fur coat

frais: il fait frais it's cool *(weather)* **4C**

un **franc** franc *(former monetary unit of France)* **3C**

ça fait… francs that's (it's) … francs **3C**

français French **1B, 11**

comment dit-on… en français? how do you say… in French? **I**

parler français to speak French **5**

le **français** French *(language)*

un **Français, une Française** French person

la **France** France **6**

en **France** in France **6**

francophone French-speaking

un **frère** brother **2C**

les **frites** *f.* French fries

un **steak-frites** steak and French fries **3A**

froid cold

il fait froid it's cold out *(weather)* **4C**

le **fromage** cheese

un **sandwich au fromage** cheese sandwich

furieux (furieuse) furious

une **fusée** rocket

G

un **garçon** boy **2A**; waiter

une **gare** train station

une **garniture** side dish

gauche left

une **gelée** jelly

généralement generally

généreux (généreuse) generous

la **générosité** generosity

génial brilliant: terrific **12**

des **gens** *m.* people **10**

gentil (gentille) nice, kind **11**; sweet

la **géographie** geography

une **girafe** giraffe **E4**

une **glace** ice cream **3A**; mirror, ice

glacé iced

un **goûter** afternoon snack

une **goyave** guava

grand tall **9**; big, large **12**

une **grande surface** big store, self-service store

grandir to get tall; to grow up

une **grand-mère** grandmother **2C**

un **grand-père** grandfather **2C**

grec (grecque) Greek

un **grenier** attic

une **grillade** grilled meat

une **grille** grid

grillé: le pain grillé toast

une **tartine de pain grillé** buttered toast

la **grippe** flu

gris gray **12**

gros (grosse) fat, big

la **Guadeloupe** Guadeloupe *(French island in the West Indies)*

une **guerre** war

une **guitare** guitar **9**

un **gymnase** gym

H

habillé dressed

habiter (à) to live (in + *city*) **7**

Haïti Haiti *(French island in the West Indies)*

un **hamburger** hamburger **3A**

la **hâte** haste

en **hâte** quickly

haut high

plus haut above

hélas! too bad!

hésiter to hesitate

l' **heure** *f.* time, hour; o'clock **4A**

… heure(s) (dix) (ten) past … **4A**

… heure(s) et demie half past … **4A**

… heure(s) et quart quarter past … **4A**

… heure(s) moins (dix) (ten) of … **4A**

… heure(s) moins le quart quarter to … **4A**

à… heures at … o'clock **6**

à quelle heure…? at what time …? **8**

à quelle heure est…? at what time is …? **4A**

il est… heure(s) it's … o'clock **4A**

par heure per hour, an hour

quelle heure est-il? what time is it? **4A**

heureux (heureuse) happy

avant-hier the day before yesterday

un **hippopotame** hippopotamus **E4**

une **histoire** story, history

l' **hiver** *m.* winter **4C**

en hiver in (the) winter **4C**
hollandais Dutch
un **homme** man **9**
honnête honest
une **horreur** horror
  quelle horreur! what a
    scandal! how awful!
un **hot dog** hot dog **3A**
un **hôte, une hôtesse** host, hostess
un **hôtel de police** police
    department
l' **huile** f. oil
huit eight **1A**
l' **humeur** f. mood
  de bonne humeur in a good
    mood
un **hypermarché** shopping center

ici here **6**
une **idée** idea
ignorer to be unaware of
il he, it **3C, 6, 10**
  il est it is **12**
  il/elle est + *nationality*
    he/she is … **2B**
  il y a there is, there are **9**
  il y a eu there was
  il n'y a pas de… there is/are
    no … **10**
  est-ce qu'il y a…? is there,
    are there …? **9**
  qu'est-ce qu'il y a…? what is
    there …? **9**
une **île** island
illustré illustrated
l' **impératif** m. imperative
    (command) mood
impoli impolite
l' **importance** f. importance
  ça n'a pas d'importance it
    doesn't matter
importé imported
impressionnant impressive
l' **imprimante** f. printer
inactif (inactive) inactive
inclure to include
l' **indicatif** m. area code
indiquer to indicate, show
indiquez… indicate …
les **informations** f. news
l' **informatique** f. computer
    science
s' **informer (de)** to find out about
un **ingénieur** engineer

un **inspecteur, une inspectrice**
    police detective
intelligent intelligent **11**
intéressant interesting **11**
l' **intérieur** m. interior, inside
l' **Internet** m. the Internet
  surfer sur l'Internet (sur le
    Net) to surf the Internet
interroger to question
interviewer to interview
inutilement uselessly
un **inventaire** inventory
un **invité, une invitée** guest
inviter to invite **7**
israélien (israélienne) Israeli
italien (italienne) Italian **11**
un **Italien, une Italienne** Italian
    person

j' (*see* **je**)
jamais ever; never
jamais le dimanche! never on
    Sunday!
la **Jamaïque** Jamaica
une **jambe** leg **E2**
janvier m. January **4B**
japonais Japanese **11**
jaune yellow **E1, 12**
jaunir to turn yellow
je I **6**
un **jeu** (*pl.* **jeux**) game
  les jeux d'ordinateur
    computer games
  les jeux télévisés TV game
    shows
  les jeux vidéo video games
jeudi m. Thursday **4B**
jeune young **9**
les **jeunes** m. young people
un **job** (part-time) job
jouer to play **7**
  jouer aux jeux vidéo to play
    video games **5**
  **jouer au tennis (volley,
    basket, foot)** to play tennis
    (volleyball, basketball,
    soccer) **5**
un **jour** day **4B**
  le Jour de l'An New Year's
    Day
  par jour per week, a week
  quel jour est-ce? what day is
    it? **8**
un **journal** (*pl.* **journaux**)
    newspaper

une **journée** day, whole day
  bonne journée! have a nice
    day!
joyeux (joyeuse) happy
juillet m. July **8**
  le quatorze juillet Bastille
    Day (*French national
    holiday*)
juin m. June **4B**
un **jumeau** (*pl.* **jumeaux**), **une
    jumelle** twin
le **jus** juice
  le jus d'orange orange juice
    3B
  le jus de pomme apple juice
    3B
  le jus de raisin grape juice **3B**
  le jus de tomate tomato juice
    3B
jusqu'à until
juste right, fair
  le mot juste the right word

un **kangourou** kangaroo **E4**
un **kilo** kilogram

l' (*see* **le, la**)
la the **2B, 10**
là here, there **6**
  là-bas over there **6**
  ça, là-bas that (one), over
    there **9**
  oh là là! uh, oh!; oh, dear!;
    wow!; oh, yes!
laid ugly
laisser (un message) to leave (a
    message)
une **lampe** lamp **9**
une **langue** language
large wide
se **laver** to wash (oneself), wash
    up
le the **2B, 10**
  le + *number* + *month* the … **4B**
  le (lundi) on (Mondays) **10**
une **leçon** lesson
lent slow
les the **10**
une **lettre** letter
se **lever: lève-toi!** stand up! **I**
    levez-vous! stand up! **I**
un **lézard** lizard **E4**

le **Liban** Lebanon *(country in the Middle East)*
libanais Lebanese
libéré liberated
une **librairie** bookstore
libre free
un **lieu** place, area
avoir lieu to take place
une **ligne** line
limité limited
la **limonade** lemon soda **3B**
un **lion** lion **E4**
* **lire** to read
comment lire reading hints
lisez... *(see* **lire***)* read ... **I**
une **liste** list
une liste des courses shopping list
un **lit** bed **9**
un **living** living room *(informal)*
un **livre** book **I, 9**
local *(m.pl.* **locaux***)* local
une **location** rental
logique logical
logiquement logically
loin d'ici far (from here)
le **loisir** leisure, free time
un **loisir** leisure-time activity
Londres London
longtemps (for) a long time
moins longtemps que for a shorter time
le **loto** lotto, lottery, bingo
un **loup** wolf **E4**
lui-même: en lui-même to himself
lundi *m.* Monday **4B**
le **Luxembourg** Luxembourg
un **lycée** high school

M

m' *(see* **me***)*
M. (monsieur) Mr. (Mister) **1C**
ma my **2C**
et voici ma mère and this is my mother **2C**
ma chambre my bedroom **9**
une **machine** machine
une **machine à coudre** sewing machine
Madagascar Madagascar *(French-speaking island off of East Africa)*
Madame (Mme) Mrs., ma'am **1C**
Mademoiselle (Mlle) Miss **1C**

un **magasin** (department) store
faire les magasins to go shopping (browsing from store to store)
magnétique magnetic
un **magnétophone** tape recorder
un **magnétoscope** VCR (videocassette recorder)
magnifique magnificent
mai *m.* May **4B**
maigre thin, skinny
un **mail** e-mail
une **main** hand **E2**
maintenant now **7**
mais but **6**
j'aime..., mais je préfère... I like ..., but I prefer ... **5**
je regrette, mais je ne peux pas... I'm sorry, but I can't ... **5**
mais oui! sure! **6**
mais non! of course not! **6**
une **maison** house
à la maison at home **6**
mal badly, poorly **1C, 7**
ça va mal things are going badly **1C**
ça va très mal things are going very badly **1C**
c'est mal that's bad **12**
malade sick
malheureusement unfortunately
malin clever
manger to eat **7**
j'aime manger I like to eat **5**
un **manteau de fourrure** fur coat
un **marchand, une marchande** merchant, shopkeeper, dealer
un **marché** open-air market
un **marché aux puces** flea market
marcher to work, to run *(for objects)* **9**; to walk *(for people)* **9**
il/elle (ne) marche (pas) bien it (doesn't) work(s) well **9**
est-ce que la radio marche? does the radio work? **9**
mardi *m.* **Tuesday 4B**
le **Mardi gras** Shrove Tuesday
le **mariage** wedding, marriage
marié married
une **marmite** covered stew pot
le **Maroc** Morocco *(country in North Africa)*
une **marque** brand (name)
une **marraine** godmother

marrant fun
marron *(inv.)* brown **12**
mars *m.* March **4B**
martiniquais from Martinique
la **Martinique** Martinique *(French island in the West Indies)*
un **match** game, (sports) match
faire un match to play a game, (sports) match **8**
les **maths** *f.* math
le **matin** in the morning
du matin in the morning, A.M. **4A**
des **matoutou crabes** *m.* stewed crabs with rice
mauvais bad **12**
c'est une mauvaise idée that's a bad idea
il fait mauvais it's bad (weather) **4C**
méchant mean, nasty **11**
un **médecin** doctor
un médecin de nuit doctor on night duty
la **Méditerranée** Mediterranean Sea
mélanger to mix, stir
même same; even
eux-mêmes themselves
les mêmes choses the same things
une **mémoire** memory
mentionner to mention
merci thank you **1C**
oui, merci yes, thank you **5**
mercredi *m.* Wednesday **4B**
une **mère** mother **2C**
mériter to deserve
la **messagerie vocale** voice mail
le **métro** subway
mexicain Mexican **11**
midi *m.* noon **4A**
mieux better
mignon (mignonne) cute **11**
militaire military
mille one thousand **2B**
une **mini-chaîne** compact stereo **9**
minuit *m.* midnight **4A**
mixte mixed
Mlle Miss **1C**
Mme Mrs. **1C**
une **mob (mobylette)** motorbike, moped **9**
la **mode** fashion
moi me **1A**
moi, je m'appelle (Marc) me, my name is (Marc) **1A**
avec moi with me **5**

donne-moi give me **3A**
donnez-moi give me **3B**
excusez-moi... excuse me ...
  13
prête-moi... lend me ... **3C**
s'il te plaît, donne-moi...
  please give me ... **3B**
un **moine** monk
moins less
  moins de less than
  ... heure(s) moins (dix) (ten)
    of ... **4A**
  ... heure(s) moins le quart
    quarter of ... **4A**
un **mois** month **4B**
  par mois per month, a
    month
mon (ma; mes) my **2C**
  mon anniversaire est le...
    my birthday is the ... **4B**
  voici mon père this is my
    father **2C**
le **monde** world
  du monde in the world
  tout le monde everyone
la **monnaie** money; change
Monsieur (M.) Mr., sir **1C**
  un monsieur (*pl.* **messieurs**)
    gentleman, man (*polite
    term*) **2A**
une **montre** watch **9**
  montre-moi (montrez-moi)
    show me **I**
un **morceau** piece
  un morceau de craie piece of
    chalk **I**
un **mot** word
une **moto** motorcycle **9**
la **moutarde** mustard
un **mouton** sheep
  moyen (moyenne) average,
    medium
  en moyenne on the average
un **moyen** means
muet (muette) silent
le **multimédia** multimedia

n' (*see* ne)
nager to swim **7**
  j'aime nager I like to swim **5**
une **nationalité** nationality **1B**
ne (n')
  ne... aucun none, not any
  ne... pas not **6**
  ne... plus no longer

n'est-ce pas? right?, no?, isn't
  it (so)?, don't you?, aren't
  you? **6**
né born
nécessaire necessary
négatif (négative) negative
négativement negatively
la **neige** snow
  neiger to snow
  il neige it's snowing **4C**
le **Net** the Internet
neuf nine **1A**
un **neveu** (*pl.* **neveux**) nephew
un **nez** nose **E2**
une **nièce** niece
un **niveau** (*pl.* **niveaux**) level
Noël *m.* Christmas
noir black **E1, 12**
un **nom** name; noun
un **nombre** number
  nombreux (nombreuses)
    numerous
nommé named
non no **1B, 6**
  non plus neither
  mais non! of course not! **6**
le **nord** north
  le nord-est northeast
normalement normally
une **note** grade
nous we **6**
la **Nouvelle-Angleterre** New
  England
la **Nouvelle-Calédonie** New
  Caledonia (*French island in
  the South Pacific*)
novembre *m.* November **4B**
  le onze novembre Armistice
    Day
la **nuit** night
un **numéro** number

objectif (objective) objective
un **objet** object **9**
une **occasion** occasion; opportunity
occupé occupied
un **océan** ocean
octobre *m.* October **4B**
une **odeur** odor
un **oeil** (*pl.* **yeux**) eye **E2**
officiel (officielle) official
offert (*p.p. of* **offrir**) offered
* **offrir** to offer, to give
oh là là! uh,oh!, oh, dear!,
  wow!, oh, yes!

un **oiseau** (*pl.* **oiseaux**) bird
une **omelette** omelet **3A**
on one, they, you
  on est... today is ...
  on va dans un café? shall we
    go to a café?
  on y va let's go
  **comment dit-on... en
    français?** how do you say
    ... in French? **I**
un **oncle** uncle **2C**
onze eleven **1B**
opérer to operate
l' **or** *m.* gold
orange (*inv.*) orange (*color*) **E1,
  12**
une **orange** orange (*fruit*)
  le jus d'orange orange juice
    3B
un **ordinateur** computer **9**
un **ordinateur portable** laptop
  computer
une **oreille** ear **E2**
organiser to organize **7**
originairement originally
l' **origine** *f.* origin, beginning
  d'origine bretonne from
    Brittany
orthographiques: les signes *m.*
  orthographiques spelling
  marks
ou or **1B, 6**
où where **6, 8**
  où est...? where is ...? **6**
oublier to forget
l' **ouest** *m.* west
oui yes **1B, 6**
  oui, bien sûr... yes, of course
    ... **5**
  oui, d'accord... yes, okay ...
    5
  oui, j'ai... yes, I have ... **9**
  oui, merci... yes, thank you
    ... **5**
  mais oui! sure! **6**
un **ouragan** hurricane
un **ours** bear **E4**
ouvert open
* **ouvrir** to open
  ouvre... (ouvrez...) open ... **I**

pâle pale
une **panne** breakdown
  une panne d'électricité
    power failure
une **panthère** panther

FRENCH-ENGLISH VOCABULARY

une **papaye** papaya
le **papier** paper
    une feuille de papier a sheet (piece) of paper **I**
par per
    par exemple for example
    par jour per day
un **parc** park
    un parc public city park
parce que (parce qu') because **8**
paresseux (paresseuse) lazy
parfait perfect
    rien n'est parfait nothing is perfect
parfois sometimes
parisien (parisienne) Parisian
parler to speak, talk **I, 7**
    parler (français, anglais, espagnol) to speak (French, English, Spanish) **5**
un **parrain** godfather
une **partie** part
 • **partir** to leave
 à **partir de** as of, beginning
partitif (partitive) partitive
pas not
    ne... pas not **6**
    pas de not a, no, not any **10**
    pas possible not possible
    pas toujours not always **5**
    pas très bien not very well
le **passé composé** compound past tense
passionnément passionately
une **pâte** dough
patient patient
le **patinage** ice skating, roller skating
une **patinoire** skating rink
une **pâtisserie** pastry, pastry shop
une **patte** foot, paw (of bird or animal)
un **pays** country
un **PC portable** laptop computer
la **peau** skin, hide
 • **peindre** to paint
peint painted
une **pellicule** film (camera)
pénétrer to enter
pénible bothersome, a pain **12**
une **pension** inn, boarding house
Pentecôte f. Pentecost
perdu (p.p. of **perdre**) lost
un **père** father **2C**
 • **permettre** to permit
un **perroquet** parrot
une **personne** person **2A**

personnel (personnelle) personal
personnellement personally
péruvien (péruvienne) Peruvian
petit small, short **9, 12**
    il/elle est petit(e) he/she is short **9**
    un petit copain, une petite copine boyfriend, girlfriend
    plus petit(e) smaller
    le petit-fils, la petite-fille grandson, granddaughter
peu little, not much
    un peu a little, a little bit **7**
    un peu de a few
peut (see **pouvoir**)
    peut-être perhaps, maybe **6**
peux (see **pouvoir**)
    est-ce que tu peux...? can you ...? **5**
    je regrette, mais je ne peux pas... I'm sorry, but I can't ... **5**
la **photo** photography
une **phrase** sentence **I**
la **physique** physics
une **pie** magpie **E4**
un **pied** foot **E2**
piloter to pilot (a plane)
une **pincée** pinch
une **pizza** pizza **3A**
un **placard** closet
plaît: s'il te plaît please (informal) **3A**; excuse me (please)
    s'il te plaît, donne-moi... please, give me ... **3B**
    s'il vous plaît please (formal) **3B**; excuse me (please)
un **plan** map
une **plante** plant
le **plat principal** main course
un **plateau** tray
pleut: il pleut it's raining **4C**
plier to fold
plumer to pluck
plus more
    plus de more than
    plus joli que prettier than
    en plus in addition
    le plus the most
    ne... plus no longer, no more
    non plus neither
plusieurs several
une **poche** pocket

l'argent m. **de poche** allowance, pocket money
une **poêle** frying pan
un **point de vue** point of view
un **poisson** fish **E4**
    un poisson rouge goldfish
    blaff de poisson fish stew
poli polite
un **politicien, une politicienne** politician
une **pomme** apple
    le jus de pomme apple juice **3B**
    une purée de pommes de terre mashed potatoes
le **porc: une côtelette de porc** pork chop
un **portable** cell phone **9**
une **porte** door **I, 9**
un **porte-monnaie** change purse, wallet
portugais Portuguese
poser: poser une question to ask a question
une **possibilité** possibility
la **poste** post office
pouah! yuck! yech!
une **poule** hen **E4**
pour for **6**
    pour que so that
    pour qui? for whom? **8**
le **pourcentage** percentage
pourquoi why **8**
pratique practical
pratiquer to participate in
des **précisions** f. details
préféré favorite
préférer to prefer, to like (in general)
    je préfère I prefer **5**
    tu préférerais? would you prefer?
un **premier(première)** first
    le premier de l'an New Year's Day
    le premier étage second floor
    le premier mai Labor Day (in France)
    c'est le premier juin it's June first **4B**
un **prénom** first name
près near
    près d'ici nearby, near here
    tout près very close
une **présentation** appearance
    la présentation extérieure outward appearance

des **présentations** *f.* introductions
pressé in a hurry
prêt ready
un **prêt** loan
  prêter à to lend to, to loan
  prête-moi... lend me... **3C**
principalement mainly
le **printemps** spring **4C**
  au printemps in the spring **4C**
un **prix** price
un **problème** problem
un **produit** product
un **prof, une prof** teacher *(informal)* **2A, 9**
un **professeur** teacher **9**
professionnel (professionnelle) professional
un **programme** program
un **projet** plan
une **romenade** walk
  faire une promenade à pied to go for a walk **8**
* **promettre** to promise
une **promo** special sale
proposer to suggest
propre own
un **propriétaire, une propriétaire** landlord/landlady, owner
la **Provence** Provence *(province in southern France)*
pu: n'a pas pu was not able to
public: un parc public city park
  un jardin public public garden
la **publicité** commercials, advertising, publicity
une **puce** flea
  un marché aux puces flea market
puis then, also
puisque since
les **Pyrénées** (the) Pyrenees *(mountains between France and Spain)*

qu' *(see que)*
une **qualité** quality
quand when **8**
  c'est quand, ton anniversaire? when is your birthday? **4B**
quarante forty **1C**
un **quart** one quarter
  ... heure(s) et quart quarter past ... **4A**

... heure(s) moins le quart quarter of ... **4A**
quatorze fourteen **1B**
quatre four **1A**
quatre-vingt-dix ninety **2B**
quatre-vingts eighty **2B**
que that, which
que veut dire...? what does ... mean? **I**
qu'est-ce que (qu') what *(phrase used to introduce a question)* **8**
  qu'est-ce que c'est? what is it? what's that? **9**
  qu'est-ce que tu veux? what do you want? **3A**
  qu'est-ce qu'il y a? what is there? **9**; what's the matter? **9**
  qu'est-ce qui ne va pas? what's wrong?
un **Québécois, une Québécoise** person from Quebec
québécois from Quebec
quel (quelle)...! what a...!
  quel âge a ta mère/ton père? how old is your mother/your father? **2C**
  quel âge a-t-il/elle? how old is he/she? **9**
  quel âge as-tu? how old are you? **2C**
  quel jour est-ce? what day is it? **4B**
  quel temps fait-il? what's (how's) the weather? **4C**
  quelle est la date? what's the date? **4B**
  quelle heure est-il? what time is it? **4A**
  à quelle heure? at what time? **4A**
  à quelle heure est...? at what time is ...? **4A**
  de quelle couleur...? what color is ...? **12**
quelques some, a few **9**
une **question** question
une **queue** tail
qui who, whom **8**
  qui est-ce? who's that (this)? **2A, 9**
  qui se ressemble... birds of a feather ...
  à qui? to whom? **8**
  avec qui? with who(m)? **8**
  c'est qui? who's that? *(casual speech)*
  de qui? about who(m)? **8**

pour qui? for who(m)? **8**
quinze fifteen **1B**
quoi? what? **9**
quotidien (quotidienne) daily
  la vie quotidienne daily life

raconter to tell about
une **radio** radio **9**
  écouter la radio to listen to the radio **5**
une **radiocassette** boom box **9**
  une radiocassette/CD boom box with CD
raisin: le jus de raisin grape juice **3B**
une **raison** reason
rapidement rapidly
un **rapport** relationship
une **raquette** racket **9**
rarement rarely, seldom **7**
un **rayon** department *(in a store)*
réalisé made, directed
récemment recently
une **recette** recipe
recherche: un avis de recherche missing person's bulletin
un **récital** *(pl.* **récitals***)* *(musical)* recital
reconstituer to reconstruct
un **réfrigérateur** refrigerator
refuser to refuse
regarder to look at, watch **I, 7**
  regarde ça look at that **9**
  regarder la télé to watch TV **5**
un **régime** diet
  être au régime to be on a diet
régional *(m.pl.* **régionaux***)* regional
regretter to be sorry
  je regrette, mais... I'm sorry, but ... **5**
régulier (régulière) regular
une **reine** queen
rencontrer to meet
une **rencontre** meeting, encounter
un **rendez-vous** date, appointment
  j'ai un rendez-vous à... I have a date, appointment at ... **4A**
la **rentrée** first day back at school in fall
rentrer to go back, come back; to return

French-English Vocabulary **R23**

réparer to fix, repair
un **repas** meal
* **repeindre** to repaint
répéter to repeat **I**
répondre (à) to answer, respond (to) **I**
 répondez-lui (moi) answer him (me)
 répondre que oui to answer yes
une **réponse** answer
un **reportage** documentary
représenter to represent
réservé reserved
une **résolution** resolution
un **restaurant** restaurant
 au restaurant to (at) the restaurant **6**
 dîner au restaurant to have dinner at a restaurant **5**
 un restaurant trois étoiles three star restaurant
rester to stay
retard: un jour de retard one day behind
en **retard** late
retourner to return; to turn over
réussir to succeed
 réussir à un examen to pass an exam
* **revenir** to come back
revoir: au revoir! good-bye! **1C**
le **rez-de-chaussée** ground floor
un **rhinocéros** rhinoceros **E4**
riche rich
rien (de) nothing
 rien n'est parfait nothing is perfect
 ne… rien nothing
une **rive** (river) bank
une **rivière** river, stream
le **riz** rice
une **robe** dress
le **roller** in-line skating
romain Roman
le **rosbif** roast beef
rose pink **12**
rosse nasty *(colloq.)*
une **rôtie** toast *(Canadian)*
rôtir to roast
une **roue** wheel
rouge red **E1, 12**
rougir to turn red
rouler to roll
roux (rousse) red-head
une **rue** street

dans la rue (Victor Hugo) on (Victor Hugo) street
russe Russian

S

sa his, her
un **sac** book bag, bag **I**; bag, handbag **9**
sais *(see* **savoir***)*
 je sais I know **I, 9**
 je ne sais pas I don't know **I, 9**
 tu sais you know
une **saison** season **4C**
 toute saison all year round (any season)
une **salade** salad **3A;** lettuce
un **salaire** salary
une **salle** hall, large room
 une salle à manger dining room
 une salle de bains bathroom
 une salle de séjour informal living room
 un salon formal living room
salut! hi!; good-bye! **1C**
une **salutation** greeting
samedi Saturday **4B**
 samedi soir Saturday night
 à samedi! see you Saturday! **4B**
 le samedi on Saturdays **10**
une **sandale** sandal
un **sandwich** sandwich **3A**
sans without
des **saucisses** *f.* sausages
le **saucisson** salami
* **savoir** to know *(information)*
 je sais I know **I, 9**
 je ne sais pas I don't know **I, 9**
 tu sais you know
un **saxo (saxophone)** saxophone
une **scène** scene, stage
les **sciences** *f.* économiques economics
les **sciences** *f.* naturelles natural science
un **scooter** motor scooter **9**
second second
seize sixteen **1B**
un **séjour** stay; informal living room
le **sel** salt
selon according to
 selon toi in your opinion

une **semaine** week **4B**
 cette semaine this week
 la semaine dernière last week
 la semaine prochaine next week
 par semaine per week, a week
semblable similar
le **Sénégal** Senegal *(French-speaking country in Africa)*
sensationnel (sensationnelle) sensational
séparer to separate
sept seven **1A**
septembre *m.* September **4B**
une **série** series
sérieux (sérieuse) serious
un **serveur, une serveuse** waiter, waitress
servi served
une **serviette** napkin
ses his, her
seul alone, only; by oneself
seulement only, just
un **short** shorts
si if, whether
si! so, yes! *(to a negative question)* **10**
un **signal** *(pl.* **signaux***)* signal
un **signe** sign
 un signe orthographique spelling mark
un **singe** monkey **E4**
situé situated
six six **1A**
le **skate** skateboarding
 faire du skate to go skateboarding
un **skate** skateboard
le **ski** skiing
le **ski nautique** waterskiing
 faire du ski to ski
 faire du ski nautique to go water-skiing
skier to ski
snob snobbish
le **snowboard** snowboarding
 faire du snowboard to go snowboarding
un **snowboard** snowboard
la **Société Nationale des Chemins de Fer (SNCF)** *French railroad system*
une **société** society
un **soda** soda **3B**
une **soeur** sister **2C**
la **soie** silk

la **soif** thirst
    avoir soif to be thirsty
    j'ai soif I'm thirsty **3B**
    tu as soif? are you thirsty? **3B**
un **soir** evening
    ce soir this evening, tonight
    demain soir tomorrow night (evening)
    du soir in the evening, P.M. **4A**
    hier soir last night
    le soir in the evening
une **soirée** (whole) evening; (evening) party
    soixante sixty **1C**, **2A**
    soixante-dix seventy **2A**
un **soldat** soldier
un **solde** (clearance) sale
    en solde on sale
la **sole** sole (fish)
le **soleil** sun
    les lunettes f. **de soleil** sunglasses
    sommes (see être)
    nous sommes... it is, today is ... (date)
    son (sa; ses) his, her
un **sondage** poll
une **sorte** sort, type, kind
   * **sortir** to leave, come out
un **souhait** wish
la **soupe** soup
une **souris** mouse (computer)
    sous under **9**
le **sous-sol** basement
    souvent often **7**
    soyez (see être): soyez
les **spaghetti** m. spaghetti
    spécialement especially
    spécialisé specialized
une **spécialité** specialty
le **sport** sports
    faire du sport to play sports
    des vêtements m. **de sport** sports clothing
    une voiture de sport sports car
    sportif (sportive) athletic **11**
un **stade** stadium
un **stage** sports training camp; internship
une **station-service** gas station
un **steak** steak **3A**
    un steak-frites steak and French fries **3A**
un **stylo** pen **I, 9**
le **sucre** sugar

le **sud** south
    suggérer to suggest
    suis (see être)
    je suis + nationality I'm ... **1B**
    je suis de... I'm from... **1B**
    suisse Swiss **11**
la **Suisse** Switzerland
    suivant following
    suivi followed
un **sujet** subject, topic
    super terrific **7**; great **12**
un **supermarché** supermarket
    supersonique supersonic
    supérieur superior
    supplémentaire supplementary, extra
    sur on **9**; about
    sûr sure, certain
    bien sûr! of course! **6**
    oui, bien sûr... yes, of course ...! **5**
    tu es sûr(e)? are you sure?
    sûrement surely
la **surface: une grande surface** big store, self-service store
    surfer to go snowboarding
    surfer sur l'Internet (sur le Net) to surf the Internet
    surtout especially
un **survêtement** jogging or track suit
un **sweat** sweatshirt
une **sweaterie** shop specializing in sweatshirts and sportswear
    sympa nice, pleasant (colloq.)
    sympathique nice, pleasant **11**
une **synagogue** Jewish temple or synagogue
un **synthétiseur** electronic keyboard, synthesizer

    t' (see te)
    ta your **2C**
une **table** table **I, 9**
    mettre la table to set the table
un **tableau** (pl. **tableaux**) chalkboard **I**
    Tahiti Tahiti (French island in the South Pacific)
une **taille** size
    de taille moyenne of medium height or size
un **tailleur** woman's suit

se **taire: tais-toi!** be quiet!
une **tante** aunt **2C**
la **tarte** pie
une **tasse** cup
un **taxi** taxi
    en taxi by taxi
    te (to) you
un **tee-shirt** T-shirt
la **télé** TV **9**
    à la télé on TV
    regarder la télé TV **5**
    télécharger to download
un **téléphone** telephone **9**
    téléphoner (à) to call, phone **5, 7**
    télévisé: des jeux m. **télévisés** TV game shows
un **temple** Protestant church
le **temps** time; weather
    combien de temps? how long?
    de temps en temps from time to time
    quel temps fait-il? what's (how's) the weather? **4C**
    tout le temps all the time
le **tennis** tennis
    jouer au tennis to play tennis **5**
    des tennis m. tennis shoes, sneakers
un **terrain de sport** (playing) field
une **terrasse** outdoor section of a café, terrace
la **terre** earth
    une pomme de terre potato
    terrifiant terrifying
    tes your
la **tête** head **E2**
le **thé** tea **3B**
    un thé glacé iced tea
un **théâtre** theater
le **thon** tuna
    tiens! look!, hey! **2A, 10**
un **tigre** tiger **E4**
    timide timid, shy **11**
le **tissu** fabric
un **titre** title
    toi you
    avec toi with you **5**
    et toi? and you? **1A**
les **toilettes** f. bathroom, toilet
un **toit** roof
une **tomate** tomato
    le jus de tomate tomato juice **3B**
un **tombeau** tomb
    ton (ta; tes) your **2C**

French-English Vocabulary *continued*

c'est quand, ton
anniversaire? when's your
birthday? **4B**
tort: avoir tort to be wrong
une **tortue** turtle **E4**
un bifteck de tortue turtle
steak
toujours always **7**
je n'aime pas toujours…
I don't always like … **5**
un **tour** turn
à votre tour it's your turn
la **Touraine** Touraine *(province in
central France)*
tourner to turn
la **Toussaint** All Saints' Day
(November 1)
tout (toute; tous, toutes) all,
every, the whole
tous les jours every day
tout ça all that
tout le monde everyone
tout le temps all the time
toutes sortes all sorts, kinds
tout completely, very
tout droit straight
tout de suite right away
tout près very close
tout all, everything
pas du tout not at all
un **train** train
tranquille quiet
laisse-moi tranquille! leave
me alone!
un **travail** *(pl.* **travaux)** job
travailler to work **5, 7**
une **traversée** crossing
treize thirteen **1B**
trente thirty **1C**
un **tréma** diaeresis
très very **11**
très bien very well **7**
ça va très bien things are
going very well **1C**
ça va très mal things are
going very badly **1C**
trois three **1A**
troisième third
en troisième ninth grade *(in
France)*
trop too, too much
trouver to find, to think of
comment trouves-tu…?
what do you think of …?;
how do you find …?
s'y trouve is there
tu you **6**
la **Tunisie** Tunisia *(country in North
Africa)*

U

un, une one **1A**; a, an **2A, 10**
unique only
uniquement only
une **université** university, college
l' **usage** *m.* use
un **ustensile** utensil
utile useful
utiliser to use
en utilisant (by) using
utilisez… use …

V

va *(see* **aller)**
va-t'en! go away!
ça va? how are you? how's
everything? **1C**
ça va! everything's fine
(going well); fine, I'm OK
1C
on va dans un café? shall we
go to a café?
on y va let's go
les **vacances** *f.* vacation
bonnes vacances! have a
nice vacation!
en vacances on vacation **6**
les grandes vacances
summer vacation
une **vache** cow
vais *(see* **aller): je vais** I'm going
la **vaisselle** dishes
faire la vaisselle to do the
dishes
valable valid
une **valise** suitcase
vanille: une glace à la vanille
vanilla ice cream
varié varied
les **variétés** *f.* variety show
vas (see **aller)**
comment vas-tu? how are
you? **1C**
vas-y! come on!, go ahead!,
do it!
le **veau** veal
une **vedette** star
un **vélo** bicycle **9**
à vélo by bicycle
faire une promenade à vélo
to go for a bicycle ride
un vélo tout terrain (un VTT)
mountain bike
un **vendeur, une vendeuse**
salesperson

vendre to sell
vendredi *m.* Friday **4B**
vendu *(p.p. of* **vendre)** sold
* **venir** to come
le **vent** wind
une **vente** sale
le **ventre** stomach **E2**
venu *(p.p. of* **venir)** came, come
vérifier to check
la **vérité** truth
un **verre** glass
verser to pour
vert green **E1, 12**
les haricots *m.* verts green
beans
une **veste** jacket
des **vêtements** *m.* clothing
des vêtements de sport
sports clothing
veut *(see* **vouloir): que veut
dire…?** what does …
mean? **I**
veux *(see* **vouloir)**
est-ce que tu veux…? do
you want …? **5**
je ne veux pas… I don't want
… **5**
je veux… I want … **5**
je veux bien… I'd love to,
I do, I want to … **5**
qu'est-ce que tu veux? what
do you want? **3A**
tu veux…? do you want …?
3A
la **viande** meat
la **vie** life
la **vie quotidienne** daily life
viens *(see* **venir)**
viens… come … oui, je viens
yes, I'm coming along with
you
vieux (vieil, vieille; *m.pl.***vieux)**
old
le **Vieux Carré** the French Quarter
in New Orleans
le **Viêt-nam** Vietnam *(country in
Southeast Asia)*
vietnamien (vietnamienne)
Vietnamese
une **vigne** vineyard
un **village** town, village
un petit village small town
une **ville** city
en ville in town, **6**
une grande ville big city,
town
le **vin** wine
vingt twenty **1B, 1C**

violet (violette) purple, violet **E1**

un **violon** violin

une **visite** visit

  rendre visite à to visit *(a person)*

  visiter to visit *(places)*

  vite! fast!, quick!

  vive: vive les vacances! three cheers for vacation!

* **vivre** to live

le **vocabulaire** vocabulary

  voici... here is, this is…, here come(s) … **2A**

  voici + du, de la *(partitive)* here's some

  voici mon père/ma mère here's my father/my mother **2C**

  voilà... there is …, there come(s) … **2A**

  voilà + du, de la *(partitive)* there's some

la **voile** sailing

  faire de la voile to sail

  la planche à voile windsurfing

* **voir** to see

  voir un film to see a movie

un **voisin, une voisine** neighbor **9**

une **voiture** car **9**

  une voiture de sport sports car

  en voiture by car

  faire une promenade en voiture to go for a drive by car

une **voix** voice

le **volley (volleyball)** volleyball

un **volontaire, une volontaire** volunteer

  comme volontaire as a volunteer

  vos your

  votre *(pl.* **vos)** your

  voudrais *(see* **vouloir): je voudrais** I'd like **3A, 3B, 5**

* **vouloir** to want

  vouloir + du, de la *(partitive)* to want some (of something)

  vouloir dire to mean

  voulu *(p.p. of* **vouloir)** wanted

  vous you **6;** (to) you

  vous désirez? what would you like? may I help you? **3B**

  s'il vous plaît please **3B**

un **voyage** trip

  bon voyage! have a nice trip!

  faire un voyage to take a trip **8**

  voyager to travel **5, 7**

  vrai true, right, real **12**

  vraiment really

le **VTT** mountain biking

  faire du VTT to go mountain biking

  un VTT mountain bike

  vu *(p.p. of* **voir)** saw, seen

une **vue** view

  un point de vue point of view

les **WC** *m.* toilet

un **week-end** weekend

  bon week-end! have a nice weekend!

  ce week-end this weekend

  le week-end on weekends

  le week-end dernier last weekend

  le week-end prochain next weekend

y there

  il y a there is, there are **9**

  est-ce qu'il y a...? is there …?, are there …? **9**

  qu'est-ce qu'il y a? what is there? **9**

  allons-y! let's go!

  vas-y! come on!, go ahead!, do it!

le **yaourt** yogurt

des **yeux** *m. (sg.* **oeil)** eyes **E3**

un **zèbre** zebra

  zéro zero **1A**

  zut! darn! **1C**

English-French Vocabulary

The English-French vocabulary contains only active vocabulary.

The numbers following an entry indicate the lesson in which the word or phrase is activated. (**I** stands for the list of classroom expressions at the end of the first Images section; **E** stands for Entracte.)

Nouns: If the article of a noun does not indicate gender, the noun is followed by *m. (masculine)* or *f. (feminine)*. If the plural *(pl.)* is irregular, it is given in parentheses.

Verbs: Verbs are listed in the infinitive form. An asterisk (*) in front of an active verb means that it is irregular. (For forms, see the verb charts in Appendix 4C.)

Words beginning with an **h** are preceded by a bullet (•) if the **h** is aspirate; that is, if the word is treated as if it begins with a consonant sound.

A

a
 a, an un, une **2A, 10**
 a few quelques **9**
 a little (bit) un peu **7**
 a lot beaucoup **7**
about whom? de qui? **8**
 are you acquainted with …? tu connais…? **2B**
afternoon: in the afternoon de l'après-midi **4A**
to **agree** *être d'accord **6**
all right d'accord **5**
also aussi **1B, 7**
always toujours **7**
 not always pas toujours **5**
A.M. du matin **4A**
am *(see* to be)
 I am … je suis + *nationality* **1B**
American américain **2**
 I'm American je suis américain(e) **1B, 11**
amusing amusant **11**
an un, une **2A, 10**
and et **1B, 6**
 and you? et toi? **1A**
annoying pénible **12**
any des, du, de, la, de l', de
 not any pas de **10**
apple juice le jus de pomme **3B**
appointment un rendez-vous
 I have an appointment at… j'ai un rendez-vous à… **4A**
April avril *m.* **4B**
are *(see* to be)
 are there? est-ce qu'il y a? **9**
 are you…? tu es + *nationality?* **1B**

there are il y a **9**
these/those/they are ce sont **12**
arm un bras **E2**
at à **6**
 at … o'clock à … heure(s) **6**
 at home à la maison **6**
 at the restaurant au restaurant **6**
 at what time? à quelle heure? **4A, 8**
 at what time is …? à quelle heure est …? **4A**
athletic sportif (sportive) **11**
attention: to pay attention *faire attention **8**
August août *m.* **4B**
aunt une tante **2C**
automobile une auto, une voiture **9**
autumn l'automne *m.*
 in (the) autumn en automne **4C**

B

back le dos **E2**
 back: in back of derrière **9**
bad mauvais **12**
 I'm/everything's (very) bad ça va (très) mal **1C**
 it's bad (weather) il fait mauvais **4C**
 that's bad c'est mal **12**
 too bad! dommage! **7**
badly mal **1C**
 things are going (very) badly ça va (très) mal **1C**
bag un sac **I, 9**

to be *être **6**
 to be … (years old) *avoir… ans **10**
 to be careful *faire attention **8**
 to be cold *(weather)* il fait froid **4C**
 to be hot *(weather)* il fait chaud **4C**
 to be hungry *avoir faim **10**
 to be thirsty *avoir soif **10**
beautiful beau (bel, belle; *m.pl.* beaux) **9**
 it's beautiful (nice) weather il fait beau **4C**
because parce que (qu') **8**
bed un lit **9**
bedroom une chambre **9**
behind derrière **9**
beverage une boisson **3B**
bicycle un vélo, une bicyclette **9**
big grand **9, 12**
birthday un anniversaire **4B**
 my birthday is (March 2) mon anniversaire est le (2 mars) **4B**
 when is your birthday? c'est quand, ton anniversaire? **4B**
bit: a little bit un peu **7**
black noir **E1, 12**
blond blond **9**
blue bleu **E1, 12**
book un livre **I, 9**
boom box une radiocassette **9**
bothersome pénible **12**
boy le garçon **2A, 2B**
brother un frère **2C,**
brown brun **9**; marron *(inv.)* **12**
but mais **5**

C

café un café **6**
  at (to) the café au café **6**
calculator une calculatrice **9**
to **call** téléphoner **7**
camera un appareil-photo (*pl.* appareils-photo) **9**
can you …? est-ce que tu peux…? **5**
  I can't je ne peux pas **5**
Canadian canadien (canadienne) **1B, 11**
  he's/she's (Canadian) il/elle est (canadien/canadienne) **2B**
cannot: I cannot je ne peux pas **5**
  I'm sorry, but I cannot je regrette, mais je ne peux pas **5**
car une auto, une voiture **9**
careful: to be careful *faire attention **8**
cat un chat **2C**
CD-ROM un cédérom (un CD-ROM)
chair une chaise **I, 9**
chalk la craie **I**
  piece of chalk un morceau de craie **I**
chalkboard un tableau (*pl.* tableaux) **I**
Chinese chinois **11**
chocolate: hot chocolate un chocolat **3B**
cinema le cinéma **6**
  to the cinema au cinéma **6**
city: in the city en ville **6**
class une classe **6**
  in class en classe **6**
classmate un (une) camarade **9**
coffee le café **3B**
cold le froid
  it's cold (*weather*) il fait froid **4C**
college student un étudiant, une étudiante **9**
color une couleur **12**
  what color? de quelle couleur? **12**
come: here comes … voici… **2A**
compact disc un compact (disc), un CD **9**

computer un ordinateur, un PC **9**
cool: it's cool (*weather*) il fait frais **4C**
to **cost** coûter
  how much does … cost? combien coûte…? **3C**
  it costs … il/elle coûte… **3C**
course: of course! bien sûr! **5**; mais oui! **6**
  of course not! mais non! **6**
cousin un cousin, une cousine **2C**
crepe une crêpe **3A**
croissant un croissant **3A**
cute mignon (mignonne) **11**

D

to **dance** danser **5, 7**
dark-haired brun **9**
darn! zut! **1C**
date la date **4B**
  I have a date at … j'ai un rendez-vous à… **4A**
  what's the date? quelle est la date? **4B**
day un jour **4B**
  what day is it? quel jour est-ce? **4B**
December décembre *m.* **4B**
desk un bureau **I, 9**
difficult difficile **12**
  to have (eat) dinner dîner **7**
  to have dinner at a restaurant dîner au restaurant **5**
to **do** *faire **8**
dog un chien **2C**
door une porte **I, 9**
downtown en ville **6**
drink une boisson **3B**
dumb bête **11**
DVD un DVD **9**

E

ear une oreille **E2**
easy facile **12**
to **eat** manger **7**
  I like to eat j'aime manger **5**
  to eat dinner dîner **7**
eight huit **1A**
eighteen dix-huit **1B**

eighty quatre-vingts **2B**
elephant un éléphant **E4**
eleven onze **1B, 3C**
English anglais(e) **1B, 11**
evening: in the evening du soir **4A**
everything tout
  everything's going (very) well ça va (très) bien **1C**
  everything's (going) so-so ça va comme ci, comme ça **1C**
  how's everything? ça va? **1C**
eye un oeil (*pl.* yeux) **E2**

F

fall l'automne **4C**
  in (the) fall en automne **4C**
false faux (fausse) **12**
family une famille **2C**
father: this is my father voici mon père **2C**
February février *m.* **4B**
few: a few quelques **9**
fifteen quinze **1B**
fifty cinquante **1C**
fine ça va **1C**
fine! d'accord **5**
  everything's fine ça va bien **1C**
  it's (June) first c'est le premier (juin) **4B**
five cinq **1A**
foot un pied **E2**
for pour **6**
  for whom? pour qui? **8**
forty quarante **1C**
four quatre **1A**
fourteen quatorze **1B**
franc (former monetary unit of France) un franc **3C**
  that's (it's) … francs ça fait…francs **3C**
France la France **6**
  in France en France **6**
  French français(e) **1B, 11**
  how do you say … in French? comment dit-on… en français? **I**
  French fries des frites *f.*
  steak and French fries un steak-frites **3A**
Friday vendredi *m.* **4B**

friend un ami, une amie **2A;** un copain, une copine **2A**
  boyfriend, girlfriend un petit copain, une petite copine
  school friend un (une) camarade **9**
from de **6**
  are you from …? tu es de…? **1B**
  I'm from … je suis de… **1B**
  front: in front of devant **9**
funny amusant **11**; drôle **12**

game un match
  to play a game (match) *faire un match **8**
gentleman un monsieur (*pl.* messieurs) **2A**
girl une fille **2A**
to **give** donner
  give me donne-moi, donnez-moi **3A, 3B**
  please give me s'il te plaît donne-moi **3B**
good bon (bonne) **12**
  good morning (afternoon) bonjour **1A**
  that's good c'est bien **12**
  the weather's good (pleasant) il fait bon **4C**
  good-bye! au revoir!, salut! **1C**
  good-looking beau (bel, belle; *m.pl.* beaux) **9, 12**
grandfather un grand-père **2C**
grandmother une grand-mère **2C**
grape juice le jus de raisin **3B**
gray gris **12**
great super **12**
green vert **E1, 12**
guitar une guitare **9**

hair les cheveux *m.* **E2**
  he/she has dark hair il/elle est brun(e) **9**
half: half past … … heure(s) et demie **4A**
  half past midnight minuit et demi **4A**

half past noon midi et demi **4A**
hamburger un hamburger **3A**
hand une main **E2**
handbag un sac **9**
handsome beau (bel, belle; *m.pl.* beaux) **9, 12**
hard difficile **12**
to **have** *avoir **10**
  do you have …? est-ce que tu as…? **9**
  I have j'ai **9**
  I have to (must) je dois **5**
  to have dinner at a restaurant dîner au restaurant **5**
he il **3C, 6, 10**
he/she is … il/elle est + *nationality* **2B**
head la tête **E2**
hello bonjour **1A, 1C**
help: may I help you? vous désirez? **3B**
her: her name is … elle s'appelle… **2B**
  what's her name? comment s'appelle-t-elle? **9**
here ici **6**
  here comes, here is voici **2A**
  here's my mother/father voici ma mère/mon père **2C**
hey! dis! **12**; tiens! **2A, 10**
  hey there! dis donc! **12**
hi! salut! **1C**
high school student un (une) élève **9**
his: his name is … il s'appelle… **2B**
  what's his name? comment s'appelle-t-il? **9**
home, at home à la maison **6**; chez (moi, toi…) **15**
homework assignment un devoir **I**
horse un cheval (*pl.* chevaux) **E4**
hot chaud **4C**
  hot chocolate un chocolat **3B**
  hot dog un •hot dog **3A**
  it's hot (*weather*) il fait chaud **4C**
how? comment? **8**
  how are you? comment allez-vous?, comment vas-tu?, ça va? **1C**

how do you say … in French? comment dit-on… en français? **I**
how much does … cost? combien coûte…? **3C**
how much is that/this/it? c'est combien?, ça fait combien? **3C**
how old are you? quel âge as-tu? **2C**
how old is he/she? quel âge a-t-il/elle? **9**
how old is your father/mother? quel âge a ton père/ta mère? **2C**
how's everything? ça va? **1C**
how's the weather? quel temps fait-il? **4C**
hundred cent **2B**
hungry avoir faim **3A**
  are you hungry? tu as faim? **3A**
  I'm hungry j'ai faim **3A**
  to be hungry avoir faim **10**

I je **6**
  I don't know je ne sais pas **I, 9**
  I have a date/appointment at … j'ai un rendez-vous à… **4A**
  I know je sais **I, 9**
  I'm fine/okay ça va **1C**
  I'm (very) well/so-so/(very) bad ça va (très) bien/comme ci, comme ça/(très) mal **1C**
ice la glace **3A**
ice cream une glace **3A**
in à **6**; dans **9**
  in (Boston) à (Boston) **6**
  in class en classe **6**
  in front of devant **9**
  in the afternoon de l'après-midi **4A**
  in the morning/evening du matin/soir **4A**
  in town en ville **6**
to **indicate** indiquer
interesting intéressant **11**
to **invite** inviter **7**
is (*see* **to be**)
  is there? est-ce qu'il y a? **9**
  isn't it (so)? n'est-ce pas? **6**

there is il y a **9**
it il, elle **6, 10**
   it's ... c'est… **2A**
   it's ... (o'clock) il est…
      heure(s) **4A**
   it's ... euros ça fait… euros
      3C
   it's fine/nice/hot/cool/
      cold/bad (*weather*) il fait
      beau/bon/chaud/frais/
      froid/mauvais **4C**
   it's (June) first c'est
      le premier (juin) **4B**
   it's not ce n'est pas **12**
   it's raining il pleut **4C**
   it's snowing il neige **4C**
   what time is it? quelle heure
      est-il? **4A**
   who is it? qui est-ce? **2A, 9**
Italian italien, italienne **11**

January janvier *m.* **4B**
Japanese japonais(e) **11**
juice le jus
   apple juice le jus
      de pomme **3B**
   grape juice le jus
      de raisin **3B**
   orange juice le jus
      d'orange **3B**
   tomato juice le jus
      de tomate **3B**
July juillet *m.* **4B**
June juin *m.* **4B**

kind gentil (gentille) **11**
know connaître (*people*); savoir
   (*facts*)
   do you know ...? tu
      connais…? **2B**
   I (don't) know je (ne) sais
      (pas) **I, 9**

lady une dame **2A**
lamp une lampe **9**
large grand **9, 12**
left gauche

---

on (to) the left à gauche **13**
leg une jambe **E2**
lemon soda la limonade **3B**
lend me prête-moi **3C**
like: what does he/she look
   like? comment est-il/elle? **9**
   what's he/she like?
      comment est-il/elle? **9**
   to like aimer **7**
   do you like? est-ce que tu
      aimes? **5**
   I also like j'aime aussi **5**
   I don't always like je n'aime
      pas toujours **5**
   I don't like je n'aime pas **5**
   I like j'aime **5**
   I like ..., but I prefer ...
      j'aime…, mais je préfère…
      5
   I'd like je voudrais **3A, 3B, 5**
   what would you like? vous
      désirez? **3B**
to listen écouter **7**
   to listen to the radio écouter
      la radio **5**
   little petit **9, 12**
   a little (bit) un peu **7**
to live habiter **7**
to look (at) regarder **7**
   look! tiens! **2A, 10**
   look at that regarde ça **9**
   what does he/she look like?
      comment est-il/elle? **9**
   lot: a lot beaucoup **7**
to love: I'd love to je veux bien **5**

to make *faire **8**
man un homme **9;** un
      monsieur (*polite term*) **2A**
many beaucoup (de) **7**
map une carte **I**
March mars m. **4B**
match un match **8**
   to play a match *faire
      un match **8**
May mai m. **4B**
maybe peut-être **6**
me moi **1A**
mean méchant **11**
   what does ... mean? que
      veut dire…? **I**
Mexican mexicain(e) **11**
midnight minuit m. **4A**
Miss Mademoiselle (Mlle) **1C**

Monday lundi m. **4B**
month un mois **4B**
moped une mob (mobylette) **9**
morning: good morning
      bonjour **1A**
   in the morning du matin **4A**
mother une mère **2C**
   this is my mother voici ma
      mère **2C**
motorbike une mob
      (mobylette) **9**
motorcycle une moto **9**
motorscooter un scooter **9**
mouth une bouche **E2**
movie theater un cinéma **6**
   at (to) the movies au
      cinéma **6**
Mr. Monsieur (M.) **1C**
Mrs. Madame (Mme) **1C**
much, very much beaucoup **7**
   how much does ... cost?
      combien coûte…? **3C**
   how much is it? ça fait
      combien?, c'est combien?
      3C
must: I must je dois **5**
my mon, ma; mes **2C**
   my birthday is (March 2)
      mon anniversaire est le (2
      mars) **4B**
   my name is ... je
      m'appelle… **1A**

name: his/her name is ...
      il/elle s'appelle... **2B**
   my name is ... je
      m'appelle… **1A**
   what's...'s name? comment
      s'appelle…? **2B**
   what's his/her name?
      comment s'appelle-t-
      il/elle? **9**
   what's your name?
      comment t'appelles-tu? **1A**
nasty méchant **11**
nationality la nationalité **1B**
neat chouette **12**
neck le cou **E2**
neighbor un voisin, une
      voisine **9**
nice gentil (gentille),
      sympathique **11**
   it's nice (beautiful) weather il
      fait beau **4C**

night: tomorrow night demain soir **4A**
nine neuf **1A**
nineteen dix-neuf **1B**
ninety quatre-vingt-dix **2B**
no non **1B, 6**
  no ... pas de **10**
  no? n'est-ce pas? **6**
noon midi *m.* **4A**
nose le nez **E2**
not ne... pas **6**
  not a, not any pas de **10**
  not always pas toujours **5**
  it's (that's) not ce n'est pas **12**
  of course not! mais non! **6**
notebook un cahier **I, 9**
November novembre *m.* **4B**
now maintenant **7**

o'clock heure(s)
  at ... o'clock à... heures **4A**
  it's ... o'clock il est... heure(s) **4A**
object un objet **9**
October octobre *m.* **4B**
of de **6**
  of course not! mais non! **6**
  of course! bien sûr **5**
  of whom de qui **8**
often souvent **7**
oh: oh, really? ah, bon? **8**
okay d'accord **5**
  I'm okay ça va **1C**
old: he/she is ... (years old) il/elle a... ans **2C**
  how old are you? quel âge as-tu? **2C**
  how old is he/she? quel âge a-t-il/elle? **9**
  how old is your father/mother? quel âge a ton père/ta mère? **2C**
  I'm ... (years old) j'ai... ans **2C**
  to be ... (years old) *avoir ... ans **10**
omelet une omelette **3A**
on sur **9**
  on Monday lundi **10**
  on Mondays le lundi **10**
  on vacation en vacances **6**
one un, une **1**
open *ouvrir

open ... ouvre... (ouvrez...) **I**
or ou **1B, 6**
orange (*color*) orange (*inv.*) **E1, 12**
  orange juice le jus d'orange **3B**
to **organize** organiser **7**
over there là-bas **6**
  that (one), over there ça, là-bas **9**
to **own** *avoir **10**

P.M. du soir **4A**
pain: a pain pénible **12**
paper le papier **I**
  sheet of paper une feuille de papier **I**
past: half past ... ... heure(s) et demie **4A**
  quarter past ... ... heure(s) et quart **4A**
to **pay: to pay attention** *faire attention **8**
pen un stylo **I, 9**
pencil un crayon **I, 9**
people des gens *m.* **10**
perhaps peut-être **6**
person une personne **2A, 9**
pet un animal (*pl.* animaux) domestique **2C**
to **phone** téléphoner **7**
piece: piece of chalk un morceau de craie **I**
pink rose **12**
pizza une pizza **3A**
to **play** jouer **7**
  to play a game (match) *faire un match **8**
  to play basketball (soccer, tennis, volleyball) jouer au basket (au foot, au tennis, au volley) **5**
pleasant sympathique **11**
  it's pleasant (good) weather il fait bon **4C**
please s'il vous plaît (*formal*) **3B**; s'il te plaît (*informal*) **3A**
  please give me ... s'il te plaît, donne-moi... **3B**
poorly mal **1C**
poster une affiche **9**
to **prefer: I prefer** je préfère + *inf.* **5**

I like ..., but I prefer ... j'aime..., mais je préfère... **5**
pretty joli **9**
pupil un (une) élève **9**
purple violet (violette) **E1**

quarter un quart
  quarter of ... ... heure(s) moins le quart **4A**
  quarter past ... ... heure(s) et quart **4A**

R

racket une raquette **9**
radio une radio **9**
  to listen to the radio écouter la radio **5**
rain: it's raining il pleut **4C**
rarely rarement **7**
rather assez **11**
really: oh, really? ah, bon? **8**
red rouge **E1, 12**
  at (to) the restaurant au restaurant **6**
  have dinner at a restaurant dîner au restaurant **5**
right vrai **12**; droite
  right? n'est-ce pas? **6**
  all right d'accord **5**
room une chambre **9**; une salle
to **run** (*referring to objects*) marcher **9**

S

salad une salade **3A**
same: the same things les mêmes choses
sandwich un sandwich **3A**
Saturday samedi *m.* **4B, 23**
  see you Saturday! à samedi! **4B**
say ... dites...
  say! dis (donc)! **12**
  how do you say ... in French? comment dit-on... en français? **I**

school friend un (une) camarade **9**

season une saison **4C**

see you tomorrow! à demain! **4B**

seldom rarement **7**

September septembre *m.* **4B**

seven sept **1A**

seventeen dix-sept **1B**

seventy soixante-dix **2A**

she elle **6, 10, 15**

sheet of paper une feuille de papier **I**

short court; petit **9, 12**
  he/she is short il/elle est petit(e) **9**

to **shut** fermer **I**

shy timide **11**

silly bête **11**

to **sing** chanter **5, 7**

sir Monsieur (M.) **1C**

sister une soeur **2C**

six six **1A**

sixteen seize **1B**

sixty soixante **1C, 2A**

small petit **9, 12**

snow: it's snowing il neige **4C**

so alors **7**
  so-so comme ci, comme ça **1C**
  everything's (going) so-so ça va comme ci, comme ça **1C**

soda un soda **3B**
  lemon soda une limonade **3B**

some des **10**; quelques **9**; du, de la, de l'

sorry: to be sorry regretter
  I'm sorry, but (I cannot) je regrette, mais (je ne peux pas) **5**

Spanish espagnol(e) **11**

to **speak** parler **7**
  to speak (French, English, Spanish) parler (français, anglais, espagnol) **5**

spring le printemps **4C**
  in the spring au printemps **4C**

steak un steak **3A**
  steak and French fries un steak-frites **3A**

stereo set une chaîne stéréo **9**

stomach le ventre **E2**

student (*high school*) un (une) élève **9**; (*college*) un étudiant, une étudiante **9**

to **study** étudier **5, 7**

stupid bête **11**

summer l'été *m.* **4C**
  in the summer en été **4C**

Sunday dimanche *m.* **4B**

supper: to have (eat) supper dîner **7**

sure bien sûr **5**
  sure! mais oui! **6**

to **swim** nager **7**
  I like to swim j'aime nager **5**

Swiss suisse **11**

table une table **I, 9**

to **take** *prendre **I**
  to take a trip *faire un voyage **8**

to **talk** parler **7**

tall grand **9, 12**

tea le thé **3B**

teacher un (une) prof **2A, 9**; un professeur **9**

telephone un téléphone **9**
  to telephone téléphoner **7**

television la télé **9**
  to watch television regarder la télé **5**

ten dix **1A, 1B**
  to play tennis jouer au tennis **5**

terrific génial **12**; super **12**

thank you merci **1C**

that is ... c'est... **9, 12**

that (one), over there ça, là-bas **9**
  that's ... c'est... **2A, 9, 12**; voilà **2A**
  that's ... euros ça fait... euros **3C**
  that's bad c'est mal **12**
  that's good (fine) c'est bien **12**
  that's not ... ce n'est pas... **12**
  what's that? qu'est-ce que c'est? **9**

the le, la, l' **2B, 10**; les **10**

then alors **11**; ensuite

there là **6**

there is (are) il y a **9**

there is (here comes someone) voilà **2A**

over there là-bas **6**

that (one), over there ça, là-bas **9**; ce...-là

what is there? qu'est-ce qu'il y a? **9**

these ces
  these are ce sont **12**

they ils, elles **6**; eux; on
  they are ce sont **12**

thing une chose
  things are going (very) badly ça va (très) mal **1C**

thirsty: to be thirsty *avoir soif
  are you thirsty? tu as soif? **3B**
  I'm thirsty j'ai soif **3B**

thirteen treize **1B**

thirty trente **1C**
  3:30 trois heures et demie **4A**

this ce, cet, cette
  this is ... voici... **2A**

those ces
  those are ce sont **12**

thousand mille **2B**

three trois **1A**

Thursday jeudi *m.* **4B**

time: at what time is ...? à quelle heure est...? **4A**
  at what time? à quelle heure? **4A**
  what time is it? quelle heure est-il? **4A**

to **à 6**; chez
  to (the) au, à la, à l', aux
  in order to pour
  to class en classe **6**
  to whom à qui **8**

today aujourd'hui **4B**
  today is (Wednesday) aujourd'hui, c'est (mercredi) **4B**

tomato une tomate
  tomato juice le jus de tomate **3B**

tomorrow demain **4B**
  tomorrow is (Thursday) demain, c'est (jeudi) **4B**
  see you tomorrow! à demain! **4B**

too aussi **1B, 7**; trop
  too bad! dommage! **7**

town un village
  in town en ville **6**
to **travel** voyager **5, 7**
  trip: to take a trip *faire un voyage **8**
true vrai **12**
Tuesday mardi *m.* **4B**
TV la télé **9**
  to watch TV regarder la télé **5**
twelve douze **1B**
twenty vingt **1B, 1C**
two deux **1A**

uncle un oncle **2C**
under sous **9**
to **understand** *comprendre
  I (don't) understand je (ne) comprends (pas) **I**
unfashionable démodé
United States les États-Unis *m.*
upstairs en • haut
us nous
  (to) us nous
to **use** utiliser

vacation les vacances *f.*
  on vacation en vacances **6**
very très **11**
  very well très bien **7**
  very much beaucoup **7**
videotape une cassette vidéo **9**
to **visit** (*place*) visiter **7**

walk une promenade
  to take (go for) a walk *faire une promenade à pied **8**
  to walk *aller à pied; marcher **9**
to **want** *avoir envie de; *vouloir
  do you want …? tu veux…? **3A**
  do you want to …? est-ce que tu veux…? **5**
  I don't want … je ne veux pas… **5**

I want … je veux… **5**
  I want to je veux bien
  what do you want? qu'est-ce que tu veux? **3A;** vous désirez? **3B**
warm chaud **4C**
  it's warm (*weather*) il fait chaud **4C**
watch une montre **9**
to **watch** regarder **7**
  to watch TV regarder la télé **5**
water l'eau *f.*
we nous **6**
to **wear** *mettre; porter
weather: how's (what's) the weather? quel temps fait-il? **4C**
  it's … weather il fait… **4C**
Wednesday mercredi *m.* **4B**
week une semaine **4B**
well bien **7**
  well! eh bien!
  well then alors **11**
  everything's going (very) well ça va (très) bien **1C**
what comment? quoi?; qu'est-ce que **8**
  what color? de quelle couleur? **12**
  what day is it? quel jour est-ce? **4B**
  what do you want? qu'est-ce que tu veux? **3A;** vous désirez? **3B**
  what does … mean? que veut dire…? **I**
  what does he/she look like? comment est-il/elle? **9**
  what is it? qu'est-ce que c'est? **9**
  what is there? qu'est-ce qu'il y a? **9**
  what time is it? quelle heure est-il? **4A**
  what would you like? vous désirez? **3B**
  what's …'s name? comment s'appelle…? **2B**
  what's he/she like? comment est-il/elle? **9**
  what's his/her name? comment s'appelle-t-il/elle? **9**
  what's that? qu'est-ce que c'est? **9**

what's the date? quelle est la date? **4B**
what's the price? quel est le prix?
what's the weather? quel temps fait-il? **4C**
what's your address? quelle est ton adresse?
what's your name? comment t'appelles-tu? **1A**
at what time is …? à quelle heure est…? **4A**
at what time? à quelle heure? **4A, 8**
when quand **8**
  when is your birthday? c'est quand, ton anniversaire? **4B**
where où **6, 8**
  where is …? où est…? **6**
white blanc (blanche) **12**
who qui **8**
  who's that/this? qui est-ce? **2A, 9**
  about whom? de qui? **8**
  for whom? pour qui? **8**
  of whom? de qui? **8**
  to whom? à qui? **8**
  with whom? avec qui? **8**
why pourquoi **8**
wife une femme
window une fenêtre **I, 9**
winter l'hiver *m.* **4C**
  in the winter en hiver **4C**
with avec **6**
  with me avec moi **5**
  with you avec toi **5**
  with whom? avec qui? **8**
woman une dame (*polite term*) **2A;** une femme **9**
to **work** travailler **5, 7;** (*referring to objects*) marcher **9**
  does the radio work? est-ce que la radio marche? **9**
  it (doesn't) work(s) well il/elle (ne) marche (pas) bien **9**
would: I'd like je voudrais **3A, 3B, 5**
wrong faux (fausse) **12**

Y

year un an, une année **4B**
  he/she is ... (years old) il/elle a... ans **2C**
  I'm ... (years old) j'ai... ans **2C**
  to be ... (years old) *avoir... ans **10**
yellow jaune **E1, 12**
yes oui **1B, 6;** (*to a negative question*) si! **10**
  yes, of course oui, bien sûr **5**
  yes, okay (all right) oui, d'accord **5**
  yes, thank you oui, merci **5**
you tu, vous **6**; on
  you are ... tu es + *nationality* **1B**
  and you? et toi? **1A**
  (to) you te, vous
  your ton, ta; tes **2C**
  what's your name? comment t'appelles-tu? **1A**
young jeune **9**

Z

zero zéro **1A**

Index

A

à 89; **à demain** 61; **à samedi** 61
activities, talking about daily 72
adjectives, agreement and formation 20, 138-139, 164-165, 166; invariable 174; of nationality 19, 167; position before and after the noun 168, 175
adverbs, in impersonal expressions 178; of quantity 165; position of 100
age   talking about your age and asking others 37
agreement, noun-adjective 166; subject-verb 84, 94, 96, 98
aller   present 24
alphabet 17
approval, expressing 100
articles *see* definite article; indefinite article
attention, how to get someone's 176
avoir, expressions with 45, 152; present 152; to tell age 37

B

body, identifying head, neck, etc. 68

C

ça va (bien; comme çi, comme ça; mal) 24
c'est 27, 53, 61, 62, 140; in impersonal expressions 178; vs. **il est** 31, 177
combien 53
cognates 122
colors, talking about 40-41, 174
commands *see* imperative compliments, expressing 186
conclusion, how to introduce 167
connaître: tu connais 31
contradict, how to contradict negative statements or questions 157

D

danser 74
dates, talking about the day and date 62, 63

days, of week 61; with definite article 63, 159
de 89; in negative sentences 156
definite article 32, 46, 153, 155; in general sense 158; with days of week 63, 159
devoir 78

E

elision 32, 89, 106
-er   verbs present 95, 98
est-ce que in information questions 106; in "yes-no" questions 86-87
être, être de 19; in descriptions 177; present 84

F

faire   expressions with 53, 65, 110; present 110
familiar vs. formal 23, 84
family members, talking about 35
food and meals, talking about 45, 49

G

gender 20, 27, 28, 46
geographical names, prepositions with 19

H

Haiti 151

I

il est 31 vs. **c'est** 177
il y a 144
imperative 45, 53; summary charts R7-R10
indefinite article 27, 28, 153, 155; in negative sentences 156
infinitive 94; after certain verbs 74, 75, 101
interrogative constructions **est-ce que** 86; information questions 106; inversion 111; **qu'est-ce que** 86, 109, 140; **qui,** and expressions with 108; "yes-no"

questions 86-87, 111; expressions 106
intonation 47, 51, 86-87, 106
invitations accepting, extending, rejecting 78
inversion, in the present 111

J

jouer à 75

L

liaison 29, 32, 36, 57, 63, 84, 89, 94, 96, 152, 153, 155, 156, 175

M

maps 4, 8-9, R1-R3
Martinique 19
money (French), talking about how much things cost; borrowing money 52, 53; expressions 53
months, of the year 62

N

nager 74
names, giving your name; asking others 11, 15, 31
nationalities, talking about 19, 167
negation, how to answer yes/no questions 87; **ne...pas** 74, 77, 78, 88, 98; **si** 157
nouns, abbreviations 23; gender: masculine/feminine 27, 28, 46, 138, 153; number: singular/plural 154; replaced by subject pronouns 53, 142; shortened forms 75
numbers, cardinal 17, 21, 25, 29, 33; in dates 63; ordinal 62; pronunciation of 33; summary chart R6

O

ouvrir 132

P

parce que 106
parts of the body 68
passé composé -er verbs 152 (TE); summary charts R7-R10
people, talking about and describing 27, 138
plural adjectives 166; articles 154-155; nouns 154-155
possession, possessive adjectives 36
possessions, talking about 142, 144, 147
preferences, expressing **j'aime, je n'aime pas, je préfère** 74
pouvoir 78
prepositions 85, 89; with cities, countries 19;
present tense 94-95; of regular verbs: *see* **-er, -ir, -re** verbs; summary charts R7 of irregular verbs: *see* individual verb listings; summary charts R8
pronouns; stress 15; subject 53, 84-85, 142, 153
pronunciation 17, 21, 25, 29, 33, 37, 47, 51, 55, 57, 84, 89, 94, 96, 101, 111, 153, 154, 155, 159, 164, 166, 169, 175, 179, summary chart R4

Q

quand 62
Quebec 31
quel, quelle quel âge… 37
qu'est-ce que 109
questions, inversion 111; "yes-no" 87
qui 108; qui **est-ce** 27, 138; expressions with 108

R

regret, expressing 100

S

salutations, asking how someone is doing 23
salut vs. **bonjour** 23
savoir 140

seasons 65

seasons 65
Senegal 105
sound-spelling correspondence summary chart R4
spelling marks 17
stress pronouns 15
subject pronouns 53, 84-85, 142, 153
surprise, mild doubt, expressing 107

T

time, how to tell 56-58; at what time? 58
tu vs. **vous** 49, 84

V

verbs regular **-er** singular 94; plural 94; negative 98: *see* **-er, -ir, -re** verbs; irregular: *see* individual verb listings; summary charts R7-R10; followed by infinitive 74-75, 77, 101
voici 27
voilà 27
vouloir, je veux/ne veux pas, je voudrais 77, 78; **tu veux** 45
vous vs. **tu** 49, 84

W

weather expressions, talking about the seasons and weather 65
wishes, expressing 77

Credits

Cover
Background and foreground photos by
Lawrence Migdale/PIX; inset: R. Krubner/ROBERTSTOCK

Illustration
Tim Foley: 74, 75 *(t)*, 80, 101, 142, 145 *(t)*, 146 (t), 148,
154, 160 *(br)*, 161 *(b)*, 182

All other illustration by:
      Yves Clarnou
      Jean-Pierre Foissy
      Elisabeth Schlossberg

Photography
All photos by Lawrence Migdale/PIX except the following:
iii Pierre Valette;**14** *(bl, br)* Owen Franken; **15** *(t)* Owen
Franken; **16** *(tl, tr)* copyright ©Albert Rene Editions; *(all
others except cr)* Owen Franken; **18** Owen Franken; **19** *(b)*
Mick Roessler/ Index Stock; **22** Owen Franken; **24** *(cr, cl)*
Owen Franken; **26** *(t)* VPG/Woods; *(b)* Owen Franken; **30**
Owen Franken; **31** *(t)* Owen Franken; *(b)* Canstock/Index
Stock; **32** Owen Franken; **34** Owen Franken; **38** *(bl)* Owen
Franken; *(br)* Carol Palmer-Andrew Brilliant, D.C. Heath;
44 J. Charlas; **56** Owen Franken; **58** *(tr)* Owen Franken;
60 Owen Franken; **58** *(t)* Owen Franken; **60** Owen
Franken; **62** *(t)* Owen Franken; **64** Owen Franken; **66** (tr)
Adine Sagalyn; **139** *(tr)* PhotoDisc; *(br)* Comstock; all oth-
ers Corbis; **105** *(tr)* Beryl Goldberg; *(cl)* Andrea
Comas/Reuters; *(cr)* Chip & Maria de la Cueva; *(bl)* School
Division, Houghton Mifflin Co.; **104** Yves Levy; **110** Yves
Levy; **123** (t) Robert Fried; *(b)* Beryl Goldberg; **124** Sophie
Reiter; **125** *(br)* Yves Levy; all others Patrick Pipard; **126** *(t)*
Self Portrait (1835), Jean-Baptiste Camille Corot. Oil on
canvas. Uffizi, Florence, Italy. Photography ©Scala/Art
Resource; *(b)* View from Chatelaine, Jean-Camille Corot.
Musee d'Art et d'Histoire, Geneva, Switzerland.
Photography ©Francis G. Mayer/Corbis; **127** Yves Levy;
129 *(b)* Michael Newman/PhotoEdit; all others Stockbyte;
131 Yves Levy; **151** *(t)* Andre Jenny/ImageState; **151** *(b)*
Manu Sassoonian/Art Resource; **162** Yves Levy; **172**
Owen Franken; **177** Patrick Pipard; **189** MBK Europe